T0189308

Lecture Notes in Computer Science 13724

More information about this series at https://link.springer.com/bookseries/558

Richard Chbeir · Helen Huang ·
Fabrizio Silvestri · Yannis Manolopoulos ·
Yanchun Zhang (Eds.)

Web Information Systems Engineering – WISE 2022

23rd International Conference
Biarritz, France, November 1–3, 2022
Proceedings

 Springer

Editors
Richard Chbeir
University of Pau and Pays de l'Adour
Anglet, France

Helen Huang
The University of Queensland
Brisbane, QLD, Australia

Fabrizio Silvestri
Sapienza Università di Roma
Rome, Italy

Yannis Manolopoulos
Open University of Cyprus
Nicosia, Cyprus

Yanchun Zhang
The New Cyber Research Department
Peng Cheng Laboratory
Shenzhen, China

Cyberspace Institute
of Advanced Technology
Guangzhou University
Cuangzhou, China

ISSN 0302-9743   ISSN 1611-3349 (electronic)
Lecture Notes in Computer Science
ISBN 978-3-031-20890-4   ISBN 978-3-031-20891-1   (eBook)
https://doi.org/10.1007/978-3-031-20891-1

This Springer imprint is published by the registered company Springer Nature Switzerland AG
The registered company address is: Gewerbestrasse 11, 6330 Cham, Switzerland

Preface

The present volume features the proceedings of the 23rd International Conference on Web Information Systems Engineering (WISE 2022), held in Biarritz, France, during November 1–3, 2022. Notably, WISE is a truly international conference as it attracts participants from the whole globe, moving year after year to different continents. In particular, previous WISE events were organized in Hong Kong, China (2000); Kyoto, Japan (2001); Singapore (2002); Rome, Italy (2003); Brisbane, Australia (2004); New York, USA (2005); Wuhan, China (2006); Nancy, France (2007); Auckland, New Zealand (2008); Poznan, Poland (2009); Hong Kong, China (2010); Sydney, Australia (2011); Paphos, Cyprus (2012); Nanjing, China (2013); Thessaloniki, Greece (2014); Miami, USA (2015); Shanghai, China (2016); Puschino, Russia (2017); Dubai, UAE (2018); Hong Kong, China (2019); Amsterdam and Leiden, The Netherlands (2020); and finally Melbourne, Australia (2021).

The series of WISE conferences aims to provide an international forum for researchers, professionals, and industrial practitioners to share their knowledge in the rapidly growing area of web technologies, methodologies, and applications. Among others, papers related to the following broad categories are welcome for submission and presentation:

- Information Retrieval and Recommendation for Web
- Web Mining and Knowledge Discovery
- Web Data Models
- Social Issues and Analysis on Web
- Distributed and Cloud Computing for Web Information Systems
- Trustworthy and Responsible Web Information Systems
- Web Applications for Economy, Society, Health, Human Beings, and Things
- Extension of the Web
- Rich Web UI and HCI
- Web Tools and Visualization
- Web Open-sourced Datasets

WISE 2022 gathered an international Program Committee from 29 countries, with members coming mainly from Australia, China, and Europe. This edition attracted a total of 94 papers that were submitted to the conference for consideration. Authors were from 25 different countries.

Each paper was reviewed by at least three reviewers (three reviews for 30 papers and four for 64 papers) in a single-blind peer review process. Finally, 30 submissions were selected as regular papers (an acceptance rate of approximately 32%), plus 14 as short papers and three as demo papers. The research papers cover the areas social media, spatio-temporal issues, query processing and information extraction, architecture and performance, graph data management, security and privacy, information retrieval and text processing, reinforcement learning, learning and optimization, spatial data processing, recommendation systems, and neural networks.

In addition to regular and short papers, the WISE 2022 program also had four keynote talks and one tutorial session. We would like to sincerely thank our keynote speakers:

- Marco Brambila (Politecnico di Milano), who delivered a talk entitled "Exploring the bi-verse: how to analyse and benefit from the digital and physical ecospheres",
- Flavius Frasincar (Erasmus University of Rotterdam), who gave a talk on "Aspect-Based Sentiment Classification",
- Sihem Amer-Yahia (CNRS Grenoble), who gave a talk on "Fairness on Online Labor Markets", and last but not least,
- Athena Vakali (Aristotle University of Thessaloniki), who delivered a talk entitled "Online Self-trails and Sensing Data Analytics".

Proudly, we emphasize the inclusion and diversity balance in respect of the above. Also, we thank our tutorialists:

- Manolis Koubarakis and Dimitris Bilidas (National and Kapodistrian University of Athens), who addressed "Data modelling and query answering for linked geospatial data".

The members of the international Program Committee and the external reviewers deserve our gratitude for a rigorous and robust reviewing process. Without "a little help from our friends", we could not have put together such a high-quality program. Thanks are due to all other members of the organizing committee, as well as the OpenCEMS research group, who contributed substantially to all phases of the conference preparation. Finally, we are also grateful to Springer and the International WISE Society for supporting this conference.

We expect that the ideas that have emerged in WISE 2022 will result in the development of further innovations for the benefit of scientific, industrial, and social communities.

November 2022

Yanchun Zhang
Yannis Manolopoulos
Richard Chbeir
Helen Huang
Fabrizio Silvestri

Preface

Message from the Diversity and Inclusion Chairs

We support Diversity and Inclusion at this conference, and we kindly ask authors to adopt inclusive language in their papers and presentations (https://dbdni.github.io/pages/inclusivewriting.html), and for all participants to follow the conference code of conduct (https://dbdni.github.io/pages/codeofconduct.html).

Diversity and Inclusion at the WISE 2022 conference supported three main actions:

(i) a plenary talk by Sihem Amer-Yahia, who leads the Diversity a Inclusion initiative for the international data management community,

(ii) a best Diversity and Inclusion WISE paper award which takes into consideration inclusive languages, and

(iii) whenever possible, a balance of gender representation as well as country of origin in conference officers including the Program Committee, session chairs, student volunteers, and award sessions.

November 2022

Wenny Rahayu
Sana Sellami

Organization

General Chairs

Yanchun Zhang   Guangzhou University, China
Yannis Manolopoulos   Open University of Cyprus, Cyprus

Program Chairs

Richard Chbeir   Universite de Pau et des Pays de l'Adour, France
Helen Huang   University of Queensland, Australia
Fabrizio Silvestri   Sapienza University of Rome, Italy

Workshops Chairs

Mirjana Ivanovic   University of Novi Sad, Serbia
Hua Wang   Victoria University, Australia

Demos Chairs

Joe Tekli   Lebanese American University, Lebanon
Apostolos Papadopoulos   Aristotle University of Thessaloniki, Greece

Tutorials Chair

Vassilis Christophides   Inria Paris, France

Diversity and Inclusion Chairs

Wenny Rahayu   La Trobe University, Australia
Sana Sellami   Aix Marseille University, France

Publicity Chair

Shiyu Yang   Guangzhou University, China

Publication Chair

Karam Bou Chaaya   Caplogy SAS, France

Treasurer

Khouloud Salameh   American University of Ras Al Khaimah, UAE

Webmasters

Elio Mansour   University of Pau and Pays Adour, France
Elie Chicha   Universite de Pau et des Pays de l'Adour, France

International Program Committee

Adam Wójtowicz   Poznań University of Economics and Business, Poland
Alessandro Bozzon   Delft University of Technology, Netherlands
Alexander Knapp   Universität Augsburg, Germany
Alfonso Pierantonio   University of L'Aquila, Italy
Allel Hadjali   ISAE-ENSMA, France
Armin Haller   Australian National University, Australia
Athman Bouguettaya   University of Sydney, Australia
Azadeh Ghari Neiat   Deakin University, Australia
Bernd Amann   Sorbonne Université, France
Bin Cao   Zhejiang University of Technology, China
Birgit Proell   Johannes Kepler University Linz, Austria
Bo Tang   Southern University of Science and Technology, China
Boualem Benatallah   DCU, Ireland
Carmen Santoro   ISTI-CNR, Italy
Chaogang Tang   China University of Mining and Technology, China
Cindy Chen   UMass Lowell, USA
Cinzia Cappiello   Politecnico di Milano, Italy
Damiano Distante   Sapienza University of Rome, Italy
Dario Colazzo   Paris Dauphine University, France
De Wang   Georgia Institute of Technology, USA
Detian Zhang   Jiangnan University, China
Devis Bianchini   University of Brescia, Italy
Dimitri Theodoratos   New Jersey Institute of Technology, USA
Dimitris Plexousakis   Institute of Computer Science, FORTH, Greece
Dimitris Sacharidis   ULB, Belgium
Djamal Benslimane   Lyon 1 University, France
Eleanna Kafeza   Athens University of Economics and Business, Greece
Epaminondas Kapetanios   University of Hertfordshire, UK
Fenglong Ma   Pennsylvania State University, USA
Filippo Ricca   Università di Genova, Italy
Flavius Frasincar   Erasmus University Rotterdam, Netherlands
Francisco Jose Dominguez   University of Seville, Spain
  Mayo
Gefei Zhang   Hochschule für Technik und Wirtschaft Berlin,
                                      Germany
George Pallis   University of Cyprus, Cyprus
George Papastefanatos   ATHENA Research Center, Greece
Georgios Kambourakis   University of the Aegean, Greece
Guanfeng Liu   Macquarie University, Australia

Gustavo Rossi	UNLP, Argentina
Guy-Vincent Jourdan	University of Ottawa, Canada
Hai Dong	RMIT University, Australia
Hanchen Wang	University of Technology, Australia
Hao Huang	Wuhan University, China
Harald Sack	Leibniz Institute for Information Infrastructure and KIT, Germany
Hayato Yamana	Waseda University, Japan
Heiko Schuldt	University of Basel, Switzerland
Hong Va Leong	The Hong Kong Polytechnic University, Hong Kong
Hongzhi Wang	Harbin Institute of Technology, China
Hua Lu	Roskilde University, Denmark
Hua Wang	Victoria University, Australia
Hui Li	Xiamen University, China
Irene Garrigos	University of Alicante, Spain
Jarogniew Rykowski	Poznan University of Economics, Poland
Javier Luis Canovas Izquierdo	UOC, Spain
Ji Zhang	University of Southern Queensland, Australia
Jiajun Liu	CSIRO, Australia
Jiangang Ma	Federation University, Australia
Jianxin Li	Deakin University, Australia
Jinli Cao	La Trobe University, Australia
Jose Ignacio Panach Navarrete	Universitat de València, Spain
Jose-Norberto Mazon	Universidad de Alicante, Spain
Jürgen Ziegler	University of Duisburg-Essen, Germany
Kai Wang	University of New South Wales, Australia
Kai Zheng	University of Electronic Science and Technology of China, China
Kari Systä	Tampere University of Technology, Finland
Katerina Tzompanaki	CY Cergy Paris University, France
Kewen Liao	Australian Catholic University, Australia
Kostas Stefanidis	Tampere University, Finland
Lei Zhao	Soochow University, China
Leong Hou U	University of Macau, China
Lina Yao	University of New South Wales, Australia
Lizhen Wang	Yunnan University, China
Lu Chen	Swinburne University of Technology, Australia
Lu Chen	Zhejiang University, China
Luciano Baresi	Politecnico di Milano, Italy
Marco Aiello	University of Stuttgart, Germany
Marco Winckler	Université Côte d'Azur, France
Marcos Baez	University of Trento, Italy
Maristella Matera	Politecnico di Milano, Italy
Markel Vigo	University of Manchester, UK

Maurizio Leotta	Università di Genova, Italy
Maxime Buron	University of Oxford, UK
Md Rafiul Hassan	King Fahd University of Petroleum and Minerals, Saudi Arabia
Michael Weiss	Carleton University, Canada
Mohamed Reda Bouadjenek	Deakin University, Australia
Mohamed-Amine Baazizi	Sorbonne Université, France
Mohammed Eunus Ali	Bangladesh University of Engineering and Technology, Bangladesh
Murali Mani	University of Michigan-Flint, USA
Nathalie Moreno	University of Malaga, Spain
Nicola Zannone	Eindhoven University of Technology, Netherlands
Nicoleta Preda	University of Versailles, France
Nora Faci	Université Lyon 1, France
Nora Koch	University of Seville, Spain
Peiquan Jin	University of Science and Technology of China, China
Peng Peng	Hunan University, China
Pieter Colpaert	Ghent University, Belgium
Ralf Klamma	RWTH Aachen University, Germany
Sajib Mistry	Curtin University, Australia
Santiago Melia	Universidad de Alicante, Spain
Schahram Dustdar	Vienna University of Technology, Austria
Sebastian Link	University of Auckland, New Zealand
Shaoxu Song	Tsinghua University, China
Shiting Wen	Zhejiang University, China
Siqiang Luo	Nanyang Technological University, Singapore
Sira Yongchareon	Auckland University of Technology, New Zealand
Stefan Tai	TU Berlin, Germany
Sven Casteleyn	Universitat Jaume I, Spain
Tanzima Hashem	Bangladesh University of Engineering and Technology, Bangladesh
Theodoros Chondrogiannis	University of Konstanz, Germany
Thomas Richter	Rhein-Waal University of Applied Sciences, Germany
Toshiyuki Amagasa	University of Tsukuba, Japan
Tsz Chan	Hong Kong Baptist University, Hong Kong
Vassilis Christophides	ENSEA, France
Verena Kantere	University of Ottawa, Canada
Vicente Pelechano	Universitat Politècnica de València, Spain
Wei Shen	Nankai University, China
Wenjie Zhang	University of New South Wales, Australia
Werner Retschitzegger	Johannes Kepler University Linz, Austria
Wieland Schwinger	Johannes Kepler University Linz, Austria
Xiangmin Zhou	RMIT University, Australia
Xiaohui Tao	University of Southern Queensland, Australia
Xiaoshuang Chen	UNSW, Australia
Xiaoye Miao	Zhejiang University, China

Xin Cao	University of New South Wales, Australia
Xin Wang	Tianjin University, China
Xun Yi	RMIT University, Australia
Yixiang Fang	The Chinese University of Hong Kong, China
Youhuan Li	Hunan University, China
Yunjun Gao	Zhejiang University, China
Zakaria Maamar	Zayed University, UAE
Zhisheng Huang	Vrije Universiteit, Netherlands
Zhiyong Peng	State Key Laboratory of Software Engineering, China
Zhu Sun	Macquarie University, Australia

Local Organizing Team

OpenCEMS, France

Contents

Architecture and Performance

Graph Data Management

Security and Privacy

Information Retrieval and Text Processing

Reinforcement Learning

Learning and Optimization

Spatial Data Processing

Recommendation

Neural Networks

Demo Papers

Social Media

Utilizing Social Media Retweeting for Improving Event Participant Prediction

Yihong Zhang[(✉)] and Takahiro Hara

Multimedia Data Engineering Lab, Graduate School of Information Science
and Technology, Osaka University, Osaka, Japan
yhzhang7@gmail.com, hara@ist.osaka-u.ac.jp

Abstract. Events have become a common way for activity organization in many digital platforms. Event participant prediction is an important problem when planning future events for these platforms. Previous works have found that cold-start recommendation techniques can
be used to solve the problem effectively. However, for many starting
platforms, training data they own is limited, and may not be sufficient
to learn accurate recommendation models. On the other hand, social
media retweeting is a kind of event participant data that can be obtained
easily. In this paper, we propose to utilize social media retweeting to
help improve event participant prediction models. Our approach uses an
entity-connect knowledge graph to bridge the social media and the target domain, assuming that event descriptions in the target domain are
written in the same language as social media tweets. Experimental evaluation with real-world event participation datasets shows that adding
social media retweeting data with our approach does steadily improve
prediction accuracy in the target domain.

Keywords: Event-based system · Social media · Graph embedding ·
Deep neural network

1 Introduction

Many digital platforms now are organizing events through the Internet. For
example, platforms such as Meetup[1] allow people to organize offline gatherings
through online registration. Flash sales run by platforms such as Gilt[2] that offer
product discounts for a limited period can be considered as events. Moreover,
retweeting viral messages of the moment in social media platforms such as Twitter[3] can be also considered as a type of event participation. Effectively predicting
event participant can provide many benefits to event organizers and participants. For example, organizers can send out invitations more effectively [14],
while potential participants can receive better recommendations [11]. Existing

---

[1] https://www.meetup.com/.
[2] https://www.gilt.com/.
[3] https://www.twitter.com.

R. Chbeir et al. (Eds.): WISE 2022, LNCS 13724, pp. 3–10, 2022.
https://doi.org/10.1007/978-3-031-20891-1_1

researches generally have a restricted context of the event, such as event-based social networks [7]. In contrast, we first consider a general definition of event proposed by Jaegwon Kim, who considered that an event consists of three parts, a finite set of objects x, a property P, and a time interval t [5]. Many social events, such as concerts, football matches, hobby classes, and flash sales, involve an organizer who would determine the activities and time of the event [6]. What they often cannot determine beforehand, though, are the participants (can be considered as x). In this paper we deal with the problem of predicting event participants before starting the event.

One problem with many newly starting event-based platforms is that they have not collected enough data to effectively learn user preference. For example, a company just began to offer hobby classes would not have a large set of participation data. On the other hand, social media platforms such as Twitter nowadays are generating huge amounts of data that are accessible publicly. A particular set of data, that is *retweeting*, which consists of a tweet id and retweeted user ids, can be seen as a type of event participant data. We argue that newly starting event-based platforms can use such data to support their own prediction models even though some restrictions are required. In this paper, we propose a method to utilize social media retweeting data in the training of event participant prediction models of a target domain, which has limited training data. We assume there is no shared users across domains, but the event descriptions in the target domains are written in the same language as the tweets. We bridge two domains by using a knowledge graph connected two domains through common entities in the text.

2   Related Work

Event participant prediction started to attract attention with the emergence of event-based social network (EBSN). Liu et al. first studied the participant prediction problem in the context of EBSN [7]. Their technique relied on the topological structure of the EBSN and early responded users. Targeting a similar problem, Zhang et al. [15] and Du et al. [3] proposed to engineer some user features and then apply machine learning such as logistic regression, decision tree, and support vector machines. Additionally, Du et al. considered the event descriptions, which were overlooked in previous works [3].

Social media has been used in various works as the support domain. For example, Wei et al. have found that Twitter volume spikes could be used to predict stock options pricing [13]. They used the tweets that contained the stock symbols. Asur and Huberman studied if social media chatter can be used to predict movie sales [1]. They conducted sentiment analysis on tweets containing movie names, and found some positive correlations. Pai and Liu proposed to use tweets and stock market values to predict vehicle sales [9]. They found that by adding the sentiment score calculated from the tweets, prediction model performance substantially increased. These works, however, only used high-level features of social media, such as message counts or aggregated sentiment scores.

In this work, we consider a more general setting in which users and events are transformed into embeddings so that more subtle information can be extracted.

3   Methodology

In this section, we will present our problem formulation, entity-connected graph construction, and event participant prediction leveraging joint user embedding.

3.1   Problem Formulation

We formulate the problem of event participant prediction leveraging social media retweeting data as the following. In the target domain, we have a set of event data E^T, and for each event $e \in E^T$, there is a number of participants $p(e) = \{u_1^T, \ldots, u_n^T\}$. In the social media retweeting data, we have a set of tweets E^S, for $e \in E^S$, we have retweeters $p(e) = \{u_1^S, \ldots, u_m^S\}$. Normally we have fewer event data in the target domain than in the retweeting data, so $|E^S| > |E^T|$. An event in the target domain is described using the same language as the tweets. Let $d(e) = \{w_i, \ldots, w_l\}$ be the words in the description of event e. If V^S and V^T are the description vocabularies in the tweets and the target domain, then $V^S \cap V^T \neq \emptyset$.

We can represent event descriptions and users as vector-form embeddings. Since the event descriptions in the target domain and the tweet texts are written in the same language, their embeddings can also be obtained from the same embeddings space. We denote $r(e)$ as the function to obtain embeddings for event e for both the target domain events and tweets, and it can be calculated as the average word2vec embedding of the words in the description $mean(word2vec(d(e)))$. In the target domain, we have base user embeddings $l^B(u)$ available through the information provided by the platform user.

Typically, a recommender system can be trained to make participation predictions given pairs of event and user embeddings $(r(e), l(u))$. We already have $r(e)$ but not $l(u)$. To leverage the retweeting data, we need to somehow connect target domain users and social media users, so that we can learn embeddings for them in the same embedding space.

3.2   Entity-Connected Graph for Learning Joint User Embedding

There exists a number of established techniques that learn embeddings from graphs [2]. Our method is to learn a joint embedding function for both target domain and social media users by deploying such techniques, after creating a graph that connects them. Based on the participation data, we can create three kinds of relations in the graph, namely, participation relation, co-occurrence relation, and same-entity relation.

The participation relation comes from the interaction data, and is set between users and events. Suppose user u participates in event e. Then we create $rel(u, w) = participation$ for each word w in $d(e)$.

The co-occurrence relation comes from the occurrence of words in the event description. We use *mutual information* [10] to represent the co-occurrence behavior. Specifically, we have $mi(w_1, w2) = log(\frac{N(w_1,w_2)|E|}{N(w_1)N(w_2)})$, where $N(w_1, w_2)$ is the frequency of co-occurrence of words w_1 and w_2, $|E|$ is the total number of events, and $N(w)$ is the frequency of occurrence of a single word w. We use a threshold ϕ to determine the co-occurrence relation, such that if $mi(w_1, w_2) > \phi$, we create $rel(w_1, w_2) = co\_occurrence$.

Two kinds of relations mentioned above are created within a single domain. We now connect the graph of two domains using the same-word relation. We create $rel(w^T, w^S) = same\_word$ if a word in the target domain and a word in the retweeting data are the same word. In this way, two separate graphs for two domains are connected through entities in the event descriptions.

Once we have the joint graph, we can use established graph embedding learning techniques to learn user embeddings. An example of such a technique is TransE [2]. In TransE, it assumes $\mathbf{h} + \mathbf{l} \approx \mathbf{t}$, where $\mathbf{h}, \mathbf{l}, \mathbf{t}$ are embeddings of entity h, relation l, and entity t, respectively. In our case, when u^T and u^S participate in events that contain a word present in both domains, they are connected indirectly and would thus have similar embeddings.

3.3 Event Participant Prediction Leveraging Joint User Embeddings

As we mentioned in the Introduction, the event participant prediction can be solved by recommendation techniques. Different from a traditional recommendation problem, though, we aim to predict participants of new events. Cold-start recommendation, on the other hand, addresses such a problem [16]. Thus we can use cold-start recommendation technique to solve our problem.

We choose the state-of-the-art cold-start recommendation technique proposed by Wang et al. [12]. It is a generalization of a neural matrix factorization (NeuMF) model [4] which originally used one-hot representation for users and items. More specifically, We use the model to learn the following function:

$$f(l(u), r(e)) = \hat{y}_{ue} \tag{1}$$

where $l(u)$ and $r(e)$ are the learned embeddings for user u and event e.

We have acquired in the previous section joint user embeddings, $l^J(u)$, from the entity-connected graph. Note that we can apply the same graph technique to learn embeddings in single domains as well, denoted as $l^S(u)$ and $l^T(u)$ respectively for the retweeting data and target domain. From problem formulation, we also have base user embedding for the target domain $l^B(u)$. A problem is that the graph embeddings $l^J(u)$ and $l^T(u)$ are only available for a small number of target domain users, because they are learned from limited participation data. When we predict participants in future events, we need to consider the majority of users who have not participated in past events. These users have base embeddings $l^B(u)$ but not graph embeddings $l^J(u)$ and $l^T(u)$.

We can use graph embeddings for training the prediction model, but in order to keep the effectiveness, the input embedding should be in the same embeddings space as in the training data. The training data embedding in our case is $l^J(u)$. So we need to map base embedding $l^B(u)$ to the embedding space of $l^J(u)$ when making the prediction. As some previous works proposed, this can be done through linear latent space mapping [8]. Essentially it is to find a transfer matrix M so that $M \times U_i^s$ approximates U_i^t, and M can be found by solving the following optimization problem

$$\min_M \sum_{u_i \in \mathbf{U}} L(M \times U_i^s, U_i^t) + \Omega(M), \tag{2}$$

where $L(.,.)$ is the loss function and $\Omega(M)$ is the regularization. After obtaining M from users who have both base embeddings and graph embeddings, we can map the base user embedding to graph user embedding $l^{J'}(u) = M \times l^B(u)$ for those users who have no graph embedding.

An alternative solution would be using the base user embedding as the input for training the model. This would then require us to map graph user embedding to target domain base user embedding. We solve it by finding the most similar target domain users for a social media user, and using their embeddings as the social media user base embedding. More specifically, we pick k most similar target domain users according to the graph embedding, and take the average of their base embedding:

$$l^{B'}(u) = \frac{1}{K} \sum_{u_i \in U^K} l^B(u_i) \tag{3}$$

where U^K is top-k target domain users most similar to the social media user u according to their graph embeddings.

4   Experimental Evaluation

We verify the effectiveness of our approach on an e-commerce domain. This target domain is a flash sales platform that allows users to participate in discount events. We also crawl actual retweeting data from Twitter as the support data.

4.1   Dataset Preparation

We prepare a retweet dataset and a target domain dataset for testing our app-roach. Both datasets are from real-world sources. For the retweet dataset, we randomly collect about two million Japanese tweets from Twitter. We cluster all retweeting tweets based on their retweeting id, and select those clusters that contain at least 10 retweets. We have 11,805 political retweeting events, and the average number of participants in one event is 40.

For the target domain dataset, we collect an e-commerce flash sales purchase dataset, which contains a number of products and the ids of users who purchased the product during the flash sales events. The dataset is of a period of four months, between June and September in 2017. In the dataset we have 10,067 flash sales events, and the average number of participants in one event is 28. The products in the purchase data are associated with text descriptions written in Japanese.

We take the text of tweets as the event description of the retweeting events, and the product description as the description of the purchase events. Since they are all written in plain Japanese, we use the same representation method for all these descriptions. Specifically, the text are tokenized and pre-trained word2vec vector is applied.

The users in the e-commerce dataset are additionally associated with embeddings generated from their browsing histories. The users in the retweeting datasets are additionally associated with user profiles, which are self-introduction texts provided by respective users. We use simply bag-of-words (BOW) representation, which are vectors indicating word counts in the text.

4.2   Experiment Setup

Based on common approaches in recommendation systems with implicit feedback [12], we create the training dataset by random negative sampling, which gives consistent information for learning the model. Specifically, for every interaction entry (u, e) in the training dataset, which is labeled as positive, we randomly pick four users who have not participated in the event, and label the pairs as negative. So the training is done on user-event pairs.

The testing, on the other hand, is event-based. For each event e in the test dataset, we label all users who participated in the event U^+ as positive. Then, for the purpose of consistent measurement, we pick $n - |U^+|$ users, labeled as negative, so that the total candidate is n. We predict the user preference score for all the n users, rank them by the score, and measure the prediction accuracy based on top k users in the rank. We use measure *Recall@K* and *Precision@K* as the performance metric. Essentially, *Recall@K* tells how many users who will participate in the event can be predicted by the method, while *Precision@K* tells how likely a user will participate in the event when targeted by the method.

We separate training and test datasets strictly by time. For building the knowledge graph and making the training dataset, we use the earliest $|E^{train}|$ events from the target domain, and the same number of retweeting events from retweeting data. In the evaluation discussion, we show results when $|E^{train}|$ is 100, 200, and 500. For making the test dataset, we use $|E^{test}|$ events from the target domain. In the evaluation, we set $|E^{test}|$ as 1,000. We ensure that E^{test} is the same for three cases of E^{train}, and that they have no overlaps.

We compare the performance of the proposed framework against single domain methods. The compared methods are single domain with target domain base embedding as the input (single base), single domain with target domain graph embedding as the input (single graph), retweet supported prediction with base embedding (rs base) and graph embedding (rs graph). In all cases, we use NeuMF described in Sect. 3.3 as the prediction model.

4.3   Evaluation Results and Discussions

The accuracy results measured in Recall@K and Precision@K are shown in Table 1. We show the results for $K = 10$, but we note that other K values give similar tendencies. Five methods are compared, and the best performing results are highlighted in bold font.

Table 1. Recall@10 and Precision@10 for purchase participation prediction

		Single base	Single graph	rs base	rs graph
Recall@10	100 train	0.044	0.057	0.044	**0.061**
	200 train	0.044	0.086	0.046	**0.093**
	500 train	0.053	**0.130**	0.053	**0.130**
Precision@10	100 train	0.100	0.136	0.101	**0.143**
	200 train	0.101	0.196	0.109	**0.205**
	500 train	0.119	0.283	0.123	**0.284**

We compare single domain methods with retweeting-supported methods. We can see that in all test cases, the supporting the target domain with graph embedding achieved the best accuracy. Compared to single domain graph embeddings, the proposed framework improves Precision@10 by about 7% when using 100 training instances. However, with 500 training instances, the improvement of the supported method is limited. This is possibly because with 500 training instances, the target domain already has sufficient data to learn a proper model, and adding more data becomes less effective.

5   Conclusion

In this paper, we study the problem of utilizing social media retweeting data in event participant prediction in a target domain. Since predicting event participants is valuable for event organizers, and many starting platforms do not have enough data to learn prediction models, leveraging open data such as those from social media is potentially beneficial. We approach the problem by proposing an entity-connected knowledge graph based on the assumption that event descriptions are written in the same language as the social media tweets. On top of it, we propose a prediction framework that leverages joint user embedding learned from the connected graph. Our experimental evaluation shows that by considering the social media retweeting data, the prediction accuracy in the target domain generally improved, especially when target domain data is limited. In some cases, the precision is increased by 7%. In the future, we would like to investigate more models that make use of social media retweeting data to further improve the prediction accuracy.

Acknowledgement. This research is partially supported by JST CREST Grant Number JPMJCR21F2.

References

1. Asur, S., Huberman, B.A.: Predicting the future with social media. In: Web Intelligence and Intelligent Agent Technology (WI-IAT), vol. 1, pp. 492–499. IEEE (2010)
2. Bordes, A., Usunier, N., Garcia-Duran, A., Weston, J., Yakhnenko, O.: Translating embeddings for modeling multi-relational data. In: Advances in Neural Information Processing Systems, vol. 26 (2013)
3. Du, R., Yu, Z., Mei, T., Wang, Z., Wang, Z., Guo, B.: Predicting activity attendance in event-based social networks: content, context and social influence. In: Proceedings of the 2014 ACM International Joint Conference on Pervasive and Ubiquitous Computing, pp. 425–434 (2014)
4. He, X., Liao, L., Zhang, H., Nie, L., Hu, X., Chua, T.S.: Neural collaborative filtering. In: Proceedings of the 26th International Conference on World Wide Web, pp. 173–182. ACM, Perth, Australia (2017)
5. Kim, J.: Events as property exemplifications. In: Brand, M., Walton, D. (eds.) Action Theory. SYLI, pp. 159–177. Springer, Dordrecht (1976). https://doi.org/10.1007/978-94-010-9074-2_9
6. Li, K., Lu, W., Bhagat, S., Lakshmanan, L.V., Yu, C.: On social event organization. In: Proceedings of the 20th ACM SIGKDD International Conference on Knowledge Discovery and Data Mining, pp. 1206–1215 (2014)
7. Liu, X., He, Q., Tian, Y., Lee, W.C., McPherson, J., Han, J.: Event-based social networks: linking the online and offline social worlds. In: Proceedings of the 18th ACM SIGKDD International Conference on Knowledge Discovery and Data Mining, pp. 1032–1040 (2012)
8. Man, T., Shen, H., Jin, X., Cheng, X.: Cross-domain recommendation: an embedding and mapping approach. In: IJCAI, vol. 17, pp. 2464–2470 (2017)
9. Pai, P.F., Liu, C.H.: Predicting vehicle sales by sentiment analysis of Twitter data and stock market values. IEEE Access **6**, 57655–57662 (2018)
10. Peng, H., Long, F., Ding, C.: Feature selection based on mutual information criteria of max-dependency, max-relevance, and min-redundancy. IEEE Trans. Pattern Anal. Mach. Intell. **27**(8), 1226–1238 (2005)
11. Qiao, Z., Zhang, P., Zhou, C., Cao, Y., Guo, L., Zhang, Y.: Event recommendation in event-based social networks. In: Proceedings of the AAAI Conference on Artificial Intelligence, vol. 28 (2014)
12. Wang, H., et al.: A DNN-based cross-domain recommender system for alleviating cold-start problem in e-commerce. IEEE Open J. Ind. Electron. Soc. **1**, 194–206 (2020)
13. Wei, W., Mao, Y., Wang, B.: Twitter volume spikes and stock options pricing. Comput. Commun. **73**, 271–281 (2016)
14. Yu, Z., et al.: Who should I invite for my party? Combining user preference and influence maximization for social events. In: Proceedings of the 2015 ACM International Joint Conference on Pervasive and Ubiquitous Computing, pp. 879–883 (2015)
15. Zhang, X., Zhao, J., Cao, G.: Who will attend?-Predicting event attendance in event-based social network. In: 2015 16th IEEE International Conference on Mobile Data Management, vol. 1, pp. 74–83. IEEE (2015)
16. Zhu, Y., et al.: Addressing the item cold-start problem by attribute-driven active learning. IEEE Trans. Knowl. Data Eng. **32**(4), 631–644 (2019)

A Domain-Independent Method for Thematic Dataset Building from Social Media: The Case of Tourism on Twitter

Maxime Masson[1(✉)], Christian Sallaberry[1], Rodrigo Agerri[2],
Marie-Noelle Bessagnet[1], Philippe Roose[1], and Annig Le Parc Lacayrelle[1]

[1] LIUPPA, E2S, University of Pau and Pays Adour (UPPA), Pau, France
{maxime.masson,christian.sallaberry,marie-noelle.bessagnet,
philippe.roose,annig.lacayrelle}@univ-pau.fr
[2] HiTZ Center - Ixa, University of the Basque Country UPV/EHU,
Donostia-San Sebastian, Spain
rodrigo.agerri@ehu.eus

Abstract. In this article, we propose a generic method to build thematic datasets from social media. Many research works gather their data from social media, but the extraction processes used are mostly *ad hoc* and do not follow a formal or standardized method. We aim at extending the processes currently used by designing an iterative, generic and domain-independent approach to build thematic datasets from social media with three modulable dimensions at its core: spatial, temporal and thematic. We experiment our method using data extracted from Twitter to build a thematic dataset about tourism in a highly touristic region. This dataset is then evaluated using both quantitative and qualitative metrics to highlight the value of this method. The application to this use case shows the effectiveness of our domain-independent method to generate thematic datasets from Twitter data.

Keywords: Social media · Dataset building · Social web analysis · Computational social science · Natural language processing

1 Introduction

Recently, we have seen a significant growth in available data sources covering many topics and the rise of user-generated content. Tourism in particular represents one of the biggest economic sectors in the world in which accurate thematic datasets are critical to better analyze and decipher trends [1].

In the domain of tourism, large datasets can have many practical use cases. On the one hand, they can be used for the purpose of supporting the decision-making process of tourism stakeholders for the improvement, development and planning of touristic cities and areas. This is done by analyzing the data to better understand the practice and needs of tourists. Such analysis is particularly useful for companies specialized in tourism marketing (such as *Destination*

© The Author(s), under exclusive license to Springer Nature Switzerland AG 2022
R. Chbeir et al. (Eds.): WISE 2022, LNCS 13724, pp. 11–20, 2022.
https://doi.org/10.1007/978-3-031-20891-1_2

Marketing Organization, DMO) where understanding the desires and expectations of tourists is key. On the other hand, tourism data can be analyzed for tourists themselves by building recommender systems. Those systems analyze the types of practices of a large number of tourists to be able to recommend better suited places, activities or tourist itineraries. Furthermore, different types of sources can be used to extract touristic data. Historically, these are mainly databases with 2 categories that stand out: (1) commercial databases, such as those from Online Travel Agencies (OTAs) and, (2) public databases, for example government issued or crowd sourced ones. The latter is a part of what is called User-Generated Content (UGC). In recent years, this category of data has grown significantly, ranging from social media (*Twitter, FourSquare*) to review sites (*TripAdvisor*).

As part of a local project, we needed to extract, analyze and present data focused on a specific theme defined by a domain expert (in our case, *tourism*). While many research works concentrate on proposing fully generic and adaptable processing pipelines to extract knowledge from flows of social media data [6] (such as NLP modules calibrated for short, informal messages), they do not propose a generic methodology to build such thematic datasets. In contrast to those previous approaches, the work presented here focuses on the upstream step of the data collection process. It aims at consolidating existing solutions when it comes to social media based Information Extraction (IE). Indeed, this contribution consists of proposing a domain-independent method to obtain high-quality data from social media to build thematic datasets. It is generic and based on an iterative and multi-dimensional (*spatial, temporal, thematic*) filtering process. It was hypothesized that representing the theme of the dataset to be built up in the form of a vocabulary can contribute to (1) an efficient thematic filtering of posts and to (2) the development of a domain independent process.

The article is organized as follows. Firstly, we introduce our project's motivations and the requirements our extraction method must meet. Secondly, we review the state of the art of the approaches used to gather data out of social media with a focus on Twitter data. Thirdly, our contribution is presented: a domain-independent, generic method for thematic dataset building from social media. We finally experiment and evaluate our method on a local touristic case.

2   Motivation

This work, carried out in the framework of a multilingual (*English, French, Spanish* and *Basque*) project, aims to collect, process, analyze and then value social media data related to the practice of tourism, visitor flows and the use of cultural heritage in the *Basque Country*, a cross-border highly touristic area.

We decided to adopt a trajectory-based analysis and therefore build multidimensional trajectories from local visitors. Our trajectory model has 3 dimensions at its core. The spatial dimension (*where*) (1) refers to the set of places (*municipalities, natural areas, etc.*) visited by tourists. The temporal dimension (*when*) (2) can be seen at different levels: the period of the trip (*season, year, month, time interval etc.*) as well as the date and duration of each activity performed. Finally, the thematic dimension (*what*) (3) is purely semantic, it describes the "*what*" of the tourist practice, such as the activities performed, the conditions of the trip, the tourist's feelings, whether they were accompanied or not, etc. We aim at moving beyond the well-known concept of spatial tracks and instead focus on trajectories where the thematic dimension has a greater weight than the spatial one, where places could be represented by themes and region by cluster of themes. Figure 1 shows an example of a trajectory in a tourist thematic space.

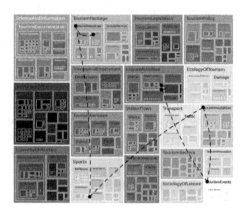

Fig. 1. Trajectory of a visitor in what could be the tourism thematic space.

With thousands of trajectories, we could run pattern analysis on it to detect affinities between types of tourist activities, categories of cultural heritage or even recurring sequences of activities. To build these thematic trajectories, social media is chosen as our primary source of data for several reasons: (1) the ease of access, no need for time-consuming collection campaigns, (2) the diversity, most tourism aspects are covered and (3) the massive amount of data available.

Although our project is mostly focused on the tourism domain, we have already identified future needs for the generation of datasets related with other specific domains such as wine culture or education. It therefore appeared necessary to move towards a method that is as independent of the domain as possible.

3   Related Work

Due to the extensive amount of research work on the subject, we focus on Twitter data that we have chosen as a main data source for our project. For the **spatial dimension (1)**, two different approaches are generally used and sometimes combined to obtain better results. First, filtering can be performed on the **spatial metadata** attached to the post, either by providing the social media API with a bounding box encompassing the area of study, or by basing it on a precise location (*referenced with a latitude/longitude*) with a radius around it (*location nearness*) [7]. The advantage of this metadata-based approach is that it is extremely accurate, as the location is generally determined using the GPS of the device. The biggest problem that arises is the low amount of posts that have metadata attached. For Twitter, it was estimated that around 1% of tweets have spatial metadata attached to them [9]. Thus, relying solely on metadata misses many potentially relevant posts. The second method is applied to the content of the post and is done via toponym filtering [7,8]. A list of place names and their associated abbreviations is compiled and all posts containing them are extracted. The big drawback of this method is the potentially large amount of noise. Disambiguation approaches are used to mitigate this problem, for example by combining this list of toponyms with exclusion lists [10].

For the **temporal dimension (2)**, the extraction is usually done according to the timestamp. It is an easy method to implement and usually quite accurate. Exchanges on social media are often done in real time, so it is not necessarily mandatory to set up a complex temporal entity extraction system.

When it comes to the **thematic dimension (3)**, multiple approaches are used. Content-based approaches use thematic keywords directly related to the theme of study (such as event names [8]), the use of too specific keywords can restrict too much the number of returned posts, so some research works associate several words together to establish filtering rules. Some social media have the concept of *hashtag* allowing to identify topics of discussion, which have often been used as a filtering tool [3]. Other thematic filtering methods are applied to the metadata and include: the language of the post, its source, etc. To reduce noise, some research work use only the posts from a pre-selected list of accounts known to validate certain desired criteria (e.g., known for speaking regularly about a specific topic [2]). Associated replies and comments can also be extracted [3].

Although, in recent years, various efforts have been made to design more generic processing techniques for social media data [6], when it comes to dataset building, each research project usually comes with its own extraction and filtering flow. While some common techniques are shared, there is not yet a fully generic and domain-independent procedure for dataset building from social media.

4   A New Method for Thematic Dataset Building from Social Media

We propose a method for creating thematic datasets from social media. It aims at formalizing a generic approach to extract social media-sourced data related to a given domain and possibly a given time period or spatial area. This method is designed around the following properties:

- **Multi-dimensional:** the method is based on 3 dimensions: spatial, temporal, thematic. One can combine two, three of them or only use one.
- **Generic:** it can be implemented with any social media that has a post system. This genericity also extends to languages.
- **Domain-independent:** it supports any target theme for the dataset.

- **Iterative, incremental:** the method is designed around an iterative and incremental process, namely, each iteration aims at refining the following iterations to have a dataset as qualitative as possible with a minimal noise.

Before proceeding with the collection process (the steps presented in Fig. 2), it is necessary to define the future dataset along the **spatial** (*territorial footprint of the data*), **temporal** (*temporal scope*) and **thematic** (*the theme, the semantics as of a vocabulary, thesaurus or ontology*) dimensions. According to our review of the state of the art, these dimensions cover the majority of use cases in dataset building. The presence of all these dimensions is not mandatory. We could therefore have only *tempo-thematic* or *spatio-thematic* datasets.

Our method being **iterative and incremental**, users can refine the dimensions later in the process, until they are satisfied with the obtained dataset. This process is semi-automatic. After this preliminary definition step, it is recommended to define a *calibration dataset*, It is a subset of the main one with a more restrictive definition used to calibrate the main, wider collection process.

4.1 Filtering the Flow of Posts

Once the dataset have been defined, we can now move on to the collection process. It is applied sequentially to 2 sets of posts with different features.

1. **Geotagged posts:** posts whose authors have activated GPS location (about 2% [9] for Twitter). This reduced set of posts is handled first (Fig. 2, ①).
2. **All posts:** posts containing a text (no image-only posts) (Fig. 2, ②).

The flow of associated media (Fig. 2, ③) is a future research axis and will therefore not be discussed in this article.

Each set is extracted following the procedure described in Fig. 2. The order of the steps is only indicative. In this sense, it is necessary to think about which steps can be delegated to the internal filtering system of the social media and which ones must necessarily be carried out locally (the latter have to be processed last). There is no universal answer to this question, it depends on the extent of the search functionality of the social media and the dimensions' complexity.

Pre-processing aims to exclude accounts, keywords or hashtags that we know should not appear in our final dataset while being prone to fit within our dimensions, for example: excluding professional, institutional or promotional accounts, excluding problematic keywords, or excluding certain languages. This step is especially useful to exclude places with the same name but actually unrelated to each other (*toponymic homonyms*), which could distort the spatial filtering process. Usually, these criteria are not known at the beginning of the process so this step is empty, although it will be filled in future iterations.

The following steps are optional and depend on the dataset definition. For a more efficient collection process, it is advisable to order the dimensions from the one believed to be the most restrictive, to the less restrictive (*in order to process as few unnecessary posts as possible*) and to delegate as much filtering as possible to the social media native API system.

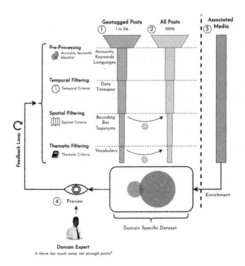

Fig. 2. Overview of the extraction process.

Temporal filtering is done using the timestamp of the posts. This method has been extensively used and covers most of the use cases. Indeed, social media are instantaneous informal exchange zones, i.e. users generally talk about the present moment. In specific cases, a temporal entity detection system could be applied on the content of the posts. This would allow to be more precise in cases where users talk about past or future events (*yesterday, next week*).

For **spatial filtering** the approach to be used differs depending on the two sets of posts described above. In the case of geotagged posts, we propose to check whether the position of the post is contained within a bounding box. This method is highly accurate because it is based on the devices' GPS. Moreover, it can usually be offsetted to the social media API. For the posts without spatial metadata attached, the approach is a bit different. We rely on the post content to do the selection. A list of toponyms contained within the area of study is provided as input and is matched within post content to determine which ones are about this area. The risk of noise is higher with this approach, but our iterative method allows to refine this step further in the process.

The objective of **thematic filtering** is to keep only the posts which are related to the theme, with the latter being defined using a given vocabulary. It is done by aligning this vocabulary with the post content (*entity linking* [4]).

4.2   Dataset Preview and Iteration

Each time an iteration of this process is performed, a dataset is obtained. We can then preview the resulting dataset and evaluate it, this step is usually performed by a domain specialist (Fig. 2, ④). Their role is to determine by reviewing a set of randomly selected posts, whether there is too much noise or not enough posts and try to identify certain types of recurring posts to exclude or that are missing. The criteria to add, remove, extend or narrow are then decided and a new iteration of the process can start using those refined criteria, and so on until the final dataset is deemed satisfactory (*feedback loop*).

5   Experimentation and Evaluation

To experiment our methodology, we chose the social media Twitter[1]. Concerning the preliminary definition step, we rely on the *Thesaurus on Tourism & Leisure* of the *WTO*[2]. This resource covers roughly 1,300 touristic concepts. For the purpose of this experiment, we reduce the spatial extent of the data. We wish to gather content from only one specific sub-area which will serve as our **spatial dimension**: the *French Basque Coast*, which is broadly considered to be among the most touristic places in the region. Also, in an effort to show the full range of our dimensions, we will focus solely on the summer of 2019.

We compute **quantitative statistics** on the collected data such as the number of users, tweets, detected concepts or locations. These quantitative metrics will allow us to determine if our method can be implemented on Twitter data and if a consistent number of tweets is collected without having too few posts or excessive noise. Then, we want to evaluate the effectiveness of our thematic filtering process. We take as reference the **context annotations** generated by Twitter. These are labels that Twitter automatically attaches to tweets based on their content. The approach used to create those is not known but among these annotations, one is about *Travel*. After reviewing them, we realized that these annotations were usually quite accurate but that many relevant tweets did not have them (e.g., *Twitter annotates well but doesn't annotate enough tweets*) making it difficult to build large datasets relying solely on them. It therefore seemed relevant to calculate what proportion of tweets suggested as related to travel by Twitter our system select. Lastly, we needed to evaluate whether all other tweets not tagged as "*Travel*" we import are relevant or just noise. We therefore perform a **qualitative** analysis on the resulting dataset. We randomly sampled 20, 50, and 100 posts of the resulting datasets and calculated the thematic accuracy @20, @50, and @100 to check the reliability of our process at each iteration. Two tourism experts will manually analyze their content and annotate whether or not they relate to tourism or not. This qualitative metric is meant to demonstrate the role of our method's multiple iterations in improving the accuracy and evaluate the overall quality of the results.

5.1   Method Implementation

The whole process (Table 1) was developed with the *Tweepy*[3] library used for the interaction with the Twitter API. We performed 3 refinement iterations and we only collected tweets in French, English and Spanish posted in summer 2019.

---

[1] https://developer.twitter.com/en/products/twitter-api/academic-research.

[2] https://www.e-unwto.org/doi/book/10.18111/9789284404551.

[3] https://www.tweepy.org.

Table 1. Application of the method using our dataset requirements.

		Iteration 1		Iteration 2		Iteration 3	
		Geotagged Posts	All Posts	Geotagged Posts	All Posts	Geotagged Posts	All Posts
Pre Processing	Criteria	Lang: FR, ES, EN. Blacklist *retweets, quotes*		− professional accounts		− blacklist G7-related keywords & #	
Temporal Filtering	Criteria	Summer 2019					
	Tweets	> 1 billion tweets					
Spatial Filtering	Criteria	Basque Bounding Box	625 Basque OSM places	Basque Bounding Box	579 Basque OSM places	Basque Bounding Box	550 Basque OSM places
	Tweets	7,003	> 2,700,000	6,689	148,860	6,127	59,878
Thematic Filtering	Criteria	Full WTO Thesaurus		Refined WTO Thesaurus		Refined++ WTO Thesaurus	
	Tweets	3,447		2,390	56,968	2,098	25,281
Stats	Hashtags (#)	3,750 hashtags	Too many tweets	3,620 hashtags	44,411 hashtags	3,341 hashtags	24,263 hashtags
	Users (@)	1,112 users		865 users	30,126 users	796 users	14,114 users
	Places	32 locations		31 locations	194 locations	31 locations	184 locations
	Mapped Concepts	462 concepts		243 concepts	540 concepts	235 concepts	458 concepts

For geotagged tweets, we simply filter on the bounding box of the area of study and get about 7,000 tweets. Those are then thematically filtered using the whole thesaurus vocabulary in conjunction with the IAM Entity Linker [4], a dictionary-based approach for semantic annotation. We get 3,447 tweets as output. For non-geotagged tweets, we use 625 multilingual toponyms extracted from OSM[4] contained within the area of study. In the first iteration, we use all of them indiscriminately to filter and therefore retrieve too many tweets (more than 2.5 million). We decide to stop the process and refine it at the next iteration.

The feedback from the 1st iteration leads us to blacklist professional or institutional accounts (not interesting for our analysis). We also refine the toponym list and remove 46 common place names (such as *Roman Theater*). Lastly, the tourism thesaurus is reduced to exclude some branches deemed irrelevant by our project domain experts. We get about 60,000 tweets at the end of the 2nd iteration and notice a large number of tweets about the G7 an important event taking place in 2019 in the region. A 3rd iteration is carried out with additional pre-processing filters to blacklist G7-related keywords and hashtags. The final dataset is made of about 2,098 geotagged tweets, 25,281 tweets in total belonging to 15,000 users and 458 unique concepts have been found in these tweets.

Fig. 3. Number of tweets annotated *"Travel"* by Twitter among those we select.

Out of those: 1,668 have the Twitter *"Travel"* annotation. In other words, only about 6% of the tweets collected were identified as relating to tourism by Twitter, that is not much and it is why we aim at collecting more than those.

---

[4] https://www.openstreetmap.org/.

5.2 Results Analysis

Figure 3 shows the different sets of tweets of the 3rd (last) iteration (*union of both geotagged non-geotagged ones*) and among these sets of tweets, the proportion of those annotated with the "*Travel*" context annotation by Twitter. We observe that among the tweets from the area of study (66,005), most of those tagged as "*Travel*" by Twitter are selected by our system (1,668 selected, 217 excluded). We get an accuracy of 0.884. We also notice a high number of selected tweets which are not tagged by Twitter (25,711) but that we select. It means that our process detects many more potentially relevant items. This can be rather a positive aspect as Twitter context annotations seem to be missing from a lot of tourism-related tweets. However, we now need to determine whether all those are just noise or other tourism-related tweets that Twitter has not annotated.

For this purpose, a qualitative analysis is set up. 100, 50 and 20 tweets are extracted randomly from the datasets at different stages of the method and manually evaluated by experts to determine whether they have been correctly or wrongfully selected. Table 2 shows the result of the evaluation done by two experts on 20, 50 and 100 tweets, randomly picked just after the thematic filtering for both sets of tweets. We compute the mean thematic accuracy between those two experts and, for the 3rd iteration @100, the associated Cohen's Kappa (κ) which measures the degree of agreement between them to mitigate subjectivity.

Table 2. Qualitative analysis of the results.

		Iteration 1		Iteration 2		Iteration 3	
		Geotagged	All	Geotagged	All	Geotagged	All
Thematic Accuracy	(@ 20)	0.75		0.60	0.30	**0.83**	**0.72**
	(@ 50)	0.64		0.60	0.30	0.77	0.74
	(@ 100)	**0.52**		**0.59**	0.35	**0.74** (κ 0.74)	**0.65** (κ 0.48)

The question asked was "*Is this tweet related to Tourism?*". We obtain a mean thematic accuracy ranging from 0.83 (@20) to 0.74 (@100) for geotagged tweets and 0.72 (@20) to 0.65 (@100) for non-geotagged ones. That means, by extrapolation, potentially 65% to 83% of the tweets not selected by Twitter might actually be relevant to the topic of tourism and our assumption that Twitter is not annotating enough content is correct.

We also observe a thematic accuracy @100 starting at 0.52 at the 1st iteration for geotagged tweets which increases to 0.59 and then 0.74 in iterations 2 and 3 which clearly highlight the effect of filter refinement and feedback loop between each iterations. Overall, experts seem to agree on the outcome as shown by the relatively high κ score. Thematic accuracy on all non-geotagged tweets is slightly lower but follow a similar increasing trend. The final dataset thematic accuracy is acceptable but could have been increased even more by doing more iterations, we limited ourself to 3 for this experiment. To go further, we observed the **same** sample of incorrect tweet from the first iteration throughout the method to see what proportion of it would get removed in future ones. We use the set of tweets used for the @100 thematic accuracy measure of the 1st iteration. The accuracy is average (0.52) which means: out of 100 tweets evaluated, 48 were incorrectly selected. The 2nd iteration removes 27 of them, so 21 are remaining. Then finally, the last iteration leaves 15 remaining. This is consistent with the accuracy we calculated on random samples previously ($\approx$70% of correct tweets).

6   Conclusion

We proposed a domain-independent and generic method for building thematic datasets from social media based on 3 dimensions. The objective is to move away from *ad hoc* collection processes and to propose a robust method to build focused datasets. We are thinking of going further by extending our dimensions by taking inspiration from the 5W1H [5] dimensions. The 5W1H is a framework widely used in problem solving and question answering based on the 6 interrogative words: *Who, What, When, Where, Why, How*. We already have the *When* (temporal), *Where* (spatial) and *What* (thematic) but we could imagine other dimensions for the *Who* (the users, the persons they are referring to), the *why* (reasoning behind an action) or the *how* (in what way is it carried out).

References

1. Aguiar, A., Szekut, A.: Big data and tourism: opportunities and applications in tourism destination management. Appl. Tour. **4**, 36 (2019)
2. Chiruzzo, L., Castro, S., Rosá, A.: HAHA 2019 dataset: a corpus for humor analysis in Spanish. In: Proceedings of the 12th Language Resources and Evaluation Conference, pp. 5106–5112 (2020)
3. Cignarella, A.T., Lai, M., Bosco, C., Patti, V., Paolo, R., et al.: Overview of the task on stance detection in Italian tweets. In: EVALITA 2020 7th Evaluation Campaign of Natural Language Processing and Speech Tools for Italian, pp. 1–10. CEUR (2020)
4. Cossin, S., Jouhet, V., Mougin, F., Diallo, G., Thiessard, F.: IAM at CLEF eHealth 2018: concept annotation and coding in French death certificates. arXiv preprint arXiv:1807.03674 (2018)
5. Han, S., Lee, K., Lee, D., Lee, G.G.: Counseling dialog system with 5W1H extraction. In: Proceedings of the SIGDIAL 2013 Conference, pp. 349–353 (2013)
6. Sathick, J., Venkat, J.: A generic framework for extraction of knowledge from social web sources (social networking websites) for an online recommendation system. Int. Rev. Res. Open Distrib. Learn. **16**(2), 247–271 (2015)
7. Scholz, J., Jeznik, J.: Evaluating geo-tagged twitter data to analyze tourist flows in Styria, Austria. ISPRS Int. J. Geo Inf. **9**(11), 681 (2020)
8. Shimada, K., Inoue, S., Maeda, H., Endo, T.: Analyzing tourism information on Twitter for a local city. In: 2011 First ACIS International Symposium on Software and Network Engineering, pp. 61–66. IEEE (2011)
9. Sloan, L., Morgan, J.: Who tweets with their location? Understanding the relationship between demographic characteristics and the use of geoservices and geotagging on Twitter. PLoS ONE **10**(11), e0142209 (2015)
10. Zenasni, S., Kergosien, E., Roche, M., Teisseire, M.: Spatial information extraction from short messages. Expert Syst. Appl. **95**, 351–367 (2018)

Domain Adversarial Training for Aspect-Based Sentiment Analysis

Joris Knoester[1], Flavius Frasincar[1], and Maria Mihaela Truşcă[2(✉)]

[1] Erasmus University Rotterdam, Burgemeester Oudlaan 50, 3062 PA Rotterdam,
The Netherlands
frasincar@ese.eur.nl
[2] Bucharest University of Economic Studies, 010374 Bucharest, Romania
maria.trusca@csie.ase.ro

Abstract. The continuously expanding digital possibilities, increasing number of social media platforms, and growing interest of companies in online marketing increase the importance of Aspect-Based Sentiment Analysis (ABSA). ABSA focuses on predicting the sentiment of an aspect in a text. In an ideal scenario, we would have labeled data for every existing domain, but acquiring annotated training data is costly. Transfer learning resolves this issue by building models that can be employed in different domains. The proposed work extends the state-of-the-art LCR-Rot-hop++ model for ABSA with the methodology of Domain Adversarial Training (DAT) in order to create a deep learning adaptable cross-domain structure, called the DAT-LCR-Rot-hop++. The major advantage of the DAT-LCR-Rot-hop++ is the fact that it does not require any labeled target domain data. The results are obtained for six different domain combinations with testing accuracies ranging from 37% up until 77%, showing both the limitations and benefits of this approach. Once DAT is able to find the similarities between domains, it produces good results, but if the domains are too distant, it is not capable of generating domain-invariant features.

Keywords: Aspect-Based Sentiment Classification · Transfer learning · Adversarial Training

1 Introduction

Ever since the introduction of the first social media platform, Six Degrees in 1997 [10], people have communicated via digital platforms. By last year, over 3.7 billion people, which accounts for 48% of the world population, have exchanged information on social media [29]. Due to the continuously growing society of Web users, more companies are becoming aware of the essential role that social media plays in brand image. The increase in users has expanded the amount of opinionated messages, which are valuable if correctly analysed.

Aspect-Based Sentiment Analysis (ABSA) classifies a person's feeling towards specific aspects [30]. ABSA is concerned with target extraction (TE),

R. Chbeir et al. (Eds.): WISE 2022, LNCS 13724, pp. 21–37, 2022.
https://doi.org/10.1007/978-3-031-20891-1_3

aspect detection (AD), and target sentiment classification (SC) [26]. This paper concentrates on the last task, SC, classifying the user's sentiment with respect to the aspects, and is called Aspect-Based Sentiment Classification (ABSC) [2]. As an example, we provide the sentence "the atmosphere and service were terrible, but the food was good". In this case, the "atmosphere", "service", and "food" are all *target words* and "terrible" and "good" are the expressions that give *context* to these target words to be able to label the targets as positive, neutral, or negative. As one can notice, the context around the target words is essential to capture the explicit aspect sentiments.

There are multiple practical applications of ABSC. By evaluating and deciding which features need improvement, a company can apply specific enhancements to their products, efficiently improving their customer services. At the same time, social media platforms such as Facebook and Twitter can implement ABSC on tweets and messages, and sell this valuable information to the marketing department of multinationals. In addition, financial firms can apply ABSC to forecast the feelings of financial individuals towards the economic market and thereby predict future stock movements. This would have been extremely beneficial for Melvin Capital before the whole GameStop phenomena at Reddit and might have prevented enormous losses [3]. Last, knowing the opinion of previous customers can help potential clients make better-informed buying decisions.

An issue that has gained much attention recently is the limited availability of labeled data. Generating new labeled data for specific domains is expensive, time-consuming, and requires manual labour. In order to decrease the dependence on labeled data, transfer learning, also called cross-domain learning, is a valuable solution [20]. This approach concentrates on training a model on a related source domain and then predicting for a different target domain. Several state-of-the-art cross-domain models rely on Domain-Adversarial Neural Networks (DANN) introduced in [8]. These neural networks are applied on diverse tasks, ranging from textual entailment analysis [14] to image classification [39]. However, little research is available on ABSA using Domain-Adversarial Training (DAT). To our knowledge, there is limited research on training domain-invariant features for Aspect-Based Sentiment Classification (ABSC) using DANN. Prior methods for sentiment classification apply a Support Vector Machine (SVM) [21] in order to predict the sentiments, but due to its shortcomings, this system was replaced by knowledge-based models [28] and deep learning algorithms [15]. Whereas the deep learning methods are flexible, knowledge-based models require more manual labour, but achieve better results [18]. Since a combination of both approaches benefits from the advantages of both solutions, several researchers merge the methods into a hybrid model [31,34].

The proposed methodology of this paper is based on the hybrid HAABSA++ model proposed in [32], a state-of-the-art ABSC approach that produces excellent results for the commonly used SemEval 2015 [23] and 2016 [24] data sets, attaining a classification accuracy of 81.7% and 87.0%, respectively. Nevertheless, our study focuses on the development of a neural network that can classify texts on multiple different domains. For this reason, the knowledge-based ontology part of the HAABSA++ approach is eliminated, leaving the LCR-Rot-hop++ model based on [42]. This model is expanded by applying the structure of DAT as proposed by [8]. More specifically, the neural network is trained concurrently on labeled instances of a source domain and unlabeled instances from a target domain. We call the newly established system Domain Adversarial Training LCR-Rot-hop++, abbreviated as DAT-LCR-Rot-hop++. All source code and data can be retrieved from https://github.com/jorisknoester/DAT-LCR-Rot-hop-PLUS-PLUS.

The main contribution of this research on the current literature is the capability of predicting aspect-based sentiment classifications on target aspects without requiring annotated target data by employing DANN. Following the general DANN approach, this paper uses both labeled source and unlabeled target domain aspects to obtain domain indiscriminative representations. To the best of our knowledge, there is limited research on extending an advanced neural network as LCR-Rot-hop++ for ABSC with DANN in a cross-domain setting.

The rest of this paper is structured as follows. First, Sect. 2 gives the relevant literature concerned with ABSC, the different components of the LCR-Rot-hop++ model, and the ideas behind transfer learning. Second, Sect. 3 provides a short description of the data together with a couple of descriptive statistics. Third, Sect. 4 concentrates on the methodology of this research for which the results are reported in Sect. 5. Last, Sect. 6 provides our conclusion and suggestions for future work.

2   Related Work

ABSC is concerned with classifying a person's sentiment towards specific aspects in a sentence. One of the first works on sentiment analysis is presented in [22] and sentiment analysis has been a hot topic ever since. While the traditional methods were mainly developed based on knowledge-based systems providing higher prediction scores for domain-specific documents [18], the more recent ones tend to rely more on deep learning solutions. Despite being considered alternative solutions, in [36] it is observed that the two approaches are in fact complementary. Consecutively, a hybrid method which incorporates both the domain ontology and a deep learning neural network is introduced in [27]. After several additional improvements, this has resulted in the HAABSA++ method [32].

HAABSA++ method has two steps so that if the ontology is unable to provide reliable results, the LCR-Rot-hop++ neural network is used as a backup. As the topic of our work is transfer learning, we focus only on the neural network. LCR-Rot-hop++ is actually a bi-directional Long Short-Term Memory (Bi-LSTM) model accompanied by an attention. This attention layer is able to put focus on specific parts of a sentence, thereby limiting the influence of the less important words. On top of this attention layer, a hierarchical attention layer is employed, enabling the model to process the text on sentence-level, bringing together the local sentence representations. The last component of the LCR-Rot-hop++ model is its rotary system that increases the interaction between targets and contexts by sharing information in order to capture the most indicative sentiment words.

Transfer learning [20] is a machine learning technique that focuses on storing information from one data set and applying this knowledge on another. Because obtaining annotated data is costly and time-consuming, new models must be developed to provide reliable results for multiple domains. The variety of methods of transfer learning is continuously expanding. One of the proposed solutions focuses on freezing the first layers of an LSTM neural network [4]. This approach is based on the fact that the source domain contains valuable universal information and higher layer neurons tend to specialize more towards the target domain, while the lower hidden layers generate more common word features [37]. A state-of-the-art method, BertMasker [38] uses the idea of masking [6] for their BERT Base network. BertMasker is able to mask domain-related words. This transforms the remaining sentence text to be domain-invariant, but at the same time still maintains its most sentiment-explicit words. Another solution scientists developed is a domain adapting network by creating counterfactual features [13]. These counterfactual depictions reduce the inductive bias of the source domain. The designed positive (negative) counterfactuals bridge the dimensional gap between the positive (negative) classified instances of the source and target domain. Different from the previous works, in this research we apply the methodology of Generative Adversarial Networks (GAN). This last solution is introduced in [9] and has shown superior performance in a broad range of scientific areas, such as image classification [5], event detection [12], and textual cross-domain sentiment classification [41]. Applying the logic of GAN, DANN is introduced in [7]. A DANN model is able to perform machine learning tasks on unlabeled target domain data, while trained on a labeled source domain with a relatively similar distribution, both in terms of polarity distribution and batch size [7]. The advantage that one does not need annotated target data makes DANN very valuable for future cross-domain deep learning problems and is therefore an important contribution to the existing machine learning techniques.

3 Data

In this paper, two different data sets are used. These are the Semantic Evaluation (SemEval) 2014 [25], and the Amazon/LibraryThing (ALT) 2019 [17]. SemEval 2014 includes information about the restaurant and laptop domain, and ALT contains the data for the book domain. The reviews of the data sets are divided into single sentences, consisting of one or more aspects and sentimental context words, which are used to classify the polarities (positive, neutral, or negative). The partitioning of the data into a training and test set is done as follows. The aspects are divided into 80% training and 20% testing. The training set consists of 80% pure training and 20% validation to compute the optimal values for the hyperparameters. The results of the split into training and test data are presented in Table 1.

Table 1. The distribution of the aspect sentiment polarities of the three domains.

	Restaurant		Laptop		Book	
	Train	Test	Train	Test	Train	Test
Positive	60.1%	65.1%	42.7%	52.4%	25.8%	32.3%
Neutral	17.7%	17.5%	19.8%	26.2%	63.1%	57.1%
Negative	22.2%	17.4%	37.5%	21.4%	11.1%	10.6%
Total	3600	1122	2250	701	2700	804

In terms of data pre-processing, the same approach is applied as introduced in [35] and [42]. The implicitly opinionated review sentences contain a sentiment, but the aspect term is missing. This makes it impossible to perform ABSC using the LCR-Rot-hop++ model. In addition to this, it could occur that an aspect has conflicting sentiments. This happens when there is both negative and positive context towards an aspect. Both the conflicting sentiment and the implicitly opinionated sentences are removed from the datasets.

DAT-LCR-Rot-hop++ requires aspects from two domains to go through the model. These domains are defined as the source domain and the target domain. Only the source domain instances have a sentiment label attached to them. As a result, during training, the aspects of the source domain consist of two labels, the domain class, d, and, the sentiment category, y, while the instances of the target domain only contain a domain class. For testing, the polarity labels of the target domain aspects are determined in order to evaluate the performance of DAT-LCR-Rot-hop++. Our proposed model is concurrently trained on one source and one target domain to obtain domain-invariant features. Results are presented for six different domain combinations, being restaurant-laptop, restaurant-book, laptop-restaurant, laptop-book, book-restaurant, and book-laptop. As an example, the restaurant-laptop model means that the restaurant data set is the source domain and the laptop data set is the target domain. When training is finished, the test instances of the target domain with sentiment labels are fed into the model for evaluation. The performance of DAT-LCR-Rot-hop++ is analysed according to its predicting sentiment accuracy of the target test aspects.

4 Framework

A GAN model [9] generally consists of two additional elements on top of the neural feature extractor, which is the LCR-Rot-hop++ model in this paper. The feature extractor transforms an input sentence to a vector representation that is ought to capture the important characteristics of the sentence. The other two extra elements are the generator and discriminator. A visual representation of our neural network is shown in Fig. 1.

The DAT method introduced in [7] is able to adapt to target domains without any labeled target data. This is done by generating deep features that are

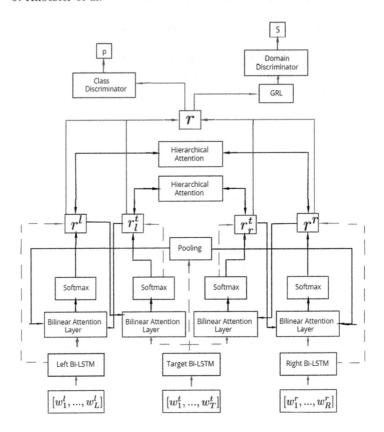

Fig. 1. A visualisation of the LCR-Rot-hop++ model. (Color figure online)

discriminative for the main learning classifying task by using the labeled sentiments of the source domain. This method ensures that these representations are invariant to shifts between the source and target domain in order to be domain in-discriminative by using the domain class of both the source and target domain. The proposed DANN solution is revisited in [8], which provides a more detailed and elaborate description of the mathematics behind the system.

The change to the GAN network in order to conform to a DANN model means replacing the generator with a Gradient Reversal Layer (GRL). GRL aims to make the task of the domain discriminator as hard as possible, which is the direct connection to GAN. In DAT-LCR-Rot-hop++, the loss of the domain discriminator is passed through GRL, which reverses the gradient before back-propagation into the feature extractor. This causes the hidden layers of LCR-Rot-hop++ to react by constructing features which will not be recognised as a certain domain by the domain discriminator. This process continues until at some point, the word vectors are completely domain-invariant, which causes the domain discriminator to be unable of distinguishing the source and target domain in the shared feature representations. The rest of this section is structured as follows. Section 4.1 describes the structure of our proposed model and Sect. 4.2 presents the training procedure for our model.

4.1   Structure

The main difference to the original LCR-Rot-hop++ model is the removal of the MLP output layer and its replacement by a domain adversarial component. After the context and target representations are concatenated into r, produced by the feature extractor, this vector is passed into two standard feed-forward MLPs, which are the class discriminator and the domain discriminator. First, the domain discriminator aims to correctly classify the domain of r. The predicted domain is given by s. Classifying the domain is a binary problem with $s = 0$ for source and $s = 1$ for target domain labels. Next, the class discriminator uses a softmax function to compute the probabilities of the sentiment of the aspect, resulting in a 1×3 output vector, p. The polarity that has the largest probability will be chosen as the final sentiment. The sigmoid function is used for the domain prediction because it shows good performance for examining binary cases and is applied by multiple researches in domain discriminators [11,40]. The DAT component is visualised by the dark purple solid arrows in Fig. 1.

The objective is reducing the error term of both the domain discriminator, denoted as $L_d(\theta_f, \theta_d)$, and the class discriminator (sentiment discriminator), denoted as $L_c(\theta_f, \theta_c)$. Here, θ represents the parameters of the feature extractor (LCR-Rot-hop++ without original MLP), the domain discriminator, and the class discriminator, defined by the underscores f, d, and c, respectively. Hence, the objection function to optimise is:

$$\min_{\theta} L_{c,d}(\theta_f, \theta_c, \theta_d) = L_d(\theta_f, \theta_d) + L_c(\theta_f, \theta_c). \tag{1}$$

However, as previously described, the GRL tries to fool the domain discriminator. After the domain is predicted and its parameters, θ_d, are updated, the loss is back-propagated into the feature extractor to change the weights accordingly. But this loss first passes through the GRL, which reverses the gradient by multiplying it with $-\lambda$ in order to hinder the performance of the domain discriminator. The reversing of the gradient forces the hidden layers of the LCR-Rot-hop++ to respond by adjusting their weights in the exact opposite way as desired by the domain discriminator, hereby making the task of the domain classifier more difficult. As a result, the features become more domain indiscriminative. This process leads to the following adjusted loss function:

$$\min_{\theta} L'_{c,d}(\theta_f, \theta_c, \theta_d) = -\lambda L_d(\theta_f, \theta_d) + L_c(\theta_f, \theta_c), \tag{2}$$

$$L_d(\theta_f, \theta_d) = -\sum_{i=1}^{N} d_i * log(s_i) + \pi_d * ||\theta_d||^2, \tag{3}$$

$$L_c(\theta_f, \theta_c) = -\sum_{i=1}^{n} y_i * log(p_i) + \pi_c * (||\theta_f||^2 + ||\theta_c||^2). \tag{4}$$

Here d_i refers to the actual domain class and y_i represents the real polarity. s_i is the predicted domain and p_i is the predicted sentiment. π represents the L2-regularisation term for the class and domain discriminator with underscore c and d, respectively. Last, n equals the source domain sample size and N is the total sample size of the source and target domain data combined. As described, both the source and target aspects are fed into the domain discriminator and only the source instances are passed into the class discriminator. As one can notice, this function is now minimised when the loss of the domain discriminator is maximised. This min-max situation resolves to:

$$\hat{\theta}_d = argmax_{\theta_d} L'_{c,d}(\hat{\theta}_f, \hat{\theta}_c, \theta_d) \tag{5}$$

$$(\hat{\theta}_f, \hat{\theta}_c) = argmin_{\theta_f, \theta_c} L'_{c,d}(\theta_f, \theta_c, \hat{\theta}_d) \tag{6}$$

At this saddle point, the parameters of the domain discriminator, θ_d (Eq. 3), minimise the domain classification error. Secondly, θ_c and θ_f are computed to optimise Eq. 2 by minimising the sentiment prediction loss and maximising the domain classification error. The hyperparameter λ regulates the balance and trade-off between both goals.

The original DANN paper [7] implements Stochastic Gradient Descent (SGD) optimisation. However, the state-of-the-art image classifying model proposed in [19] shows that utilising the faster momentum method [16] instead of SGD also produce accurate results. In each iteration, the parameters of the neural network will be updated according to this method:

$$v_t \longleftarrow \gamma * v_{t-1} + \eta * \nabla_{\theta_k} L(\theta_k) \tag{7}$$

$$\theta_k \longleftarrow \theta_k - v_t. \tag{8}$$

Here, the hyperparameters are the learning rate, η, and momentum factor, γ. In addition, the parameter θ_k represents the weights and biases for the domain discriminator, the feature extractor, and the class discriminator, with $k = d$, $k = f$, and $k = c$, respectively. Last, L represents the corresponding loss function.

4.2   Training Procedure

After constructing the feature representations by the feature extractor, both the source and target domain aspects are passed into the domain discriminator. But, only the source instances are fed into the class discriminator. In our research, the aspects of the target domain also contain a sentiment polarity, but this information is not used in the training and remains unknown to the model up until the moment of testing. The performance of the DAT-LCR-Rot-hop++ is evaluated based on this testing accuracy. The benefit of being able to employ a model, which is trained only on the labels of a source domain, on a target domain gives the DANN approach an advantage over other methods.

The weights and biases are improved using the combined loss function, given by Eq. 2. This equation includes the $-\lambda$ multiplication in order to create senti-ment discriminative and domain indiscriminate features. The domain discrimina-tor uses ascending gradient to maximise this loss function, whereas the feature extractor and the class discriminator use descending gradient to minimise it. The exact training procedure is shown in Algorithm 1. The stopping condition is $max(acc_{t-1}, acc_{t-2}) - acc_{t-3} > \epsilon$, which specifies that if the maximum of the accuracy of the previous epoch and the epoch before minus the loss of three epochs ago is larger than ϵ continue with training. In other words, we continue if there is still a significant improvement.

Algorithm 1. Training procedure of Domain-Adversarial Learning

---

$\epsilon = 0.50\%$
while stopping condition is not met do **do**
    for each epoch **do**
        for each iteration i **do**
    – Sample approximately identical percentage batch of source domain, $S(x_i, y_i, d_i)$, and target, $T(x_i, y_i, d_i)$, data. n denotes the source domain batch size and N is the total batch size (source and domain combined).
    – Feed input into feature extractor to obtain instance representations (r).
    – Pass both $S(x_i, y_i, d_i)$ and $T(x_i, y_i, d_i)$ into domain discriminator and forecast the actual domain d_i. The predicted domain is defined as s_i. Afterwards update the parameters of the discriminator, θ_d, according to the loss function with ascending gradient:

$$\nabla_{\theta_d} [-\lambda(-\frac{1}{N} \sum_{i=1}^{N} d_i * \log(s_i) + \pi_d * ||\theta_d||^2)]$$

    – Last, feed $S(x_i, y_i, d_i)$ in class discriminator and predict the real label, y_i. The predicted sentiment is represented by p_i. Finally, adjust the parameters of both the feature extractor, θ_f, and sentiment classifier, θ_c, using the previously estimated domain discriminator parameters, $\hat{\theta}_d$, with descending gradient:

$$\nabla_{\theta_f, \theta_c} [-\lambda(-\frac{1}{N} \sum_{i=1}^{N} d_i * \log(s_i) + \pi_d * ||\theta_d||^2]) +$$

$$-\frac{1}{n} \sum_{i=1}^{n} y_i * \log(p_i) + \pi_f * (||\theta_f||^2 + ||\theta_c||^2)]$$

        end for
    end for
end while

The other hyperparameters besides λ in DAT-LCR-Rot-hop++ are the learning rates, η_k, the momentum terms, γ_k, the L2-regularisation terms, π_k, and the dropout rate. $k = d$ for the domain discriminator and $k = c$ for the feature extractor and class discriminator. First, η determines the rate at which the momentum optimiser converges. In addition, γ determines the influence of past gradient values on the current instance. Furthermore, π reduces overfitting. Fourth, as previously described, λ is a parameter that balances the trade-off between the discriminative objectives of the class and domain discriminator. Last, the dropout probability regulates the number of layer outputs to be randomly dropped from the network in order to prevent overfitting.

Because the dropout rate does not differ between the methods proposed in [32] and [33], this variable is kept at 0.3 in this research. The remaining hyperparameters (η_k, γ_k, π_k, and λ) are determined by a Tree-structured Parzen Estimator (TPE), which replaces the distribution of the initial observations with a non-parametric distribution by applying a threshold that splits the observations based on different densities [1].

As in the research performed in [32] and [33], the dimension of the word embeddings, $1 \times d$, is equal to 1×768. For convenience, the number of nodes in the Bi-LSTMs, bilinear, and hierarchical attention layer are the same as in [32]. These are 300, 600, and 600, respectively. The number of hidden layers and cells in both the class and domain discriminator is optimised by TPE. The weights of the layers are initialised randomly using a normal distribution with a zero mean. The biases are set to zero at the start.

After the hyperparameters are initialised, DAT-LCR-Rot-hop++ is trained on the training set. The sentiment accuracy of the validation set is used to decide which combination of hyperparameters achieves the best performance. We decided to let the program run 15 times for each source-target domain combination with different settings for the structure and the hyperparameters. Each run includes 50 epochs. The hyperparameter fine-tuning occurs twice. In the first step, λ is excluded, because we want to show the effect of λ on the cross-domain performance of the model. A higher λ should increase the domain-invariance of the features. As a result, λ will first be set to a value of 1.0 [8] in order to find the optimal values for the other parameters. After that the influence of λ is analysed, all hyperparameters, including λ, are fine-tuned to define the best possible configuration. This setting is applied for the final training optimisation with a maximum of 200 epochs.

5   Evaluation

In Sect. 5.1, we first describe the influence of λ on the performance of DAT-LCR-Rot-hop++. Then in Sect. 5.2, the results for the final optimisation are shown.

5.1   Impact of λ

First, the optimal number of hidden layers and neurons together with the values for the hyperparameters are computed. DAT-LCR-Rot-hop++ is run for 7 incrementing values of λ with these settings, starting from 0.5 up until 1.1 with a step of 0.1 for each domain combination (Fig. 2). The impact of the balance hyperparameter λ is visualised by the six graphs that follow in this section. In these graphs, the dark blue line represents the labeling accuracies of the test set of the target domain, while the light orange line shows the base performance when the majority group of the test sample was selected. The model uses a maximum of 50 epochs.

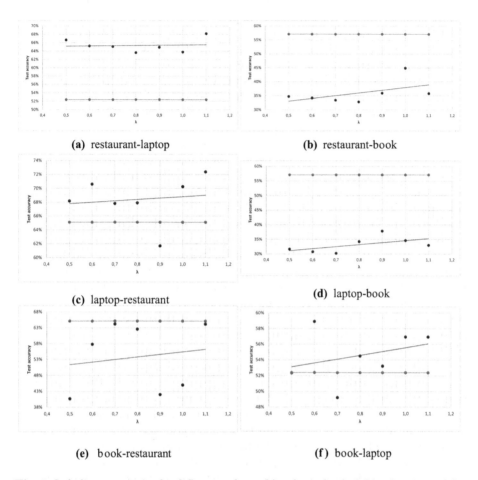

(a) restaurant-laptop

(b) restaurant-book

(c) laptop-restaurant

(d) laptop-book

(e) book-restaurant

(f) book-laptop

Fig. 2. Labeling accuracies for different values of λ, where the dark blue line is used for the target domain classification by our model and the light orange line for the target domain classification by the majority classifier. (Color figure online)

When analysing Fig. 2a and 2c, we observe that the classifying accuracy for the restaurant-laptop and laptop-restaurant domain combination is significantly higher than for the other four. Since the similarities between laptops and restaurants do not seem more prevalent than those between books and laptops, this might come across as a surprising result. However, both the laptop and restaurant domain are taken from the SemEval 2014 dataset [25] while the book domain is retrieved from the ALT 2019 [17]. First of all, these datasets share common context and target text with words such as "service" and "quality". Whereas the ALT 2019 dataset contains these target words 6 and 0 times, respectively, the words occur 59 and 85 times in the laptop set and 420 and 85 times in the restaurant domain, respectively. In addition, the (digital) language might have changed throughout these 5 years. Last, the fraction of neutral aspects in the book data test set is significantly higher than the neutral percentage in the training sets of both the restaurant and laptop domain with a percentage of 63.1 as compared to 17.7, and 19.8, respectively. This causes emotional phrases, for example "awesome", to appear 5 times in the book domain as compared to 30 and 16 times in the laptop and restaurant domain, respectively. On these grounds, it is expected that the predicting score of the book domain in combination with either laptop or restaurant will result in lower scores compared to laptop-restaurant or restaurant-laptop.

Furthermore, the accuracy of book as a target domain is worse than applying book as a source domain. Because each domain has a disproportionate training set, it causes the neurons of the model to start with predicting the sentiment that occurs most often, especially in the early iterations. So, for both the restaurant and laptop domain this results in predicting a positive sentiment, which leads to a low score for the book target domain. On the other hand, using book as a source domain does lead to acceptable performance. Not surprisingly, most neutral aspects are correctly classified in the book-restaurant and book-laptop combinations, with an average accuracy of 65% and 81%, respectively. Next, DAT-LCR-Rot-hop++ focuses on the second largest polarity percentage, the positive sentiments, which is the majority in both the restaurant and laptop domain. The drawback of this is the bad score for the negative polarities with an average accuracy of 3.2% and 0%, respectively.

When looking at Fig. 2a, we observe a scattered graph with an almost flat regression line. Accordingly, the coefficient of the OLS slope is 0.61, which means that increasing λ with 1.0 increases the testing accuracy by 61%. The same holds for Fig. 2c, which has a slope of 2.04. One reason for this could be the previously mentioned overlap between the restaurant and laptop domain, thereby decreasing the difficulty of the cross-domain task and hence, making λ less important. Besides this result, the restaurant-laptop combination does beat the base performance line at 52% with an average of 65%. The same applies to the laptop-restaurant for which the observation at $\lambda = 0.9$ appears to be an outlier. In contrast to the flat regression lines of the restaurant-laptop and laptop-restaurant, restaurant-book depicts a clear positive linear trend with a slope of 9.73 in Fig. 2b. The same applies to the graph in Fig. 2d, which has a slope of 6.91, showing the effect of λ.

As previously stated, employing book as the target domain produces a poor labeling accuracy. Especially, the positive outlier in Fig. 2b is an observation that proves the effect of the disproportionate data sets. Only during this run, DAT-LCR-Rot-hop++ was capable of predicting neutral sentiments correctly, which results in a neutral accuracy of 26%. As compared to a maximum of 5% for the other runs with book as a target domain. The competence to classify the neutral aspects precisely immediately leads to a significantly better performance with an accuracy of 45%, as compared to approximately 35%. The disproportionate sets cause DAT-LCR-Rot-hop++ to overfit on the training set and focus only on the major two polarities, resulting in low scores for the restaurant-book and laptop-book combination. Whereas there is a clear ascending performance for the training set, reaching percentages up until 92%, the maximum accuracy of the target domain is reached after approximately 100 epochs. The statistic then moves around this number with some large outliers into both directions, but never really improving. After some time, the accuracy starts to drop. The model becomes too much specified towards the information of the training set.

Both book-restaurant and book-laptop in Fig. 2e and 2f, provide an ascending line with a slope coefficient of 7.04 and 4.88, respectively. However, the data points in Fig. 2e are scattered, causing a standard deviation of 10%. Therefore, this positive relationship might be questioned in this case.

5.2   Final Optimisation

The final values of the hyperparameters for the final optimisation with 200 iterations are defined in Table 2. Each domain combination is tested for the final prediction using these parameter settings. The results are shown in Table 3. As expected, the accuracies improve for each source and target domain model as compared to the previous run with 50 epochs. The training label accuracy increases from 84% up until 92% for the book-laptop domain. In addition, the maximum testing accuracy of 80% for the restaurant-laptop is a 9 percentage points improvement from the previous 71%. The ratios of correctly predicted polarities follow the previously seen distribution.

Table 2. Values for hyperparameter optimisation.

Hyperparam	re-la	re-bo	la-re	la-bo	bo-re	bo-la
lr_d	0.01	0.03	0.03	0.01	0.01	0.03
$lr_{c,f}$	0.005	0.005	0.03	0.01	0.005	0.03
mom_d	0.90	0.85	0.80	0.90	0.85	0.90
$mom_{c,f}$	0.90	0.90	0.85	0.85	0.85	0.85
$l2 - term$	0.001	0.001	0.001	0.001	0.001	0.0001
structure	2400-600	2400-0	2400-600	2400-600	2400-0	2400-600
λ	1.1	0.8	1.1	0.6	1.1	0.6

"re", "la", and "bo" represent restaurant, laptop, and book domain, respectively

The performance of the restaurant-laptop domain increased significantly, which results in a total test accuracy of 77%. The relevance of not requiring any labeled target data should not be underestimated when comparing it with other research, because this ability reduces labeling costs significantly. Specifically, the outcomes for the book-restaurant are promising. Both domains are not closely related in terms of sentiment distribution, but the model achieves an encouraging test accuracy of 72%, which is an improvement of 8% points

Table 3. Test accuracies for DAT-LCR-Rot-hop++ model.

	test	train	max	base	pos	neu	neg
rest-lapt	77%	87%	80%	52%	94%	38%	83%
rest-book	37%	88%	48%	57%	71%	9%	88%
lapt-rest	74%	83%	78%	65%	90%	9%	85%
lapt-book	42%	90%	52%	57%	86%	11%	72%
book-rest	72%	88%	76%	65%	78%	81%	40%
book-lapt	60%	92%	66%	52%	75%	79%	0%

"base" is the majority classifier in the target domain
test set, "pos", "neu", and "neg" are sentiment labels

as compared to the value after the previous runs. Interestingly, the fraction of correctly labeled sentiments is more balanced, instead of one polarity that is driving the results.

6   Conclusion

The prominent role of digital online media increases the relevance of ABSA, and in particular ABSC. Since obtaining labeled target data is extremely costly, new models should be developed that can be employed on a variety of domains, a concept known as transfer learning. [8] introduces a method known as DANN, which is a specification of GAN as defined by [9] for transfer learning. The major benefit of this approach is the fact that it does not need any labeled target data at all.

The state-of-the-art LCR-Rot-hop++ structure from [32] forms the basis of our proposed DAT-LCR-Rot-hop++, which adds an adversarial component based on DANN. It consists of a domain discriminator, a class discriminator, and a GRL module. The GRL module reverses the loss of the domain discriminator before back-propagation, which enforces the earlier layers to generate domain-invariant features. At the same time, the class discriminator is trained on the labels of the source domain. This results in label-discriminative features.

Increasing λ (domain invariance) improves, in general, the performance of the target, especially for domains that are distant. Furthermore, the model is not able to correctly predict the sentiments of the restaurant-book and laptop-book models. The benchmark of predicting the majority class of the test set is not reached for both domain combinations. This is the outcome of multiple factors of which the most essential one is the disproportionate data set in terms of polarity distribution of the three domains. The high percentage of neutral aspects in the book domain causes the model to perform poorly. Nevertheless, the produced models are better than a random classifier, which shows that even in these extreme conditions our approach is able to detect useful signals.

On the other hand, the accuracy score for the restaurant-laptop, laptop-restaurant, and book-restaurant all exceed 72%. So in half of the cases, DAT-LCR-Rot-hop++ is able to properly classify polarities, but it depends on which combination of domains is used. Domains with similar polarity distributions seem to benefit the most from the proposed approach.

In order to further improve our method, we propose two adaptions. The first one covers the difficulty of predicting three kinds of classes. We would like to investigate the performance of the model for only the binary case. Classifying neutral aspects appears to be a harsh task for the neural network, looking at the results, as this class is poorly represented in two out of our three domains. Our second extension includes transforming the LCR-Rot-hop++ component. In some cases, the model becomes overfitted on the training data, so a less complicated feature extractor might help prevent this. One way to reduce the complexity is to reduce the dimensionality of the internal network layers.

References

1. Bergstra, J., Bardenet, R., Bengio, Y., Kégl, B.: Algorithms for hyper-parameter optimization. In: 25th Annual Conference on Neural Information Processing Systems (NIPS 2011), pp. 2546–2554. Curran Associates (2011)
2. Brauwers, G., Frasincar, F.: A survey on aspect-based sentiment classification. ACM Comput. Surv. **1**, 35 (2022)
3. Chapman, B.: GameStop: reddit users claim victory as \$13bn hedge fund closes position, accepting huge losses (2021). https://www.independent.co.uk/news/business/gamestop-share-price-reddit-hedge-fund-melvin-capital-b1793543.html
4. Chen, Y., Tong, Z., Zheng, Y., Samuelson, H., Norford, L.: Transfer learning with deep neural networks for model predictive control of HVAC and natural ventilation in smart buildings. J. Clean. Prod. **254**, 119866 (2020)
5. Ciresan, D., Meier, U., Schmidhuber, J.: Multi-column deep neural networks for image classification. In: 2012 IEEE Conference on Computer Vision and Pattern Recognition (CVPR 2012), vol. 1, pp. 3642–3649. IEEE Computer Society (2012)
6. Devlin, J., Chang, K., Lee, K., Huang, D., Toutanova, K.: BERT: pre-training of deep bidirectional transformers for language understanding. In: 2019 Conference of the North American Chapter of the Association for Computational Linguistics (NAACL-HLT 2019), pp. 4171–4186. ACL (2019)
7. Ganin, Y., Lempitsky, V.: Unsupervised domain adaption by backpropagation. In: 32nd International Conference on Machine Learning (ICML 2015), vol. 37, pp. 1180–1189. PMLR (2015)
8. Ganin, Y., et al.: Domain-adversarial training of neural networks. J. Mach. Learn. Res. **17**, 59:10–59:35 (2016)
9. Goodfellow, I., et al.: Generative adversarial networks. In: 28th Annual Conference on Neural Information Processing Systems (NIPS 2014), pp. 2672–2680 (2014)
10. Hendricks, D.: Complete history of social media: then and now (2013). https://smallbiztrends.com/2013/05/the-complete-history-of-social-media-infographic.html
11. Hong, W., Wang, Z., Yang, M., Yuan, J.: Conditional generative adversarial network for structured domain adaption. In: 8th IEEE International Conference on Computer Vision and Pattern Recognition (CVPR 2018), vol. 12, pp. 1335–1344. IEEE (2018)
12. Hong, Y., Zhou, W., Zhang, J., Zhu, Q., Zhou, G.: Self-regulation: employing a generative adversarial network to improve event detection. In: 56th Annual Meeting

of the Association for Computational Linguistics (ACL 2018), pp. 515–526. ACL (2018)

13. Johansson, F., Shalit, U., Sontag, D.: Learning representations for counterfactual inference. In: 33rd International Conference on Machine Learning (ICML 2016). JMLR Workshop and Conference Proceedings, vol. 48, pp. 3020–3029. JMLR (2016)

14. Kamath, S., Gupta, S., Carvalho, V.: Reversing gradients in adversarial domain adaption for question deduplication and textual entailment tasks. In: 57th Annual Meeting of the Association for Computational Linguistics (ACL 2019), pp. 5545–5550. ACL (2019)

15. Lai, S., Xu, L., Liu, K., Zhao, J.: Recurrent convolutional neural networks for text classification. In: 29th Conference on Artificial Intelligence (AAAI 2015), vol. 29, pp. 2267–2273. AAAI Press (2015)

16. Liu, C., Belkin, M.: Accelerating SGD with momentum for over-parameterized learning. In: 8th International Conference on Learning Representations (ICLR 2020). OpenReview.net (2020)

17. Álvarez-López, T., Fernández-Gavilanes, M., Costa-Montenegro, E., Bellot, P.: A proposal for book oriented aspect based sentiment analysis: comparison over domains. In: Silberztein, M., Atigui, F., Kornyshova, E., Métais, E., Meziane, F. (eds.) NLDB 2018. LNCS, vol. 10859, pp. 3–14. Springer, Cham (2018). https://doi.org/10.1007/978-3-319-91947-8_1

18. Maat, E.D., Krabben, K., Winkels, R.: Machine learning versus knowledge based classification of legal texts. In: 23rd Annual Conference on Legal Knowledge and Information Systems (JURIX 2010), vol. 223, pp. 87–96. IOS Press (2010)

19. Mauro, M., Mazzia, V., Khalil, A., Chiaberge, M.: Domain-adversarial training of self-attention based networks for land cover classification using multi-temporal sentinel-2 satellite imagery. arXiv preprint arXiv:2104.00564 (2021)

20. Pan, S., Yang, Q.: A survey on transfer learning. IEEE Trans. Knowl. Data Eng. **22**, 1345–1359 (2009)

21. Pang, B., Lee, L.: A sentimental education: sentiment analysis using subjectivity summarization based on minimum cuts. In: 42nd Annual Meeting of the Association for Computational Linguistics (ACL 2004), pp. 271–278. ACL (2004)

22. Pang, B., Lee, L., Vaithyanathan, S.: Thumbs up? Sentiment classification using machine learning techniques. In: 2002 Conference on Empirical Methods in Natural Language Processing 2002 (EMNLP 2002), pp. 79–86. ACL (2002)

23. Pontiki, M., Galanis, D., Papageorgiou, H., Androutsopoulos, I., Manandhar, S.: SemEval-2015 task 12: aspect based sentiment analysis. In: 9th International Workshop on Semantic Evaluation (SemEval 2015), pp. 486–495. ACL (2015)

24. Pontiki, M., et al.: SemEval-2016 task 5: aspect based sentiment analysis. In: 10th International Workshop on Semantic Evaluation (SemEval 2016), pp. 19–30. ACL (2016)

25. Pontiki, M., Galanis, D., Pavlopoulos, J., Papageorgiou, H., Androutsopoulos, I., Manandhar, S.: SemEval-2014 task 4: aspect based sentiment analysis. In: 8th International Workshop on Semantic Evaluation (SemEval 2014), pp. 27–35. ACL (2014)

26. Schouten, K., Frasincar, F.: Survey on aspect-level sentiment analysis. IEEE Trans. Knowl. Data Eng. **28**, 813–880 (2016)

27. Schouten, K., Frasincar, F.: Ontology-driven sentiment analysis of product and service aspects. In: Gangemi, A., et al. (eds.) ESWC 2018. LNCS, vol. 10843, pp. 608–623. Springer, Cham (2018). https://doi.org/10.1007/978-3-319-93417-4_39

28. Taboada, M., Brooke, J., Tofiloski, M., Voll, K., Stede, M.: Lexicon-based methods for sentiment analysis. Comput. Linguist. **37**, 267–307 (2011)
29. Tankovska, H.: Social media - statistics and facts (2021). https://www.statista.com/topics/1164/social-networks/
30. Thet, T., Na, J., Khoo, C.: Aspect-based sentiment analysis of movie reviews on discussion boards. J. Inf. Sci. **36**, 823–848 (2010)
31. Towell, G., Shavlik, J.: Knowledge-based artificial neural networks. Artif. Intell. **70**, 119–165 (1994)
32. Truşcă, M.M., Wassenberg, D., Frasincar, F., Dekker, R.: A hybrid approach for aspect-based sentiment analysis using deep contextual word embeddings and hierarchical attention. In: Bielikova, M., Mikkonen, T., Pautasso, C. (eds.) ICWE 2020. LNCS, vol. 12128, pp. 365–380. Springer, Cham (2020). https://doi.org/10.1007/978-3-030-50578-3_25
33. Wallaart, O., Frasincar, F.: A hybrid approach for aspect-based sentiment analysis using a lexicalized domain ontology and attentional neural models. In: Hitzler, P., et al. (eds.) ESWC 2019. LNCS, vol. 11503, pp. 363–378. Springer, Cham (2019). https://doi.org/10.1007/978-3-030-21348-0_24
34. Wang, F., Zhang, Q.: Knowledge-based neural models for microwave design. IEEE Trans. Microw. Theory Tech. **45**, 2333–2343 (1997)
35. Wang, Z., Huang, M., Zhao, L., Zhu, X.: Attention-based LSTM for aspect-level sentiment classification. In: 2016 Conference on Empirical Methods in Natural Language Processing (EMNLP 2016), pp. 606–615. ACL (2016)
36. Yanase, T., Yanai, K., Sato, M., Miyoshi, T., Niwa, Y.: bunji at SemEval-2016 task 5: neural and synctactic models of entity-attribute relationship for aspect-based sentiment analysis. In: 10th International Workshop on Semantic Evaluation (SemEval 2016), pp. 289–295. ACL (2016)
37. Yosinski, J., Clune, J., Bengio, Y., Lipson, H.: How transferable are features in deep neural networks? In: 27th Annual Conference on Neural Information Processing Systems (NIPS 2014), vol. 27, pp. 3320–3328. Curran Associates (2014)
38. Yuan, J., Zhao, Y., Qin, B., Liu, T.: Learning to share by masking the non-shared for multi-domain sentiment classification. arXiv preprint arXiv:2104.08480 (2021)
39. Zhang, W., Ouyang, W., Li, W., Xu, D.: Collaborative and adversarial network for unsupervised domain adaption. In: 2018 Conference on Computer Vision and Pattern Recognition (CVPR 2018), pp. 3801–3809. IEEE (2018)
40. Zhang, Y., Qiu, Z., Yao, T., Liu, D., Mei, T.: Fully convolutional adaption networks for semantic segmentation. In: 2018 International Conference on Computer Vision and Pattern Recognition (CVPR 2018), pp. 6810–6818. IEEE (2018)
41. Zheng, L., Zhang, Y., Wu, Y., Wei, Y., Yang, Q.: End-to-end adversarial memory network for cross-domain sentiment classification. In: 26th International Joint Conference on Artificial Intelligence (IJCAI 2017), pp. 2237–2243. IJCAI (2017)
42. Zheng, S., Xia, R.: Left-center-right separated neural network for aspect-based sentiment analysis with rotatory attention. arXiv preprint arXiv:1802.00892 (2018)

Social Community Evolution Analysis and Visualization in Open Source Software Projects

Jierui Zhang, Liang Wang[(✉)], Zhiwen Zheng, and Xianping Tao

State Key Laboratory for Novel Software Technology, Nanjing University,
Nanjing 210023, China
{jieruizhang,zwzheng}@smail.nju.edu.cn, {wl,txp}@nju.edu.cn

Abstract. The importance of social communities around open-source software projects has been recognized. Despite that a lot of relevant research focusing on this topic, understanding the structures and dynamics of communities around open-source software projects remains a tedious and challenging task. As a result, an easily accessible and useful application that enables project developers to gain awareness of the status and development of the project communities is desirable. In this paper, we present MyCommunity, a web-based online application system to automatically extract communication-based community structures from social coding platforms such as GitHub. Based on the detected community structures, the system analyzes and visualizes the community evolution history of a project with a set of semantic-rich events, and quantify the strength of community evolution with respect to different events with a series of indexes. Built-in support to quantitative analysis and machine learning tasks based on the quantitative evolutionary events are provided. We demonstrate the usefulness of the system by presenting its ability in predicting project success or failure with the community evolution features. The results suggest the system achieves a prediction accuracy of 88.5% with commonly available machine learning models.

Keywords: Web-based application · Open source community analysis · Community evolution

1 Introduction

Open source software (OSS) developers form implicit collaborative social networks [2], i.e., developer social networks (DSNs) [10], when working together on social coding platforms like GitHub. In [10], the authors discover that community evolution events originally proposed for general social networks (GSNs) [13,15], including community *split*, *shrink*, *merge*, *expand*, *extinct*, and *emerge*, are also feasible in understanding community evolution in DSNs. They also discover that events of community evolution in DSNs correspond to the developing stages and important events in OSS projects. As a result, keeping aware of the structure and dynamics of DSNs around OSS projects is important for OSS maintainers due

R. Chbeir et al. (Eds.): WISE 2022, LNCS 13724, pp. 38–45, 2022.
https://doi.org/10.1007/978-3-031-20891-1_4

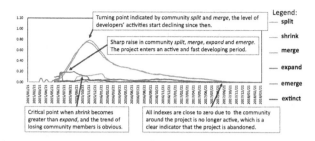

Fig. 1. Quantified community evolution events over time for GitHub project *google/material-design-lite*, with a moving average over 20 data points. It can be seen that the proposed approach can provide useful information about the dynamics of communities around the project, as well as the project's status. Better viewed in color.

to the strong correlation between the health of social communities and project viability [1, 3, 8–10].

In summary, this paper makes the following contributions. And our application can easily extend to commits and PRs.

1. We present a web-based online application called MyCommunity for community evolution analysis for OSS projects that implements a complete workflow from data collection, community detection, evolution analysis, and visualization, with high usability and integrity.
2. We extend existing approaches for community evolution event detection and provide quantitative analysis to the strength of community evolution with respect to the events.
3. We demonstrate the usefulness of the analysis results, and the functions of the proposed application in supporting intelligent analysis for OSS projects by predicting project success and failure with the quantified community evolution events and machine learning techniques.

2 Related Work

Existing studies show that community evolution in developer social networks and general social networks can be described by a set of semantic-rich events [10, 13, 15]. Community detection algorithms such as the Clauset-Newman-Moore (CNM) algorithm [14], clique percolation method (CPM) [15], etc, are proposed to discover communities inside social networks. Despite that community evolution can potentially provide valuable insights about the current and future status of OSS projects [10, 12], performing community evolution analysis requires a lot of tedious work.

With respect to web-based systems, there are many applications and services developed to understand OSS projects. INFOX [17] is a web-based application to automatically identify non-merged features in forks and generate an overview of fork status of the project. OSR [11] is a visualization application to identify OSS developers' practices and generate biographies for them. However, applications that focus on understanding community evolution in OSS projects are rare. In this paper, we present the MyCommunity application to fill the niche and bridge the gap between community evolution research [10,13,15] and web-based services for OSS projects.

3   System Architecture

This section shows MyCommunity's architecture (see Fig. 2) which consists of three components. Each part is described as follows.

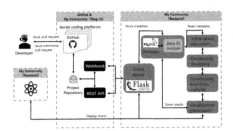

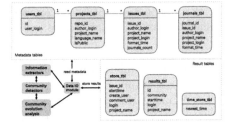

Fig. 2. Overview of system architecture.

Fig. 3. Overview of database.

3.1   MyCommunity GitHub Plug-in

The third-party application has two mechanisms to obtain repository data on GitHub. The MyCommunity GitHub Plug-in, which establishes the connection between GitHub and the MyCommunity backend, is responsible for providing data and creating webhooks from GitHub. In addition, the MyCommunity GitHub plug-in gets all the data since the repository was built, and will provide a crawler function to help the application get the communication of this repository before setting up the webhook.

Users can connect our applications to different social coding platforms and databases by selecting different MyCommunity Plug-ins (see Fig. 4).

3.2   MyCommunity Backend

The backend of MyCommunity has four components: read/write data from a database, information extraction, community detection, and visualization generation (see Fig. 2). In particular, we made an image of our application based on image *tiangolo/uwsgi-nginx-flask:python3.9*[1], which can run Flask web applications in a single container with uWSGI and Nginx.

Data IO module uses a relational database to store data (see Fig. 3). The connection in the metadata table box represents the foreign key relationship.

---

[1] https://github.com/tiangolo/uwsgi-nginx-flask-docker.

Table 1. Rules to determine the evolution events of a community c detected in one time step, e.g., community i in time t (adopted from [10, 16]).

Event	Community evolution event detection
extinct	Community c has no matching community in the next step. This event marks a massive exodus of developers from the community
emerge	Community c has no matching community in the prior step. This mode marks the rise of community discussion and may also represent new issues to be discussed
split	Community c has at least two communities matched to it in the next step. Members of the community have dispersed interests and are no longer working towards a common goal
shrink	Community c has only one community matched in the next step, and the size of the matching community is less than the size of $c^{\dagger}$. This event represents a shrinking community size and users are attracted to other communities
merge	Community c has at least two matching communities in the previous time step. This mode represents the integration of multiple communities, perhaps users have a common interest or solve a shared bug
expand	Community c only matches with one community in the previous step, and the size of the prior community is less than the size of c. This event represents an increase in the size of the community and new members are drawn into the community

$\dagger$ We modify the rule in [10] to match c with communities detected in the next step when determining community *shrink*. With this modification, there are even numbers of evolution events potentially associated with a community when matching communities in the previous and next time steps, respectively— community *extinct*, *split*, and *shrink* associated with communities in the next step, and community *emerge*, *merge*, and *expand* by matching communities in the previous step.

We use the user's login name and project name to uniquely identify a project, and use *issue_id* to uniquely identify an issue of the same project. Information extraction module, prepare data for subsequent community detection, can extract information from metadata and write results to the database using the Data IO module. In visualization generation module, the results of the calculation will be formatted in the form required for the presentation of the chart.

The algorithm in the application is described as follows.

Community Detection: Community detection uses the extension of the Clauset-Newman-Moore (CNM) algorithm [4, 14], which can be used on weighted graphs using the strength of connections between the nodes indicated by edge weights. Input is all communication content in a time slice of a project for detection.

We apply an overlapping sliding window with a length of a month that slides temporally forward one week at a time. Then we obtain a series of segments $S = \langle s_1, s_2, \ldots, s_T \rangle$. We then use a weighted, undirected graph $G_t = \langle V_t, E_t, U_t, W_t \rangle$ to model the structure of a developer social network (DSN) in the segment $s_t \in S$, where V_t includes all the participants of conversations in s_t, and E_t is the set of edges representing the relationship between users in V_t. For each edge $e_{ij} \in E_t$, there is a edge weight $w_{ij} \in W_t$ that quantifies the strength of interactions between user v_i and v_j. And we assign a weight $u_i \in U_t$ to quantify the importance of user v_i.

Finally, we execute the community detection algorithm and get a set of non-overlapping communities $C_t = \{c_{t,1}, c_{t,2}, \cdots, c_{t,n}\}$ $(c_{t,i} \subseteq V_t)$ in graph G_t of the t-th snapshot.

Community Evolution Analysis: U_i^k represents the weight of the node k if it belongs to community i. And in Eq. 2, $S_{i,j}$ calculates the similarity between community i and community j.

$$U_i^k = \begin{cases} 0, k \notin c_i \\ u_i^k, k \in c_i \end{cases} \tag{1}$$

$$S_{i,j} = \frac{\sum_{k=0}^{p} max(U_i^k, U_j^k)}{min(\sum_{l=0}^{q} max(U_i^l, U_j^l), \sum_{m=0}^{r} max(U_i^m, U_j^m))} \tag{2}$$

where p is the set of the common nodes of community i and j, q and r are the node sets of the two communities before and after.

We filter out irrelevant communities by comparing $S_{i,j}$ with threshold $\varepsilon=0.3$ [10,16]. We obtained the predecessor community set $C_{prior_i}^t = \{c_{prior_i}^{t,1}, c_{prior_i}^{t,2} \cdots\cdots c_{prior_i}^{t,n}\}$ and the successor community set $C_{next_i}^t = \{c_{next_i}^{t,1}, c_{next_i}^{t,2} \cdots\cdots c_{next_i}^{t,n}\}$ of each community through the calculation of community tracer.

We adopt the six events used in [10,13,16] to determine the evolution of each community c by matching the communities detected in time steps before and after c is detected following the rules defined in Table 1. An evolutionary event vector is taken at time t-th denoted as V_t, is obtained by:

$$V_t = 0.001 * \left[\sum_{i=0}^{n} \left(P_i^t * W_{next_i}^t \right) + \sum_{j=0}^{m} \left(P_j^{t+1} * W_{prior_j}^{t+1} \right) \right] \tag{3}$$

where P_i^t is the event label of i-th community in t-th snapshot, $W_{prior_i}^t$ and $W_{next_i}^t$ represent its weight relative to its prior and post communities. Finally, the values and scales for each event are displayed inline and in pie charts, as shown in Fig. 5. We standardize all values to keep them in range $[0, 1]$.

3.3   MyCommunity Frontend

Fig. 4. The configuration page where users can: (a) list existing repositories; (b) add new repositories from a specified data source.

Fig. 5. Visualization of community evolution events with interactive charts provided by the frontend.

The frontend of our application consists of a series of HTML files returned by the backend.

There are three parts that users can operate MyCommunity directly: configuring settings, selecting a repository that you can view, and viewing the results of the analysis for a specific project.

Users can configure the owner and project name of a repository to get a convenient and unique identification (see Fig. 4). Then the application will crawl all communication information by GitHub REST API as well as waiting for a callback to be triggered. After the configuration process is completed, users can view their repository in the list of repositories and click the table item they want to check.

There are four charts on the exhibit page (see Fig. 5). We use *echarts*[2] combined with JavaScript files to generate charts. Event line charts are a higher level of abstraction of the community evolution map, quantitatively reflecting the evolutionary history of the community. We can look at the lines from two dimensions: the event proportion and the overall trend. The overall trend chart can be observed by the line chart below Fig. 5, while the event scale can be seen in the pie chart above Fig. 5. We explain an example of a project which is once active and has stopped developing, *google/material-design-lite*, in Fig. 1, and show the overall trend of the project and the continuous decline of certain indices (e.g. Continued decline in a split and merge means less active project members and reflects the continued increase in the project's risk of failure) may indicate the future success or failure of the project.

4   Predict Project Success or Failure

To demonstrate the usefulness of the proposed system, and to help developers to gain information about the future trend of their projects, we provide in our system a function to predict the success or failure of a project based on the time series of quantified community evolution events as shown in Fig. 6. As illustrated in Fig. 1, the curve trend of the project community model has some practical significance, representing certain specific events, and the occurrence of these specific times ultimately affects the success or failure of the project. We built and evaluated the model based on a dataset of 339 successful projects and 192 failed projects. We used the number of stars to measure popularity and selected some of the most popular projects from GitHub. Next we label these projects as *success* and *failure*. The failed projects are selected following the steps proposed in [7], which are projects without receiving commits for a year and declared as no longer maintained in the documents (or manually checked by authors).

First, we extract features from the sequential data for each of the community evolution events using the *tsfresh* package [6]. To filter features, we use Fisher's exact test to determine whether the feature is strongly or weakly correlated with the resulting label (based on Scalable Hypothesis tests) [5]. Additionally, we store the filtered feature dict for later use on the test set. We use the number n to denote the final count of features. For a project j, we generate a $n + 1$-dimensional vector using *tsfress*: $M_j = \left\langle f_1^j, f_2^j, \ldots, f_i^j, \ldots, f_n^j, L_j \right\rangle$, where f_i^j

---

[2] https://echarts.apache.org/zh/index.html.

Fig. 6. An example of predicting results of the future success or failure of a project.

Table 2. Accuracy of different classification models

Model	Accuracy	Precision	Recall	F1
Decision Tree Classifier	0.840 ± 0.056	0.783	0.771	0.777
Random Forest Classifier	0.885 ± 0.041	0.849	0.823	0.836
SVM	0.828 ± 0.078	0.755	0.802	0.778
K-Neighbors Classifier	0.871 ± 0.035	0.815	0.849	0.832

represents the i-th feature and L_j represents the label of the jth project. The label marks the success or failure of a given project.

Next, we use the 10-fold-cross-validation to compare and select a suitable model. Cross-validation is a resampling procedure used to evaluate machine learning models on a limited data sample. We compared the efficiency of several models (see Table 2) and finally chose Random Forest Classifier.

Finally, we evaluate the model and give the project in the application a success or failure prediction result. It can be seen that the results obtained by the random forest classifier are most consistent with the true values. The overall mean accuracy of our model is 88.5%. Precision, which is the fraction of relevant instances among the retrieved instances, is 84.9%. While recall, which is the fraction of relevant instances that were retrieved, is 82.3%. And F1 score, which is the harmonic mean of precision and recall, is 83.6%.

5   Conclusion

We introduce the MyCommunity application which is a community metrics application seamlessly integrated with GitHub to assist developers in monitoring project communication status and notify them of the probability of project success. MyCommunity's main contribution is the ability to support the quantitative and automatic analysis of how the developers evolved in the project.

Our future work involves support for a more accurate predictive model and more systematic evaluation. During the evaluation, we identified the need for further improvements in our predictions such as obtaining a larger dataset.

Acknowledgement. This work is supported by the National Key R&D Program of China under Grant No. 2018AAA0102302, the NSFC under Grant No. 62172203, and the Collaborative Innovation Center of Novel Software Technology and Industrialization.

References

1. Antwerp, M.V., Madey, G.: The importance of social network structure in the open source software developer community. In: 2010 43rd Hawaii International Conference on System Sciences (HICSS) (2010)
2. Begel, A., Khoo, Y.P., Zimmermann, T.: Codebook: discovering and exploiting relationships in software repositories. In: ACM/IEEE International Conference on Software Engineering (2010)
3. Catolino, G., Palomba, F., Tamburri, D.A., Serebrenik, A., Ferrucci, F.: Gender diversity and women in software teams: how do they affect community smells? In: 2019 IEEE/ACM 41st International Conference on Software Engineering: Software Engineering in Society (ICSE-SEIS) (2019)
4. Chakraborty, T., Dalmia, A., Mukherjee, A., Ganguly, N.: Metrics for community analysis: a survey. ACM Comput. Surv. (CSUR) **50**(4), 1–37 (2017)
5. Christ, M., Kempa-Liehr, A.W., Feindt, M.: Distributed and parallel time series feature extraction for industrial big data applications (2016)
6. Christ, M., Braun, N., Neuffer, J., Kempa-Liehr, A.W.: Time Series FeatuRe Extraction on basis of Scalable Hypothesis tests (tsfresh - a Python package). Neurocomputing **307**, 72–77 (2018)
7. Coelho, J., Valente, M.T.: Why modern open source projects fail. In: Proceedings of the 2017 11th Joint Meeting on Foundations of Software Engineering, pp. 186–196 (2017)
8. Ducheneaut, N.: Socialization in an open source software community: a socio-technical analysis. Comput. Support. Coop. Work **14**(4), 323–368 (2005)
9. Hannemann, A., Klamma, R.: Community dynamics in open source software projects: aging and social reshaping. In: Petrinja, E., Succi, G., El Ioini, N., Sillitti, A. (eds.) OSS 2013. IAICT, vol. 404, pp. 80–96. Springer, Heidelberg (2013). https://doi.org/10.1007/978-3-642-38928-3_6
10. Hong, Q., Kim, S., Cheung, S.C., Bird, C.: Understanding a developer social network and its evolution. In: 2011 27th IEEE International Conference on Software Maintenance (ICSM), pp. 323–332. IEEE (2011)
11. Jaruchotrattanasakul, T., Yang, X., Makihara, E., Fujiwara, K., Iida, H.: Open source resume (OSR): a visualization tool for presenting OSS biographies of developers. In: 2016 7th International Workshop on Empirical Software Engineering in Practice (IWESEP), pp. 57–62 (2016). https://doi.org/10.1109/IWESEP.2016.17
12. Le, Q., Panchal, J.H.: Analysis of the interdependent co-evolution of product structures and community structures using dependency modelling techniques. J. Eng. Des. **23**(10–11), 807–828 (2012)
13. Lin, Y.R., Sundaram, H., Chi, Y., Tatemura, J., Tseng, B.L.: Blog community discovery and evolution based on mutual awareness expansion. In: IEEE/WIC/ACM International Conference on Web Intelligence (WI 2007), pp. 48–56. IEEE (2007)
14. Newman, M.E.: Analysis of weighted networks. Phys. Rev. E **70**(5), 056131 (2004)
15. Palla, G., Barabási, A.L., Vicsek, T.: Quantifying social group evolution. Nature **446**(7136), 664–667 (2007)
16. Wang, L., Li, Y., Zhang, J., Tao, X.: Quantitative analysis of community evolution in developer social networks around open source software projects. arXiv preprint arXiv:2205.09935 (2022)
17. Zhou, S., Stanciulescu, S., Leßenich, O., Xiong, Y., Wasowski, A., Kästner, C.: Identifying features in forks. In: 2018 IEEE/ACM 40th International Conference on Software Engineering (ICSE), pp. 105–116. IEEE (2018)

Spatial and Temporal Issues

Hop-Constrained *s-t* Simple Path Enumeration in Billion-Scale Labelled Graphs

Xia Li[1], Kongzhang Hao[1(✉)], Zhengyi Yang[1], Xin Cao[1], Wenjie Zhang[1],
Long Yuan[2], and Xuemin Lin[3]

[1] The University of New South Wales, Sydney, Australia
{xia.li,k.hao,zhengyi.yang,xin.cao,wenjie.zhang}@unsw.edu.au
[2] Nanjing University of Science and Technology, Nanjing, China
longyuan@njust.edu.cn
[3] Shanghai Jiao Tong University, Shanghai, China

Abstract. Hop-constrained *s-t* simple path (HC-s-t path) enumeration is a fundamental problem in graph analysis. Existing solutions for this problem focus on unlabelled graphs and assume queries are issued without any label constraints. However, in many real-world applications, graphs are edge-labelled and the queries involve label constraints on the path connecting two vertices. Therefore, we study the problem of labelled hop-constrained s-t path (LHC-s-t path) enumeration in this paper. We aim to efficiently enumerate the HC-s-t paths using only edges with provided labels. To achieve this goal, we first demonstrate the existence of unnecessary computation specific to the label constraints in the state-of-the-art HC-s-t path enumeration algorithm. We then devise a novel online index to identify the fruitless exploration during the enumeration. Based on the proposed index, we design an efficient LHC-s-t path enumeration algorithm in which unnecessary computation is effectively pruned. Extensive experiments are conducted on real-world graphs with billions of edges. Experiment results show that our proposed algorithms significantly outperform the baseline methods by over one order of magnitude.

Keywords: Graph · Labelled graph · Path enumeration

1 Introduction

Graphs have been widely used to represent relationships of entities in many areas including social networks, web graphs, and biological networks [6,11,12,24]. With the proliferation of graph applications, research efforts have been devoted to many fundamental problems in analyzing graph [18,21–23]. Among them, the problem of hop-constrained s-t simple path (HC-s-t path) enumeration receives considerable attention and has been well-studied in the literature [3,5,15–17,19]. Given an unweighted directed graph G, a source vertex s, a target vertex t, and a hop constraint k, HC-s-t path enumeration computes all the simple paths (i.e.,

© The Author(s), under exclusive license to Springer Nature Switzerland AG 2022
R. Chbeir et al. (Eds.): WISE 2022, LNCS 13724, pp. 49–64, 2022.
https://doi.org/10.1007/978-3-031-20891-1_5

paths without repeated vertices) from s to t such that the number of hops in each path is not larger than k.

Remarkably, all of the existing algorithms for HC-s-t path enumeration focus on unlabelled graphs and assume queries are issued without any label constraints. However, in many real-world applications, graphs are edge-labelled graphs [1,4,8,14,26], i.e., edges are associated with labels to denote different types of relationships between vertices, and the HC-s-t path enumeration for labelled graphs often involves label constraints on the path connecting two vertices. As a result, we study the problem of labelled hop-constrained s-t path (LHC-s-t path) enumeration in this paper. Specifically, given a labelled directed graph G, a source vertex s, a destination vertex t, a hop constraint k and a subset L of the set of all edge labels $\mathcal{L}$ of G, we aim to efficiently enumerate the HC-s-t paths using only edges with labels in L.

Applications. LHC-s-t path enumeration can be used in many applications, for example:

- *Fraud detection in E-commerce transaction networks.* A cycle in a E-commerce transaction network is a strong indication of a fraudulent activity [25]. A recent study from Alibaba group presents that the HC-s-t path enumeration is used to report all newly formed cycles to detect fraudulent activities [16]. In real world scenarios, transactions are usually associated with labels demonstrating their types, such as "bank_transfer" or "credit_card", and users may be interested in querying specific types of transactions (e.g. limiting the edge label to "credit_card" in credit card fraud detection). This gives rise to the need for LHC-s-t path enumeration.
- *Pathway queries in biological networks.* Pathway queries are a fundamental tool in biological networks analytics [7,10]. [10] shows that HC-s-t path enumeration is one of the most important pathway queries that can figure out the chains of interactions between two substances. Since there are many different types of interactions between two substances, the pathway queries are often issued with certain constraints on the types of interactions along the path, suggesting the utility of label constraints.
- *Path ranking in knowledge graphs.* Path ranking algorithms enumerate the paths from one entity to another in a knowledge graph and use these paths as features to train a model for missing fact prediction [2,9,13]. As real-world knowledge graphs (e.g., RDF graphs) are usually associated with rich labels, LHC-s-t path enumeration is used to enumerate paths with meaningful labels defined by users to more precisely predict the missing relations between entities.

Motivation and Challenges. To address this important problem, the most straightforward way is to directly process a LHC-s-t path query using the state-of-the-art HC-s-t path enumeration algorithm in the literature [19] (i.e. referred to as BaseEnum) and then remove the invalid results that violate the label constraints. However, although BaseEnum works well on general HC-s-t path queries, it is inefficient and unscalable to solve the problem of LHC-s-t path enumeration especially on large-scale graphs. The reasons are as follows: (1) since BaseEnum is designed for general HC-s-t path queries, it does not consider the possible pruning opportunities to reduce unnecessary computation specific to the label constraints, while pruning such unnecessary computation has crucial effects on the enumeration performance as proved in our experiments; (2) as the results of BaseEnum may violate the label constraints, each HC-s-t path found by BaseEnum needs to be verified individually to ensure that the labels of edges in the path are within the given set of labels, which leads to a high verification cost.

Motivated by this, we aim to develop an efficient algorithm tailored for the problem of LHC-s-t path enumeration in large graphs. The algorithm should not only have the ability of pruning unnecessary computation specific to the label constraints during the enumeration, but also avoid the costly verification of the results at the end of the enumeration.

Contributions. The main contributions of our paper are summarized as follows:

(A) The first work to study the LHC-s-t path *enumeration.* To the best of our knowledge, this is the first work to study the problem of LHC-s-t path enumeration in large graphs, which has many real-world applications.

(B) An efficient and scalable algorithm for LHC-s-t path *enumeration.* By revisiting the missing pruning opportunities in the state-of-the-art HC-s-t path enumeration algorithm, we first propose an online label-based index based on which the fruitless exploration can be effectively identified. After that, we propose an efficient LHC-s-t path enumeration algorithm in which the identified unnecessary computation is effectively pruned, which can significantly improve the enumeration performance by reducing the search space.

(C) Extensive performance studies on real-world datasets. We conduct extensive performance studies on real-world graphs with various graph properties. The experiment results demonstrate that our proposed algorithm is efficient and scalable regarding processing HC-s-t path enumeration queries in large graphs.

2   Preliminary

Let $G = (V, E, \mathcal{L}, \lambda)$ denote a labelled directed graph, where $V(G)$ is the set of vertices, $E(G)$ is a set of directed edges, $\mathcal{L}(G)$ is the set of edge labels, and λ is the function that assigns each edge $e \in E(G)$ a label $\lambda(e) \in \mathcal{L}(G)$. We use n and m to denote the number of vertices and edges, respectively. For a vertex $v \in V(G)$, we use $G.\mathrm{nbr}^-(v)/G.\mathrm{nbr}^+(v)$ to denote the in-neighbors/out-neighbors of v in G. We omit G in the notations when the context is self-evident. Given a graph G, the reverse graph of G, denoted by $G_r = (V, E_r)$, is the graph generated by reversing the direction of all edges in G.

A path from vertex u to vertex v, denoted by $p(u, v)$, is a sequence of vertices $\{u = v_0, v_1, \ldots, v_h = v\}$ such that $(v_{i-1}, v_i) \in E(G)$ for every $1 \le i < h$. Given two paths p_A and p_B, p_A is a partial path of p_B if p_A makes up part of P_B, denoted by $p_A \subseteq p_B$. A simple path is a loop-free path where there are no repetitions of vertices and edges. By $|p|$ and $p[i]$, we denote the length of path

p and the ith vertex of p, respectively. We call the intermediate path of a query during its enumeration as its prefix. Given two vertices u and v, the shortest distance from u to v, denoted by $\mathsf{dist}_G(u, v)$, is the length (i.e., the number of hops in this paper) of the shortest path from u to v on G, we omit G in the notations when the context is self-evident. Given a pre-defined hop constraint k, we say a path p is a hop-constrained path if $|p| \leq k$. We call a traversal on G as a forward search and on G_r as a backward search. The results of a LHC-s-t path query q are denoted as $P(q)$.

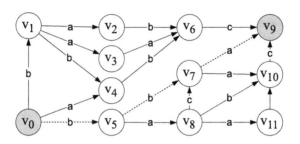

Fig. 1. Labelled graph G

Problem Statement. Given a labelled directed graph G and a LHC-s-t path query $q(s, t, k, L)$, we aim to *efficiently* enumerate the LHC-s-t path $P(q)$ from s to t on G using only edges with labels in L such that the number of hops in each path is not larger than k.

Example 1. Consider a labelled directed graph G shown in Fig. 1. Given a LHC-s-t path query $q(v_0, v_9, 4, \{a, b\})$, one LHC-s-t path can be found, namely $p = (v_0, v_5, v_7, v_9)$, which is demonstrated by the dashed arrows in Fig. 1.

3   The Baseline Solution

In this section, we introduce the state-of-the-art algorithm, PathEnum [19], for HC-s-t path enumeration query and present a straightforward baseline solution BaseEnum for LHC-s-t path query processing based on PathEnum. Given a HC-s-t path query q from s to t with hop constraint k, the main idea of PathEnum is to prune any vertex v visited during the enumeration if the shortest distance $\mathsf{dist}(v, t)$ from v to t exceeds the remaining hop budget.

Based on PathEnum, the baseline solution for LHC-s-t path query processing is as follows: since the results computed by PathEnum contain all the results for LHC-s-t path enumeration, it is immediate that all LHC-s-t paths for q can be correctly enumerated by filtering the HC-s-t paths that violate the label constraints. Algorithm 1 illustrates the baseline solution BaseEnum for LHC-s-t path query processing.

Algorithm 1: BaseEnum(G, q)

---

1 Find $\text{dist}_{G_r}(q.\text{t}, v)$ for each $v \in V(G)$ by a BFS;
2 Search$(G, P, (q.\text{s}), q)$;
3 $P \leftarrow$ Verify(P, q);
4 **foreach** $p \in P$ **do**
5 $\quad$ Output p;
6 **Procedure** Search(G, P, p, q)
7 $\quad$ $v' \leftarrow p[|p|]$; **if** $v' = q.\text{t}$ **then** $P.\text{add}(p)$;
8 $\quad$ **if** $|p| = q.\text{k}$ **or** $v' = q.\text{t}$ **then return**;
9 $\quad$ **foreach** $v'' \in \text{nbr}^+(v')$ *s.t.* $|p| + \text{dist}_{G_r}(q.\text{t}, v'') < k$ **do**
10 $\quad\quad$ **if** $v'' \notin p$ **then** Search$(G, P, p \bigcup\{v''\}, q)$;
11 **Procedure** Verify(P, q)
12 $\quad$ $P' \leftarrow \emptyset$;
13 $\quad$ **foreach** $p \in P$ **do**
14 $\quad\quad$ **foreach** $i \in 0..|p| - 1$ **do**
15 $\quad\quad\quad$ **if** $\lambda((p[i], p[i+1])) \notin q.\text{L}$ **then**
16 $\quad\quad\quad\quad$ **continue**;
17 $\quad\quad\quad$ $P'.\text{add}(p)$;
18 $\quad$ **return** P';

Given a graph G and a LHC-s-t path query q, BaseEnum first computes the distance between t and all vertices in G by running a BFS (line 1). Then the enumeration for LHC-s-t paths is conducted (line 2). The paths obtained by the search are then verified to ensure that only paths with valid labels are output (lines 3–5). Procedure Search enumerates the paths with a hop constraint of k recursively (lines 6–10). Specifically, if a path p ends with vertex $q.\text{t}$ is found, p is a candidate result, which is immediately added to P (line 8). If p's length has reached $q.\text{k}$ or p ends with vertex $q.\text{t}$, the search terminates (line 9). Otherwise, for the out-neighbor v'' of v' which meets the hop constraint and has not been explored in p, BaseEnum adds v'' in p and continues the search (line 9–10). In procedure Verify, the paths found by Search are examined in a row, such that any path that contains invalid labels are filtered and the rest are returned as the final results for q (lines 11–18).

Remark. As a bidirectional search could improve the enumeration performance, PathEnum conducts a forward search from s on G and a backward search from t on G_r concurrently, and concatenates the paths explored during the bidirectional search to obtain the final results by a hash join. Since the optimization is orthogonal to the label constraints in our problem and can be easily adapted to our approach, we follow the single direction search when introducing BaseEnum and our approach in Sect. 4. In Sect. 7, both of these methods are evaluated in our experiments.

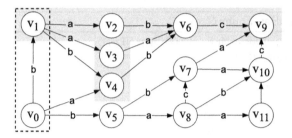

Fig. 2. Main observation of our approach

4 Our Approach

4.1 Overview

Given a LHC-s-t path query, BaseEnum prunes the unnecessary computation during enumeration by examining the vertices' reachability based on the existence of edges, which misses the possible pruning opportunities specific to the label constraints. In fact, there still exists a huge amount of fruitless exploration attributed to the label constraints, which can be identified and avoided to significantly reduce the search space. Consider the enumeration procedure of BaseEnum regarding $q(v_0, v_9, 4, \{a, b\})$ in Fig. 1. Initially, the search by BaseEnum starts from v_0. Because $|(v_0)| + \mathsf{dist}(v_1, v_9) = 4 \leq q.\mathsf{k}$, the search following v_1 is determined to be promising and hence v_1 is explored, resulting in the search prefix (v_0, v_1) shown in Fig. 2 by the dashed box. After this, because it is found by looking up the index that for each $v \in \{v_2, v_3, v_4\}$, $|(v_0, v_1)| + \mathsf{dist}(v, v_9) = 4 \leq q.\mathsf{k}$, all three out-neighbors of v_1 are considered to be promising and therefore explored, resulting in the enumerated prefixes $\{(v_0, v_1, v_2), (v_0, v_1, v_3), (v_0, v_1, v_4)\}$. Subsequently, v_6 and v_9 are explored in a row. However, when verifying the correctness of the three found paths $\{(v_0, v_1, v_2, v_6, v_9), (v_0, v_1, v_3, v_6, v_9), (v_0, v_1, v_4, v_6, v_9)\}$, it is noticed that all these results are invalid because $\lambda((v_6, v_9)) = c$ and thus the label constraint $q.\mathsf{L} = \{a, b\}$ fails on edge (v_6, v_9) in all of these paths. As a result, all the computation in this example is fruitless and therefore unnecessary, which is represented by the shaded area in Fig. 2.

According to this example, it is clear that there exists a huge amount of unnecessary computation specific to label constraints in LHC-s-t path enumeration, while pruning them in advance can considerably reduce the search space and avoid the expensive final verification, which consequently improves the enumeration performance. To achieve this goal, we first define a label-based index, which is constructed online to effectively identify the fruitless exploration. Based on the devised index, we propose an efficient LHC-s-t path enumeration algorithm which can maximally prune the unnecessary computation, and thus improve the whole performance.

4.2   Label-Based Index

As discussed in Sect. 4.1, given a LHC-s-t path query q, pruning the exploration that violates the label constraints can significantly reduce the search space. However, it is infeasible to prune such exploration by dynamically checking each explored edge during the enumeration to ensure that its label is in q.L. Consider the same example in Fig. 2, where the prefix (v_0, v_1) explores v_2, v_3 and v_4 by extending the edges (v_1, v_2), (v_1, v_3) and (v_1, v_4). Because $\lambda((v_1, v_2)) = a$, $\lambda((v_1, v_3)) = a$ and $\lambda((v_1, v_4)) = b$, all these three edges have valid labels contained by q.L, which means the search on them should continue normally. However, it has been demonstrated in Sect. 4.1 that the enumeration following them is fruitless. According to this contradiction, it is obvious that the fruitless computation attributed to the label constraints cannot be trivially identified and pruned by dynamically checking the labels of explored edges. As a result, the following question arises: is it possible to design an approach such that the fruitless exploration regarding LHC-s-t path enumeration can be effectively identified and pruned? In this section, we aim to answer this questions and introduce our approach to prune the unpromising search in LHC-s-t path enumeration.

Reconsider the example of running $q(v_0, v_9, 4, \{a, b\})$ on G by BaseEnum shown in Fig. 2, we observe that the enumeration following (v_0, v_1) is fruitless because v_1 is not reachable to v_9 due to the label constraint, which only allows edges labelled a and b to be explored during the search. Based on this observation, if the reachability regarding the query constraints on both labels and hops can be efficiently retrieved, the pruning can be effectively done during the enumeration. Following the idea, we define:

Definition 1 (Label-constrained Distance $\mathcal{D}$). *Given a graph G, two vertices v_0, v_1 and a set of labels L, the label-constrained distance from v_0 to v_1 with labels L, denoted by $\mathcal{D}_G(v_0, v_1, L)$, is the length of the shortest path from v_0 to v_1 on G using only the labels in L. G is omitted in the notation when the context is self-evident.*

Based on the definition of label-constrained distance, we then prove the following lemmas on which our index is based:

Lemma 1. *Given a graph G, a LHC-s-t path query q and a vertex $v \in V(G)$, if there exists a LHC-s-t path p from s to t with $|p| \leq k$ and constrained label set L, then for any $p[i] = v$ where $0 \leq i < |p|$, $\mathcal{D}_G(s, v, L) \leq i$ and $\mathcal{D}_{G_r}(t, v, L) \leq k - i$.*

Proof. Based on the definition of LHC-s-t path, if $0 \leq i < |p|$, then $v[i]$ must be reachable from $v[0]$ (i.e. s) and reachable to $v[|p|]$ (i.e. t) within i and $|p| - i$ hops, respectively, using only the labels in q.L. Moreover, given that $|p| \leq k$ and $v[i]$ must be reachable to $v[|p|]$ (i.e. t) within $k - i$ hops using only the labels in q.L, $v[i]$ should also be reachable to t within $k - i$ hops regarding q.L. □

According to Lemma 1, we further define the following lemmas to demonstrate how the vertices can be pruned during the search to reduce unnecessary computation:

Algorithm 2: ConstructIndex(G, q)

---

1 $S_v \leftarrow \{q.\mathsf{s}\}$; $end \leftarrow$ False;
2 $\mathcal{D} \leftarrow \emptyset$; $\mathcal{D}(q.\mathsf{s}, q.\mathsf{s}, q.\mathsf{L}) = 0$;
3 **while** $|S_v| \neq 0$ *and* $!end$ **do**
4 $\quad$ $v \leftarrow S_v[0]$; $S_v.\mathsf{remove}(v)$;
5 $\quad$ **foreach** $v' \in \mathsf{nbr}^+{}_G(v)$ *s.t.* $\lambda((q.\mathsf{s}, v')) \in q.\mathsf{L}$ **do**
6 $\quad\quad$ **if** $(q.\mathsf{s}, v', q.\mathsf{L}) \notin \mathcal{D}$ **then**
7 $\quad\quad\quad$ **if** $q.\mathsf{k} < \mathcal{D}(q.\mathsf{s}, v, q.\mathsf{L}) + 1$ **then**
8 $\quad\quad\quad\quad$ $end =$ True; **break;**
9 $\quad\quad\quad$ $\mathcal{D}(q.\mathsf{s}, v', q.\mathsf{L}) = \mathcal{D}(q.\mathsf{s}, v, q.\mathsf{L}) + 1$;
10 $\quad\quad\quad$ $S_v.\mathsf{add}(v')$;
11 **return** $\mathcal{D}$;

Lemma 2. *Given a graph G, a vertex $v \in V(G)$ and a* LHC-s-t path *query q, if $\mathcal{D}_G(q.\mathsf{s}, v, q.\mathsf{L}) + \mathcal{D}_{G_r}(q.\mathsf{t}, v, q.\mathsf{L}) > q.k$, then $\nexists p \in P(q)$ s.t. $v \in p$.*

Proof. Based on Lemma 1, if $\mathcal{D}_G(q.\mathsf{s}, v, q.\mathsf{L}) + \mathcal{D}_{G_r}(q.\mathsf{t}, v, q.\mathsf{L}) > q.k$, then when v exists in a LHC-s-t path p from s to t, the length $|p|$ of p must be larger than $q.\mathsf{k}$, thus p obviously cannot be a valid result for q, which proves $\nexists p \in P(q)$ s.t. $v \in p$. $\qquad\square$

According to Lemma 2, given a LHC-s-t path query q, it is clear that for any vertex $v \in V(G)$, if $\mathcal{D}_G(q.\mathsf{s}, v, q.\mathsf{L}) + \mathcal{D}_{G_r}(q.\mathsf{t}, v, q.\mathsf{L}) > q.k$, then vertex v can never appear in a valid LHC-s-t path and thus does not need to be explored at all during the enumeration, which can be removed from $V(G)$ before the enumeration begins. Moreover, the pruning can also take place during the enumeration, as shown in the following lemma:

Lemma 3. *Given a graph G, a prefix p' and a* LHC-s-t path *query q, if $|p'| + \mathcal{D}_{G_r}(q.\mathsf{t}, p'[|p'|], q.\mathsf{L}) > q.k$, then $\nexists p \in P(q)$ s.t. $p' \subseteq p$.*

Proof. Based on Lemma 1, if $|p'| + \mathcal{D}_{G_r}(q.\mathsf{t}, p'[|p'|], q.\mathsf{L}) > q.k$, then p' requires at least $q.k - |p'| + 1$ hops to explore $q.\mathsf{t}$, which obviously exceeds the hop budget left. As a result, $\nexists p \in P(q)$ s.t. $p' \subseteq p$. $\qquad\square$

According to Lemma 3, given a LHC-s-t path query q and a prefix p', if $|p'| + \mathcal{D}_{G_r}(q.\mathsf{t}, p'[|p'|], q.\mathsf{L}) > q.k$, then p' requires to proceed more hops to reach $q.\mathsf{t}$ than its remaining hop budget. Hence the enumeration procedure following p' is fruitless and can be directly pruned.

Based on the observations, given a graph G and a LHC-s-t path query q, in order to reduce unnecessary computation during the enumeration, we want to build an index to support instant lookup on both $\mathcal{D}_G(q.\mathsf{s}, v, q.\mathsf{L})$ and $\mathcal{D}_{G_r}(q.\mathsf{t}, v, q.\mathsf{L})$ for $v \in V(G)$, which gives rise to our index construction algorithm ConstructIndex.

Algorithm. Algorithm 2 illustrates the procedure of the index construction on G, as the same procedure on G_r can be achieved similarly. Given a graph G and a LHC-s-t path query q, ConstructIndex performs a BFS exploration on G while updating the label-constrained distance $\mathcal{D}$ from q.s to each visited vertex.

Specifically, ConstructIndex first creates a queue S_v to store the current set of vertices whose out-neighbors need to be explored, which initially only contains q.s. Boolean variable *end* is created to record if the index construction needs to terminate, which happens when the allowed hop budget has been exhausted (line 1). Then, $\mathcal{D}$ is initialized and the label-constrained distance between q.s and itself is set to 0 (line 2). After this, ConstructIndex iteratively explores the vertices while following the label constraints in G in a BFS order, updating the label-constrained distance $\mathcal{D}$ for them, which terminates when no more vertices can be explored or the distance has exceeded the hop constraint (lines 3–10). At the start, the first vertex v in S_v is popped out and v's out-neighbors v' such that the label of edge (v, v') is in q.L are visited (lines 4–5). When the distance between q.s and v' is not recorded, if the new distance to be assigned, $\mathcal{D}(q.s, v, q.L) + 1$, is greater than q.k, then the assigned distance has exceeded the hop constraint. Therefore, the procedure of ConstructIndex will terminate (lines 6–8). Otherwise, $\mathcal{D}(q.s, v', q.L)$ is updated and v' is added to S_v for further exploration (lines 9–10). Finally, $\mathcal{D}$ is returned (line 11).

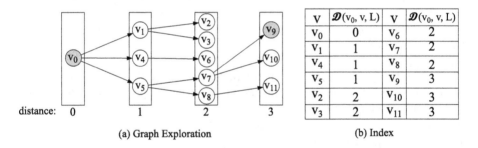

(a) Graph Exploration   (b) Index

Fig. 3. Example of ConstructIndex

Example 2. Reconsider the graph G and the LHC-s-t path query $q(v_0, v_9, 4, \{a, b\})$ in Fig. 1. We demonstrate the example of running Algorithm 2 on (G, q) in detail, where the vertices explored at each size of the label constraint distance are shown in Fig. 3(a). The vertices q.s and q.t are marked in grey. Additionally, Fig. 3(b) demonstrates the index constructed on $\mathcal{D}$, which shows the label-constrained distance between s (i.e. v_0) and each $v \in V(G)$ that is reachable from s within the hop budget.

Initially, the search starts from v_0 because $S_v = \{v_0\}$. Then, the out-neighbors of v_0, namely $\{v_1, v_4, v_5\}$, are visited as they follow the label constraint, resulting in the new label-constraint distances $\mathcal{D}(v_0, v_1, q.L) = \mathcal{D}(v_0, v_4, q.L) = \mathcal{D}(v_0, v_5, q.L) = 1$, which are inserted into the index. After this, the vertices in S_v, namely $\{v_1, v_4, v_5\}$, are extended by their out-neighbors $\{v_2, v_3, v_6, v_7, v_8\}$ and their label-constraint distances from v_0 are also updated to 2. Finally, because the

---

Algorithm 3: LabelledEnum(G, q)

---

1   $\mathcal{D} \leftarrow$ ConstructIndex$(G/G_r, q)$;
2   ReduceGraph$(G, q, \mathcal{D})$; $P \leftarrow \emptyset$;
3   Search$(G, P, (q.\mathsf{s}), q)$;
4   **foreach** $p \in P$ **do**
5 | Output p;
6   **Procedure** ReduceGraph$(G, q, \mathcal{D})$
7 | **foreach** $v \in V(G)$ **do**
8 | | **if** $\mathcal{D}_G(q.\mathsf{s}, v, q.\mathsf{L}) + \mathcal{D}_{G_r}(q.\mathsf{t}, v, q.\mathsf{L}) > q.k$ **then**
9 | | | $V(G)$.remove(v);
10 | | | **foreach** $e \in E(G)$ s.t. $v \in e$ **do**
11 | | | | $E(G)$.remove(e);
12 **Procedure** Search(G, P, p, q)
13 | $v' \leftarrow p[|p|]$; **if** $v' = q.\mathsf{t}$ **then** P.add(p);
14 | **if** $|p| = q.k$ **or** $v' = q.\mathsf{t}$ **then return**;
15 | **foreach** $v'' \in \mathsf{nbr}^+(v')$ s.t. $|p| + \mathcal{D}_{G_r}(q.\mathsf{t}, v') < k$ **do**
16 | | **if** $v'' \notin p$ **then** Search$(G, P, p \bigcup \{v''\}, q)$;

---

label of edge (v_6, v_9) is c which violates the label constraint, vertex v_9 cannot be extended from v_6. Instead, v_9 and v_{10} are extended from v_7, and v_{11} is extended from v_8, leading to $\mathcal{D}(v_0, v_9, q.\mathsf{L}) = \mathcal{D}(v_0, v_{10}, q.\mathsf{L}) = \mathcal{D}(v_0, v_{11}, q.\mathsf{L}) = 3$.

Theorem 1. *The time complexity of* ConstructIndex *is* $O(|V(G)| + |E(G)|)$.

Proof. The time complexity of ConstructIndex is $O(|V(G)| + |E(G)|)$ because a breadth-first search is performed during the construction procedure, which visits each vertex and edge in G once.   □

4.3   LHC-s-t Path Enumeration

Given a graph G and a LHC-s-t path query q, after constructing the index on the label-constrained distances from $q.\mathsf{s}/q.\mathsf{t}$ to each $v \in V(G)$ (the label-constrained distance to vertices that are not visited in ConstructIndex are treated as ∞.), we can identify the fruitless exploration during the enumeration based on Lemma 2 and Lemma 3, and thus accelerate the LHC-s-t path query processing by pruning them. According to Lemma 2, it is obvious that there exist many vertices in $V(G)$ that will never be a part of a valid LHC-s-t path due to the label and hop constraints. As a result, to minimize the unnecessary computation, we remove such vertices in $V(G)$ and their corresponding edges in $E(G)$ in advance, which effectively reduces the graph size and search space before the enumeration procedure begins. Additionally, based on Lemma 3, it can be determined early that the vertices explored during the enumeration will be fruitless. Therefore, we dynamically verify the explored vertices to ensure that the search following them must be promising. The detailed algorithm, LabelledEnum, is shown in Algorithm 3.

Algorithm. For a LHC-s-t path query q, LabelledEnum first constructs the index on both G and G_r, to compute $\mathcal{D}_G(q.\mathsf{s}, v)$ and $\mathcal{D}_{G_r}(q.\mathsf{t}, v)$ for all $v \in V(G)$ (line

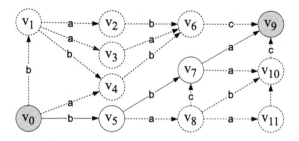

Fig. 4. Example of ConstructIndex

1). After this, LabelledEnum reduces the search space by removing the vertices and edges in G that will never be a part of a valid LHC-s-t path (line 2). P is then initialized to store the LHC-s-t paths found during the enumeration, which is conducted in a DFS manner with procedure search (line 3). For each path p obtained during the search, p is output as a valid LHC-s-t path (lines 4–5). In procedure ReduceGraph, each vertex $v \in V(G)$ such that $\mathcal{D}_G(q.s, v, q.L) + \mathcal{D}_{G_r}(q.t, v, q.L) > q.k$ will be removed directly based on Lemma 2 (lines 7–9). Any edge that contains such v is also removed (lines 10- 11). Procedure Search enumerates the LHC-s-t paths with a hop constraint of k based on the index recursively (lines 12–16). Specifically, if a path p with length $q.k$ is found, p is added into P (line 14). Otherwise, for the out-neighbor v'' of v' which meets both the label and hop constraint according to Lemma 3 and has not been explored in p, LabelledEnum adds v'' in p and continues the search (line 15–16).

Example 3. Reconsider the graph G and LHC-s-t path query q in Fig. 1. We demonstrate the example of running LabelledEnum on G and q. After constructing the index, the dashed vertices and edges in Fig. 4 are those removed in procedure ReduceGraph due to the violation of label and hop constraints. The search starts from prefix (v_0) and explores v_5 because $|(v_0)| + \mathcal{D}_{G_r}(v_9, v_5) = 2 < q.k$. Similarly, v_7 and v_9 are subsequently explored, resulting in the found LHC-s-t path (v_0, v_5, v_7, v_9).

Theorem 2. *Given a graph G and a* LHC-s-t path *query q, Algorithm 3 enumerates all* LHC-s-t paths *for q in G correctly.*

Proof. Based on the correctness of PathEnum, it is direct that q's LHC-s-t paths on G are enumerated correctly if no pruning is done on the label constraints. Moreover, according to Lemma 2 and Lemma 3, a vertex is not pruned unless it cannot be a part of a valid LHC-s-t path. As a result, Algorithm 3 enumerates all LHC-s-t paths for q in G correctly. □

5   Evaluation

In this section, we evaluate the efficiency of the proposed algorithms. All the experiments are performed on a machine with one 20-core Intel Xeon CPU E5-2698 and 512 GB main memory running Red Hat Linux 7.3, 64 bit.

Table 1. Statistics of the datasets

Dataset	Name	$|V|$	$|E|$	d_{avg}	d_{max}
Epinsion	EP	75K	508K	13.4	3,079
LiveJournal	LJ	4M	69M	17.9	20,333
Twitter-2010	TW	42M	1.46B	70.5	2,997,487
Friendster	FS	65M	1.81B	27.5	5,214

Datasets. We evaluate our algorithms on four real-world graphs, which are shown in Table 1. Among them, Epinsion is a who-trust-whom online social network of consumer review site Epinions.com. LiveJournal is a free online community based social network. Twitter-2010 is a web graph crawled from Twitter. Friendster is a social network retrieved from Friendster. Twitter-2010 is downloaded from LAW[1] and the rest are downloaded from SNAP[2]. As all the datasets come with no edge labels, we use the method in [20] to synthetize the edge labels, while the number of labels $|\mathcal{L}(G)|$ is set to 8.

Algorithms. We compare the following algorithms:

- BaseEnum: Algorithm 1 where PathEnum runs in a single direction (Sect. 3).
- BaseEnum+: Algorithm 1 where PathEnum runs with an optimized bidirectional search order (Sect. 3).
- LabelledEnum: Algorithm 3 (Sect. 4.3).
- LabelledEnum+: LabelledEnum with an optimized bidirectional search order introduced by BaseEnum+ (Sect. 3).

Settings. All the algorithms are implemented in Rust 1.43. In the experiments, the time cost is measured as the amount of wall-clock time elapsed during the program's execution.

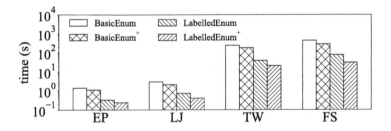

Fig. 5. Processing time on all datasets

---

[1] https://law.di.unimi.it/index.php.
[2] https://snap.stanford.edu/data/.

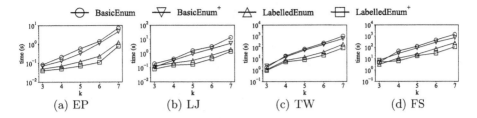

Fig. 6. Processing time when varying k

Exp-1: Efficiency on Different Datasets. In this experiment, we evaluate the processing time of four algorithms (i.e. BaseEnum, BaseEnum$^+$, LabelledEnum, LabelledEnum$^+$) on all four graphs. We randomly generate 100 random LHC-s-t path query $q(s, t, k, L)$ on each graph where source vertex s could reach target vertex t in k hops with the given label set L. We set $k = 6$ and $|L| = 4$ by default. The results are reported in Fig. 5.

As can be seen in Fig. 5, our proposed LHC-s-t path enumeration algorithms LabelledEnum and LabelledEnum$^+$ always outperform the other two algorithms on all of the graphs. For example, on graph FS, LabelledEnum is 5.6× faster than BaseEnum and 3.5× faster than BaseEnum$^+$. Comparatively, LabelledEnum$^+$ demonstrates a better performance, which is 12.9× faster than BaseEnum and 8.1× faster than BaseEnum$^+$. This is because the pruning technique used in our proposed algorithms can significantly reduce the search space and the fruitless exploration attributed to the label constraints is avoided. For LabelledEnum and LabelledEnum$^+$, LabelledEnum$^+$ always outperforms LabelledEnum on all datasets, this is because by using the bidirectional search, some computed paths can be shared during the enumeration, which is consistent with the analysis in [19].

Exp-2: Efficiency When Varying Hop Constraint k. In this experiment, we evaluate the efficiency when varying hop constraint k from 3 to 7. For each hop constraint k, we randomly generate 50 queries. The average processing time for each query is shown in Fig. 6.

As shown in Fig. 6, as the hop constraint k increases, the processing time of all algorithms increases as well. This is because as k increases, the number of LHC-s-t paths also increases. Furthermore, LabelledEnum and LabelledEnum$^+$ always outperform the other two algorithms, and the performance gap increases as the hop constraint k increases. For example on TW, when $k = 4$, LabelledEnum is 2.4× faster than BaseEnum and 2.1× faster than BaseEnum$^+$; in contrast, when k increases to 7, LabelledEnum becomes 5.6× faster then BaseEnum and 3.5× faster than BaseEnum$^+$. This is because when the search space grows larger due to the increase of k, the fruitless exploration in the baseline algorithms increases accordingly while these fruitless exploration can be significantly avoided due to index-based pruning on the label constraints in LabelledEnum and LabelledEnum$^+$.

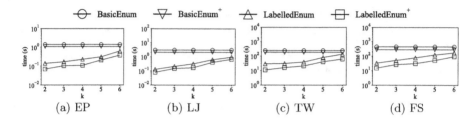

Fig. 7. Processing time when varying $|L|$

Exp-3: Efficiency When Varying Label Set Size $|L|$. In this experiment, we evaluate the efficiency when varying the label set size $|L|$ from 2 to 6. For each label set size $|L|$, we randomly generate 50 queries. The average processing time for each query is shown in Fig. 7.

As shown in Fig. 7, as the label set size $|L|$ increases, the processing time of our proposed algorithms increases while the time of the two baseline algorithms remain the same. This is because as $|L|$ increases, the size of fruitless computation that can be pruned becomes smaller. For example on TW, when $|L| = 2$, LabelledEnum is 8.3× faster than BaseEnum and 6.3× faster than BaseEnum$^+$; in contrast, when $|L|$ increases to 6, LabelledEnum becomes 1.8× faster then BaseEnum and 1.4× faster than BaseEnum$^+$. The time of the two baseline algorithms remain the same because they always have to first enumerate all the paths that follow the hop constraint.

6 Related Work

HC-s-t path enumeration is a fundamental problem in graph analysis and several algorithms have been proposed [3,15–17,19] for this problem. We divided them into two categories, which are *pruning-based algorithms* [3,15,17] and *index-based algorithms* [19]. Pruning-based algorithms typically adopt a backtracking strategy based on a depth-first search based framework. During the enumeration, [17] and [3] dynamically compute the shortest path distance from v to t and prunes v if it is unreachable to t, while [15] dynamically maintains a lower bound of hops to the target vertex t for the vertices visited and prunes v if the current remaining hop budget is smaller than the lower bound of hops required. For the index-based algorithm, [19] finds that the pruning-based algorithms typically suffer from severe performance issues caused by the costly pruning operations during enumeration. Therefore, BaseEnum builds a light-weight index to reduce the number of edges involved in the enumeration. Thanks to the index structure, BaseEnum significantly outperform pruning-based algorithms as demonstrated in [19]. Hence, we also adopt the index-based approach in this paper.

7   Conclusion

In this paper, we study the problem of LHC-s-t path enumeration. To address this problem, we observe that there exists a huge amount of unnecessary computation due to the label constraints and the processing performance can be significantly improved if these unnecessary computation can be effectively pruned. Following this observation, we first propose a label-based index to identify the fruitless exploration. Based on the constructed index, we design an efficient algorithm to process the given query by pruning the fruitless computation related to both the label and hop constraints. Experiment results on real-world datasets demonstrate the efficiency of our proposed algorithms.

References

1. Chen, Z., Yuan, L., Lin, X., Qin, L., Yang, J.: Efficient maximal balanced clique enumeration in signed networks. In: WWW 2020: The Web Conference 2020, Taipei, Taiwan, 20–24 April 2020, pp. 339–349. ACM/IW3C2 (2020)
2. Freitas, A., da Silva, J.C.P., Curry, E., Buitelaar, P.: A distributional semantics approach for selective reasoning on commonsense graph knowledge bases. In: Métais, E., Roche, M., Teisseire, M. (eds.) NLDB 2014. LNCS, vol. 8455, pp. 21–32. Springer, Cham (2014). https://doi.org/10.1007/978-3-319-07983-7_3
3. Grossi, R., Marino, A., Versari, L.: Efficient algorithms for listing k disjoint st-paths in graphs. In: Bender, M.A., Farach-Colton, M., Mosteiro, M.A. (eds.) LATIN 2018. LNCS, vol. 10807, pp. 544–557. Springer, Cham (2018). https://doi.org/10.1007/978-3-319-77404-6_40
4. Hao, K., Yang, Z., Lai, L., Lai, Z., Jin, X., Lin, X.: PatMat: a distributed pattern matching engine with cypher. In: Proceedings of the 28th ACM International Conference on Information and Knowledge Management, CIKM 2019, pp. 2921–2924 (2019)
5. Hao, K., Yuan, L., Zhang, W.: Distributed hop-constrained s-t simple path enumeration at billion scale. Proc. VLDB Endow. **15**(2), 169–182 (2021)
6. Hao, Y., Zhang, Y., Cao, J.: A novel QoS model and computation framework in web service selection. World Wide Web **15**(5), 663–684 (2012)
7. Krishnamurthy, L., et al.: Pathways database system: an integrated system for biological pathways. Bioinform. **19**(8), 930–937 (2003)
8. Lai, L., et al.: Distributed subgraph matching on timely dataflow. Proc. VLDB Endow. **12**(10), 1099–1112 (2019)
9. Lao, N., Cohen, W.W.: Relational retrieval using a combination of path-constrained random walks. Mach. Learn. **81**(1), 53–67 (2010)
10. Leser, U.: A query language for biological networks. In: ECCB/JBI 2005 Proceedings, Madrid, Spain, 28 September–1 October 2005, p. 39 (2005)
11. Li, L., Xu, G., Yang, Z., Dolog, P., Zhang, Y., Kitsuregawa, M.: An efficient approach to suggesting topically related web queries using hidden topic model. World Wide Web **16**(3), 273–297 (2013)
12. Liu, B., Yuan, L., Lin, X., Qin, L., Zhang, W., Zhou, J.: Efficient (a, β)-core computation: an index-based approach. In: The World Wide Web Conference, WWW 2019, San Francisco, CA, USA, 13–17 May 2019, pp. 1130–1141. ACM (2019)
13. Mazumder, S., Liu, B.: Context-aware path ranking for knowledge base completion. In: Sierra, C. (ed.) IJCAI, pp. 1195–1201. ijcai.org (2017)

14. Peng, Y., Lin, X., Zhang, Y., Zhang, W., Qin, L.: Answering reachability and K-reach queries on large graphs with label-constraints. VLDB J. **31**, 1–25 (2021)
15. Peng, Y., Zhang, Y., Lin, X., Zhang, W., Qin, L., Zhou, J.: Hop-constrained s-t simple path enumeration: towards bridging theory and practice. Proc. VLDB Endow. **13**(4), 463–476 (2019)
16. Qiu, X., et al.: Real-time constrained cycle detection in large dynamic graphs. Proc. VLDB Endow. **11**(12), 1876–1888 (2018)
17. Rizzi, R., Sacomoto, G., Sagot, M.-F.: Efficiently listing bounded length st-paths. In: Kratochvíl, J., Miller, M., Froncek, D. (eds.) IWOCA 2014. LNCS, vol. 8986, pp. 318–329. Springer, Cham (2015). https://doi.org/10.1007/978-3-319-19315-1_28
18. Sun, R., Chen, C., Liu, X., Xu, S., Wang, X., Lin, X.: Critical nodes identification in large networks: the inclined and detached models. World Wide Web **25**(3), 1315–1341 (2022)
19. Sun, S., Chen, Y., He, B., Hooi, B.: PathEnum: towards real-time hop-constrained s-t path enumeration. In: Proceedings of SIGMOD, pp. 1758–1770 (2021)
20. Valstar, L.D.J., Fletcher, G.H.L., Yoshida, Y.: Landmark indexing for evaluation of label-constrained reachability queries. In: SIGMOD, pp. 345–358. ACM (2017)
21. Wang, K., Lin, X., Qin, L., Zhang, W., Zhang, Y.: Accelerated butterfly counting with vertex priority on bipartite graphs. VLDB J. 1–25 (2022)
22. Wang, K., Zhang, W., Lin, X., Qin, L., Zhou, A.: Efficient personalized maximum biclique search. In: 2022 IEEE 38th International Conference on Data Engineering (ICDE), pp. 498–511. IEEE (2022)
23. Yang, Z., Lai, L., Lin, X., Hao, K., Zhang, W.: HUGE: an efficient and scalable subgraph enumeration system. In: Li, G., Li, Z., Idreos, S., Srivastava, D. (eds.) SIGMOD 2021: International Conference on Management of Data, Virtual Event, China, 20–25 June 2021, pp. 2049–2062. ACM (2021)
24. Yao, W., He, J., Huang, G., Cao, J., Zhang, Y.: A graph-based model for context-aware recommendation using implicit feedback data. World wide web **18**(5), 1351–1371 (2015)
25. Yue, D., Wu, X., Wang, Y., Li, Y., Chu, C.H.: A review of data mining-based financial fraud detection research. In: 2007 International Conference on Wireless Communications, Networking and Mobile Computing, pp. 5519–5522. IEEE (2007)
26. Zhang, J., Yuan, L., Li, W., Qin, L., Zhang, Y.: Efficient label-constrained shortest path queries on road networks: a tree decomposition approach. Proc. VLDB Endow. **15**(3), 686–698 (2021)

Complex Question Answering
Over Temporal Knowledge Graphs

Shaonan Long[1], Jinzhi Liao[2(✉)], Shiyu Yang[1], Xiang Zhao[2], and Xuemin Lin[3]

[1] Guangzhou University, Guangzhou, China
shaonanlong@e.gzhu.edu.cn, syyang@gzhu.edu.cn
[2] National University of Defense Technology, Changsha, China
{liaojinzhi12,xiangzhao}@nudt.edu.cn
[3] Antai College of Economics and Management, Shanghai Jiao Tong University,
Shanghai, China

Abstract. A temporal knowledge graph (TKG) comprises facts aligned with timestamps. Question answering over TKGs (TKGQA) finds an entity or timestamp to answer a question with certain temporal constraints. Current studies assume that the questions are fully annotated before being fed into the system, and treat question answering as a link prediction task. Moreover, the process of choosing answers is not interpretable due to the implicit reasoning in the latent space. In this paper, we propose a semantic parsing based method, namely **AE-TQ**, which leverages abstract meaning representation (AMR) for understanding complex questions, and produces question-oriented semantic information for explicit and effective temporal reasoning. We evaluate our method on `CronQuestions`, the largest known TKGQA dataset, and the experiment results demonstrate that **AE-TQ** empirically outperforms several competing methods in various settings.

Keywords: Temporal knowledge graphs · Question answering ·
Abstract meaning representation

1 Introduction

Temporal knowledge graph (temporal KG or TKG) is a multi-relational graph, consisting of facts associated with timestamps. A fact in a TKG, or a *temporal fact*, is expressed in a quadruple form as (*subject, relation, object, timestamp*), where the timestamp can be a time *point* or *interval*. Consider the temporal fact that (`Barack Obama, held the position of, President of USA, 2009--2017`). It states that `Barack Obama` held the position of `President of USA` during the years of 2009--2017.

Compared with the triplet form (*subject, relation, object*) in conventional KGs, the timestamp of a temporal fact indicates the effective or occurrence time of the fact, which makes the stored information more accurate and time-sensitive. As a consequence, recent efforts have been devoted to TKGs, and made progress

R. Chbeir et al. (Eds.): WISE 2022, LNCS 13724, pp. 65–80, 2022.
https://doi.org/10.1007/978-3-031-20891-1_6

on the representation and completion of TKGs [5,12–14], as well as question answering over TKGs (TKGQA) [15,17,18].

TKGQA is the task of answering natural language questions based on TKGs. Distinct from question answering over conventional KGs, the questions contain temporal constraints, and the supporting data resource is a TKG.

Example 1. Consider a question "Who was the President of USA before Obama?" On the basis of a TKG, the question necessitates a few temporal facts, including (George W. Bush, held the position of, President of USA, 2001--2009), and (Barack Obama, held the position of, President of USA, 2009--2017), to construct a supporting set of facts from the TKG. By reasoning among the facts, the system returns George W. Bush as the answer.

TKGQA requires the system to be able to resolve the temporal logic imposed by the question. The current system CronKGQA [17] utilizes an encoder to acquire representations of entities (e.g., President of USA) and timestamp (e.g., 2010) in the question, then searches for the most similar entity/timestamp in the TKG according to the scoring function of TComplEx [12]. CronKGQA is shown to perform well on *simple* questions, in which a single fact is necessary to locate the missing entity or timestamp.

In real life, however, time-involved questions usually require more complicate logic reasoning, such that answer generation is a process of semantically synthesizing multiple temporal facts. CronKGQA is apt to fall short when dealing with complex questions like in Example 1. To be more specific, it cannot tell the temporal constraint (i.e., before) in the question, and simply embeds the query into the high-dimensional vector space. And due to the lack of temporal reasoning capability, it may mistakenly return the object that is merely "closest" to the question in the vector space. The latest model TempoQR [15], which utilizes the embedding of entities and timestamps to enhance the representation of questions, substantially improves the performance.

Nevertheless, both CronKGQA and TempoQR implement question answering in the vector space, and their reasoning process is not interpretable. Moreover, there is a strong *premise* held by both of CronKGQA and TempoQR that the questions come with full annotations of each entity and timestamp, which unveil the roles of the entities (e.g., head or tail) and timestamps. Thus, they eventually reduce the problem into a link prediction task over TKG [16]. This can be less realistic, since manual labeling of temporal questions is expensive, meanwhile current automatic annotation is still inadequate [19]. On all accounts, a desirable solution is free from such annotations, meanwhile the reasoning process is interpretable over basic facts.

In response, we present a semantic parsing based approach to complex question answering over TKGs, which leverages effective semantic parsing (and temporal reasoning) using abstract meaning representations (AMR) [1]. AMR graph is a labeled rooted directed acyclic graph, which abstracts away from syntactic idiosyncrasies and captures the underlying semantic information of a sentence. Specifically, we introduce AMR as an effective semantic parser for understand-

ing complex questions, and design an algorithm to obtain semantic information and temporal relationship from the AMR graph. Then, the nodes in the
semantic information are aligned with the underlying TKG to obtain a semantic
information structure (SIS) similar to the quadruple in TKG. Thus, a complex
question can be represented by one or two SISs, based on which temporal reasoning is carried out using a pre-trained TKG embedding model while retaining
interpretability. The proposed techniques are assembled into a novel solution
named AE-TQ (AMR enhanced TKGQA), which is comprehensively evaluated
on benchmark data.

Contribution. In summary, the contribution of our work is at least three-fold:

- We propose to investigate question answering over TKGs in a realistic setting,
  where annotations of entities and timestamps are not provided;
- By introducing AMR, we present a semantic parsing based solution, namely
  AE-TQ, which is exploited to obtain semantic information and temporal constraints of questions, while keeping AE-TQ interpretable; and
- Equipped with a pre-trained TKG embedding model, AE-TQ is shown to
  empirically outperform several competing methods in various settings.

Organization. The rest of the paper is structured as follows. We provide the
background of the work in Sect. 2. Section 3 presents our method, followed by
experiments in Sect. 4. We conclude the paper in Sect. 5.

2   Background

2.1   Problem Definition

In a temporal knowledge graph $\mathcal{G} = (\mathcal{E}, \mathcal{R}, \mathcal{T}, \mathcal{F})$, $\mathcal{E}$ is a set of entities, $\mathcal{R}$ is a
set of relations, $\mathcal{T}$ is a set of timestamps, and $\mathcal{F}$ is a set of facts. Each fact
$(s, r, o, t) \in \mathcal{F}$ is a quadruple, where $s, o \in \mathcal{E}$ represent subject and object entity
respectively, $r \in \mathcal{R}$ represents the relation between them, and $t \in \mathcal{T}$ indicates
when this fact is valid.

Given a TKG $\mathcal{G} = (\mathcal{E}, \mathcal{R}, \mathcal{T}, \mathcal{F})$ and a natural language question q, the task
of question answering over TKGs is to predict an entity $\epsilon \in \mathcal{E}$ or a timestamp
$t \in \mathcal{T}$, which can answer the question q correctly.

2.2   Related Work

We discuss related work from two aspects.

Temporal Question Answering Over KGs. TempQuestions [8] is the first
KGQA dataset specifically aimed at temporal question answering. Based on
TempQuestions, TEQUILA was developed [9], which uses hand-crafted templates to decompose and rewrite the question into non-temporal sub-questions
with temporal constraints, and candidate answers to the sub-questions are then
retrieved using some conventional KGQA model, which are further confined
using the temporal constraints to derive the final answer. EXAQT [10] is the first

end-to-end system for answering complex temporal questions over large-scale knowledge graphs, which applies fine-tuned BERT models and convolutional graph networks to identify relevant facts for answering complex temporal questions. It is worth noting that TEQUILA and EXAQT are based on conventional KGs rather than TKGs, which are inapplicable to handling TKGQA.

Recently, a large temporal question answering dataset CronQuestions was proposed [17], which consists of a temporal KG and natural language questions (with annotations). Based on it, CronKGQA provides a learnable temporal reasoning solution [17] that exploits recent advances in TKG embeddings. As CronKGQA does not explicitly consider the temporal constraints in the question, it is sub-optimal when dealing with complex temporal questions that require reasoning. The latest contribution is from TempoQR [15], which is based on EaE [4] and incorporates TKG embeddings to combine the textual representation of a question with embeddings of entities and timestamps. TempoQR achieves state-of-the-art on CronQuestions. It has to be noted that both CronKGQA and TempoQR rely on question annotations of entities and timestamps, and regard question answering as a link prediction task over TKG.

Temporal KG Embedding. Temporal KG embedding learns to embed temporal facts of TKGs into vector spaces, serving as the basis of many downstream tasks, e.g., to predict the missing element in a temporal fact. Specifically, most of the models are adapted from their counterparts for conventional KGs. For instance, TTransE [13] is an extension of TransE [3] by adding a timestamp embedding into the score function. TA-DistMult [5] utilizes recurrent neural networks to learn time aware representations of relation types and scores the facts using the scoring function of DistMult [20]. Recently, inspired by the canonical decomposition of tensors of order four, TComplEx was proposed [12], which embeds temporal facts by complex vectors. In our implementation, TComplEx was used to perform entity and timestamp prediction.

3   Methodology

Given a natural language question and a TKG, it needs to effectively 1) associate the free text of the question with the structured facts in the TKG, and 2) identify and reason over the candidate facts with the temporal constraints, in order to reach an answer entity/timestamp. In this light, as overviewed in Fig. 1, our method AE-TQ comprises three steps—AMR parsing, SIS generation and temporal reasoning, where the first two steps establish the association, and the third step performs the reasoning.

To this end, we propose to leverage AMR parsing to understand the question with regard to the given TKG. In particular, we parse the question into a structured form, namely semantic information structures (SISs), and for each SIS with unknown elements, we query the TKG to obtain candidate answers, which are then reasoned together with the temporal constraints in pursuit of the final answer. In the sequel, we explain each step in detail.

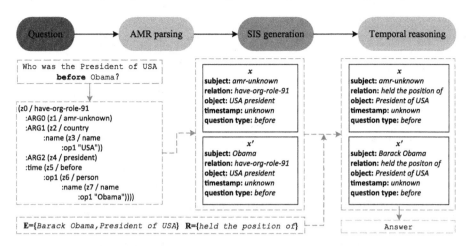

Fig. 1. Overview of our proposed method AE-TQ.

3.1 AMR Parsing

Our method utilizes AMR parsing to analyze and identify the components of semantics structure of the question.

Abstract meaning representation (AMR) is a semantic representation language, and an AMR graph is a rooted, directed, acyclic graph expressing "who is doing what to whom". Nodes in an AMR graph represent concepts that are either English words (e.g., "boy"), PropBank framesets [11] (e.g., "want-01"), or special keywords including special entity types (e.g., "date-entity", "ordinal-entity"), quantities (e.g., "monetary-quantity", "distance-quantity"), and logical conjunctions (e.g., "and"). Edges in an AMR graph represent relations between concepts, including PropBank conventions [11] (e.g., ":ARG0", ":ARG1"), general semantic relations (e.g., ":accompanier", ":direction", ":domain"), relations for date-entities (e.g., ":day", ":month", ":year", ":weekday", ":time") and so on. The `amr-unknown` node in the AMR graph refers to the concept that indicates the answer to the given question.

Example 2. The parsing result of the sample question in Example 1 is shown in Fig. 2(a). The temporal signal word "before" is clearly identified through AMR parsing, which means that `amr-unknown` holding the position of `the President of USA` needs to be earlier than `Obama`. For ease of understanding, the parsing result in graph form is supplied in Fig. 2(b).

The incorporation of AMR parsing brings about several advantages, and the most important one is that it enables the proposed solution free from question annotations. It can be seen that AMR is able to disambiguate natural language questions by generating the same semantic structure of the questions with the same basic meaning. Moreover, AMR can also recognize the temporal signal words (e.g., "before", "after", "first", "last", and "date"), which help unveil the

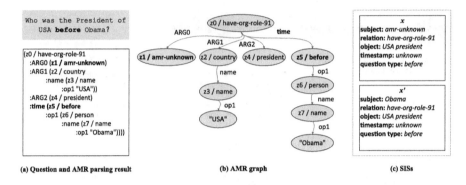

(a) Question and AMR parsing result   (b) AMR graph   (c) SISs

Fig. 2. AMR parsing result, AMR graph and SISs of sample question.

temporal order among facts. As a consequence, AMR parsing serves as a pre-processing of TKGQA, such that the system captures the temporal constraint of the complex question, as well as understands its underlying semantics.

In our implementation, we resorted to an extension of the pre-trained Transformer encoder-decoder model SPRING [2] for effective AMR parsing.

3.2   Semantic Information Generation

AMR graph is a structured form of the question, but not presented with respect to the TKG. With AMR graphs, the system cannot easily retrieve relevant facts from the TKG. In other words, it is necessary to further transform AMR graphs into temporal knowledge graph quadruples, such that relevant facts can be found in the TKG. Subsequently, we propose an algorithm to analyze the semantic features of the complex question based on an AMR graph and generate question-oriented semantic information structures (SISs).

Formally, a question-oriented SIS is defined as

$$ss = \{subject, relation, object, timestamp, question\ type\}.$$

All elements in a SIS can be parsed from the AMR graph, and the "question type" represents the temporal relationship, which is of particular importance for the subsequent temporal reasoning.

To fulfill the transformation, we present Algorithm algo1, which uses the rules of PropBank conventions (e.g., ":ARG0", ":ARG1") to identify the subject, relation and object in the question (Lines 5–6), and then uses the edge (e.g., ":ord") in the AMR graph to identify the chronological order of the answer, and the question type (Line 7). Edge ":time" plays an important role in the AMR graph. The subgraph rooted at the end node of edge ":time" is used to indicate the temporal constraint of the question (Lines 8–20), which can be an explicit time or another fact. For the other edges, complement the subject or object based on the concept of their start node and edge (Lines 21–22). Finally, if a question contains two facts, return ss and ss', otherwise ss' is empty.

Algorithm 1: Question-oriented SISs generation

Input : $\mathcal{A} = (\mathcal{V}, \mathcal{E})$: AMR graph of question q; $\mathcal{V}$ represents the node set $\{u_1, u_2, ..., u_n\}$ in $\mathcal{A}$, $\mathcal{E}$ represents the set of edges in $\mathcal{A}$, each edge has the start node and the label, and the end node;

Output : ss, ss': SISs of q, where ss' can be empty;

1 $ss \leftarrow ss' \leftarrow \varnothing$, $ss.timestamp \leftarrow$ unknown;

2 **foreach** $u_i \in \mathcal{V}$ **do**

3   **foreach** edge $(u_i, e, v_j) \in \mathcal{E}$ **do**

4   **switch** e **do**

5   **case** ARG0 **do** $ss.subject \leftarrow v_j$;

6   **case** ARG1 **do** $ss.object \leftarrow v_j$; $ss.relation \leftarrow u_i$;

7   **case** :ord **do** identify question type of ss using the concept of v_j ;

8   **case** :time **do**

9   **if** the concept of v_j is amr-unknown **then**

10                      $ss.timestamp \leftarrow$ amr-unknown;

11   **else if** the concept of v_j is a explicit time **then**

12                      $ss.timestamp \leftarrow$ the concept of v_j;

13   **else**

14   identify question type of ss based on the concept of v_j;

15                      $\mathcal{A}' = (\mathcal{V}', \mathcal{E}')$ is a subgraph rooted at v_j;

16   **if** there is another fact in $\mathcal{A}'$ **then**

17                          $ss'.timestamp \leftarrow$ unknown;

18   C;

19   om $ss', ss'' \leftarrow$ Question-oriented SISs generation$(\mathcal{A}')$

20   delete $\mathcal{V}'$ and $\mathcal{E}'$ from $\mathcal{A}$;

21   use ss to complete missing information in ss' ;

22   **otherwise do**

23   set v_j as complement of ss based on the concept of u_i and e;

24 **return** ss, ss';

As shown in Algorithm 1, each node and its adjacent edges will be visited once (Lines 2–3), and the nodes and edges in the subgraph will not be visited repeatedly (Line 19), so the time complexity of Algorithm 1 is $O(|\mathcal{V}| + |\mathcal{E}|)$. Since the time complexity of Algorithm 1 is linear and the scale of the AMR graph is small. The effectiveness of the Algorithm 1 is mainly reflected by the accuracy of question answering.

As a rule-based procedure, it is interpretable. Since the questions in the existing TKGQA dataset [17] only involve at most two facts and a temporal constraint, so Algorithm 1 is designed for the existing situation. But as a rule-based procedure, it is easy to extend for questions involving more facts and time constraints. Next, we continue with Examples 1 and 2 to illustrate the algorithm.

Example 3. As shown in the AMR graph in Fig. 2(b), the PropBank frameset "have-org-role-91" is used to describe the relation "held the position of" abstractly; this frameset has four out-going edges, in which the first out-going edge "ARG0" indicates that node $z1$ is the subject, the second out-going edge "ARG1" indicates that node $z2$ is the object, and "ARG2" can be seen as a

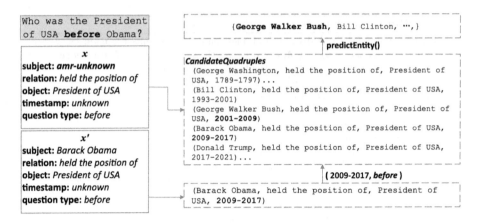

Fig. 3. Temporal reasoning process based on SISs.

complement to the object. The out-going edge "time" and the node $z5$ indicate that the question type is "before".

Hence, we can first generate a SIS of x (Fig. 2(c)) as

$x = \{subject : \texttt{amr-unknown}, relation : \texttt{have-org-role-91},$

$object : \texttt{USA president}, timestamp : \texttt{unknown}, question\ type : \texttt{before}\}.$

Nonetheless, x is not enough to express the complete semantic information of the question, because the node $z5(before)$ and $z6(person)$ indicate that there is another fact in the question and the timestamp in x must predate the time of another fact. Therefore, we should also derive an additional x' as a complement to the semantic information of the question according to the concepts of $z7(person)$ and "Obama", such that in the reasoning phase, the timestamp of x' can be used to find the time constraint of x.

$x' = \{subject : \texttt{Obama}, relation : \texttt{have-org-role-91},$

$object : \texttt{USA president}, timestamp : \texttt{unknown}, question\ type : \texttt{before}\}.$

Before reasoning, there could be mismatches of expressions of entities/relations in SISs and those in the TKG. Thus, it is necessary to align them. In our implementation, we used a BERT-based system[1] to encode both the elements in a SIS and the entity $e \in \mathbf{E}$ ($\mathbf{E}$ is a set of entities extracted from the question), and Cosine similarity is used to guide the alignment.

After obtaining the entity $e' \in \mathbf{E}$ that is most similar to the SIS element, we replace it (except `amr-unknown` and `unknown`) with the entity e'. The same procedure is applicable to relations. After alignment, all the entities and relations in SISs are expressed in entities and relations from the underlying TKG, such as x and x' in Fig. 3.

---

[1] https://github.com/hanxiao/bert-as-service.

Algorithm 2: Temporal reasoning using SISs

Input : ss, ss': SISs; $\mathcal{G}$: a TKG;
Output : ans: answer, either an entity e or a timestamp t;
1   $\mathbb{C} \leftarrow$ getCandQuadruples$(ss, \mathcal{G})$;
2   **if** $ss \neq \varnothing \wedge ss' = \varnothing$ **then**
3   **if** $ss.timestamp =$ amr-unknown **then**
4       $ans \leftarrow$ predictTime$(\mathbb{C}, ss)$
5   **else**
6       $t \leftarrow$ getTimeConstraint$(\mathbb{C}, ss.timestamp, ss.type)$;
7   **if** $ss.subject$ or $ss.object$ is amr-unknown **then**
8         $ans \leftarrow$ predictEntity$(\mathbb{C}, ss, t)$;

9   **else if** $ss \neq \varnothing \wedge ss' \neq \varnothing$ **then**
10     $ss'.timestamp \leftarrow$ predictTime$(\mathbb{C}, ss')$;
11     $t \leftarrow$ getTimeConstraint$(\mathbb{C}, ss'.timestamp, ss.type)$;
12   **if** $ss.subject$ or $ss.object$ is amr-unknown **then**
13       $ans \leftarrow$ predictEntity$(\mathbb{C}, ss, t)$;

14   **return** ans;
    Function getTimeConstraint$(\mathbb{C}, timestamp, type)$
1     $t \leftarrow$ find the time constraint using $timestamp$ and $type$;
2   **return** t;

3.3 Temporal Reasoning

To ensure that the reasoning is interpretable, we conceive a two-step procedure for temporal reasoning: 1) the first step is to generate candidate quadruples based on a SIS, which finds quadruples relevant to the question and helps to find the time constraint; and 2) the second step is to implement reasoning based on the time constraint and SISs.

In our implementation, we employed the state-of-the-art TKG embedding model, namely TComplEx [12], to execute entity and timestamp prediction. TComplEx is a tensor factorization method that embeds entities, relations, and timestamps in the complex space, the scoring function of which is

$$\phi(s, r, o, t) = \Re\left(\langle \boldsymbol{u}_s, \boldsymbol{v}_r \odot \boldsymbol{w}_t, \boldsymbol{u}_o^\star \rangle\right), \tag{1}$$

where $\Re(\cdot)$ denotes the real part of a complex vector, $\boldsymbol{u}_o^\star$ is the complex conjugate of the object embedding vector, and $\odot$ is the element-wise product.

The whole procedure is encapsulated in Algorithm 2. In specific, take the quadruples in TKG that intersect with ss as candidate quadruples and generate a set $\mathbb{C}$ (Line 1). If the question can be represented by one SIS, then it executes Lines 2–8. For questions with two SIS, first, according to the question type and the timestamp of ss' (predicted by TComplEx), find the time constraint t in $\mathbb{C}$ (Lines 10–11), which represents a timestamp in $\mathbb{C}$ that satisfies the temporal constraint of the question. Finally, use this time constraint t and ss to infer the final answers (Lines 12–13).

Table 1. Number of different types of questions in CronQuestions.

Type	Train	Dev	Test
Before/After	23,869	1,982	2,151
First/Last	118,556	11,198	11,159
Time Join	55,453	3,878	3,832
Total	197,878	17,058	17,142

Let us denote the number of quadruples in the underlying TKG as $|N_Q|$. It requires $O(|N_Q|)$ time to generate $\mathbb{C}$ (Line 1). In the worst case, it also requires $O(|\mathbb{C}|)$ time to find the time constraint (Line 6 or Line 11). So the time complexity of Algorithm 2 is $O(|N_Q| + |\mathbb{C}|)$.

Example 4. Continue our running example. As shown in Fig. 3, we have SISs x and x' after entity and relation alignment. And there is a fact in the TKG that is (Barack Obama, held the position of, President of USA, 2009--2017), we can infer the timestamp (i.e., 2009--2017) of x' via TComplEx. Next, the timestamp (2009--2017) and the question type (*before*) are used to find the time constraint in the candidate quadruples of x. As the timestamp (i.e., 2001--2009) exists, it is earlier than 2009--2017, so this timestamp (2001--2009) is regarded as the time constraint of x, which can represent the temporal relationship between facts. Finally, the answer George Walker Bush can be inferred by the time constraint (2001--2009) and the object (President of USA), relation (held the position of) of x.

4 Experiments

This section reports our experiment studies.

Dataset. We evaluated the performance of our method using the (only) TKGQA dataset—CronQuestions [17]. It contains 232K complex questions that are further categorized into

- Before/After type: e.g., Who was the President of USA before Obama?,
- First/Last type: e.g., Who was the first President of USA?, and
- Time Join type: e.g., Which club did Cristiano Ronaldo play for when Messi played for FC Barcelona?

In CronQuestions, each question contains a set of gold answers. The statistics of the dataset are detailed in Table 1.

Baselines. Our method is compared with the following baselines.

- EmbedKGQA [18] leverages KG embedding to perform multi-hop KGQA but it can only deal with non-temporal KGs and single entity questions.

Table 2. Comparison with other baselines on `CronQuestions` dataset, Hits@1 and Hits@3 for different reasoning type questions. The bold denotes the best results and the underline denotes the comparable second ones.

Methods	Hits@1			Hits@3		
	Before/After	First/Last	Time Join	Before/After	First/Last	Time Join
EmbedKGQA	0.199	0.324	0.223	0.492	0.523	0.690
T-EaE-add	0.256	0.285	0.175	0.405	0.442	0.302
T-EaE-replace	0.256	0.288	0.168	0.417	0.453	0.316
CronKGQA	0.288	0.371	0.511	0.500	0.581	0.701
TempoQR	**0.670**	<u>0.570</u>	**0.894**	**0.829**	<u>0.733</u>	**0.937**
CronKGQA *	0.158	0.370	0.278	0.281	0.579	0.438
TempoQR *	<u>0.585</u>	0.507	0.719	<u>0.780</u>	0.694	<u>0.867</u>
AE-TQ	0.542	**0.762**	<u>0.737</u>	0.701	**0.793**	0.767

- T-EaE-add [17] uses the element-wise sum of BERT and entity/time embedding as the input.
- T-EaE-replace [17] replaces the BERT embedding with the entity/time embedding from a pre-trained TKG embedding model. T-EaE-add and T-EaE-replace are based on EaE [4].
- CronKGQA [17] is an extension of EmbedKGQA, which leverages Temporal KG Embedding [12] to perform TKGQA.
- TempoQR [15] exploits TKG embeddings to ground the question to the specific entities and time scope it refers to and utilizes the score function of TKG embedding model for answer prediction.

As mentioned above, these methods are highly dependent on the annotations in the dataset. Representatively, TempoQR treats the annotation (e.g., head entity, tail entity, and timestamp) as a component to enrich the input.

For a fairer comparison of experimental results, we modify the inputs of CronKGQA and TempoQR to make them less dependent on annotations of the dataset and concentrate on the question (i.e., natural language sentence). In detail, we use a Named Entity Recognition (NER) system [7] to extract entities and timestamps from the question sentence, and then align them with the supported TKG. The head and tail entities are determined by the order in which the entities appear in the question. In the experiment, these modified methods are marked with *.

Metrics and Implementation. Hits@1 and Hits@3 are used to evaluate the experimental results. We use TComplEx embedding model as implemented in [12]. All baselines follow the original parameter settings. Our method uses Penman (a Python library and tool for AMR graphs) [6] to parse the AMR graph.

4.1 Main Results

We compare the performance of these methods on the complex questions of `CronQuestions`. As recorded in Table 2, AE-TQ outperforms EmbedKGQA, T-

Table 3. Results of different types of complex questions.

Type	Correct	Sum	Accuracy
Before/After	1,197	1,993	**0.600**
First/Last	7,455	9,150	**0.814**
Time Join	2,351	3,156	**0.744**
Total	11,003	14,299	**0.769**

EaE-add, T-EaE-replace, and CronKGQA on all types and metrics. Compared with CronKGQA, the relative improvements at Hits@1 reach 88.1%, 105.3% and 44.2%, respectively. The reason might be that CronKGQA ignores the temporal logic unveiled by a question, since it only employs the head entity, tail entity, and timestamp (given by the annotation) as the basic units to model a time-sensitive framework. Notably, the temporal words (i.e., *before* and *last*) identified by AE-TQ are able to explicitly indicate the temporal logic inside the question. After that, combined with our temporal reasoning module, the generation of the answer works more accurately.

Compared with TempoQR, our method leads by 19.2% at Hits@1 and 6.0% at Hits@3 in "First/Last" type, while meets gaps in "Before/After" and "Time Join". As mentioned before, different from the ground truth of "First/Last", the gold labels of these two types consist of different entities. AE-TQ can effectively locate the most suitable answer, proved by the result in "First/Last", but fails to exploit features of similar candidates. Nevertheless, TempoQR fuses entities and timestamps from annotations into the representation of the question, and trains on question-answer pairs. The procedure encourages it to explore entities with semantics-similarity, making TempoQR cover more potential answers.

As shown in Table 2, the performance of both CronKGQA and TempoQR degrades significantly after removing the annotations from the inputs. The results illustrate that they are too dependent on the experimental setting, which contradicts the practical application. Our method beats TempoQR * on "First/Last" and "Time Join" type at Hits@1, the relative improvement reaches 50.2% and 2.5%, respectively. For "First/Last" type, our method also outperforms TempoQR * by 14.2% at Hits@3. As TempoQR * still equips with an end-to-end training framework, with enough training samples supporting, it can acquire some superiority in some metrics.

In conclusion, AE-TQ exhibits competitive performance in more realistic settings, which proves that the proposed AMR graph-based semantic parsing method is effective in complex question answering over TKG.

4.2   Performance w.r.t. Different Question Types

Distinct from other approaches, AE-TQ can directly achieve the graph search over the provided TKG to locate the ideal entity based on the generated AMR graph. To evaluate the search, we apply the entity and timestamp specified in *ss* and ss' to match temporal quadruples instead of using TComplEx to calculate the similarity scores.

As shown in Table 3, for questions in "First/Last" type, as AE-TQ can effectively determine the earliest or latest timestamp from the candidates, the accuracy gets the highest score. When it comes to the questions of type "Before/After", though AE-TQ can identify the question type, the temporal logic necessitates further reasoning. It is more difficult to parse semantic information. Therefore, the accuracy of this type is also the lowest. Overall, our method achieves 76.9% accuracy on complex question answering, which proves that our proposed AMR graph-based question parsing method is effective.

4.3   Performance w.r.t. Question Type Identification

The type of question plays a crucial role in the temporal reasoning stage since it associates with different time constraints leading to the corresponding process. In our method, we utilize the AMR graph to identify the question type.

For "Before/After" type questions, AMR graph can effectively identify the temporal signal words (i.e., before and after). Similarly, for questions in "First/Last" type, the "ordinal-entity:value 1" or "ordinal-entity:value -1" are used to indicate the chronological order of the answers in the AMR graph. Therefore, the question type of these questions can be determined by their features. In "Time Join" type, the question may not a signal word but comprise two facts or an explicit timestamp, which supports the typing of such questions.

We perform the experiments on mentioned types and the result is illustrated in Table 4. The results show that the identification accuracy for "Before/After" and "Time join" is more than 85%. The overall accuracy is more than 88%, which shows that the identification method based on AMR graph is effective.

Table 4. Results of question type prediction.

Type	Corr.	Sum	Acc
Before/After	1,834	2,151	**0.852**
First/Last	9,564	11,159	**0.857**
Time Join	3,752	3,832	**0.979**
Total	15,150	17,142	**0.883**

Table 5. Results of answer type prediction.

Type	Corr.	Sum	Acc
Before/After	1,929	1,993	**0.967**
First/Last	8,469	9,150	**0.925**
Time Join	2,983	3,156	**0.945**
Total	13,381	14,299	**0.935**

4.4   Performance w.r.t. Answer Type Identification

The answer type potentially benefits the answer generation. For instance, with a "timestamp" answer type, the model can filter non-numeric candidates. As an essential component of AE-TQ, we evaluate the prediction's accuracy.

Specifically, after AMR parsing, there is an `amr-unknown` node in the graph whose position indicates the answer type of the related question. If the subject or

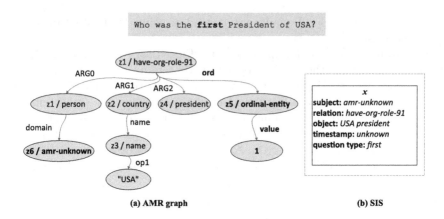

Fig. 4. Case study of a "First/Last" type question.

object in SIS is the `amr-unknown` node, then the answer type of the question must be a non-numeric entity. And if the timestamp in SIS is the `amr-unknown` node, then the answer is numeric. We experimentally demonstrate that our method can effectively discriminate the answer types of questions. As shown in Table 5, experimental results show that our method achieves more than 93% identification accuracy on three types of questions.

4.5   Case Study

We further report a case study by looking into a sample question of "First/Last" type to demonstrate the interpretability of the proposed method. Consider a complex question ''`Who was the first President of USA?`'', the corresponding AMR graph is shown in Fig. 4(a), node *(z5/ordinal-entity:value 1)* indicates that `amr-unknown` must be the subject corresponding to the earliest timestamp in the candidate quadruples. Based on Algorithm 1, we can get a SIS, as shown in Fig. 4(b), after entity and relation alignment, this SIS can be expressed by y.

$y \leftarrow \{subject : $ `amr-unknown`$, relation : $ `held the position of`,

$object : $ `President of USA`$, timestamp : $ `unknown`$, question\ type : $ `first`$\}$,

Next, we feed y into Algorithm 2 to find the correct answer. As shown in Fig. 3, the earliest timestamp is (1789--1797) in the candidate quadruples, so we treat (1789--1797) as the time constraint of y, and the answer `George Washington` can be inferred by (1789--1797) and the object (`President of USA`), relation (`held the position of`) of y.

5   Conclusion

In this paper, we have proposed a novel method for complex question answering over TKGs, which does not pre-labeling of the questions, and hence, substantially reduces the burden of a real-life question answering system. In particular, we introduce AMR parsing to identify the temporal signal words in the question, as well as the temporal relationships among facts. We also conceive the concept of question-oriented semantic information structure, which is derived from AMR graphs for determining semantic roles and question types. Then, temporal reasoning is performed using the structures to obtain the final answers. The experiment results show that it empirically outperforms several competing methods in various settings.

Acknowledgements. This work is supported by Guangzhou Basic and Applied Basic Research Foundation (Grant No. 202201020131), GuangDong Basic and Applied Basic Research Foundation 2019B1515120048, and NSFC under grants No.61872446.

References

1. Banarescu, L., et al.: Abstract meaning representation for sembanking. In: LAW-ID@ACL, pp. 178–186 (2013)
2. Bevilacqua, M., Blloshmi, R., Navigli, R.: One SPRING to rule them both: symmetric AMR semantic parsing and generation without a complex pipeline. In: AAAI, pp. 12564–12573 (2021)
3. Bordes, A., Usunier, N., García-Durán, A., Weston, J., Yakhnenko, O.: Translating embeddings for modeling multi-relational data. In: NIPS, pp. 2787–2795 (2013)
4. Févry, T., Soares, L.B., FitzGerald, N., Choi, E., Kwiatkowski, T.: Entities as experts: sparse memory access with entity supervision. In: EMNLP, pp. 4937–4951 (2020)
5. García-Durán, A., Dumancic, S., Niepert, M.: Learning sequence encoders for temporal knowledge graph completion. In: EMNLP, pp. 4816–4821 (2018)
6. Goodman, M.W.: Penman: an open-source library and tool for AMR graphs. In: ACL, pp. 312–319 (2020)
7. Honnibal, M., Montani, I., Van Landeghem, S., Boyd, A.: spaCy: industrial-strength natural language processing in python (2020)
8. Jia, Z., Abujabal, A., Roy, R.S., Strötgen, J., Weikum, G.: Tempquestions: a benchmark for temporal question answering. In: WWW, pp. 1057–1062 (2018)
9. Jia, Z., Abujabal, A., Roy, R.S., Strötgen, J., Weikum, G.: TEQUILA: temporal question answering over knowledge bases. In: CIKM, pp. 1807–1810 (2018)
10. Jia, Z., Pramanik, S., Roy, R.S., Weikum, G.: Complex temporal question answering on knowledge graphs. In: CIKM, pp. 792–802 (2021)
11. Kingsbury, P.R., Palmer, M.: From treebank to propbank. In: LREC (2002)
12. Lacroix, T., Obozinski, G., Usunier, N.: Tensor decompositions for temporal knowledge base completion. In: ICLR (2020)
13. Leblay, J., Chekol, M.W.: Deriving validity time in knowledge graph. In: WWW, pp. 1771–1776 (2018)
14. Liu, Y., Hua, W., Zhou, X.: Temporal knowledge extraction from large-scale text corpus. World Wide Web **24**(1), 135–156 (2021). https://doi.org/10.1007/s11280-020-00836-5
15. Mavromatis, C., et al.: Tempoqr: temporal question reasoning over knowledge graphs. In: AAAI, pp. 5825–5833(2022)

16. Portisch, J., Heist, N., Paulheim, H.: Knowledge graph embedding for data mining vs. knowledge graph embedding for link prediction - two sides of the same coin? Semantic Web **13**(3), 399–422 (2022)
17. Saxena, A., Chakrabarti, S., Talukdar, P.P.: Question answering over temporal knowledge graphs. In: ACL/IJCNLP, pp. 6663–6676 (2021)
18. Saxena, A., Tripathi, A., Talukdar, P.P.: Improving multi-hop question answering over knowledge graphs using knowledge base embeddings. In: ACL, pp. 4498–4507 (2020)
19. Trivedi, P., Maheshwari, G., Dubey, M., Lehmann, J.: LC-QuAD: a corpus for complex question answering over knowledge graphs. In: d'Amato, C., et al. (eds.) ISWC 2017. LNCS, vol. 10588, pp. 210–218. Springer, Cham (2017). https://doi.org/10.1007/978-3-319-68204-4_22
20. Yang, B., Yih, W., He, X., Gao, J., Deng, L.: Embedding entities and relations for learning and inference in knowledge bases. In: ICLR (2015)

Hotspots Recommender: Spatio-Temporal Prediction of Ride-Hailing and Taxicab Services

Huan Huang$^{(\boxtimes)}$, Basem Suleiman⦿, and Waheeb Yaqub⦿

School of Computer Science, The University of Sydney, Sydney, NSW 2006, Australia
hhua9871@uni.sydney.edu.au,
{basem.suleiman,waheeb.faizmohammad}@sydney.edu.au

Abstract. The complexity of predicting hotspot areas for taxicab services has recently increased with the popularity of ride-hailing services such as Uber and Lyft. In this paper, we first reveal that passengers in certain areas prefer ride-hailing services over taxicab services at certain times, and propose an enhanced LSTM model for predicting the hotspots areas of ride-hailing and taxicab services. It learns the spatio-temporal aspects of ride-hailing and taxicab services' pickup and drop-off orders to predict future orders every 10-min, based on which, a hotspot recommender system that comprises a pipeline of recommending the best hotspot areas to taxicab drivers by taking both regional passenger's preference and the distance of the driver's current location into account. The evaluation of our approach on real datasets of five ride-hailing and taxicab service providers in New York City (NYC) demonstrated sensible accuracy which is comparable to baseline models. We demonstrate the benefits of our hotspot recommender algorithm over two scenarios considering the NYC dataset and our demand and supply prediction model in terms of suggesting the best hotspots taxicab drivers should target.

Keywords: Machine learning · Taxicab services · Ride-hailing services · Hotspots · Recommender system

1 Introduction

In the US, ride-hailing services such as Uber and Lyft have attracted the majority of passengers of the traditional taxicab services (e.g., Yellow and Green taxis) and therefore have significantly challenged the long-existing traditional taxicab services [2]. On-demand ordering of ride-hailing services relies mainly on location-based services that naturally grants ride-sharing service providers a competitive advantage given the data collected from the passengers' orders and trips. In particular, ride-hailing providers use orders and trip data to forecast hotspot areas where there is high demand for passenger orders and less supply of drivers. Therefore, ride-sharing providers could optimize the allocation of the nearest drivers to the hotspots, and even share hotspot areas with their drivers (often

© The Author(s), under exclusive license to Springer Nature Switzerland AG 2022
R. Chbeir et al. (Eds.): WISE 2022, LNCS 13724, pp. 81–94, 2022.
https://doi.org/10.1007/978-3-031-20891-1_7

through systems such as Uber's Surge[1]) so they can target profitable areas ahead of time. With such a competitive advantage, traditional taxicab service providers are challenged with the need to intelligently predict not only the hotspot areas in terms of demand but also the supply of other traditional and ride-hailing service providers. This problem can even be more complex, given the variable passenger preferences over location and time. Passengers may prefer ride-hailing services at certain times, and locations are given the dynamic pricing of these services (charges can become more expensive at certain times and/or from certain busy locations). For example, as illustrated in Fig. 1, region 235 is a hotspot for Uber, while it is not for Green and Yellow cabs[2]. The opposite also holds where ride-hailing services can be cheaper than taxicab services when there is low demand (number of pickups) and high supply (number of drop-offs) of services. There have been many studies on forecasting hotspot areas for taxicab services on an hourly basis. Some studies used road sensor data to identify hotspots with recurrent neural network (RNN) models [12,22,26], or Convolution neural network (CNN) models [27], and some others used pedestrian trajectory [6]. However, such studies considered traffic data (such as taxicabs and road sensor data) but failed to account for the actual demand (number of pickup orders) and supply (number of drop-offs). It also did not consider the availability of other competitors (e.g., Uber, Lyft, and other traditional taxicab services). Furthermore, these studies predicted hotspots hourly. Prediction at fine granular levels (e.g. 10 min) can be more useful given the dynamic changes in the number of pickups and dropoffs over time [7].

In this paper, we address the above-discussed problem of predicting hotspot areas considering multiple ride-hailing and taxicab services. We first reveal that there is a spatio-temporal difference in terms of the passengers' preference, such as region 265 (Fig. 1) which had plentiful supplies of Uber and Lyft over the summer season in 2019, while only a few yellow taxicabs were in demand. This suggests that taxicab drivers should consider moving to other regions and thus it should be considered when recommending hotspot areas. We present our novel spatio-temporal and context-aware approach that learns the demand and supply of taxicab and ride-hailing services based holistically on real data (pick-up and drop-off orders) from five service providers, namely, Yellow cabs, Green cabs, Uber, Lyft, and Via. By embedding orders of all regions at the same timestamp, fine-granular time intervals (i.e., every 10-min) as one input for a long-short-term memory (LSTM) model to predict the potential demand and supply of these five service providers, the resulting prediction will contain demand and supply with spatio-temporal aspects. Based on this model, we further propose a hotspot recommender system that recommends areas of potentially higher probability to gain passengers. The result shows that this approach is promising and competitive with other state-of-the-art algorithms.

---

[1] https://www.uber.com/blog/courier-surge-intro/.

[2] Based on historical pickups and drop-offs of five ride-hailing and taxicab service providers across 265 regions in New York City.

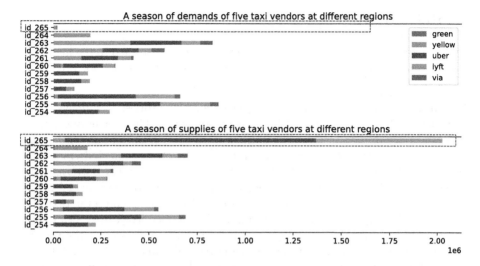

Fig. 1. A comparison of the total orders of five taxi vendors in a season at all regions in the New York City.

The contributions of our proposed approach are twofold[3]:

- we reveal that there is a spatio-temporal difference in terms of the passengers' preference, such as region 235 in Fig. 1 was a hotspot for Uber, while it is not for Green and Yellow cabs. This suggests that the taxicab drivers should consider moving to other regions.
- Spatio-temporal prediction models consisting of hotspots classifier and hotspots recommender for taxicab and ride-hailing services. Unlike existing approaches which consider one service provider at a time and aggregate the prediction on an hourly basis, our models predict the demand and supply of the five service providers (ride-hailing and traditional taxicabs) in all regions at every 10-min time interval. This provides a more fine-granular prediction which can help taxicab drivers to consider different hotspots more frequently (rather than every hour) [7].

The rest of this paper is organized as follows. Section 2 presents analysis of related work in the literature. Section 3 presents our proposed Hotspot recommender method and algorithms. The experiments and evaluation results of our proposed hotspot recommender and baseline models are introduced in Sect. 4. Two scenarios of how to use our hotspot recommender are also discussed in Sect. 4. Section 5 concludes with key summary and future work.

---

[3] The datasets used in our study, the implementation of our algorithms and models, and supplementary results and materials can be accessed from the project repository https://github.com/BasemSuleiman/HotspotRecommender.

2   Related Work

The taxi data recommendation problem has been widely studied in the literature [11]. Research can be divided into two groups: different methods for predicting the hotspots and exploring for higher accuracy.

Hotspot Prediction Methods: Zhang et al. [28] propose a framework for predicting hotspots' demand for the recommendation. The framework utilizes historical taxicab data, assigning a hotness score to each timestamp with a proposed algorithm, then recommends the top-k^{th} hotspots to taxicab drivers. Li et al. [10] and Moreira-Matias et al. [13] investigate human mobility patterns using an improved ARIMA model to predict the spatial-temporal passengers' distribution in a hotspot. Xu et al. [23] map a trajectory graph based on the taxicabs' frequency, they have used HotSpotScan and Preference Trajectory Scan algorithms. This enables them to calculate the probability and forecast the waiting time for getting a taxi. In addition, Kernel Density Estimation can be applied to detect hotspots statistically, as Zheng et al. [29] demonstrated in their research, and Chan et al.'s method can effectively visualize the results from A to B [3].

Hotspot Prediction Accuracy: Some studies emphasized the design of more efficient algorithms for ride-hailing services [20]. Simonetto et al. [16] cast the ride-hailing problem as a linear assignment problem between fleet vehicles and passenger trip requests within a federated optimization architecture, to achieve a faster, almost real-time suggestion. Furthermore, most of the literature addresses prediction by learning taxicab GPS traces and mobility pattern of passengers, some use it to build a recommendation system [14,25], some simply predict with time series models [19,22]. Others provide only statistical results on market shares between Uber, Lyft, and taxicabs [9], or unilaterally analyze the major ride-hailing company [5,17]. Some researchers proposed ideas to help this traditional taxicab sector remain competitive [24], but did not yet provide recommendation services based on hotspot prediction and game theory as we propose. Moreover, we discuss in Sect. 4.5 to justify whether it is worthy to struggle for a higher accuracy by several percentages in the real-world problem like taxi demands forecasting.

   In summary, previous studies rarely investigated the interaction between different ride-hailing and taxicab service providers when predicting hotspots. Besides, they did not consider spatio-temporal prediction at the fine-granular level (10-min) and a game theory-based recommender to support competing taxicab drivers in targeting hotspot areas and increasing their profit.

3   Method - Hotspot Recommender for Taxicab and Ride-Hailing Services

Our proposed Hotspot Recommender includes a number of notations that are used to describe the prediction model. These notations are summarised in Table 1.

Table 1. Notations used in this study

Notation	Definition
$D^{p_k}_{t_i,l_j}$	The number of demands at location l_j, timestamp t_i for the service provider p_k
$S^{p_k}_{t_i,l_j}$	The number of supplies at location l_j, timestamp t_i for the service provider p_k
$D^{p_k}_{t_i}$	A j-dimensional vector indicating the demands of all regions at timestamp t_i for the service provider p_k. Similarly, the supply cases: $S^{p_k}_{t_i}$
D^{p_k}	A sequence of demand vectors with the length $= i$ for the service provider p_k. Similarly, the supply cases: S^{p_k}
D	The demand dataset of all service providers. Similarly, the supply dataset is denoted as S
D'	The predicted demand dataset of all service providers. Similarly, the predicted supply dataset is denoted as S'
$dist\_mx$	A matrix maintaining the distance between all locations
$hotspot\_list$	The hotspots identified by the hotspot identifier (Algorithm 1)
$prefer\_list$	A list of location IDs where the taxicabs' market share rates are higher than 1%
$src, dest$	The source location when the driver sends the request and the suggested location

Predicting hotspot areas requires historical taxi order data from different ride-hailing and taxicab services. In this study, we use the New York City Taxi and Limousine Commission (TLC) Trip Record dataset[4]. The dataset is based on statistical pickup and drop-off orders organized by region. As such, we consider the centroid of a region to be the location of all vehicles within that area. We aim to predict the hotspot areas at 10-min intervals. In the scope of our study, we assume there is no difference between vehicles on traffic conditions, vehicle speeds, and price during the fine-granular 10-min time window, and that there is no denial trip due to the passenger's willingness.

The overall structure of our proposed Hotspots Recommender, including key components and models, is depicted in Fig. 2.

Demand and Supply Models: We model the demand and supply are as follows. Let $D^{p_k}_{t_i,l_j}$ denote the historical demand (number of pickups) in location l_j at timestamp t_i for the service provider p_k, where i is the index of timestamp, $j \in [1, 265]$ being the index of location id, $k \in [0, 5)$ is the index of taxi providers. Similarly, the corresponding supply (number of drop-offs) is $S^{p_k}_{t_i,l_j}$.

Location Embedding Model: A taxicab moves from location A and arrives at location B over time. Hence, the pickup and drop-off orders of different locations are not strictly independent, they are spatial-temporally correlative. We combined all orders in separated regions $l_1, l_2, \ldots, l_j$, at the same timestamp, into one j-dimensional input. For example, if there are three locations with demand orders (4, 2, 6) at timestamp t_i, the 3-dimensional vector will be $D_{t_i} = \{4, 2, 6\}$. Thus, the resulting demand vector at timestamp t_i, provider

---

[4] https://www1.nyc.gov/site/tlc/about/tlc-trip-record-data.page.

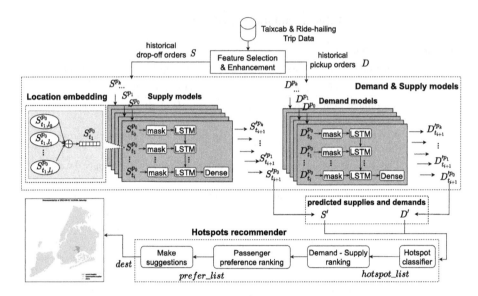

Fig. 2. Proposed Hotspot Recommender framework. Three components are described above, feature embedding, time series model, hotspots recommender service.

p_k, is $D_{t_i}^{p_k} = \{D_{t_i,l_1}^{p_k} || D_{t_i,l_2}^{p_k} || \ldots || D_{t_i,l_j}^{p_k}\}$. Similarly, the corresponding embedded supply vector is $S_{t_i}^{p_k} = \{S_{t_i,l_1}^{p_k} || S_{t_i,l_2}^{p_k} || \ldots || S_{t_i,l_j}^{p_k}\}$.

Demand and Supply Prediction: LSTM [8] is a variant of the recurrent neural network. As part of our proposed model, a mask layer was added before it. Because there were occasions that all locations had no orders, it automatically skips these cases during the training process, to avoid training bias. Given a set of historical demands after location embedding D^{p_k}, the mask layer initializes it as $(D^{p_k})_m$. Then the data is fed to the LSTM cell recurrently to update the model. The output of this cell is the last hidden state h_{t+1}. Later it is fed to the dense layer to calculate the most probable value $D_{t_{i+1}}'^{p_k}$ in the nearest future timestamp t_{i+1}:

$$D_{t_{i+1}}'^{p_k} = \text{LSTM}(\{D_{t_0}^{p_k}, D_{t_1}^{p_k}, \ldots, D_{t_i}^{p_k}\}) \tag{1}$$

The structure of the supply model is the same, only the input is changed from D^{p_k} to S^{p_k}, and the corresponding output. (We also tested the GRU [4], and the performance is very similar to the LSTM. Thus, we used LSTM in our approach.)

Hotspots Classifier: Areas such as the central business district during rush hours, and around the famous clubs during midnight on weekends are representative examples of hotspots. Our goal is to first predict the demand and supply as described above so that we can identify hotspot areas. As some areas could be more intense (the ratio of demand is much higher than supply), we need to classify the level of hotspot areas. Algorithm 1 takes in the predicted demands of all regions and classifies every one of them into ("low", "low to medium", "medium",

---

Algorithm 1. Proposed hotspots classifier

Input: D'
Output: $hotspot\_list$
$U \leftarrow$ find unique values of D'
$bin \leftarrow \max(U)/5$, each bin represent one category of low, low to medium, medium, medium to high, high
initial an empty list variable $hotspot\_list$
for all d in D' **do**
    check which bin category d falls in
    push d-bin pair to $hotspot\_list$
end for
return $hotspot\_list$

"medium to high", "high"), then returns a list variable $hotspot\_list$ encompassing locationID - category pairs.

Demand-Supply Ranking: We capture the interaction between taxicab/ride-hailing drivers and passengers as two groups of participants [1]. Based on our hotspot classification, the choices for a driver can be: "high demand rank", "low supply rank", or "high demands - supplies gap rank". However, it has been reported that the dominant reasons passengers choose ride-hailing services are "Trip cost (fare)", "Travel time", "Ease of payment" [18]. Also, it was reported that the "Trip cost (fare)" and "Ease of payment" were the advantages of ride-hailing taxi services. Therefore, a driver can only choose the location with the highest "high demands - supplies gap" to gain the largest probability of attaining a passenger.

Passenger Preference: Some passengers prefer certain taxi service providers in some regions and at certain times (as illustrated in the Introduction section, Fig. 1). We refer to this phenomenon as the indicator of "passenger preference", and mathematically calculate it using the ratio of the taxicabs' market share in the total market share in the respective region – if the ratio was less than 1% in a region, we say the passengers in this region were unwilling to take on a taxicab, and the region should not be recommended to the taxicab drivers whatsoever. This locationID - ratio pairs are stored as $prefer\_list$.

Based on the above models, the logic of our proposed hotspots recommender (shown in Fig. 2) is summarized as follows. First, the historical pickup and drop-off data, $D_{t_i,l_j}^{p_k}, S_{t_i,l_j}^{p_k}$, are arranged to the nearest 10-min time slot, e.g. from '2019-06-01 09:29:46' to '2019-06-01 09:20:00'. Second, the location embedding method is applied to transform the data into j-dimensional vectors, $D_{t_i}^{p_k}, S_{t_i}^{p_k}$ as individual location can be influenced by other locations and dependencies. Third, the sequences $D_{t_i}^{p_k}, S_{t_i}^{p_k}$ are then fed each as input for the corresponding time series model (each service provider had its own model) so that each taxi provider can learn its own regional latent correlation with individual models, to produce the potential future demand and supply predictions at $t = i + 1$, $D_{t_{i+1}}'^{p_k}, S_{t_{i+1}}'^{p_k}$. Furthermore, the framework can be extended to accommodate new taxi service

---

Algorithm 2. Proposed hotspots recommender

Input: $D', S', dist\_mx, hotspot\_list, prefer\_list, src$
Output: suggested location id
$W_d, W_h, W_g \leftarrow$ create new lists
$R_{src} \leftarrow$ the index row of src in $dist\_mx$
for all $dist$ in R_{src} **do**
    $x \leftarrow \ln(dist + 1)/10$ scale down the distance value to be comparable with other weights
    insert x to W_d
end for
for all d in D', s in S' **do**
    $x \leftarrow \ln(max(d - s, 1))$
    insert x to W_g
    if d is in hotspot_list and in prefer_list **then**
        $y \leftarrow 1$
    else
        $y \leftarrow 0$
    end if
    insert y to W_h
end for
$dest \leftarrow max(W_d + W_h + W_g)$
return the index of the $dest$

---

providers by adding its time series model. Forth, the predicted demand and supply for all regions at a 10-min interval, are passed as input D', S' into the hotspot recommender, where the hotspots are identified by hotspot identifier Algorithm 1 and stored as *hotspot_list*. And the distance weights between source *src* and other locations are converted from the distance matrix *dist_mx* since hotspots with shorter distances should rank higher. Both *hotspot_list* and *dist_mx* are used as the inputs and determine the location for recommendation (Algorithm 2). In the Algorithm 2, the predicted demand-supply gaps $(D' - S')$ are converted to Demand-supply weights. Because the raw number of demand-supply gaps is confounding, for example, a location with 41(demand) - 40(supply) vs another with 1(demand) - 0(supply), the former location should rank higher. The same rule applies to the ratio. Then the recommender checks if each ranked location is in the *prefer_list*. As a result, the *dest* is computed as the location with the maximum weight and considered the best hotspot for the taxicab driver.

4   Experiment and Results

4.1   Datasets

We use the New York City Taxi and Limousine Commission (TLC) Trip Record Dataset[5] to evaluate our proposed demand and supply prediction model and

---

[5] https://www1.nyc.gov/site/tlc/about/tlc-trip-record-data.page.

hotspot recommender. These taxi/ride-hailing service data were obtained by the meters embedded in the taxicabs and the associated mobile ride-hailing application records. As the dataset consists of tens of millions of records, we focus on the summer season which is often the busiest season of the year. We also used 2019 data which is before Covid-19. The common features are *pickup datetime, pickup location, drop-off datetime, drop-off location, vehicle type, quantity.* The models used the "Roll Forward" method to predict the future one point using the previous whole week's data points. For example, to predict the 1008_{th} data point, the input is 0_{th} to 1007_{th}, then for the 1009_{th}, the input is 1_{th} to 1008_{th}. Hence, historical data from '2019-06-01 00:00:00' to '2019-06-06 23:59:50' was trained to predict '2019-06-07 00:00:00'. We predicted a week of data for evaluation, the input was from '2019-06-01 00:00:00' to '2019-06-13 23:59:50'[6].

4.2 Experiments Setup

We implemented our cleaning procedure and models with Python 3.7 in Google Colab, which was Linux 5.4.109+. Then a visualization platform was built with R (version 4.0.5 (2021-03-31)). We evaluated the performance of our prediction model by comparing it with baseline models namely auto-regressive integrated moving average (ARIMA), and Holt-Winter's exponential smoothing (Holt-Winters ES). These models demonstrated good performance for short-term spatio-temporal demand and supply prediction problems [15].

ARIMA is a generalization of an autoregressive moving average (ARMA) model. We implemented our proposed prediction using the ARIMA model with the parameters set as ($p = 1, d = 0, q = 2$) to adapt to the 10-min prediction interval (in contrast to hourly time intervals [19]).

The Holt-Winters ES model estimates the future time-series data by combining the exponential smoothing influences of value, trend, and seasonality. We implemented the Holt-Winters ES model and set the "seasonal_periods" parameter to a day (=6*24, as there are 6 10-min intervals in an hour, 24 h a day).

Besides, we implemented our proposed demand and supply prediction and recommender using LSTM. The model input is $shape = (none, 1008, 265)$, masking layer $shape = (none, 1008, 265)$ for both input and output, one layer LSTM with input $shape = (none, 1008, 265)$, output $shape = (none, 512)$, lastly, the dimensional conversion dense layer with input $shape = (none, 512)$ (512 neurons) and output $shape = (none, 265)$.

4.3 Evaluation Metrics

We evaluate the prediction accuracy of the models using Root Mean Square Error (RMSE) and Mean Absolute Error (MAE) [21, 22].

---

[6] The datasets used in our study, the implementation of our algorithms and models, and supplementary results and materials can be accessed from the project repository https://github.com/BasemSuleiman/HotspotRecommender.

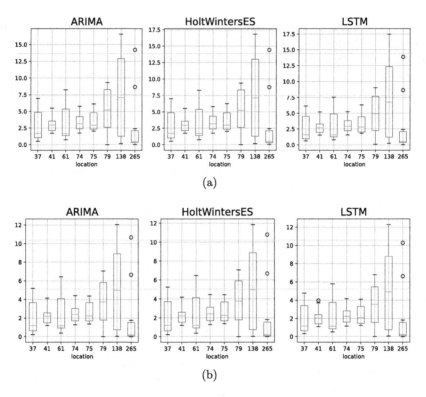

Fig. 3. Two boxplots, (a) RMSE (b) MAE, with selected regions on x-axis, and RMSE/MAE values on y-axis, indicating the evaluation metrics.

4.4　Results

The three models (LSTM, ARIMA, and Holt-Winters ES) are implemented to predict the demand and supply every 10-min across the 265 regions in New York City. Figure 3 shows the box plots of the RMSE and MAE of the three prediction models across eight locations. These locations demonstrate significant trip and order activities. The box plots show that the RMSE and MAE of the three models are quite similar.

Table 2 shows the breakdown of the average accuracy of demand and supply accuracy across the eight locations for the five taxicab and ride-hailing providers. As it can be noticed, the overall performance of the LSTM model is 5.98% higher than the ARIMA model in RMSE and 5.23% higher than Holt-Winters ES. The prediction of ARIMA and Holt-Winters ES models followed the fluctuation of the real data, while that of the LSTM model tended to predict more stably.

Based on these results, the LSTM is chosen as the base model for our time-series prediction component (in Fig. 2) to predict the demand and supply every

10-min interval. These predictions are then fed to the Hotspots Recommender Algorithm 2 to recommend the best hotspot areas for taxi drivers[7].

Table 2. MAE and RMSE of ARIMA, Holt-Winters ES and LSTM models

		ARIMA		HoltWinters ES		LSTM	
Service provider	Type	MAE	RMSE	MAE	RMSE	MAE	RMSE
Green	Demand	1.00	1.49	1.03	1.52	**0.93**	**1.39**
	Supply	0.89	1.40	0.89	1.40	**0.85**	**1.30**
Lyft	Demand	3.15	4.24	3.15	4.28	**2.97**	**4.02**
	Supply	3.84	5.16	3.87	5.20	**3.64**	**4.87**
Uber	Demand	5.33	7.14	5.34	7.21	**5.17**	**6.96**
	Supply	6.36	8.68	6.42	8.76	**5.97**	**8.14**
Via	Demand	1.10	1.57	1.11	1.58	**1.00**	**1.40**
	Supply	1.09	1.61	1.09	1.62	**1.03**	**1.49**
Yellow	Demand	3.30	4.60	3.30	4.62	**3.16**	**4.40**
	Supply	2.90	4.04	2.92	4.07	**2.78**	**3.88**

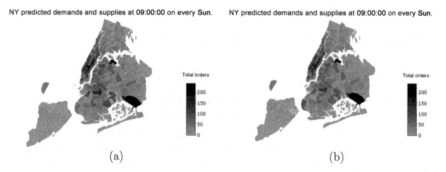

(a)   (b)

Fig. 4. The recommended area (yellow region) on Sunday morning at 9:00 am when the driver is at (red circled)(a) East New York (b) Arrochar/Fort Wadsworth (Color figure online)

4.5 Discussion

Based on the demand and supply prediction models and algorithm described above, we discuss two scenarios to demonstrate how our recommender algorithm suggests the best hotspot areas for taxi drivers.

---

[7] The datasets used in our study, the implementation of our algorithms and models, and supplementary results and materials can be accessed from the project repository https://github.com/BasemSuleiman/HotspotRecommender.

Scenario 1: Recommended hotspot within preference list

Given a taxicab driver at location src = East New York on Sunday at 8:45 AM. Our prediction model forecasted the src's demand of all taxicab and ride-hailing providers to be 41, and the supply of all providers to be 43 at 9:00 am. This is illustrated in Fig. 4 (a). Here, the competition was very high given the Demand-supply weight = 1.69. Our Algorithm 1 classified the $hotspot\_list$ at 9:00 am and the hotspot recommender Algorithm 2 suggested that Canarsie ranked top (with Demand-supply weight = 3.53) and it was within the $prefer\_list$. Therefore, Canarsie was recommended to be the $dest$. The driver is 8 min away from the recommended hotspot.

Scenario 2: Recommended hotspot not within preference list

Given a taxicab driver at location src = Arrochar/Fort Wadsworth on Sunday at 8:45 am. The hotspot classifier Algorithm 1 ranked the predicted Demand-supply weights of all hotspots nearby, while the hotspot recommender Algorithm 2 found that the top-five locations (namely 'Grymes Hill/Clifton', 'Heartland Village/Todt Hill', 'South Beach/Dongan Hills', 'Stapleton', 'Westerleigh', 'West Brighton') should not be recommended as passengers did not prefer taxicab service (from the historical data) in these five locations at 9:00 am. Instead, it recommended the sixth hotspot (Bay Ridge) to the taxicab driver which is 11 min away from the src (see Fig. 4(b))[8].

5   Conclusion and Future Work

We proposed a novel approach to recommend hotspots at 10-min intervals for the taxicab drivers considering the demand and supply of different taxicab and ride-hailing services at different locations and times. We propose an enhanced spatio-temporal LSTM model that predicts the demand and supply of competing taxicab and ride-hailing services. We also propose our hotspots recommender algorithm that ranks all hotspot locations every 10-min and considers passengers' preferences given the time and location. Our experimental evaluation of five taxicab and ride-hailing trips data within New York city demonstrated adequate prediction performance. Our demand and supply prediction model outperforms baseline models across most of the locations. Over two scenarios, we showed how our hotspots recommender algorithm would help taxicab drivers to target the best hotspot locations considering the demand and supply of the competing ride-hailing drivers and passengers' preferences at certain times and locations.

In future work, it could be interesting to investigate the impact of weather conditions on the demand and supply of both taxicab and ride-hailing providers, including other factors such as trip fare, distance, and time in our hotspots recommender algorithm could be another interesting aspect to study. With regards

---

[8] The datasets used in our study, the implementation of our algorithms and models, and supplementary results and materials can be accessed from the project repository https://github.com/BasemSuleiman/HotspotRecommender.

to the deep learning model, it is possible to dive into Transformer based architecture such as the spatio-temporal attention layer on top of the LSTM layer to further improve the performance.

References

1. Bai, Z., Huang, M., Bian, S., Wu, H.: A study of taxi service mode choice based on evolutionary game theory. J. Adv. Transp. **2019** (2019). https://doi.org/10.1155/2019/8607942
2. Calcea, N.: Uber and Lyft are cutting even further into the taxi market during the pandemic, August 2020
3. Chan, T.N., Cheng, R., Yiu, M.L.: QUAD: quadratic-bound-based Kernel density visualization. In: Proceedings of the 2020 ACM SIGMOD International Conference on Management of Data. ACM, June 2020. https://doi.org/10.1145/3318464.3380561
4. Cho, K., et al.: Learning phrase representations using RNN encoder-decoder for statistical machine translation (2014). https://doi.org/10.48550/arXiv:1406.1078
5. Cramer, J., Krueger, A.B.: Disruptive change in the taxi business: the case of Uber. Am. Econ. Rev. **106**(5), 177–182 (2016). https://doi.org/10.3386/w22083
6. Gharineiat, A., Bouguettaya, A., Ba-Hutair, M.N.: A deep reinforcement learning approach for composing moving IoT services. IEEE Trans. Serv. Comput. 1 (2021). https://doi.org/10.1109/TSC.2021.3064329
7. Guo, J., Williams, B.M., Smith, B.L.: Data collection time intervals for stochastic short-term traffic flow forecasting. Transp. Res. Rec. (2007). https://doi.org/10.3141/2024-03
8. Hochreiter, S., Schmidhuber, J.: Long short-term memory. Neural Comput. **9**(8), 1735–1780 (1997). https://doi.org/10.1162/neco.1997.9.8.1735
9. Jiang, S., Chen, L., Mislove, A., Wilson, C.: On ridesharing competition and accessibility: evidence from Uber, Lyft, and taxi. In: The 2018 World Wide Web Conference, WWW 2018, pp. 863–872. International World Wide Web Conferences Steering Committee, Republic and Canton of Geneva, CHE (2018). https://doi.org/10.1145/3178876.3186134
10. Li, X., et al.: Prediction of urban human mobility using large-scale taxi traces and its applications. Front. Comput. Sci. **6**(1), 111–121 (2012). https://doi.org/10.1007/s11704-011-1192-6
11. Lyu, T., Wang, P.S., Gao, Y., Wang, Y.: Research on the big data of traditional taxi and online car-hailing: a systematic review. J. Traffic Transp. Eng. (Engl. Ed.) (2021). https://doi.org/10.1016/j.jtte.2021.01.001
12. Ma, X., Yu, H., Wang, Y., Wang, Y.: Large-scale transportation network congestion evolution prediction using deep learning theory. PloS One **10**(3), e0119044 (2015). https://doi.org/10.1371/journal.pone.0119044
13. Moreira-Matias, L., Gama, J., Ferreira, M., Mendes-Moreira, J., Damas, L.: Predicting taxi-passenger demand using streaming data. IEEE Trans. Intell. Transp. Syst. **14**(3), 1393–1402 (2013). https://doi.org/10.1109/TITS.2013.2262376
14. Rong, H., Zhou, X., Yang, C., Shafiq, Z., Liu, A.: The rich and the poor: a Markov decision process approach to optimizing taxi driver revenue efficiency. In: The 25th ACM International Conference on Information and Knowledge Management (2016). https://doi.org/10.1145/2983323.2983689

15. Schwemmle, N.: Short-term spatio-temporal demand pattern predictions of trip demand. Ph.D. thesis, KU Leuven, February 2021
16. Simonetto, A., Monteil, J., Gambella, C.: Real-time city-scale ridesharing via linear assignment problems. Transp. Res. Part C: Emerg. Technol. **101**, 208–232 (2019). https://doi.org/10.1016/j.trc.2019.01.019
17. Subham, S., Singh, S., Kumar, A., Fatima, F., Geetha, G.: Improving taxi revenue using reinforcement learning. Int. J. Eng. Res. Technol. **8** (2020). https://doi.org/10.17577/IJERTCONV8IS11037
18. Tirachini, A.: Ride-hailing, travel behaviour and sustainable mobility: an international review. Transportation **47**(4), 2011–2047 (2019). https://doi.org/10.1007/s11116-019-10070-2
19. Wan, X., Ghazzai, H., Massoud, Y.: A generic data-driven recommendation system for large-scale regular and ride-hailing taxi services. Electronics **9**(4) (2020). https://doi.org/10.3390/electronics9040648
20. Wang, H., Yang, H.: Ridesourcing systems: a framework and review. Transp. Res. Part B: Methodol. **129**, 122–155 (2019). https://doi.org/10.1016/j.trb.2019.07.009
21. Xu, J., Rahmatizadeh, R., Bölöni, L., Turgut, D.: A sequence learning model with recurrent neural networks for taxi demand prediction. In: 2017 IEEE 42nd Conference on Local Computer Networks (LCN), pp. 261–268. IEEE (2017). https://doi.org/10.1109/LCN.2017.31
22. Xu, J., Rahmatizadeh, R., Bölöni, L., Turgut, D.: Real-time prediction of taxi demand using recurrent neural networks. IEEE Trans. Intell. Transp. Syst. **19**(8), 2572–2581 (2018). https://doi.org/10.1109/TITS.2017.2755684
23. Xu, X., Zhou, J., Liu, Y., Xu, Z., Zhao, X.: Taxi-RS: taxi-hunting recommendation system based on taxi GPS data. IEEE Trans. Intell. Transp. Syst. **16**(4), 1716–1727 (2014). https://doi.org/10.1109/TITS.2014.2371815
24. Yıldızgöz, K., Çelik, H.M.: Critical moment for taxi sector: What should be done by traditional taxi sector after the TNC disruption? In: Nathanail, E.G., Karakikes, I.D. (eds.) CSUM 2018. AISC, vol. 879, pp. 453–460. Springer, Cham (2019). https://doi.org/10.1007/978-3-030-02305-8_55
25. Yuan, J., Zheng, Y., Zhang, L., Xie, X., Sun, G.: Where to find my next passenger. In: The 13th International Conference on Ubiquitous Computing, pp. 109–118 (2011). https://doi.org/10.1145/2030112.2030128
26. Zhang, J., Zheng, Y., Qi, D.: Deep spatio-temporal residual networks for citywide crowd flows prediction. In: 31st AAAI Conference on Artificial Intelligence (2017). https://doi.org/10.5555/3298239.3298479
27. Zhang, J., Zheng, Y., Qi, D., Li, R., Yi, X.: DNN-based prediction model for spatio-temporal data. In: The 24th ACM SIGSPATIAL International Conference on Advances in Geographic Information Systems, pp. 1–4 (2016). https://doi.org/10.1145/2996913.2997016
28. Zhang, K., Feng, Z., Chen, S., Huang, K., Wang, G.: A framework for passengers demand prediction and recommendation. In: 2016 IEEE International Conference on Services Computing (SCC), pp. 340–347. IEEE (2016). https://doi.org/10.1109/SCC.2016.51
29. Zheng, Y., Jestes, J., Phillips, J.M., Li, F.: Quality and efficiency for Kernel density estimates in large data. In: Proceedings of the 2013 International Conference on Management of Data - SIGMOD 2013. ACM Press (2013). https://doi.org/10.1145/2463676.2465319

Query Processing and Information Extraction

Towards a Co-selection Approach for a Global Explainability of Black Box Machine Learning Models

Khoula Meddahi[1], Seif-Eddine Benkabou[2(✉)], Allel Hadjali[1], Amin Mesmoudi[2],
Dou El Kefel Mansouri[3], Khalid Benabdeslem[4], and Souleyman Chaib[5]

[1] ISAE-ENSMA (LIAS), Chasseneuil-du-Poitou, France
allel.hadjali@ensma.fr
[2] Université de Poitiers (LIAS), Poitiers, France
{seif.eddine.benkabou,amin.mesmoudi}@univ-poitiers.fr
[3] University Ibn Khaldoun Tiaret, Tiaret, Algeria
douelkefel.mansouri@univ-tiaret.dz
[4] Université de Lyon (LIRIS), Lyon, France
khalid.benabdeslem@univ-lyon1.fr
[5] École Supérieure d'Informatique (ESI-SBA), Sidi Bel Abbès, Algeria
s.chaib@esi-sba.dz

Abstract. Recently, few methods for understanding machine learning model's outputs have been developed. SHAP and LIME are two well-known examples of these methods. They provide individual explanations based on feature importance for each instance. While remarkable scores have been achieved for individual explanations, understanding the model's decisions globally remains a complex task. Methods like LIME were extended to face this complexity by using individual explanations. In this approach, the problem was expressed as a submodular optimization problem. This algorithm is a bottom-up method aiming at providing a global explanation. It consists of picking a group of individual explanations which illustrate the global behavior of the model and avoid redundancy. In this paper, we propose CoSP (Co-Selection Pick) framework that allows a global explainability of any black-box model by selecting individual explanations based on a similarity preserving approach. Unlike submodular optimization, in our method the problem is considered as a co-selection task. This approach achieves a co-selection of instances and features over the explanations provided by any explainer. The proposed framework is more generic given that it is possible to make the co-selection either in supervised or unsupervised scenarios and also over explanations provided by any local explainer. Preliminary experimental results are made to validate our proposal.

Keywords: Machine learning models · Explicability · Local explanation · Global aggregation

1   Introduction

Nowadays, a wide range of real-life applications such as computer vision [5,11], speech processing, natural language understanding [6], health [14], and military fields [2,4] make use of Machine Learning (ML) models for decision making or prediction/classification purpose. However, those models are often implemented as black boxes which make their predictions difficult to understand for humans. This nature of ML-models limits their adoption and practical applicability in many real world domains and affect the human trust in them. Making ML-models more explainable and transparent is currently a trending topic in data science and artificial intelligence fields which attracts the interest of several researchers.

Explainable AI (XAI) refers to the tools, methods, and techniques that can be used to make the behavior and predictions of ML models to be understandable to human [3]. Thus, the higher the interpretability/explainability of a ML model, the easier it is for someone to comprehend why certain decisions or predictions have been made.

Multiple interpretability approaches are based on additive models where the prediction is a sum of individual marginal effects like feature contribution [16], where a value (denoting the influence on the output) is assigned to each feature. One of the latest proposed methods is based on mathematical Shapeley Values and was introduced by Scott et al. [9] as SHAP (for SHapley Additive exPlanations). It relies on combining ideas from cooperative game theory and local explanations [8].

Let us also mention the LIME (Local Interpretable Model-agnostic Explanations) method which is one of the most famous local explainable models [13].

LIME explains individual predictions of any classifier or regressor in a faithful and intelligible way, by approximating them locally with an interpretable model (e.g., linear models, decision trees). However, having a global explanation of the model can be challenging as it is more complicated to maintain a good fidelity - interpretability trade off. To this end, authors in [13] proposed an approach, called submodular Pick which is an algorithm aiming to maximize a coverage function of total feature importance for a set of instances. While maximizing the coverage function is NP-Hard, authors make use of a greedy algorithm which adds iteratively instances with the highest marginal coverage to the solution set, offering a constant-factor approximation to the optimum. The selected set is the most representative, non-redundant individual explanations of the model.

In this paper, our aim is to introduce a new approach to select individual instances (explanations) to be considered for global explanation to ensure that the picked group reflects the global behavior of the black-box model. Unlike submodular optimization proposed in [13], we advocate to consider the problem of picking representative instances as a co-selection task. The idea is to apply a similarity preserving co-selection approach to select a set of instances and features on the explanations provided by any explainer.

The paper is structured as follows. Section 2 provides a necessary background on LIME method. In Sect. 3, we present our approach allowing for a global explanation of black box ML models. Section 4 shows the preliminary experiments done to validate our proposal. In Sect. 5, we conclude the paper and draw some research lines for future work.

2 Background on LIME

Interpretability of ML models reflects the ability to provide meaning in understandable terms to human. It is crucial to trust the system and get insights based on its decisions. Quality of an explanation could be improved by making it more Interpretable, Faithful, and model-agnostic [12]. Faithfulness represents how the explanation is describing the reality of the model. Model-agnostic methods are used for any type of model. LIME introduced by Ribeiro et al [13], is one of the well-known examples of such methods. It is a framework which explains a prediction by approximating it locally using an interpretable model (Algorithm 1).

Algorithm 1. Sparse Linear Explanations LIME

Require: Classifier f, Number of samples N
Require: Instance x, and its interpretable version x'
Require: Similarity kernel π_x, Lengths of explanation K
1: $Z \longleftarrow \{\}$
2: **for** ($i \in \{1, 2, 3, ..., N\}$) **do**
3:     $z_i' \longleftarrow$ sample-around(x')
4:     $Z \longleftarrow Z \cup \langle z_i', f(z_i), \pi_x(z_i) \rangle$
5: **end for**
6: $w \longleftarrow K$-Lasso(Z, K), z_i' as features, $f(z)$ as target
7: **return** w

The basic idea of LIME is to replace a data instance x by its interpretable representations x' thanks to a mapping function $\Phi(x)$. For example, an image will be represented as a group of super-pixels, a text as binary vectors indicating the presence or the absence of a word. The interpretable representations are more easily understandable and close to human intuition. Then, x' is perturbed to generate a set of new instances. The black box model is used to make predictions of generated instances from x' which are weighted according to their dissimilarity with x'. Now, for the explanation purpose, an interpretable model, such as linear models, is trained on weighted data to explain prediction locally.

2.1 LIME: Fidelity-Interpretability Trade-off

Authors in [13] define an explanation as a model $g \in G$, where G is a class of potentially interpretable models (e.g., linear models, decision trees). Let $\Omega(g)$ be a measure of complexity (as opposed to interpretability) of the explanation g. For example, for linear models $\Omega(g)$ may be the number of non-zero weights. The model being explained is denoted by $f : \mathbb{R}^d \longrightarrow \mathbb{R}$. Let now π_x defines a locality around x and $\mathcal{L}(f; g; x)$ be a measure of how unfaithful g is in approximating f in the locality π_x. The explanation produced by LIME is then obtained by the following minimization problem [13]:

$$\xi(x) = \underset{g \in G}{\operatorname{argmin}} \mathcal{L}(f; g; \pi_x) + \Omega(g) \qquad (1)$$

2.2 Explaining Global Behavior

LIME explains a single prediction locally. Then, it picks K explanations which "must be representative" to show to the user. The *Submodular Pick* explained in Algorithm 2 is used to choose instances to be inspected for global understanding. The quality of selected instances is critical to get insights from the model in a reasonable time.

Algorithm 2. Submodular Pick (SP)

1: **Require:** Instances X, Budget **B**
2: **for** (all x_i in X) **do**
3:     $\mathbf{W}_i \longleftarrow explain(x_i, x_i')$ {Using LIME}
4: **end for**
5: **for** $j \in 1...d'$ **do**
6:     $I_j \longleftarrow \sqrt{\sum_{i=1}^{n} |\mathbf{W}_{ij}|}$ {Compute the feature importance}
7: **end for**
8: $V \longleftarrow \{\}$
9: **while** $|V| < \mathbf{B}$ **do**
10:     $V \longleftarrow V \bigcup argmax_i \ \ c(V \bigcup \{i\}, \mathbf{W}, I)$
11: **end while**
12: return

Let $\mathbf{X}$ (with $|\mathbf{X}| = n$) be the set of instances to explain, Algorithm 2 calculates $\mathbf{W} \in \mathbb{R}^{n \times d'}$ an explanation matrix using each individual explanation given by Algorithm 1. Then, it computes (I_j) global feature importance for each column j in W, such that the highest importance score is given to the feature explaining an important number of different instances. Submodular Pick aims then at finding the set of instances V, $|V| < \mathbf{B}$ that scores the highest coverage, defined as the function which calculates total importance of features in at least one instance. Finally, greedy algorithm is used to build V by adding the instance with highest marginal coverage gain.

3   Proposed Approach

The approach we propose in this paper consists of two sequential phases (see Fig. 1). The first is to use LIME (without loss of generality, any other explainer can be used) to obtain the explanations of the predictions for the test data. While the second phase focuses on global explainability by co-selecting the most important test instances and features. Thus, we provide a global understanding of the black-box model.

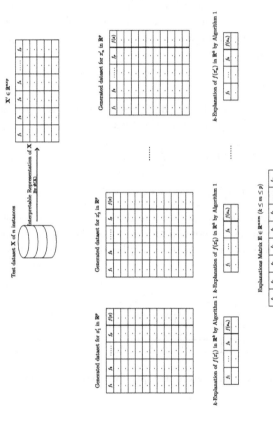

Fig. 1. The proposed framework for a global explanation using a co-selection of features and instances.

3.1   Explanation Space

Let f be a black box model, and $\mathbf{X}$ a test dataset of n instances and $\varPhi(\mathbf{X}) = \mathbf{X}'$ its interpretable representation in $\mathbb{R}^p$. First, to obtain an individual explanation of the prediction made by f for each instance x_i we use LIME by fitting a linear model on a generated dataset around x'_i, the interpretable representation of x_i. Thus, for each instance x_i, we obtain an explanation of length k $(k < p)$. It is worthy to note that the length is a parameter set by the user and corresponds to the number of features retained.

Once the individual explanations have been obtained, we construct an explanation space represented by $\mathbf{E} \in \mathbb{R}^{n \times m}$, where the dimension m of the explanations space corresponds to the union of the k features of each explanation. We illustrate this step with the following example:

Example 1

Let $\mathbf{X}'$ be the interpretable representation of 3 instances in $\mathbb{R}^{500}$, and $k = 3$ be the length of the explanation desired for these three instances. By performing LIME algorithm on $\mathbf{X}'$, we obtain 3 explanations of length 3:

$$e_i = \begin{cases} e_1 = \{(f_1, 0.5), (f_{25}, 0.9), (f_4, 0.1)\} \\ e_2 = \{(f_{17}, 0.2), (f_6, 0.3), (f_{78}, 0.4)\} \\ e_3 = \{(f_{500}, 0.8), (f_{25}, 0.7), (f_1, 0.25)\} \end{cases} \tag{2}$$

where e_1, e_2, and e_3 are the explanations of x'_1, x'_2 and x'_3 respectively. Thus, the matrix $\mathbf{E} \in \mathbb{R}^{3 \times 7}$ can be seen as the concatenation of all the explanations and the union of the set of features obtained by each explanation. Note that the dimension m here is equal to 7.

	f_1	f_4	f_6	f_{17}	f_{25}	f_{78}	f_{500}
x_1	0.5	0.1	0	0	0.9	0	0
x_2	0	0	0.3	0.2	0	0.4	0
x_3	0.25	0	0	0	0.7	0	0.8

Fig. 2. Explanation matrix $\mathbf{E}$ (this matrix is given as input for CoSP Algorithm 3)

3.2   Global Explicability by Co-selection

Understanding the model's decisions globally remains a complex task. In fact, some approaches like LIME were extended to face this complexity by only picking a group of individual explanations. In this paper, we advocate a method allowing global explainability by co-selecting the most important instances and features over the explanations provided by any explainer. The idea is to find a residual matrix $\mathbf{R}$ and a transformation matrix $\mathbf{W}$, which transforms high-dimensional explanations data $\mathbf{E}$ to low dimensional data $\mathbf{EW}$, to maximize the global similarity between $\mathbf{E}$ and $\mathbf{EW}$. After the optimal $\mathbf{W}$ and $\mathbf{R}$ have been obtained, the original features and instances are ranked, based on the $\ell_{2,1}$-norm values of the rows of $\mathbf{R}$ and $\mathbf{W}$, and the top features and instance are selected accordingly.

3.3   Notation

First, we present the notation we use in this paper. Let $\mathbf{E}$ be an explanation matrix of n instances and m features. The $l_{2,1}$-norm of $\mathbf{E}$ is:

$$\| \mathbf{E} \|_{2,1} = \sum_{i=1}^{m} \| \mathbf{E}_i \|_2 = \sum_{i=1}^{m} \sqrt{\sum_{j=1}^{n} \mathbf{E}_{ij}^2} \qquad (3)$$

and its Frobenius norm ($l_{2,2}$) is:

$$\| \mathbf{E} \|_F = \left(\sum_{i=1}^{m} \| \mathbf{E}_i \|_2^2 \right) = \left(\sum_{i=1}^{m} \left(\sum_{j=1}^{n} \mathbf{E}_{ij}^2 \right) \right)^{1/2} \qquad (4)$$

Table 1. Summary of symbols and notations

Symbol	Definition
n	Number of instances
m	Number of features
h	Dimension of the low dimensional space
$\mathbf{E} \in \mathbb{R}^{n \times m}$	Explanation matrix
$\mathbf{A} \in \mathbb{R}^{n \times n}$	Pairwise similarity matrix over $\mathbf{E}$
$\mathbf{R} \in \mathbb{R}^{n \times h}$	Instance coefficient matrix
$\mathbf{W} \in \mathbb{R}^{m \times h}$	Feature coefficient matrix
$\mathbf{Z} \in \mathbb{R}^{n \times h}$	Eigen-decomposition of $\mathbf{A}$
$\| \cdot \|_F ; \| \cdot \|_{2,1}$	Matrix norms

3.4   Co-Selection Pick (CoSP)

To perform a co-selection of instances and features on the explanations matrix, we must minimize the following problem as pointed out in [1]:

$$\min_{\mathbf{W},\mathbf{R}} \| \mathbf{EW} - \mathbf{R}^T - \mathbf{Z} \|_F^2 + \lambda \| \mathbf{W} \|_{2,1} + \beta \| \mathbf{R} \|_{2,1} \qquad (5)$$

where:

– $\mathbf{Z}$ is the eigen-decomposition of the pairwise similarity matrix, $\mathbf{A}$, computed over the explanation matrix $\mathbf{E}$. Note that the similarity matrix $\mathbf{A}$ can be calculated in supervised fashion (e.g. adjacency matrix, fully binary matrix) if the labels of test instances are available, or in unsupervised mode as follows:

$$\mathbf{A}_{ij} = e^{-\frac{\|e_i - e_j\|^2}{2\delta^2}} \tag{6}$$

– $\mathbf{R} = \mathbf{W}^T\mathbf{E}^T - \mathbf{Z}^T - \Theta.$, is a residual matrix and Θ is a random matrix, usually assumed to be multi-dimensional normal distribution [15]. Note that the matrix $\mathbf{R}$ is a good indicator of outliers and less important and irrelevant instances in a dataset according to [17,18].
– λ and β are regularization parameters, used to control the sparsity of $\mathbf{W}$ and $\mathbf{R}$ respectively; and δ is a parameter for the RBF kernel used to compute the matrix $\mathbf{A}$ in the unsupervised mode in Eq. (6).

The first term of the objective in Eq. (5) exploits the $\mathbf{E}$ structure by preserving the pairwise explanations similarity while the second and third terms are used to perform feature selection and instance selection, respectively. In order to minimize Eq. (5), we adopt an alternating optimization over $\mathbf{W}$ and $\mathbf{R}$ as in [1], by solving two reduced minimization problems:

Problem 1: Minimizing Eq. (5) by fixing $\mathbf{R}$ to compute $\mathbf{W}$ (for feature selection). To solve this problem, we consider the lagrangian function of Eq. (5):

$$\mathcal{L}_\mathbf{W} = trace(\mathbf{W}^T\mathbf{E}^T\mathbf{E}\mathbf{W} - 2\mathbf{W}^T\mathbf{E}^T(\mathbf{R}^T + \mathbf{Z})) + \lambda \parallel \mathbf{W} \parallel_{2,1}. \tag{7}$$

Then, we calculate the derivative of $\mathcal{L}_W$ w.r.t $\mathbf{W}$:

$$\frac{\partial \mathcal{L}_\mathbf{W}}{\partial \mathbf{W}} = 2\mathbf{E}^T\mathbf{E}\mathbf{W} - 2\mathbf{E}^T(\mathbf{R}^T + \mathbf{Z}) + 2\lambda\mathcal{D}_\mathbf{W}\mathbf{W}. \tag{8}$$

where $\mathcal{D}_W$ is a $(m \times m)$ diagonal matrix with the ith element equal to $\frac{1}{2\|\mathbf{W}(i,:)\|_2}$. Subsequently, we set the derivative to zero to update $\mathbf{W}$:

$$\mathbf{W} = (\mathbf{E}^T\mathbf{E} + \lambda\mathcal{D}_\mathbf{W})^{-1}\mathbf{E}^T(\mathbf{R}^T + \mathbf{Z}) \tag{9}$$

Problem 2: Minimizing Eq. (5) by fixing $\mathbf{W}$ to compute the solution for $\mathbf{R}$ (for explanation selection). To solve this problem, we consider the Lagrangian function of Eq. (5):

$$\mathcal{L}_\mathbf{R} = trace(\mathbf{R}^T\mathbf{R} - 2\mathbf{R}^T(\mathbf{E}\mathbf{W} - \mathbf{Z})) + \beta \parallel \mathbf{R} \parallel_{2,1}. \tag{10}$$

Then, we calculate the derivative of $\mathcal{L}_\mathbf{R}$ w.r.t $\mathbf{R}$:

$$\frac{\partial \mathcal{L}_\mathbf{R}}{\partial \mathbf{R}} = 2\mathbf{R}^T - 2(\mathbf{E}\mathbf{W} - \mathbf{Z}) + 2\beta\mathcal{D}_\mathbf{R}\mathbf{R}^T. \tag{11}$$

where $\mathcal{D}_\mathbf{R}$ is a $(n \times n)$ diagonal matrix with the ith element equal to $\frac{1}{2\|\mathbf{R}^T(i,:)\|_2}$.

Subsequently, we set the derivative to zero to update $\mathbf{B}$:

$$\mathbf{R} = (\mathbf{EW} - \mathbf{Z})^T ((\mathbf{I} + \beta \mathcal{D}_{\mathbf{R}})^{-1})^T \tag{12}$$

where $\mathbf{I}$ is a $(n \times n)$ identity matrix. All of the above developments are summarized on Algorithm 3.

Algorithm 3. Co-Selection Pick (CoSP)

1: **Require:** Instances $\mathbf{X}$, Budget $\mathbf{B}$ and $\mathbf{L}$, hyper-parameters: $\lambda, \beta, \delta, h$.
2: **for** (all x_i in $\mathbf{X}$) **do**
3:    $e_i \longleftarrow explain(x_i, x_i')$ {Using LIME}
4: **end for**
5: Build the explanations matrix $\mathbf{E}$ (see Fig. 2).
6: Calculate $\mathbf{A}$ {according to Eq. (6) for unsupervised mode or as adjacency matrix for supervised mode}.
7: Eigen-decomposition of $\mathbf{A}$ such as $\mathbf{A} = \mathbf{ZZ}^T$.
8: Initialize $\mathcal{D}_W$ and $\mathcal{D}_{\mathbf{R}}$ as identity matrices.
9: **repeat**
10:    Update $\mathbf{W}$ by $(\mathbf{E}^T\mathbf{E} + \lambda \mathcal{D}_W)^{-1}\mathbf{E}^T(\mathbf{R}^T + \mathbf{Z})$
11:    Update $\mathbf{R}$ by $(\mathbf{EW} - \mathbf{Z})^T((\mathbf{I} + \beta \mathcal{D}_{\mathbf{R}}))^{-1})^T$
12:    Update $\mathcal{D}_{\mathbf{R}}$ and $\mathcal{D}_W$.
13: **until** *Convergence*
14: Rank the features according to $\| \mathbf{W}(j,:) \|_2$ in descending order, and the instances according to $\| \mathbf{R}(:,i) \|_2$ in ascending order.
15: Pick the top $\mathbf{B}$ instances and the top $\mathbf{L}$ features.

3.5   Algorithm Analysis

In the Algorithm 3, the final user expects a selection of $\mathbf{B}$ instances (e.g., explanations) and $\mathbf{L}$ features which are most relevant to provide global explanation of the model. In order to achieve this, CoSP requires four hyper-parameters λ, β, δ and h that will be used later on to build the set of chosen instances and features. Firstly, we build the explanations matrix $\mathbf{E}$ using any explainer, in our case we use LIME. Secondly, we compute the similarity matrix $\mathbf{A}$ either in supervised mode (as adjacency matrix or a binary matrix) or in an unsupervised way according to the availability of the labels of the test instances $\mathbf{X}$. Then, we eigen-decompose $\mathbf{A}$ to find $\mathbf{Z}$. From line 9 to line 13 $\mathbf{W}$ and $\mathbf{R}$ are updated until convergence according to Eqs. (9) and (12). Following the alternate optimization, we rank the instances and the features according to $\mathbf{R}$ and $\mathbf{W}$ respectively. So, the higher the norm of $\| \mathbf{R}(:,j) \|_2$, the more the jth explanation is not representative, while the higher the norm $\| \mathbf{W}(i,:) \|_2$, the more the ith feature is important.

4   Experiments

In this section, we conduct some experiments to validate our framework[1] on some known sentiment datasets.

4.1   Datasets

We use a binary sentimental classification dataset. Sentimental analysis is the task of analyzing people's opinions, reviews, and comments presented as textual data. It gives intuition about different points of view and feedback by detecting relevant words used to express specific sentiments [10]. Today, companies rely on sentimental analysis to improve their strategy. People's opinions are collected from different sources like Facebook, Tweets, product reviews and processed in order to understand customer's needs and improve marketing plans. When the sentiment is divided into positive and negative ones, it is called binary sentimental analysis which is the most common type and the one used in our case. While multi-class sentiment analysis classifies text into groups of possible labels. We use multi-Domain Sentiment Dataset[2], which contains multiple domains reviews (books and dvd) from Amazon.com, where for each type of product there are hundred of thousands of collected reviews. Then, we use an experiment introduced in [13] which aims to evaluate if explanations could help a simulated user to recognize the best model from a group of models having the same accuracy on validation set. In the order to do this, a new dataset will be generated by adding 10 artificial features to the train and validation set from original public dataset (reviews). For the train examples, each of those features appears in 10% of instances in one class and in 20% of the other class. In the test examples, an artificial feature appears in 10% of examples in both classes. This represents the case of having spurious correlations in the data introduced by none informative features.

4.2   Evaluation and Results

We train pairs of classifiers until their validation accuracy is within 0.1% of each other. However, their test accuracy should differ by at least 5% which will make one classifier better than the other. Then, we explain global behaviors of both classifiers using our proposed approach **CoSP**.

To validate our approach, we use the same experimental setting introduced in [7] by selecting top five important features per class chosen as most relevant ones to be considered for the classification task. Global approach is validated if it selects distinguishing features. Results shown in Figs. 3 and 4 were produced by applying **CoSP** with its hyper-parameters: $\lambda \approx 2.11$, $\beta \approx 61.79$, $\delta = 1$ and $h = 17000$ (which stands for the number of features selected by CoSP). First, the displayed perception contains words that are meaningful in order to judge the

---

[1] https://github.com/KhaoulaBF/CoSPIctai.

[2] https://www.cs.jhu.edu/~mdredze/datasets/sentiment/.

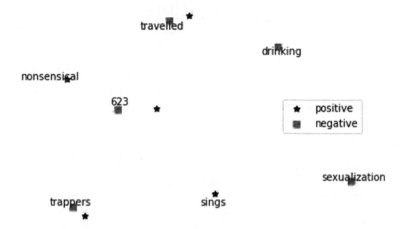

Fig. 3. Top 5 features per class picked by CoSP global approach for review's binary classification on books dataset

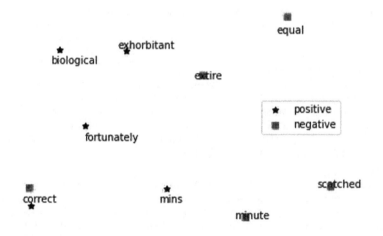

Fig. 4. Top 5 features per class picked by CoSP global approach for review's binary classification on kitchen dataset

type of comment. Features are aligned with human intuition and words with no representative meaning like stop words were not selected. Second, noisy features labeled with prefix "FAKE" added to the dataset were not deemed important.

5   Conclusion

In this paper, we presented CoSP, a generic framework aiming to select individual instances in order to provide global explanation for machine learning models.

We used Co-selection based on similarity as foundation to build global understanding of the black box internal logic over any local explainer. Furthermore, we
conducted some experiments showing that CoSP offers representative insights.
This study is a another step towards understanding machine learning models
globally. For future work, we would like to explore this methods in the context
of time series data, as it is a challenging to find representative illustration for
this type of data.

References

1. Benabdeslem, K., Mansouri, D.E.K., Makkhongkaew, R.: sCOs: semi-supervised
   co-selection by a similarity preserving approach. IEEE Trans. Knowl. Data Eng.
   34(6), 2899–2911 (2022). https://doi.org/10.1109/TKDE.2020.3014262
2. Bistron, M., Piotrowski, Z.: Artificial intelligence applications in military systems and their influence on sense of security of citizens. Electronics **10**(7) (2021).
   https://www.mdpi.com/2079-9292/10/7/871
3. Guidotti, R., Monreale, A., Ruggieri, S., Turini, F., Giannotti, F., Pedreschi, D.:
   A survey of methods for explaining black box models. ACM Comput. Surv. **51**(5)
   (2018)
4. Gunning, D., Aha, D.: DARPA's explainable artificial intelligence (XAI) program.
   AI Mag. **40**(2), 44–58 (2019)
5. Holm, E.A., et al.: Overview: computer vision and machine learning for microstruc-
   tural characterization and analysis. CoRR abs/2005.14260 (2020). https://doi.org/
   10.1007/s11661-020-06008-4
6. Kłosowski, P.: Deep learning for natural language processing and language modelling. In: 2018 Signal Processing: Algorithms, Architectures, Arrangements,
   and Applications (SPA), pp. 223–228 (2018). https://doi.org/10.23919/SPA.2018.
   8563389
7. Linden, I.V.D., Haned, H., Kanoulas, E.: Global aggregations of local explanations
   for black box models. CoRR abs/1907.03039 (2019). https://arxiv.org/abs/1907.
   03039
8. Lundberg, S., et al.: Explainable AI for trees: from local explanations to global
   understanding. ArXiv abs/1905.04610 (2019)
9. Lundberg, S., Lee, S.: A unified approach to interpreting model predictions. In:
   Advances in Neural Information Processing Systems, pp. 4765–4774 (2017)
10. Minaee, S., Kalchbrenner, N., Cambria, E., Nikzad, N., Chenaghlu, M., Gao, J.:
    Deep learning-based text classification. ACM Comput. Surv. (CSUR) **54**, 1–40
    (2021)
11. Mohaghegh, F., Murthy, J.: Machine learning and computer vision techniques to
    predict thermal properties of particulate composites. CoRR abs/2010.01968 (2020).
    https://arxiv.org/abs/2010.01968
12. Ribeiro, M., Singh, S., Guestrin, C.: Fairness, accountability, and transparency in
    machine learning, paper 'why should i trust you?' Explaining the predictions of any
    classifier (2016). https://www.fatml.org/schedule/2016/presentation/why-should-
    i-trust-you-explaining-predictions
13. Ribeiro, M., Singh, S., Guestrin, C.: "Why should I trust you?": Explaining the
    predictions of any classifier. In: Krishnapuram, B., et al. (eds.) Proceedings of the
    22nd ACM SIGKDD International Conference on Knowledge Discovery and Data
    Mining, San Francisco, CA, USA, 13–17 August 2016, pp. 1135–1144. ACM (2016).
    https://doi.org/10.1145/2939672.2939778

14. Shailaja, K., Seetharamulu, B., Jabbar, M.A.: Machine learning in healthcare: a review. In: 2018 Second International Conference on Electronics, Communication and Aerospace Technology (ICECA), pp. 910–914 (2018). https://doi.org/10.1109/ICECA.2018.8474918

15. She, Y., Owen, A.B.: Outlier detection using nonconvex penalized regression. CoRR abs/1006.2592 (2010). https://arxiv.org/abs/1006.2592

16. Štrumbelj, E., Kononenko, I.: Explaining prediction models and individual predictions with feature contributions. Knowl. Inf. Syst. **41**(3), 647–665 (2013). https://doi.org/10.1007/s10115-013-0679-x

17. Tang, J., Liu, H.: CoSelect: feature selection with instance selection for social media data. In: Proceedings of the 13th SIAM International Conference on Data Mining, 2–4 May 2013. Austin, Texas, USA, pp. 695–703. SIAM (2013)

18. Tong, H., Lin, C.: Non-negative residual matrix factorization with application to graph anomaly detection. In: Proceedings of the Eleventh SIAM International Conference on Data Mining, SDM 2011, 28–30 April 2011, Mesa, Arizona, USA, pp. 143–153. SIAM/Omnipress (2011)

A Multi-Threading Algorithm for Constrained Path Optimization Problem on Road Networks

Kousik Kumar Dutta[(⊠)], Ankita Dewan, and Venkata M. V. Gunturi

Indian Institute of Technology Ropar, Rupnagar, India
kousik.21csz0004@iitrpr.ac.in

Abstract. The constrained path optimization (CPO) problem takes the following input: (a) a road network represented as a directed graph, where each edge is associated with a "cost" and a "score" value; (b) a source-destination pair and; (c) a budget value, which denotes the maximum permissible cost of the solution. Given the input, the goal is to determine a path from source to destination, which maximizes the "score" while constraining the total "cost" of the path to be within the given budget value. CPO problem has applications in urban navigation. However, the CPO problem is computationally challenging as it can be reduced to an instance of the arc orienteering problem, which is known to be NP-hard. Given its heavy computational nature, the current state-of-the-art algorithms for this problem explore only a limited amount of search space to come up with a solution within a reasonable amount of execution time (around a few seconds). As a result, these algorithms often miss out on promising candidates and thus, result in low solution quality. In contrast, this paper proposes a novel algorithm called *Parallel-Spatial-RG*, which explores a much larger search space and obtains a significantly better solution quality. By using multiple threads, *Parallel-Spatial-RG* keeps the execution time within feasible limits by smartly distributing the total workload evenly among all the available threads. Moreover, *Parallel-Spatial-RG* is also able to demonstrate an almost linear speed-up with an increase in the number of cores.

Keywords: Spatial network routing algorithms · Road networks

1 Introduction

The problem of finding a path in road networks has been of great importance. Given the significance of this problem area, several researchers (e.g., [1,3]) have explored it from different aspects. Among these, the most fundamental is computing a path between a source and destination under a given preference metric. The preference metric of choice has typically been the minimization of distance (e.g., [16]), time (e.g., [3]), or fuel (e.g., [11]).

However, the increasing proliferation of mobility-based Big Data [7] enables one to ask for much more nuanced routing queries such as: "Determine the path

R. Chbeir et al. (Eds.): WISE 2022, LNCS 13724, pp. 110–118, 2022.
https://doi.org/10.1007/978-3-031-20891-1_9

which goes through wide roads while constraining the total length of the path to be at most 5km longer than the shortest path?" or "Determine a path which can be easily followed (refer [9]) while constraining the total length of the path to be at most 5km longer than the shortest path." The central theme of both these queries is that they have the notion of both an optimizing metric and a constraining metric. The aim here is to determine a path that maximizes on the optimizing metric (e.g., road width, navigability) while constraining the path according to the constraining metric (e.g., distance). We refer to such problems as *Constrained Path Optimization (CPO)* problems.

An instance of the constrained path optimization (CPO) problem can be reduced to an instance of the arc orienteering problem (AOP), which is known to be an NP-hard problem [2,5]. Moreover, any typical urban road network would have hundreds of thousands of road segments and road intersections. Thus, scalability is vital for any potential solution for the CPO problem. To maintain scalability, the current state-of-the-art [9,10,13] proposed heuristic metrics to reduce the search space of the algorithm. Consequently, they achieve good execution times (around a few seconds). However, they fail to obtain high solution quality due to the reduced search space.

In contrast, our proposed algorithm uses a recursive greedy approach to explore a significantly higher search space to find out a much better solution. And to maintain scalability, we adopt parallel computing for this problem. To the best of our knowledge, this work is a first such attempt for the CPO problem. The proposed parallel algorithm also efficiently utilizes all available resources and achieves an almost linear speed-up by its intelligent task scheduling policy. This paper makes the following contributions:

(a) We propose a novel parallel approach, called *Parallel-Spatial-RG*, for the CPO problem on road networks.

(b) *Parallel-Spatial-RG* uses **intelligent task assignment policy and demonstrates an almost linear speed-up** with an increase in the number of cores.

(c) Experimentally evaluate *Parallel-Spatial-RG* on real road networks.

(d) Our results indicate that *Parallel-Spatial-RG* obtains significantly better solution quality than the current state-of-the-art [9,13] while maintaining comparable (or lower) running times.

The rest of the paper is organized as follows: Sect. 3 presents some basic concepts and formally defines the CPO problem. Section 4 presents our proposed approach. We experimentally evaluate our proposed approach and compare it with alternatives in Sect. 5. Finally, we conclude in Sect. 6.

2 Related Work

Researchers from theoretical computer science [2] proposed a quasi-polynomial algorithm that yields a $O(\log OPT)$[1] approximation for the orienteering problem which can be reduced to the arc orienteering problem [5].

---

[1] OPT implies the optimal solution quality.

Research work done in the area of parallel algorithms for shortest paths (e.g., [1,15]) has focused on developing path-finding algorithms that optimize routes based on a single preference metric (e.g., distance or time).

The work done in the area of constraint shortest path (CSP) problem [12,16] determines the shortest path between a source-destination pair subject to certain constraints. Note that the CSP problem is a *minimization based problem* and cannot be mapped to our problem which focuses on maximization ([10]).

Following two works (ILS*(CEI) and MSWBS) are most relevant to our problem:

ILS*(CEI): *ILS*(CEI)* [13] first computes a candidate arc set (CAS) by performing a spatial range query on the road network. It then determines and removes infeasible edges from CAS using spatial filters. Thereafter, *ILS*(CEI)* tries to replace the current segment by an edge with best *Quality Ratio* value (a metric defined by the authors) in CAS. Following this, they iteratively improve the solution by replacing its segments with low score values using a similar procedure. From the perspective of solution quality, *ILS*(CEI)* limits its search space by making a greedy choice of selecting the best edge in the current CAS and proceeding forward to replace low score segments in the resulting path. In contrast, our approach would exhaustively evaluate all options in CAS and choose the best option. Our approach builds the solution in a bottom-up approach instead of making heuristic choices.

MSWBS: *MSWBS* [9,10] algorithm first uses a procedure called weighted bidirectional search (WBS) to find a replacement for each segment of the initial seed path. WBS is more "goal-oriented" in the sense that edges that have higher score values and are spatially oriented toward the goal are chosen to continue the search. WBS directs the search frontiers from source and destination to each other (using its forward and backward reachability metrics) rather than conducting a more open-ended search. Hence, WBS limits the search space of MSWBS as well as the solution quality. Following this, *MSWBS* employs a DP-based approach to determine the replacements which can fit inside the budget.

3   Basic Concepts

Score: We define the score value associated with each edge as the preference value of that edge. If we are considering the landmarks of a particular segment, then scores should be positive (segments with more landmarks are preferable). If there are no landmarks on an edge, then its score would be 0.

Optimizing Metric $(\Gamma())$: Given any directed path P_i, $\Gamma(P_i)$ returns the total "score" collected by P_i. In its simplest form, $\Gamma(P_i)$ can be defined as a sum of the score values of all the edges constituting the path P_i.

Constraining Metric $(\Phi())$: Given any directed path P_i, $\Phi(P_i)$ returns the total "cost" consumed by P_i. We define $\Phi(P_i)$ as the sum of the cost values of all the edges constituting the path P_i.

3.1 Problem Definition

Input: consists of the following:
(1) A road network, $G(V, E)$, where each node $v \in V$ is associated with certain spatial coordinates and each edge $e \in E$ associated with a cost and a score value.
(2) A source $s \in V$ and a destination $d \in V$.
(3) A positive value *overhead*. We define the term *budget* as the sum of overhead and the cost of the shortest path between s and d.

Output: A directed path $P*$ between s and d.

Objective function: Maximize $\Gamma(P*)$

Constraint: $\Phi(P*) \leq budget$
**Please refer [4] for detailed steps for generalizing our proposed algorithms for minimization case, i.e., the objective function is to Minimize $\Gamma(P*)$.

4 Proposed Approach

Due to lack to space, we are only presenting a brief summary of our proposed approach. Please refer to [4] for a detailed presentation of our algorithms.

4.1 Spatial Recursive Greedy Approach for CPO Problem

The key idea over here is to first find an initial seed path (shortest path) between the given source and destination nodes and, then recursively determine its better replacements. In our implementation, we used A* algorithm with *euclidean distance* as the heuristic function [6] for determining the initial seed path.

A pseudocode of the algorithm is presented in Algorithm 1. Each call to the algorithm primarily takes the following input: (i) "source node" u, (ii) "destination node" v and (iii) remaining budget β. In the first call to the *Spatial-RG* algorithm, u, v, and β would be set according to the input values given while defining the CPO query. Thereafter, u, v, and β would change during the course of the recursion calls.

In each recursion, Algorithm 1 first iterates (outer loop on line 9) over all edges e which satisfy the following two filters: (a) $\Gamma(e) > 0$ and, (b) e is inside the ellipse formed by u and v as the foci and β as the major axis length. It is important to note that the filter proposed in (a) may affect the quality of the final solution. Nevertheless, we use it to gain performance. Correctness of filter (b) was established in [10,13].

Suppose an edge $e = (x, y) \in E$ is being considered in the outer loop (line 9). This means that the current path between u and v would be replaced by a path which is the combination of the following three sub-paths: (1) a path P_1 between u and x, (2) edge $e = (x, y)$ and, (3) a path P_2 between y and v. Both P_1 and P_2 are determined recursively inside the inner loop on line 11 as described next.

The inner loop of Algorithm 1 loops over a set of feasible budget values. In each iteration of this inner loop, P_1 and P_2 are determined recursively for different budget values (line 12 and 13). For each pair of P_1 and P_2 (as returned by their respective recursive calls), we determine P_{new} as $P_1 \cup e \cup P_2$ (joining P_1, e, and P_2 in same order). We store P_{new} if it has better score value than the original path between u and v (determined on line 1). Thus, at the termination of the inner while loop, we would have the "best possible" P_1 and P_2 which can be attached with e (current edge being considered on outer loop) to obtain the "best possible" replacement for the current path between u and v. It is important to note that budget values sent into the recursive calls for determining P_1 and P_2 (line 12 and line 13) are not entirely independent of each other. More precisely, if a budget value of b is given to determine P_1, then a maximum value of β - b - $\Phi(e)$ budget can be given to determine P_2.

And lastly, the set of feasible budget values (b) for the inner while loop would range from $b = Euclidean\_Distance\,(u, x)$ to $b = \beta - \Phi(e) - Euclidean\_Distance\,(y, v)$. Correctness of these values can be easily proved by considering the fact *shortest network distance over a graph would always be greater than or equal to the Euclidean distance*. Details omitted due to lack of space.

Spatial Indexing: We use *Uniform Grid Indexing* [14] to efficiently determine the edges present in $ellipse(u, v, \beta)$ on line 9 of Algorithm 1.

Algorithm 1. Spatial-RG Algorithm

Input: (a) Input graph $G(V, E)$; (b) source node u; (c) destination node v; (d) Remaining budget β; (e) current *level*; (f) maximum recursion depth θ.
Output: (a) A directed path P between u and v

1: $P \leftarrow$ minimum cost path between u and v
2: **if** $\Phi(P) > \beta$ **then**
3:     Return Null
4: **end if**
5: **if** level $= \theta$ **then** /*Maximum recursion depth reached*/
6:     Return P
7: **end if**
8: $s_p \leftarrow \Gamma(P)$ /*stores value of optimizing metric of P */
9: **for all** edge $e = (x, y) \in E$ with $\Gamma(e) > 0$ and e inside ellipse(u,v,β) **do**
10:     $b \leftarrow$ Euclidean_Distance(u,x)
11:     **while** $b \leq \beta - \Phi(e) -$Euclidean_Distance(y, v) **do**
12:         $P_1 \leftarrow$ Spatial-RG $(u, x, b, level + 1)$
13:         $P_2 \leftarrow$ Spatial-RG $(y, v, \beta - b - \Phi(e), level + 1)$
14:         $P_{new} \leftarrow P_1 \cup e \cup P_2$
15:         **if** $(P_1 \cap P_2) = null$ & $\Gamma(P_{new}) > s_p$ **then**
16:             $P \leftarrow P_{new}$ and $s_p \leftarrow \Gamma(P_{new})$
17:         **end if**
18:         $b \leftarrow b + 1$
19:     **end while**
20: **end for**
21: Return P

4.2   Parallel Algorithm for CPO Problem

Spatial-RG algorithm has a huge search space as compared to existing heuristics [9,13]. While *Spatial-RG* algorithm uses several strategies for gaining performance, its running time is still impractical for meeting the real-world expectation of getting a solution within a few seconds. To this end, a parallel version of *Spatial-RG* algorithm is developed which can harness the increasingly available multi-core systems to **improve execution time while still maintaining the same solution quality as *Spatial-RG*.**

Details of Parallel-Spatial-RG Algorithm: *Spatial-RG* algorithm has some inherent parallelism at the following three places: (a) Outer loop (For loop on line 9 in Algorithm 1), (b) Recursion calls on line numbers 12 and 13 (in Algorithm 1) and (c) Inner While loop (on line 11 in Algorithm 1). However, an approach which is solely dependent on unpacking the recursion (followed by simultaneous independent exploration by threads) would have poor CPU utilization (refer to [4] for more details on this aspect).

Parallel-Spatial-RG first creates a *threadpool* with thread count same as the number of available cores. Here, we use the following key strategy: In each recursion call, the current thread creates further tasks for exploring its designated search space, but those tasks may not always be executed in parallel. Instead, they are stored in its local *job pool*. After creating jobs, the current thread would look for free threads. If no free threads are found, then the current thread would start picking up jobs from its own job pool (while still actively looking for free threads). With the intent to simplify the notations, the term "primary thread" refers to the thread that creates the job pool in a recursion call. There would be only one "primary thread" per call.

In our parallel algorithm, a separate task is created for each iteration of the outer loop (on line 9 in Algorithm 1) and kept in a *job pool*. Each task in this pool corresponds to a executing a instance of the while loop on line 11 of the *Spatial-RG* algorithm. Now, whenever a thread t_i is executing a task from this job pool, it creates two further tasks for each iteration of while loop (on line 11 in Algorithm 1), corresponding to the two recursive calls on line numbers 12 and 13 of the *Spatial-RG* algorithm, which are kept in the *job pool* of t_i.

Parallel-Spatial-RG maintains a *result set* for each *job pool*. Jobs from any *job pool* may assigned to any idle thread, but these threads would report their respective results only to the associated *result sets*. In our implementation, each job in the *job pool* is assigned a unique location in its respective *result set*. This allows all the threads to access the *result set* simultaneously and avoids a critical section. Consequently, we get better CPU utilization. Please refer to [4] for the detail pseudocode of the *Parallel-Spatial-RG* algorithm.

Time Complexity Analysis of Parallel-Spatial-RG: In the worst case, an instance of *Parallel-Spatial-RG* algorithm would iterate over m feasible edges, and for each iteration, it would again iterate for β times. Following this, it would have two recursion calls inside the inner loop. Thus, the time complexity for one recursion depth is $O(2m\beta)$. For a maximum recursion depth of θ, the total time complexity of *Parallel-Spatial-RG* would be $O((2m\beta)^{\theta})$.

5   Experimental Analysis

Dataset: We conducted experimental analysis on the real road networks of London, Delhi, and Buenos Aires (obtained from [8]). Due to lack of space, we are presenting only a summary of our results in this paper. Please refer to [4] for a detailed experimental analysis. In this paper, we present our results on the London dataset. This dataset has 285050 nodes and 749382 edges. Edges are selected uniformly at random from across the network and are assigned (randomly) a score value between 1 and 15. Other edges has 0 score value.

Candidate Algo: *(a) Parallel-Spatial-RG (b) ILS*(CEI)* [13], *(c) MSWBS* [9].

Variable Parameters: *(a) Overhead, (b) Path Length*[2]*, (c) Recursion Depth* *(θ), (d) Number of Threads (n) and (e) Number of edges with a non-zero score.*

Metrics Measured: *(a) Execution time of the algorithm. (b) Score gain over the score of the shortest path.*

Experimental Setup: All the algorithms are implemented in JAVA11. We use an Ubuntu machine with Intel Xeon Platinum 8280M CPU and 2048 GB RAM. Each core has a clock speed of 2.70 GHz (with a max frequency of 4.00 GHz).

5.1   Sensitivity Analysis

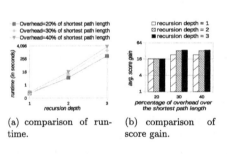

(a) comparison of run-time.   (b) comparison of score gain.

Fig. 1. Illustrating performance of Parallel-Spatial-RG for different recursion depths and for different overheads. 40% of edges with non-zero score value. Y-axis is in log_4 scale.

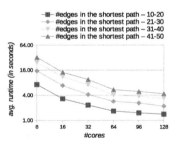

Fig. 2. Evaluating Parallel-Spatial-RG for different number of threads. Y-axis is in log_4 scale.

Effect of Recursion Depth (θ): The run-time of *Parallel-Spatial-RG* increases exponentially with an increase in the recursion depth (Fig. 1(a)). Therefore, we

---

[2] We define the path length as the number of edges in the shortest path. Experiments were conducted for different path lengths. While compiling the results for different path lengths, we have bucketed them into different ranges, and reported the average value of 100 source-destination pairs for each bucket.

consider a smaller instance of Delhi road network (9401 nodes and 25941 edges) and path length range of 11–20 for this experiment. Figure 1(b) shows that there is little gain with regards to score improvement as we increase the recursion depth. To this end, we set θ to 1 in our remaining experiments.

Effect of Number of Cores: Figure 2 shows that *Parallel-Spatial-RG* gives an almost linear scale up when we increase the number of cores. In this experiment, overhead was 30% over the shortest path cost, and 40% of edges has non-zero score value. For shorter path lengths (11–20), the improvement gets saturated with the increase in the number of cores. This is because of two reasons: (a) runtime is already in around one second; (b) the number of sub-tasks created is less than the number of cores available.

5.2 Other Sensitive Analysis

Our experiments indicate that both the run-time and the score gain of *Parallel-Spatial-RG* increases as we increase the overhead and the density of the edges with non-zero score values. Please refer to [4] for more details on this experiment.

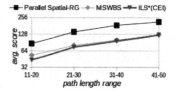

5.3 Comparison with the State-of-the-Art

Figure 3 shows that *Parallel-Spatial-RG* obtains a significantly better score than both *MSWBS* and *ILS*(CEI)*. Runtime of *Parallel-Spatial-RG* was more than *MSWBS*. Runtime of *ILS*(CEI)* was in some occasions smaller than *Parallel-Spatial-RG*. In summary, our algorithm had a average running of runtime of 2.9 s across all path lengths. Please refer to [4] for more details.

Fig. 3. Comparison of Parallel-Spatial-RG, MSWBS, and ILS*(CEI). 30% overhead over the shortest path cost, 40% of edges with non-zero score and recursion depth 1. Y-axis is in log_2 scale.

6   Conclusion

This paper studies the problem of the Constrained Path Optimization (CPO) problem on road networks. CPO problem has value addition potential in the domain of urban navigation. However, the current state-of-the-art solutions (approximation algorithms and heuristic solutions) either fail to scale up to real-world road networks or have poor solution quality. In contrast, our proposed algorithm *Parallel-Spatial-RG* shows promising results in terms of both scalability and solution quality. In the future, we will continue to explore the potential of hierarchical routing techniques for improving the scalability of *Parallel-Spatial-RG* and establish a formal approximation ratio for the algorithm.

Acknowledgement. IIT Ropar and Microsoft India R&D (MAGP 2021 grant).

References

1. Chakaravarthy, V.T., et al.: Scalable single source shortest path algorithms for massively parallel systems. IEEE Trans. PDS **28**(7), 2031–2045 (2017)
2. Chekuri, C., et al.: A recursive greedy algorithm for walks in directed graphs. In: Proceedings of the Symposium on Foundations of Computer Science, pp. 245–253. IEEE (2005)
3. Demiryurek, U., Banaei-Kashani, F., Shahabi, C., Ranganathan, A.: Online computation of fastest path in time-dependent spatial networks. In: Pfoser, D., et al. (eds.) SSTD 2011. LNCS, vol. 6849, pp. 92–111. Springer, Heidelberg (2011). https://doi.org/10.1007/978-3-642-22922-0_7
4. Dutta, K.K., Dewan, A., Gunturi, V.M.V.: A multi-threading algorithm for constrained path optimization problem on road networks. CoRR abs/2208.02296 (2022). https://doi.org/10.48550/arXiv.2208.02296
5. Gavalas, D., et al.: Approximation algorithms for the arc orienteering problem. Inf. Process. Lett. **115**(2), 313–315 (2015)
6. Gunturi, V.M.V., Shekhar, S.: Spatio-Temporal Graph Data Analytics. Springer, Cham (2017). https://doi.org/10.1007/978-3-319-67771-2
7. Henke, N., et al.: The Age of Analytics: Competing in a Data-Driven World. Mckinsey Global Institute, December 2016. https://tinyurl.com/yb7vytkg
8. Karduni, A., et al.: A protocol to convert spatial polyline data to network formats and applications to world urban road networks. Sci. Data **3**(160046) (2016)
9. Kaur, R., Goyal, V., Gunturi, V.M.V.: Finding the most navigable path in road networks: a summary of results. In: Hartmann, S., Ma, H., Hameurlain, A., Pernul, G., Wagner, R.R. (eds.) DEXA 2018. LNCS, vol. 11029, pp. 440–456. Springer, Cham (2018). https://doi.org/10.1007/978-3-319-98809-2_27
10. Kaur, R., et al.: Finding the most navigable path in road networks. Geoinformatica **25**(1), 207–240 (2021)
11. Li, Y., et al.: Physics-guided energy-efficient path selection: a summary of results. In: Proceedings of the 26th ACM SIGSPATIAL, pp. 99–108 (2018)
12. Liu, Z., et al.: Efficient constrained shortest path query answering with forest hop labeling. In: IEEE 37th ICDE, pp. 1763–1774 (2021)
13. Lu, Y., Shahabi, C.: An arc orienteering algorithm to find the most scenic path on a large-scale road network. In: Proceedings of the 23rd SIGSPATIAL. ACM (2015)
14. Shekhar, S., Chawla, S.: A Tour of Spatial Databases. Prentice Hall, Upper Saddle River (2003)
15. Vishwakarma, Kartik, Gunturi, Venkata M. V..: Impromptu rendezvous based multi-threaded algorithm for shortest Lagrangian path problem on road networks. In: Wen, Sheng, Zomaya, Albert, Yang, Laurence T.. (eds.) ICA3PP 2019. LNCS, vol. 11944, pp. 201–222. Springer, Cham (2020). https://doi.org/10.1007/978-3-030-38991-8_14
16. Wang, S., et al.: Effective indexing for approximate constrained shortest path queries on large road networks. Proc. VLDB Endow. **10**(2), 61–72 (2016)

An Unsupervised Approach to Genuine Health Information Retrieval Based on Scientific Evidence

Rishabh Upadhyay[iD], Gabriella Pasi[iD], and Marco Viviani[✉][iD]

Department of Informatics, Systems, and Communication (DISCo), Information and
Knowledge Representation, Retrieval, and Reasoning (IKR3) Lab, Edificio ABACUS,
University of Milano-Bicocca, Viale Sarca, 336, 20126 Milan, Italy
{rishabh.upadhyay,gabriella.pasi,marco.viviani}@unimib.it
https://ikr3.disco.unimib.it/

Abstract. In contemporary society, more and more people refer to
information they find online to meet their information needs. In some
domains, such as health information, this phenomenon has been particularly on the rise in recent years. On the one hand, this could have a positive impact in increasing people's so-called health literacy, which would
benefit the health of the individual and the community as a whole. On
the other hand, with a significant amount of health misinformation circulating online, people and society could face very serious consequences. In
this context, the purpose of this article is to investigate a solution that
can help online users find health information that is relevant to their
information needs, while at the same time being genuine. To do so, in
the process of retrieval of estimated relevant information, the genuineness
of the information itself is taken into consideration, which is evaluated
by referring to scientific articles that can support the claims made in
the online health information considered. With respect to the literature,
the proposed solution is fully unsupervised and does not require any
human intervention. It is experimentally evaluated on a publicly accessible dataset as part of the TREC 2020 Health Misinformation Track.

Keywords: Health misinformation · Information Retrieval ·
Information genuineness · Multidimensional relevance · Health literacy

1 Introduction

It has now been demonstrated how, especially in recent years, people increasingly rely on information they find online about various tasks and contexts [21].
One may want to find news about specific events, to retrieve people's opinions
with respect to certain products or services, to seek information about diseases,
symptoms, and treatments, etc. In the latter area, we refer specifically to *Consumer Health Search* (CHS), which indicates search conducted by laypersons
looking for health advice online [32]. As early as 2013, the *Pew Research Center*,

© The Author(s), under exclusive license to Springer Nature Switzerland AG 2022
R. Chbeir et al. (Eds.): WISE 2022, LNCS 13724, pp. 119–135, 2022.
https://doi.org/10.1007/978-3-031-20891-1_10

a "nonpartisan *fact tank* informing the public about issues, attitudes and trends shaping the world",[1] was highlighting how a large proportion of the U.S. population searched and consulted health information online, even going so far as to exclude the figure of the doctor when making decisions with respect to their own health [14]. By means of a recent *Eurostat* survey,[2] it was shown that also in Europe online health information seeking has been steadily increasing over the years, especially among young people.

Such a phenomenon must take into account the problem that a great deal of information disseminated online actually turns out to be *false* or *misleading* [35]; this, especially in the case of an area as sensitive as health, can have even very serious repercussions both at the individual level and at the level of society as a whole; let us think, for example, of the proposition of "miracle cures" for cancer or other diseases, or the amount of non-genuine information that has occurred with respect to COVID-19 in recent years [3,12]. In most cases, laypeople are unable to discern genuine health information from non-genuine one, because of their insufficient level of *health literacy* [5,30]; this latter concept was included in the glossary of the *World Health Organization* (WHO) in 1988, and indicates "the ability of a citizen to obtain, process, and understand basic health information in order to make informed choices" [16]. At the same time, clinical experts cannot take charge of evaluating every single piece of information that appears online, because of the volume and speed with which it is constantly generated. This is why it is necessary to develop automated solutions or tools that can support non-expert users in avoiding behaviors that are harmful to their health when they come into contact with *misinformation*.

In this article, we refer to this latter concept which, in the literature, we believe to be the most general one compared to that of *disinformation*, which often refers to false or misleading information that is generated *on purpose* [36]. In fact, we do not aim at estimating the purpose for which non-genuine information is disseminated, but we aim at investigating a solution that can somehow help users limit access to *health misinformation*, intended as "a health-related claim of fact that is currently false due to a lack of scientific evidence" [7]. To do this, we propose the development of a *retrieval model* that takes into account both the *topical relevance* of health-related content with respect to user queries and the *genuineness* of the information itself, by comparing such content with what is reported in scientific articles, which we consider as a reputed source of scientific evidence. In this work, information genuineness is also considered a query-dependent dimension of relevance, and it is computed in a totally unsupervised manner, requiring no human intervention w.r.t. the definition of indicators of information genuineness or the formal definition of knowledge bases. The proposed model is evaluated against data made publicly accessible as part of the *Health Misinformation Track* at TREC 2020, and against a baseline and various experimental model configurations that demonstrate its potential effectiveness.

---

[1] https://www.pewresearch.org/.

[2] https://ec.europa.eu/eurostat/web/products-eurostat-news/-/edn-20220406-1 (accessed on May 25, 2022).

2   Related Work

The scientific community has rather recently begun to propose solutions to the growing health misinformation circulating online. A good portion of them started from works that addressed the problem of misinformation detection in general (e.g., fake news detection, opinion spam detection, etc.), and used their solutions applied to the health domain. These are mainly works that treat misinformation detection as a *binary classification* task [35]. Other works have addressed the problem by attempting to take more account of the point characteristics of the health domain and developing ad hoc solutions. Again, these are mainly supervised solutions acting on both health-related content in the form of Web pages [17,33] and social media content [2,28,38].

However, since health information can be somewhat verified against the presence of experts, prior knowledge, and/or quality content, a recent research direction is investigating how to automatically use such different forms of "scientific evidence" in the context of health misinformation detection. In this context, some work has involved *experts* and, in general, *human assessors* in evaluating health information genuineness. For example, DISCERN [6] is a brief questionnaire, developed within the DISCERN Project,[3] which aims at providing users with a possible reliable way of assessing the quality of written information on treatment choices for a health problem. The *Health on the Net foundation* (HON) [4] has issued a code of conduct and quality label for medical sites by considering different attributes such as: disclosure of authorship, sources, updating of information, disclosure of editorial and publicity policy, as well as confidentiality.[4] The approach known as HC-COVID [18] focuses on COVID-related health misinformation detection by employing a crowdsourcing-based knowledge graph, used as a source of evidence, built by leveraging the collaborative efforts of expert and non-expert crowd workers. The drawbacks characterizing these approaches are mainly related to the high level of human intervention needed, e.g., to manually assign quality indicators to each new piece of content, to recruit expert and non-expert crowd workers, to guarantee the quality of annotations, etc.

Other work has formalized evidence-based health-related concepts into *knowledge bases* (through the use of ontologies or knowledge graphs) to compare online health-related claims against such knowledge. For example, in *Med-Fact* [28], the authors develop an algorithm for checking social media post based on the so-called *Evidence-Based Medicine* [27], i.e., integrating individual clinical expertise with the best available external clinical evidence from systematic research and trusted medical information sources such as the *Turning Research Into Practice* (TRIP) database.[5] In another pretty recent model named DETER-

---

[3] http://www.discern.org.uk/.

[4] According to HON, "the HONcode is not an award system, nor does it intend to rate the quality of the information provided by a Web site. It only defines a set of rules to: (*i*) hold Web site developers to basic ethical standards in the presentation of information; (*ii*) help make sure readers always know the source and the purpose of the data they are reading". https://www.hon.ch/HONcode/.

[5] https://www.tripdatabase.com/home.

RENT [11], the authors focus on explainable healthcare misinformation detection by leveraging a medical knowledge graph named *Knowlife* [13], built on top of medical content extracted from *PubMed*,[6] and other health portals such as *Mayo Clinic*,[7] *RxList*,[8] the *Wikipedia Medicine Portal*,[9] and *MedlinePlus*.[10] The potential disadvantages of these latter approaches lie mainly in the complexity of the knowledge base formalization, which is difficult to build automatically, and subject to constant updating issues.

All the above-mentioned works do not address the problem as an Information Retrieval task. Only some recent works are starting to be proposed in this area, to produce a *ranking* of search results within an *Information Retrieval System* (IRS) while also taking into consideration as a relevance criterion that of information genuineness. Among them, Vera [23] is a solution that identifies *harmful* and *helpful* documents by considering a multi-stage ranking architecture. Specifically, the top-ranked topically relevant documents – retrieved by means of the BM25 retrieval model [26] – are re-ranked by using the mono-T5 and duo-T5 retrieval models [24], by exploiting the passages with the highest probability of being relevant within the documents; subsequently, a label prediction model is trained using the TREC 2019 Decision (Medical Misinformation) Track data [1] to consider information genuineness (referred as *credibility* in the paper) and to re-rank again documents based also on this criterion. In [29] the authors consider, beyond topical relevance computed using BM25, another relevance dimension related to information genuineness, i.e., *information quality*. In this work, quality estimation is performed by training a multi-label classifier that returns a probabilistic score for ten quality criteria considered (e.g., Does the story adequately quantify the benefits of the intervention? Does the story establish the availability of the treatment/test/product/procedure?, etc.).[11] Specifically, a RoBERTa-based model is trained on the *Health News Review* dataset presented in [39], labeled with respect to the above-mentioned quality criteria. Once distinct rankings are obtained on the basis of topical relevance and information quality scores, they are merged by means of *Reciprocal Rank Fusion* [9]. The work described in [25], in the context of social search, uses the *query likelihood model* [10] to calculate topical relevance, a *Multi Criteria Decision Making* (MCDM) approach to calculate information genuineness [34], and a simple linear combination to obtain the final relevance value. The works just illustrated suffer from: (*i*) the need to have labeled datasets available to calculate information genuineness scores [23,29], which can be unavailable or characterized by bias related to domain dependence or to choices made during the labeling process (first and foremost the subjectivity of human assessors), and (*ii*) the need for human intervention in defining the computational model of information genuineness [25].

---

[6] https://pubmed.ncbi.nlm.nih.gov/.

[7] https://www.mayoclinic.org/.

[8] https://www.rxlist.com/.

[9] https://en.wikipedia.org/wiki/Portal:Medicine.

[10] https://medlineplus.gov/.

[11] https://www.healthnewsreview.org/about-us/review-criteria/.

3 Considering Information Genuineness Based on Scientific Evidence in Health Information Retrieval

The proposed solution, which aims to address the various problems associated with the approaches presented in the previous section, is based on the development of a *retrieval model* capable of considering both *topical relevance* and *information genuineness* in providing access to health-related content. The model focuses, in particular, on the idea of calculating the second criterion on the basis of comparing health claims in distinct health documents and medical journal articles, which are considered reliable sources of scientific evidence for a given query. In this way, we obtain two *query-dependent* relevance scores related to each distinct criterion, which are combined through a suitable *aggregation strategy* for obtaining the final *Retrieval Status Value* (RSV), based on which the estimated relevant documents are ranked. Neither human intervention, nor complex knowledge bases, nor labeled datasets are needed for this purpose. The architecture of the proposed model is illustrated in Fig. 1.

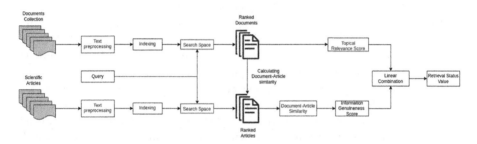

Fig. 1. The proposed retrieval model, considering both topical relevance and information genuineness (based on scientific evidence in the form of medical journal articles).

3.1 Computing Topical Relevance

Topical relevance constitutes the core relevance dimension in any IRS, and assesses how well the content of a document topically meets the information needs of users, which are usually expressed by means of a query [10]. There are several approaches in literature to estimate topical relevance, one of the most effective is still Okapi BM25 [26], which is a lexical-based unsupervised model, a strong baseline for distinct IR tasks, based on a probabilistic interpretation of how terms contribute to the relevance of a document and uses easily computed statistical properties such as functions of term frequencies, document frequencies, and document lengths. Using BM25, the *topical relevance score* of a document d with respect to a query q, denoted as $trs(d, q)$, is calculated as follows:

$$trs(d, q) = \sum_{t \in q, d} \log \frac{N - df(t) + 0.5}{df(t) + 0.5} \cdot \frac{tf(t, d) \cdot (k_1 + 1)}{tf(t, d) + k_1 \cdot (1 - b + b \frac{l_d}{L})} \tag{1}$$

The left part of the equation allows to compute the *inverse document frequency* of a term with respect to the entire document collection; specifically, N denotes the total number of documents in the collection, and $df(t)$ refers to the *document frequency* for the term t, i.e., the number of documents in which t appears. In the second part, $tf(t, d)$ denotes the *term frequency*, i.e., the number of times the term t appears in the document d. Since document collections usually are constituted by documents with different lengths, length normalization is performed in the denominator; specifically, l_d refers to length of the document d, L refers to the average document length, while k_1 (a positive tuning parameter that calibrates the document term frequency scaling) and b (determines the document length scaling) are internal BM25 parameters.

3.2 Computing Information Genuineness

Various approaches have been proposed in the literature to evaluate *information genuineness*,[12] whether health-related or not, whether applied to IR or not. As illustrated in Sect. 2, most of them need either human intervention, or hand-built knowledge bases, or datasets labeled for the purpose.

Without using any of these solutions, in the proposed approach we initially indexed open-source articles extracted from reputed medical journals,[13] such as the *Journal of the American Medical Association* (JAMA),[14] and *eLife*,[15] considered as sources of trustworthy scientific evidence. From these articles, we employed BM25 to retrieve topically relevant ones by considering as queries those extracted from the dataset employed in this work for evaluation purposes, illustrated in Sect. 4. Each retrieved journal article was compared with each retrieved document for the considered query, by using *cosine similarity*. To represent both documents and journal articles, we used two BERT-based textual representation models, one pre-trained on MSMarco,[16] and the other on the *Pubmed* and *PubMed Central* (PMC) datasets.[17] We obtained, this way, dense vector representations based on chunks of 512 tokens, along with a sliding-window of 500 words (to keep context of the past passage) on the whole document. For the top-n retrieved documents and the top-k retrieved journal articles,[18] we obtained an $n \times k$ *similarity matrix*, where rows represent the documents, columns the journal articles, and each cell of the matrix contains the similarity score between the document and the journal article, as shown in Fig. 2.

---

[12] Although there are numerous terms that have been used in the literature, to refer to this dimension of relevance (e.g., *credibility, veracity, truthfulness*, etc.), in this and other works we prefer to use the concept of *genuineness* as an abstract term that can grasp various aspects of the above concepts.

[13] https://openmd.com/guide/finding-credible-medical-sources.

[14] https://jamanetwork.com/.

[15] https://elifesciences.org/.

[16] https://huggingface.co/sentence-transformers/msmarco-distilbert-base-v4.

[17] https://github.com/dmis-lab/biobert.

[18] Where $k << n$, to keep the focus on document retrieval and consider only the most relevant journal articles.

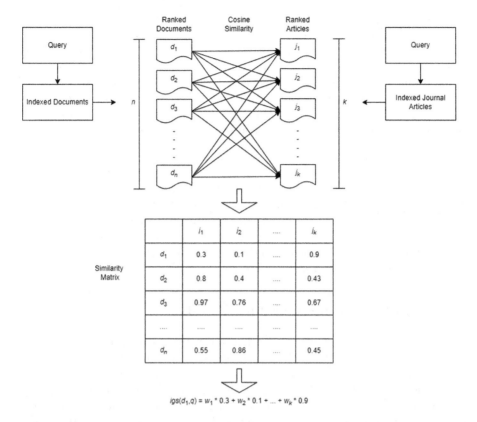

Fig. 2. Information genuineness score calculation. q denotes the query that is used to retrieve both documents and journal articles.

The *information genuineness score* for each document d with respect to a query q, denoted as $igs(d, q)$, is obtained by *linearly combining* the similarity scores among d and the top-k journal articles j_i that were estimated relevant for the same query for which d was retrieved, by considering distinct weights proportional to the positions in the *ranking* of the retrieved journal articles. Formally:

$$igs(d, q) = w_1 * \cos(d, j_1) + w_2 * \cos(d, j_2) + \ldots + w_k * \cos(d, j_k) \qquad (2)$$

In Eq. 2, $w_1, w_2, \ldots, w_k$ denote the weights assigned to each similarity score, such that $\sum w_i = 1$ and $w_i \geq w_{i+1}$ $(1 \leq i \leq k-1)$. This second condition serves to consider the position in the rank in which the journal articles were positioned with respect to the similarity to the documents retrieved (i.e., the higher the position, the higher the weight). The way in which the w_i weights are actually assigned, for evaluation purposes, is illustrated in detail in Sect. 4.3.

3.3   Computing the Retrieval Status Value

Once the two relevance dimension scores have been obtained, both of which in this case are dependent on the query formulated by the user, it was necessary to aggregate them to obtain the *Retrieval Status Value*, denoted as $\text{RSV}(d, q)$, which represents the final relevance score of a document with respect to a query given topical relevance and information genuineness. In this case, we also opted for a *linear combination* among the scores. Formally:

$$\text{RSV}(d, q) = w_{trs} * trs(d, q) + w_{igs} * igs(d, q) \tag{3}$$

In Eq. 3, w_{trs} denotes the weight assigned to the topical relevance score, and w_{igs} denotes the weight assigned to the information genuineness score. Also in this case, each weight w_{**s} is actually assigned, for evaluation purposes, as illustrated in Sect. 4.3. In the same section, the solution adopted to normalize the two relevance dimension scores in the same numerical range is also explained, since they are calculated in different ranges.

4   Evaluation Framework and Results

This section describes the experimental evaluation framework that was set up to assess the effectiveness of the retrieval model presented in this article. A BM25 baseline and several model configurations are evaluated on a public dataset and by means of suitable evaluation metrics.[19] The purpose of this experimental evaluation is to punctually assess the effectiveness of such configurations of the proposed approach in using external reputed sources (medical journal articles) to consider information genuineness as a query-dependent dimension of relevance, compared to the simple baseline chosen that uses topical relevance alone. Comparison with IR solutions that consider information genuineness (or related concepts) in the context of supervised or requiring human intervention solutions (see Sect. 2) is currently under study.

4.1   The TREC Health Misinformation Track Dataset

The TREC *Health Misinformation Track* fosters research on retrieval methods that promote reliable and correct information over misinformation for health-related decision-making tasks.[20] In this work, we used a subset of the dataset provided by the Track in its 2020 edition [8]. The original dataset is constituted by *CommonCrawl news*,[21] sampled from January, 1st 2020 to April 30th, 2020, which contains health-related news articles from all over the world. For our experiments, given the large volume of the original dataset, we selected 219,245

---

[19] Materials and documentation for reproducing the experiments are available at the following link: https://github.com/ikr3-lab/misinformation-wise2022.

[20] https://trec-health-misinfo.github.io/.

[21] https://commoncrawl.org/2016/10/news-dataset-available/.

English news related to COVID-19. The dataset has a fixed structure, organized into *topics*. Each topic includes a *title*, a *description*, which reformulates the title as a question, a *yes/no answer*, which is the actual answer to the description field based on the provided evidence, and a *narrative*, which describes helpful and harmful documents in relation to the given topic. For example, for the topic title field: 'ibuprofen COVID-19', the value of the other attributes in the dataset are, for the description: 'Can ibuprofen worsen COVID-19?', for the yes/no answer: 'no', and for the narrative: 'Ibuprofen is an anti-inflammatory drug used to reduce fever and treat pain or inflammation'.

The considered dataset also consists of an *evaluation set* of 5,340 labeled data. The data is labeled with respect to *usefulness, answer,* and *credibility.* Usefulness corresponds to topical relevance, answer indicates if the document provides an answer to the query contained in the description field, and credibility is the concept that, in the document collection, is used to indicate information genuineness. In this work, we just considered as labels usefulness and credibility. Both of them are provided on a binary scale, i.e., useful or non-useful, and credible or non-credible.

4.2 Evaluation Metrics

The TREC Health Misinformation Track, in addition to provide publicly available data, also provides an evaluation tool in which standard IR evaluation measures are implemented, especially when referring to multiple dimensions of relevance, which we have therefore also used for our experiments. The measures considered in this work are *Average Precision* (AP) and *Normalized Discounted Cumulative Gain* [15] on the first 10 results (NDCG@10), both computed by means of the MM *evaluation framework* for multidimensional relevance estimation [22], and two different implementations of the *Convex Aggregating Measure* (CAM) [20], one based on *Mean Average Precision* (MAP) [15], and the other on NDCG@n, for a distinct number of n results retrieved. Specifically:

- The MM framework for multidimensional relevance evaluation allows to incorporate distinct relevance criteria in the assessment of the effectiveness of an IRS along with topical relevance. In such a framework, firstly the evaluation results for each dimension of relevance are calculated separately using distinct evaluation measures. Taking inspiration from the measures used by the TREC Decision Track 2019 [1], we considered both *Average Precision* and NDCG@10. Finally, these scores are combined into a measure using the *weighted harmonic mean*. As the weighted harmonic mean is particularly sensitive to a single lower-than-average value, thus it will reward systems that are consistently more effective across all relevance dimensions.
- The *Convex Aggregating Measure* (CAM) is defined as the *convex sum* of the distinct evaluation results computed with respect to each relevance dimension considered. Formally:

$$\mathrm{CAM}(r) = \lambda_{rel}M_{rel}(r) + \lambda_{cred}M_{cre}(r) \tag{4}$$

where r denotes the number of documents, and M_{rel}, and M_{cre} denote the relevance (i.e., topical relevance), and credibility (i.e., information genuineness) evaluation measures considered. In our work, we applied both Mean Average Precision and NDCG@n. In the equation, λ denotes a weight to assign more importance to one of the two relevance dimensions, under the condition that $\lambda_{rel} + \lambda_{cred} = 1$. For our evaluation, we set the value of λ for each dimension to 0.5, as performed in the TREC 2020 Health Misinformation Track.

4.3   Implementation Technical Details

This section provides some technical details related to the implementation of the proposed solution, regarding indexing and other basic IR operations, the assignment of weights for the calculation of information genuineness and RSV, and the normalization of topical relevance and information genuineness scores into a single numerical range.

Basic IR Operations. To index documents, compute topical relevance scores, and implementing BM25-based retrieval models, we employed the implementation of BM25 provided in *PyTerrier*,[22] with default parameters. To retrieve documents, we used the description of the topic in the considered TREC 2020 dataset as the query. The same procedure was also adopted to find the journal articles related to the query considered, which are used to calculate the information genuineness score, as illustrated in Sect. 3.2.

Assignment of Weights. For assigning both w_i and w_{**s} weights, different solutions can be adopted. One can choose these values heuristically, or on the basis of greedy strategies, or on other ad hoc models. It is not the purpose of this article to determine which solution is best. Exclusively for evaluation purposes, it was decided to employ the weight assignment solution mentioned in [37] in the Information Retrieval field for computing the w_i weights; with this solution, ten queries were randomly selected, and a *grid search* strategy was performed with distinct weights to assess the best results, in computing both $trs(d, q)$ and $igs(d, q)$, in terms of CAM_{MAP}.[23] This latter is the official metric used in TREC 2020 Health Misinformation Track [8], fully described in Sect. 4.1. Regarding the calculation of the w_{**s} weights, it was decided to heuristically consider the case where equal importance is given to both dimensions of relevance, i.e., $w_{trs} = w_{igs} = 0.5$, the case where topical relevance is considered more important, i.e., $w_{trs} = 0.6$ and $w_{igs} = 0.4$, and the case where information genuineness is considered more important, i.e., $w_{trs} = 0.4$ and $w_{igs} = 0.6$.

---

[22] PyTerrier is a Python-based retrieval framework for simple and complex information retrieval (IR) pipelines by making use of Terrier IR platform for basic document indexing and retrieval. https://github.com/terrier-org/pyterrier.

[23] This choice does not impact the general unsupervised nature of the solution proposed in this article. It is only the simplest, least expensive, and already used in the IR literature solution to be able to provide an initial experimental evaluation.

Normalization of Relevance Dimension Scores. Topical relevance scores are computed using Eq. 1, which does not return values in a predetermined numerical range. In contrast, information genuineness scores, obtained by Eq. 2, take values in the range [0,1]. Hence, to make sure that both relevance scores are in the same numerical range, we normalized topical relevance scores using the *min-max normalization* [19]. Formally:

$$trs'(d, t) = \frac{trs(d, q) - \min_{trs(q)}}{\max_{trs(q)} - \min_{trs(q)}} \qquad (5)$$

where $trs'(d, q)$ and $trs(d, q)$ are the normalized and original topical relevance scores of a document d for a query q; $\min_{trs(q)}$ and $\max_{trs(q)}$ are the minimum and maximum topical relevance scores for all documents retrieved for q.

4.4 Results and Discussion

This section illustrates and discusses the results obtained by considering a simple BM25 retrieval model as a baseline, with respect to different model configurations proposed in this paper, against the considered evaluation metrics. In particular, the differences in model configurations aim to assess the impact of different textual representation of documents and journal articles (i.e., BERT vs BioBERT) and the relevance dimensions considered (we recall that distinct weights were heuristically attributed to topical relevance and information genuineness). The results are illustrated in Tables 1, 2, and 3, where:

- **BM25** denotes the baseline model, based on just topical relevance;
- **Model (1)** denotes the proposed retrieval model in which we compute topical relevance scores using BM25, and information genuineness scores by considering documents and top-10 journal articles as scientific evidence, both represented as BERT embeddings. In this model, the RSV is calculated by linearly combining (Eq. 3) topical relevance and information genuineness scores with equal weights (i.e., $w_{trs} = 0.5$ and $w_{igs} = 0.5$);
- **Model (2)** denotes the proposed retrieval model which differs from the previous one only in that RSV is calculated by assigning different weights to different relevance dimensions in the linear combination, specifically 0.6 to topical relevance, and 0.4 to information genuineness;
- **Model (3)** differs from Model (2) because, in the linear combination, a weight equal to 0.4 is assigned to topical relevance, and to 0.6 to information genuineness;
- **Model (4)** differs from Model (1) because documents and top-10 journal articles are represented as BioBERT embeddings;
- **Model (5)** differs from Model (2) because documents and top-10 journal articles are represented as BioBERT embeddings;
- **Model (6)** differs from Model (3) because documents and top-10 journal articles are represented as BioBERT embeddings.

Table 1. Experimental results obtained by using the MM evaluation framework in terms of Average Precision (AP) ad NDCG@10. Evaluations are performed by considering the same number of top-k journal articles, i.e., $k = 10$, as scientific evidence. Statistically significant results ($p < 0.05$ using the t-test [31]) are denoted with $*$.

Model	w_{trs}	w_{igs}	AP	NDCG@10	Embeddings
BM25	–	–	0.461	0.8601	–
Model (1)	0.5	0.5	0.469	0.8676	BERT
Model (2)	0.6	0.4	0.474	0.8701	BERT
Model (3)	0.4	0.6	0.476	0.8747	BERT
Model (4)	0.5	0.5	0.479	0.8785*	BioBERT
Model (5)	0.6	0.4	0.481*	0.8813*	BioBERT
Model (6)	0.4	0.6	0.493*	0.8951*	BioBERT

Table 1, which summarizes the effectiveness results of model configurations in terms of both AP and NDCG@10, shows that joint consideration of two relevance criteria in computing the final RSV improves system performance compared with topical relevance alone (BM25), regardless of the specific model configuration selected. Again for all the proposed models, analysis of the results suggests that assigning a higher weight to information genuineness leads to slightly higher performance. Finally, we can observe that Models (4), (5), and (6) are the best performing, all of which are based on the BioBERT representation. This suggests how taking into account the medical scientific vocabulary within (semantic- and context-aware) textual representation can actually improve health search results even in terms of information genuineness.

The greater effectiveness of models that are based on the BioBERT representation compared with the BERT representation, almost under each model configuration, also emerges from Table 2, which summarizes results in terms of both CAM_{MAP} and $CAM_{NDCG@n}$. This observation remains valid for whatever the number of documents retrieved from the system (in this case we chose to consider $n = 5$, 10, 15 and 20 retrieved documents). Also with respect to these measures, it can be observed that assigning higher weights to information genuineness produces slightly better results. The results in terms of these measures are even more significant because of the very nature of the two metrics, which explicitly combine assessments related to the two distinct dimensions of relevance.

Finally, to test the effectiveness of both textual representations as the number of articles taken as scientific evidence increases, i.e., for $k = 5$, 10, and 15, we kept fixed the number of retrieved documents on which the assessments were made (specifically, $n = 20$), and employed both Model (3) and Model (6), which are the ones who provided the best results in Table 2 for the BERT and BioBERT representations. From Table 3, summarizing these results in terms of both CAM_{MAP} and $CAM_{NDCG@20}$, we can observe that increasing the number of journal articles taken into account as scientific evidence actually contributes positively to the improved results obtained. Also in this case, the superiority of

Table 2. Experimental results in terms of Convex Aggregating Measure (CAM), w.r.t. both Mean Average Precision (MAP) and NDCG@n, for the top-n documents (# n docs) considered in different runs. The number of top-k journal articles considered as scientific evidence (# k j.arts) is fixed, i.e., $k = 10$. Statistically significant results.

Model	# n docs	w_{trs}	w_{igs}	# k j.arts	CAM$_{\text{MAP}}$	CAM$_{\text{NDCG@}n}$	Embeddings
BM25		1	–	–	0.0631	0.1435	–
Model (1)		0.5	0.5	10	0.0641	0.1434	BERT
Model (2)		0.6	0.4	10	0.0685	0.1475	BERT
Model (3)	5	0.4	0.6	10	0.0697	0.1495	BERT
Model (4)		0.5	0.5	10	0.0701	0.1487	BioBERT
Model (5)		0.6	0.4	10	0.0721	0.1500	BioBERT
Model (6)		0.4	0.6	10	**0.0894**	**0.1688**	BioBERT
BM25		1	–	–	0.1047	0.2052	–
Model (1)		0.5	0.5	10	0.1073	0.2057	BERT
Model (2)		0.6	0.4	10	0.1085	0.2084	BERT
Model (3)	10	0.6	0.4	10	0.1145	0.2151	BERT
Model (4)		0.5	0.5	10	0.1124	0.2112	BioBERT
Model (5)		0.6	0.4	10	0.1177	0.2161	BioBERT
Model (6)		0.4	0.6	10	**0.1249**	**0.2299**	BioBERT
BM25		1	–	–	0.0631	0.1435	–
Model (1)		0.5	0.5	10	0.1399	0.249	BERT
Model (2)		0.6	0.4	10	0.1435	0.2535	BERT
Model (3)	15	0.4	0.6	10	0.1485	0.2552	BERT
Model (4)		0.5	0.5	10	0.1489	0.2541	BioBERT
Model (5)		0.6	0.4	10	0.1507	0.259	BioBERT
Model (6)		0.4	0.6	10	**0.1597**	**0.2702**	BioBERT
BM25		1	–	–	0.1676	0.285	–
Model (1)		0.5	0.5	10	0.1649	0.2845	BERT
Model (2)		0.6	0.4	10	0.1726	0.2905	BERT
Model (3)	20	0.4	0.6	10	0.1797	0.2945	BERT
Model (4)		0.5	0.5	10	0.1753	0.2902	BioBERT
Model (5)		0.6	0.4	10	0.1783	0.2948	BioBERT
Model (6)		0.4	0.6	10	**0.1978**	**0.3102**	BioBERT

the model based on the BioBERT representation is confirmed, regardless of the number of journal articles considered.

Table 3. Comparison of Model (3) and Model (6) by considering the same number, i.e., $n = 20$, of retrieved documents and a different number of top-k journal articles (# k j.arts), as scientific evidence. Statistically significant results.

Model	# k j.arts	CAM_{MAP}	$CAM_{NDCG@20}$	Embedding
Model (3)	5	0.1698	0.285	BERT
Model (6)		**0.1787**	**0.2953**	BioBERT
Model (3)	10	0.1797	0.2945	BERT
Model (6)		**0.1978**	**0.3102**	BioBERT
Model (3)	15	0.1810	0.2912	BERT
Model (6)		**0.1975**	**0.3109**	BioBERT

5   Conclusions and Further Research

In the context of the spread of increasingly health misinformation online, in this article we addressed the problem of how to provide online users with topically relevant yet genuine information by proposing a retrieval model that considers scientific evidence in the form of reputed medical international journal articles in calculating so-called information genuineness.

Unlike other approaches that have been presented in the literature, which rely on the use of experts, or manually constructed knowledge bases, or labeled datasets and supervised approaches to assess the genuineness of information in retrieval models, in this article we have attempted to give a simple yet effective unsupervised solution to compare health content circulating online directly with the content of scientific articles, thereby succeeding in providing an automatic and non-time-consuming solution.

The results obtained showed that this approach is indeed effective when considering together topical relevance (calculated by state-of-the-art methods) and information genuineness calculated as in the proposed method. In particular, it can be seen that if the documents in the collection and the articles taken as scientific evidence are represented by embeddings related to the domain under consideration, the proposed solution is even more effective.

As for future developments to consider, there is first of all the comparison with other literature baselines in IR, both in terms of effectiveness and efficiency. It will also be necessary to further study the impact of individual relevance dimensions on the final results, as in this article we have only begun this investigation by heuristically testing a few configurations addressing this issue (which, in any case, have made it possible to observe that information genuineness can have a non-negligible impact in calculating the best Retrieval Status Value). Automated methods will also have to be considered to build knowledge bases that can actually exploit more semantic information than simply comparing textual representations between documents and reference articles.

Acknowledgment. This work was supported by the EU Horizon 2020 ITN/ETN on Domain Specific Systems for Information Extraction and Retrieval (H2020-EU.1.3.1., ID: 860721).

References

1. Abualsaud, M., et al.: Overview of the TREC 2019 Decision Track (2020)
2. Bal, R., et al.: Analysing the extent of misinformation in cancer related tweets. In: Proceedings of the International AAAI Conference on Web and Social Media, vol. 14, pp. 924–928 (2020)
3. Barua, Z., et al.: Effects of misinformation on COVID-19 individual responses and recommendations for resilience of disastrous consequences of misinformation. Prog. Disaster Sci. **8**, 100119 (2020)
4. Boyer, C., Selby, M., Appel, R.: The health on the net code of conduct for medical and health websites. In: Proceedings of the 9th World Congress on Medical Informatics, vol. 2, pp. 1163–1166. IOS Press (1998)
5. Chang, Y.S., Zhang, Y., Gwizdka, J.: The effects of information source and eHealth literacy on consumer health information credibility evaluation behavior. Comput. Hum. Behav. **115**, 106629 (2021)
6. Charnock, D., et al.: DISCERN: an instrument for judging the quality of written consumer health information on treatment choices. J. Epidemiol. Commun. Health **53**(2), 105–111 (1999)
7. Chou, W.Y.S., Oh, A., Klein, W.M.: Addressing health-related misinformation on social media. JAMA **320**(23), 2417–2418 (2018)
8. Clarke, C.L.A., et al.: Overview of the TREC 2020 Health Misinformation Track (2020). https://trec.nist.gov/pubs/trec29/papers/OVERVIEW.HM.pdf
9. Cormack, G.V., Clarke, C.L., Buettcher, S.: Reciprocal rank fusion outperforms Condorcet and individual rank learning methods. In: Proceedings of the 32nd International ACM SIGIR Conference on Research and Development in IR, pp. 758–759 (2009)
10. Croft, W.B., Metzler, D., Strohman, T.: Search Engines: Information Retrieval in Practice, vol. 520. Addison-Wesley Reading (2010)
11. Cui, L., et al.: DETERRENT: knowledge guided graph attention network for detecting healthcare misinformation. In: Proceedings of the 26th ACM SIGKDD International Conference on Knowledge Discovery & Data Mining, pp. 492–502 (2020)
12. Enders, A.M., et al.: The different forms of COVID-19 misinformation and their consequences. Harv. Kennedy Sch. Misinf. Rev. (2020)
13. Ernst, P., et al.: KnowLife: a knowledge graph for health and life sciences. In: 2014 IEEE 30th International Conference on Data Engineering, pp. 1254–1257. IEEE (2014)
14. Fox, S., Duggan, M.: Health online 2013. Health **2013**, 1–55 (2013)
15. Järvelin, K., Kekäläinen, J.: IR evaluation methods for retrieving highly relevant documents. In: ACM SIGIR Forum, vol. 51, pp. 243–250. ACM, New York (2017)
16. Kickbusch, I.S.: Health literacy: addressing the health and education divide. Health Promot. Int. **16**(3), 289–297 (2001)
17. Kinkead, L., Allam, A., Krauthammer, M.: AutoDiscern: rating the quality of online health information with hierarchical encoder attention-based neural networks. BMC Med. Inform. Decis. Mak. **20**(1), 1–13 (2020)

18. Kou, Z., Shang, L., Zhang, Y., Wang, D.: HC-COVID: a hierarchical crowdsource knowledge graph approach to explainable COVID-19 misinformation detection. In: Proceedings of the ACM on Human-Computer Interaction, vol. 6, no. GROUP, pp. 1–25 (2022)
19. Lee, J.H.: Analyses of multiple evidence combination. In: Proceedings of the 20th Annual International ACM SIGIR Conference on Research and Development in IR, pp. 267–276 (1997)
20. Lioma, C., Simonsen, J.G., Larsen, B.: Evaluation measures for relevance and credibility in ranked lists. In: Proceedings of the ACM SIGIR International Conference on Theory of Information Retrieval, pp. 91–98 (2017)
21. Metzger, M.J., Flanagin, A.J.: Psychological approaches to credibility assessment online. In: The Handbook of the Psychology of Communication Technology, pp. 445–466 (2015)
22. Palotti, J., Zuccon, G., Hanbury, A.: MM: a new framework for multidimensional evaluation of search engines. In: Proceedings of the 27th ACM International Conference on Information and Knowledge Management, pp. 1699–1702 (2018)
23. Pradeep, R., Ma, X., Nogueira, R., Lin, J.: Vera: prediction techniques for reducing harmful misinformation in consumer health search. In: Proceedings of the 44th International ACM SIGIR Conference on Research and Development in IR, pp. 2066–2070 (2021)
24. Pradeep, R., Nogueira, R., Lin, J.: The expando-mono-duo design pattern for text ranking with pretrained sequence-to-sequence models. arXiv preprint arXiv:2101.05667 (2021)
25. Putri, Divi Galih Prasetyo., Viviani, Marco, Pasi, Gabriella: Social search and task-related relevance dimensions in microblogging sites. In: Aref, S., et al. (eds.) SocInfo 2020. LNCS, vol. 12467, pp. 297–311. Springer, Cham (2020). https://doi.org/10.1007/978-3-030-60975-7_22
26. Robertson, S., Zaragoza, H.: The Probabilistic Relevance Framework: BM25 and Beyond. Now Publishers Inc. (2009)
27. Sackett, D.L.: Evidence-based medicine. In: Seminars in Perinatology, vol. 21, pp. 3–5. Elsevier (1997)
28. Samuel, Hamman, Zaïane, Osmar: MedFact: towards improving veracity of medical information in social media using applied machine learning. In: Bagheri, Ebrahim, Cheung, Jackie C. K.. (eds.) Canadian AI 2018. LNCS (LNAI), vol. 10832, pp. 108–120. Springer, Cham (2018). https://doi.org/10.1007/978-3-319-89656-4_9
29. Schlicht, I.B., de Paula, A.F.M., Rosso, P.: UPV at TREC Health Misinformation Track 2021 Ranking with SBERT and Quality Estimators. arXiv preprint arXiv:2112.06080 (2021)
30. Schulz, P.J., Nakamoto, K.: The perils of misinformation: when health literacy goes awry. Nat. Rev. Nephrol. 1–2 (2022)
31. Smucker, M.D., Allan, J., Carterette, B.: A comparison of statistical significance tests for information retrieval evaluation. In: Proceedings of the Sixteenth ACM Conference on Information and Knowledge Management, pp. 623–632 (2007)
32. Suominen, H., et al.: Overview of the CLEF eHealth evaluation lab 2021. In: Candan, K.S., et al. (eds.) CLEF 2021. LNCS, vol. 12880, pp. 308–323. Springer, Cham (2021). https://doi.org/10.1007/978-3-030-85251-1_21
33. Upadhyay, R., Pasi, G., Viviani, M.: Health misinformation detection in web content: a structural-, content-based, and context-aware approach based on Web2Vec. In: Proceedings of the Conference on Information Technology for Social Good, pp. 19–24 (2021)

34. Viviani, Marco, Pasi, Gabriella: A multi-criteria decision making approach for the assessment of information credibility in social media. In: Petrosino, Alfredo, Loia, Vincenzo, Pedrycz, Witold (eds.) WILF 2016. LNCS (LNAI), vol. 10147, pp. 197–207. Springer, Cham (2017). https://doi.org/10.1007/978-3-319-52962-2_17

35. Viviani, M., Pasi, G.: Credibility in social media: opinions, news, and health information-a survey. Wiley Interdiscip. Rev.: Data Mining Knowl. Discov. **7**(5), e1209 (2017)

36. Wardle, C., et al.: Thinking about 'information disorder': formats of misinformation, disinformation, and mal-information. In: Ireton, C., Posetti, J. (eds.) Journalism, 'Fake News' & Disinformation, pp. 43–54. UNESCO, Paris (2018)

37. Wu, S., et al.: Assigning appropriate weights for the linear combination data fusion method in information retrieval. Inf. Process. Manag. **45**(4), 413–426 (2009)

38. Zhao, Y., Da, J., Yan, J.: Detecting health misinformation in online health communities: incorporating behavioral features into machine learning based approaches. Inf. Process. Manag. **58**(1), 102390 (2021)

39. Zuo, C., Zhang, Q., Banerjee, R.: An empirical assessment of the qualitative aspects of misinformation in health news. In: Proceedings of the Fourth Workshop on NLP for Internet Freedom: Censorship, Disinformation, and Propaganda, pp. 76–81 (2021)

Explaining Unexpected Answers of SPARQL Queries

Louise Parkin[1([✉])], Brice Chardin[1], Stéphane Jean[2], and Allel Hadjali[1]

[1] ISAE-ENSMA, LIAS, Chasseneuil-du-Poitou, France
{louise.parkin,brice.chardin,allel.hadjali}@ensma.fr
[2] Université de Poitiers, LIAS, Poitiers, France
stephane.jean@univ-poitiers.fr

Abstract. *"Why am I not getting the right answer?"* is a question many Knowledge Base users may ask themselves. In particular, novice users can easily make mistakes and find differences between the answer they expected and the answer they got. This problem is known as the unsatisfactory answer problem. A subproblem, where no answers are returned, has been widely studied and identifying failure causes can help users modify their queries to fit their requirements. But users may be unhappy with their results for multiple other reasons: they may be overwhelmed by too many answers, expect a particular answer that is not included, or even encounter a combination of these problems. In this paper, we classify the various types of unsatisfactory answers, and propose algorithms to compute generalized failure causes. We evaluate the performance of our algorithms and show that they perform comparably to existing problem-specific methods, while being more extensive.

Keywords: Knowledge bases · SPARQL · Unexpected answers · MFIS · XSS

1 Introduction

A Knowledge Base (KB) is a solution for storing data as RDF triples (subject, predicate, object). KBs are widely used in industry and academia. Well-known examples of KBs are DBpedia [16] and Google's Knowledge Vault [6]. Users unfamiliar with the technology are likely to need to extract information from a KB. Specific interfaces can allow for text based searching, but the most common method for retrieving information from a KB is the SPARQL query language [11].

Novice users can struggle to write queries, inaccurately describing their requirements. Therefore, *mistakes* or *misconceptions* may appear, causing unexpected or unsatisfactory answers. Mistakes refer to the user incorrectly writing their query, for example misspelling a term. Misconceptions refer to a user's incorrect understanding of a KB [27]. There are five unexpected answers problems, each linked to a why-question: no answers (*why empty*), too few answers

(a) Knowledge base D

subject	predicate	object
p_1	age	25
p_1	suffersFrom	brokenArm
p_1	suffersFrom	flu
p_1	ward	ICU
p_1	status	Dead
p_2	age	47
p_2	suffersFrom	stroke
p_2	ward	ER
n_1	worksIn	ICU
n_1	treats	p_3
n_2	worksIn	ER
n_2	treats	p_2
n_2	treats	p_3
n_3	worksIn	ICU
n_3	treats	p_1
n_3	treats	p_2

(a) Knowledge base D

```
SELECT * WHERE {
?p ward ICU .          #t1
?p status Dead .       #t2
?n treats ?p .         #t3
?n ward ICU .          #t4
?p suffersFrom ?i }    #t5
No answers
```

(b) Query $Q = t_1 t_2 t_3 t_4 t_5$

```
SELECT * WHERE {
?p ward ICU .       #t1
?p status Dead .    #t2
?n treats ?p .      #t3
?n ward ICU .  } #t4
No answers
```

(c) $Q' = t_1 t_2 t_3 t_4$

```
SELECT * WHERE {
?p ward ICU .          #t1
?p status Dead .       #t2
?n ward ICU .          #t4
?p suffersFrom ?i }    #t5
Too many answers
```

(d) Query $Q'' = t_1 t_2 t_3 t_5$

```
SELECT * WHERE {
?p ward ICU .          #t1
?p status Dead .       #t2
?p suffersFrom ?i }    #t5
Satisfactory answers
```

(e) $Q''' = t_1 t_2 t_5$

Fig. 1. A Knowledge Base, SPARQL queries and their results

(*why so few*), too many answers (*why so many*), missing answers (*why not*), and unwanted answers (*why so*). So far each problem has been studied separately, so combined problems are difficult to handle. These can occur if fixing one type of unexpected answer creates another (i.e. turning an insufficiently restricted query into a too restrictive one), or in situations with precise cardinality requirements.

Consider the example of a hospital KB, and a user who wants information on the patients who died in the intensive care unit (ICU) and suppose the user expects around 100 answers based on their knowledge of the hospital. A section of the KB and succession of query attempts are shown in Fig. 1. The user writes a SPARQL query (b), but receives no answers. From their contextual knowledge, the user determines there must be a mistake somewhere. However they have no way of knowing what is causing the problem, as there are several possibilities. There could be an inappropriate term within the query (ICU rather than Intensive Care Unit), or some incompatible properties (dead patients are not being treated by anyone). Once the user manages to produce some results (d), they find over 10,000 answers, which is far too many to be able to deal with. Again they will wonder where the mistake is, as they have fixed the initial problem, but created another. Some possible explanations for the overabundant answers are having two triple patterns whose combination causes a multiplication of the number of answers (illness and the people treating a patient) or having an insufficiently constrained variable. All in all, a user faced with unsatisfactory answers must undergo a time-consuming and frustrating trial and error process to fix their query without a guarantee to receive the expected answers in the end.

To help a user facing an unexpected answer, there are two approaches: explain what is causing these answers, or suggest changes to the query. Existing work focusing on a specific type of unexpected answers has mainly explored the query modification solution [18, 23]. The answer explanation strategy has been successfully used to deal with empty answers [8] and was shown to increase the performance of subsequent query modification steps [2, 7, 14]. Figure 2 shows how identifying failure causes would help to deal with the previous query by studying its con-

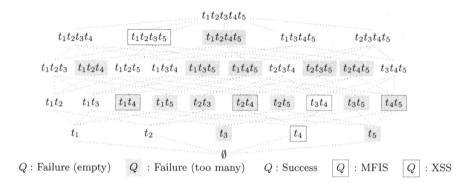

Fig. 2. Lattice of subqueries of Q

stituent parts. The lattice shows the successful queries, and those that fail either because they have empty answers or too many answers (for a threshold of 200 in this example). We are interested in providing the MFIS (Minimal Failure Inducing Subqueries) and XSS (maXimal Succeeding Subqueries). The MFIS are the smallest parts of the query that induce unexpected answers if they are part of a query and the XSS are largest parts of the query that produce acceptable answers. Here, the MFIS show that the inclusion of triple pattern t_4 : ?n ward ICU with any other triple pattern causes unexpected answers (either because there will be empty answers if t_3 is also included, or because there will be too many answers with another triple pattern). Indeed, the user has used the property *ward* which applies to a patient, but with subject n which in the context of the query is meant to indicate a member of the hospital staff. This query could be fixed by removing triple pattern t_4, therefore replacing the query with the XSS $t_1t_2t_3t_5$, or by modifying the predicate in t_4 from *ward* to *worksIn*. The interpretation of MFIS and XSS to fix a query is beyond the scope of this paper.

In this paper, we apply the failure cause definition used for the why empty and why so many problems, called Minimal Failure Inducing Subquery (MFIS) to the other elementary problems in order to propose a generalized system to deal with unsatisfactory answers. We will show that our method can cope with combinations of unexpected answers and we will perform experimental evaluation to determine its usability on real data from DBpedia along with real queries from the *Linked SPARQL Queries Dataset* [22].

We start by exploring related work for each unexpected answer problem in Sect. 2. In Sect. 3, we give the elementary notions of RDF, and introduce a classification for unexpected answers and related properties. Section 4 presents the algorithms for computing failure causes. We perform experimental evaluation of our algorithms in Sect. 5 and conclude with future prospects in Sect. 6.

2   Related Work

Unexpected answers have been studied using both a data based and a query based approach. The data based approach provides information on data provenance: operations that led to missing information [12] or the data source producing problematic answers [28]. These methods can help database providers enhance data quality, but rarely help end users with no control over the KB content. On the other hand, the query based approach uses the hypothesis that the user incorrectly specified their query so it does not match their requirement.

To fix the unexpected answer problem, most query-based methods modify the user query by removing, changing or adding triple patterns. Various modification strategies have been used for specific problems. For the why empty and why so many problems in graph queries, maximum common connected subgraphs are computed by removing parts of the initial query to create the largest succeeding query graph [25]. For the same problems in KBs, maXimal Succeeding Subqueries are computed by triple pattern suppression [9]. For the why not problem in relational databases, a similarity metric based on edit distance is used to rank modified queries [24]. Exact algorithms and heuristics are used for the why not and why so problems in knowledge graphs, to change a query step by step to include new answers [23]. To deal with the why so many problem with fuzzy queries, intensification techniques can be used [18]. New queries are found via an exhaustive search [23,25], or using semantic information to chose more relevant queries [24]. New queries may still produce unexpected answers, so finding queries that return the desired answers remains a trial and error process.

To address this issue, some query based techniques identify the reasons for unexpected answers. Failure causes were introduced for the why empty problem: false presuppositions are returned to the user if their query produces no answers [15,19]. Minimal Failing Subqueries (MFS) have then been used to describe the smallest parts of a query that lead to empty answers [5,7,9]. A related notion, Minimal Failure Inducing Subquery, is used for the why so many problem [20]. Failure causes have also been used in the why not problem in relational databases [1], and KBs [26] to identify the triple pattern or SPARQL operator responsible for an absent answer. To our knowledge, no query based failure causes have been studied for the why so few and why so problems, or combined problems.

Failure causes can be used to enhance query modification by focusing changes on the parts responsible for unexpected answers. MFS have been used in automated query modification systems dealing with empty answers [2,14] and in interactive query rewriting frameworks, where users can select parts to be relaxed [14,17]. In RDF, a hybrid method balances the MFS computation cost and the gain of not executing modified queries [7]. Thus, the efficiency of query modification methods can be improved if unexpected answers have been explained first.

3   Problem Formalization

We start by describing the formalism and semantics of RDF and SPARQL necessary for the paper, using notations and definitions from Pérez et al. [21]. We then give definitions for unexpected answers and introduce related properties. For space considerations, some proofs are not provided here.

3.1   Basic Notions

Data Model. We consider three pairwise disjoint infinite sets: I the set of IRIs, B the set of blank nodes, and L the set of literals. An *RDF triple* is a triple (subject, predicate, object) $\in (I \cup B) \times I \times (I \cup B \cup L)$. An *RDF database* stores a set of RDF triples. We also consider V a set of variables disjoint from $I \cup B \cup L$.

RDF Queries. A triple t (subject, predicate, object) $\in (I \cup L \cup V) \times (I \cup V) \times (I \cup L \cup V)$ is a *triple pattern*. We denote by $s(t)$, $p(t)$, $o(t)$, and $var(t)$ the subject, predicate, object and variables of t. In this paper, we will consider *RDF queries* defined as conjunctions of triple patterns $Q = SELECT \; * \; WHERE \; t_1 \cdots t_n$, which we write as $Q = t_1 \cdots t_n$. We write that t is a triple pattern appearing in a query Q by $t \in Q$. The variables of a query are $var(Q) = \bigcup var(t_i)$. We define an order on queries using triple pattern inclusion. Given $Q = t_1 \cdots t_n$, $Q' = t_i \cdots t_j$ is a *subquery* of Q, denoted by $Q' \subseteq Q$, iff $\forall t \in Q', t \in Q$. Then Q is a *superquery* of Q'. For a query $Q = t_1 \cdots t_n$ and a triple pattern $t \notin Q$, we denote the addition of t to Q by $Q \wedge t = t_1 \cdots t_n t$. This notation is extended to queries, so $Q \wedge Q'$ refers to the conjunction of Q and Q'. Conversely for $t' \in Q$, removing t from Q is denoted by $Q - t$.

Query Evaluation. A mapping μ from V to T is a partial function $\mu : V \to T$. For a triple pattern t, we denote by $\mu(t)$ the triple obtained by replacing the variables in t according to μ. The domain of μ, $dom(\mu)$, is the subset of V where μ is defined. The restriction of a mapping μ to a subset of variables $var \subseteq V$ is denoted by $\mu_{|var}$ and defined as a partial function $\mu_{|var} : var \to T$, where $\forall x \in var, \mu_{|var}(x) = \mu(x)$. Two mappings μ_1 and μ_2 are *compatible* if $\forall x \in dom(\mu_1) \cap dom(\mu_2), \mu_1(x) = \mu_2(x)$. The join of two sets of mappings Ω_1 and Ω_2 is: $\Omega_1 \bowtie \Omega_2 = \{\mu_1 \cup \mu_2 \mid \mu_1 \in \Omega_1, \mu_2 \in \Omega_2 \text{ are compatible mappings}\}$. The *evaluation* of a triple pattern t over a KB D, is $[[t]]_D = \{\mu \mid dom(\mu) = var(t) \wedge \mu(t) \in D\}$. The evaluation of a query $Q = t_1 \cdots t_n$ over D is $[[Q]]_D = [[t_1]]_D \bowtie \cdots \bowtie [[t_n]]_D$.

Boolean Function. A boolean function of n variables is a function on B^n into B, where B is the set $[0,1]$, n is a positive integer, and B^n denotes the n-fold cartesian product of the set B with itself [3].

3.2   Unexpected Answers

There are many reasons why a user may be unsatisfied by the answer to their query. To formalize this, we define a *failure condition*, using the formalism of boolean functions, which takes as entry a query Q, and returns a boolean value describing whether its answer is satisfactory or not when executed on a given KB. The boolean function has n variables, $(x_1, ..., x_n)$ where n is the number of triple patterns of the initial query, and $\forall i, x_i = 1 \iff Q$ contains t_i.

For a query Q and a KB D, we denote this property: $FAIL(Q, D)$. There are five elementary types of query failure [13]. They are based on the query result $[[Q]]_D$, and can be split into cardinality based, and content based properties.

Cardinality based failure conditions depend on the number of answers of a query. As such, it is not necessary to know the content of the answers to determine if the query succeeds or fails. The failure conditions will be based on a threshold value K to be determined by the user or the system. They are:

- *Why so many*: $FAIL_{>K}(Q, D) = (|[[Q]]_D| > K)$ for $K \geq 0$.
- *Why so few*: $FAIL_{<K}(Q, D) = (|[[Q]]_D| < K)$ for $K > 0$.
- *Why empty*: $FAIL_{\emptyset}(Q, D) = (|[[Q]]_D| = 0)$. This is a special case of *Why so few* with K=1.

Example 1. $FAIL_{<2}(Q, D)$ is a failure property denoting that queries with under 2 answers fail. In the example in Fig. 1, $t_1 t_3 t_4$ and $t_2 t_5$ fail with respectively 0 and 1 answer. $t_4 t_5$ and $t_1 t_2 t_5$ succeed with respectively 3 and 2 answers.

Content based failure conditions are based on the content of the answers. In particular, a user is interested in obtaining or avoiding a particular mapping. The failure conditions will be based on a provided mapping μ_w. They are:

- *Why not* : $FAIL_{\not\subseteq \mu_w}(Q, D) = (\forall \mu \in [[Q]]_D : \mu_w$ and μ are not compatible)
- *Why so* : $FAIL_{\subseteq \mu_w}(Q, D) = (\exists \mu \in [[Q]]_D : \mu_w$ and μ are compatible)

For the content based failure condition to have meaning, the variables of the mapping must all be included in the query. As such, $FAIL_{\not\subseteq \mu_w}(Q, D)$ and $FAIL_{\subseteq \mu_w}(Q, D)$ are undefined if $dom(\mu_w) \not\subseteq var(Q)$. So when studying subqueries obtained by removing triple patterns, we will eliminate from the search space any query which does not respect this condition.

Example 2. For μ_w, where $dom(\mu_w) = \{p\}$ and $\mu_w(p) = p_2$, $FAIL_{\not\subseteq \mu_w}(Q, D)$ is a failure property denoting that queries where no answer has p_2 as the value for variable p fail. In Fig. 1, $t_1 t_3$ and $t_2 t_5$ fail, and $t_4 t_5$ succeeds. t_4 is not a valid query for this problem, as variable p from the mapping is missing.

For μ_w, where $dom(\mu_w) = \{n\}$ and $\mu_w(n) = p_2$, $FAIL_{\subseteq \mu_w}(Q, D)$ is a failure property denoting that queries where an answer has p_2 as the value for variable n fail. In Fig. 1, $t_1 t_2 t_3 t_4 t_5$ succeeds, and $t_2 t_4$ fails. t_1 is not a valid query for this problem, as variable n is missing.

These five elementary unexpected answers can be combined using the basic logical operators conjunction ($\wedge$), disjunction ($\vee$) and negation ($\neg$).

Negation. For each problem, the negation can be expressed as another problem:

- $\neg(FAIL_{>K}(Q, D)) = FAIL_{<K+1}(Q, D)$
- $\neg(FAIL_{\subseteq \mu_w}(Q, D)) = FAIL_{\not\subseteq \mu_w}(Q, D)$
- $\neg(FAIL_{\emptyset}(Q, D)) = FAIL_{>0}(Q, D)$

Conjunction and Disjunction. We define conjunction and disjunction based on the failure conditions:

- $(FAIL_1 \wedge FAIL_2)(Q, D) = FAIL_1(Q, D) \wedge FAIL_2(Q, D)$
- $(FAIL_1 \vee FAIL_2)(Q, D) = FAIL_1(Q, D) \vee FAIL_2(Q, D)$

3.3 Relations Between Problems

The why not problem can be transformed into a why empty problem. We consider a query Q and a why not question μ_w mapping some variables v to $\mu_w(v)$. We build a new query Q', based on Q by replacing the variables v with their mappings according to μ_w. This technique was used to deal with the why not problem in KBs [26]. The following property transforms a failure of Q into a failure of Q':

Property 1. Consider a query Q, a why not question μ_w, and Q' built by replacing each $v \in dom(\mu_w) \cap var(Q)$ by $\mu_w(v)$. $FAIL_{\not\subseteq \mu_w}(Q, D) = FAIL_\emptyset(Q', D)$

Proof. If $FAIL_{\not\subseteq \mu_w}(Q, D) = true$, suppose $\exists \mu' \in [[Q']]_D$. From the definition of Q', $dom(\mu') \cap dom(\mu_w) = \emptyset$, so μ' and μ_w are compatible. So $\mu = \mu' \cup \mu_w$ is a mapping, $\mu \in [[Q]]_D$, and μ and μ_w are compatible which contradicts $\not\exists \mu \in [[Q]]_D$, μ and μ_w are compatible. So $[[Q']]_D = \emptyset$ and $FAIL_\emptyset(Q', D) = true$.

If $FAIL_\emptyset(Q', D) = true$, suppose $\exists \mu \in [[Q]]_D$ such that μ_w and μ are compatible. From the definition of Q', $\mu_{|var(Q')} \in [[Q']]_D$ which contradicts $[[Q']]_D = \emptyset$. So $\not\exists \mu \in [[Q]]_D$, μ and μ_w are compatible, and $FAIL_{\not\subseteq \mu_w}(Q, D) = true$.

Similarly, a why so problem can be transformed into a why so many problem (with a threshold K=1).

Property 2. Consider a query Q, a why not question μ_w, and Q' built by replacing each $v \in dom(\mu_w) \cap var(Q)$ by $\mu_w(v)$. $FAIL_{\subseteq \mu_w}(Q, D) = FAIL_{>1}(Q', D)$

3.4 Monotony of the Failure Condition

A particular type of boolean functions are Monotone Boolean Functions (MBF) [3]. A boolean function f is *positive* if for each of its variables x, $f_{x=0} \leq f_{x=1}$. In that case, we call the associated failure condition *positive*, meaning that if a query fails, all its superqueries fails, and therefore if a query succeeds, all its subqueries succeed. More formally, $FAIL(Q', D) \wedge Q'' \subseteq Q' \implies FAIL(Q'', D)$. Considering the partial order of queries based on triple pattern inclusion, the failure condition is upward closed. A boolean function f is *negative* if for each of its variables x, $f_{x=0} \geq f_{x=1}$. In that case, we call the associated failure condition *negative*, meaning that if a query succeeds, all its superqueries succeed, and if a query fails, all its subqueries fail. A *monotonic* failure condition is either a positive or a negative failure condition.

Property 3. $FAIL_\emptyset$ and $FAIL_{\not\subseteq \mu_w}$ are positive properties.

As $\neg(FAIL_{\subseteq \mu_w}(Q, D)) = FAIL_{\not\subseteq \mu_w}(Q, D)$, it follows that the why so problem has a negative failure condition. We show that the why so few and why so many problems do not have monotonic failure conditions with a counter-example.

Example 3. We use KB D and query Q from Fig. 1, failure causes $F_1(Q, D) = FAIL_{>1}(Q, D)$, $F_2(Q, D) = FAIL_{<2}(Q, D)$ and subqueries $Q_1 = t_3$, $Q_2 = t_2 t_3$, $Q_3 = t_1 t_2 t_3 t_5$. $|[[Q_1]]_D| = 5$, $|[[Q_2]]_D| = 1$, $|[[Q_1]]_D| = 2$. As $Q_1 \subseteq Q_2 \subseteq Q_3$ and $F_1(Q_1, D) = true$, $F_1(Q_2, D) = false$, $F_1(Q_3, D) = true$, F_1 is not monotnic. As $F_2(Q_1, D) = false$, $F_2(Q_2, D) = true$, $F_2(Q_3, D) = false$, F_2 is not monotonic.

problem	cardinality or content	failure condition	monotonic
why empty	cardinality	$[[Q]]_D = \emptyset$	positive
why so many	cardinality	$|[[Q]]_D| > K$	no monotony
why so few	cardinality	$|[[Q]]_D| < K$	no monotony
why not	content	$\forall \mu \in [[Q]]_D \mu_w \not\subseteq \mu$	positive
why so	content	$\exists \mu \in [[Q]]_D \mu_w \subseteq \mu$	negative

Fig. 3. The five elementary failure conditions

Figure 3 summarises the characteristics of all five elementary failure conditions. Some combinations of failure properties can also be monotonic.

Property 4. A conjunction or disjunction of positive (resp. negative) properties is positive (resp. negative).

4 Failure Causes

Having defined what a user can consider a query failure, we want to provide tools describing the parts of the query responsible for query failure. These notions should be computed quickly to improve user experience. To that end we suggest algorithms to determine failure causes that execute as few queries as possible.

4.1 Definitions

Our aim is to identify the parts of a query responsible for its failure. Building on the Minimal Failing Subquery (MFS) and maXimal Succeeding Subqueries (XSS) introduced in the why empty problem, the following definitions have been proposed to deal with the why so many answers problem [20].

Definition 1. *A Failure Inducing Subquery (FIS) of a query is one of its failing subqueries whose superqueries all fail. The set of FIS of a query Q is:*

$$fis(Q, D, FAIL) = \{Q^* \mid Q^* \subseteq Q \land FAIL(Q^*, D) \land$$
$$\forall Q' \subseteq Q, \ Q^* \subset Q' \Rightarrow FAIL(Q', D)\}$$

Definition 2. *A Minimal Failure Inducing Subquery (MFIS) of a query is one of its failure inducing subqueries such that none of its subqueries are FIS. The set of MFIS of a query Q is:*

$$mfis(Q, D, FAIL) = \{Q^* \in fis(Q, D, FAIL) \mid \nexists Q' \subset Q^*, \ Q' \in fis(Q, D, FAIL)\}$$

Definition 3. *A maXimal Succeeding Subquery (XSS) of a query is a succeeding subquery whose superqueries are all FIS. The set of XSS of a query Q is:*

$$xss(Q, D, FAIL) = \{Q^* \mid Q^* \subseteq Q \land \neg FAIL(Q^*, D) \land$$
$$\forall Q', Q^* \subset Q' \Rightarrow Q' \in fis(Q, D, FAIL)\}$$

These definitions do not rely on the monotony of the failure condition. In this paper we apply them in a general setting, for any unexpected answer problem. In the case of a negative failure condition (for the why so problem), if the initial query fails then all its subqueries fail. This means that there are no XSS, and that the MFIS are all the smallest subqueries that contain the variables of the missing mapping. The notions of MFIS and XSS are therefore not very useful to solve problems with a negative failure condition. They can however be used if that failure condition is a part of a disjunction in a bigger failure condition. We will now consider methods for identifying the MFIS and XSS of a query.

4.2   Computation

Finding the queries that succeed and fail can be accomplished by executing them on the KB and analyzing the answer or by applying deduction rules based on the answers of related queries. To measure the cost of finding MFIS, we will start by using the metric of number of queries executed. The number of query executions is measured relative to n, the number of triple patterns in the initial query, as the search space, i.e. the number of subqueries is equal to $2^n - 1$. For any problem, a baseline method, called BASE is to execute every subquery, and check if it succeeds or fails using the failure property.

In the general case, finding all the MFIS and XSS can require an exponential number of operations, as a query can have up to $\binom{n}{\lfloor n/2 \rfloor}$ MFIS and XSS [9]. However for some problems, we can apply properties to execute fewer queries.

Positive Failure Properties. If the failure property is positive, the Lattice Based Algorithm (LBA) proposed by Fokou [8] based on the a_mel_fast algorithm by Godfrey [9] can be used to compute the MFIS. It uses the following property:

Property 5. Consider a positive failure property $FAIL$, queries Q and Q_i and triple pattern t_i with $Q = Q_i \wedge t_i$. If $FAIL(Q, D)$ and $\neg FAIL(Q_i, D)$, every MFIS of Q contains t_i.

The LBA algorithm finds a first MFIS Q^* by removing triple patterns from the initial query Q one by one. For a triple pattern t_i, and Q_i where $Q = Q_i \wedge t_i$, if Q_i succeeds, t_i is added to Q^*. LBA continues, replacing Q with $Q_i \wedge Q^*$. A first MFIS Q^* is found once all triple patterns have been removed. The process is repeated over the largest subqueries of Q that do not contain the found MFIS.

Pruning Properties. To reduce the number of query executions, some query properties can be leveraged. A general property can be applied to all problems [20]:

Property 6. If a subquery Q' succeeds and $Q'' \subset Q'$, Q'' is not an MFIS or XSS.

Using this property, subqueries of XSS do not need to be studied, so we start by checking that the query does not have a succeeding query, and only study its failure if that is the case. The why so many study also introduces properties that use the failure of a query to determine the failure of another query [20]. We have adapted these to be useful to any cardinality based problem.

Property 7. Given a query Q and triple pattern t, if $var(Q \wedge t) = var(Q)$ then $|[[Q \wedge t]]_D| \leq |[[Q]]_D|$.

Definition 4. *The global minimum and maximum cardinality of a predicate p in a dataset D are [4]:*

$$\text{card}_{\min}(p, D) = \min_{s | \exists\, p,o:(s,p,o) \in D} |\{(s,p,o) \mid (s,p,o) \in D\}|$$

$$\text{card}_{\max}(p, D) = \max_{s | \exists\, p,o:(s,p,o) \in D} |\{(s,p,o) \mid (s,p,o) \in D\}|$$

Property 8. Given a query Q, and a triple pattern t with a fixed predicate $p(t)$, a variable object $o(t) \notin var(Q)$ and $s(t) \in var(Q)$, if $\text{card}_{\max}(p(t), D) = 1$ then $|[[Q \wedge t]]_D| \leq |[[Q]]_D|$ and if $\text{card}_{\min}(p(t), D) = 1$ then $|[[Q \wedge t]]_D| \geq |[[Q]]_D|$.

These properties are useful to determine an upper or lower bound of the number of answers to a query if the number of answers of another query is known. For cardinality based problems they can be used to determine success or failure of queries without executing them. In a top-down algorithm, these properties can be used to determine the status of a query Q, knowing $Q \wedge t$, but for an algorithm with another execution order, they can be applied in the other direction.

Dealing with Combined Problems. When considering a combined problem, there are two possibilities for finding the MFIS. The first option is to execute an algorithm for each elementary part of the failure cause, then combine the results. The second option is to execute a single algorithm as previously, applying the combined failure definition when considering a query execution. In the first case, we should consider whether the knowledge of the MFIS and XSS for two failure properties is sufficient to determine the MFIS and XSS for their combination. The MFIS and XSS of a query for a conjunction of failure properties can be computed from the MFIS and XSS of the query for each property.

Property 9. Consider a query Q, a failure condition $FAIL = F_1 \wedge F_2$, Q' an MFIS of Q for $FAIL$ and Q'' an XSS of Q for $FAIL$. Q' is a superquery of an MFIS of Q for F_1 and a superquery of an MFIS of Q for F_2. Q'' is an XSS of Q for F_1 or for F_2.

Proof. Consider Q' an MFIS of Q for $FAIL$. Since $Q' \in mfis(Q, D, FAIL)$, then $Q' \in fis(Q, D, FAIL)$. So $Q' \in fis(Q, D, F_1)$ and $Q' \in fis(Q, D, F_2)$. From the MFIS definition, $\exists Q_1 \in mfis(Q, D, F_1)$ and $\exists Q_2 \in mfis(Q, D, F_2)$ such that $Q_1 \subseteq Q'$ and $Q_2 \subseteq Q'$.

Consider Q' an XSS of Q for $FAIL$. Suppose Q' is not an XSS of Q for F_1. Either $\exists Q'', Q' \subseteq Q'' \wedge F_1(Q'', D) = false$, which means $FAIL(Q'', D) = false$ and contradicts the assertion that Q' is an XSS of Q for $FAIL$ or $F_1(Q', D) = true$. Since $FAIL(Q', D) = false$, then $F_2(Q', D) = false$. Suppose $\exists Q''', Q' \subseteq Q''' \wedge F_2(Q''', D) = false$, meaning $FAIL(Q''', D) = false$ and contradicting the assertion that Q' is an XSS of Q for $FAIL$. So Q' is an XSS of Q for F_2.

To show that this is not the case for a disjunction of failure properties, consider the introduction example. The failure cause was $FAIL = FAIL_\emptyset \vee FAIL_{>200}$. For the initial query Q, we have $FAIL_{>200}(Q, D) = false$. So Q is the XSS and there are no MFIS for $FAIL_{>200}$. But $FAIL_{>200}$ is significant for finding the MFIS and XSS for $FAIL$. So for a disjunction of failure properties, we need to know the entire status of the lattice. The previous algorithms must therefore be adapted to return the status of the whole lattice rather than the MFIS and XSS.

5   Experimentation

We propose two sets of experiments. The first will compare variations of our algorithms to illustrate the various improvements from the use of the properties introduced in Sect. 4. The second will compare our generic algorithm, Shiny, with specific solutions proposed for the why empty [7], why so many [20], and why not [26] problems. We will observe the performance cost of a general method compared with specific solutions, and compare the proposed failure causes.

5.1   Experimental Setup

Hardware. Our experiments were run on a Ubuntu Server 16.04 LTS system with Intel(R) Xeon(R) CPU E5-2630 v3 @ 2.40 GHz and 32 GB RAM. The results presented are the average of five consecutive runs of the algorithms. To prevent a cold start effect, a preliminary run is performed but not included in the results.

Algorithms. The algorithms are implemented in Oracle Java 1.8 64 bits and run on top of Jena TDB. To compare the generic solution to specific methods from the state of the art, we have used the QARS system [7] (why empty), the TMA4KB system [20] (why so many), and the ANNA system [26] (why not). We used the reference implementations for the first two systems[1,2], and we re-implemented the ANNA algorithm as a reference implementation was not available.

Dataset and Queries. We downloaded the DBpedia dataset (the English 3.9 version) which contains 812M triple patterns and used conjunctive queries from the LSQ project [22] for our first experiments. Minor adaptations were made as some original queries used URIs incompatible with DBpedia v.3.9. Values for content-based questions were taken from the domain of one of the triple patterns of query in order to have plausible missing answers.

   To compare with state of the art methods, we have used the datasets and queries from the initial papers: 7 queries on the LUBM dataset [10] for why empty, 9 queries on DBpedia for why so many, 5 queries with 6 missing mappings on DBpedia for why not.

---

[1] https://forge.lias-lab.fr/projects/qars.
[2] https://forge.lias-lab.fr/projects/tma4kb.

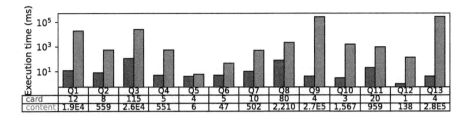

	Q1	Q2	Q3	Q4	Q5	Q6	Q7	Q8	Q9	Q10	Q11	Q12	Q13
card	12	8	115	5	4	5	10	80	4	3	20	1	4
content	1.9E4	559	2.6E4	551	6	47	502	2,210	2.7E5	1,567	959	138	2.8E5

Fig. 4. Execution time for WhyNot queries with cardinality or content method

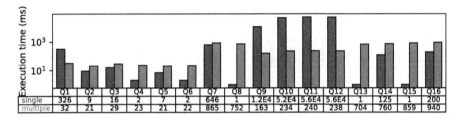

	Q1	Q2	Q3	Q4	Q5	Q6	Q7	Q8	Q9	Q10	Q11	Q12	Q13	Q14	Q15	Q16
single	326	9	16	2	7	2	646	1	1.2E4	5.2E4	5.6E4	5.6E4	1	125	1	200
multiple	32	21	29	23	21	22	865	752	163	234	240	238	704	760	859	940

Fig. 5. Execution time for combined failure causes with single or multiple algorithms

5.2 Results

Content-Based Problems. Figure 4 shows the execution times for finding the MFIS and XSS for 13 why not questions. The card method uses the transformation to an equivalent why empty problem, whereas the content method searches for the expected mapping in the query answers. Dealing with the why not problem by transforming it into a cardinality problem is a significant improvement. Execution times are reduced by up to five orders of magnitude. On average, the card method runs in 7% of the content method's time. For the content method the execution time is related to the size of the result set as determining that an answer is missing requires checking every other answer. In the card method, we only need to know if a query produced an answer, without examining all the answers. By transforming the content problem to a cardinality problem, results unrelated to the mapping of interest are not generated and most of the processing is performed by the underlying triplestore.

Combined Problems. Figure 5 shows the execution times for finding the MFIS and XSS for 16 combinations of two failure causes. All odd numbered executions are disjunctions, and even numbered executions are conjunctions. The single method uses one algorithm execution, using the BASE algorithm and leveraging Property 6, and determines failure based on the conjunction of failure conditions. The multiple method executes one algorithm per failure condition then combines the results, either combining the MFIS and XSS for a conjunction or the complete lattices for a disjunction. In most cases, the single execution performs better, in particular for conjunctions. When executing the single algorithm, a success with

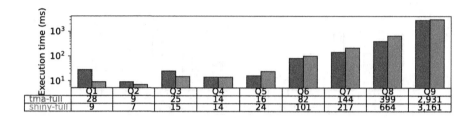

Fig. 6. Execution time for why so many problem with TMA4KB and Shiny algorithms

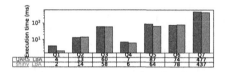

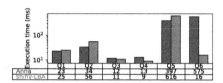

Fig. 7. Execution time for why empty problem with QARS and Shiny algorithms

Fig. 8. Execution time for why not problem with ANNA and Shiny algorithms

Initial query	SELECT * WHERE {?f dbo:director ?dir . ?f dbo:starring ?dir . ?dir dbp:name ?name . ?f dbp:name ?fname . ?dir dbp:gender Female . ?dir dbp:awards dbr:Academy_Award_for_Best_Picture}
Mapping	?fname → Argo
XSS	SELECT * WHERE {?f dbo:director ?dir . ?f dbo:starring ?dir . ?dir dbp:name ?name . ?f dbp:name ?fname}
ANNA modification	SELECT * WHERE {?f dbo:director ?dir . ?f dbo:starring ?dir . ?dir dbp:name ?name . ?f dbp:name ?fname . ?dir ?v0 dbr:Academy_Award_for_Best_Picture}

Fig. 9. Results for Q6 in the why not experiment

a conjunction is detected faster, since only one failure condition needs to be false for a query to succeed. For queries 9 to 12, the failure condition involves a why not failure condition. In the multiple execution method, this is dealt with by transforming the why not failure condition into a cardinality failure condition, which is a significant performance improvement as shown previously. Here the multiple execution method performs up to three orders of magnitude better.

Comparison with State of the Art Algorithms. Figure 6 shows the execution time to identify the MFIS and XSS in the why so many problem, using TMA4KB [20], and our generic algorithm. Figure 7 shows the time to identify the MFS and XSS using QARS [7], and to find the MFIS and XSS with our algorithm. For the empty answer problem, MFIS and MFS are the same. For the why not problem,

Fig. 8 shows the execution time to produce modified queries using ANNA [26], and to identify the MFIS and XSS with our algorithm. An example of the results returned is given in Fig. 9. The modified answer returned by ANNA is similar to an XSS, but may differ slightly if one of the triple patterns has been relaxed. For all the experiments, the execution times are close, our system is on average 1% slower than ANNA, 13% faster than QARS, and 8% slower than TMA4KB. Overall, the added genericity does not have a major impact on performance.

6   Conclusion

In this paper, we have addressed the problem on unexpected answers in the context of RDF. While the specific problem of empty answers has received much attention in existing work, no solution for a problem with multiple unsatisfactory aspects has yet been proposed. Through the study of specific problems, we have proposed a framework for unexpected answers and identified existing definitions of MFIS and XSS which can be applied to the general problem.

Using existing algorithms for specific problems, we studied adaptations to deal with any unsatisfactory answers. We have shown the benefits of the adaptations experimentally, and compared the performance of our generic method with three specialized algorithms. Our methods perform on average 1% faster than the specialized algorithms execution time, and are faster in 55% of cases.

Our next goal is to use the MFIS in a query modification process. So far, our algorithms only allow modification through triple pattern removal, but the MFIS could help identify triple patterns for relaxation. In the comparison with ANNA, we saw that the XSS provided by our method are similar to the modified queries provided to deal with the why not problem, but that modifying the content of triple patterns can provide a finer tuning of the user's queries.

References

1. Bidoit, N., Herschel, M., Tzompanaki, K.: Query-based why-not provenance with NedExplain. In: Extending Database Technology (EDBT) (2014). https://doi.org/10.5441/002/edbt.2014.14

2. Bosc, P., Hadjali, A., Pivert, O.: Incremental controlled relaxation of failing flexible queries. J. Intell. Inf. Syst. **33**(3), 261 (2009). https://doi.org/10.1007/s10844-008-0071-6

3. Crama, Y., Hammer, P.L.: Boolean Functions: Theory, Algorithms, and Applications. Cambridge University Press, Cambridge (2011)

4. Dellal, I.: Management and exploitation of large and uncertain knowledge bases. Ph.D. thesis, ISAE-ENSMA - Poitiers (2019)

5. Dellal, I., Jean, S., Hadjali, A., Chardin, B., Baron, M.: On addressing the empty answer problem in uncertain knowledge bases. In: DEXA 2017, pp. 120–129 (2017). https://doi.org/10.1007/978-3-319-64468-4_9

6. Dong, X., et al.: Knowledge vault: a web-scale approach to probabilistic knowledge fusion. In: SIGKDD 2014, pp. 601–610 (2014). https://doi.org/10.1145/2623330.2623623

7. Fokou, G., Jean, S., Hadjali, A., Baron, M.: RDF query relaxation strategies based on failure causes. In: Sack, H., Blomqvist, E., d'Aquin, M., Ghidini, C., Ponzetto, S.P., Lange, C. (eds.) ESWC 2016. LNCS, vol. 9678, pp. 439–454. Springer, Cham (2016). https://doi.org/10.1007/978-3-319-34129-3_27

8. Fokou, G., Jean, S., Hadjali, A., Baron, M.: Cooperative techniques for SPARQL query relaxation in RDF databases. In: Gandon, F., Sabou, M., Sack, H., d'Amato, C., Cudré-Mauroux, P., Zimmermann, A. (eds.) ESWC 2015. LNCS, vol. 9088, pp. 237–252. Springer, Cham (2015). https://doi.org/10.1007/978-3-319-18818-8_15

9. Godfrey, P.: Minimization in cooperative response to failing database queries. Int. J. Coop. Inf. Syst. 6(2), 95–149 (1997). https://doi.org/10.1142/S0218843097000070

10. Guo, Y., Pan, Z., Heflin, J.: LUBM: a benchmark for OWL knowledge base systems. J. Web Semant. 3(2–3), 158–182 (2005). https://doi.org/10.1016/j.websem.2005.06.005

11. Harris, S., Seaborne, A.: SPARQL 1.1 query language. W3C Recommendation (2013). https://www.w3.org/TR/sparql11-query/

12. Huang, J., Chen, T., Doan, A., Naughton, J.F.: On the provenance of non-answers to queries over extracted data. Proc. VLDB Endow. 1(1) (2008). https://doi.org/10.14778/1453856.1453936 https://doi.org/10.14778/1453856.1453936

13. Jagadish, H.V., et al.: Making database systems usable. In: SIGMOD 2007, pp. 13–24 (2007). https://doi.org/10.1145/1247480.1247483

14. Jannach, D.: Techniques for fast query relaxation in content-based recommender systems. In: Freksa, C., Kohlhase, M., Schill, K. (eds.) KI 2006. LNCS (LNAI), vol. 4314, pp. 49–63. Springer, Heidelberg (2007). https://doi.org/10.1007/978-3-540-69912-5_5

15. Kaplan, S.J.: Cooperative responses from a portable natural language query system. Artif. Intell. 19(2), 165–187 (1982). https://doi.org/10.1016/0004-3702(82)90035-2

16. Lehmann, J., et al.: DBpedia - a large-scale, multilingual knowledge base extracted from Wikipedia. Semant. Web 6(2), 167–195 (2015). https://doi.org/10.3233/SW-140134

17. McSherry, D.: Incremental relaxation of unsuccessful queries. In: Funk, P., González Calero, P.A. (eds.) ECCBR 2004. LNCS (LNAI), vol. 3155, pp. 331–345. Springer, Heidelberg (2004). https://doi.org/10.1007/978-3-540-28631-8_25

18. Moises, S.A., do Pereira, S.L.: Dealing with empty and overabundant answers to flexible queries. J. Data Anal. Inf. Process. 12–18 (2014). https://doi.org/10.4236/jdaip.2014.21003

19. Motro, A.: SEAVE: a mechanism for verifying user presuppositions in query systems. ACM Trans. Inf. Syst. (TOIS) 4(4), 312–330 (1986). https://doi.org/10.1145/9760.9762

20. Parkin, L., Chardin, B., Jean, S., Hadjali, A., Baron, M.: Dealing with plethoric answers of SPARQL queries. In: Strauss, C., Kotsis, G., Tjoa, A.M., Khalil, I. (eds.) DEXA 2021. LNCS, vol. 12923, pp. 292–304. Springer, Cham (2021). https://doi.org/10.1007/978-3-030-86472-9_27

21. Pérez, J., Arenas, M., Gutierrez, C.: Semantics and complexity of SPARQL. ACM Trans. Database Syst. 34(3) (2009). https://doi.org/10.1145/1567274.1567278

22. Saleem, M., Ali, M.I., Hogan, A., Mehmood, Q., Ngomo, A.N.: LSQ: the linked SPARQL queries dataset. In: ISWC 2015, pp. 261–269 (2015). https://doi.org/10.1007/978-3-319-25010-6_15

23. Song, Q., Namaki, M.H., Wu, Y.: Answering why-questions for subgraph queries in multi-attributed graphs. In: ICDE 2019, pp. 40–51 (2019). https://doi.org/10.1109/ICDE.2019.00013

24. Tran, Q.T., Chan, C.Y.: How to conquer why-not questions. In: Proceedings of the 2010 ACM SIGMOD International Conference on Management of Data (2010). https://doi.org/10.1145/1807167.1807172

25. Vasilyeva, E., Thiele, M., Bornhövd, C., Lehner, W.: Answering "Why empty?" and "Why so many?" Queries in graph databases. JCSS **82**(1), 3–22 (2016). https://doi.org/10.1016/j.jcss.2015.06.007

26. Wang, M., Liu, J., Wei, B., Yao, S., Zeng, H., Shi, L.: Answering why-not questions on SPARQL queries. Knowl. Inf. Syst. **58**(1), 169–208 (2018). https://doi.org/10.1007/s10115-018-1155-4

27. Webber, B.L., Mays, E.: Varieties of user misconceptions: detection and correction. In: IJCAI 1983, vol. 2, pp. 650–652 (1983)

28. Woodruff, A., Stonebraker, M.: Supporting fine-grained data lineage in a database visualization environment. In: ICDE, pp. 91–102. IEEE (1997). https://doi.org/10.1109/ICDE.1997.581742

Architecture and Performance

Bitcoin Transaction Confirmation Time Prediction: A Classification View

Limeng Zhang[1,2], Rui Zhou[1(✉)], Qing Liu[2], Jiajie Xu[3], and Chengfei Liu[1]

[1] Swinburne University of Technology, Melbourne, Australia
{limengzhang,rzhou,cliu}@swin.edu.au
[2] Data61, CSIRO, Hobart, Australia
Q.Liu@data61.csiro.au
[3] Soochow University, Suzhou, China
xujj@suda.edu.cn

Abstract. With Bitcoin being universally recognised as the most popular cryptocurrency, more Bitcoin transactions are expected to be populated to the Bitcoin blockchain system. As a result, many transactions can encounter different confirmation delays. One of the most demanding requirements for users is to estimate the confirmation time of a newly submitted transaction. In this paper, we argue that it is more practical to predict the confirmation time as falling into a time interval rather than falling onto a specific timestamp. After dividing the future into a set of time intervals (i.e. classes), the prediction of a transaction's confirmation can be considered as a classification problem. Consequently, a number of mainstream classification methods, including neural networks and ensemble learning models, are evaluated. For comparison, we also design a baseline classifier that considers only the transaction feerate. Experiments on real-world blockchain data demonstrate that ensemble learning models can obtain higher accuracy, while neural network models perform better on the f1-score, especially when more classes are used.

Keywords: Transaction confirmation time · Bitcoin · Blockchain · Ensemble learning · Neural network

1 Introduction

Bitcoin, invented by Satoshi Nakamoto in 2008 [23], has become one of the most popular cryptocurrencies, with its market capitalization reaching 1100 billion in August 2021[1]. Meanwhile, many worldwide businesses, like Paypal, Microsoft, Overstock, etc., have embraced Bitcoin as one method of payment. As a result, more Bitcoin transactions are anticipated to be propagated into the Bitcoin blockchain system. However, the bulk of new transactions cannot be included together in the next block due to the limited capacity of a block. Transactions submitted to the Bitcoin system, therefore, incur confirmation delays. Concerned

---

[1] https://www.coindesk.com/price/bitcoin.

R. Chbeir et al. (Eds.): WISE 2022, LNCS 13724, pp. 155–169, 2022.
https://doi.org/10.1007/978-3-031-20891-1_12

by this, it becomes vital to help a user to understand how long it may take for a transaction to be confirmed in the Bitcoin blockchain.

Most previous attempts on estimating the confirmation time for a transaction focus on predicting a specific timestamp or predicting the number of blocks a transaction needs to wait for before it is confirmed [3,7,10,12,13,18,32,33]. However, it is usually more practical to predict the confirmation time as falling into which time interval in future (e.g., within 1 h, between 1 h and 4 fours, and more than 4 h). Users also find such prediction informative and helpful. When estimating a specific timestamp, the first drawback to consider is the confirmation time variance, particularly for transactions that will be confirmed in the next block. Their confirmation times are affected by the remaining waiting time before the next block is generated. Even transactions with the highest fees need to consume such periods before get confirmed. This means, due to later submission, a transaction with a higher fee may take longer confirmation time than one with a lower fee in the same block. The second factor is that the mining time of a new block is unpredictable (ten minutes is in average [1]), so a relatively long time interval may correspond to different number of blocks in reality, resulting in another type of estimation variation. When utilizing the block interval as the confirmation time, the primary issue is the unbalanced distribution of transactions throughout each confirmation time (block interval), which may cause the estimation to be heavily dependent on a single transaction, particularly when transactions are scarce for a given block interval. For example, for the transactions confirmed in the block range 621001–621500, the maximum confirmation time is 162 blocks. 85% of transactions are confirmed within 5 blocks, with the remaining 15% scattered among the remaining 157 blocks. Consequently, a transaction falling in one of the remaining 157 blocks could have a considerable impact on the estimation result for that particular block. Furthermore, when the estimated confirmation time (in terms of both a time interval and a block interval) surpasses a certain level, users usually choose to pay a higher transaction fee in order to accelerate transaction confirmation. In conclusion, we argue that as long as the confirmation time falls within an acceptable range, a confirmation time range offered to system users is more practical. In this scenario, the prediction task can be considered as a classification problem.

Existing efforts on transaction confirmation estimation suffer from the following four types of drawbacks: (1) Estimation is not tailored for an individual transaction. The works in [12,13,33] estimate the confirmation time for a group of transactions as opposed to a single transaction. Among them, [12,13] estimate the average confirmation time of high-feerate class transactions and low-feerate transactions. Zhao et al. [33] estimate the average confirmation time of all unconfirmed transactions. (2) Models proposed in [7,16] only predict whether a transaction can be confirmed in the next block, addressing the issue as a binary classification problem. They might not be sufficient in practice because they are unable to provide more confirmation information. (3) Some assumptions are not realistic. The confirmation process is modeled as a steady-state queueing system [15], with the assumption that system transactions arrive at a slower rate than they are confirmed, and each time a fixed number of transactions can be confirmed [3,10,12,13,18,33]. In fact, there can be different number of transactions in a block, and the submission rate of transactions establishes a periodic pattern for each day and each week[2], and the rate of submission can exceed the rate of confirmation. (4) There is insufficient utilisation of information on transactions, blocks, and mempool, which can provide further information on the current blockchain system. For example, information in the block sequence can disclose the size and generation rate of future blocks.

In this paper, we compare the prediction performance of three different classification techniques. The first are neural network models, which have been demonstrated to be promising in a range of classification tasks [2,6,11,19,29,31]. It classifies based on neuron layers to discover intrinsic patterns among features. The second are ensemble learning models, which are another type of powerful classification techniques [25]. It makes predictions by combining the results of multiple classifiers. The final is a feerate-ranking baseline classifier that classifies transactions simply based on feerate.

To summarize, we have made the following contributions: (1) summarize and extract features related to transaction confirmation; (2) propose a strategy for discretizing confirmation time; (3) compare the performance of neural network models, ensemble learning models, and a baseline classifier in predicting transaction confirmation time; and (4) demonstrate the importance of incorporating additional features, such as block and mempool features.

The rest of this paper is organized as follows: Sect. 2 reviews the related work on transaction confirmation time estimation. In Sect. 3, we define the problem studied in this paper. In Sect. 4, we outline the selected confirmation features, confirmation time discretization strategy, and the studied classification models. Section 5 presents the classification performance of different models, and Sect. 6 concludes this paper.

2   Related Work

In the Bitcoin blockchain, a transaction will be broadcast across all system nodes once it is submitted to the blockchain system. If a transaction meets the requirements for validity [1], the miner nodes will add it to the mempool. Transactions in the mempool compete to be included in each miner node's candidate block. Then, each miner node will compete to link its own candidate block to the blockchain, a process known as "mining". Once a new block is successfully linked to the blockchain, its transactions are confirmed and its miner is rewarded. These transactions will then be removed from the miners' mempool [21]. In the Bitcoin blockchain, some works have been done on estimating transaction confirmation time. In some studies [7,16], the estimation issue has been modeled as a binary classification problem, predicting whether a transaction could be confirmed in the following block. Then, a number of traditional machine learning algorithms, including Support Vector Machine, Random Forest, AdaBoost, etc., are tested.

---

[2] Blockchain.com, https://www.blockchain.com/charts/transactions-per-second.

Some studies [3,10,12,13,18,33] choose to base their predictions on analysing the distribution of the transaction submission and transaction confirmation. Among them, the authors of [12,13] approach this estimation problem by modeling it as a bulk service queueing system $M/G^B/1$, with transaction arrival following the Poisson distribution and batches of transactions (B) being confirmed at a rate with a specified distribution. Balsamo et al. [3] describe it as another type of bulk service queueing systems, $M/M^B/1$, with transaction arrival following the Poisson distribution and the confirmation of batches following an exponential distribution. Zhao et al. [33] introduce a possible zero-transaction service to the traditional bulk queueing system, which adds the case of a zero-transaction block in the model. It assumes that transaction arrival follows a Poisson distribution and the batch confirmation follows a stochastic density function. Except for the queueing system solutions, researchers in [10,18] model the confirmation process as a Cramér-Lundberg process with a fixed rate of transaction arrival and an exponential distribution for the confirmation of a fixed number of transactions. Existing works provide insights on estimating the confirmation time based on different source of information. However, these solutions are constrained by either the model's preliminary assumptions or insufficient consideration of the balance between output precision and user expectations. To address these issues, we discretize the original transaction confirmation time into several intervals and do estimations based on these intervals.

3   Problem Definition

The confirmation of a transaction is a complex procedure affected by multiple factors, including the transaction itself, unconfirmed transactions in the mempool, mining policy, and system resources. Given a newly submitted transaction $\hat{tx}$, the studied problem is to predict its confirmation time interval $y \in \{y_1, \cdots, y_n\}$, where $\{y_1, \cdots, y_n\}$ are a set of non-overlapping confirmation time intervals, and they together constitute the future. The goal is to find a function $\mathcal{F}$ that can predict in which time interval a submitted transaction will be confirmed, based on various sources of information. We mainly consider three types of features listed below:

$$y = \mathcal{F}(\text{FeaInfo } (\hat{tx}), \text{BlockInfo}, \text{MemInfo})$$

- **FeaInfo** ($\hat{tx}$) describes the transaction itself, including transaction feerate, transaction weight, transaction inputs, submission time, etc.
- **BlockInfo** refers to the characteristics of mined blocks. It maintains the information of prior blocks, such as historical transactions feerate, block size, block generation speed, etc., implicitly reflecting the volume and speed of future mining information.
- **MemInfo** provides information on unconfirmed transactions in the mempool, revealing the competition among the unconfirmed transactions in the mempool.

4   Methodology

This section starts with a summary of the transaction confirmation features. The technique of discretization is then utilised to discretize the confirmation time. Finally, neural network models, ensemble learning models, and a feerate-ranking baseline classifier are described for this prediction problem.

4.1   Feature Selection

Based on the confirmation process in the Bitcoin blockchain, we summarize three factors that contribute to transaction confirmation:

- **Transaction features** describe the unique details of a submitted transaction.
  - *transaction weight* measures transaction size owing to the Segwit upgrade[3].
  - *transaction feerate* is the transaction fee per size unit (each unit is approximately equivalent to a quarter of a transaction weight unit). Typically, transactions with a higher feerate are considered confirmed earlier than those with a lower feerate.
  - *number of inputs* and *number of outputs* are related to the validation cost. Miners need to check the legitimacy of the assets stated in each transaction input.
  - *transaction first-seen time* is the first time that a transaction is noticed by the blockchain. The first-seen time is used since it is difficult to determine the exact submission time of a transaction.
  - *mempool position* indicates the unconfirmed transactions that are typically expected to be processed earlier than this one. It sums up the weight of unconfirmed transactions with higher feerates.
- **Block states** reflect the characteristics of the mined blocks, including block size, block generation speed, transaction confirmation distribution, etc.:
  - *block weight* and *number of transactions* represent the capacity of a block in terms of transaction weight and transaction number included in this block.
  - *difficulty* refers to the mining difficulty, which is related to the computational cost of a miner node.
  - *block interval* is the interval between this block and the previous one, indicating the rate at which blocks are generated.
  - *average feerate* is the average feerate of transactions included in this block. It is calculated by dividing the total transaction fee by one-fourth of the total transaction weight. By introducing this feature, we aim to capture the feerate trend in continuous blocks.

---

[3] Segwit transactions relocate the unlocking script (witness) from within the transaction to an external data structure, resulting a smaller size in terms of its raw data.

- *transaction confirmation distribution* is the distribution, in terms of transaction weight, of transactions in this block at each feerate interval.
- **Mempool states** indicate the competition among the unconfirmed transactions. It is modeled in terms of the weight of these unconfirmed transactions at each feerate interval, due to the limited capacity of a block and the precedence of transactions with greater feerates.

4.2   Confirmation Time Discretization

First of all, we choose to discretize the future time according to block intervals, rather than time intervals. This is mainly due to the unpredictability of a block's mining time, which records the confirmation time of many transactions confirmed together within a single block. For example, Fig. 1 illustrates the time range of all confirmed transactions with a 2-block confirmation interval. We can find that the duration of the 2-block interval could range from a few seconds to several hundred seconds, causing the time interval to potentially overlap with other block intervals. In addition, the index of block interval can handle submission time fluctuation. Due to later submission, a transaction with a higher feerate may take longer confirmation time than one with a lower feerate in the same block.

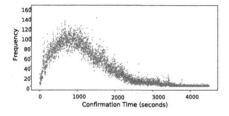

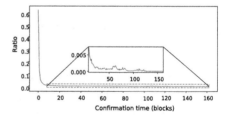

Fig. 1. The frequency of each confirmation time (seconds) with 2-block interval

Fig. 2. The ratio of confirmation time (blocks) distribution in the blockchain

We design two guidelines to discrete the future time into a set of classes. The first is to make the number of transactions balanced for each class. The Bitcoin blockchain system exhibits the long-tail effect of transaction confirmation time, as shown in Fig. 2. Few transactions are confirmed after 10 blocks, with the majority of transactions being confirmed within 10 blocks. The second is that transactions with the same confirmation block interval are better to be grouped in the same class.

Specifically, the discretization is done in the following steps: (1) Initiate the remaining intervals using the required intervals k and the smallest confirmation time by a 1-block interval. (2) Determine the split ratio to classify the unclassified confirmation time range. It is calculated by dividing the remaining proportions by the remaining intervals. (3) Create a new discretized confirmation interval by adding the ratios beginning with the shortest confirmation time until their sum reaches the split ratio from step 2. (4) Replace the shortest confirmation time with the next confirmation time and reduce the remaining intervals by one. (5) Repeat steps 2–4 until k-1 intervals are obtained, at which point the remaining confirmation time range corresponds to the last discretization interval.

4.3   Classification Methods

Baseline Classifier (Baseline). The baseline classifier assumes that a transaction with a higher feerate will be confirmed earlier than one with a lower feerate. Specifically, it operates by first sorting historical confirmed transactions by feerate and then classifying them based on the fraction of the related class. For example, according to Table 1, transactions in Class 1 (1-block confirmation time) account for 62%, indicating that 62% of transactions are confirmed in the next block after submission. The baseline classifier will then assume that 62% of transactions with the highest fees are confirmed in the next block. Therefore, the criteria for classification will be based on the lowest feerate, 22.24, generated by the top 62% of transactions. Thus, a new transaction with a feerate higher than 22.24 will be classified as Class 1.

Table 1. Prediction results of Baseline under 4 classes

Classes	Discretization		Baseline
	Range_block	Ratio	(corresponding feerates)
Class 1	1	62%	$\geq$22.24
Class 2	2	13%	[17.59, 22.24)
Class 3	3–7	13%	[7.09, 17.59)
Class 4	$\geq$8	11%	<7.09

Neural Network Models (NN). Deep neural networks (DNNs) have emerged as a major force in the machine learning community, with applications in many areas [19,31], such as speech recognition, image classification, medical diagnosis, etc. DNNs are known for their capacity to discover complicated structures and acquire high-level concepts in data. Additionally, DNN makes it easier to incorporate additional information owing to its structure flexibility. Consequently, we adopt three major types of deep neural networks: the first is a fully connected network, Multi-Layer Perceptron (MLP), which predicts only based on transaction features, and the other models are neural networks with Long Short-Term Memory (LSTM) [11] and attention mechanisms [2,6,29]. LSTM and attention mechanisms are applied to capture inherent patterns in blocks and mempool, and both have showed remarkable performance in the processing of time series data

[8, 22, 26]. LSTM aggregates information on a token-by-token basis in sequential order, whereas attention mechanisms attempt to capture the relationships between different positions of a single sequence to generate a representation for the sequence. In this work, we employ three popular attention mechanisms: additive attention (Adv) [2], self attention (Self) [29] and weighted attention (Wht) [6].

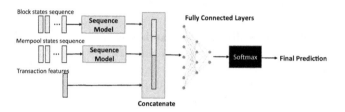

Fig. 3. The general architecture of neural network models.

The general structure of neural network models is shown in Fig. 3. It comprises two models: a feature extraction module and a prediction module. The function of the feature extraction module is to extract inherent patterns from transaction features, block states, and mempool states. Specifically, sequence processing models (only applicable in LSTM and attention models) are initially employed to derive patterns from historical block states and mempool states. The last time-step features derived from both block and mempool state sequence are then combined with transaction characteristics (only transaction features are involved in MLP) for further prediction. In the prediction module, fully-connected layers are stacked to handle the combined features from the feature extraction module. Then a softmax function is applied to generate the classification results.

Ensemble Learning Models (EL). Ensemble learning is known as the crowd wisdom of machine learning techniques. It enhances the performance of prediction by training multiple estimators and integrating their predictions. Figure 4 provides a general illustration of the structure. When each base classifier has finished producing a prediction result, output fusion is used to integrate all of the base model outputs into a single output [25]. In this paper, we study the classification performance of four state-of-the-art ensemble approaches: XGBoost [5], lightGBM [14], Random Forest (RF) [4] and Rotation Forest (RoF) [24], all of which are well-known for their outstanding performance in handling classification tasks. XGBoost is a cutting-edge gradient boosting framework of decision trees, which gains popularity in the 2015 Kaggle classification challenge. Compared to XGBoost, LightGBM employs histogram-based algorithms to reduce execution time and memory consumption. RF, ensembling decision trees based on the bagging technique, is popular owing to its generalized performance, high prediction

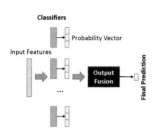

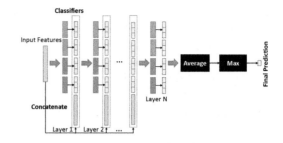

Fig. 4. The general architecture of ensemble learning models.

Fig. 5. The framework of deep forest (each level is composed of two random forests (grey) and two extremely randomized trees (yellow)) (Color figure online)

accuracy, and quick operation speed. Meanwhile, RoF has been demonstrated to score much better on classification tests than other ensemble approaches such as Bagging, AdaBoost, and Random Forest [24].

In addition, extensive studies have been made on the coupling of ensemble learning models with DNN techniques, driven by the outperformance of the neural networks and ensemble learning methods [17,20,30,36]. Among these methods, deep forest (DF) [36] has been proven effective in handling a range of classification tasks, including crop detection [34], medical diagnosis [27,28], software defect prediction [35], etc. Figure 5 illustrates the general framework of Deep forest (DF). It maintains the layer structure of DNN while replacing the neurones in the fully connected layers with base estimators (some ensemble learning models). In the work [9], the based estimators consist of two random forest models and two extremely randomised trees classifiers. In addition, it combines the output of the previous layer with the raw input feature as the new input for the subsequent layer. Finally, DF makes its prediction based on the prediction results of each base estimator in the final layer. In the training process, DF adaptively controls its layer complexity by terminating training when the required accuracy is achieved.

Further, among existing attempts with DF, The work [20] addresses the problem of price prediction, which is analogous to confirmation time prediction. Inspired by it, we adapt its framework as well as its penalty mechanism (DF_cost). The penalty mechanism operates as follows: if a sample of one class i is misclassified as class j, the model will incur a misclassification cost c_{ij}. The predicted class $\hat{y}$ is acquired by optimizing the objective function as follows:

$$\hat{y} = \underset{\hat{y} \in \{I_1, I_2, \dots I_n\}}{argmin} \mathcal{L}(y, \hat{y}) \tag{1}$$

$$\mathcal{L}(y, \hat{y}) = \sum_{i=1}^{n} p(\hat{y}|y) c_{ij} \tag{2}$$

$$c_{i,j} = |o_i - o_j| \tag{3}$$

where I_j denotes misclassifying class i as class j, and $p(\hat{y}|y)$ refers to the posterior probability of predicting the class y as $\hat{y}$. Meanwhile, $c_{ij} = c_{ji}$ and $c_{ii} = 0$. The cost c_{ij} is determined by the distance from the class centre (the mean of samples in each class), and the classification cost for the model is the overall cost of misclassification for all samples.

5   Experiments

5.1   Experiment Settings

Datasets. We collect transaction data from block range 621001–622500 via Blockchain.com[4]. Each dataset consists of 225 continuous blocks picked from every 250 blocks. The first 80% blocks in each dataset are utilised for training (about 400,000 transactions), while the remaining 20% are used for testing (about 100,000 transactions). The information regarding testing can be found in Table 2. In the experiments, only newly submitted transactions are selected for both training and testing.

Table 2. Testing data

Interval	Block information	Interval	Block information
1	621185–621229	4	621935–621979
2	621435–621479	5	622185–622229
3	621685–621729	6	622435–622479

Evaluation Metrics. To evaluate the performance of different models, we calculate the overall accuracy:

$$\text{accuracy (acc)} = \frac{\text{TP}+\text{TN}}{\text{TP}+\text{TN}+\text{FP}+\text{FN}} \tag{4}$$

We also utilise the macro-averaged f1-score, which is the arithmetic mean of all the per-class f1-score, as an indicator of classification performance:

$$\text{recall} = \frac{\text{TP}}{\text{TP}+\text{FN}} \tag{5}$$

$$\text{precision} = \frac{\text{TP}}{\text{TP}+\text{FP}} \tag{6}$$

$$\text{f1-score} = \frac{2\text{recall} \times \text{precision}}{\text{recall} + \text{precision}} \tag{7}$$

where TP (true positive), FP (false positive), FN (false negative), and TN (true negative) are observed classification results.

---

[4] https://www.blockchain.com/api/blockchain_api.

Compared Methods

- **NN** stands for neural network models.
  - **MLP** is a neural network model which only takes transaction features as input.
  - **Lstm** employs LSTM to extract patterns in block states and mempool states.
  - **Adv**, **Wht** and **Self** correspond to using different attention techniques to extract features from block states and mempool states: additive attention [2], weighted attention [6] and self attention [29].
- **EL** stands for ensemble learning models.
  - **RF**, **RoF**, **xgBoost** and **lightGBM** are four state-of-the-art ensemble learning models.
  - **DF** and its variants
    * **DF** refers to deep forest [9], with two random forest classifiers and two extremely randomized tree classifiers in each layer.
    * **DF_cost** introduces penalty into DF for misclassification [20].
    * **DF_xg** and **DF_xgRF** replace the base estimators in each layer of DF with four xgBoost classifiers and two random forest classifiers along with two xgBoost classifiers.
- **Baseline** stands for the baseline classifier.

Discretization. As shown in Table 3, we discretize the transaction confirmation time range into four different class sizes: $k = 2$, $k = 4$, $k = 6$, and $k = 8$. For $k = 2$, confirmation time is split into two categories: confirmed in 1 block interval and confirmed in more than 1 block (≥ 2 blocks). In such case, the problem can be considered as predicting whether a transaction will be confirmed in the next block [7,16]. Considering that transactions confirmed beyond 50 blocks are very rare at each confirmation time as shown in Fig. 2, and Class 8 in $k = 8$ in Table 3 has included transactions confirmed beyond 59-block interval, we stop discretizing the confirmation time into more classes.

Table 3. Confirmation time discretization (block intervals falling in each class)

Classes	$k = 2$		$k = 4$		$k = 6$		$k = 8$	
	Range	Ratio	Range	Ratio	Range	Ratio	Range	Ratio
Class 1	1	62.2%	1	62.2%	1	62.2%	1	62.2%
Class 2	≥ 2	37.8%	2	13.2%	2	13.2%	2	13.2%
Class 3			3–7	13.2%	3–4	8.5%	3	5.2%
Class 4			≥ 8	11.5%	5–8	5.5%	4–5	5.5%
Class 5					9–28	5.3%	6–9	4.0%
Class 6					≥ 29	5.3%	10–18	3.4%
Class 7							19–58	3.4%
Class 8							≥ 59	3.2%

Model Configuration. In the neural networks, the sequence processing model is configured with 8 hidden units and a sequence length of 3. Fully connected layers are a three-layer fully-connected neural network with 64 and 8 hidden units for the first two levels, and then the specified class size. The batch size is set to 1000 if applicable and models are optimised using stochastic gradient descent (SGD) with the Adam optimizer. In the ensemble learning models, RF, RoF and extremely randomized tree classifiers are set with 100 trees.

5.2   Result Analysis

Comparison on Classification Models. The accuracy and f1-score shown in Table 4 are the average of the results obtained from the six datasets. As class size increases, both the accuracy and f1-score performances of each model decrease. xgBoost achieves the most competitive performance among all discretization results, while Baseline performs the worst. The Baseline's worst performance exposes the complexity of the transaction confirmation mechanism, in contrast to the simplicity of the transaction priority.

Table 4. An overall performance of models on 6 datasets

Methods		k = 2		k = 4		k = 6		k = 8	
		acc	f1-score	acc	f1-score	acc	f1-score	acc	f1-score
NN	MLP	91.52%	86.70%	82.85%	57.02%	79.20%	43.53%	77.29%	33.79%
	Adv	91.98%	87.61%	84.06%	60.43%	79.42%	**45.65%**	77.45%	36.27%
	Wht	91.89%	87.33%	83.39%	58.15%	78.80%	44.89%	77.38%	**37.37%**
	Self	91.99%	87.86%	82.45%	54.75%	78.82%	38.22%	76.49%	33.98%
	Lstm	91.74%	86.42%	81.11%	51.29%	77.13%	33.63%	76.78%	32.68%
EL	RF	96.03%	94.72%	86.31%	62.51%	82.07%	42.97%	80.29%	32.69%
	RoF	92.76%	89.82%	81.78%	55.62%	77.62%	38.62%	75.87%	29.14%
	xgBoost	**96.23%**	**94.92%**	**86.70%**	63.16%	**82.84%**	44.17%	**81.15%**	33.84%
	lightGBM	96.10%	94.67%	86.38%	62.73%	82.29%	43.20%	80.44%	32.52%
	DF	95.21%	94.49%	82.65%	63.14%	77.87%	45.03%	75.38%	34.02%
	DF_cost	–	–	82.64%	**63.25%**	77.69%	45.06%	73.88%	36.35%
Baseline		62.30%	56.61%	49.54%	29.10%	46.93%	19.87%	45.67%	14.70%

xgBoost, followed by lightGBM and RF, achieves the highest accuracy among all models on all four classification tests. In particular, when $k = 2$, its accuracy and f1-score are superior to those of other models. As the class size increases ($k \in \{4, 6, 8\}$), however, its f1-score advantage over DF and DF_cost diminishes. In addition, based on the performance of RF, DF and DF_cost, the strategy of assembling RF within their framework surpasses RF in terms of f1-score but fails to achieve superior prediction accuracy.

Despite the fact that neural network models perform poorly in terms of accuracy and f1-score on smaller class size ($k \in \{2, 4\}$), Adv achieves a very competitive f1-score on larger class size ($k \in \{6, 8\}$). Moreover, among all neural network models, Adv has the highest prediction accuracy. Moreover, the higher performance of Adv in comparison to MLP demonstrates the importance of block and mempool information.

Performance of DF Variants. This set of experiments aims to test the performance of DF variants by replacing the base estimators in each layer. According to Table 4, XgBoost fails to achieve comparable f1-score performance. However, by assembling RF into DF, DF can achieve a better f1-score than RF. Therefore, we attempt to incorporate xgBoost into DF. Specially, we substitute the original four estimators in DF with two random forests and two xgBoost classifiers (DF_xgRF) or four xgBoost classifiers (DF_xg) in each layer. According to results shown in Fig. 6(a) and Fig. 6(b), DF and its two variants outperform xgBoost in terms of f1-score but still fall short in terms of accuracy. In addition, we find that substituting estimators have no positive effect on the accuracy or f1-score of the DF framework.

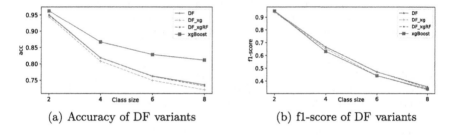

(a) Accuracy of DF variants   (b) f1-score of DF variants

Fig. 6. Prediction performance of DF variants

6   Conclusion

In this study, we compare the performance of neural networks, ensemble learning models and a feerate-ranking baseline classifier on the prediction of transaction confirmation time as a classification problem. In terms of prediction accuracy, xgBoost provides the best classification results, whereas the neural network model applying additive attention delivers increasingly competitive f1-score performance as class size increases. In addition, we demonstrate that block and mempool information has a positive effect on improving neural networks prediction performance. Our future work will focus on two areas: incorporating block and mempool information into ensemble learning methods and boosting the predictive accuracy of neural network models.

Acknowledgements. This research is supported by Data61, Australian Research Council Discover (Grant No. DP170104747, No. DP180100212 and No. DP200103700) and National Natural Science Foundation of China (Grant No. 61872258).

References

1. Antonopoulos, A.M.: Mastering Bitcoin: Programming the Open Blockchain. O'Reilly Media, Inc., Sebastopol (2017)
2. Bahdanau, D., Cho, K., Bengio, Y.: Neural machine translation by jointly learning to align and translate. arXiv preprint arXiv:1409.0473 (2014)
3. Balsamo, S., Marin, A., Mitrani, I., Rebagliati, N.: Prediction of the consolidation delay in blockchain-based applications. In: Proceedings of the ACM/SPEC International Conference on Performance Engineering, pp. 81–92 (2021)
4. Breiman, L.: Random forests. Mach. Learn. **45**(1), 5–32 (2001)
5. Chen, T., et al.: XGBoost: extreme gradient boosting. R Package Version 0.4-2 **1**(4), 1–4 (2015)
6. Felbo, B., Mislove, A., Søgaard, A., Rahwan, I., Lehmann, S.: Using millions of emoji occurrences to learn any-domain representations for detecting sentiment, emotion and sarcasm. arXiv preprint arXiv:1708.00524 (2017)
7. Fiz, B., Hommes, S., State, R.: Confirmation delay prediction of transactions in the bitcoin network. In: Park, J.J., Loia, V., Yi, G., Sung, Y. (eds.) CUTE/CSA -2017. LNEE, vol. 474, pp. 534–539. Springer, Singapore (2018). https://doi.org/10.1007/978-981-10-7605-3_88
8. Fu, R., Zhang, Z., Li, L.: Using LSTM and GRU neural network methods for traffic flow prediction. In: 2016 31st Youth Academic Annual Conference of Chinese Association of Automation (YAC), pp. 324–328. IEEE (2016)
9. Geurts, P., Ernst, D., Wehenkel, L.: Extremely randomized trees. Mach. Learn. **63**(1), 3–42 (2006)
10. Gundlach, R., Gijsbers, M., Koops, D., Resing, J.: Predicting confirmation times of bitcoin transactions. ACM SIGMETRICS Perform. Eval. Rev. **48**(4), 16–19 (2021)
11. Hochreiter, S., Schmidhuber, J.: Long short-term memory. Neural Comput. **9**(8), 1735–1780 (1997)
12. Kasahara, S., Kawahara, J.: Effect of bitcoin fee on transaction-confirmation process. J. Ind. Manag. Optim. **15**(1), 365 (2019)
13. Kawase, Y., Kasahara, S.: Priority queueing analysis of transaction-confirmation time for bitcoin. J. Ind. Manag. Optim. **16**(3), 1077 (2020)
14. Ke, G., et al.: LightGBM: a highly efficient gradient boosting decision tree. In: Advances in Neural Information Processing Systems, vol. 30 (2017)
15. Kleinrock, L.: Theory, vol. 1. Queueing Systems (1975)
16. Ko, K., Jeong, T., Maharjan, S., Lee, C., Hong, J.W.-K.: Prediction of bitcoin transactions included in the next block. In: Zheng, Z., Dai, H.-N., Tang, M., Chen, X. (eds.) BlockSys 2019. CCIS, vol. 1156, pp. 591–597. Springer, Singapore (2020). https://doi.org/10.1007/978-981-15-2777-7_48
17. Kontschieder, P., Fiterau, M., Criminisi, A., Bulo, S.R.: Deep neural decision forests. In: Proceedings of the IEEE International Conference on Computer Vision, pp. 1467–1475 (2015)
18. Koops, D.: Predicting the confirmation time of bitcoin transactions. arXiv preprint arXiv:1809.10596 (2018)
19. LeCun, Y., Bengio, Y., Hinton, G.: Deep learning. Nature **521**(7553), 436–444 (2015)
20. Ma, C., Liu, Z., Cao, Z., Song, W., Zhang, J., Zeng, W.: Cost-sensitive deep forest for price prediction. Pattern Recogn. **107**, 107499 (2020)
21. Ma, Y., Sun, Y., Lei, Y., Qin, N., Lu, J.: A survey of blockchain technology on security, privacy, and trust in crowdsourcing services. World Wide Web **23**(1), 393–419 (2020)

22. McNally, S., Roche, J., Caton, S.: Predicting the price of bitcoin using machine learning. In: 2018 26th Euromicro International Conference on Parallel, Distributed and Network-Based Processing (PDP), pp. 339–343. IEEE (2018)

23. Nakamoto, S.: Bitcoin: a peer-to-peer electronic cash system. In: Decentralized Business Review, p. 21260 (2008)

24. Rodriguez, J.J., Kuncheva, L.I., Alonso, C.J.: Rotation forest: a new classifier ensemble method. IEEE Trans. Pattern Anal. Mach. Intell. **28**(10), 1619–1630 (2006)

25. Sagi, O., Rokach, L.: Ensemble learning: a survey. Wiley Interdisc. Rev.: Data Min. Knowl. Discov. **8**(4), e1249 (2018)

26. Srivastava, N., Mansimov, E., Salakhudinov, R.: Unsupervised learning of video representations using LSTMs. In: International Conference on Machine Learning, pp. 843–852 (2015)

27. Su, R., Liu, X., Wei, L., Zou, Q.: Deep-Resp-Forest: a deep forest model to predict anti-cancer drug response. Methods **166**, 91–102 (2019)

28. Sun, L., et al.: Adaptive feature selection guided deep forest for COVID-19 classi-fication with chest CT. IEEE J. Biomed. Health Inform. **24**(10), 2798–2805 (2020)

29. Vaswani, A., et al.: Attention is all you need. In: Advances in Neural Information Processing Systems, pp. 5998–6008 (2017)

30. Wen, G., Hou, Z., Li, H., Li, D., Jiang, L., Xun, E.: Ensemble of deep neural net-works with probability-based fusion for facial expression recognition. Cogn. Com-put. **9**(5), 597–610 (2017)

31. Zhang, G.P.: Neural networks for classification: a survey. IEEE Trans. Syst. Man Cybern. Part C (Appl. Rev.) **30**(4), 451–462 (2000)

32. Zhang, L., Zhou, R., Liu, Q., Xu, J., Liu, C.: Transaction confirmation time esti-mation in the bitcoin blockchain. In: Zhang, W., Zou, L., Maamar, Z., Chen, L. (eds.) WISE 2021. LNCS, vol. 13080, pp. 30–45. Springer, Cham (2021). https://doi.org/10.1007/978-3-030-90888-1_3

33. Zhao, W., Jin, S., Yue, W.: Analysis of the average confirmation time of trans-actions in a blockchain system. In: Phung-Duc, T., Kasahara, S., Wittevrongel, S. (eds.) QTNA 2019. LNCS, vol. 11688, pp. 379–388. Springer, Cham (2019). https://doi.org/10.1007/978-3-030-27181-7_23

34. Zhong, L., Hu, L., Zhou, H.: Deep learning based multi-temporal crop classification. Remote Sens. Environ. **221**, 430–443 (2019)

35. Zhou, T., Sun, X., Xia, X., Li, B., Chen, X.: Improving defect prediction with deep forest. Inf. Softw. Technol. **114**, 204–216 (2019)

36. Zhou, Z.H., Feng, J.: Deep forest: towards an alternative to deep neural networks. In: IJCAI (2017)

Offworker: An Offloading Framework for Parallel Web Applications

An-Chi Liu and Yi-Ping You[(⊠)] [iD]

Department of Computer Science, National Yang Ming Chiao Tung University,
Hsinchu, Taiwan
acliu@cs.nycu.edu.tw, ypyou@nycu.edu.tw

Abstract. More and more applications are shifting from traditional
desktop applications to web applications due to the prevalence of mobile
devices and recent advances in wireless communication technologies. The
Web Workers API has been proposed to allow for offloading computation-
intensive tasks from applications' main browser thread, which is responsible for managing user interfaces and interacting with users, to other
worker threads (or web workers) and thereby improving user experience. Prior studies have further offloaded computation-intensive tasks to
remote servers by dispatching web workers to the servers and demonstrated their effectiveness in improving the performance of web applications. However, the approaches proposed by these prior studies expose
potential vulnerabilities of servers due to their design and implementation and do not consider multiple web workers executing in a concurrent
or parallel manner. In this paper, we propose an offloading framework
(called *Offworker*) that transparently enables concurrent web workers to
be offloaded to edge or cloud servers and provides a more secure execution environment for web workers. We also design a benchmark suite
(called *Rodinia-JS*), which is a JavaScript version of the Rodinia parallel benchmark suite, to evaluate the proposed framework. Experiments
demonstrated that Offworker effectively improved the performance of
parallel applications (with up to 4.8x of speedup) when web workers
were offloaded from a mobile device to a server. Offworker introduced
only a geometric mean overhead of 12.1% against the native execution
for computation-intensive applications. We believe Offworker offers a
promising and secure solution for computation offloading of parallel web
applications.

Keywords: Offloading · JavaScript · Parallelism · Web workers

1 Introduction

More and more desktop applications (e.g., Google Earth[1], Stellarium[2], and
Autodesk[3]) are moving to the mobile market in the form of web applications.

---

[1] https://earth.google.com/web/.

[2] https://stellarium-web.org/.

[3] https://www.autodesk.com/solutions/cloud-based-online-cad-software.

© The Author(s), under exclusive license to Springer Nature Switzerland AG 2022
R. Chbeir et al. (Eds.): WISE 2022, LNCS 13724, pp. 170–185, 2022.
https://doi.org/10.1007/978-3-031-20891-1_13

Web applications for machine learning, gaming, and extended reality are getting more attractive since mobile devices as an input/output interface for end users become ubiquitous. However, these applications usually require high computation power and involve mass interactive activities, and sometimes demand a good internet connection for fast data download. These requirements can be problems for mobile devices, even for premium mobile devices, since heavy computation can drain their battery quickly, not to mention for mid-range or low-cost devices, which are usually not equipped with powerful processing units.

The Web Worker API[4] has been introduced to enable parallel JavaScript programming on the web. Many prior studies have shown that offloading computation-intensive tasks in web applications from mobile devices to edge or cloud servers can greatly enhance device performance without requiring the devices to have advanced compute capabilities or high connection bandwidth [3, 6, 8]. This was done by offloading the computation-intensive tasks to worker threads (or web workers for short), which are spawned to run concurrently with the main thread in JavaScript, and dispatching the web workers to remote servers. Nevertheless, these studies only addressed the benefits of offloading serial web workers, and almost none of them have examined the viability of offloading concurrent or parallel web workers. This is probably attributed to the fact that the Web Workers API has been primarily used for offloading tasks from the main browser thread so as to prevent the main browser thread from being blocked by the tasks, thereby providing a better user experience. However, with the advance of multi-core mobile devices, we believe parallel web applications are gaining more attention and popularity, and offloading parallel web workers to edge or cloud servers is a demanding task. To our best knowledge, Puffin Web Browser[5] (or Puffin for short), a commercial web browser developed by CloudMosa, is the only work that enables parallel web workers to run remotely. Essentially, Puffin is basically a "thin-client" browser that renders webpages, including JavaScript code that operates using web workers, in the cloud. However, this type of offloading scheme is inherently incapable of supporting numerous interactions with user interface components because each user action request must be transferred to the cloud for processing and then back to the client, resulting in long response times.

In this paper, we propose a framework (called *Offworker*[6]) that enables offloading parallel web workers to edge or cloud servers so as to enhance the execution of web applications on mobile devices, particularly on mid-range or low-cost devices. The Offworker framework comprises two main components: (1) a front-end library (FL), which exposes Web Workers APIs and forwards requests to remote servers, and (2) a back-end manager (BM) for launching web workers on the remote servers. Offworker is designed to improve web worker applications in four aspects: (1) faster execution, (2) improved user experience, (3) secure execution environment, and (4) transparent programmability. As an offloading framework, Offworker aims to improve the execution performance of web worker appli-

---

[4] https://developer.mozilla.org/en-US/docs/Web/API/Web_Workers_API.

[5] https://www.puffin.com/web-browser.

[6] https://github.com/nycu-sslab/offworker.

cations by offloading heavy computation, which may involve multiple web workers running in parallel, or communication to edge or cloud servers. Offworker also delivers a better user experience than other offloading framework (e.g., Puffin) for applications that frequently interact with users since it offloads only web workers, which are typically computationally intensive, rather than the whole rendering process of webpages. Moreover, with Offworker, a separate V8 isolate, which is an isolated JavaScript environment using the V8 JavaScript engine[7], is created on the remote site for each offloaded web worker, and each offloaded web worker run within the V8 isolate; therefore, Offworker provides a more secure environment for web workers. Furthermore, Offworker is partly designed and implemented as a library that conforms to the Web Workers APIs, so ordinary web worker applications can directly take advantage of Offworker without modifying any code, thereby providing a transparent offloading mechanism.

2   Related Work

There have been many prior studies focusing on offloading computation-intensive tasks in web applications from mobile devices to servers. The Web Workers API has been considered the most common interface for web application developers to implement a complex computation task without interfering the user interface. Therefore, there have been several studies (with the same objective as this study) that aimed to offload web workers to servers in order to improve the execution performance of web applications [4–8]. Most of these studies proposed a roughly same architecture as proposed in this study, which includes a front-end library, which accepts computation requests on the client, and a back-end manager, which enables web workers to execute on the server.

Hwang and Ham proposed a framework, called WWF [5], that allows web workers (with some modifications to the original application) to be offloaded to servers and whose BM was implemented based on the Node.js library[8], but how web workers operates on the server was not clearly stated. Zbierski and Makosiej proposed a similar framework like WWF but without requiring modifications to the application. They also proposed an offloading decision model according to CPU and memory usages and network conditions [8]. However, the implementation details of the proposed framework and decision model were not elaborated in details. Gong et al. proposed a framework, called WWOF [3], which is also similar to WWF, but web workers are executed on servers using the VM module of Node.js. Jeong et al. introduced a different offloading scenario that allows a running web worker to migrate from a mobile device to a server—though with a larger offloading overhead [6]. They implemented a snapshot mechanism that enables web worker migration, using the subprocess module of Node.js to execute web workers on the server.

Although the aforementioned studies have demonstrated their success in offloading web workers to servers, the libraries they use for executing web work-

---

[7] https://v8.dev/.
[8] https://nodejs.org/.

ers on servers, such as the VM and the subprocess modules of Node.js, may expose vulnerability to the servers. In contrast, Offworker adopts the isolated-vm library[9], which guarantees an offloaded web worker to execute within a sandbox, thereby providing a more secure offloading environment. More details about the potential security issues and how Offworker addresses these issues are discussed in Sect. 3.2. In addition, these prior studies considered only applications without concurrent web workers, whereas in this study we address the issues in offloading concurrent web workers and evaluate the proposed approach with a set of parallel web applications.

3   Design and Implementation of Offworker

The Offworker framework comprises two main components: (1) the FL and (2) the BM. The FL, which is included in web applications, exposes web worker-related APIs to the applications and passes web worker requests—such as the creation of web workers and communication between web workers—to the BM. The BM, which is designed as a service daemon running on an edge or cloud server, is responsible for fulfilling web worker requests so that web workers can run on the server and communicate with one another properly. Figure 1 illustrates the workflows of the native execution and offloading execution of a web worker application, respectively, and also the conceptual architecture of the Offworker framework. We briefly introduce the two workflows and then focus on how a web work task is offloaded to the server using Offworker. It is worth mentioning that parallelism for web applications is commonly implemented using the proxy pattern[10], in which parallel worker threads are created by a proxy thread, which is created by the main thread and interacts with the worker threads. This proxy pattern avoids the main browser thread (which is typically the main application thread) from constantly synchronizing with other worker threads (i.e., web workers) and allows the main browser thread to focus on rendering and handling user interactions. In this study, we presume that parallelism is expressed in parallel web applications using the proxy pattern.

For both the native and offloading execution of the web applications in Fig. 1, the workflow starts with the initial HTTP requests from a client who intends to launch a web application, and then the web server responds to the client with the web application, which contains HTML pages with CSS formatting and JavaScript codes. Using the Web Workers API, computation-intensive tasks (sometimes referred to as *kernels*) of the web application can be offloaded onto a separate web worker or several web workers that are launched by a proxy web worker. During the native execution of a kernel, all web workers are created and run natively on the client side (i.e., the browser), and the web workers may request resources from the web server during their execution. In contrast, when the FL is included in the application, Offworker is activated, and the kernel, including the proxy web worker and its associated parallel web workers, can be

---

[9] https://github.com/laverdet/isolated-vm.
[10] https://emscripten.org/docs/porting/pthreads.html#proxying.

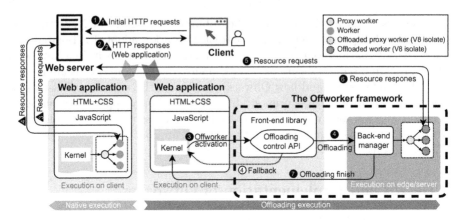

Fig. 1. The workflows of the native execution and offloading execution (using Off-worker) of a web worker application, respectively.

offloaded to the server depending on the developer's decision. The proxy web worker is created either natively, in which case the kernel is executed with the same workflow as the native execution, or on the server, in which case the request for creating the proxy web worker is sent to the BM. In the latter case, the BM creates the proxy web worker and its associated parallel web workers as separate V8 isolates on the server, and these workers can directly communicate with the web server. Lastly, the BM sends back the results to the client when all web workers finished.

3.1   The Front-End Library

The FL is an implementation of the Web Worker API and allows a web worker to be created and run remotely. The FL overrides the Worker class, in which the constructor, communication-related methods or properties (e.g., postMessage() and onmessage), and other class members are implemented in a way that they work with the BM. More specifically, once developers have included the front-end Offworker library and created a proxy web worker object with the Worker class, the constructor of Worker uses the WebSocket API[11] to create connections between the FL and the BM so as to pass the request for worker creation and the worker creation argument (the script that the worker will execute) to the BM and allow for communication between the main browser thread and the proxy web worker. How the communication is processed is discussed in detail in Sect. 3.2.

3.2   The Back-End Manager

The BM is a server-side daemon process that receives and handles requests from the FL and is responsible for creating web workers on the server and managing communication among the main browser thread and the web workers being

---

[11] https://developer.mozilla.org/en-US/docs/Web/API/WebSockets_API.

offloaded to the server. In essence, the BM enables the functionality to run web workers on the server and can be implemented by adopting a server-side JavaScript library that allows web workers to run on the server. The simplest and most intuitive way to run web workers on the server is by using the *worker threads* module in the Node.js library, which is almost the counterpart of the Web Workers API in Node.js. However, such an implementation of the BM exposes vulnerability of the server since worker threads (i.e., web workers created on the server using the worker threads module) are able to invoke system calls to access privileged system information and resources by using the Node.js APIs. Moreover, the BM will be unable to fully manage worker threads—for example, to control resources used by worker threads in order to prevent resource starvation attacks—, unless modifying the Node.js library. These effects also occur when using other modules, such as the *child process* or *VM* modules, in the Node.js library as the basis for implementing the BM.

In view of this, we propose to create web workers on the server by using the *isolated-vm* library, which allows code to run within an isolated environment that conforms to a V8 isolate. In other words, a V8 isolate is created for each offloaded web worker and used to run the corresponding task in a web worker. Furthermore, since a V8 isolate is an isolated instance of the V8 JavaScript engine, which runs only core JavaScript (i.e., ECMAScript[12]) code but not client- or server-side JavaScript code, an offloaded worker is guaranteed to execute within a sandbox with configurable resource limitations and unable to access any resources on the server or even call web APIs, thereby solving the aforementioned potential security issues.

Nevertheless, the fact that each offloaded worker runs as a V8 isolate also raises another two issues: creating V8 isolates within an existing V8 isolate is not feasible, and communication between V8 isolates is not possible without a proper runtime system. Therefore, the BM must serve as a proxy for isolate creation and further implement a communication mechanism that manages possible communication among different isolates. The BM involves three main components: (1) an isolate creator, which creates web workers as V8 isolates on the server, (2) a message handler, which enables the message passing mechanism between the client and the server and between V8 isolates, and (3) a shared memory manager, which allows memory to be shared between V8 isolates. The BM also implements some web APIs for V8 isolates to facilitate functionality of web applications. We elaborate in detail how the three components work by demonstrating how web workers are offloaded and created onto the server and how communication between the client and server and communication between web workers function in the following paragraphs.

Creation of Web Workers on the Server. As stated at the beginning of Sect. 3, the hypothesis underlying this study is that web applications express parallelism using the proxy pattern. Hence, each kernel is always activated by creating a proxy web worker, which further creates parallel web workers. Figure 2

---

[12] https://tc39.es/ecma262.

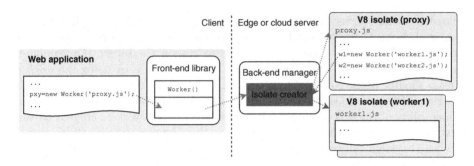

Fig. 2. The workflows of creating web workers (V8 isolates) on the server using Off-worker. (Color figure online)

illustrates how a kernel is offloaded to the server by showing the workflows of how V8 isolates, which act as web workers on the server, are created. There are two types of workflows: (1) the client's web application creates a proxy web worker, as shown in red text and red dotted arrows in the figure, and (2) the proxy web worker (or any other worker) creates another web worker, as shown in blue text and blue dotted arrows. In the former case, when the client's web application calls "new Worker()" to create a proxy web worker, the FL passes the request of the proxy worker creation to the BM, and then the isolate creator in the BM creates a V8 isolate to execute the proxy worker. In the latter case, when a web worker calls "new Worker()" to create another web worker, the isolate creator, which is registered as an event handler for the "new Worker()" event in V8 isolates, creates another V8 isolate to execute the newly created worker.

Communication Management. Apart from creating V8 isolates (i.e., web workers on the server), the other primary task of the BM is to enable communication, which involves a V8 isolate on one end. For parallelism using the proxy pattern, there are only two scenarios of communication to consider: (1) the communication between the client's web application and a proxy V8 isolate and (2) the communication between V8 isolates. Since the communication can be done by using the message passing (via postMessage() and onmessage) or shared-memory (via SharedArrayBuffer) mechanisms, the BM must guarantee that both the two communication mechanisms work correctly when web workers are offloaded to the server. We discuss how these two communication mechanisms are managed by the BM, respectively.

Figure 3 shows how communication using message passing is performed in Offworker. The BM implements a message handler, which is essentially an event handler, for all communication requests made in both of the aforementioned scenarios. In the first scenario, it is illustrated in red text and red dotted arrows how the client's web application sends a message to a proxy V8 isolate—the FL passes the sending request to the BM, which then directs the message to the proxy V8 isolate—, while in blue text and blue dotted arrows how it goes in reverse. The client–server communication (between the FL and the BM) is

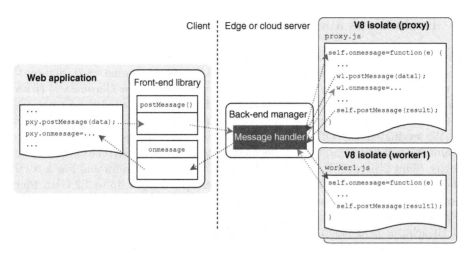

Fig. 3. Communication between the client and server and communication among web workers using message passing in Offworker. (Color figure online)

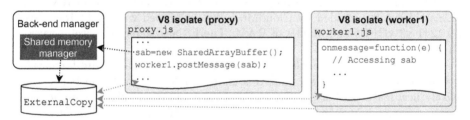

Fig. 4. Communication among web workers using shared memory in Offworker.

enabled by the WebSocket connection established when creating a proxy V8 isolate (as discussed in Sect. 3.1), and `MessageChannel` in JavaScript is used to communicate between the BM and the proxy V8 isolate. Communication in the second scenario, which can be seen in green/orange text and green/orange dotted arrows, is similar to communication in the first scenario, but all of the communication happens on the server.

Figure 4 depicts how communication using shared memory is processed in Offworker. It is worth mentioning that for parallelism using the proxy pattern, shared-memory communication typically occurs only between web workers (either proxy or regular), so only the second scenario is considered in this case. The BM deploys a shared-memory manager, which is registered as an event handler for the "new `SharedArrayBuffer()`" event in V8 isolates. When a new `SharedArrayBuffer()` request is made, the shared-memory manager allocates an `ExternalCopy` object, which is implemented by the isolated-vm library and treated as the standard shared memory that is accessible to any V8 isolate, so as to allow shared-memory communication among V8 isolates.

4 Evaluations and Discussion

We implemented the proposed Offworker framework in JavaScript, based on isolated-vm v4.2 and Node.js v14.16 (with V8 JavaScript engine v8.4), and evaluated the framework with web applications running on Google Chrome v91 (with V8 JavaScript engine v9.1). And Node.js v14.16, and evaluated the framework with web applications running on Google Chrome v91.

We evaluated the Offworker framework in different scenarios in order to examine its effectiveness. Unless specified, web applications ran on a client mobile device (Sony Xperia 10), which was located in Hsinchu, Taiwan and has a total of eight CPU cores with four Cortex-A53 cores operating at up to 2.2 GHz, four Cortex-A53 cores operating at up to 1.8 GHz, and 3 GB of RAM. The BM of Offworker was deployed on three different servers: an edge server (ES) located in Hsinchu, a near cloud server (NCS) in Hong Kong, and a far cloud server (FCS) in the United States. The ES was equipped with an Intel quad-core i3-10100 processor operating at 3.6 GHz and 32 GB of RAM; the NCS was hosted in an Amazon EC2 t3.2xlarge instance, which was equipped with eight Intel Xeon Platinum 8259CL vCPUs operating at 2.5 GHz and 32 GB of RAM; the FCS, which was provided by CloudMosa, was equipped with eight Intel Xeon E3-1241 v3 vCPUs and 32 GB of RAM. The ES also acted as a web server in all experiments conducted in this work.

To our best knowledge, there is no JavaScript benchmark suite for parallel web applications. We believe that this is attributed to parallelism being a relatively new feature in JavaScript and many computation-intensive applications have not yet moved to the web. In order to evaluate the effectiveness of Offworker, especially in terms of its capability of running parallel web applications, we manually ported the Rodinia benchmark suite (version 1) [2], a popular benchmark suite for heterogeneous computing, from OpenMP programs into JavaScript programs, where the computation-intensive parts of the programs (i.e., kernels) were expressed by using the Web Workers API with the proxy pattern, and workers synchronize via a barrier at the end of a kernel. All Rodinia applications have been successfully ported, except *Leukocyte Tracking*, *Stream Cluster*, and *Similarity Score* due to their large code size (over 3,000 lines of code). We call this new benchmark suite *Rodinia-JS*.

The Rodinia benchmark suite includes default datasets, but their size is too large for client-side web applications, which fetch external data from the web server rather than from the local file system, since data fetching is likely to become a major task of the applications. We scaled down the datasets to meet the following criteria: (1) the total running time of an application on the mobile device takes less than seven seconds while the time spent in data fetching is less than two seconds, which is more reasonable for web applications as more than half of visits are abandoned if a mobile site takes over three seconds to load[13], and (2) the time spent in computation is greater than the overhead time incurred by creating workers, which makes sense for parallelization to be beneficial.

---

[13] https://developer.chrome.com/blog/search-ads-speed/.

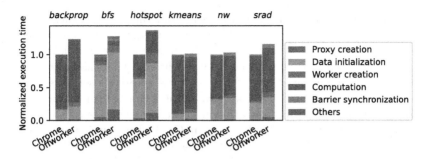

Fig. 5. Normalized execution times for the Rodinia-JS benchmark suite on the ES when running natively on Chrome and using Offworker.

We also used the Hopscotch micro-benchmark suite [1] to further evaluate the performance difference in manipulating shared memory between Offworker and Chrome. 14 (out of 16) types of memory access patterns were ported to JavaScript. Two types of patterns (r_rand_pchase and w_seq_memset) were excluded due to no pointers and "memset" in JavaScript.

4.1 Overhead Analysis

Figure 5 displays the breakdown of normalized execution times for the Rodinia-JS applications without kernel parallelization (i.e., only one web worker for computing a kernel task) when running the applications natively on the headless Chrome browser and using Offworker, respectively. Both the client and server ran on the same machine (ES) so that we could better identify the performance overhead due to the proposed Offworker framework. Each execution time is divided into six parts in our measurements: (1) proxy creation, which fetches the script of the proxy web worker and initializes the proxy worker, (2) data initialization, which fetches input data and constructs data structures, (3) worker creation, which fetches the script of the worker and initializes the worker, (4) computation, which is the main task of a kernel, (5) barrier synchronization, which is necessary at the end of each kernel due to the fork-join model of OpenMP being adopted, and (6) others, which do not belong to any of the aforementioned five parts. Overall, Offworker introduced a (geometric) mean overhead of 12.1% for computation-intensive applications (*backprop, kmeans, nw,* and *srad*) and 18.5% for all applications in Rodinia-JS. *bfs* and *hotspot* had a larger percentage overhead since they had a short application time on ES (only around 160 and 260 ms, respectively)—although they took around one and two seconds to execute on the mobile device, respectively—, and they are I/O-intensive applications.

One of the main overhead sources lied in the creation of the proxy web worker (geometric mean of 4.5%) and regular web workers initialization (6%), which involves additional HTTP connections to fetch the script of web workers, creating workers, and initializing workers. Offworker added an additional overhead of around 20 ms for each worker creation (excluding worker initialization). Another main overhead source was from the barrier synchronization (2.2%), which was implemented using the message passing mechanism, because each message passing operation between web workers was around 0.7 ms slower when using Offworker than running natively on Chrome. This slight overhead was attributed to an implementation difference, where a worker's script is executed on the Node.js platform and non-core JavaScript API calls (including message passing) are implemented in JavaScript in Offworker, whereas all the script is executed by Chrome (which is implemented in C++) when running natively. This implementation difference also leaded to some overheads in data initialization (5.2%). For example, *bfs* and *hotspot* had a larger overhead in data initialization (7.5% and 15.8%, respectively) since they both invoked the `split` function, which splits a string into substrings, where a `split` function call was around 70 ms slower on Node.js than on Chrome. Each HTTP connection was also around 30 ms slower when using Offworker than on Chrome. The computation parts also showed slight variations between the two platforms due to the implementation difference. Offworker performed slightly better than Chrome with respect to the computation part for *nw*, but worse than Chrome for *backprop* and *kmeans*. We discuss these variations in details in Sect. 4.2.

4.2   Effectiveness in Running Parallel Applications

As mentioned in Sect. 1, a significant novelty of this study is to examine the viability of offloading parallel web workers to servers; therefore, we evaluated the effectiveness of Offworker in terms of running parallel web workers. We do not discuss how Offworker could scale different Rodinia-JS applications since the scalability of an application is highly dependent on its design. Instead, we focus on the execution time differences of applications between running on Chrome and Offworker, and therefore both the client and server were on the ES.

Figure 6 shows the execution time ratios of Offworker over Chrome for the Rodinia-JS applications when different numbers of web workers were used. As observed in Fig. 5, when using Offworker, all applications (with only one web worker being created for each kernel) had longer execution time due to the extra offloading manipulation. The inferiority of Offworker persisted for applications with more parallelism and went slightly up as the number of web workers increased for most applications. The ratios for *backprop* stayed roughly the same when increasing the number of web workers, whereas the ratios for *kmeans* grew more significantly as the number of web workers increased. We further investigated the contributing components of the execution time differences between Offworker and Chrome for each application in order to identify why Offworker performed differently.

Figure 7 illustrates the execution time differences in terms of their contributing components between Offworker and Chrome for the Rodinia-JS benchmark suite when different numbers of web workers were used. A positive difference represents that Chrome was better than Offworker. We observed that the time differences for the proxy creation, data initialization, and other parts were less

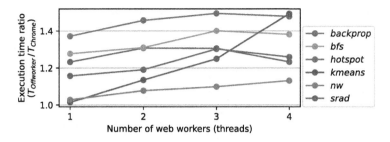

Fig. 6. Execution time ratios of Offworker over Chrome for the Rodinia-JS benchmark suite on the ES when different numbers of web workers were used.

than 50 ms and consistent for different numbers of web workers since these components were irrelevant to parallelization. The time differences for the barrier synchronization part were also almost identical when different numbers of web workers were used since there are no more than 300 barriers required for each Rodinia-JS application, and the overhead added by Offworker for each barrier synchronization was insignificant. The time differences for the worker creation part grew slightly with the number of web workers due to more worker initialization costs when using Offworker. This effect was more obvious for *backprop* and *kmeans* because they required more initialization work than others. However, different applications showed different trends in time differences for the computation part. This abnormal phenomenon was believed to result from the differences in handling arithmetic and shared-memory access operations between Offworker (which is based on isolated-vm and Node.js) and Chrome.

Figure 8 displays execution time ratios of Offworker over Chrome for 14 memory access patterns in the Hopscotch micro-benchmark suite on a large (or small) array when using different numbers of web workers. We observed that the execution times for each micro benchmark operating on a large shared-memory array (of length 10^4–10^8) were similar between using Offworker and running natively on Chrome; however, the execution time ratios of Offworker over Chrome were up to five when operating on a small shared-memory array (of length 10^0–10^4). As indicated in Fig. 7, the computation time differences between Offworker and Chrome (CTDs for short) were larger for *backprop* since there were five memory access patterns on six small and two large shared-memory arrays, and more time was spent accessing these small arrays. The CTDs grew up greatly with the number of web workers for *kmeans* since r_seq_reduce on small arrays provided the majority of shared-memory access patterns. The shared-memory access patterns in *bfs*, *nw*, and *srad* also explained their trend of CTDs, respectively: r_seq_ind and w_seq_fill on six small arrays, r_tile on two large arrays, and r_rand_ind and w_seq_fill on four small arrays and seven large arrays provided the majority of shared-memory access patterns for *bfs*, *nw*, and *srad*, respectively. Despite these negative consequences, we believe isolated-vm still provides an adequate solution for offloading JavaScript applications due to its secure nature.

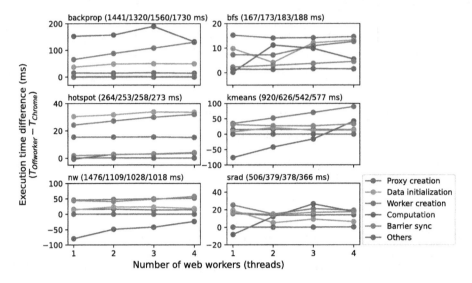

Fig. 7. Execution time differences between Offworker and Chrome for the Rodinia-JS benchmark suite on the ES when different numbers of web workers were used. The values follow a benchmark name indicate the execution times of the benchmark for 1–4 workers, respectively, when using Offworker.

4.3   Effectiveness in Different Server Capabilities

Figure 9 illustrates the execution times for the Rodinia-JS benchmark suite on the client when using five different offloading decisions: (1) mobile, in which web workers ran natively on the client, (2) ES-Offworker, in which web workers ran on the ES using Offworker, (3) NCS-Offworker, in which web workers ran on the NCS using Offworker, (4) FCS-Offworker, in which web workers ran on the FCS using Offworker, and (5) FCS-Puffin, in which almost an entire application (including web workers) ran on the FCS using Puffin, which is a commercial browser developed by CloudMosa based on Chromium v79 and renders webpages on the cloud.

ES-Offworker had the best performance (2.8–4.8x faster than Mobile) among all offloading decisions, while NCS-Offworker came second (0.9–2.6x faster than Mobile). These results were expected because both the ES and NCS had more powerful computing capabilities than the client mobile device and were located close to the client mobile device—the round-trip time (RTT) between the client and the ES or NCS was sufficiently low to allow for offloading web workers to the ES or NCS with benefit—, and because the ES was physically closer to the client than the NCS.

Despite the fact that the FCS might not be a good candidate for offloading operations, we conducted evaluations for FCS-Offworker in order to compare Offworker with Puffin, while the FCS, which had similar hardware configurations with the NCS, was the only platform that worked for both Offworker and

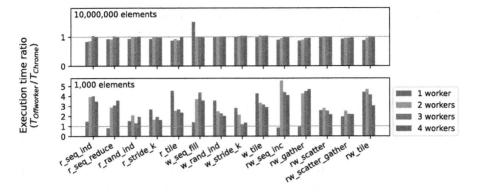

Fig. 8. Execution time ratios of Offworker over Chrome for 14 memory access patterns on a large (or small) array when different numbers of web workers were used.

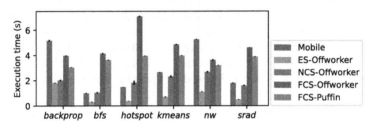

Fig. 9. Execution times for the Rodinia-JS benchmark suite on the client when using different offloading decisions, mostly in terms of server capabilities.

Puffin. Both FCS-Offworker and FCS-Puffin suffered from the problem of long RTTs between the FCS and the web server (hosted on the ES) such that they did not perform well for some applications, especially for I/O-intensive applications (*bfs* and *hotspot*), which involve fetching massive resources from the web server. Nevertheless, this negative effect may disappear or even be reversed if the FCS is close to the web server due to lower RTTs. In general, Offworker performed slightly worse than Puffin because Puffin was implemented based on Chromium, which is an open-source browser that Chrome is built on, and Chrome performed slightly better than Offworker, as discussed in Sect. 4.1. FCS-Offworker performed poorly for *hotspot* because *hotspot* included massive HTTP connections, and the implementation for handling HTTP connections in Offworker was not optimized and did not performed well.

While Puffin performed better than Offworker for the Rodinia-JS benchmark suite, it has some weaknesses when used with applications that require extensive user interaction. These weaknesses are attributed to the design of Puffin, which offloads an entire web page to the server, and consequently the delay time between firing a user action and receiving its corresponding rendering results from the server can significantly decrease the user experience. This application scenario with high user interaction will become common as more and more desktop applications are converted into web applications (e.g., online image editors). Compared with Puffin's coarse-grained offloading approach, Offworker provides a fine-grained offloading mechanism that allows users to offload tasks on demand, thereby achieving wider applicability.

5   Conclusion

We have proposed a framework, called Offworker, for transparently offloading parallel web workers to edge or cloud servers. To our best knowledge, this is the first work that supports inter-worker communication (with message passing or shared memory) for offloaded web workers. Furthermore, Offworker ensures that each offloaded web worker runs within a sandbox (V8 isolate) so as to provide a more secure execution environment for web workers and servers. We have also presented a parallel JavaScript benchmark suite, called Rodinia-JS, and evaluated Offworker with Rodinia-JS. The experimental results show that Rodinia-JS applications with Offworker enabled ran up to five times faster than they running natively on a mobile device, and Offworker had a small overhead (mean of 12.1%) for computation-intensive Rodinia-JS applications. We believe our proposed solution best serves the needs for parallel web applications. We consider to support WebAssembly threads in JavaScript applications and propose an offloading decision model in the future.

Acknowledgements. This study was partially supported by the Ministry of Science and Technology of Taiwan under Grant No. MOST 110-2221-E-A49-030-MY3. We would like to thank CloudMosa, Inc. for providing supports and hardware resources for benchmarking.

References

1. Ahmed, A., Skadron, K.: Hopscotch: a micro-benchmark suite for memory performance evaluation. In: Proceedings of the International Symposium on Memory Systems, MEMSYS 2019, pp. 167–172 (2019)
2. Che, S., et al.: Rodinia: a benchmark suite for heterogeneous computing. In: Proceedings of the 2009 International Symposium on Workload Characterization, pp. 44–54 (2009)
3. Gong, X., Liu, W., Zhang, J., Xu, H., Zhao, W., Liu, C.: WWOF: an energy efficient offloading framework for mobile webpage. In: Proceedings of the 13th International Conference on Mobile and Ubiquitous Systems: Computing, Networking and Services, pp. 160–169 (2016)
4. Hwang, I., Ham, J.: Cloud offloading method for web applications. In: Proceedings of the 2nd International Conference on Mobile Cloud Computing, Services, and Engineering, pp. 246–247 (2014)
5. Hwang, I., Ham, J.: WWF: web application workload balancing framework. In: Proceedings of the 28th International Conference on Advanced Information Networking and Applications Workshops, pp. 150–153 (2014)

6. Jeong, H.J., Shin, C.H., Shin, K.Y., Lee, H.J., Moon, S.M.: Seamless offloading of web app computations from mobile device to edge clouds via HTML5 web worker migration. In: Proceedings of the ACM Symposium on Cloud Computing 2019, pp. 38–49 (2019)
7. Wang, Z., Deng, H., Hu, L., Zhu, X.: HTML5 web worker transparent offloading method for web applications. In: Proceedings of the 18th International Conference on Communication Technology, pp. 1319–1323 (2018)
8. Zbierski, M., Makosiej, P.: Bring the cloud to your mobile: transparent offloading of HTML5 web workers. In: Proceedings of the 6th International Conference on Cloud Computing Technology and Science, pp. 198–203 (2014)

High-Performance Transaction Processing for Web Applications Using Column-Level Locking

Xiaodong Zhang and Jing Zhou[(⊠)]

Shanghai Jiao Tong University, 800 Dongchuan Road, Shanghai, China
{xdzhang97,zhoujing2021}@sjtu.edu.cn

Abstract. Column-level concurrency control allows higher concurrency but also brings additional coordination overhead. Therefore, many relational database systems usually coordinate transactions at the row level. However, our observation based on real-world web applications suggests that row-level coordination can sometimes be too coarse. It can cause web applications to suffer reduced throughput due to false conflicts. To address this issue, we introduce an application-side column-level lock management system called CLL in this paper. It allows applications to choose the concurrency control granularity adaptively. With CLL, accesses to highly contended data items can now be executed in parallel without false conflicts caused by row-level coordination. Our evaluation shows that, in both synthetic and real-world workloads, CLL can help to improve performance significantly and achieve at most 64%/33% higher throughput, respectively.

Keywords: Web applications · Concurrency control · Object–Relational Mapping

1 Introduction

Web applications usually rely on the concurrency control of database management systems (DBMSs) to coordinate concurrent transactions. There is a trade-off between the degree of concurrency achieved and the coordination overhead. More precise coordination allows higher concurrency at the cost of increased management overhead (e.g., storage and computation) and complicated system architecture [9]. Nowadays, popular DBMSs provide row-level or even coarser-grained coordination [1,2,7,11] to avoid unnecessary overhead.

However, row-level coordination sometimes is not optimal. Take Broadleaf[1], a popular open-source e-commerce web framework, as an example. In Fig. 1, with row-level coordination, two transactions will conflict with each other when accessing the same row. This conflict is unnecessary since they require different columns. A recent study [12] has confirmed that some applications implement

---

[1] https://github.com/BroadleafCommerce/BroadleafCommerce.

© The Author(s), under exclusive license to Springer Nature Switzerland AG 2022
R. Chbeir et al. (Eds.): WISE 2022, LNCS 13724, pp. 186–193, 2022.
https://doi.org/10.1007/978-3-031-20891-1_14

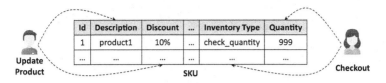

Fig. 1. In Broadleaf, transaction Checkout and Update Product access different columns of SKU.

Fig. 2. New Order and Payment transactions in TPC-C may block each other because of false conflicts. Colors distinguish columns accessed by different transactions. (Color figure online)

their own application-level coordination, bypassing the DBMSs to avoid such false conflicts. Nevertheless, in the absence of systematic design, these ad hoc coordinations are usually error-prone and can not improve performance efficiently.

Therefore, we designed CLL, an application-side column-level lock management system. It allows web applications to choose the appropriate coordination granularity for better performance while preserving correctness, i.e., transaction serializability. For SQL statements suffering from false conflicts, applications can coordinate at the finer-grained column level to improve transaction processing parallelism. As for other SQL statements, applications can still use database systems' existing mechanisms without adding any overhead.

In building CLL, two techniques are essential. First, to accurately identify the locks to be acquired, we use *Optimistic/Pessimistic Lock Location Prediction* (O/PLLP) [13] to prefetch data needed by scan SQL statements. Second, to mitigate the effect of database exclusive row locks when coordinating at the column level, we use *deferred writes* to defer the write operations until the commit phase. Our evaluation shows that CLL can bring up to 64%/33% throughput improvements respectively in TPC-C [3] and Broadleaf workloads.

2   Background

2.1   False Conflicts Caused by Row-Level Coordination

Existing DBMSs usually coordinate transactions at multiple granularities [5] for flexible concurrency control. For example, MySQL and PostgreSQL support

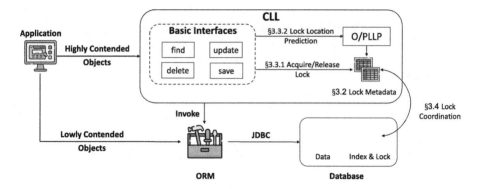

Fig. 3. The architecture of CLL

both page and row-level locks. However, among them, the finest granularity is usually the row level, which may make transactions suffer from false conflicts.

Figure 2 gives a detailed example in TPC-C. Although New Order and Payment transactions access different columns of warehouse and district tables, they may still block each other because of row-level conflicts. They are the two most frequent transactions in TPC-C. Therefore the false conflicts between them will hurt performance significantly.

2.2 Object–Relational Mapping

Object-Relational Mapping (ORM) [8] is widely used as middleware between web applications and backend storage systems. ORMs usually fetch full rows (i.e., a SELECT * FROM ... statement) from databases for simplicity [15]. Therefore DBMSs may be unaware of the needed columns, and implementing column-level locks inside database systems helps little in reducing false conflicts. This fact motivates us to design and build the column-level lock management system on the application side. Then developers can choose the granularity of concurrency control flexibly based on the applications' business logic characteristics.

3   Design and Implementation

3.1   System Overview

Figure 3 shows the architecture of CLL. SQL statements accessing highly contended data, such as ones in warehouse and district tables of TPC-C, are more likely to suffer from false conflicts. Therefore developers can utilize CLL for finer-grained coordination. As for other data, developers can directly access them through ORMs without adding unnecessary coordination overhead. CLL provides basic interfaces for CRUD, which are similar to ORMs'. With CLL, developers can specify columns to be locked for concurrency control. The lock metadata is stored in the memory of the server. To handle SQL statements scanning multiple rows, CLL uses the Optimistic/Pessimistic Lock Location Prediction (O/PLLP) to prefetch the primary keys of the result set for locking.

3.2 Application-Maintained Data Structures

For each column in a table, CLL keeps a hashmap to store lock metadata. The key of a hashmap is the row's primary key, and the corresponding value is a read-write lock. SQL statements accessing highly contended data can acquire column-level locks to avoid false conflicts. These locks will be removed after being released by the last holder without causing a lot of storage overhead.

3.3 Identifying the Data for Locking

Handling SQL Statements Using Primary Key Equality in Conditions. Acquiring locks for SQL statements using the primary key equality in conditions is easy. According to the table and columns accessed, CLL first tries to find the primary key in the corresponding hashmap. If the key exists, the current statement can directly try to acquire the lock. The key absent means that no transaction is accessing the same column of the same row. Then CLL will atomically create the lock and get it granted for the statement.

Handling SQL Statements Using Other Conditions. We handle statements using other conditions in different ways. For statements with an index (non-primary key) equality in conditions, we use Optimistic Lock Location Prediction (OLLP) to identify the primary key of rows and get locks. OLLP will issue a non-blocking read-only query to retrieve the primary key set of required rows first. With index equality in conditions, such reconnaissance queries will not bring much overhead. Then we try to get column-level locks according to the primary keys of rows in the read/write set. After the locks are granted, we need to execute the statement again and validate whether the read/write set is the same as the reconnaissance query. If validation fails, we must retry the above procedure or abort the whole transaction.

For statements that may perform the sequential or index range scan, we apply Pessimistic Lock Location Prediction (PLLP), which acquires column locks for all rows through wildcard. The reasons are twofold. On the one hand, these statements involving many rows will bring significant overhead to column-level lock management. On the other hand, their read/write sets are likely changed after the reconnaissance query. Using OLLP may cause a lot of failed validation.

3.4 Lock Coordination

For SQL statements using column-level locks, we must prevent them from acquiring database row-level locks. Therefore we use weak isolation levels (Read Committed or Repeatable Read) for transactions. We can acquire row-level locks explicitly (e.g., such as for share/update) when the finer-grained coordination is

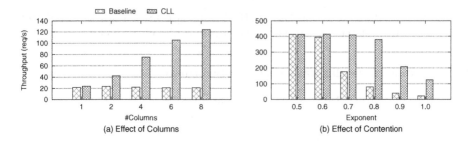

Fig. 4. The evaluation result with microbenchmark

unnecessary. However, in some databases, write SQL statements acquire exclusive row-level locks by default. To reduce the impact of these database locks, we defer write operations until the commit phase. So exclusive row-level locks will be held for little time and hardly cause write-write false conflicts.

3.5   Correctness and Consistency

CLL can be integrated with applications while preserving correctness and consistency. SQL statements using CLL are also wrapped in database transactions, so the atomicity and durability are guaranteed. Each statement will acquire locks from either database or CLL and release them until committed to guarantee the serializable isolation. When the application server crashes, we assume all ongoing transactions have failed. Therefore, the loss of column-level locks caused by a crash does not matter. After a restart, the system is still in a consistent state.

4   Evaluation

We evaluate CLL to answer the following questions: 1) In what workloads is CLL more effective? 2) How much benefit can CLL bring by avoiding false conflicts? 3) Will CLL decrease performance in workload without false conflicts?

4.1   Experimental Setup

Configuration. We build the application server based on the Spring framework with Hibernate-5.4.32 as ORM. CLL can work with DBMSs that supports weak isolation level and explicit locks, such as PostgreSQL and MySQL. We apply MySQL-8.0.25[2] for evaluation. The database and web server are deployed in independent physical machines. Both have 2×12 2.20 GHz cores (Intel Xeon Processor E5-2650 v4), 128 GiB DDR4 memory, and a 1 Gbit/s NIC.

Comparison. We compare CLL with the baseline that relies on DBMSs' row-level concurrency control. They both use a weak isolation level (Read Committed). The baseline acquires row-level locks explicitly for correctness. CLL replaces them with column-level locks when accessing highly contended data.

---

[2] For Broadleaf, we use MySQL-5.7.35 as suggested.

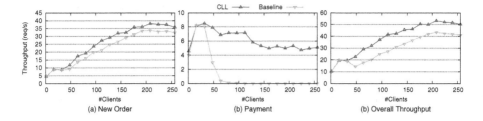

Fig. 5. The evaluation result with standard TPC-C

4.2   Microbenchmarks

The benefit of CLL is related to the contention and the number of no-overlapping column subsets accessed by transactions. To show their effect and answer the first question, we designed the following microbenchmark. A table is initialized with 100,000 rows, each of which has eight columns. Concurrent transactions read or update different columns of a row chosen from a Zipfian distribution.

The result is shown in Fig. 4. When the contention is low and most transactions access the same columns, CLL performs similar to the baseline. As the contention and the columns used increase, transactions using row-level coordination are more likely to suffer from false conflicts. Thus CLL can bring more performance benefits and achieve at most 5.4× higher throughput.

4.3   Macrobenchmarks

To answer the second question, we first compare CLL with baseline in TPC-C workload with one warehouse. Among the five transactions, the New Order (45%) and Payment(43%) can benefit from CLL. The result is shown in Fig. 5. As the number of clients increases (contention becomes higher), the Payment throughput of the baseline approaches zero, making CLL significantly better. The reason is that TPC-C specifies the upper limit of transaction response time. Under high contention, in the baseline, most Payment transactions are timed out due to false conflicts. Similarly, with CLL, the throughput of New Order transactions can be improved by at most 28% (112 clients). As for the overall throughput, CLL can achieve at most 64% (64 clients) higher than the baseline.

To answer the third question, we evaluate CLL with TPC-C New Order transaction only, in which row-level locks cause no false conflicts. As shown in Fig. 6, CLL brings a little overhead and has at most 8.9% lower throughput. Therefore, to avoid unnecessary overhead, we should not use column-level locks in workloads with little or without false conflicts.

4.4   Performance Improvement in Real-World Applications

Broadleaf is a framework used for e-commerce applications. As we mentioned, Checkout and Update Product may suffer from false conflicts caused by row-level

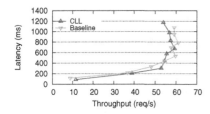
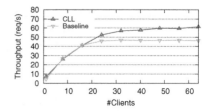

Fig. 6. The evaluation result with TPC-C New Order only (#clients from 1 to 64)

Fig. 7. The evaluation result with Broadleaf

coordination. We integrated CLL into Broadleaf with little engineering effort to address this issue. To simulate the high contention, we keep one seller updating the hottest product and many customers buying it concurrently. The result in Fig. 7 shows that CLL can improve the throughput up to 33%.

5   Related Work

Some DBMSs already provide column-level coordination. PostgreSQL [2] supports For Key Share and For No Key Update hints. Nevertheless, such column-level coordination can only be used for the primary key. Google F1 [10] fully supports column-level locks. However, it creates a separate lock column for each column to store timestamp, which may bring significant storage overhead. Furthermore, F1 is built for Google AdWords business, and it is not open-source. Our CLL can fully support column-level locks. It creates lock only when the data is accessed, thus causing little memory overhead. Finally, its design does not rely on specific databases or ORMs so that it can be deployed with most applications.

Some works focus on the optimization of concurrency control. Graefe et al. [4] proposed ghost records (logically deleted records) to avoid false conflicts caused by gap locks. Grechanik et al. [6] combine static analysis and run-time monitoring to detect and prevent database deadlocks in applications efficiently. To handle contended workloads, Wang et al. [14] designed interleaving constrained concurrency control (IC3), which allows parallel execution for transactions under contention while preserving serializability. These works optimize concurrency control in other ways rather than improving concurrency control granularity.

6   Conclusion

In this work, we propose CLL, an application-side column-level lock management system to avoid false conflicts caused by row-level concurrency control. With CLL, developers can choose finer-grained coordination granularity for highly contended access to improve parallelism. The evaluation shows that it can improve throughput significantly in both synthetic and real-world workloads.

Acknowledgement. We appreciate the anonymous reviewers for their constructive feedback and suggestions.

References

1. MySQL. https://www.mysql.com/. Accessed 18 Aug 2022
2. PostgreSQL. https://www.postgresql.org/. Accessed 18 Aug 2022
3. TPC-C Benchmark. https://www.tpc.org/tpcc/. Accessed 18 Aug 2022
4. Graefe, G.: Hierarchical locking in B-tree indexes. In: On Transactional Concurrency Control. SLDM, pp. 45–73. Springer, Cham (2019). https://doi.org/10.1007/978-3-031-01873-2_3
5. Gray, J.N., Lorie, R.A., Putzolu, G.R.: Granularity of locks in a shared data base. In: Proceedings of the 1st International Conference on Very Large Data Bases, VLDB 1975, pp. 428–451. Association for Computing Machinery, New York, NY, USA (1975). https://doi.org/10.1145/1282480.1282513
6. Grechanik, M., Hossain, B.M.M., Buy, U., Wang, H.: Preventing database deadlocks in applications. In: Proceedings of the 2013 9th Joint Meeting on Foundations of Software Engineering, ESEC/FSE 2013, pp. 356–366. Association for Computing Machinery, New York, NY, USA (2013)
7. Huang, D., et al.: TiDB: a raft-based HTAP database. Proc. VLDB Endow. **13**(12), 3072–3084 (2020). https://doi.org/10.14778/3415478.3415535
8. O'Neil, E.J.: Object/relational mapping 2008: hibernate and the entity data model (EDM). In: Proceedings of the 2008 ACM SIGMOD International Conference on Management of Data, SIGMOD 2008, pp. 1351–1356. Association for Computing Machinery, New York, NY, USA (2008)
9. Ries, D.R., Stonebraker, M.: Effects of locking granularity in a database management system. ACM Trans. Database Syst. **2**(3), 233–246 (1977). https://doi.org/10.1145/320557.320566
10. Shute, J., et al.: F1: a distributed SQL database that scales. Proc. VLDB Endow. **6**(11), 1068–1079 (2013). https://doi.org/10.14778/2536222.2536232
11. Taft, R., et al.: CockroachDB: the resilient geo-distributed SQL database. In: Proceedings of the 2020 ACM SIGMOD International Conference on Management of Data, SIGMOD 2020, pp. 1493–1509. Association for Computing Machinery, New York, NY, USA (2020). https://doi.org/10.1145/3318464.3386134
12. Tang, C., et al.: Ad hoc transactions in web applications: the good, the bad, and the ugly. In: Proceedings of the 2022 International Conference on Management of Data, SIGMOD 2022, pp. 4–18. Association for Computing Machinery, New York, NY, USA (2022). https://doi.org/10.1145/3514221.3526120
13. Thomson, A., Diamond, T., Weng, S.C., Ren, K., Shao, P., Abadi, D.J.: Calvin: fast distributed transactions for partitioned database systems. In: Proceedings of the 2012 ACM SIGMOD International Conference on Management of Data, SIGMOD 2012, pp. 1–12. Association for Computing Machinery, New York, NY, USA (2012). https://doi.org/10.1145/2213836.2213838
14. Wang, Z., Mu, S., Cui, Y., Yi, H., Chen, H., Li, J.: Scaling multicore databases via constrained parallel execution. In: Proceedings of the 2016 International Conference on Management of Data, SIGMOD 2016, pp. 1643–1658. Association for Computing Machinery, New York, NY, USA (2016). https://doi.org/10.1145/2882903.2882934
15. Yang, J., Subramaniam, P., Lu, S., Yan, C., Cheung, A.: How not to structure your database-backed web applications: a study of performance bugs in the wild. In: Proceedings of the 40th International Conference on Software Engineering, ICSE 2018, pp. 800–810. Association for Computing Machinery, New York, NY, USA (2018). https://doi.org/10.1145/3180155.3180194

sGrid++: Revising Simple Grid Based Density Estimator for Mining Outlying Aspect

Durgesh Samariya[1(✉)], Jiangang Ma[1], and Sunil Aryal[2]

[1] School of Engineering, Information Technology and Physical Sciences, Federation University, Churchill, VIC, Australia
{d.samariya,j.ma}@federation.edu.au
[2] School of Information Technology, Deakin University, Geelong, VIC, Australia
sunil.aryal@deakin.edu.au

Abstract. In this paper, we address the problem of outlying aspect mining, which aims to identify a set of features (subspace(s) a.k.a aspect(s)) where a given data object stands out from the rest of the data. To detect the most outlying aspect of a given data object, outlying aspect mining algorithms need to compare and rank subspaces with different dimensionality. Thus, they require a fast and dimensionally unbias scoring measure. Existing measures use density or distance to compute the outlyingness of the query in each subspace. Density and distance are dimensionally bias, i.e. density decreases as the dimension of subspace increases. To make them comparable (dimensionally unbias), Z-score normalization is used in the previous works. However, to compute Z-score normalization, we need to compute the outlyingness of each data point in each subspace, which adds significant computational overhead on top of the already expensive density or distance computation.

Recently developed measure called sGrid is a simple and efficient density estimator which allows a fast systemic search. While it is efficient compared to other distance and density-based measures, it is also a dimensionally bias measure and it requires to use Z-score normalization to make it dimensionality unbiased, which makes it computationally expensive. In this paper, we propose a simpler version of sGrid called **sGrid++** that is not only efficient and effective but also dimensionality unbiased. It does not require Z-score normalization. We demonstrate the effectiveness and efficiency of the proposed scoring measure in outlying aspect mining using synthetic and real-world datasets.

Keywords: Outlying aspect mining · Dimensionality-unbiased score · Outlier explanation · Histogram · Density estimation

1 Introduction

Anomaly detection (**AD**) is one of the crucial tasks of data mining, besides clustering and classification, which detects anomalous data points in a data set

R. Chbeir et al. (Eds.): WISE 2022, LNCS 13724, pp. 194–208, 2022.
https://doi.org/10.1007/978-3-031-20891-1_15

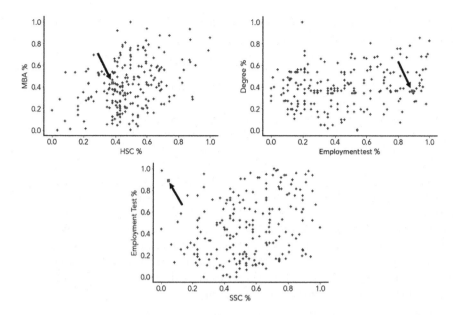

Fig. 1. University students performance on SSC %, HSC %, Degree %, MBA % and Employment test %. The red square point represents candidate A. (Color figure online)

automatically. Anomalies (also refers to as outliers) are data points that are significantly different from the other points in the data set. AD has applications in various domains such as fraud detection, medical or public health, intrusion detection, and machine fault detection [2,13]. While there are wide range of algorithms proposed in the literature to detect anomalies/outliers, they cannot explain why those outliers are flagged.

Lately, as an attempt to provide such explanation, researchers are interested in *Outlying Aspect Mining* (**OAM**) [3,9–12,14,15], where the task is to identify on what aspects (subset of features) a given anomaly/outlier exhibits the most outlying characteristics. In other words, OAM is the task of identifying feature subset(s), where a given query is significantly inconsistent with the rest of the data.

OAM has many real-world applications. For example, when evaluating job applications, recruitment team wants to know strengths/weaknesses of each candidate, i.e., they want to know in what aspect a candidate is outstanding among the applicants. Let's have a look at the example of 215 candidates data[1] with their scores in percentage (%) in their secondary school (SSC), higher secondary (HSC), undergraduate degree, MBA and Employment test. As shown in Fig. 1(c),

---

[1] Data set is available at https://www.kaggle.com/benroshan/factors-affecting-campus-placement.

Candidate A scored very high percentage in the Employment test while having quite low percentage in SSC.

Another example, assume that you are a football coach or commentator and you want to highlight the strengths and/or weaknesses of a player in the most recent game. Moreover, when the doctor wants to know in which aspect a given patient's condition is not normal [10].

OAM algorithm requires two techniques – (i) scoring measure and (ii) subspace search technique, to detect outlying aspect of a given query. Distance or density-based scoring measures are widely used in the OAM algorithms. The main drawback of these types of measures in OAM is that such measures are computationally expensive and dimensionality biased. Vinh et al. [14] proposed to use Z-score normalization to make density-based scoring measures dimensionality unbiased so that they can be compared to rank subspaces with different dimensionality. It requires computing outlier scores of each data point in each subspace. It adds significant computational overhead making OAM algorithms making them infeasible to run in large and/or high-dimensional datasets.

To summarise, most OAM scoring measures do not work well in practical application due to the following main reasons:

- **High time complexity:** Existing scoring measure uses distance or density, and the known weakness of these measures is, that they are computationally expensive.
- **Dimensionality unbiasedness:** In OAM, subspaces with different dimensionalities are compared to find the best subspace. Thus, we need a measure that is dimensionally unbiased to rank those subspaces. Existing density or distance-based measures are dimensionally biased.

This paper makes the following contributions:

- Propose a new scoring measure for outlying aspect mining algorithm based on sGrid density estimator. We extend the sGrid density estimator and make it dimensionally unbiased measure, thus it does not require any additional normalization. We called the proposed measure sGrid++.
- Compare sGrid++ against three existing OAM scoring measures using synthetic and real-world datasets.
- Through our empirical evaluation, we demonstrate that sGrid++ is a dimensionality unbiased measure. In addition to that, it is faster than existing scoring measures.

The rest of the paper is organized as follows. Section 2 provides a summary of previous work on outlying aspect mining. The proposed scoring measure is presented in Sect. 3. Empirical evaluation results are provided in Sect. 4. Finally, conclusions are provided in Sect. 5.

2   Related Work

Let $\mathcal{O} = \{o_1, o_2, \cdots, o_N\}$ be a collection of N data objects in M-dimensional real domain. Each object **o** is represented as M-dimensional vector

$\langle o.1, o.2, \cdots, o.M \rangle$. The feature set $\mathcal{F} = \{F_1, F_2, \cdots, F_M\}$ denotes the full feature space and $\mathcal{S}_\mathcal{F} = \{S_1, S_2, \cdots, S_n\}$ is the set of all possible subspaces (i.e., $|\mathcal{S}_\mathcal{F}| = 2^M$). The problem of OAM is to identify $S_i \in \mathcal{S}_\mathcal{F}$ in which a given query object $o_i \in \mathcal{O}$ is significantly different from the rest of the data.

2.1 Problem Formulation

Definition 1 (Problem definition). *Given a set of N instances $\mathcal{O}$ ($\|\mathcal{O}\| = N$) in M dimensional space, a query $\mathbf{q} \in \mathcal{O}$, a subspace S is called outlying aspect of $\mathbf{q}$ iff,*

- *outlyingness of $\mathbf{q}$ in subspace S is higher than other subspaces; and*
- *there is no other subspace with same or higher outlyingness.*

The main aim of outlying aspect mining is to identify a minimal outlying aspect of a given query.

2.2 Outlying Aspect Mining Techniques

Duan et al. (2015) [3] employs depth-first search [8] with kernel density estimation (KDE) based outlying measure, called OAMiner. For a given query $\mathbf{q}$ and data set $\mathcal{O}$, OAMiner computes outlyingness as follows:

$$f_S(\mathbf{q}) = \frac{1}{N(2\pi)^{\frac{m}{2}} \prod_{i \in S} h.i} \sum_{x \in \mathcal{O}} e^{-\sum_{i \in S} \frac{(\mathbf{q}.i - x.i)^2}{2h.i^2}}$$

where, $f_S(\mathbf{q})$ is a kernel density estimation of $\mathbf{q}$ in subspace S ($|S| = m$), $h.i$ is the kernel bandwidth in dimension i.

OAMiner first ranks a data point based on the density of each data point in each subspace. After ranking the data point in each subspace, it sorts the subspace in ascending order based on the score. Lastly, it returns the top-ranked subspace(s) as an outlying aspect of a given query $\mathbf{q}$.

Vinh et al. (2016) [14] discussed the issue of using density rank as an outlying measure in OAM and provided some examples of where it can be counterproductive. They suggested to use Z-score normalized density to compare subspaces of different dimensionalities. Z-score computes the outlyingness of query $\mathbf{q}$ in subspace S as:

$$Z(f_S(\mathbf{q})) \triangleq \frac{f_S(\mathbf{q}) - \mu_{f_S}}{\sigma_{f_S}}$$

where μ_{f_S} and σ_{f_S} are the mean and standard deviation of densities of all data instances in subspace S, respectively.

They formulate the concept of dimensionality unbiasedness and proposed to use Z-score normalization to convert any dimensionality-biased measure to unbiased one. Authors have combined the Beam search with the density Z-score measure to identify outlying aspects of a given query.

Wells and Ting (2019) [15] proposed sGrid density estimator, which is a smoothed variant of the traditional grid-based estimator (a.k.a histogram). They also used Z-score normalization to make the score dimensionality unbiased. Because sGrid density can be computed faster than KDE, it allows Beam search OAM to run orders of magnitude faster.

Samariya et al. (2020) [9] proposed a **S**imple **I**solation score using **N**earest **N**eighbor **E**nsemble (SiNNE in short) measure. SiNNE constructs t ensemble of models $(\mathcal{M}_1, \mathcal{M}_2, \cdots, \mathcal{M}_t)$. Each model $\mathcal{M}_i$ is constructed from randomly chosen sub-samples $(\mathcal{D}_i \subset \mathcal{O}, |\mathcal{D}_i| = \psi < N)$. Each model has ψ hyperspheres, where radius of hypersphere is the euclidean distance between a $(a \in \mathcal{D}_i)$ to its nearest neighbor in $\mathcal{D}_i$.

The outlying score of $\mathbf{q}$ in model $\mathcal{M}_i$, $I(\mathbf{q}\|\mathcal{M}_i) = 0$ if $\mathbf{q}$ falls in any of the balls and 1 otherwise. The final outlying score of $\mathbf{q}$ using t models is:

$$\text{SiNNE}(\mathbf{q}) = \frac{1}{t} \sum_{i=1}^{t} I(\mathbf{q}\|\mathcal{M}_i)$$

2.3   Desired Properties of Outlying Scoring Measure

In this section, we provide some desired properties for an ideal outlying aspect mining scoring measure. In Table 1, we summarize the desired properties of existing scoring measures.

Dimensionality Unbiasedness. As we are comparing subspaces with different dimensionality, a scoring measure needs to be unbiased w.r.t. dimensionality. An example of a dimensionally bias scoring measure is the density measure, which decreases as dimension increases. As a result, density is biased towards higher-dimensional subspaces.

Efficiency. To find an outlying aspect of a given query, OAM algorithms are expected to search through a large number of subspaces. Thus, it is essential to have an efficient scoring measure to evaluate subspace efficiently. The efficiency of the scoring measure can be analyzed in terms of time complexity.

Effectiveness. To find the most outlying aspects of a given query, the OAM algorithm ranks each subspace based on its score. Thus, the scoring measure should be effective for getting better outlying aspects. The effectiveness of the scoring measure can be analyzed in terms of the quality of discovered subspaces.

3   sGrid++: The New Proposed Measure

Wells and Ting (2019) [15] introduced a simple and effective alternative of kernel density estimator called sGrid, which allows systematic search method to run faster in outlying aspect mining domain. sGrid is smoothed variant of the grid (a.k.a histogram) based density estimator. sGrid computes the density of multi-dimensional subspace as a multi-dimensional grid. The grid's width is set based on the bin width in one dimension.

Table 1. Summary of desired properties for scoring measures. Time complexity of estimating one query in a subspace is presented. (N = data size; m = dimensionality of subspace; ψ = sub-sample size; t = number of set; w = block size for bit set operation).

Scoring measure	Unbiasedness	Time complexity
Density	✗	✗($O(Nm)$)
Density rank	✔	✗($O(N^2m)$)
Density Z-score	✔	✗($O(N^2m)$)
sGrid	✗	✔($O(Nm/w)$)
sGrid Z-score	✔	✔($O(N^2m/w)$)
SiNNE	✔	✔($O(t\psi^2 + t\psi)$)

sGrid computes the outlying score of a given data point based on a grid in which the point falls and its neighboring grids. sGrid measure is two orders of magnitude faster than kernel density estimation [15]. However, sGrid is dimensionally biased, i.e., sGrid density tends to decreases as dimensions increases. Thus, the authors used Z-score normalization on top of sGrid, which makes sGrid computationally expensive. In addition to that, Samariya et al. [9] shows that Z-normalization is biased towards subspace having high variance. Moreover, Z-score normalization adds additional computation overhead on a measure. Thus, sGrid with Z-score normalization is not effective and due to dimensionality biasedness, it can not be used directly.

Motivated by these limitations, we proposed sGrid++, a simple yet effective variant of sGrid which is dimensionally unbiased in its raw form thus it does not require any additional normalization.

The proposed method consists of two stages. In the first stage (training stage), g number of grids are generated. The second stage is the evaluation stage, which evaluates the outlyingness of a given data point $\mathbf{q}$ in each subspace. Let $\mathcal{O}$ be a M dimensional data set in $\Re^M$, and $S \subset \mathcal{S}_{\mathcal{F}}$ be a subspace of m, where $m = |S|$ dimensions and $m \leq M$.

For each dimension, the proposed measure first creates equal-width univariate bins. We used the Freedman-Diaconis rule [4] to set the bin width and number of bins in each dimension automatically for a given data set, which means sGrid++ creates b equal width bins overvalue range.

Definition 2 (Histogram). *A histogram is a set of b equal width bins, $H = \{B_1, B_2, \cdots, B_b\}$.*

Once a histogram is created, the proposed measure calculates the mass of each histogram.

Definition 3. *A mass is defined as the number of data points that falls into the region.*

Definition 4. *A mass of a data instance $o \in \Re^M$ with respect to B_i is estimated as follows.*

$$\bar{mass}\Big(B_i(o)\Big) = \begin{cases} \textbf{mass}, & \textit{where } \textbf{mass} \textit{ is the mass of bin } B_i \textit{ in which } o \textit{ falls into} \\ 0, & \textit{otherwise} \end{cases}$$

sGrid++ computes density as follows.

$$\text{sGrid++}(\mathbf{q}) = \frac{\bar{mass}(\mathcal{G}_S(\mathbf{q}))}{v(\mathcal{G}_S(\mathbf{q}))} \tag{1}$$

where $\mathcal{G}_S(\mathbf{q})$ is a mass of grid (cell) in which $\mathbf{q}$ falls into and $v(\mathcal{G}_S(\mathbf{q}))$ is a volume of grid $\mathcal{G}_S(\mathbf{q})$.

Assuming that, data is normalized and in the range of $[0, 1]$. sGrid++ creates equal width histogram in each dimension thus it creates b^m grids (cells) of the same volume because they are in same range ($[0, 1]$). So, volume of each cell in subspace S is

$$v(\mathcal{G}_S(\mathbf{q})) = 1/b^m \tag{2}$$

Plugging Eq. 2 into Eq. 1, sGrid++ density of a query $\mathbf{q}$ is estimated as follows.

$$\text{sGrid++}(\mathbf{q}) = \bar{mass}(\mathcal{G}_S(\mathbf{q})) \cdot b^m \tag{3}$$

Let $\mathcal{G}_{(i,j,k)}(\mathbf{q})$ is a grid in which $\mathbf{q}$ falls into and has indices of $(i, j, k) \in \{(1, 1, 1), \cdots, (b_1, b_2, b_3)\}$ in their respective dimensions in 3-dimensional space. To estimate the final outlying score of query $\mathbf{q}$, sGrid++ uses the mass of the grid in which $\mathbf{q}$ falls into. The mass of grid in which $\mathbf{q}$ falls is computed by bit set intersection operation $\mathcal{G}_{(i,j,k)} = b_i \cap b_j \cap b_k$.

$$\bar{mass}(\mathcal{G}_S(\mathbf{q})) = \bigcap_{i \in m} B_i(\mathbf{q}) \tag{4}$$

The final outlying score of query $\mathbf{q}$ in subspace S is computed as:

$$grid_S(\mathbf{q}) = \bar{mass}(\mathcal{G}_S(\mathbf{q})) \cdot b^m \tag{5}$$

where $\mathcal{G}_S(\mathbf{q})$ is grid in which $\mathbf{q}$ falls into subspace S. $\bar{mass}(\mathcal{G}_S(\cdot))$ is the mass of grid $\mathcal{G}_S(\cdot)$, which is computed as shown in Eq. 4.

A working example of the proposed measure in a two-dimensional space is shown in Fig. 2. The $grid_S(x)$ is 3 while $grid_S(y)$ is 1. Thus, point y is considered more outlying.

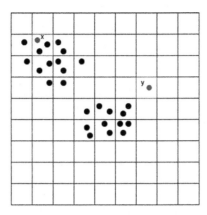

Fig. 2. Example of the new proposed method. The red highlighted regions shows the bins used to estimate outlyingness of two instances x and y. (Color figure online)

Proposition 1. *If point q falls within grid $\mathcal{G}_S$ which has higher mass then subspace S is not an outlying aspect of a query q.*

Theorem 1. *The proposed measure $grid_S(q)$ is dimensionally-unbiased as per dimensionality unbiasedness definition [14, Definition 4].*

Proof. Given a data set $\mathcal{O}$ of N data instances drawn from a uniform distribution $\mathcal{U}([0,1]^M)$.

As data is drawn from the uniform distribution, each grid has the same mass,

$$m\bar{a}ss(\cdot) = \frac{N}{g}$$

where g is total number of grid ($g = b^M$).

If we substitute mass in Eq. 5, for query q, final outlying score is,

$$grid(\mathbf{q}) = \frac{N}{g} \cdot b^M$$

$$= \frac{N}{g} \cdot g = N$$

Thus, an average value of the sGrid++ scoring measure is,

$$E[grid(\mathbf{q})|\mathbf{q} \in \mathcal{O}] = \frac{1}{N} \sum_{\mathbf{q} \in \mathcal{O}} grid(\mathbf{q})$$

$$= \frac{1}{N} \sum_{\mathbf{q} \in \mathcal{O}} N$$

$$= \frac{1}{N} N \cdot N = N, constant \; w.r.t \; |S|$$

The proposed measure is scalable to both huge datasets and high dimensions. We will prove this by our empirical evaluation.

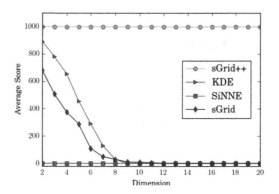

Fig. 3. Dimensionality unbiasedness.

4   Experiments

A series of experiments were performed to answer the following questions:

- **Dimensionality unbiasedness:** Does the proposed measure dimensionally unbiased?
- **Effectiveness:** How accurate is the proposed method?
- **Efficiency:** Does the proposed method scalable compared to its competitor w.r.t. data set size and dimensionality?

We first provided the experimental setup details before detailing our findings.

4.1   Experimental Setup

Algorithm Implementation and Parameters. All measures were implemented in Java using WEKA [5]. We implemented the proposed measure by making the required changes in the Java implementation of sGrid provided by the authors. We used sGrid and SiNNE Java implementations made available by [15] and [9], respectively.

$Z(\text{KDE})$ is performed by using a Gaussian kernel with default bandwidth. sGrid uses the default recommended parameter block size for a bit set operation w as 64. In terms of SiNNE, the sub-sample size $\psi = 8$ and ensemble size $t = 100$. sGrid++ also uses parameter block size for bit set operation $w = 64$.

All experiments were conducted in a macOS machine with a 2.3 GHz 8-core Intel Core i9 processor and 16 GB memory running on macOS Monterey 12.4. We run all jobs for 24 h and killed all uncompleted jobs.

4.2   Desired Properties

Dimensionality Unbiasedness. We generated 19 synthetic datasets, each data set contains 1000 data points from uniform distribution $\mathcal{U}([0,1]^M)$, where

Table 2. Comparison of the proposed measure and its three contenders on five synthetic datasets. q-id represents query index, GT represents ground truth. The numbers in a bracket are feature indices (i.e. subspaces).

	q-id	GT	sGrid++	Z(KDE)	Z(sGrid)	SiNNE
Synth_10D	172	{8, 9}	**{8, 9}**	{8, 9}	{8, 9}	{8, 9}
	245	{2, 3, 4, 5}	**{2, 3, 4, 5}**	{2, 3, 4, 5}	{3, 4, 5}	{2, 3, 4, 5}
	577	{2, 3, 4, 5}	**{2, 3, 4, 5}**	{6, 7}	{2, 3, 4, 5}	{2, 3, 4, 5}
Synth_20D	43	{0, 1, 2}	**{0, 1, 2}**	{0, 1, 2}	{0, 1, 2}	{0, 1, 2}
	86	{18, 19}	**{18, 19}**	{18, 19}	{18, 19}	{18, 19}
	665	{0, 1, 2}	**{0, 1, 2}**	{0, 1, 2}	{0, 1, 2}	{0, 1, 2}
Synth_50D	121	{21, 22, 23}	**{21, 22, 23}**	{21, 22, 23}	{21, 22, 23}	{21, 22, 23}
	248	{13, 14, 15}	**{13, 14, 15}**	{13, 14, 15}	{13, 14, 15}	{13, 14, 15}
	427	{5, 6, 7, 8}	**{5, 6, 7, 8}**	{8, 9, 48}	{48, 49}	{5, 6, 7, 8}
Synth_75D	69	{6, 7, 8}	**{6, 7, 8}**	{6, 7, 8}	{6, 7, 8}	{6, 7, 8}
	145	{0, 1}	**{0, 1}**	{0, 1}	{0, 1}	{0, 1}
	214	{9, 10}	**{9, 10}**	{9, 10}	{9, 10}	{9, 10}
Synth_100D	80	{17, 18}	**{17, 18}**	{17, 18}	{17, 18}	{17, 18}
	105	{10, 11}	**{10, 11}**	{10, 11}	{10, 11}	{10, 11}
	258	{43, 44}	**{43, 44}**	{43, 44}	{43, 44}	{43, 44}

M varied from 2 to 20. We computed the average score of all instances using sGrid++, SiNNE, sGrid, and KDE. The result is presented in Fig. 3. The flat line for the proposed measure and SiNNE shows that both measures are dimensionally unbiased, whereas sGrid and KDE (without Z-score normalization) are not. Note that, in [14], it is shown that using ranks and Z-score normalization, makes any score dimensionally unbiased. Hence, we did not include them in our experiment.

4.3   Mining Outlying Aspects on Synthetic Datasets

We evaluate the performance of sGrid++ and three contending scoring measures on 5 synthetic datasets[2], where number of instances (N) are 1,000 and number of dimensions (M): 10 to 100.

Table 2 summarised the discovered subspaces of three queries[3] by the contending measures on five synthetic datasets. In terms of exact matches, sGrid++ and SiNNE are the best performing measures that detect the ground truth of all 15 queries. Whereas Z(sGrid) and Z(KDE) produced exact matches for 14 queries.

---

[2] The synthetic datasets are from Keller et al. (2012) [6]. Available at https://www. ipd.kit.edu/~muellere/HiCS/.

[3] We reported three queries only due to page limitation.

Table 3. Comparison of the proposed measure and its three contenders on *student performance* data set. **q**-id represents query index. The numbers in the bracket are feature indices (i.e. subspaces).

q-id	sGrid++	Z(KDE)	Z(sGrid)	SiNNE
5	{1, 3, 4}	{4}	{1}	{1, 3, 4}
52	{0, 3, 4}	{0}	{0}	{0, 2, 4}
68	{0, 1}	{1}	{1}	{0, 1, 2}
156	{0, 3, 4}	{0, 4}	{0, 4}	{0, 3, 4}
197	{2, 3}	{2}	{2}	{1, 2, 3}

4.4 Mining Outlying Aspects on Student Performance Data Set

While evaluating job applications, the recruiting team wants to know in which aspects an applicant is different than other applicants. Considering this example as a case study, we detect outlying aspects of all top k outlier/anomaly students[4]. We used campus placement data set[5] which has 15 features, and we removed non-numerical features and all data points with a missing value.

For each query **q**, we apply the Beam search strategy with four different scoring measures. Table 3 summarizes the outlying aspects found by four different scoring measures on the student data set.

In absence of better quality measures for outlying aspects, we visually present 3 queries in Table 4. Visually, we can say that the sGrid++ and SiNNE detects better subspaces than Z-score based scoring measures – Z(KDE) and Z(sGrid).

4.5 Mining Outlying Aspects on NBA2020 Data Set

Let's assume that, you are an NBA coach, commentator, or agent and you may want to know the strengths or weaknesses of a particular player, using the OAM application one can detect and find that easily. We mine data from Foxsports[6] to prepare technical statistics on *shooting, assists* and *defence* stats of NBA 2020.

Table 5 summarizes the outlying aspects found by sGrid++ and three contending measures on 3 NBA datasets – *assists, defence* and *shooting*. We visually present the results of one query from each data set in Table 6. Visually we can say that out of three sGrid++ detects better subspaces whereas Z-score based measures Z(KDE) and Z(sGrid) are unable to detect best subspaces. SiNNE also detects better subspace as sGrid++. However, SiNNE is slower than sGrid++.

---

[4] We used a state-of-the-art anomaly detection algorithm called LOF [1] to identify top $k = 5$ anomalies; and used them as queries.

[5] Available at https://www.kaggle.com/benroshan/factors-affecting-campus-placement.

[6] https://www.foxsports.com/nba/stats.

Table 4. Visualization of discovered subspaces by sGrid++, Z(KDE), Z(sGrid) and SiNNE in the *student performance* data set.

q-id	sGrid++	Z(KDE)	Z(sGrid)	SiNNE

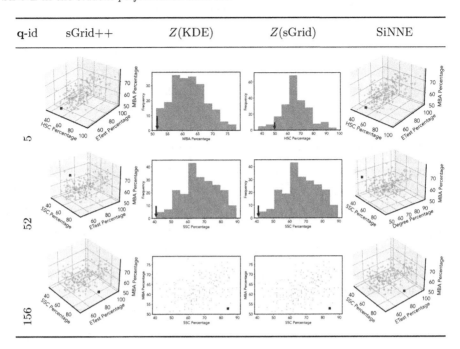

4.6   Scale-up Test

We conducted a scale-up test of these four measures w.r.t. (i) increasing data sizes (N) and (ii) increasing dimensionality (M), using synthetic datasets. We generated three equal-sized Gaussian's with random mean $\mu = [-10, 10]$ and variance $\sigma = 1.0$ in each dimension using Python Scikit-Learn [7] library. For each data set, we randomly pick 10 data points as queries and presented the average runtime. Note that, for a fair comparison we set the maximum dimensionality of subspace (ℓ) = 3.

Increasing Data Size. In this scale-up test, we examined the efficiency of the contending scoring measures w.r.t. the number of data sizes (N). A wide range of N values from 100 to 5 million is used and dimension M is fixed to 5. Figure 4a shows the average runtime on 10 queries of the contending measures w.r.t. increasing data set sizes. Note that the runtime and data set size is plotted using a logarithmic scale. sGrid++ and SiNNE are the only measures to finish scale-up test for each data set. However, SiNNE is order of magnitude slower than sGrid++. Z(sGrid) is unable to finish for data set having 5 million data points in 24hrs, whereas Z(Beam) is able to finish upto data set having 50 thousand data points. Overall, sGrid++ is order of magnitude faster than SiNNE, two orders of magnitude faster than Z(sGrid) and four orders of magnitude faster than Z(KDE).

Table 5. Comparison of sGrid++ and its three contenders on *NBA 2020* technical statistics. **q-id** represents query index. The numbers in the bracket are feature indices (i.e. subspaces).

	q-id	sGrid++	Z(KDE)	Z(sGrid)	SiNNE
assists	19	{0,1}	{3, 6}	{0, 7, 8}	{1, 6, 7}
	35	{2, 7}	{0, 8}	{1, 2, 5}	{0, 2, 3}
	52	{4}	{4}	{4}	{0, 3, 9}
defence	51	{2, 3, 4}	{4}	{4}	{4, 5, 12}
	131	{11}	{4}	{13}	{5, 7, 11}
	339	{0, 2, 5}	{0, 1, 5}	{2, 5}	{2, 4, 6}
shooting	4	{11, 21}	{6}	{11, 21}	{4, 6, 11}
	34	{5, 18}	{1}	{1}	{1, 6, 14}
	96	{10, 18}	{12}	{12}	{12, 17, 18}

Table 6. Visualization of discovered subspaces by sGrid++, Z(KDE), Z(sGrid) and SiNNE in the *NBA 2020* data set.

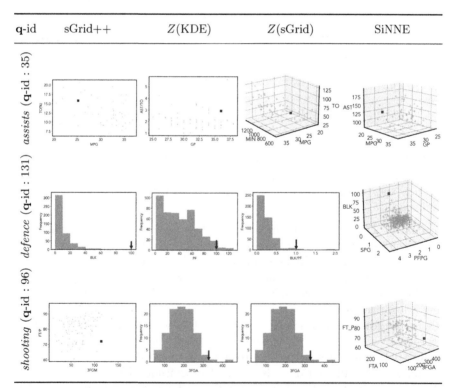

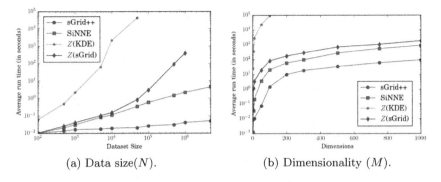

(a) Data size(N).   (b) Dimensionality (M).

Fig. 4. Scale-up test.

Increasing Dimensionality. In this scale-up test, we examined the efficiency of the contending measures w.r.t. the increasing number of dimensions. A wide range of M values from 2 to 1000 and a data set size of 10,000 was used. Figure 4b shows the average runtime on 10 queries of the contending measure w.r.t. increasing data set dimensions. Except Z(KDE) all other measures are able to finish scale-up test for each data set with in 24 h. sGrid++ is the fastest measure compare to its contenders followed by SiNNE and Z(sGrid). sGrid++ is order of magnitude faster than SiNNE and Z(sGrid).

5   Conclusion

In this paper, we discussed the issue of existing scoring measures, specifically the existing density estimator sGrid. We proposed a simple yet effective solution for making existing dimensionally biased measure to unbiased. sGrid++ creates univariate histograms in each dimension of subspace. Afterwards, the mass of the grid in which a given data point falls is used to compute the outlyingness of the query in that subspace. Our extensive experiments shows that the proposed scoring measure is dimensionally unbiased and is the fastest measure compared to all its competitors.

Acknowledgments. This work is supported by Federation University Research Priority Area (RPA) scholarship, awarded to Durgesh Samariya. Dr Sunil Aryal is supported by an Air Force Office of Scientific Research (AFOSR) research grant under award number FA2386-20-1-4005.

References

1. Breunig, M.M., Kriegel, H.P., Ng, R.T., Sander, J.: LOF: identifying density-based local outliers. In: Proceedings of the 2000 ACM SIGMOD International Conference on Management of Data, SIGMOD 2000, pp. 93–104. Association for Computing Machinery, New York (2000). https://doi.org/10.1145/342009.335388

2. Chandola, V., Banerjee, A., Kumar, V.: Anomaly detection: a survey. ACM Comput. Surv. **41**(3), 1–58 (2009). https://doi.org/10.1145/1541880.1541882

3. Duan, L., Tang, G., Pei, J., Bailey, J., Campbell, A., Tang, C.: Mining outlying aspects on numeric data. Data Min. Knowl. Disc. **29**(5), 1116–1151 (2015). https://doi.org/10.1007/s10618-014-0398-2

4. Freedman, D., Diaconis, P.: On the histogram as a density estimator: L 2 theory. Zeitschrift für Wahrscheinlichkeitstheorie und verwandte Gebiete **57**(4), 453–476 (1981)

5. Hall, M., Frank, E., Holmes, G., Pfahringer, B., Reutemann, P., Witten, I.H.: The WEKA data mining software: An update. SIGKDD Explor. Newsl. **11**(1), 10–18 (2009). https://doi.org/10.1145/1656274.1656278

6. Keller, F., Muller, E., Bohm, K.: HiCS: high contrast subspaces for density-based outlier ranking. In: 2012 IEEE 28th International Conference on Data Engineering, pp. 1037–1048 (2012). https://doi.org/10.1109/ICDE.2012.88

7. Pedregosa, F., et al.: Scikit-learn: machine learning in python. J. Mach. Learn. Res. **12**, 2825–2830 (2011)

8. Russell, S., Norvig, P.: Artificial Intelligence: A Modern Approach, 3rd edn. Prentice Hall Press, Upper Saddle River (2009)

9. Samariya, D., Aryal, S., Ting, K.M., Ma, J.: A new effective and efficient measure for outlying aspect mining. In: Huang, Z., Beek, W., Wang, H., Zhou, R., Zhang, Y. (eds.) WISE 2020. LNCS, vol. 12343, pp. 463–474. Springer, Cham (2020). https://doi.org/10.1007/978-3-030-62008-0_32

10. Samariya, D., Ma, J.: Mining outlying aspects on healthcare data. In: Siuly, S., Wang, H., Chen, L., Guo, Y., Xing, C. (eds.) HIS 2021. LNCS, vol. 13079, pp. 160–170. Springer, Cham (2021). https://doi.org/10.1007/978-3-030-90885-0_15

11. Samariya, D., Ma, J.: A new dimensionality-unbiased score for efficient and effective outlying aspect mining. Data Sci. Eng. **7**, 1–16 (2022). https://doi.org/10.1007/s41019-022-00185-5

12. Samariya, D., Ma, J., Aryal, S.: A comprehensive survey on outlying aspect mining methods. arXiv preprint arXiv:2005.02637 (2020)

13. Samariya, D., Thakkar, A.: A comprehensive survey of anomaly detection algorithms. Ann. Data Sci. 1–22 (2021). https://doi.org/10.1007/s40745-021-00362-9

14. Vinh, N.X., et al.: Discovering outlying aspects in large datasets. Data Min. Knowl. Disc. **30**(6), 1520–1555 (2016). https://doi.org/10.1007/s10618-016-0453-2

15. Wells, J.R., Ting, K.M.: A new simple and efficient density estimator that enables fast systematic search. Pattern Recogn. Lett. **122**, 92–98 (2019). https://doi.org/10.1016/j.patrec.2018.12.020, http://www.sciencedirect.com/science/article/pii/S0167865518309371

LinGBM: A Performance Benchmark for Approaches to Build GraphQL Servers

Sijin Cheng[(✉)] and Olaf Hartig

Department of Computer and Information Science (IDA), Linköping University,
Linköping, Sweden
{sijin.cheng,olaf.hartig}@liu.se

Abstract. GraphQL is a popular new approach to build Web APIs that enable clients to retrieve exactly the data they need. Given the growing number of tools and techniques for building GraphQL servers, there is an increasing need for comparing how particular approaches or techniques affect the performance of a GraphQL server. To this end, we present LinGBM, a GraphQL performance benchmark to experimentally study the performance achieved by various approaches for creating a GraphQL server. In this paper, we discuss the design considerations of the benchmark and describe its main components (data schema; query templates; performance metrics). Thereafter, we present experimental results obtained by applying the benchmark in two different use cases, which demonstrate the broad applicability of LinGBM.

Keywords: GraphQL · Benchmark · Performance · Testbed · Experiments

1 Introduction

GraphQL is a new approach to build data access APIs for Web and mobile applications [7]. Since its first published specification in 2015, the approach has become highly popular with a flourishing ecosystem of related software tools and programming libraries [15], and many adopters. For instance, an early-2019 study of open source projects identified more than 37,000 code repositories that depend on the GraphQL reference implementation (which is just one of several implementations of the approach) [10]. A similar study found 8,399 unique GraphQL API schemas on Github [17]. Besides open source projects, many companies are adopting GraphQL for their commercial software applications, including household names such as Airbnb, AWS, Expedia, IBM, Paypal, and Twitter [14].

What makes GraphQL interesting from a systems research perspective is that it is based on a declarative query language which enables clients to define precisely the data they want to retrieve. In comparison to REST interfaces, this approach reduces the number of requests that need to be issued and the amount of data transferred from server to client [2,3]. Leveraging this advantage, however, requires GraphQL servers that can process such query requests efficiently.

While there exists a plethora of Web tutorials and blog posts, as well as several books (e.g., [4,5,8,11,12,16]), that all describe approaches to implement a

GraphQL server and to avoid typical performance pitfalls, studies that show or even compare how using particular approaches may affect the performance of the resulting GraphQL server are rare and remain often anecdotal. Yet, understanding the pros and cons of different solutions is crucial for building an *efficient* GraphQL server that provides an optimal performance for a given application.

Achieving such an understanding requires performance tests, for which suitable experimentation frameworks, methods, and tooling are needed. Although there are a few performance-related test suites for specific GraphQL tools (cf. Sect. 2) and some basic experimental results [13], we observe that there does not exist any methodological approach to thoroughly evaluate and compare the performance of approaches to create a GraphQL server. In this paper we introduce a GraphQL performance benchmark called LinGBM to fill this gap.

Contributions and Organization of the Paper: Our main contribution in this paper is LinGBM, that is, a benchmark to experimentally study and compare the performance achieved by various approaches to create a GraphQL server. The benchmark consists of[1] i) a data schema for creating benchmark datasets at different scales, ii) 16 query templates that cover different performance-related challenges of GraphQL, iii) performance metrics and execution rules, and iv) the necessary tooling to conduct experiments with the benchmark (e.g., dataset and query workload generators, test drivers). Before describing these elements of the benchmark in detail (Sect. 4), we discuss the design considerations for the benchmark, including the design methodology and design artifacts (Sect. 3).

Given the benchmark, we make further contributions by demonstrating several microbenchmarking use cases in which we apply LinGBM (Sect. 5). In particular, we show that LinGBM can be used i) to evaluate the effectiveness of optimization techniques for GraphQL servers and ii) to study approaches that focus on improving the read scalability of GraphQL servers. In this context, we also present experimental results that highlight the pros and cons of selected techniques, and we outline further application scenarios for the benchmark.

Due to space limitations, this paper assumes familiarity with GraphQL. In an extended version of this paper we provide an overview of GraphQL and of approaches to create GraphQL servers, and discuss LinGBM in more detail [6].

2   Existing Test Suites

While there is no work on GraphQL benchmarks in the research literature, there exist a few performance-related test suites (cf. Table 1). These test suites are GraphQL variations of HTTP load testing tools such as wrk and vegeta[2]. Each of them consists of a specific dataset (of a comparably small size), a few GraphQL queries, and a test driver that records and visualizes throughput measurements obtained by issuing these queries to a GraphQL server built over the dataset.

---

[1] All the material related to LinGBM is available online (including, e.g., files with the query templates, the source code of tools, and documentation). In the related parts of this paper we provide links to the relevant Web pages.

[2] https://github.com/wg/wrk and https://github.com/tsenart/vegeta.

Table 1. Comparison of existing GraphQL test suites.

Test suite	Number of datasets	Number of queries	Design method
gbench	https://github.com/graphql-quiver/gbench		
	1 (100 empty objects and 1 string)*	5 queries	Unclear
The Benchmarker framework	https://github.com/the-benchmarker/graphql-benchmarks		
	1 (10 tuples)*	1 query	Unclear
PostGraphile's GraphQL Bench	https://github.com/benjie/graphql-bench-prisma		
	1 (15,607 tuples)	9 queries	Unclear
Hasura's GraphQL Bench	https://github.com/hasura/graphql-bench		
	1 (23,288 tuples)	3 queries	Unclear
GraphQL server benchmark	https://github.com/tsegismont/graphql-server-benchmark		
	1 (60 tuples)	4 templates with up to 10 instances each	Unclear
LinGBM *(our proposal)*	https://github.com/LiUGraphQL/LinGBM		
	Unlimited (unbounded scale factor)	16 templates with, 100–1M+ instances each	Choke-point based

need to be hardcoded in the resolver functions of the tested servers

We argue that these test suites are insufficient for benchmarking the performance achieved by different approaches to build GraphQL servers. By focusing on a single (small) dataset, these test suites cannot be used to study the behavior of GraphQL server implementations at scale. By using only a small number of fixed queries, it is not possible to extensively test or compare the throughput of systems that may apply caching on various levels. Additionally, it is not clear whether the few selected queries test all important aspects of approaches to build GraphQL servers. Our work in this paper addresses the limitations of the existing test suites and, more generally, the lack of a well-designed performance benchmark for evaluating and comparing approaches to build GraphQL servers.

3   Design of the Benchmark

The aim of our benchmark is to provide a framework that can be used to test and to compare the performance that can be achieved by different approaches to build GraphQL servers. To make this aim more concrete we identified two use case scenarios for the benchmark. Given these scenarios, we developed the benchmark by applying the design methodology for benchmark development of the Linked Data Benchmark Council [1]. The main artifacts created by the process of applying this methodology are i) a data schema, ii) a workload of operations to be performed by the system under test, iii) performance metrics, and iv) benchmark execution rules. A crucial aspect of the methodology is to identify key technical challenges, so-called *choke points*, for the types of systems for which the benchmark is designed. These choke points then inform the creation of the aforementioned artifacts. In this section we describe the two use case scenarios and provide an overview of the choke points defined for our benchmark. The benchmark artifacts shall then be introduced in the next section.

3.1   Use Case Scenarios

Scenario 1 represents use cases in which data from a *legacy database* has to be exposed as a *read-only* GraphQL API with a *user-specified GraphQL schema*. Hence, this scenario focuses primarily on tools and techniques to implement GraphQL servers manually.

Scenario 2 represents use cases in which data from a *legacy database* has to be exposed as a *read-only* GraphQL API provided by an *automatically generated GraphQL server*. Hence, this scenario focuses on tools that auto-generate all artifacts necessary to set up a GraphQL API over a legacy database. Notice that such tools do not support the first scenario out of the box because any GraphQL API created by such a tool is based on a tool-specific generated GraphQL schema (not a user-specified one).

Due to the space limitation, the rest of this paper focuses primarily on Scenario 1.

3.2   Choke Points

As mentioned before, we have applied a choke-point based methodology [1] for designing our benchmark. To this end, we have identified 16 choke points for GraphQL servers. As per our two benchmark scenarios (which capture read-only use cases), these choke points focus only on queries. Table 2 (left-hand side) lists these choke points, which are grouped into the following five classes.[3]

Choke Points Related to Attribute Retrieval: Queries may request the retrieval of multiple attributes (scalar fields) of the data objects selected by the queries. The technical challenge captured by the corresponding choke point is to fetch these attributes from the underlying data source using a single operation rather than performing a separate fetch operation for each attribute.

Choke Points Related to Relationship Traversal: One of the main innovations of GraphQL in comparison to REST APIs is that it allows users to traverse the relationships between data objects in a single request. Supporting such a traversal in a GraphQL server may pose different challenges, which are captured by the choke points in this class. For instance, choke point CP 2.4 captures the challenge to avoid unnecessary operations in cases in which relationships between requested objects form directed cycles. Queries that traverse along these relationships may come back to an object that has been visited before on the same traversal path. A naive implementation may end up requesting the same data multiple times from the underlying data source. Even a more sophisticated solution that caches and reuses the results of such requests may end up repeating the same operations over the cached data.

Choke Points Related to Ordering and Paging: Since an exhaustive traversal of a sequence of 1:N relationships may easily result in reaching a prohibitively

---

[3] For a detailed description of all 16 choke points covered by our benchmark we refer to our wiki: https://github.com/LiUGraphQL/LinGBM/wiki/Choke-Points.

Table 2. Choke points of LinGBM and their coverage by the 16 query templates.

QT		1	2	3	4	5	6	7	8	9	10	11	12	13	14	15	16
Attribute retrieval																	
CP 1.1	Multi-attribute retrieval	X							X		X						X
Relationship traversal																	
CP 2.1	Traversal of 1:N relationship types	X	X		X	X	X	X		X			X	X	X		
CP 2.2	Traversal of 1:1 relationship types	X		X	X	X	X	X		X		X					
CP 2.3	Traversal with retrieval of intermediate object data			X	X	X						X	X	X	X		
CP 2.4	Traversal of relationship cycles						X										
CP 2.5	Acyclic relationship traversal that visits objects repeatedly				X		X	X		X		X		X	X		
Ordering and paging																	
CP 3.1	Paging without offset								X	X							
CP 3.2	Paging with offset							X									
CP 3.3	Ordering								X	X							
Searching and filtering																	
CP 4.1	String matching									X				X	X		
CP 4.2	Date matching														X		
CP 4.3	Subquery-based filtering												X	X	X		
CP 4.4	Subquery-based search											X					
CP 4.5	Multiple filter conditions														X		
Aggregation																	
CP 5.1	Calculation-based aggregation																X
CP 5.2	Counting															X	

large number of objects, providers of GraphQL APIs aim to protect their servers from queries that cause such resource-intensive traversals. A common solution in this context is to enforce clients to use paging when accessing 1:N relationships, which essentially establishes an upper bound on the maximum possible fan-out at every level of the traversal. A feature related to paging is to allow users to specify a particular order over the objects visited by traversing a 1:N relationship. This class of choke points focuses on implementing these features efficiently.

Choke Points Related to Searching and Filtering: Field arguments in GraphQL queries are powerful not only because they can be used as a flexible approach to expose paging and ordering features. Another use case, which is perhaps even more interesting from a data retrieval point of view, is to expose arbitrarily complex search and filtering functionality. The choke points in this class capture different challenges related to this use case.

Choke Points Related to Aggregation: Another advanced feature that GraphQL APIs may provide is to execute aggregation functions over the queried data. Challenges in this context are to compute aggregations efficiently (CP 5.1)—e.g., by pushing their computation into the underlying data source—and to recognize that for counting, the corresponding objects/values may not actually have to be retrieved from the underlying data source (CP 5.2).

4   Elements of the Benchmark

4.1   Data Schema

The data schema of the benchmark[4] consists of i) a database schema for synthetic datasets that can be generated in the form of an SQL database or an RDF graph database, ii) rules for generating such datasets in different sizes, iii) a GraphQL schema for a GraphQL server that may provide access to any version of the benchmark dataset, and iv) a schema mapping that defines how the elements of the GraphQL schema map to the database schema.

Datasets. Instead of creating a new dataset generator from scratch, LinGBM reuses the dataset generator of the Lehigh University Benchmark (LUBM) [9]. LUBM is a popular benchmark in the Semantic Web community for evaluating the performance of storage and reasoning systems for RDF data. The generated datasets capture a fictitious scenario of universities with departments, different types of faculty (lecturers, assistant professors, etc.), students, courses, research publications, and other related types of entities as well as corresponding relationships between them. It is easy to imagine different Web or mobile applications in such a scenario that enable students or researchers to browse and interact with the data, where these applications access the data via a GraphQL API. Hence, these datasets are a suitable starting point for a GraphQL benchmark.

In order *"to make the data[sets] as realistic as possible,"* the dataset generator applies *"restrictions [that] are [...] based on common sense and domain investigation"* [9]. For instance, each university has 15–25 departments, each department has 7–10 full professors, and the undergraduate student/faculty ratio per department is between 8 and 14, whereas the graduate student/faculty ratio is between 3 and 4.[5] The actual cardinalities are selected from these ranges uniformly at random. Similarly, when generating relationships between generated entities, the entities to be connected are selected uniformly at random from the corresponding pool of possible entities. Depending on the type of relationship, this pool of possible entities is either context specific (e.g., students may take courses only from their department) or global (e.g., grad students may have their undergraduate degree from any university). The advantage of using uniform distributions for the data is that different queries of the same query template have the same predictable performance footprint; that is, they are roughly the same in terms of properties such as intermediate result sizes and overall result sizes.

In addition to being sufficiently realistic and diverse in terms of different types of relationships, another important property for our purposes is that these datasets can be generated at different sizes where the number of universities to be created serves as the *scale factor*. That is, the smallest dataset, at scale factor 1, consist of the data about one university. Yet another important property is that the data generation process is both deterministic and monotonic; hence, all data that is generated at a smaller scale factor is guaranteed to be contained

---

[4] https://github.com/LiUGraphQL/LinGBM/wiki/Data-Schema-of-the-Benchmark.
[5] http://swat.cse.lehigh.edu/projects/lubm/profile.htm.

in every dataset generated with the same random seed at a greater scale factor. Due to these properties, we consider the LUBM datasets as a suitable basis for our benchmark. The fact that LUBM has been designed for a different purpose is not an issue in this context because its focus on reasoning systems is reflected mainly in the queries defined for LUBM, not in its datasets.

The only relevant limitation of the LUBM datasets is that they can be created only as RDF data. For LinGBM we wanted to also support SQL databases as underlying data sources for the tested GraphQL servers. Therefore, we have defined a relational database schema[6] that resembles the concepts and relationships of the LUBM ontology, and we have developed a mapping from the generated RDF graphs to SQL databases that are instances of our database schema.

GraphQL Schema. In addition to the benchmark datasets, LinGBM introduces a GraphQL schema for exposing any version of these datasets as a GraphQL API. Essentially, this schema contains an object type for each type of entities in the benchmark dataset (universities, departments, graduate students, etc.). The fields of each such object type match both the attributes of the corresponding entity type and its relationships to other entity types. For example, the object type `GraduateStudent` in the LinGBM GraphQL schema has fields such as `emailAddress` and `memberOf` where the former is for the email-address attribute of each graduate student in the generated datasets and the latter is for the relationship that such students have to the department they belong to. Hence, the value type of this `memberOf` field is the object type `Department` which, in turn, contains a field called `graduateStudents`, with a `GraduateStudent` list as value type, to allow for GraphQL queries that traverse the relationship in the reverse direction.

In addition to the object types that we created by this straightforward translation of the database schema into a GraphQL schema, we added a few more fields and types to the GraphQL schema in order to cover all the aforementioned choke points of the benchmark. For example, some fields were extended with arguments to express filter conditions or requirements for sorting and paging. The complete LinGBM GraphQL schema can be found online[7], and we also provide a definition of the mapping[8] between this GraphQL schema and the schema of the benchmark datasets. Notice that this GraphQL schema is relevant only for Scenario 1 of the benchmark (cf. Sect. 3.1). GraphQL schemas as used in Scenario 2 are auto-generated by the corresponding systems under test.

Statistics. The size of each LinGBM dataset depends on the corresponding scale factor. Table 3 presents these statistics for scale factors 1, 10,

Table 3. Dataset sizes at different scale factors.

	$sf = 1$	$sf = 10$	$sf = 100$	$sf = 150$
File size	12 MB	161 MB	1.66 GB	2.60 GB
Overall rows	43,319	542,467	5,707,958	8,490,274
Overall objects	17,195	207,426	2,179,766	3,243,523

---

[6] https://github.com/LiUGraphQL/LinGBM/wiki/Datasets.

[7] https://github.com/LiUGraphQL/LinGBM/tree/master/artifacts.

[8] https://github.com/LiUGraphQL/LinGBM/wiki/Schema-Mapping.

100, and 150, using three different metrics: i) the file size of the generated SQL import scripts, ii) the sum of the number of rows across all tables of the generated SQL database, and iii) the sum of the overall number of objects for all types of the LinGBM GraphQL schema. As can be observed from these numbers, for each of the three metrics, the dataset size increases linearly with the scale factor.

4.2   Query Templates

As a basis for creating query workloads, we have hand-crafted a mix of 16 templates of GraphQL queries such that, on one hand, these queries cover the choke points identified in the initial design phase of our benchmark (cf. Sect. 3.2). At the same time, given the university scenario represented by the benchmark datasets, the queries capture data retrieval requests that may be issued by Web or mobile applications built for such a scenario. We emphasize that these queries are completely independent of the queries considered by the aforementioned LUBM benchmark. Although we adopt (and extend) the dataset generator of LUBM, the queries of that benchmark are irrelevant for our purpose because they have been created with a focus on testing RDF stores and reasoners. In contrast, the mix of query templates that we have created for LinGBM focuses on GraphQL servers and their specific choke points. Table 2 illustrates the coverage of these choke points by our LinGBM query templates.

Each such template is a GraphQL query that contains at least one placeholder for specific values that exist in the generated benchmark datasets. To instantiate such a template into an actual query, every placeholder has to be substituted by one of the possible values. For some placeholders, the number of possible values depends on the scale factor (bigger versions of the benchmark datasets may contain more possible values), whereas other placeholders are independent of the scale factor. For query templates with a placeholder of the former type, the number of possible instances of the template increases with the scale factor. Table 4 lists these numbers for each template at different scale factors.

Table 4. Number of query instances at different scale factors.

	$sf = 1$	$sf = 10$	$sf = 20$
QT1	540	6,843	14,457
QT2	1,000	1,000	1,000
QT3	224	2,827	6,032
QT4	93	1,128	2,399
QT5	15	189	402
QT6	1,000	1,000	1,000
QT7	48,950	493,250	989,250
QT8	15,000	15,000	15,000
QT9	2,000	2,000	2,000
QT10	27,077	344,750	728,208
QT11	1,000	1,000	1,000
QT12	14,685	1,864,485	7,953,570
QT13	899,701	113,921,020	480,241,305
QT14	6,297,907	797,447,140	3,361,689,135
QT15	1,000	1,000	1,000
QT16	1,000	1,000	1,000

While all 16 templates can be found online[9], including a detailed description of each of them[10], in the following, we describe one of them as an example.

---

[9] https://github.com/LiUGraphQL/LinGBM/blob/master/artifacts/ queryTemplates.

[10] https://github.com/LiUGraphQL/LinGBM/wiki/Query-Templates.

```
query qt5($departmentID:ID) {
  department(nr:$departmentID) {
    id
    subOrganizationOf {
      id
      undergraduateDegreeObtainedBystudent {
        id
        emailAddress
        memberOf {
          id
          subOrganizationOf {
            id
            undergraduateDegreeObtainedBystudent {
              id
              emailAddress
              memberOf { id }
} } } } } } }
```

Fig. 1. Query template QT5.

Figure 1 presents query template QT5, which is a typical example of queries that traverse relationships in cycles and that, thus, may come back to the same objects multiple times. In the particular case of QT5, the traversal starts from a given department, retrieves the university of this department, then proceeds to retrieve all graduate students with an undergraduate degree from this university, and then to the departments that these students are members of. This cycle is repeated two times. Hence, QT5 covers choke point CP 2.4. Additionally, by requesting the students' email addresses along the way, the template also covers choke point CP 2.3. Furthermore, the template covers CP 2.1 (because of the traversal from a university to graduate students) and CP 2.2 (because of the traversal from departments to their respective university, as well as from each graduate student to their department). The placeholder of this query template is $departmentID, which is used to select a department based on its number as a starting point for the traversal. Hence, for any benchmark dataset, all department numbers in this dataset can be used to instantiate QT5 in order to obtain queries that can be used for the dataset, as well as for all datasets generated with scale factors greater than the given dataset.

4.3 Performance Metrics

The performance metrics considered by LinGBM are defined based on the following two notions: i) *Query execution time (QET)* is the amount of time that passes from the begin of sending a given query request to the GraphQL server under test until the complete query result has been received in return. ii) *Throughput* is the number of queries that are processed completely by a GraphQL-based client-server system within a specified time interval, where a query is considered to be processed completely after its complete result has been received by the client that requested the execution of the query.

Then, for **single queries**, we define the metric aQETq as the average of the QETs measured when executing an individual query multiple times with the GraphQL server under test. When reporting this metric, the corresponding standard deviation has to be reported as well.

For whole **query templates**, we define the following two metrics: i) QETt is the distribution of the individual QETs measured for multiple queries of the same template and ii) aTPt is the average of the throughput measured when running the same query workload multiple times, where the queries in the workload are all from the same template.

For **mixed workloads** with queries from multiple templates, i) aTPw is the average of the throughput measured when running the same mixed query workload multiple times and ii) aTPm is the average of the throughput measured for multiple mixed workloads, where each such workload is run once.

4.4 Tools

To enable users to perform experiments with the benchmark we have developed a number of tools, including a dataset generator, a query generator, and test drivers for both throughput and QET experiments. For more information about them refer to the github repository of the benchmark.[11]

5 Application of the Benchmark

In this section we demonstrate the applicability of LinGBM for two different microbenchmarking use cases and present corresponding experimental results.

5.1 General Experiments Setup

All experiments described in the following have been performed on a server machine with two 8-core Intel Xeon E5-2667 v3@3.20 GHz CPUs and 256 GB of RAM. The machine runs a 64-bit Debian GNU/Linux 10 server operation system. On this machine, we use Docker (v9.03.6) to run all components of the experiment setups in a separate, virtual environment (e.g., the GraphQL server under test, the database server used as data source, and the LinGBM test driver).

All GraphQL servers that we implemented manually for the experiments are node.js (v10.21.0) applications that use the Apollo Server package (v2.17.0) and, for database access, the knex.js package (v0.20.15). As database server we use PostgreSQL (v12.1, default configuration options), given as a public Docker image, for which we limit the available resources to two vCPUs and 1 GB RAM. To obtain the relevant measurements we used the LinGBM test drivers.

Based on preliminary tests, we selected the following default parameters for the experiments. Unless specified otherwise, we use scale factor 100 and, to connect to the database server, the manually-implemented GraphQL servers use connection pooling with up to 10 parallel connections. Most experiments focus on average throughput per template (aTPt, cf. Sect. 4.3) with one client, for which we always do six runs of 60 secs where the first run is regarded as warm-up and the number of successfully completed queries per each of the other five runs are averaged. To have a sufficiently high number of distinct queries for these throughput runs, we generated 5000 queries for every template for which this is possible at scale factor 10 (which is the smallest scale factor used in our experiments), and for the other templates we used the maximum possible (cf. Table 4).

---

[11] https://github.com/LiUGraphQL/LinGBM/tree/master/tools.

5.2   Evaluation of Optimization Techniques

The aim of our first use case is to evaluate the effectiveness of two prominent optimization techniques used in GraphQL servers, and to show which choke points each of these techniques can address. The techniques are called server-side caching and batching.[12] The idea of *server-side caching* is to cache the response to every request that the resolver functions in the GraphQL server make to the underlying data source, and if the exact same request is made again within the scope of executing a given GraphQL query, then use the response from the cache instead of accessing the data source again. The idea of *batching* is to combine multiple similar requests to the underlying data source into a single request. Typically, this can be done for the requests issued by the same resolver function based on different inputs. A popular tool to implement this form of server-side request batching is called DataLoader[13] which also supports server-side caching.

For this evaluation we have developed a GraphQL server for Scenario 1 of the benchmark by using a straightforward implementation in which resolver functions for the elements of the GraphQL schema issue SQL queries to fetch the relevant data from the underlying database. This GraphQL server implementation represents the baseline for the evaluation and we call it the *naive* server. Thereafter, we have extended this server in three different ways to obtain three additional test servers: As a first variation, we have integrated server-side caching using memoization. For the second variation, we have replaced the naive resolvers by resolvers that use DataLoader to implement both server-side caching and batching. The third variation is a version of the second with caching disabled in DataLoader (i.e., it uses only batching). The source code for these four test servers (the naive one plus the three extended variations) is available online.[14]

Initial Macro-Level Comparison. We begin by comparing the test servers based on the aTPm metric using six different mixed workloads. Each of them is a randomly sorted sequence of 100 queries from each template (i.e., 1600 queries per workload in total). We have measured aTPm with one client and a runtime of 600 s per workload.[15] For each tested server, the first workload was used as a warm-up and the throughputs achieved for the other five workloads were averaged to calculate aTPm. In this experiment, naive server achieved an average throughput of 200 queries; for the server with caching, it is 312; with batching, 729; and with both batching and caching together, 735. These numbers show that i) both optimization techniques improve upon the baseline of the naive server, ii) batching is significantly more effective than caching, and iii) adding caching to batching does not lead to a significant improvement over batching alone. While this experiment, with its diverse mix of queries, gives us a general idea of the effectiveness of the two optimization techniques, it does not allow

---

[12] https://graphql.org/learn/best-practices/#server-side-batching-caching.

[13] https://github.com/graphql/dataloader.

[14] https://github.com/LiUGraphQL/LinGBM-OptimizationTechniquesExperiments.

[15] We use a longer duration for these runs (600 s rather than 60 s) to ensure that the tested servers have to process a greater selection of queries from each template.

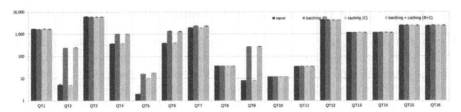

(a) aTPt (one client) for each query template as achieved with different optimizations

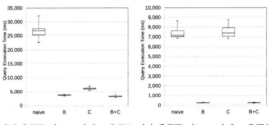

(b) QETt (in ms) for QT5   (c) QETt (in ms) for QT9

Fig. 2. Comparison of GraphQL server implementations with different optimization techniques, in terms of average throughput with one client (a) and execution times of 100 queries of template QT5 (b) and QT9 (c), at scale factor 100.

us to derive more detailed insights about them. To gain such insights we can leverage the template-specific and query-specific metrics of LinGBM as follows.

Experiments. As a first microbenchmarking experiment, we have measured the aTPt that the four test servers achieve for each of the 16 query templates at scale factor 100 with one client. Figure 2a illustrates these measurements (error bars represent one standard deviation). Thereafter, we have measured the corresponding QETt required by the test servers for a single run with 100 randomly selected queries per template. The box plots in Figs. 2b–2c illustrate these measurements for templates QT5 and QT9, respectively.[16] As a last experiment, we have increased the scale factor from 100 to 125, and then to 150, and measured aQETq for five randomly selected queries per template, as illustrated in Fig. 3 for five queries of QT5.

General Observations. A first, expected observation is that smaller query execution times result in a greater throughput, as can be seen in Fig. 2 by comparing the aTPt and the corresponding QETt that each test server achieves for QT5 and QT9. We also observe that, for the queries of some query templates, the execution times increase significantly at increasing scale factors (e.g., QT5, cf. Fig. 3), whereas for other templates the changes are less substantial. We explain these differences by differences in how the respective query result sizes increase

---

[16] The complete set of QETt charts for all templates can be found in a companion document in the aforementioned github repository with the four test servers.

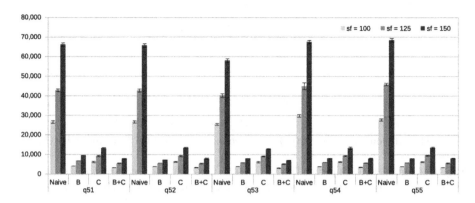

Fig. 3. aQETq (in ms) for individual queries of QT5 at increasing scale factors.

at greater scale factors (i.e., for some templates the result sizes increase more than for others).

Server-Side Caching. In our experiment, server-side caching has a major impact only for QT5. The reason why executions of QT5 queries can leverage caching is because the template captures choke point CP 2.4 (traversal of relationships that form cycles). More precisely, these queries retrieve data about particular graduate students once, and then come back to these graduate students later in a subquery; additionally, for these graduate students, the queries retrieve data about the students' departments and multiple students belong to the same department. Server-side caching enables the GraphQL server to avoid fetching the same data for these students and departments multiple times from the database.

Server-Side Batching. The idea to combine multiple requests to the underlying database helps to increase the throughput for queries of QT2, QT4–QT7, and QT9 (cf. Fig. 2a). The choke point that is common to these query templates is CP 2.1 which captures traversals of 1:N relationship types. The execution of such queries involves at least two resolvers where the first one returns an array of objects and then, for each of these objects, the second resolver is invoked once. If this second resolver performs an SQL request in the context of the given input object, these requests for the different input objects from the array can be batched, and that is exactly the case for the aforementioned templates.

While the same is true also for templates QT12–QT14, batching has no effect for queries of these templates. The reason is that these templates contain filter conditions regarding the objects in the corresponding array, and only few objects satisfy this condition. As a result, the number of SQL requests that are batched in these cases is just too small to make a difference.

A question that remains is why QT1 is not affected by batching although it covers CP 2.1 as well. The reason is that, in this case, none of the resolvers that are invoked multiple times issues any SQL requests (the data they use has already been fetched by parent resolvers). Hence, we conclude that batching

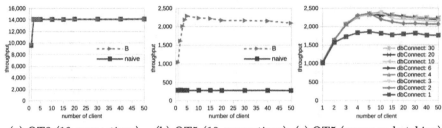

(a) QT3 (10 connections)   (b) QT5 (10 connections) (c) QT5 (server w. batching)

Fig. 4. Average throughput (aTPt, $sf = 100$) for multiple concurrent clients, where the test servers in (a)–(b) use a max of 10 connections to the underlying DB.

addresses CP 2.1 for queries in which any subquery that follows a traversal of a 1:N relationship requires further requests to the underlying data source.

5.3   Evaluation of Connection Pooling

With the second use case we aim to demonstrate that LinGBM can be employed to evaluate the effectiveness of approaches to achieve read scalability of a GraphQL server. While there is a wide range of options to this end, we consider a simple option for demonstrating this use case, namely, the option to vary the number of connections between the GraphQL server to the database server.

Experiments. As a first experiment, to understand how the number of clients affects the performance of our manually-implemented GraphQL servers, we have repeated the earlier throughput experiment with an increasing number of clients that issue sequences of GraphQL queries concurrently (first two clients, then three, four, five, ten, 15, 20, 30, 40, and 50). Figures 4a–4b illustrate these measurements for both the naive server and the server with batching, for the queries of QT3 and QT5, respectively. Thereafter, for the server with batching, we have repeated this experiment with different values for the maximum number of database connections. Figure 4c illustrates these measurements for the queries of QT5 (note that the x-axis in this chart is stretched to better see the measurements for smaller numbers of clients). For these experiments we used a smaller dataset ($sf = 10$) because, in some cases for the bigger dataset, the test servers became overloaded when serving multiple clients; in particular, this was the case for queries that have much bigger results at greater scale factors (e.g., QT5).

Observations. For QT3, and both server variants, we observe that the throughput increases when going from one to two clients, but then it does not increase further when adding more clients. We explain this behavior as follows: QT3 queries traverse along three N:1 relationship types and, thus, have results that consist of a single leaf node, and batching cannot be leveraged for these queries. During the execution of each such query, the GraphQL server issues four SQL requests to the database server, one after the other. Hence, with the default connection pool size of 10, the queries of two clients can be served concurrently without any interference. However, when aiming to serve three clients or more, the executions of the concurrent queries are competing for the available database connections and, thus, the throughput stagnates.

For QT5, without batching, the naive test server issues several hundred SQL requests per GraphQL query. In this case, the limited number of available database connections becomes a bottleneck already for one client. In contrast, when using batching, the test server needs only three SQL requests for each QT5 query and, thus, the throughput starts to increase when serving more than one client concurrently. In comparison to QT3, however, for QT5 queries, fetching data from the database is not the only major task of the test server but, instead, the fetched data also needs to be combined into larger result trees. As a consequence, even if concurrent query executions compete for the available database connections, the overall throughput increases up to five clients. However, when increasing the number of concurrent clients beyond five, the throughput starts to drop slightly. At this point, since each of the batched SQL requests fetches more data, constantly switching between requests for different concurrent queries means that the waiting times of each concurrent query execution are affected more and more as the number of concurrent query executions increases.

If we now consider the option to vary the connection pool size (cf. Fig. 4c), we make two observations in our setting for QT5: First, a connection pool size that is smaller than the default value of 10 causes the throughput to drop already for smaller numbers of clients, which is not unexpected of course. Second, however, increasing the connection pool size does not help to improve the throughput anymore. At this point, the database server becomes the bottleneck.

6   Concluding Remarks

This paper introduces LinGBM, a benchmark to evaluate the performance that can be achieved by various approaches to build a GraphQL server over an existing database. LinGBM captures key technical challenges ("choke points") to be addressed when building such server. After introducing LinGBM, we have demonstrated its applicability for two different microbenchmarking use cases.

We emphasize, however, that these are not the only types of use cases for which LinGBM can be employed. For instance, our experiments may be extended to setups in which multiple machines are used (e.g., to study the effect of remote database servers or to analyze different load-balancing approaches for GraphQL servers). Moreover, given that the benchmark datasets can also be generated in the form of RDF graphs, approaches to provide GraphQL-based access to such RDF data—and to graph databases in general—can be tested with the benchmark. Further use cases may focus on stress testing of systems by using mixed workloads from multiple selected templates (e.g., all templates that cover a particular choke point). In fact, the definition of mixed workloads may go beyond considering only an equal and uniform distribution of queries from different templates (as done in Sect. 5.2). LinGBM provides everything needed to design and run experiments with a specific mix of queries that is typical in a particular application scenario (where some types of queries are more frequent than others).

One of our future work tasks is to define and evaluate such workloads for selected application scenarios. Another task will be to extend the benchmark with update operations and possible read-write workloads.

Acknowledgements. This work was funded by the Swedish Research Council (Vetenskapsrådet, project reg. no. 2019-05655), by CUGS (the National Graduate School in Computer Science, Sweden), and by the CENIIT program at Linköping University (project no. 17.05). We also thank Lukas Lindqvist, David Ångström, and Markus Larsson for contributing to the development of LinGBM-related software.

References

1. Angles, R., et al.: The linked data benchmark council: a graph and RDF industry benchmarking effort. SIGMOD Rec. **43**(1), 27–31 (2014)
2. Brito, G., Mombach, T., Valente, M.T.: Migrating to GraphQL: a practical assessment. In: Proceedings of the 26th International Conference on Software Analysis, Evolution and Reengineering (SANER) (2019)
3. Brito, G., Valente, M.T.: REST vs GraphQL: a controlled experiment. In: Proceedings of the 2020 IEEE International Conference on Software Architecture (ICSA) (2020)
4. Buna, S.: Learning GraphQL and Relay. Packt Publishing, Birmingham (2016)
5. Buna, S.: GraphQL in Action. Manning Publications (2020)
6. Cheng, S., Hartig, O.: LinGBM: a performance benchmark for approaches to build GraphQL servers (extended version). CoRR abs/2208.04784 (2022). https://arxiv.org/abs/2208.04784
7. Facebook Inc: GraphQL (2018). http://spec.graphql.org/June2018
8. Grebe, S.: Hands-on Full-Stack Web Development with GraphQL and React. Packt Publishing, Birmingham (2019)
9. Guo, Y., Pan, Z., Heflin, J.: LUBM: a benchmark for OWL knowledge base systems. J. Web Semant. **3**(2–3), 158–182 (2005)
10. Kim, Y.W., Consens, M.P., Hartig, O.: An empirical analysis of GraphQL API schemas in open code repositories and package registries. In: Proceedings of the 13th Alberto Mendelzon International Workshop on Foundations of Data Management (2019)
11. Kimokoti, B.: Beginning GraphQL. Packt Publishing, Birmingham (2018)
12. Porcello, E., Banks, A.: Learning GraphQL: Declarative Data Fetching for Modern Web Apps. O'Reilly Media, Inc., Sebastopol (2018)
13. Roksela, P., Konieczny, M., Zielinski, S.: Evaluating execution strategies of GraphQL queries. In: Proceedings of the 43rd International Conference on Telecommunications and Signal Processing (TSP) (2020)
14. The GraphQL Foundation: 2019 Annual report (2019). https://graphql.org/foundation/annual-reports/2019/
15. The GraphQL Foundation: GraphQL Landscape (2021). https://landscape.graphql.org
16. Williams, B., Wilson, B.: Craft GraphQL APIs in Elixir with Absinthe. The Pragmatic Programmers, LLC (2018)
17. Wittern, E., Cha, A., Davis, J.C., Baudart, G., Mandel, L.: An empirical study of GraphQL schemas. In: 17th International Conference on Service-Oriented Computing (2019)

A Service-Based Framework for Adaptive Data Curation in Data Lakehouses

Firas Zouari[1]([⊠])[iD], Chirine Ghedira-Guegan[1], Khouloud Boukadi[3],
and Nadia Kabachi[2]

[1] Univ Lyon, Université Jean-Moulin Lyon 3, LIRIS UMR5205,
iaelyon School of Management, Lyon, France
`firas.zouari@univ-lyon3.fr`
[2] Univ Lyon, Université Claude Bernard Lyon 1, ERIC UR 3083, Lyon, France
[3] University of Sfax, Sfax, Tunisia

Abstract. Data lakehouses are novel data management designs intended to hold disparate batch and streaming data sources in a single data repository. These data sources could be retrieved from different sources, including sensors, social networks, and open data. Because the data carried in data lakehouses is heterogeneous and complicated, data curation is required to improve its quality. Most existing data curation systems are static, require expert intervention, which can be error-prone and time-consuming, do not meet user expectations, and do not treat real-time data. Given these constraints, we propose a service-based framework for adaptive data curation in data lakehouses that encompasses five modules: data collection, data quality evaluation, data characterization, curation services composition, and data curation. The curation services composition module, which leverages several curation services to curate multi-structured batch and streaming data sources, is the focus of this work. A reinforcement learning-based method is provided for adaptively extracting the curation services composition scheme based on the data source type and the end user's functional and non-functional requirements. The experimental findings validate the proposal's effectiveness and demonstrate that it outperforms the First Visit Monte Carlo and Temporal Learning algorithms in terms of scalability, execution time, and alignment with functional and non-functional requirements.

Keywords: Data curation · Service composition · Machine learning · Reinforcement learning · Data lakehouse

1 Introduction

Big data gave birth to diverse concepts such as cloud computing, smart services, data lakes, and most recently, data lakehouses to carry and manage this amount of data. Data lakehouses are data management architectures that present a new generation of unified data platforms. They combine the strengths of data warehouses and data lakes and can hold a variety of data structures (i.e., structured,

R. Chbeir et al. (Eds.): WISE 2022, LNCS 13724, pp. 225–240, 2022.
https://doi.org/10.1007/978-3-031-20891-1_17

semi-structured, or unstructured), as well as batch and streaming data in a well-organized way using metadata. Data lakehouses can be an effective solution in today's urgent contexts and situations, such as crises, that require real-time data collection and analysis. Nevertheless, data heterogeneity and complexity remain critical challenges for data lakehouses. Thus, data cleaning is necessary to enhance data quality before performing data analysis or visualization. For this purpose, data curation ensures managing and promoting data use from its point of creation by enriching or updating it to keep it fit for a specific purpose [7]. It provides more information about the provenance of the data, the original context of measurement and use, and the object of observation to facilitate the re-use of the data [6]. However, the existing data curation approaches are no longer sufficient to curate data in multi-structured data lakehouses and collected from multiple sources (i.e., batch and streaming data) [13]. Besides, the data curation process may be affected by factors such as the data source characteristics and the decision context. Indeed, critical decision contexts, such as crises, are generally evolving and impose restrictions on the execution time and the accuracy of information system outcomes. Therefore, it is paramount to consider the data characteristics and usage context to identify and perform the suitable data curation [1]. Besides, the value of data is never settled, as its semantics are continuously changing, which forces the data curation process to be re-arranged and changed over time [11]. Hence, the data curation needs to be aware of the changing decision process features to optimize the quality of the decision process outcomes, its execution time, and to align with user expectations. We deem *it is challenging to identify the convenient data curation tasks and rearrange them regarding the data source characteristics, the decision context, and the user expectation.* Yet, most existing data curation approaches are static and do not consider the abovementioned features. The latter are handicapping the decision-makers (i.e., those dealing with critical situations) who want to make decisions in a timely and effective manner. Besides, some existing approaches require human intervention, which can be time-consuming and error-prone. Accordingly, we propose a new adaptive data curation framework for batch and streaming data sources to overcome these limitations. The proposed global framework is service-based and encompasses the data curation stages (i.e., data source collection, data quality evaluation, data source characterization, and data curation) as modules. The data curation process encompasses curation services composition and data curation modules that employ a library of curation services in which each service presents a curation task. The curation service composition module composes the curation services adaptively to the decision process features to optimize the data curation process in terms of execution time and alignment to user needs. Subsequently, the data curation module invokes the composing services. To compose curation services, our original contribution relies on artificial intelligence techniques, particularly machine learning, for adaptive generation of data curation services composition scheme according to functional requirements such as the data source characteristics and non-functional requirements like the user preferences and constraints and the decision context. Mainly, our proposed framework takes advantage of reinforcement learning as a practical solution that can learn over time to make increasingly effective decisions in a dynamic environment like the one of the data lakehouse. This paper presents an overview of the adaptive data curation framework, focusing on the curation services composition module. The remainder of this paper is structured as follows: Sect. 2 presents the related work. Section 3 overviews the proposed framework. Section 4 details the data source characterization and curation services composition modules. Section 5 presents the elaborated experiments and the obtained results. Finally, Sect. 6 concludes the paper and presents some future endeavors.

2   Related Work

Data management in general and data curation, in particular, has attracted the attention of many researchers. Several works in the literature addressing the data curation process exist. Some of them target the sequencing and the dynamic orchestration of data preparation and cleansing automatically combined with semi-automated steps of curation such in [2] for social data via a pool of services, and in [4] which is dedicated only to structured data source curation via loosely coupled data preparation components. In the same vein, some architectures and frameworks were proposed, such as KAYAK [8] that lies between users/applications and the file system (i.e., data storage location), and exposes a set of primitives and tasks for data preparation represented as a Direct Acyclic Graph. Also, [3] details the use of Vadalog, which is a Knowledge Graph Management System dedicated to data science tasks such as data wrangling (i.e., information extraction, stemming, entity resolution, etc.). By analyzing the existing works, we noticed that most proposed approaches could not be generalized to treat at the same time all data source structures (i.e., unstructured, semi-structured, or structured). Yet, data lakehouses contain various data source formats, which require sophisticated tools to curate. Regarding curation process automation, several approaches are not fully automatic. However, the intervention of the human actor is error-prone and time-consuming. Besides, we investigated the flexibility of the studied approaches. Most of them are static regarding the decision process features, and if considered, they ensure a low level of adaptation to end-user needs. Finally, and to our knowledge, all the examined approaches consider only batch data sources.

Considering the above approaches' limits, it is essential to propose a solution that aims to overcome them by performing data curation adaptively. Specifically, our solution should perform data curation for batch and streaming data simultaneously, adaptively to the decision context, the user profile, constraints and preferences, and the type of the considered data source.

3   Adaptive Data Curation Framework

Data lakehouses contain multi-structured data stored as batch and streaming data sources. Hence, data curation is an essential step that needs to be applied before analyzing data sources to enhance the quality of outcomes. Curating these data sources while simultaneously considering heterogeneous batch and streaming data is challenging. To address this challenge, we propose an adaptive data curation framework for batch and streaming data sources to optimize the further data analysis steps in terms of execution time and alignment with user needs. As depicted in Fig. 1, our framework encompasses the following four layers: data collection, data quality control, data treatment, and data curation layers. Our framework ensures adaptability from the moment of data collection. Indeed, the data collection layer ingests batch and streaming data sources and information about streaming data, data providers, location, and temporal information as metadata. Then, the framework assesses the quality of batch and streaming data via the data quality evaluation module and data streaming monitoring module. The data quality module assesses the data quality and the data source's quality dimensions, such as data accuracy, timeliness, believability, verifiability, and reputation. According to the evaluated quality dimension values, the data curation framework judges whether the data source needs to be curated or not. Specifically, data curation is performed for each data source and follows the data evaluation process when one of the evaluated data quality dimensions is below a threshold β. This threshold can be fixed and modified by the user. Following the data evaluation process, the values of the data quality dimensions and the data source are transmitted to the data characterization module, which we define in the data treatment layer. The data source characterization module extracts the data source characteristics required for the data curation process, like its format, data source type, and specific data curation tasks (See Sect. 4). Based on the extracted features, the user profile, and the decision context, the data curation layer selects the most convenient curation services from a library of curation services to perform a data curation process. Indeed, each curation service ensures a curation task (e.g., removing duplicate records, anomaly detection, etc.). These curation tasks could be combined in a specific way to curate a data source. Hence, we propose to execute the data curation tasks as a service composition while aligning with end-user expectations. Our framework relies on artificial intelligence mechanisms and, more precisely, machine learning techniques to address the challenges mentioned above related to data source heterogeneity, decision context instability, restriction in terms of execution time, and the accuracy of outcomes. Machine learning algorithms can automate curation tasks organization as well as gain experience as they improve accuracy and efficiency to make better decisions. Thus, the curation services composition is enhanced as the learning algorithms gain experience each time. Technically, we deploy our framework following the service-oriented architecture since it is a reliable, scalable, and loosely coupled architecture. The rest of the paper sheds light on the service composition for adaptive data curation.

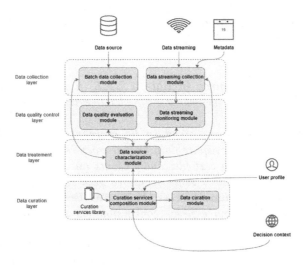

Fig. 1. Adaptive data curation framework

4 Towards an Adaptive Curation Service Composition Method

To attempt our aforementioned objectives, we propose an adaptive curation service composition method that encompasses two steps, namely data characterization and curation services composition scheme generation. We formalize and illustrate our method and the main features of each step in what follows.

4.1 Data Source Characterization Step

The data source characterization step extracts the data source's characteristics required for the curation services composition scheme generation step. Indeed, the data source characteristics may impact the curation services selection, which influences, consequently, the composition of the overall services. We assume a particular data source includes URLs within its attributes. Accordingly, a service named URL extraction service needs to be invoked to fetch information from the data present in the web pages. We formally define a data source as:

$$\mathbf{D} = <DN, DAtt, Do, MAtt, DCh>$$

where:

- **DN** is the data source name
- **DAtt** represents the data attributes
- **Do** represents the data records
- **MAtt** is the set of attributes taken from a Metadata M
- **DCh** represents the extracted data source characteristics needed for adaptive data curation. The following features characterize a data source:

– *The data source format (structured (S), semi-structured (SS), or unstructured (US)):* This feature guides the service composition module to select the suitable curation services according to the type of the source.

– *Does the data source include a URL in its data values ?:* This feature helps determine whether the URL extraction service should be invoked.

– *Does the data source need to be converted to another format ?:* Some data sources require data format conversion before being curated. For example, a plain text file that presents an unstructured data source could be converted into a semi-structured data source (e.g., an XML file) to enhance the curation process. Using this feature, we can distinguish whether the data source needs conversion via the "Converter Service" invocation.

– *Does the data source need to undergo a PoS Tagging process?:* Some data sources contain paragraphs that need to be annotated via a POS Tagging to enrich them semantically. Indeed, POS Tagging is the association of words in a text with the corresponding grammatical information, such as the gender. Hence, this feature allows identifying whether the data source contains paragraphs that need to be annotated via the POS Tagging process.

– *Is it streaming data ?:* This feature identifies batch and streaming data to invoke the convenient curation services for each data type.

A Metadata is defined as :

$$M = <Mn, MAtt, MVal>$$

where:

– **Mn** is the metadata name
– **MAtt** represents the metadata attributes
– **MVal** represents the data objects

Illustration. We assume a JSON dataset named DSPop, which includes demographic information. This dataset also consists of an attribute that contains links to personal web pages.

This dataset can be represented as D = <"DSPop", ("Name", "Age", "Location", " Personal webpage"), {("Alice", 25, "USA", "http://..."), ...}, {("Author", "Charlie"), ("Creation Date", "25/03 /2020"), ("Format", "JSON"), ("Publisher", "Eve")}, ("SS", True, False, False, False)>.

The dataset D is linked with a Metadata M presented as M = <("Author", "Charlie"), ("Creation Date", "25/03/2020"), ("Format", "JSON"), ("Publisher", "Eve")>.

4.2 Curation Services Composition Scheme Generation Step

Following data characterization, the next step generates the convenient curation services composition scheme. Each curation service ensures a specific curation task. The curation tasks are combined to perform a curation process. By analyzing the existing curation works, we propose the taxonomy of the main batch and streaming data curation task categories, depicted in Fig. 2. These curation tasks ensure the necessary operations for data curation. We point out that concept drift detection is devoted to streaming data curation. Concept drift tasks detect the deviation of captured streaming data due to a sensor failure. Yet, the curation tasks within the other categories could be applicable for both batch and streaming data. It is worth noting that we considered this taxonomy when designing the curation services library.

As our proposed method relies on several curation services, we extend the reasoning proposed in [12] for service composition, which has proven to be effective. Yet, the work presented by Wang et al. takes into account only user preferences and QoS to perform service composition. In the proposed work, we consider the various factors implied in curation services composition, namely the non-functional requirements such as user preferences, constraints, and QoS, as well as the functional requirements like the structure (i.e., structured, unstructured, etc.) and the type (i.e., batch or streaming) of the treated data source. Specifically, we adopt reinforcement learning since our proposed method is designed to deal with dynamic environments [10].

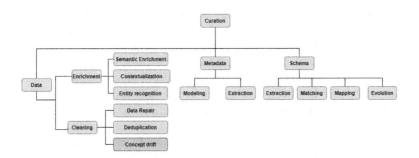

Fig. 2. Taxonomy of data curation tasks.

Thus, and as depicted in Fig. 3, the first process is a training one that identifies the optimal policy to compose curation services. In contrast, the composition process extracts the curation services composition scheme using the generated policy. The training process, in its turn, relies on three tasks: environment initialization, exploration, and exploitation. The initialization task prepares the environment to be explored/exploited by the learning agent to identify the optimal curation services composition scheme (i.e., a set of transition actions). This scheme is generated according to the user's functional and non-functional requirements. To do so, the proposed method uses the Q-Learning algorithm, one of the most popular algorithms for reinforcement learning, to learn the optimal curation services composition scheme adaptively, which optimizes the execution time and outcomes accuracy. The Q-Learning algorithm is a model-free reinforcement algorithm that defines an agent interacting with an environment (usually, a Markov Decision Process) to learn the optimal actions to be taken for the transition from one state to another. Following this logic, we assign weights to actions to guide the learning agent during the learning process. The weights present rewards accumulated at each transition. Hence, we treat the curation service composition as a gain maximization problem.

We represent the curation services in a Markov Decision Process (MDP) in which each transition action presents a curation service. Thus, in the MDP environment, we present all the valid possible compositions of all the curation services for all data source types regardless of user requirements and environmental factors. As curation services are devoted to curating either semi-structured, unstructured, or structured data sources, the environment adapts itself during the initialization task by disabling some actions (i.e., representing curation services) that are not convenient for the treated data source type. For this purpose, the environment initializes the reward returned by the disabled actions to a negative value. Since we deal with a gain maximization problem, the agent will avoid these actions and select only the transition actions worthing a positive reward value. We propose Eq. 1 to compute the transition rewards. The proposed equation relies on curation services QoS, user preferences, and constraints (e.g., The QoS response time value >90%) to compute the reward value. Equation 1 supports the use of several QoS dimensions together to compute the reward. Regarding user preferences, they could be defined as weights to promote a QoS dimension over another. For example, a user may be more interested in accuracy than response time. Thus, the accuracy quality dimension may receive a higher weight than the response time. We note that it is possible to define constraints over QoS values by setting a minimum threshold M that should be satisfied to invoke a service. For instance, a user may invoke only services with an accuracy quality dimension higher than 80%. By considering the QoS, user preferences, and constraints, the reward function (i.e., Eq. 1) returns a positive value when all users' constraints are satisfied. Otherwise, the function returns a negative value. Since the service composition is a gain maximization problem, the negative rewards prevent the agent from choosing curation services that do not fit the user's constraints. The first part of Eq. 1 computes the difference between user-imposed constraints and QoS values. It returns either 1 if all user constraints are fulfilled or -1 otherwise. Equation 1 relies on Eq. 2 to compute the difference between one QoS dimension and the threshold M defined by the user. Subsequently, the value of Eq. 2 is normalized to -1 or 1 according to the obtained value. The second part allows assigning user preferences to QoS dimensions. Therefore, the preferences are defined as weights to multiply the evaluated QoS dimensions' values. Afterward, the multiplication of the two parts of the equation returns the reward value according to user preferences, constraints, and QoS values.

$$R(s) = \underbrace{\frac{\sum_{i=1}^{m} X(i) - 1 + \phi}{\sum_{i=1}^{m} |X(i) - 1 + \phi|}}_{\text{Part1}} * \underbrace{\sum_{k=1}^{m} w_k * D_k}_{\text{Part2}} \qquad (1)$$

$$X(k) = \frac{\sum_{i=1}^{m} |D_k - M_k + \phi|}{D_k - M_k + \phi} \qquad (2)$$

where:

- **w** represents user preferences regarding a QoS, defined as weight ranging from 0 to 1
- **D** is a normalized value of QoS dimension evaluation ranging from 0 to 1
- **M** represents a minimum threshold set by the user for QoS that needs to be fulfilled to invoke the service. The value of M ranges from 0 to 1.
- ϕ a normalization value that needs to be strictly higher than 0 and lower than 1.

As the reward function relies mainly on the QoS, user preferences, and constraints, we illustrate the inputs of the training process (See Fig. 3), which contain these characteristics. Specifically, we formally describe the curation services, the library of services, and the user profile. Each curation service CS is characterized by an ID, a name, its quality (QoS), and an operation. We define a curation service as:

$$\textbf{CS} = \textbf{<Id, CSN, QoS, Op>}$$

where:

- **Id** represents the curation service Id
- **CSN** is the curation service name
- **QoS** is a set of evaluated QoS dimensions. It contains QoS dimension **QoS$_D$** and the evaluated QoS value **QoS$_V$** presented as couples and assigned for each assessed QoS dimension
- **Op** is the operation name to be executed following a service invocation.

The user profile encompasses the user preferences and the user group preferences. A user can be a part of a group of users. Each group of users can have group preferences aggregated from users' preferences. During the training process, the user can use either his own preferences or his group preferences to promote a QoS dimension over another. Indeed, group preferences allow sharing information about specified preferences between the users, saving efforts, and learning from other members. Thus, we define a user profile as:

$$\textbf{U} = \textbf{<Np, Pru, G>}$$

where:

- **Np** represents the user profile name

- **Pru** is a set that represents the user's preferences regarding a decision context **C**
- **G** represents a group of user profiles. A group is characterized by group name **Ng** and group preferences **Prg** concerning a decision context **C**.

We define the decision context that represents the user's surroundings as:

$$C = <Nc,Tc>$$

where:

- **Nc** represents the name of the context
- **Tc** is the decision context type (e.g., crisis, ordinary situation, etc.). We rely on the proposal in [5] to design the characteristics of the decision context.

We implement the different steps of the curation services composition scheme generation method as modules of the adaptive data curation framework.

Illustration. To illustrate the idea behind the proposed method, we assume that the adaptive data curation framework is implemented in a crisis management system that relies on different data management stages, including data curation. We suppose that Alice, Deputy Senior Defense and Security Officer at the Ministry of Health, and Bob, an infectious disease specialist, use this system to predict and manage health crises. Assume that Alice uses the system in a crisis context, while Bob uses it in an ordinary situation. Hence, they may have different needs regarding the accuracy of outcomes and the system's response time. Indeed, response time may be significant for Alice, while it is not as important as outcomes accuracy in Bob's case. We assume they use this system to deal with multi-structured data sources ingested in batch and streaming modes from different providers (e.g., web, sensors, social networks, etc.). Considering this crisis management system, we focus, in the following example, on data curation. We suppose that Alice wants to decide on a critical health crisis using various data sources, including sensors. To curate the data streams, our proposed data curation framework collects data using the data streaming collection module and monitors the data streams via the data streaming monitoring module. Subsequently, the framework extracts data characteristics using the data source characterization module. This latter identifies several characteristics, among which data are collected from streaming sources in JSON Format. Since the curation service composition module deals with streaming semi-structured data, it initializes the MDP environment by disabling the transition actions referencing improper services, such as the ones for batch or structured data curation. Then, during the exploration/exploitation process, the learning agent learns the optimal composition service policy π^* using Eq. 1. Subsequently, using the learned policy π^*, the module composes the curation services that fit Alice's needs by selecting services with a high response time QoS value. Later, the curation service composition scheme is transmitted to the data curation module to invoke the curation services and perform data curation. In another context, we assume that Alice uses the system in an ordinary situation to get some statistics from the system. Accordingly, she has other preferences regarding the decision context. Hence, the curation services composition module adapts itself and generates another scheme to meet Alice's needs. As for Bob, we assume that he is using the crisis management system to check the last recommendations to treat a new infectious disease. Thus, the system collects data from diverse sources like health institutions to generate these recommendations. We consider, in this example, the databases provided by health institutions. Accordingly, the curation service composition module initializes the MDP environment differently than in Alice's case by enabling curation services for batch and structured data curation, since Bob is more interested in the accuracy of the results. The curation services composition module adjusts Eq. 1 weights during the exploration/exploitation process to promote accuracy over response time. Hence, it generates a different curation service composition scheme that meets Bob's needs.

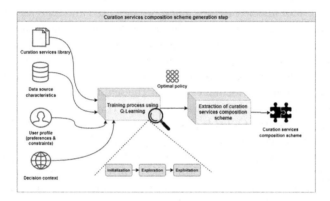

Fig. 3. Illustration of the curation services composition scheme generation step

5   Experiments and Results

In this section, we present the conducted experiments to assess the effectiveness and the performance of the curation service composition module. These experiments extend those that we presented in [14], which assess the reinforcement learning performance and adaptivity to changes. Specifically, in this paper, we evaluate the scalability of our approach regarding (1) the number of users, (2) the number of services, and (3) the adaptivity and the alignment with user requirements that we measure using cumulative rewards and evaluation scenarios. To do so, we applied our proposed method to generate curation services composition scheme for an unstructured dataset[1], a semi-structured dataset[2], and a structured dataset[3]. Then, we compared the obtained results with the First-visit Monte Carlo, and Temporal-difference Learning [9], two well-known reinforcement learning algorithms, which we use to tackle the service composition problem. We adjusted the hyperparameters (e.g., learning rate) of each algorithm using several tests to identify the optimal configuration. Moreover, we assess the adaptivity of our approach regarding the changing data source characteristics, user preferences, and constraints using the cumulative reward.

Curation Services Composition Scalability. These experiments examine the scalability of our curation service composition method according to the number of simultaneous users and curation services. For this purpose, we relied on multithreading to simulate the curation services composition by several users. Thus, we developed threads, and each one simulates the curation service composition by one user. We defined the same input parameters (i.e., user preferences, constraints, etc.) for all the threads. Then, we executed and increased the number of threads progressively to examine the response time to these queries. Indeed, we considered the average execution time as a result. Figure 4a depicts the overall execution time according to the number of threads. Since we used different datasets to elaborate the experiments, we noticed that the data source type does not affect our approach performance. As for the scalability according to the number of services, we executed the curation services composition process for several services by increasing the Q-Table size. Indeed, as each entry of the Q-Table corresponds to one service, increasing the Q-Table size simulates the rising number of service instances. At each iteration, we executed the service composition three times and took the average execution time as a result. Consequently, the elaborated experiments showed that the service composition scheme is generated in near real-time using 12000 services. However, in our case, the Monte Carlo and Temporal-difference algorithms cannot generate a service composition scheme for more than 200 services. Following the experimental results, we noticed that our curation services composition method is scalable according to the number of users' queries and the curation services. Moreover, we can see that our proposed method outperforms the two reinforcement learning algorithms.

Cumulative Rewards. We conducted experiments on the abovementioned datasets to assess our curation service composition method's alignment with user expectations. As we adopted the reinforcement learning paradigm, we rely on the returned reward to evaluate the adaptivity of our proposed method to the QoS, user preferences, and constraints. Accordingly, we highlight that as the value of the reward increases, the composition method becomes more aligned with user needs. To do so, we designed a library of 17 existing services for structured

---

[1] https://archive.ics.uci.edu/ml/datasets/Health+News+in+Twitter: A dataset that contains health news from more than 15 major health news agencies such as BBC.

[2] https://www.ncbi.nlm.nih.gov/datasets/coronavirus/genomes/: A dataset provided by the National Center for Biotechnology Information (NCBI) that contains data about COVID-19 genomes.

[3] https://github.com/LogIN-/fluprint: A structured dataset about Flu.

and unstructured/semi-structured data curation. Afterward, we defined similar experimental settings for all the tested algorithms. Specifically, we defined similar user preferences, QoS values, decision context, user constraints, and data source format. Considering these parameters, we executed our curation service composition method using the Q-Learning, the First-visit Monte Carlo, and the Temporal-difference learning algorithms to generate a curation services composition scheme for the three datasets. Then, we took the average of the rewards gained for the three datasets and presented them in Fig. 4b. As depicted in the Figure, our curation service composition aligns better with user needs than the First-visit Monte Carlo and Temporal-difference Learning algorithms, since it returns a higher cumulative reward. Indeed, the cumulative reward gained by our service composition method exceeds 9, while the maximum rewards returned by the other reinforcement learning algorithms are less than 6. We also investigated the adaptivity of our approach via the definition of evaluation scenarios. Through these scenarios, we generated curation services composition schemes for different data source types according to different user requirements. We examine the validity of the curation services composition scheme via the investigation of the convenience of its services according to the functional and non-functional requirements. To do so, we rely on the library of services described above that contains curation services for structured, semi-structured, and unstructured data sources. Specifically, we evaluated our approach's adaptivity according to (i) data source type, (ii) QoS and user preferences, and (iii) data source characteristics. Regarding the data source type, our approach has generated different services composition schemes for each data source type. For instance, the composition scheme for the semi-structured data source contains (Entity Extraction Service → Linking Service → Synonym Service), which is different from the one generated for the structured data source (Metadata Extraction Service → Descriptive Statistics Service → Missing Values Service → Terminology Extraction Service → Lexical Service → Rules Extraction Service → Entity Extraction Service → Linking Service → Synonym Service). Thus, the experiment results show that our approach generates convenient curation services schemes for each data source type (i.e., structured, semi-structured, unstructured). Regarding user preferences, we extended the library of services by defining three curation services for each curation task (e.g., PoS Tagging). Indeed, each curation service has different QoS values that are measured using the accuracy, availability, reliability, response time, reputation, and security quality dimensions. We treat in the first evaluation scenario a semi-structured data source, and we assume that the user expresses more interest in response time via the definition of the following preferences (Accuracy: 10%, Availability: 10%, Reliability: 10%, Response Time: 50%, Reputation: 10%, Security: 10%). Accordingly, our approach generated the following scheme (Stem Extraction Service → Synonym Extraction Service). Subsequently, we examined the services that constituted the scheme to check whether our service composition method has selected the most convenient services according to the user preferences. As we defined three curation services corresponding to each curation task, our method generates a composition scheme that contains the least costly services in terms of response time. We consider the stem extraction services ST1, ST2, ST3, and the synonym extraction services SY1, SY2, SY3 which are candidates to constitute the abovementioned scheme. Hence, our method selected ST2 and SY1 which have the most Response Time QoS (i.e., ST1: 71%, ST2: 85%, ST3: 50%, SY1: 99%, SY2: 78%, SY3: 84%). Following this experiment, we changed the user preferences by promoting the accuracy dimension (Accuracy: 50%, Availability: 10%, Reliability: 10%, Response Time: 10%, Reputation: 10%, Security: 10%) to check whether this will have an impact on the curation services composition scheme. Hence, the generated composition scheme is constituted from ST3 and SY3 which are the most accurate services (i.e., ST1: 48%, ST2: 66%, ST3: 77%, SY1: 77%, SY2: 40%, SY3: 98%). Thus, based on the cumulative rewards values and the evaluation scenarios, we can deduce that our method aligns well with user requirements. We also investigated the alignment of our method with the treated data source characteristics. As we illustrated in Sect. 3, our framework extracts the characteristics of the data sources that are required for scheme generation. Following the characterization of a semi-structured data source containing URLs, the scheme generated by our method (Stem Extraction Service → URL Extraction Service → Entity Extraction Service → Synonym Extraction Service) contains a service dedicated to fetching data from URLs. We present another evaluation scenario in which we treat streaming data. By investigating the scheme generated for the streaming data (Streaming Concept Drift Service → Stem Extraction → Entity Extraction → Linking Service), we noticed that the generated scheme is different from the other schemes generated for batch data since it contains a service dedicated to streaming data. Hence, the results reveal our method ensures adaptivity since it aligns with the functional and non-functional requirements for data curation services scheme generation.

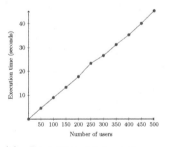 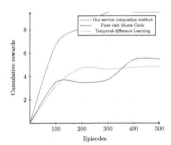

(a) Execution time per number of users

(b) Cumulative rewards by each algorithm

Fig. 4. Experiments results

Following the obtained results, we conclude that our method outperforms the Monte Carlo and Temporal-difference algorithms in terms of scalability, alignment with user needs, and execution time. We also noticed that our method has the same performance for the different data source types. As a result, we believe it is appropriate for use in systems that handle heterogeneous data for different user needs in various decision contexts. Hence, it aligns with their needs to generate personalized outcomes. Moreover, it can be suitable in critical contexts since it is lightweight and fast. We highlight that the scope of our experiments covers only the service composition scheme generation and not services invocation.

6 Conclusion

We presented an original framework for batch and streaming data curation in data lakehouses. This paper sheds light on a novel adaptive curation services composition scheme generation method that constitutes the core of the presented framework. Hence, the originality of this work is the adaptivity throughout the entire process, starting from data collection to data curation passing by data quality evaluation, and data source characterization. The proposed method relies on the reinforcement learning algorithm to retrieve the convenient curation services composition according to the functional and non-functional requirements thanks to a reward function that considers the data source type, the decision context, the QoS values, and the users' preferences and constraints as well. We conducted several experiments to present the deterministic aspect of our proposal and illustrate its performance in comparison to well-known reinforcement learning algorithms, namely, First Visit Monte Carlo and Temporal difference algorithms. Experimental results show that our method outperforms the evaluated algorithms in terms of alignment with user expectations, the quality of the outcomes, and overall execution time. In future work, we plan to consider the trade-off between adaptive data curation services outcome and the accuracy of data analysis. The goal is to investigate data analysis scenarios within a data lakehouse to evaluate the effectiveness and accuracy of their curation.

References

1. Akoka, J., Comyn-Wattiau, I., Laoufi, N.: Research on big data - a systematic mapping study. Comput. Stan. Interfaces **54**, 105–115 (2017)
2. Beheshti, A., Vaghani, K., Benatallah, B., Tabebordbar, A.: CrowdCorrect: a curation pipeline for social data cleansing and curation. In: Mendling, J., Mouratidis, H. (eds.) CAiSE 2018. LNBIP, vol. 317, pp. 24–38. Springer, Cham (2018). https://doi.org/10.1007/978-3-319-92901-9_3
3. Bellomarini, L., et al.: Data science with Vadalog: knowledge graphs with machine learning and reasoning in practice. Futur. Gener. Comput. Syst. **129**, 407–422 (2022)
4. Konstantinou, N., et al.: VADA: an architecture for end user informed data preparation. J. Big Data **6**(1), 1–32 (2019). https://doi.org/10.1186/s40537-019-0237-9
5. Lauras, M., Truptil, S., Bénaben, F.: Towards a better management of complex emergencies through crisis management meta-modelling. Disasters **39**(4), 687–714 (2015)

6. Leonelli, S.: Classificatory theory in data-intensive science: the case of open biomedical ontologies. Int. Stud. Philos. Sci. **26**(1), 47–65 (2012)

7. Lord, P., Macdonald, A., Lyon, L., Giaretta, D.: From data deluge to data curation. In: In Proceedings of the 3th UK e-Science All Hands Meeting, pp. 371–375 (2004)

8. Maccioni, A., Torlone, R.: KAYAK: a framework for just-in-time data preparation in a data lake. In: Krogstie, J., Reijers, H.A. (eds.) CAiSE 2018. LNCS, vol. 10816, pp. 474–489. Springer, Cham (2018). https://doi.org/10.1007/978-3-319-91563-0_29

9. Sutton, R.S., Barto, A.G.: Reinforcement Learning: An Introduction, 2nd edn. The MIT Press, Cambridge (2018)

10. Szepesvári, C.: Algorithms for reinforcement learning, vol. 9 (2010)

11. Tempini, N.: Data curation-research: practices of data standardization and exploration in a precision medicine database. New Genet. Soc. **40**, 73–94 (2020)

12. Wang, H., Zhou, X., Zhou, X., Liu, W., Li, W., Bouguettaya, A.: Adaptive service composition based on reinforcement learning. In: Maglio, P.P., Weske, M., Yang, J., Fantinato, M. (eds.) ICSOC 2010. LNCS, vol. 6470, pp. 92–107. Springer, Heidelberg (2010). https://doi.org/10.1007/978-3-642-17358-5_7

13. Weatherall, J., et al.: Clinical trials, real-world evidence, and digital medicine. In: The Era of Artificial Intelligence. Machine Learning, and Data Science in the Pharmaceutical Industry, pp. 191–215. Academic Press, Cambridge (2021)

14. Zouari, F., Ghedira, C., Kabachi, N., Boukadi, K.: Towards an adaptive curation services composition based on machine learning. In: IEEE International Conference on Web Services (ICWS), pp. 73–78 (2021)

Retrofitting Industrial Machines with WebAssembly on the Edge

Otoya Nakakaze[1]([✉]) [iD], István Koren[2] [iD], Florian Brillowski[3] [iD],
and Ralf Klamma[1] [iD]

[1] Chair of Databases and Information Systems, RWTH Aachen University, Aachen,
Germany
otoya.nakakaze@rwth-aachen.de, klamma@dbis.rwth-aachen.de
[2] Chair of Process and Data Science, RWTH Aachen University, Aachen, Germany
koren@pads.rwth-aachen.de
[3] Institut für Textiltechnik, RWTH Aachen University, Aachen, Germany
florian.brillowski@ita.rwth-aachen.de

Abstract. Tapping into previously inaccessible data sources promises
new potential for value creation in the manufacturing industry. However,
asset-heavy shopfloors, long machine replace cycles, and equipment heterogeneity demand major investments to achieve smart manufacturing,
which small businesses struggle with. Retrofitting is a sustainable means
of equipping aged machines with low-cost sensors and microcontrollers
to read and forward machine data. In this paper, we present a concept
and a prototype to retrofit industrial scenarios using lightweight web
technologies on the edge. We propose using WebAssembly as a new byte-
code standard that runs on browsers and bare-metal hardware alike, thus
providing a uniform development environment from cloud to edge. We
confirm its applicability by achieving near-native performance together
with modularity known from container-based service architectures. Our
prototype is evaluated with a real industrial robot within a showcase
factory, including measurements of data exchange with a state-of-the-art
data lake setup. We are convinced that our groundwork paves the way
to an easier-to-implement and more sustainable Industry 4.0.

Keywords: Industry 4.0 · Retrofitting · Edge computing ·
WebAssembly

1 Introduction

The digital transformation infused by the fourth industrial revolution (Industry 4.0) [14] promises huge opportunities based on new data-driven capabilities.
The concept recommends interconnected information technologies such as Internet of Things (IoT) to exploit previously inaccessible data sources. Data can

Supplementary Information The online version contains supplementary material
available at https://doi.org/10.1007/978-3-031-20891-1_18.

help companies target areas where they can improve their processes to make their manufacturing operations more efficient. By tracking data on energy use, water use, and other resources, companies can identify areas where they can make reductions in their consumption. Lastly, sensors and actuators can be used to address issues of robot-human collaboration. Altogether, Industry 4.0 creates growing pressure on manufacturing companies to quickly transform factories. However, in today's shopfloors, long-term investments in legacy machines without networking capabilities prevail. Replacing an entire machine shop with new equipment is costly, results in unwanted downtime, and is also unsustainable. In particular, SMEs struggle with the upfront cost and implementation challenges associated with smart manufacturing settings. *Retrofitting* refers to the low-cost upgrade of existing equipment [32]. It allows for efficient upgrades by attaching devices, enabling rapid modernization and extending the life of machines. For instance, by monitoring the vibrations of legacy machines with cheap sensors, machine learning models are able to predict breakdowns caused by faulty parts [2]. In addition, existing production lines and know-how can continue to be used without retraining employees.

In practice, it is not easy to retrofit production lines, as they consist of different control systems and electromechanical components [8]. There is currently no one-stop solution that can be deployed in a modular and uniform manner. Existing retrofitting examples are either specialized on a particular use case (e.g., [8,21]) or too general (e.g., the commercial *Bosch XDK*[1]); both cannot be easily fitted to custom use cases with heterogeneous machine interfaces. Web technologies, in turn, are excellent in addressing device heterogeneity. For instance; JavaScript runs on front- and backend alike. However, JavaScript is not ideal for running on microcontrollers, as features such as dynamic typing incur a large overhead. We therefore propose the use of WebAssembly (in the following, we use the term's abbreviation Wasm interchangeably) [34]. It is a low-level language with a compact binary format that gets processed with near-native performance in a sandboxed execution environment. Although WebAssembly is a relatively new technology, it is already utilized for many use cases like serverless computing [10,23], and resource-constrained embedded systems [12].

In this paper, we present retrofitting with Wasm and investigate its capability to access machine interfaces and performing data processing tasks on the edge. Our architecture follows a state-of-the-art data lake setup, involving edge-based sensors, a cloud-based message broker, and a time-series database for long-term storage. We describe the conceptual design, demonstrate the implementation and analyze it using a laptop, a single-board computer, and a microcontroller in a real-life setting in a showcase factory. The structure of this paper is as follows. First, Sect. 2 presents related work, discussing challenges of retrofitting and a technical background on Wasm. The conceptual design is subject of Sect. 3. Section 4 discusses the performance of our prototype. Finally, Sect. 5 concludes the paper and discusses possible future research directions.

---

[1] cf. https://developer.bosch.com/products-and-services/sdks/xdk.

2   Related Work

Industrial applications for data processing and control systems require latencies that distant cloud-based services cannot offer. Edge computing is a paradigm for data processing that takes place at or near the edge of a network, as opposed to in a centralized data center. Commonly, it is associated with the Internet of Things, especially when it comes to sensors and actuators [5]. The edge paradigm is also suitable for real-time data analytics tasks [28], like Edge AI [30]. Therefore, an edge architecture with processing power next to industrial machines is a prime target for retrofitting industrial machines. In the following, we first look at use cases and systems for retrofitting. We then discuss WebAssembly as runtime for edge-oriented data processing.

2.1   Retrofitting in Industry

Instead of buying new equipment, retrofitting can meet digitalization demands by installing cost-effective devices and sensors on existing machines. It allows for seamless updates when technology advances and thereby extends the machine's life [32], rendering it particularly effective for SMEs [1,15]. Sustainability including economic, environmental and social aspects is mentioned as a major reason for retrofitting by Ilari et al. [11]. The authors present a methodology to evaluate new purchase vs. smart upgrades and discuss different types of retrofitting. A review by Jaspert et al. criticizes that despite obvious reasons, sustainability aspects are largely neglected by academic literature [13].

Guerreiro et al. [8] mention that many old industrial parks are not technologically prepared for the concepts of Industry 4.0. In a testbed, they installed external embedded devices for a tool wear measurement of a drilling process in an actual manufacturing plant. The measurement results are stored in a database, and employees can get real-time data with augmented reality (AR) glasses. AR glasses are also the target of another study by Mourtzis et al. [25]. Lins and Rabelo Oliveira [21] propose the standardization of retrofitting based on the RAMI 4.0 architecture for cyber-physical production systems [4]. They modernize the robot arm ED-7220C from ED Corporation by using the Linux-based single-board computer Beagle Bone Blue (BBBlue), the Open Platform Communications Unified Architecture (OPC-UA) for communication, and the programming language Python. As a result, the retrofit brought improvements in energy consumption and response time. However, the suitability for other industrial equipment is not explained in detail, and the heterogeneity of the machines is not fully considered.

Amongst commercial solutions, *Bosch XDK* is a prototyping board including various sensors and wireless network interfaces costing around €200. One of the advertised use cases is its mounting on a robotic arm to capture motion data over its built-in gyroscope, and forward it to a database in the cloud. To the best of our knowledge, there is no uniform, standardized way to tackle retrofitting. Either solutions are too specific, targeting a one-of-its-kind use case, or they are too general, merely acceptable for prototyping. We postulate that the further adoption of retrofitting is also hindered by a lack of ready-made toolkits and software development kits. In the next section, we analyze the recent WebAssembly byte code standard that is able to run on different hardware platforms and is therefore a good candidate for edge-oriented sensor data processing.

2.2   WebAssembly and Its Use Cases

WebAssembly [9] is a portable compact binary format that gets processed with near-native performance in a sandbox environment. Wasm can be compiled from many programming languages[2]. This feature allows software written in multiple high-level programming languages to run on the web. The WebAssembly Text Format (WAT), is a human-readable format available to see the compilation results. Listing 1.1 shows an exemplary "add" function.

Listing 1.1. WebAssembly text format: *Add* example [26]

```
1  (module
2    (func (export "add") (param i32 i32) (result i32)
3      local.get 0
4      local.get 1
5      i32.add))
```

The basic unit of code in WebAssembly, both binary and WAT, is a module [26]. Wasm's design places particular emphasis on portability and security, and Wasm binaries are developed to run in an isolated environment independent of the device's system environment. The WebAssembly System Interface (WASI) extension allows Wasm to interact with the underlying operating system.

AssemblyScript (AS) is a strict variant of TypeScript for Wasm (https://www.assemblyscript.org/). Developers can write code with the syntax of JavaScript or TypeScript, both of which are highly popular programming languages [7]. Since AS is compiled into statically typed Wasm binaries ahead of time, dynamic typing is not usable. As Wasm runs without parsing and re-optimizing, its execution is faster than JavaScript. In particular, one must give explicit types for arguments and outputs of functions. Therefore, compiling from TypeScript or JavaScript to the low-level language is not possible, i.e., any libraries for them are incompatible.

While WebAssembly was first designed for applications with high processing requirements in the web browser, its use has now spread into non-browser applications such as serverless computing and Internet of Things. Due to its memory and execution safety guarantees, WebAssembly is inherently tailored to short-lived functions for serverless applications. For instance, Hall and Ramachandran present a runtime [10], but the framework does not integrate dynamic deployment capabilities. *Sledge* is an optimized runtime for serverless functions running with WebAssembly [6]. A performance benchmark is presented by Mendki, measuring faster startup times compared to service containers, but slower speed than native applications [23]. Similarly, Napieralla [27] investigates performance

---

[2] cf. https://github.com/appcypher/awesome-wasm-langs.

for edge computing. The WASI-based virtualization has an advantage in startup time and size; in contrast, it suffers from overhead during operation. To this end, *Wasmachine* is a WebAssembly operating system with ahead-of-time compilation to native binary that speeds up the execution of commonly-used IoT and fog applications by up to 11% compared to Linux [33]. Other work focuses on binary code analysis for security and language analysis optimizations [19,31]. A number of commercial vendors now offer edge-oriented runtimes for WebAssembly, e.g., *Cloudflare*, *Fastly* and *wasmCloud*.

WebAssembly has been successfully used on wearable devices, like a pulse sensor [12]. Mäkitalo et al. discuss WebAssembly as enabler for liquid Internet of Things applications [22]. Their runtime allows live code migration within IoT settings. The *WiProg* approach has similar goals and uses ESP32 devices and the wasm3 library, like our prototype [20]. A list of projects using WebAssembly is compiled on the *Made with WebAssembly* website[3]. For instance, it contains use cases like CAD, PDF viewers and whole database implementations. The *Awesome Wasm* repository available on GitHub[4] lists a number of runtimes and embeddings outside the browser. However, we are not aware of any related work that employs WebAssembly with industrial machines. Along with the pressure on companies to align their production with sustainability goals, we see enormous potential for this technology. It can offer a way to extend asset-heavy industrial machines using familiar programming languages and tools, to share code between machines in an agile way.

3 Collision Detection System Running with WebAssembly

This section introduces our conceptual design and prototype for retrofitting legacy industrial machines using Wasm. To give background information on our design, we first present our industrial showcase *human-robot collision detection* and derive requirements. For instance, the communication between the device and a machine uses RS-232 as the most common serial interface amongst industrial equipment (alongside RS-422 and RS-485). For our edge device, an RS-232 port or a corresponding converter is necessary. In addition, a runtime for the Wasm module is mandatory on the edge hardware.

3.1 Showcase: Industrial Robot Collision Detection

The class of modern small robotic arms (also called as Cobots) usually has sensors for collision detection and safety measures such as stopping the robot when it hits the human body. However, this is not the case for large robots. Attaching communication devices, sensors, and cameras to such robots allows to collect data needed to calculate the real-time distance between a person and the robot. To measure the real-world applicability of our concept and prototype, we selected

---

[3] cf. https://madewithwebassembly.com/.
[4] cf. https://github.com/mbasso/awesome-wasm.

Gantry robot
with linear axis

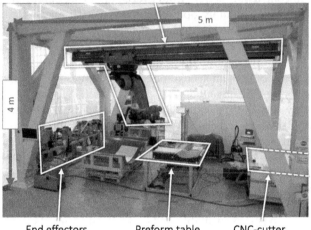

End effectors   Preform table   CNC-cutter

Fig. 1. Preform workshop with industrial robot.

the use case of a robotic arm within a demonstration factory at the institute for textile engineering at our university. Figure 1 shows the workshop, a KUKA KR-150-2 robot arm [16] and a KR C2 controller. The robot's movement area is five meters wide and four meters high, as it assists humans in moving textile material between preform table and CNC-cutter. It has six axes and is designed for a maximum load of 150 kg. The stretched arm's length is 2700 mm. KR C2 runs a program written in KUKA Robot Language to get and send axis values in byte sequences over a RS-232 9-Pin D-Sub serial port. The controller has a submit interpreter to perform other tasks in parallel with the main task. The device receives values of axes as byte sequences and converts them to numeric types.

In the current setup, an anti-collision system for the robot KUKA KR 150-2 is running on a standalone PC developed in Java. The system uses an infrared camera and a time-of-flight camera to locate the person's position and then uses the axis data sent from the robot's controller to calculate the distance. Since the robot is moving between sending these data and the stop order, a safety distance must be kept from workers. This distance that depends on the communication latency and the calculation speed is proportional to the robot's speed. If the current minimal space falls below the distance, the systems stops the robot. One of the main problems with this implementation is latency. It needs an impractical long safety distance because of the time of the data transmission. The length depends on the movement speed of the robot; it is about 3.6 m for 1 m/s. As humans and robots work in shifts, collaboration is impossible with this latency. The used robot is a typical legacy machine that requires serial communication for sending data. For these reasons, this use case fits to realize and demonstrate the retrofitting using WebAssembly. We implement the transmission of axis data of the KUKA robot using an inexpensive device and calculate the distance between the arm and an object for collision prevention in the same environment.

3.2 Requirements for Retrofitting with Edge Devices

Based on the general motivation of data-intensive Industry 4.0 use cases, and the capabilities needed for retrofitting, we derive the following requirements:

Low-level Hardware Access: Many aged industrial Programmable Logic Controllers (PLCs) provide at least a serial communication interface. Therefore, any retrofitting framework must be able to interface with it.

Networking Interface: In order to be able to forward the acquired sensor data, (wireless) communication interfaces must be available.

Agile Updates: The fast-changing smart manufacturing landscape requires rapid update cycles resulting in, e.g., software improvements and bugfixing.

Standard-based Solution: Our top-most premise is a lightweight approach leading to a more usable, more useful, and less fragmented Internet of Things. This excludes proprietary runtimes and libraries.

Our design should be capable of standardizing the serial data format before forwarding. This conversion is required as one of the tasks to be performed by the device. Finally, the processed data is stored in a data lake, a data repository in which raw data from sources are stored without structuring [29]. However, network communication is power- and resource-consuming and can be a heavy burden for less powerful devices. Therefore, the communication overhead must be as low as possible. The program for the device must be lightweight enough to run in a restricted environment.

As shown in the previous section, industrial machines can be retrofitted by proprietary embedded systems, but these do not offer the demanded flexibility. To realize agile changes in manufacturing, we intend to build on the strength of web technologies regarding heterogeneous device access. To this end, we consider WebAssembly an effective means for the computation of edge devices due to its size and performance.

3.3 Conceptual Architecture

Figure 2 shows the conceptual architecture for retrofitting an industrial robot. The workflow of can be divided into three phases: data reading through serial communication, data processing, and data transmission. Generally, industrial machinery employs Programmable Logic Controllers (PLCs). The controller also manages data transmission and reception; it reads the data from the machine and sends it to the device through the serial port. Thus, our device communicates with the PLC. Usually, the controller's task is implemented using a controller-specific programming language. The device connected to the serial port monitors its interface and detects data arrival. The received data is filtered, structured, and computed, before the results are sent via MQTT. On the data lake side, to account for many machines sending data in parallel, our design employs software for data stream ingestion.

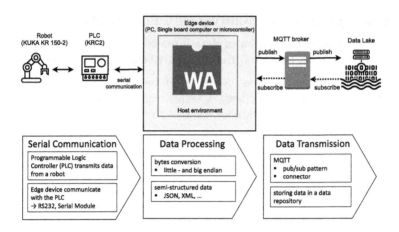

Fig. 2. Conceptual retrofitting architecture.

3.4 Realization

We implemented prototypes for single-board computers and microcontrollers as open source software[5]. As single-board computer, we use a Raspberry Pi 4 with Raspberry Pi OS, a 1.5 GHz quad-core CPU, and 8 GB of RAM (around €30). The used microcontroller is an ESP32, often used for IoT projects (around €4). Despite its low cost, it has a dual-core CPU, 512 KB of RAM, and 4 MB of flash memory. WASI does not yet support I/O and network sockets, we thus decided to bypass it by using a Wasm runtime that provides respective interfaces. Our prototype for Raspberry Pi uses a NodeJS runtime. The restricted microcontroller is insufficient for a full JavaScript engine, the binary code therefore runs with the wasm3 interpreter (https://github.com/wasm3).

Single-Board Computer Host. Figure 3 shows the component diagram of the single-board computer host implementation. To run the Wasm module on NodeJS, it needs to be instantiated. The *AssemblyScript Loader* based on *Wasm JavaScript API* (https://www.w3.org/TR/wasm-js-api-2/) performs instantiation and memory operations. The exchange of high-level data types such as strings between JavaScript and Wasm uses a shared linear memory. Our prototype uses the *as-bind* library (https://github.com/torch2424/as-bind) to simplify the exchange of high-level data types. A `SerialPort` (https://serialport.io/) instance is used to access the USB port. Our implementation that uses AssemblyScript for data processing handles data conversion from bytes to number, error value detection, and creating JSON data. Each time the serial communication event listener detects new data, it calls a method in the Wasm module. The implementation of sending data uses MQTT.js (https://github.com/mqttjs/MQTT.js).

---

[5] cf. https://github.com/internet-of-production/WasmRetrofittingESP32

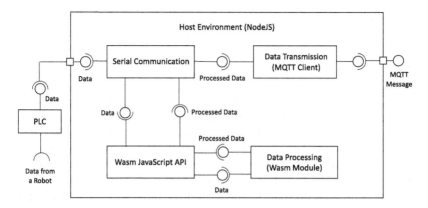

Fig. 3. Components of the edge device implementation for single-board computer

Microcontroller Host. We wrote the runtime host for the microcontroller in the Arduino programming language. The implementation uses wasm3, a library of the WebAssembly interpreter for Arduino. Regarding their tasks, there is no difference to the single-board host. However, the Wasm file for a single-board computer is not runnable on a microcontroller because the AssemblyScript Loader targets only the NodeJS environment. Besides, supporting the AS standard library by wasm3 is not complete; for example, two-dimensional arrays declared like `Array<Array<f64>>` cause an allocation out of the defined memory. Therefore, we implemented the distance calculation and the JSON conversion in other ways for our use case. In future versions of the library, this distinction will likely change and enable fully isomorphic code [24] between all hosts.

`Serial` included in the Arduino programming language standard library is used to communicate with the controller. If data arrives, it calls the Wasm module with the corresponding call function. The conversion of JSON data uses methods written in the Arduino programming language because the conversion targeting String and the concatenation of String in AS are not fully supported by the interpreter yet. After converting the byte data, Wasm passes the keys and values for JSON to Arduino. In this process, it passes pointers and uses a method written in C++ that converts a string with a fixed length of UTF-16 to UTF-8. Also, by using this method, a string of JSON data, including settings such as SSID and broker IP for WiFi and MQTT connections, is passed from Wasm to Arduino. Instead of `Array` types, we use `load` and `store` functions. WiFiClientSecure, a library of the Arduino core for the ESP32, is used for the network connection using TLS, and PubSubClient (https://pubsubclient. knolleary.net/) is used for MQTT communication.

Data Stream Ingestion. The edge device sends processed data to the MQTT broker; our implementation uses the open-source *Eclipse Mosquitto*. It is only used as a middleware between the client and server, making a data stream ingestion mechanism in the cloud necessary to cope with the expected high amount of data. We use an Apache Kafka endpoint, which is a popular open-source distributed messaging system (https://kafka.apache.org/). It is used for handling high throughput, low latency messaging. In order to receive data from Mosquitto, Kafka must subscribe to a specific topic. Therefore, we connected it to the open-source *Fluentd* (https://www.fluentd.org/) as data collector. Fluentd has high throughput and low resource consumption, and more than 500 community-contributed plugins are available. The plugins used here are fluent-plugin-kafka (https://github.com/fluent/fluent-plugin-kafka) and Fluent::Plugin::Mqtt::IO (https://github.com/toyokazu/fluent-plugin-mqtt-io). We deployed InfluxDB (https://www.influxdata.com/) as time-series database in the data lake. Fluentd also connects Kafka and the data lake with the plugin influxdb-plugin-fluent (https://github.com/influxdata/influxdb-plugin-fluent). Furthermore, our prototype uses Docker containers and Kubernetes, an open-source container orchestration; Kafka, InfluxDB, and Fluentd are deployed in our cloud cluster.

In this section, we discussed the conceptual design and prototype realization for the microcontroller and single-board hosts. Currently, the runtime of the former has a number of limitations making slightly different byte code necessary. We expect this limitation to cease soon, once the runtimes get settled and fully implemented. In the next section, we discuss the evaluation of our prototypes.

4   Evaluation of WebAssembly on the Edge

This section evaluates our implementation in a production setting. First, we measured the performance of the distance calculation and the required program size. In addition, we tested the round-trip time (RTT) between the edge device and the data lake to evaluate the feasibility of our edge scenario. Finally, we discuss the reusability and limitations of our prototype.

4.1   Performance of the Distance Calculation

We implemented the distance calculation between a point in space and the robot arm's end as a base for collision prevention. This calculation is done with a product of 4×4 matrices according to homogeneous transformation [3,17]. Application performance on edge devices with different computation power was investigated; a laptop is an example with sufficient computation power (running the single-board computer implementation), Raspberry Pi is a lightly restricted hardware, and ESP32 is a strictly limited device example. The used laptop was a MacBook Pro 2020 with macOS Big Sur version 11.2.1, a 1.4 GHz Quad-Core processor, and 16 GB of RAM. The KRC2 sends each axis data numbered one to six and external one separately but in a fixed order every loop. Since all the axis data is needed to calculate the spatial coordinates of the robot, it checks the number of saved items after every reading and conversion cycle. In this computation, we used a simulation of previously recorded data that we replayed via serial communication. The data were randomly generated within the specified value range and therefore contained no errors; ESP32 sent bytes at the measurement on the laptop and the Raspberry Pi 4, and a JavaScript program transmitted values through the USB port for the microcontroller. The laptop executed the single-board computer implementation. We sent the machine data 100 times for each device. It did not perform JSON conversion and transmission of the results during these measurements. Table 1 shows the measurements.

Table 1. Time measurements of distance calculation on three device types.

Device	Messages #	Average (ms)	First Call (Max.) (ms)
Laptop	100	0.230	1.451
RasPi	100	1.060	5.800
ESP32	100	3.093	9.576

On average, the laptop was the fastest at 0.23 ms, the Raspberry Pi 4 at 1.06 ms, and the ESP32 consumed about three times the average processing time of Raspberry Pi. The maximum processing time is due to the first call of the function. NodeJS, an execution environment built on V8, a JS engine that performs JIT compilation, and wasm3, an interpreter, decode and compile Wasm when calling the function. These runtimes cause the overhead of calling function but Wasm does not need the optimization by a JIT compiler.

In the implementation of our previous work, 1 ms is required in proportion to the number of spheres to reflect the axis values to the robot model. The time required to calculate the distance between the robot's end and a fixed point in space using the Raspberry Pi in this paper is 1.06 ms on average. Assuming the calculation is in proportion to the number of coordinate points set on robot parts, the same level of processing speed is achievable by using Wasm.

4.2   Storage Usage of Our Program

The single-board computer host requires NodeJS, which takes about 100 MB to install, and the Wasm file is 22 KB in size, including both JSON conversion and coordinate calculation. The main JS file is 4 KB, but the dependencies require a large 26.6 MB. The implementation for microcontrollers uses about 800 KB of ESP32 external flash. The size of the written program is about 750 KB, and the global variables are about 50 KB. Since the overall capacity for storing variables is 320 KB and reserved, the remaining flash memory of approximately 2.9 MB is available for RAM and the file system.

4.3   Latency Between Edge and Data Lake

We measured the round-trip time between the device connected to the KRC2 and Apache Kafka running in the data lake to confirm the need for edge computing in the highly latency-sensitive collision use case. A cable connected to the RS-232 serial port, further extended by a USB converter cable, linked the KRC2 and the edge device. Sending messages from the device to a local laptop used MQTTS. HTTPS was used between the computer and the data lake. Each device subscribed to a specific topic to record the arrival time of the response.

First, we executed the single-board computer host implementation on the local laptop to perform the measurements. In this case, Eclipse Mosquitto and Fluentd ran on the same platform. Second, we measured the RTT with a Raspberry Pi 4. The MQTT messages were sent to the broker on the laptop through the Ethernet cable. The on-site download speed was 82 Mbps, and the upload speed was 76 Mbps at the time of measurement, but the rate was not always stable. The average RTT was about 60 ms for both edge devices. In the previous work, all collision prevention processes were done at the machine, and the RTT from the data transmission to the stop operation were around 50 ms in total. Therefore, an improvement of the response time with calculating at the centralized data lake is impossible.

4.4   Reusability and Limitations of Our Prototype

The implementation based on NodeJS uses only JavaScript and AssemblyScript. AS also uses the Node project environment with common tools such as the Node package manager (npm). In particular, as-bind enables the exchange of high-level data types between the two languages, thus simplifying programming. We realized JSON conversion and distance calculation using only AssemblyScript. Therefore, if the same execution engine is available, the Wasm file is reusable. Furthermore, when calling new external functions in JavaScript, it is possible to import them by simply using modules of Wasm instances. The AS library provides a developer-friendly coding environment, and using it can simplify and improve the readability of source code, but it also creates dependencies. The implementation for microcomputers using wasm3 does not include dependencies on such language-specific libraries. However, the interpreter is still under development and does not fully support all the possibilities of AS. For example, developers using two-dimensional arrays for matrix calculation have to manage linear memory using store and load functions due to opcode detection issues.

Our prototype shares common limitations of WebAssembly. For example, Wasm does currently not allow hardware-specific features like GPU-based matrix multiplication [10]. Although ESP32 has a dual-core processor, the runtime does not support threads. Wasm uses linear memory and does not support unmapped pages, so any read or write within the allocated space will succeed; an attacker does not need to consider page faults at the memory access [18].

The results of our evaluation, especially with regard to latency to the data lake, must be taken with a grain of salt. Collision detection frameworks using machine learning will inevitably have different requirements, which in turn will lead to adapted recommendations for placement at the edge or in the cloud. For instance, we did not perform long-term operations over several weeks and in changing environmental conditions like hot temperatures, which may lead to overheating issues with our microcontroller hardware. Our showcase study clearly focuses on the KUKA industrial robot. However, its communication architecture with an attached PLC is a well-established pattern in machine shops. We are therefore confident that results are transferable to other production equipment; we are currently targeting further use cases within the workshops of our university and associated industry partners.

5 Conclusions

In this paper, we presented a conceptual design and prototypical implementation of retrofitting industrial machines on the edge using WebAssembly. To the best of our knowledge, it is the first open implementation using WebAssembly to make data available directly from proprietary, legacy industrial machines that do not have an own network connection. Our prototype uses AssemblyScript and the associated binding generator to pass high-level structures between the runtime and the Wasm module. Because certain features of AssemblyScript are not supported by the wasm3 interpreter, we added the necessary bindings with function calls written in C++ and Arduino. By comparing devices with distance calculation times, we found that the first function call caused overhead on all of them due to the interpreter and the JIT compiler, which an ahead-of-time compiler could improve [33]. Running Wasm on the Raspberry Pi showed that the byte code has near-native performance for our distance calculation. As future work, we plan to extend our showcase to other industrial machines within our demonstration factory. In addition to that, evaluation for more complex calculations and longer operation time is needed. The WASI standard will likely become the backbone of our implementation work, once socket connections are available. We are confident that WebAssembly will become a core component in data processing pipelines, as it can target any place in the edge-cloud continuum. In the long run, Wasm can become the catalyst in achieving a uniform development and deployment environment for Industry 4.0 and beyond.

Acknowledgement. Funded by the Deutsche Forschungsgemeinschaft (DFG, German Research Foundation) under Germany's Excellence Strategy - EXC-2023 Internet of Production - 390621612.

References

1. Burresi, G., et al.: Smart retrofitting by design thinking applied to an industry 4.0 migration process in a steel mill plant. In: 2020 9th Mediterranean Conference on Embedded Computing (MECO) (2020). https://doi.org/10.1109/MECO49872. 2020.9134210
2. Carvalho, T.P., Soares, F., Vita, R., Da Francisco, R.P., Basto, J.P., Alcalá, S.G.S.: A systematic literature review of machine learning methods applied to predictive maintenance. Comput. Indus. Eng. **137**, 106024 (2019). https://doi.org/10.1016/j.cie.2019.106024
3. Craig, J.J.: Introduction to Robotics: Mechanics and Control, 3rd edn. Pearson-/Prentice Hall, Hoboken (2005)

4. DIN: 91345: reference architecture model industrie 4.0 (RAMI4.0) (2016)
5. Dustdar, S., Murturi, I.: Towards IoT processes on the edge. In: Aiello, M., Bouguettaya, A., Tamburri, D.A., van den Heuvel, W.-J. (eds.) Next-Gen Digital Services. A Retrospective and Roadmap for Service Computing of the Future. LNCS, vol. 12521, pp. 167–178. Springer, Cham (2021). https://doi.org/10.1007/978-3-030-73203-5_13
6. Gadepalli, P.K., McBride, S., Peach, G., Cherkasova, L., Parmer, G.: SLEdge: a serverless-first, light-weight wasm runtime for the Edge. In: Proceedings of the 21st International Middleware Conference, pp. 265–279. ACM, Delft Netherlands (2020). https://doi.org/10.1145/3423211.3425680
7. GitHub Inc: the state of the Octoverse (2020). https://octoverse.github.com
8. Guerreiro, B.V., Lins, R.G., Sun, J., Schmitt, R.: Definition of smart retrofitting: first steps for a company to deploy aspects of industry 4.0. In: Hamrol, A., Ciszak, O., Legutko, S., Jurczyk, M. (eds.) Advances in Manufacturing. LNME, pp. 161–170. Springer, Cham (2018). https://doi.org/10.1007/978-3-319-68619-6_16
9. Haas, A., et al.: Bringing the web up to speed with WebAssembly. In: Cohen, A., Vechev, M. (eds.) Proceedings of the 38th ACM SIGPLAN Conference on Programming Language Design and Implementation - PLDI 2017, pp. 185–200. ACM Press, New York (2017). https://doi.org/10.1145/3062341.3062363
10. Hall, A., Ramachandran, U.: An execution model for serverless functions at the edge. In: Landsiedel, O., Nahrstedt, K. (eds.) Proceedings of the International Conference on Internet of Things Design and Implementation, pp. 225–236. ACM, New York, NY, USA (2019). https://doi.org/10.1145/3302505.3310084
11. Ilari, S., Carlo, F.D., Ciarapica, F.E., Bevilacqua, M.: Machine tool transition from industry 3.0 to 4.0: a comparison between old machine retrofitting and the purchase of new machines from a triple bottom line perspective. Sustainability **13**(18), 10441 (2021). https://doi.org/10.3390/su131810441
12. Jacobsson, M., Willén, J.: Virtual machine execution for wearables based on WebAssembly. In: Sugimoto, C., Farhadi, H., Hämäläinen, M. (eds.) BODYNETS 2018. EICC, pp. 381–389. Springer, Cham (2020). https://doi.org/10.1007/978-3-030-29897-5_33
13. Jaspert, D., Ebel, M., Eckhardt, A., Poeppelbuss, J.: Smart retrofitting in manufacturing: a systematic review. J. Clean. Prod. **312**, 127555 (2021). https://doi.org/10.1016/j.jclepro.2021.127555
14. Kargermann, H., Wahlster, W., Helbig, J.: Recommendations for implementing the strategic initiative INDUSTRIE 4.0: final report of the INDUSTRIE 4.0 working group (2013). https://en.acatech.de/wp-content/uploads/sites/6/2018/03/Final_report__Industrie_4.0_accessible.pdf
15. Kolla, S.S.V.K., Lourenço, D.M., Kumar, A.A., Plapper, P.: Retrofitting of legacy machines in the context of industrial internet of things (IIoT). Proc. Comput. Sci. **200**, 62–70 (2022). https://doi.org/10.1016/j.procs.2022.01.205
16. KUKA Roboter GmbH: KUKA Serie 2000: the all-rounders in the high payload range (2020). https://www.kuka.com/-/media/kuka-downloads/imported/6b77eecacfe542d3b736af377562ecaa/pf0020_kr_1502_en.pdf
17. LaValle, S.M.: Planning Algorithms. Cambridge University Press, Cambridge (2006). https://doi.org/10.1017/CBO9780511546877
18. Lehmann, D., Kinder, J., Pradel, M.: Everything old is new again: binary security of WebAssembly. In: 29th USENIX Security Symposium (USENIX Security 20), pp. 217–234. USENIX Association (2020)

19. Lehmann, D., Pradel, M.: Wasabi: a framework for dynamically analyzing WebAssembly. In: Bahar, I., et al. (eds.) Proceedings of the Twenty-Fourth International Conference on Architectural Support for Programming Languages and Operating Systems, pp. 1045–1058. ACM, New York (2019). https://doi.org/10.1145/3297858.3304068
20. Li, B., Dong, W., Gao, Y.: WiProg: a WebAssembly-based approach to integrated IoT programming. In: IEEE INFOCOM 2021 - IEEE Conference on Computer Communications, pp. 1–10. IEEE (2021). https://doi.org/10.1109/INFOCOM42981.2021.9488424
21. Lins, T., Rabelo Oliveira, R.A.: Cyber-physical production systems retrofitting in context of industry 4.0. Comput. Indus. Eng. **139**, 106193 (2020). https://doi.org/10.1016/j.cie.2019.106193
22. Mäkitalo, N., et al.: WebAssembly modules as lightweight containers for liquid IoT applications. In: Brambilla, M., Chbeir, R., Frasincar, F., Manolescu, I. (eds.) ICWE 2021. LNCS, vol. 12706, pp. 328–336. Springer, Cham (2021). https://doi.org/10.1007/978-3-030-74296-6_25
23. Mendki, P.: Evaluating Webassembly enabled serverless approach for edge computing. In: 2020 IEEE Cloud Summit, pp. 161–166. IEEE, Harrisburg (2020). https://doi.org/10.1109/IEEECloudSummit48914.2020.00031
24. Mikkonen, T., Pautasso, C., Taivalsaari, A.: Isomorphic internet of things architectures with web technologies. Computer **54**(7), 69–78 (2021). https://doi.org/10.1109/MC.2021.3074258
25. Mourtzis, D., Angelopoulos, J., Panopoulos, N.: Recycling and retrofitting for industrial equipment based on augmented reality. Proc. CIRP **90**, 606–610 (2020). https://doi.org/10.1016/j.procir.2020.02.134
26. Mozilla and individual contributors: understanding WebAssembly text format (2021). https://developer.mozilla.org/en-US/docs/WebAssembly/Understanding_the_text_format
27. Napieralla, J.: Considering WebAssembly containers for edge computing on hardware-constrained IoT devices. Master thesis, Blekinge Institute of Technology, Karlskrona, Sweden (2020). https://www.diva-portal.org/smash/get/diva2:1451494/FULLTEXT02
28. Nastic, S., et al.: A serverless real-time data analytics platform for edge computing. IEEE Internet Comput. **21**(4), 64–71 (2017). https://doi.org/10.1109/MIC.2017.2911430
29. Quix, C., Hai, R.: Data lake. In: Sakr, S., Zomaya, A. (eds.) Encyclopedia of Big Data Technologies, pp. 1–8. Springer, Cham (2018). https://doi.org/10.1007/978-3-319-63962-8_7-1
30. Rausch, T., Hummer, W., Muthusamy, V., Rashed, A., Dustdar, S.: Towards a serverless platform for edge AI. In: 2nd USENIX Workshop on Hot Topics in Edge Computing (HotEdge 19). USENIX Association, Renton, WA (2019)
31. Stievenart, Q., de Roover, C.: Compositional information flow analysis for WebAssembly programs. In: 2020 IEEE 20th International Working Conference on Source Code Analysis and Manipulation (SCAM), pp. 13–24. IEEE (2020). https://doi.org/10.1109/SCAM51674.2020.00007

32. Stock, T., Seliger, G.: Opportunities of sustainable manufacturing in industry 4.0. Proc. CIRP **40**, 536–541 (2016). https://doi.org/10.1016/j.procir.2016.01.129
33. Wen, E., Weber, G.: Wasmachine: bring iot up to speed with a WebAssembly OS. In: 2020 IEEE International Conference on Pervasive Computing and Communications Workshops (PerCom Workshops), pp. 1–4. IEEE (2020). https://doi.org/10.1109/PerComWorkshops48775.2020.9156135
34. World Wide Web Consortium: WebAssembly Core Specification (2019). https://www.w3.org/TR/wasm-core-1/

Graph Data Management

Attention-Based Relation Prediction of Knowledge Graph by Incorporating Graph and Context Features

Shanna Zhong[1,2], Kun Yue[1,2(✉)], and Liang Duan[1,2]

[1] School of Information Science and Engineering, Yunnan University,
Kunming, China
zsn@mail.ynu.edu.cn, {kyue,duanl}@ynu.edu.cn
[2] Yunnan Key Laboratory of Intelligent Systems and Computing, Kunming, China

Abstract. As the vital resource for various applications like question answering and recommendation system, knowledge graph (KG) often suffers from incompleteness. The task of relation prediction in KG aims to infer the relations between entities, which depend on the structure of the query-specific subgraph but also the neighborhood as context. In this paper, we propose an attention-based joint model for relation prediction by incorporating the graph and context features of entities and relations. First, we extract the subgraph and entity context from KG, and adopt the attention mechanism to capture the most relevant graph and context features, which we leverage to generate the enhanced representations. Then, we give the joint loss function to guarantee the unified representation including the relevant graph and context features simultaneously. Finally, we fulfill model training for relation prediction. Experimental results on real-world datasets demonstrate that our proposed approach outperforms the state-of-the-art competitors.

Keywords: Knowledge graph · Relation prediction · Attention mechanism · Context feature · Representation learning

1 Introduction

Knowledge graph (KG) is a kind of directed graph, which contains nodes denoting entities and edges denoting relationships [1]. A fact in KG is expressed as a triplet (h, r, t), where r indicates a relationship between head entity h and tail entity t. In recent years, a variety of large-scale KGs have been created, such as Freebase [2], Wordnet [3] and YAGO [4]. KG has been beneficial for many artificial intelligence tasks [5], including recommendation systems [6,7] and question answering [8,9]. However, KG often suffers from incompleteness [10,11], since there exist unknown relations between entities in KG, as well as numerous entities outside KG with missing relations to the entities inside KG. To this end, researchers propose various approaches for relation prediction to discover new relations between entities. From the practical perspective of relation prediction

© The Author(s), under exclusive license to Springer Nature Switzerland AG 2022
R. Chbeir et al. (Eds.): WISE 2022, LNCS 13724, pp. 259–273, 2022.
https://doi.org/10.1007/978-3-031-20891-1_19

of KG, the relations could be unknown for the entities inside or outside KG. As shown in Fig. 1, the relation between *Steve Jobs* and *Bill Gates* (inside KG) is unknown, while the relation between *Satya Nadella* (outside KG) and *Bill Gates* is unknown. Thus, it is necessary to predict the missing relations between entities no matter they are inside or outside KG.

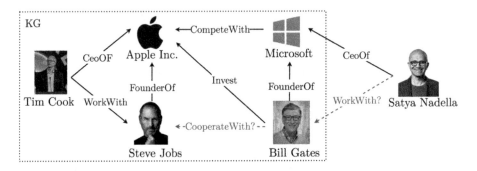

Fig. 1. An example of relation prediction. Dark solid lines represent relations between entities. Red dash lines represent relations to be predicted. (Color figure online)

In the past few years, a large amount of knowledge graph embedding (KGE) methods [12–14] have been proposed to relation prediction successfully. These methods intend to learn low-dimensional embedding vectors of each entity and relation by minimizing a predefined loss function on all embeddings, so that the geometric operations over these embeddings could be used to detect new knowledge. However, most of them treat the triplets in KG individually, ignoring the association among them. Some approaches [21–24] attempt to incorporate external resources, like text description and types of entities, to predict relations between entities by additional computations on external resources. Some researchers [25–30] find graph or context feature around entities and relations critical for relation prediction, but only use either graph or context feature, which may lead to information loss.

Different kinds of surrounding information of entities and relations carry different surrounding features. For instance, as shown in Fig. 1, the graph of (*Satya Nadella, ?, Bill Gates*) and (*Tim Cook, WorkWith, Bill Gates*) have similar graph structures, which indicate that these two graphs may share similar interactions. Moreover, *Bill Gates* has two neighbors *Microsoft* and *Apple Inc.* and *Satya Nadella* has one neighbor *Microsoft*. These contexts indicate that there may exist a relation between *Bill Gates* and *Satya Nadella* as they share a common neighbor *Microsoft*. The ability of new fact mining could be improved if the graph and context features are considered simultaneously, since graph contains logical evidence and context contains syntactic interactions concerned in relation prediction.

It is known that the attention mechanism [20] enables the model to assign the highest weight to the most relevant information. As shown in Fig. 2, we consequently propose an attention-based model by incorporating both graph and context features to find new relations between entities w.r.t. the query triplet including at least one entity in KG. First, we extract the subgraph of the triplet to obtain its corresponding graph feature, which is aggregated into the representation of the head, tail and relation, respectively. By this way, the graph-enhanced representation of each entity and relation could be obtained. Next, we use the attention mechanism to obtain the most relevant context, since not all the contexts have important impacts on relation prediction. Thus, the context-enhanced representation of entities could be learned via merging these weighted contexts. Then, we give the joint loss function to guarantee that the most relevant graph and context features could be described by the unified representation of entities and relations. Finally, we fulfill model training for relation prediction.

Generally, our contributions are summarized as follows:

- We give the attention-based aggregation strategy to obtain the two kinds of enhanced representations via leveraging the surrounding graph and context features respectively.
- We give the joint loss function to achieve the unified representation of entities and relations to describe the most relevant graph and context features simultaneously.
- We conduct experiments to demonstrate that our method outperforms some state-of-the-art competitors for relation prediction.

The rest of this paper is organized as follows: Sect. 2 introduces related work. Section 3 presents our methodology. Section 4 shows experiments and performance studies. Section 5 concludes and discusses future work.

2   Related Work

Knowledge Graph Embedding. Knowledge graph embedding [12–19] aims to map entities and relations into continuous vector space to learn corresponding real-valued representation of entities and relations. Most of KGE methods have been successfully applied to relation prediction. TransE [12] learns the embedding of entity and relation by minimizing a predefined scoring function, $f_r(h, t) = -||\mathbf{h} + \mathbf{r} - \mathbf{t}||_2^2$, which indicates that the tail embedding $\mathbf{t}$ should be similar to the sum of head embedding $\mathbf{h}$ and relation embedding $\mathbf{r}$. TransH [13] models relations as hyperplanes and projects head and tail entities to the relational-specific hyperplane to form embeddings. TransR [14] models embeddings of entities and relations in distinct semantic spaces, and then projects entities into corresponding relation space to learn the transformation. These models could be trained easily, but they treat triplets individually, ignoring the rich surrounding information around triplets.

Relation Prediction by Exploiting Text Description. To obtain representation of entities outside KG, some researchers incorporate external resources.

ConMask [21] combines entity name and part of its text-description into entity embedding so as to connect entities outside KG. MIA [22] uses the attention mechanism to learn interactive features between head entity name, head entity description, relation name and candidate tail entity description to form enriched representation. OWE [23] aggregates word embeddings into entity embedding by pre-training and builds a transformation to project the embeddings of an entity name and description into the graph-based embedding space. DKRL [24] explores continuous bag-of-words and deep convolutional neural models to encode semantics of entity descriptions. These approaches could be well generalized to predict the facts with entities outside KG, but require sufficient computation over large additional resources. Moreover, the graph or context features around entities and relations have not been fully used.

Relation Prediction by Exploiting Association Information. Some approaches attempt to find association information inside KG to fulfill relation prediction. OOKB [25] exploits limited contextual knowledge including entity neighbors to compose representation of entity outside KG. AggrE [26] integrates multi-hop contextual information into embedding of each entity and relation respectively. A2N [27] combines graph neighbors around the entity to learn the query-dependent entity representation. SAGNN [28] finds latent association from structural information including in-degree, out-degree and co-occurrence frequency to learn the enriched representation of each entity. GRAIL [29] uses the graph structure of triplets to learn entity-independent relational semantics, which could be generalized to entities outside KG. TACT [30] exploits the topology-aware surrounding between relations in an entity-independent manner under the assumption that the semantic surrounding between two relations is highly correlated to their topological structure in KG. By these methods, external entities could be well incorporated, but only a single type of association information around entities and relations is exploited.

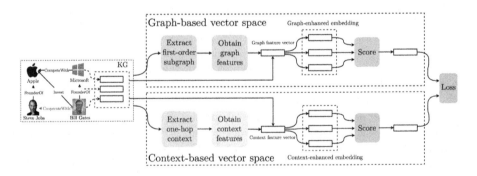

Fig. 2. Framework of our model.

3   Methodology

In this section, we introduce definitions and present our proposed method for relation prediction.

3.1   Definitions and Problem Formulation

First, we give the symbols and notations in Table 1.

Table 1. Notations.

Notation	Description
$\mathcal{G}$	The KG
$\mathcal{E}$	The set of entities in KG
$\mathcal{R}$	The set of relationships in KG
$\mathcal{T}$	The set of positive triplets in KG
$\mathcal{T}_{neg}$	The set of negative triplets not in KG
$\mathcal{G}_{aux}$	The auxiliary KG
$\mathcal{E}_{aux}$	The set of entities in auxiliary KG
$\mathcal{R}_{aux}$	The set of relationships in auxiliary KG
$\mathcal{T}_{aux}$	The set of positive triplets in auxiliary KG
C_e	The set of entity contexts of the given entity e
$\mathcal{G}'_{(h,r,t)}$	The first-order subgraph of the given triplet (h,r,t)
$\mathcal{S}(h_q, r_q, t_q)$	The ranking list of candidate triplets w.r.t. (h_q, r_q, t_q)

Then, we define some concepts as the basis of later discussions.

Definition 1. *A KG is denoted as* $\mathcal{G} = \langle \mathcal{E}, \mathcal{R}, \mathcal{T} \rangle$, *where* $\mathcal{E}$ *and* $\mathcal{R}$ *denote the sets of all entities and relationships in KG respectively, and* $\mathcal{T} = \{(h,r,t) | h \in \mathcal{E}, t \in \mathcal{E}, r \in \mathcal{R}\}$.

Definition 2. *An auxiliary KG is denoted as* $\mathcal{G}_{aux} = \langle \mathcal{E}_{aux}, \mathcal{R}_{aux}, \mathcal{T}_{aux} \rangle$, *where* $\mathcal{E}_{aux} \not\subset \mathcal{E}$, $\mathcal{R}_{aux} \subseteq \mathcal{R}$, *and* $\mathcal{T}_{aux} = \{(h,r,t) | r \in \mathcal{R}_{aux}, (h \in \mathcal{E} \wedge t \notin \mathcal{E}) \vee (h \notin \mathcal{E} \wedge t \in \mathcal{E})\}$.

Definition 3. *The first-order subgraph of the given triplet* (h,r,t) *is denoted as* $\mathcal{G}'_{(h,r,t)} = \langle \mathcal{E}', \mathcal{R}' \rangle$, *where* $\mathcal{E}' \subset \mathcal{E} \cup \mathcal{E}_{aux}$ *is the set of entities directly connected to* h *or* t, *and each edge* $\overline{e_i e_j} \in \mathcal{R}'(e_i, e_j \in \mathcal{E}', i \neq j)$ *indicates the association between* e_i *and* e_j.

Definition 4. *The one-hop entity context of the given entity* e *is denoted as* $C_e = \langle \mathcal{N}_e, \mathcal{N}_{e,t} \rangle$, *where* $\mathcal{N}_e \subset \mathcal{E}$ *is the set of entities directly connected to* e, *and* $\mathcal{N}_{e,t} \subseteq \mathcal{R}$ *is the set of relations between* $e(e \in \mathcal{E} \cup \mathcal{E}_{aux})$ *and* $t(t \in \mathcal{N}_e)$.

We now formulate the problem to be solved in this paper. Given the query triplet (h_q, r_q, t_q), we replace r_q with every r' in KG to generate candidate triplets. For each (h, r, t) as a candidate triplet, we extract its first-order subgraph $\mathcal{G}'_{(h,r,t)}$ and one-hop entity context C_h and C_t. Then, we aggregate $\mathcal{G}'_{(h,r,t)}$, C_h and C_t into the representation of h, r and t respectively to obtain the corresponding graph-enhanced representation and context-enhanced representation. Upon these two kinds of enhanced representations, we calculate the score of each candidate triplet and output the ranking list of candidate triplets $\mathcal{S}(h_q, r_q, t_q)$ w.r.t. the query triplet (h_q, r_q, t_q).

3.2 Graph Feature Learning

We assume that the first-order subgraph contains the most relevant logical information required for relation prediction. Given a triplet (h, r, t), we generate its first-order subgraph $\mathcal{G}'_{(h,r,t)}$ from KG to obtain the graph structure, which could be well represented by the following Laplacian matrix of $\mathcal{G}'_{(h,r,t)}$.

$$\mathbf{M} = \mathbf{D} - (\mathbf{A} + \mathbf{I}) \tag{1}$$

where $\mathbf{M}$, $\mathbf{D}$, $\mathbf{A}$ and $\mathbf{I}$ denote the Laplacian matrix of $\mathcal{G}'_{(h,r,t)}$, degree matrix of $\mathcal{G}'_{(h,r,t)}$, adjacency matrix of $\mathcal{G}'_{(h,r,t)}$ and identity matrix, respectively.

Given two identical head-tail entity pairs, we generate two identical first-order subgraphs. To distinguish the relations in each subgraph, we introduce different relational-specific weight matrixes for different relations. Then, we combine the Laplacian matrix of $\mathcal{G}'_{(h,r,t)}$, the initial embeddings of all the entities in $\mathcal{G}'_{(h,r,t)}$ and the weight matrix of r together to capture the structural interactions between entities. Thus, we give the pooling-based function to obtain the graph feature of $\mathcal{G}'_{(h,r,t)}$ as follows

$$\mathbf{w}_g = Pool(\mathbf{MHW}_r) \tag{2}$$

where $\mathbf{w}_g$, $Pool()$, $\mathbf{H}$ and $\mathbf{W}_r$ denote the representation of $\mathcal{G}'_{(h,r,t)}$, sum-pooling function, initial embedding matrix of all entities in $\mathcal{G}'_{(h,r,t)}$ and relation-specific weight matrix of r, respectively.

As the external entities are unseen in training time, the representation of the external entities largely depend on its corresponding graph feature. Therefore, we give the following function to aggregate the graph feature into the representation of each element e in the triplet (h, r, t), where h and t could be inside or outside KG.

$$\mathbf{e}_g = \mathbf{e} \odot \mathbf{w}_g \odot \mathbf{w}_g \tag{3}$$

where $\mathbf{e}_g$, $\mathbf{e}$ and $\odot$ denote the graph-enhanced embedding of e, initial embedding of e and hadamard product, respectively.

To estimate the score of the given triplet (h, r, t) and model the structure information, we use the following scoring function based on TransE [12].

$$f_g(h, r, t) = -\|\mathbf{h}_g + \mathbf{r}_g - \mathbf{t}_g\|_2^2 \tag{4}$$

where $f_g(h, r, t)$, $\mathbf{h}_g$, $\mathbf{r}_g$ and $\mathbf{t}_g$ denote the score of (h, r, t) over the graph-based vector space, graph-enhanced embedding of h, graph-enhanced embedding of r and graph-enhanced embedding of t, respectively.

3.3 Context Feature Learning

We assume that the one-hop entity context contains the most relevant syntactic associations required for relation prediction. Thus, given an entity e, we select its one-hop entity context C_e from KG to obtain the context feature.

Attention mechanism [20] enables the model to focus on the most relative information w.r.t a specific task. Intuitively, different entities have different impacts on entity, and the weights of different relations between the same head-tail entity pair should be identical. Thus, we give an attention function in Eq. (5) to obtain the attention score of C_e.

$$\mathbf{w}_{c_e} = \frac{1}{|\mathcal{N}_e|} \sum_{t_k \in \mathcal{N}_e} \alpha_{t_k} \mathbf{w}_{t_k}' \tag{5}$$

where α_{t_k} denotes the weight of t_k, and could be computed by Eq. (6)

$$\alpha_{t_k} = \frac{1}{|\mathcal{N}_{e,t_k}|} \sum_{r_i \in \mathcal{N}_{e,t_k}} \mathbf{w}_{r_i} \tag{6}$$

where $\mathbf{w}_{c_e}$, $\mathcal{N}_e$, $|\mathcal{N}_e|$, α_{t_k}, $\mathcal{N}_{e,t_k}$, $|\mathcal{N}_{e,t_k}|$, $\mathbf{w}_{r_i}$, $\mathbf{w}_{t_k}'$ and $\odot$ denote the representation of the one-hop entity context C_e, the set of entities in C_e, the number of $\mathcal{N}_e$, the attention score of t_k, the set of relations between e and t_k, the number of relations in $\mathcal{N}_{e,t_k}$, the weight vector of relation r_i, the weight vector of entity t_k and hadamard product, respectively.

To guarantee our method could be well generalized to external entities, we aggregate the context feature into the representation of each entity. The aggregation function is given as follows

$$\mathbf{e}_c = \mathbf{e} \odot \mathbf{w}_{c_e} \odot \mathbf{w}_{c_e} \tag{7}$$

where $\mathbf{e}_c$, $\mathbf{e}$ and $\odot$ denote the context-enhanced embedding of e, initial embedding of e and hadamard product, respectively.

To calculate the score of the given triplet (h, r, t), we assume that the combinational representation of h and r should be as close as possible to the representation of t in the context-based vector space. Thus, we give a context-aware scoring function in Eq. (8) upon the relational-specific weight matrix of r.

$$f_c(h, r, t) = -\|\mathbf{h}_c \mathbf{W}_r' \mathbf{r} - \mathbf{t}_c \mathbf{W}_r'\|_2^2 \tag{8}$$

where $f_c(h, r, t)$, $\mathbf{h}_c$, $\mathbf{r}$, $\mathbf{W}'_r$ and $\mathbf{t}_c$ denote the score of (h, r, t) over the context-based vector space, context-enhanced embedding of h, initial embedding of r, relational-specific weight matrix of r and context-enhanced embedding of t, respectively.

3.4   Training Algorithm

The hinge loss [31] is a linear learning-to-rank loss function, which requires the score of the positive triplet to be at least γ lower than the score of the negative triplet. Therefore, we construct a group of negative triplets $\mathcal{T}_{neg} = \{(h, r', t) | (h, r', t) \notin \mathcal{T}, h \in \mathcal{E}, t \in \mathcal{E}, r' \in \mathcal{R}\}$ and use the hinge loss over the graph-based vector space, defined as

$$\mathcal{L}_g = \sum_{(h,r,t) \in \mathcal{T}} \sum_{(h,r',t) \in \mathcal{T}_{neg}} \max\{0, f_g(h, r, t) + \gamma - f_g(h, r', t)\} \tag{9}$$

Likewise, the hinge loss over the context-based vector space is expressed as

$$\mathcal{L}_c = \sum_{(h,r,t) \in \mathcal{T}} \sum_{(h,r',t) \in \mathcal{T}_{neg}} \max\{0, f_c(h, r, t) + \gamma - f_c(h, r', t)\} \tag{10}$$

To guarantee that the two kinds of enriched representations could accurately capture the useful latent interactions between entities, we use a trade-off weight factor to bridge the gap between $\mathcal{L}_g$ and $\mathcal{L}_c$. Meanwhile, we add a regularization term to the loss function to avoid overfitting. Thus, our loss function is given as follows

$$\mathcal{L} = \mathcal{L}_g + \lambda \mathcal{L}_c + \frac{\mu}{2} \|\Theta\|_2^2 \tag{11}$$

where γ, λ, μ, $\| \cdot \|_2^2$ and Θ denote the constant, the trade off factor between $\mathcal{L}_g$ and $\mathcal{L}_c$, the hyperparameter, the L_2 regularization and the set of parameters, respectively.

To minimize $\mathcal{L}$, we first sample m positive triplets, denoted as $\mathcal{A}_{batch}$. For each triplet in $\mathcal{A}_{batch}$, we generate a negative triplet. We merge these positive and negative triplets to generate the set $\mathcal{B}_{batch}$ for training. Next, for each positive and negative triplet in $\mathcal{B}_{batch}$, we randomly extract σ entity neighbors to obtain the first-order subgraph and the one-hop entity context. Then, we use the batch gradient descent algorithm for parameter optimization, and the training process is depicted in Algorithm 1.

4   Experiments

In this section, we present experimental results upon three real-world datasets to evaluate the performance of our proposed method. We first introduce experimental settings, and then design three experiments: (1) relation prediction with entities inside KG, (2) relation prediction with entities outside KG, and (3) impacts of the number of entity neighbors, to evaluate our method compared with existing methods.

Algorithm 1. Training

Input: Training set $\mathcal{T}_{train}$, relation set $\mathcal{R}$, epoch n, learning rate η, batch size m, parameter set Θ, margin γ, number of entity neighbors σ
Output: Updated Θ
1: For Each $\theta \in \Theta$ Do //Initialize parameters
2:     $\theta \leftarrow normal(0, 1)$
3: End For
4: For $i = 1$ To n Do
5:     For $j = 1$ To $\frac{|\mathcal{T}_{train}|}{m} + 1$ Do
6:         $\mathcal{A}_{batch} \leftarrow sample(\mathcal{T}_{train}, m)$ //Randomly sample a set of m positive triplets
7:         $\mathcal{B}_{batch} \leftarrow \phi$
8:         For Each $(h, r, t) \in \mathcal{A}_{batch}$ Do //Sample a set of m negative triplets
9:             Randomly choose r' from $\mathcal{R}$
10:             While $r' = r$ Do
11:                 Randomly choose r' from $\mathcal{R}$
12:             End While
13:             $\mathcal{B}_{batch} \leftarrow \mathcal{B}_{batch} \cup \{((h, r, t), (h, r', t))\}$
14:         End For
15:         For Each $((h, r, t), (h, r', t)) \in \mathcal{B}_{batch}$ Do
16:             Calculate $f_g(h, r, t)$ and $f_g(h, r', t)$ by Eq. (4)
17:             Calculate $f_c(h, r, t)$ and $f_c(h, r', t)$ by Eq. (8)
18:         End For
19:         Calculate batch loss $\mathcal{L}$ by Eq. (11)
20:         Calculate batch gradient $\frac{\partial \mathcal{L}}{\partial \Theta}$
21:         $\Theta \leftarrow \Theta - \eta \frac{\partial \mathcal{L}}{\partial \Theta}$ //Back propagation
22:     End for
23: End for
24: Return Θ

4.1 Experiment Settings

Datasets. Our experiments conducted on three real-world datasets, whose statistics were shown in Table 2.

Next, we extracted nine datasets from FB15k, FB15k-237 and WN11 to evaluate the performance in relation prediction with external entities. We selected 1000/3000/5000 entities from FB15k, FB15k-237 and WN11 test files as external entities respectively. Using the selected external entities, we first filtered out triplets containing the external entities from the original training dataset as new Train dataset, and then we selected triplets from the original validation dataset as Aux dataset with one external entity and one entity in new Train dataset. Finally, we selected triplets from the original test dataset as new Test dataset with one entity in new Train dataset and one external entity.

The details of these generated datasets are shown in Table 3, denoted as Both-1000/Both-3000/Both-5000, where 1000/3000/5000 indicates the number of external entities concerned in the test.

Table 2. Statistics of datasets. #Relation, #Entity, #Train, #Valid and #Test denote the number of relation, entity, training triplets, validation triplets and test triplets, respectively.

Dataset	#Relation	#Entity	#Train	#Valid	#Test
FB15k	1,345	14,951	483,142	50,000	59,071
FB15k-237	237	14,541	272,115	17,535	20,466
WN11	11	38,584	112,581	2,609	10,544

Table 3. Statistics of the nine generated datasets. #Train, #Aux and #Test denote the number of training triplets, auxiliary triplets and test triplets, respectively.

Dataset	Both-1000			Both-3000			Both-5000		
	#Train	#Aux	#Test	#Train	#Aux	#Test	#Train	#Aux	#Test
FB15k	283,556	18,345	21,741	132,489	26,844	30,531	67,518	24,312	26,790
FB15k-237	158,466	7,930	9,003	81,386	9,829	10,196	44,444	8,597	7,663
WN11	92,997	578	2,126	70,837	966	2,982	56,132	1,092	2,766

Metrics. We used two common ranking metrics in our experiments: (1) Hits@k ($k = 1, 3$), which measures the proportion of correct triplets in the top k. (2) Mean Reciprocal Rank (MRR), the average of the inverse of correct triplets ranks. Higher value of Hits@k and MRR means better performance of relation prediction.

Comparison Methods. We compared our proposed method with four state-of-the-art ones, including TransE [12], TransH [13], TransR [14] and OOKB [25]. The first three models are traditional relation prediction methods by modeling the translation between entities and relations, while the OOKB model could be generalized to the entities outside KG by exploiting limited auxiliary knowledge.

Implementation. Our proposed method was implemented in Pytorch and trained on a single GPU (NVIDIA GeForce RTX 3090) with 24 GB video memory and 128 GB RAM. We used Adam optimization with the learning rate of 0.01. The batch size, embedding dimension of entities and relations were set as 1,024, 100 and 100, respectively. The margin γ, weight factor λ, and number of entity neighbors σ in the loss function were set to 8, 1, and 16, respectively. In all experiments, the training epochs were set as 10.

4.2 Experimental Results

Exp-1: Relation Prediction with Entities Inside KG. To test the performance of relation prediction, we first corrupted each test triplet by replacing the correct r with every r' in FB15k, FB15k-327 and WN11 respectively as candidate triplets. Then, we calculated the score of these candidate triplets by our method and ranked them by their score. Hits@1, Hits@3 and MRR were shown as Table 4. The results tell us that (1) our method improves Hits@1, Hits@3 and MRR by 1.2%, 1.1%, and 0.1% over the second-highest method on FB15k respectively, (2) our method improves Hits@1, Hits@3 and MRR by 0.5%, 0.3%, and 0.6% over the second-highest method on FB15k-237 respectively, and (3) our method improves Hits@1, Hits@3 and MRR by 18.8%, 8.7%, and 12.2% over the second-highest method on WN11 respectively.

Table 4. Hits@1, Hits@3 and MRR on FB15k, FB15k-237 and WN11.

Method	FB15k			FB15k-237			WN11		
	Hits@1	Hits@3	MRR	Hits@1	Hits@3	MRR	Hits@1	Hits@3	MRR
TransE	0.577	0.823	0.715	0.791	0.911	0.858	0.707	0.849	0.795
TransH	0.598	0.851	0.736	0.793	0.917	0.861	0.708	0.856	0.798
TransR	0.487	0.749	0.637	0.802	0.930	0.870	0.705	0.870	0.802
OOKB	0.147	0.345	0.298	0.432	0.718	0.598	0.577	0.871	0.733
OUR	**0.605**	**0.860**	**0.737**	**0.806**	**0.933**	**0.875**	**0.841**	**0.947**	**0.900**

Exp-2: Relation Prediction with Entities Outside KG. To test the performance of relation prediction w.r.t each test triplet including one entity unseen in training, we first corrupted each test triplet by replacing the correct r with every r' in Both-1000, Both-3000 and Both-5000 extracted from FB15k, FB15k-327 and WN11 respectively as candidate triplets. Then, we calculated the score of these candidate triplets by our method and ranked them by their score.

Hits@1, Hits@3 and MRR on the datasets extracted from FB15k were shown as Table 5. The results tell us that (1) our method improves Hits@1, Hits@3 and MRR by 434.9%, 280%, and 271% over the second-highest method on Both-1000 respectively, (2) our method improves Hits@1, Hits@3 and MRR by 106.8%, 90.9%, and 86.1% over the second-highest method on Both-3000 respectively, and (3) our method improves Hits@1, Hits@3 and MRR by 25.8%, 32.1%, and 28.2% over the second-highest method on Both-5000 respectively.

Hits@1, Hits@3 and MRR on the datasets extracted from FB15k-237 were shown as Table 6. The results tell us that (1) our method improves Hits@1, Hits@3 and MRR by 119.1%, 50.6%, and 67% over the second-highest method on Both-1000 respectively, (2) our method improves Hits@1, Hits@3 and MRR by 188.2%, 82.7%, and 95.7% over the second-highest method on Both-3000 respectively, and (3) our method improves Hits@1, Hits@3 and MRR by 279.1%, 123.1%, and 128.3% over the second-highest method on Both-5000 respectively.

Hits@1, Hits@3 and MRR on the datasets extracted from WN11 were shown as Table 7. The results tell us that (1) our method improves Hits@1, Hits@3 and

Table 5. Hits@1, Hits@3 and MRR on datasets extracted from FB15k.

Method	Both-1000			Both-3000			Both-5000		
	Hits@1	Hits@3	MRR	Hits@1	Hits@3	MRR	Hits@1	Hits@3	MRR
TransE	0.084	0.146	0.140	0.095	0.169	0.156	0.103	0.175	0.165
TransH	0.086	0.155	0.145	0.103	0.176	0.165	0.103	0.182	0.168
TransR	0.068	0.138	0.125	0.081	0.162	0.144	0.081	0.170	0.150
OOKB	0.056	0.129	0.141	0.067	0.166	0.161	0.047	0.122	0.126
OUR	**0.460**	**0.589**	**0.538**	**0.213**	**0.336**	**0.307**	**0.130**	**0.241**	**0.215**

Table 6. Hits@1, Hits@3 and MRR on datasets extracted from FB15k-237.

Method	Both-1000			Both-3000			Both-5000		
	Hits@1	Hits@3	MRR	Hits@1	Hits@3	MRR	Hits@1	Hits@3	MRR
TransE	0.075	0.136	0.128	0.084	0.154	0.143	0.091	0.140	0.144
TransH	0.084	0.144	0.139	0.093	0.153	0.148	0.098	0.145	0.154
TransR	0.084	0.140	0.138	0.099	0.158	0.156	0.095	0.153	0.150
OOKB	0.267	0.437	0.379	0.170	0.313	0.279	0.093	0.201	0.188
OUR	**0.585**	**0.658**	**0.633**	**0.490**	**0.572**	**0.546**	**0.372**	**0.448**	**0.429**

MRR by 213.6%, 20.3%, and 82.2% over the second-highest method on Both-1000 respectively, (2) our method improves Hits@1, Hits@3 and MRR by 221.7%, 27%, and 84.3% over the second-highest method on Both-3000 respectively, and (3) our method improves Hits@1, Hits@3 and MRR by 243.6%, 28.8%, and 85.7% over the second-highest method on Both-5000 respectively.

Table 7. Hits@1, Hits@3 and MRR on datasets extracted from WN11.

Method	Both-1000			Both-3000			Both-5000		
	Hits@1	Hits@3	MRR	Hits@1	Hits@3	MRR	Hits@1	Hits@3	MRR
TransE	0.258	0.655	0.476	0.244	0.633	0.461	0.232	0.603	0.443
TransH	0.250	0.683	0.478	0.217	0.637	0.446	0.228	0.619	0.445
TransR	0.215	0.672	0.466	0.189	0.664	0.441	0.223	0.669	0.466
OOKB	0.186	0.760	0.476	0.226	0.711	0.464	0.183	0.710	0.439
OUR	**0.809**	**0.914**	**0.871**	**0.785**	**0.903**	**0.855**	**0.797**	**0.915**	**0.865**

Exp-3: Impacts of the Number of Entity Neighbors. To evaluate the impacts of the number of entity neighbors σ on Both-5000 extracted from FB15k, FB15k-237 and WN11 respectively, we set σ to 1/2/4/8/16, and tested the

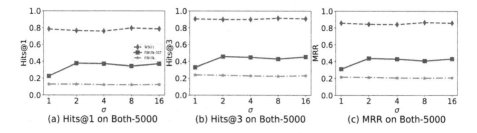

Fig. 3. Results of impacts of σ.

Hits@1/Hits@3/MRR with different σ. The results were reported in Fig. 3(a)–Fig. 3(c), respectively. The results tell us that the Hits@1/Hits@3/MRR on Both-5000 extracted from FB15k, FB15k-237 and WN11 remains relatively stable when varying σ, which demonstrates that our method could capture the most useful surrounding features.

Summary: The above experimental results are summarized as follows:

- In Exp-1, Hits@1, Hits@3 and MRR increase on average by 6.8%, 3.3% and 4.3% respectively compared with other comparison methods.
- In Exp-2, Hits@1, Hits@3 and MRR increase significantly on average by 197.3%, 56.3% and 92.5% respectively compared with other comparison methods. Specifically, MRR increases significantly on average by 121.8%, 90.1% and 84.0% on Both-5000 extracted from FB15k, FB15k-237 and WN11 respectively compared with other comparison methods.

5   Conclusions and Future Work

In this paper, we propose a method to find new facts regardless of entities inside or outside KG. By incorporating both graph and context features around entities and relations, the representation of external entities could be obtained to improve the relation prediction of KG, which facilitates the discovery of knowledge outside KG.

However, our method just considers the first-order subgraph and one-hop entity context features around the given entity, while more orders of subgraphs and more hops of context features are worthwhile to further explore to improve the capability of external fact mining. Moreover, zero-shot knowledge graph completion could be conducted based on our method.

Acknowledgements. This paper was supported by the National Natural Science Foundation of China (Nos. U1802271, 62002311); Program of Yunnan Key Laboratory of Intelligent Systems and Computing (No. 202205AG070003); Science Foundation for Distinguished Young Scholars of Yunnan Province (No. 2019FJ011); Major Science and Technology Special Foundation of Yunnan Province (No. 202202AD080001).

References

1. Liu, P., Wang, X., Fu, Q., Yang, Y., Li, Y., Zhang, Q.: KGVQL: a knowledge graph visual query language with bidirectional transformations. Knowl. Based Syst. **250**, 108870 (2022). https://doi.org/10.1016/j.knosys.2022.108870
2. Bollacker, K., Evans, C., Paritosh, P., Sturge, T., Taylor, J.: Freebase: a collaboratively created graph database for structuring human knowledge. In: Proceedings of the ACM SIGMOD International Conference on Management of Data, pp. 1247–1250. ACM, Vancouver (2008)
3. Miller, G.A.: Wordnet: a lexical database for English. Commun. ACM **38**(11), 39–41 (1995)
4. Suchanek, F. M., Kasneci, G., Weikum, G.: Yago: a core of semantic knowledge. In: Proceedings of the 16th International Conference on World Wide Web, pp. 697–706. ACM, Banff (2007)
5. Song, Y., et al.: Optimizing subgraph matching over distributed knowledge graphs using partial evaluation. World Wide Web J. (2022). https://doi.org/10.1007/s11280-022-01075-6
6. Chicaiza, J., Valdiviezo-Diaz, P.: A comprehensive survey of knowledge graph-based recommender systems: technologies, development, and contributions. Information **12**(6), 232 (2021)
7. Lin, Z., Feng, L., Yin, R., Xu, C., Kwoh, C.K.: GLIMG: global and item graphs for top-n recommender systems. Inf. Sci. **580**, 1–14 (2021)
8. Huang, X., Zhang, J., Li, D., Li, P.: Knowledge graph embedding based question answering. In: Proceedings of the 12th ACM International Conference on Web Search and Data Mining, pp. 105–113. ACM, Melbourne (2019)
9. Shin, S., Lee, K.: Processing knowledge graph-based complex questions through question decomposition and recomposition. Inf. Sci. **523**, 234–244 (2020)
10. Dong, X., et al.: Knowledge vault: a web-scale approach to probabilistic knowledge fusion. In: Proceedings of the 20th ACM SIGKDD International Conference on Knowledge Discovery and Data Mining, pp. 601–610. ACM, New York (2014)
11. Borrego, A., Ayala, D., Hernández, I., Rivero, C.R., Ruiz, D.: CAFE: knowledge graph completion using neighbor-aware feature. Eng. Appl. Artif. Intell. **103**, 104302 (2021)
12. Bordes, A., Usunier, N., Garcia-Duran, A., Weston, J., Yakhnenko, O.: Translating embeddings for modeling multi-relational data. In: Proceedings of the 27th Annual Conference on Neural Information Processing Systems, pp. 2787–2795. MIT Press, Lake Tahoe (2013)
13. Wang, H., Zhang, J., Feng, J., Chen, Z.: Knowledge graph embedding by translating on hyperplanes. In: Proceedings of the 28th AAAI Conference on Artificial Intelligence, pp. 1112–1119. AAAI, Québec (2014)
14. Lin, Y., Liu, Z., Sum, M., Liu, Y., Zhu, X.: Learning entity and relation embeddings for knowledge graph completion. In: Proceedings of the 29th AAAI Conference on Artificial Intelligence, pp. 2181–2187. AAAI, Austin (2015)
15. Cai, H., Zheng, V.W., Chang, K.C.C.: A comprehensive survey of graph embedding: problems, techniques, and applications. IEEE Trans. Knowl. Data Eng. **30**(9), 1616–1637 (2018)
16. Rossi, A., Barbosa, D., Firmani, D., Matinata, A., Merialdo, P.: Knowledge graph embedding for link prediction: a comparative analysis. ACM Trans. Knowl. Discov. Data **15**(2), 14:1–14:49 (2021)

17. Li, Z., Liu, X., Wang, X., Liu, P., Shen, Y.: TransO: a knowledge-driven representation learning method with ontology information constraints. World Wide Web J. (2022). https://doi.org/10.1007/s11280-022-01016-3
18. Li, J., Yue, K., Duan, L., Li, J.: Ranking associative entities in knowledge graph by graphical modeling of frequent patterns. In: Jensen, C.S., et al. (eds.) DASFAA 2021. LNCS, vol. 12681, pp. 224–239. Springer, Cham (2021). https://doi.org/10.1007/978-3-030-73194-6_16
19. Mao, X., Wang, W., Xu, H., Wu, Y., Lan, M.: Relational reflection entity alignment. In: Proceedings of the 29th ACM International Conference on Information and Knowledge Management, pp. 1095–1104. ACM (2020)
20. Bahdanau, D., Cho, K., Bengio, Y.: Neural machine translation by jointly learning to align and translate. In: Proceedings of the 3rd International Conference on Learning Representations, ICLR, San Diego (2015)
21. Shi, B., Weninger, T.: Open-world knowledge graph completion. In: Proceedings of the 32nd AAAI Conference on Artificial Intelligence, pp. 1957–1964. AAAI, New Orleans (2018)
22. Fu, C., et al.: Multiple interaction attention model for open-world knowledge graph completion. In: Cheng, R., Mamoulis, N., Sun, Y., Huang, X. (eds.) WISE 2020. LNCS, vol. 11881, pp. 630–644. Springer, Cham (2019). https://doi.org/10.1007/978-3-030-34223-4_40
23. Shah, H., Villmow, J., Ulges, A., Schwanecke, U., Shafait, F.: An open-world extension to knowledge graph completion models. In: Proceedings of the 33rd AAAI Conference on Artificial Intelligence, pp. 3044–3051. AAAI, Honolulu (2019)
24. Xie, R., Liu, Z., Jia, J., Luan, H., Sun, M.: Representation learning of knowledge graphs with entity descriptions. In: Proceedings of the 30th AAAI Conference on Artificial Intelligence, pp. 2659–2665. AAAI, Phoenix (2016)
25. Hamaguchi, T., Oiwa, H., Shimbo, M., Matsumoto, Y.: Knowledge transfer for out-of-knowledge-base entities: a graph neural network approach. In: Proceedings of the 26th International Joint Conference on Artificial Intelligence, pp. 1802–1808. Morgan Kaufmann, Melbourne (2017)
26. Qiao, Z., Ning, Z., Du, Y., Zhou, Y.: Context-enhanced entity and relation embedding for knowledge graph completion. In: Proceedings of the 35th AAAI Conference on Artificial Intelligence, pp. 15871–15872. AAAI (2021)
27. Bansal, T., Juan, D., Ravi, S., McCallum, A.: A2N: attending to neighbors for knowledge graph inference. In: Proceedings of the 57th Conference of the Association for Computational Linguistics, pp. 4387–4392. Association for Computational Linguistics, Florence (2019)
28. Wang, J., Wang, X., Luo, X., Qin, W.: Open-world relationship prediction. In: Proceedings of the 32nd IEEE International Conference on Tools with Artificial Intelligence, pp. 323–330. IEEE, Baltimore (2020)
29. Teru, K., Denis, E., Hamilton, W.: Inductive relation prediction by subgraph reasoning. In: Proceedings of the 37th International Conference on Machine Learning, pp. 9448–9457. PMLR (2020)
30. Chen, J., He, H., Wu, F., Wang, J.: Topology-aware correlations between relations for inductive link prediction in knowledge graphs. In: Proceedings of the 35th AAAI Conference on Artificial Intelligence, pp. 6271–6278. AAAI (2021)
31. Rosset, S., Zhu, J., Hastie, T.: Margin maximizing loss functions. In: Proceedings of the Advances in Neural Information Processing Systems, vol. 16, pp. 1237–1244. MIT Press, Vancouver and Whistler (2003)

Rumor Detection in Social Network via Influence Based on Bi-directional Graph Convolutional Network

Lifu Chen, Junhua Fang$^{(\boxtimes)}$, Pingfu Chao, An Liu, and Pengpeng Zhao

School of Computer Science and Technology, Soochow University, Soochow, China
20204227034@stu.suda.edu.cn, {jhfang,pfchao,anliu,ppzhao}@suda.edu.cn

Abstract. Nowadays, social media has become a convenient and prevalent platform for users to communicate with others and share their opinions publicly. In the meantime, due to the rapid growth of social media,
the circulation of untrue and irresponsible statements is also boosted,
making it harder to detect rumors in the massive amount of social data.
Existing deep learning-based approaches detect rumors by modeling the
way they spread or their semantic features. However, most of them ignore
the different levels of influence when various users participate in the
spread of rumors. Hence, we define the influence power of users, which
is related to the popularity of their posts, as influence factors, and users
with higher influence factors are more likely to determine the direction
of public opinion, which can also make rumors spread more quickly and
widely. In this paper, we propose a novel graph model named Influence-
based Bi-Directional Graph Convolutional Network (IBi-GCN) to capture the influence of users and the way a rumor spreads. First, our model
uses an information entropy-based approach to calculate the local and
global influence of users, respectively, and obtain the overall influence
factors of users in the form of a weighted sum. Second, we combine the
overall influence factor with the two main features of rumor propagation
and diffusion. Finally, we use a bi-directional graph convolutional neural
network to learn a high-level representation for rumor detection.

Keywords: Data mining · Graph convolutional network · Rumor
detection · Social network · Rumor clustering

1 Introduction

The rapid growth of social media makes it easier for groups of users to access
information, share their opinions, and communicate with each other online.
These online platforms help promote the latest information or news among people, but at the same time, they also breed rumors unintentionally. Due to the
large scale and the convenience of social media, rumors can spread widely and
quickly, causing social unrest and massive economic losses [1,27]. For example,
the outbreak of COVID-19 provides fertile ground for the emergence of various

© The Author(s), under exclusive license to Springer Nature Switzerland AG 2022
R. Chbeir et al. (Eds.): WISE 2022, LNCS 13724, pp. 274–289, 2022.
https://doi.org/10.1007/978-3-031-20891-1_20

rumors and conspiracy theories, and their quick propagation on social media undermines the peace and stability of society. What is worse, many politicians and celebrities even consider it as a tool to get people's attention or control public opinion. They claim that "Wearing a mask to prevent the spread of COVID-19 is unnecessary". These statements are widely spread without confirmation, causing the public to have a wrong perception of epidemic prevention. Therefore, to prevent the social harm caused by rumors, an effective method to detect social media rumors is urgently needed. [5,12]

In social psychology, rumors are defined as stories or statements of false or unconfirmed truth value and they are designed to attract more attention and discussions than normal information [6]. The purpose of rumor detection is to identify suspicious statements without validating their truthfulness physically. Traditional approaches to rumor detection use supervised classifiers based on feature engineering for textual feature mining from social media [9,13,29]. However, feature engineering-based approaches require significant time and labor overheads. Recent research in representation learning-based approaches identifies rumors by mining more advanced representations from their propagation paths and features. Bi-directional graph convolutional network (Bi-GCN) [3] uses a bidirectional convolutional neural network to capture both ways of rumor propagation and learn higher-order rumor feature vectors. Recurrent neural network (RvNN) [19] uses a recurrent neural network to capture the features of rumor propagation. And a transformer-based method [16] selectively focuses on the corresponding tweets to enhance the representation learning of rumor-indicating features.

Although these methods consider the semantic and structural features in rumor detection, none of them takes into account the impact of users' influence when it comes to boosting the propagation. In general, two problems still remain in the existing methods: 1) In social networks, influencers such as stars or Internet celebrities can lead to the widespread circulation of rumors [2,8,10]. Their influence ability is generally tied to the retweets, mentions, etc. of posts [21]. Figure 1 shows an example. When the influencer U_0 makes a subjective statement that is not validated, a large number of his followers, such as U_1-U_6, will support him/her by making the same call blindly, which leads to a quick spread of unconfirmed news. Moreover, they may even abuse those who express doubt or holds different opinions about it. Besides, influencers are not only rumor spreaders, but also rumor makers sometimes, which may cause massive social panic and Internet violence; 2) The structure of spreading is one of the key influencing factors in the task of rumor detection. Existing approaches treat all users equally and model the propagation structure in terms of relationships between users with directions. Such an approach severely neglects the influence of influencers on the propagation structure. As shown in Fig. 1, an influencer such as U_0 has a significantly higher influence on rumors in the propagation structure than the common users U_1-U_6. So there is still a lack of a framework for rumor detection that combines user influence factors and spreading structures.

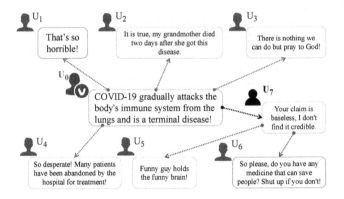

Fig. 1. The affect of influencer.

The two problems mentioned above not only make it more difficult to detect rumors, but also deepen the level of harm they can cause. In this paper, we propose a bi-directional graph convolutional neural network model based on users' influence (IBi-GCN). In our model, we calculate the influence factor of each user node to estimate their effect on the spread of rumors and combine it with two structural information of rumor propagation. And the high-level representation of rumors will be extracted from it by using GCN. In addition, we propose an effective solution to the above problem: 1) we refer to the idea of information entropy to calculate the local influence entropy and global influence entropy of each user node, and finally obtain the influence coefficient by a weighted sum of the two to represent the overall influence ability of users; 2) we use a tree structure to represent the two ways of rumor propagation [3], and combine it with the overall influence factor as a novel rumor detection framework. We conduct extensive experiments on the large-scale Twitter15 and Twitter16 corpus [18]. The experimental results show that IBi-GCN has a better performance compared with multiple baselines. In general, we summarize our main contributions as follows:

- We propose a novel way to generate the user influence by the information entropy-based approach. This method calculates the local and global influence of each user and returns an overall influence factor in the form of a weighted sum, representing the user's influence capacity.
- We design a novel rumor detection framework based on GCN that combines the user influence coefficient and the rumor propagation structure. More complete feature information allows our model to detect rumors more accurately.
- Extensive experimental results on large-scale real datasets show that the model has an excellent performance in the task of social rumor detection.

2   Related Work

In this section, we will introduce the existing rumor detection schemes. A special note here is that in this paper, we define rumors to include, but are not limited to, false statements, fake news, false comments, etc. The existing work of rumor detection can be divided into the following tow main categories:

2.1   Methods Based on Manual Feature Engineering

Previous research in automatic rumor detection focuses on extracting rumor features from text content, user profiles, and propagation structures to learn supervised classifiers from labelled data. The text content usually refers to long text. Castillo et al. [4] propose a manual feature engineering-based decision tree classifier that uses a large number of manually annotated datasets for supervised classifier training. Popat et al. [22] detect rumors by modelling language styles such as lexicality, factual/assertive verbs and subjectivity as a credibility judgment of message text. Potthast et al. [23] propose a classifier for detecting fake news based on writing style. They compare the text writing style and similarity of current news and fake news, which is used to determine the authenticity of current news. User profiles include retweets, relationships, posting times, etc. Liu et al. [13] add different belief groups in an event as new features to the feature set for classifier training to better detect rumors. Yang et al. [28] propose a RBF kernel-based SVM classifier. It uses the client usage and the event location as two new features to train the classifier. Ma et al. [17] use a time-series based SVM classifier to capture contextual time series and combine it with social context information. The propagation structure of rumors in social networks is also a key feature of rumor detection tasks. Ma et al. [18] build a kernel-based approach to capture the similarity between the propagation tree structures that distinguish different types of rumors. Sampson et al. [26] use the implicit information during message propagation to detect burst rumors. They define implicit information as conversation structures with certain similarities and use them as features to train a rumor classifier. Most of these methods use manual feature engineering to extract feature information sets. It does not only consumes a large number of time but also affects the quality of the feature set due to manual errors, which causes large rumor detection errors.

2.2   Methods Based on Neural Networks

In recent years, the rapid development of neural networks brings more significant improvements to rumor detection tasks. Ma et al. [19] propose a tree structure-based recursive neural network. It uses the non-sequential propagation structure of tweets to learn features of tweet content and generate more powerful representations to identify different types of rumors. Bian et al. [3] use a bi-directional graph convolutional neural network to simulate two ways of rumor propagation and learn the high-level representation of rumors from it. Lin et al. [11] represent the session threads completely with undirected interaction graphs, and then use graph neural network to capture multi-level rumor indication features. This method enhances the interaction of opinions between users and performs well on early rumor detection tasks. Lu et al. [15] first extract user features and word embeddings. Then they construct a graph to model potential interactions between users and put them into GCN to learn graph-aware representations of user interactions.

Although the deep learning-based methods show a good performance in rumor detection, it does not take into account the user's influence in the community, which has been convinced as an essential factor in social media [20,24]. Our

IBi-GCN method uses information entropy to calculate the overall influence of users in social networks after taking into account the structure of rumor propagation, which enhances the characteristics of user nodes in the rumor propagation tree. At the same time, we use the powerful information aggregation capability of GCN to achieve high accuracy of rumor detection.

3 Preliminaries

In this section, we will introduce the problem definition and the framework of our model.

3.1 Problem Definition

Definition 3.1 (Social Event Set). The social event set is defined as $C = \{c_1, c_2, ..., c_n\}$, where c_i denotes the i-th event in the event set and n represents the number of events. Each c_i is defined as $c_i = \{s_i, k_1^i, k_2^i, ..., k_m^i\}$, where s_i represents the root post, and k_j^i refers to the j-th relevant responsive post of s_i.

Definition 3.2 (Propagation Structure Graph). Two propagation structures of rumor are defined as $G_{O2M} = \langle V_i, E_i \rangle$ and $G_{M2O} = \langle V_j, E_j \rangle$, where G_{O2M} refers to the propagation along a relationship chain from one to many, and G_{M2O} refers to the propagation along a relationship chain from many to one. V denotes the message node set and E denotes the set of directed edges.

Definition 3.3 (Feature Extraction). Given an event c_i, the feature extraction converts each post into feature matrix X_i, which is defined as $X_i = \{x_0^{i\top}, x_1^{i\top}, x_2^{i\top}, ..., x_m^{i\top}\}^{\top}$. The x_0^i denotes the feature vector of s_i, x_m^i denotes the feature vector of k_m^i where m is decided by the number of vectors.

Definition 3.4 (Rumor Detection Model). The rumor detection model regards the task of rumor detection as a supervised classification problem, which learns a classifier from labeled events. It is defined as $f(C, \sigma) = Y$, where σ denotes the parameter of model and Y denotes the label classes. Different from the labels for dichotomous task, we utilize the labels of four finer-grained classes {N, F, T, U} (i.e., Non-rumor, False rumor, True rumor, and Unverified rumor) [18].

According to Definition 3.4, to design a better classifier for rumor detection, the main objectives of this paper are to improve the quality of c_i, i.e. the events in dataset. We optimize parameter σ to get correct results by adding information on user influence, which is defined as influence factor in this paper. Therefore, we propose a model named IBi-GCN to address it, which will be introduced in the next section.

3.2 Framework Overview

The Algorithm 1 shows the framework of our IBi-GCN model. It takes the set of social events C as input and a probability vector for event label $\hat{y}$ as output.

Algorithm 1. IBi-GCN

Input: A social event set: $C = \{c_1, c_2, ..., c_n\}$
Output: The vector of event label: $\hat{y}$
Begin:
1: /* **Generate the features** */
2: /* z represents two types of propagation way named O2M and M2O */
3:   $G_z \leftarrow$ Create the propagation graph(C)
4:   $G_z' \leftarrow$ DropEdge(G_z)
5: **for** $i = 1, 2, 3, ..., n$ **do**
6:     **for** $j = 1, 2, 3, ..., m - 1$ **do**
7:       $x_j^i \leftarrow$ generate the feature vector(k_j^i)
8:       $\hat{x}_j^i \leftarrow$ influence factor enhanced(x_j^i)
9:     **end for**
10: **end for**
11: /* **Representation Learning** */
12: **for** $L = 1, 2, ...$ **do**
13:    $H_z^{(l+1)} = \sigma\left(\tilde{D}^{-\frac{1}{2}}\tilde{A}_z\tilde{D}^{-\frac{1}{2}}H_z^{(l)}W_z^{(l)}\right)$
14:    $\hat{H}_z^{(l)} \leftarrow$ root feature concat$\left(\left(H_z^{(l-1)}\right)^{root}\right)$
15: **end for**
16: $R_{O2M}, R_{M2O} \leftarrow$ mean-pooling($\hat{H}_{O2M}, \hat{H}_{M2O}$)
17: $R = $concat($R_{O2M}, R_{M2O}$)
18: $\hat{y} = Softmax(FC(R))$
19: **return** probability vector of event labels $\hat{y}$

We use z to represent the two propagation ways. The whole process is divided into two parts. In part of the feature generation phase, we first construct graphs for both propagation ways and process these graphs with the DropEdge method (**Line 2–5 in Algorithm 1**). And next, we construct feature vectors x_j^i with posts k_j^i in social events and add influence factors to enhance them (**Line 6–10 in Algorithm 1**). In part of the representation learning phase, we first use graph convolutional neural network to aggregate node information and learn higher representations. (**Line 13–18 in Algorithm 1**) And in each layer, we cascade root post feature from the previous layer with the feature in current layer as an extra complementary feature (**Line 15 and Line 17 in Algorithm 1**). Then, we cascade the representation vectors after the mean-pooling operation (**Line 19–20 in Algorithm 1**). Finally, we pass the representation vector through the fully connected and softmax layers to obtain the probability vector of event labels (**Line 21 in Algorithm 1**).

4   IBi-GCN Rumor Detection Model

The architectures of our models are shown in Fig. 2. Our method aims at improving the accuracy of rumor detection by (1) proposing the user influence factor based on information entropy to better capture the feature information of social network users and (2) getting more accurate representation by combining the

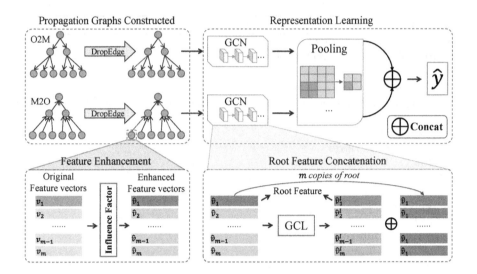

Fig. 2. The rumor detection model IBi-GCN. The two ways of rumor propagation are expressed as graphs and the DropEdge method will be used to delete edges randomly. Each feature vector of nodes in graphs will be reinforced by the influence factor. In the representation learning phase, except for the first layer in GCN, the vectors of each layer concatenate the root feature which comes from the previous layer. We represent the impact of the root feature on each response feature by replicating m copies of the root post from the previous layer.

enhanced feature information with the structure of rumor propagation. In this section, we elaborate on the details of our proposed model.

4.1 Influence Factor Based on Information Entropy

A person's influence in the spread of rumors is related to the influence of a particular rumor tweet or their own influence on social networks. Information entropy is a concept in information theory that was originally proposed by Claude Elwood Shannon in his 1948 book "A Mathematical Theory of Communication". It is used to measure the amount of information contained in each message received. In the information field, the higher the information entropy, the more information is transmitted, and vice versa. In this paper, we use information entropy to model the local influence factor as well as the global influence factor of a user, which models the amount of information carried by a user and how the user can affect the propagation of a particular event or all events in general, respectively. We count the number of times a user is mentioned in an event and a collection of events as the user's local influence and global influence respectively. The local influence factor and the global influence factor are then calculated using information entropy. It is expressed in the formula as follows:

$$I_L = -\sum_i^n \frac{1}{h_i} \log_{10} \frac{1}{h_i} \tag{1}$$

$$I_G = -\sum_i^n \frac{1}{H_i} \log_{10} \frac{1}{H_i}, \tag{2}$$

where I_L and I_G denote the local and global influence factor, respectively. h_i denotes the number of times the i-th user is mentioned in the current event, while H_i denotes the corresponding number in all events. n represents the total number of users to be calculated.

And in order to combine two different grained influence factors, we define two weighting coefficients and return an Overall Influence Factor (OIF) in the form of a weighted sum of the two impact factors. It is expressed as:

$$I_O = \omega I_L + \varphi I_G, \tag{3}$$

where ω and φ satisfy $\omega + \varphi = 1$.

To verify the influence of OIF on rumors. We multiply all the feature vectors $x_m^{i\top}$ in the feature matrix X_i by their respective OIFs. It is formulated as:

$$\hat{x}_j^{i\top} = \left(1 + I_{jO}^i\right) \cdot x_j^{i\top}, \tag{4}$$

where $\hat{x}_j^{i\top}$ denotes the feature vector of i-th event which added the information of users' influence, I_{jO}^i denotes the OIF of j-th feature vector in i-th event, and $x_j^{i\top}$ denotes the j-th feature vector in i-th event.

4.2 Construct Propagation Graphs

In social networks, it is common to use a graph with directional edges to represent interactions among users. But such a structure does not perform the spread structure of social rumors. To express such characteristics, we classify the propagation nature of rumors into two categories according to the actual situation of rumor propagation in social networks, which are the way based on one to many and the way based on many to one. We use two kinds of directed graph structures with different directions to represent the propagation characteristics of rumors.

One to Many (O2M): In social media, a message is retweeted and commented on heavily, which leads to some subjective statements being spread as rumors. It is a one-to-many process. As shown in Fig. 3 (a), when an influencer U_1 makes an unconfirmed statement, he may mention people he knows such as U_2 and U_3. U_2 and U_3 comment on the message subjectively and retweet it or mention more people. This results in a one to many propagation pattern with the influencer as a root node.

Many to One (M2O): Thomas [27] argues that the collective efficacy of communities increases the impact of rumors on individuals. The misfortunes of some groups are amplified through collective efficacy, causing other individuals to overreact to the misfortunes and thus evolve into rumors for dissemination. It is a many to one process. As an example in Fig. 3 (b), victims U_1, U_2, U_3 may suffer

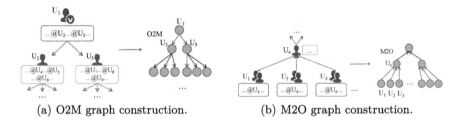

(a) O2M graph construction.   (b) M2O graph construction.

Fig. 3. The graph construction on two propagation ways.

from natural or man-made disasters. So, They exaggerate the damage they have suffered and pass it on to others through social networks. Their comments are often radicalised by their strong subjective impressions of an event or a person, which breeds untrue claims that cause social crisis and panic.

As shown in Fig. 3, we construct an O2M graph and an M2O graph based on the two ways of rumor propagation. We represent our graph structure by $G = \langle V, E \rangle$, where the nodes set $V = \{s_i, k_1^i, k_1^i, ..., k_m^i\}$, directed edges $E = \{e_{wj}^i | w, j = 0, 1, 2, ..., m - 1\}$. We define the retweet, mention, etc. between message nodes as their connections. When a directed edge exist between nodes, such as $k_1^i \rightarrow k_2^i$, it is denoted as e_{12}^i. We use A_{wj}^i represents the adjacency matrix of the i-th event. It is expressed by the formula:

$$A_{wj}^i = \begin{cases} 1, & \text{if } e_{wj}^i \in E_i \\ 0, & \text{otherwise} \end{cases} \tag{5}$$

4.3 Representation Learning

We perform DropEdge [25] operations on both constructed graphs, multiplying the extracted feature vector x_i by the corresponding overall influence factor. Then, we use graph convolutional neural network to learn higher-level representations of the two propagation structures. It is expressed as:

$$H_z^{(l+1)} = \sigma \left(\tilde{D}^{-\frac{1}{2}} \tilde{A}_z \tilde{D}^{-\frac{1}{2}} H_z^{(l)} W_z^{(l)} \right), \tag{6}$$

where H_z denotes the l-th layer representations and z denotes the type of two rumor spreading structures named $O2M$ and $M2O$, if $l = 0$, the $H_z^0 = X_z$. $\tilde{A} = A + I_N$ denotes the adjacency matrix with self-connections added. $\tilde{D}$ represents the degree matrix of $\tilde{A}$, $\tilde{D}_{ii} = \Sigma_j \tilde{A}_{ij}$. $W^{(l)} \in \mathbb{R}^{n \times n}$ denotes trainable parameters. $\sigma()$ represents an activation function, such as a ReLU function.

We also consider the influence of root posts in rumor detection [3]. The root post has abundant information and makes a widespread impact. Therefore, it is necessary to include information about the root node in the representation learning. We concatenate the hidden feature vectors of the l-th layer with the hidden feature vector of the root node of the $(l - 1)$-th layer to construct a new feature matrix. It is expressed as:

$$\widehat{H}^{(l)} = concat\{H^{(l)}, \left(H^{(l-1)} \right)^{root}\}, \tag{7}$$

where $\widehat{H}^{(l)}$ denotes the l-th layer hidden feature vector with information of root post, $H^{(l)}$ denotes the l-th layer hidden feature vector, $\left(H^{(l-1)}\right)^{root}$ denotes the $(l-1)$-th layer hidden feature vector of root post, and $concat\{\}$ denotes the function to concatenate two feature vectors.

Pooling operations are generally used to compress data, perform feature selection and reduce the number of features. Here, we choose a mean-pooling operation to aggregate the node representations from these two groups. It is formulated as:

$$R_z = MeanP\left(\widehat{H}_z\right) \tag{8}$$

Then, concatenating the two rumor spreading structures pooled vectors to denote the final representation. It is formulated as:

$$R = concat\{R_{O2M}, R_{M2O}\} \tag{9}$$

The fully connected layer classifies the pooled vector representation R and then uses the softmax function to compute the probability vector for event label prediction. It is formulated as:

$$\hat{y} = Softmax(FC(R)), \tag{10}$$

where $\hat{y} \in \mathbb{R}^{1 \times n}$ represents the probability vector of all classes used to predict the event labels.

5   Experiments

In this section, we first compare the performance of baselines and our proposed IBi-GCN model in the rumor detection task. Then, we also study three variants of our proposed influence factor and perform ablation experiments.

5.1   Datasets

We use two large-scale, publicly available datasets, namely Twitter15 and Twitter16, for our experiments. Both datasets are preprocessed by the providers to remove duplicate and invalid data for better data quality. In both datasets, nodes refer to users, edges indicate forwarding or response relationships, and features are the first 5000 words extracted. They also contain four types of labels: Non-rumor (N), False rumor (F), True rumor (T), and Unverified-rumor (U). Table 1 shows the statistics of datasets.

Table 1. Statistics of datasets.

Datasets	Posts	Users	Events	T	F	U	N
Twitter15	331,612	276,663	1490	374	205	374	372
Twitter16	204,820	173,487	818	370	205	2 03	205

5.2 Baselines and Metrics

We select some state-of-the-art methods of recent years as baselines to compare with our model, including:

RvNN [19]: A tree structure-based recursive neural network. It uses the non-sequential propagation structure of tweets to learn features of tweet content and generate more powerful representations to identify different types of rumors.

DTC [4]: A manual feature engineering-based decision tree classifier. It uses a large number of manually annotated datasets and employs supervised learning to train a classifier, which can automatically evaluate the credibility of information to detect rumors.

SVM-TS [17]: A time-series-based SVM classifier. It captures contextual time series and combines them with social context information. It is used for rumor detection in the early stage of message propagation.

SVM-TK [18]: A propagation Tree Kernel-based SVM classifier. This method distinguishes different types of rumors by modelling the rumor propagation structure and evaluating the similarity between the propagation tree structures.

SVM-RBF [28]: A RBF kernel-based SVM classifier. It uses client usage and event location as two new features to train the classifier and uses it to detect rumors automatically.

PPC-RNN + CNN [14]: A time series classifier based on recurrent and convolutional networks. It models the story propagation path as a multivariate time series to represent user features. And the recurrent network and convolutional network can be used to learn the global and local variations on it, respectively, which are used to determine if the event is a rumor.

Bi-GCN [3]: Bi-directional graph convolutional neural network. It uses graph convolutional neural network to learn two modes of rumor propagation.

IBi-GCN: the GCN model we proposed based on influence factor.

We use Keras to implement PPC-RNN+CNN, scikit-learn to implement DTC and SVM-based model and PyTorch to implement RvNN and our proposed model. To evaluate the performance of all models, we use the following metrics:

(Acc.): It denotes the number of correctly classified samples as a percentage of the total number of samples. **(F_1.)**: It denotes the summed average of precision and recall.

5.3 Experimental Setup and Results

We use the Adam algorithm to optimize our proposed model. And the parameters of IBi-GCN are updated using stochastic gradient descent. The dropping rate of DropEdge is set to 0.2, the rate of dropout is set to 0.5, the dimension of the hidden feature vector of each node is set to 64, and the epoch of training is set to 200. The training stopped early when the validation loss stops decreasing by 10 epochs.

Table 2. Experimental results on Twitter 15.

Method	Acc.	F1			
		N	F	T	U
RvNN	0.713	0.662	0.743	0.821	0.645
DTC	0.452	0.403	0.372	0.721	0.324
SVM-TS	0.541	0.802	0.471	0.394	0.476
SVM-TK	0.743	0.793	0.688	0.752	0.721
SVM-RBF	0.308	0.214	0.081	0.432	0.226
PPC-RNN + CNN	0.482	0.342	0.491	0.306	0.632
Bi-GCN	0.885	0.883	0.918	0.890	0.836
IBi-GCN	**0.905**	**0.907**	**0.924**	**0.941**	**0.860**

Table 2 and Table 3 show the performance of our method and baseline on two datasets, respectively. Our proposed IBi-GCN method has a significant advantage over all types of baselines. Among all the baselines, we observe that the experimental results of Bi-GCN, RvNN and PPC-RNN+CNN are significantly better than the others. It is because the deep learning-based methods can capture various features better by learning the higher-level representation of rumors. Besides, other baselines such as DTC, SVM-TK, SVM-WS and SVM-RBF are based on manual feature engineering. The large error of manually labelled data usually tends to cause instability in the experimental results. However, our model achieves optimal results in all performance metrics. PPC-RNN + CNN focuses on textual and temporal information, ignoring the important feature of how rumors spread; RvNN is based on the relationship of textual context, but cannot capture

Table 3. Experimental results on Twitter 16.

Method	Acc.	F1			
		N	F	T	U
RvNN	0.724	0.657	0.752	0.813	0.725
DTC	0.465	0.253	0.072	0.174	0.466
SVM-TS	0.552	0.764	0.424	0.562	0.513
SVM-TK	0.721	0.711	0.701	0.827	0.663
SVM-RBF	0.546	0.653	0.073	0.121	0.354
PPC-RNN + CNN	0.532	0.582	0.531	0.403	0.6 64
Bi-GCN	0.902	0.859	0.907	0.935	0.910
IBi-GCN	**0.934**	**0.879**	**0.933**	**0.985**	**0.939**

additional features; Bi-GCN combines two ways of rumor spreading, but does not consider the influence of users. However, our proposed method takes into account the structure of rumor propagation, incorporates the user's influences, which allows for achieving better results than any other baselines in the experiments.

5.4 Ablation Study

To analyze the impact factor effect qualitatively, we compare our model with its two variants. Both variants use only the local influence factor and the global influence factor, respectively. The results on both data sets are shown in Fig. 4. From the figure, we can see that the role of the local influence factor is slightly greater than the role of the global influence factor in all the different datasets. In both datasets, the number of response nodes for a single event is much larger than the number of events in the event set, leading to a larger effect of the local influence factor. We can conclude that the accuracy of rumor detection can only be maximized with the combined effect of local and global influence factors. This trend illustrates from one side that in the rumor detection task, the influence ability of various aspects of the user determines the breadth of rumor propagation.

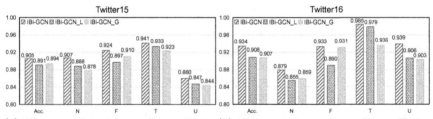

(a) The experimental result on Twitter15.

(b) The experimental result on Twitter16.

Fig. 4. The ablation study on two datasets.

5.5 Early Detection

Early rumor detection (ERD) is an important metric of the quality of rumor detection models [7]. It evaluates the performance of the model for rumor detection in an early limited, incomplete and noisy message environment. Therefore, we divide the data according to specific time intervals and check the early detection experiments of rumors on these time intervals. It should be noted here that we did not perform experiments with PPC-RvNN+CNN for early detection. In the early detection experiments, the sizes of the data volume in fixed time intervals are largely skewed. However, the PPC-RvNN+CNN model is difficult to adapt to data with inconsistent length, which causes the experimental results to fluctuate widely and lose reference value.

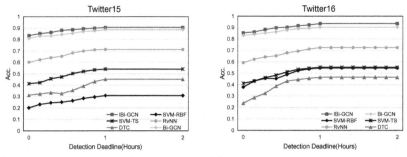

(a) The experimental result on Twitter15.

(b) The experimental result on Twitter16.

Fig. 5. Early detection results on two datasets.

The Fig. 5 shows the performances of our IBi-GCN model versus Bi-GCN, RvNN, SVM-TS, SVM-RBF and DTC at various deadlines for the datasets of Twitter15 and Twitter16. Deep learning methods such as our IBi-GCN, Bi-GCN and RvNN show high accuracy in the early stages of rumor detection, this depends on the ability of the neural network to accurately learn high-level representations from the initial aggregation of features. However, methods based on manual feature engineerings such as SVM-TS, SVM-RBF and DTC only give very low accuracy in the early stages of rumor detection. This is due to the large errors in the human labelled data, which results in a very poor detection as the classifier cannot be trained with accurate data at the beginning. In the subsequent training phase, due to the poor accuracy of the data, the classification results of the classifier are always at a relatively low value. In general, the figures show that our proposed IBi-GCN model achieves high detection accuracy at the early stage after message propagation. These exciting experimental results show that our model can effectively and quickly exploit the influence of users in the rumor spreading process to detect rumors more accurately compared to other baselines.

6   Conclusions

In this paper, we proposed a new model named IBi-GCN which combined an information entropy-based influence factor with GCN that enhanced features of influential users in rumor detection. Our model first counted the number of mentions of users in different scenarios, then calculated the local influence factor and global influence factor for all users separately using the information entropy-based method, and finally returned the overall influence factor in the form of a weighted sum. The advantage of the IBi-GCN model was it combined the rumor propagation mode and the user influence factor in using the GCN model to learn more advanced feature representations that help rumor detection. In addition, we constructed two variants of IBi-GCN, namely IBi-GCN-L and IBi-GCN-G, to model user influence patterns. Experimental results on two large-scale datasets showed that our proposed method outperformed the state-of-the-art baseline in terms of accuracy for both rumor detection.

Acknowledgments. This work was supported by National Natural Science Foundation of China under grant (No. 61802273, 62102277), Postdoctoral Science Foundation of China (No. 2020M681529), Natural Science Foundation of Jiangsu Province (BK20210703), China Science and Technology Plan Project of Suzhou (No. SYG202139), Postgraduate Research & Practice Innovation Program of Jiangsu Province (SJCX2_11342), Project Funded by the Priority Academic Program Development of Jiangsu Higher Education Institutions.

References

1. Ahsan, M., Kumari, M., Sharma, T.: Rumors detection, verification and controlling mechanisms in online social networks: A survey. OSNM (2019)
2. Alahmadi, D.H., Zeng, X.J.: Ists: Implicit social trust and sentiment based approach to recommender systems. Expert Systems with Applications (2015)
3. Bian, T., Xiao, X., Xu, T.: Rumor detection on social media with bi-directional graph convolutional networks. In: Proceedings of the AAAI conference on artificial intelligence. vol. 34, pp. 549–556 (2020)
4. Castillo, C., Mendoza, M., Poblete, B.: Information credibility on twitter. In: Proceedings of the 20th international conference on World Wide Web (2011)
5. Chen, X., Deng, L., Zhao, Y., Zhou, X., Zheng, K.: Community-based influence maximization in location-based social network. World Wide Web **24**(6), 1903–1928 (2021). https://doi.org/10.1007/s11280-021-00935-x
6. DiFonzo, N., Bordia, P.: Rumor, gossip and urban legends. Diogenes (2007)
7. Gao, J., Han, S., Song, X., Ciravegna, F.: Rp-dnn: A tweet level propagation context based deep neural networks for early rumor detection in social media. arXiv preprint arXiv:2002.12683 (2020)
8. Khoo, L.M.S., Chieu: Interpretable rumor detection in microblogs by attending to user interactions. In: Proceedings of the AAAI Conference on Artificial Intelligence. vol. 34, pp. 8783–8790 (2020)
9. Kwon, S., Cha, M., Jung, K.: Prominent features of rumor propagation in online social media. In: 2013 IEEE 13th international conference on data mining
10. Li, Q., Liu, X., Fang, R.: User behaviors in newsworthy rumors: A case study of twitter. In: Proceedings of the International AAAI Conference on Web and Social Media. pp. 627–630 (2016)
11. Lin, H., Ma, J., Cheng, M.: Rumor detection on twitter with claim-guided hierarchical graph attention networks. arXiv preprint arXiv:2110.04522 (2021)
12. Liu, G., Liu, Y., Zheng, K.: MCS-GPM: multi-constrained simulation based graph pattern matching in contextual social graphs. IEEE TKDE. pp. 1050–1064 (2018)
13. Liu, X., Nourbakhsh, A., Li, Q.: Real-time rumor debunking on twitter. In: Proceedings of the 24th ACM international on conference on information and knowledge management. pp. 1867–1870 (2015)
14. Liu, Y., Wu, Y.F.: Early detection of fake news on social media through propagation path classification with recurrent and convolutional networks. In: Proceedings of the AAAI conference on artificial intelligence. vol. 32 (2018)

15. Lu, Y.J., Li, C.T.: Gcan: Graph-aware co-attention networks for explainable fake news detection on social media. arXiv preprint arXiv:2004.11648 (2020)
16. Ma, J., Gao, W.: Debunking rumors on twitter with tree transformer. ACL (2020)
17. Ma, J., Gao, W., Wei, Z.: Detect rumors using time series of social context information on microblogging websites. In: Proceedings of the 24th ACM international on conference on information and knowledge management. pp. 1751–1754 (2015)
18. Ma, J., Gao, W., Wong, K.F.: Detect rumors in microblog posts using propagation structure via kernel learning. Association for Computational Linguistics (2017)
19. Ma, J., Gao, W., Wong, K.F.: Rumor detection on twitter with tree-structured recursive neural networks. Association for Computational Linguistics (2018)
20. Peng, S., Yang, A., Cao, L.: Social influence modeling using information theory in mobile social networks. Information Sciences **379**, 146–159 (2017)
21. Peng, S., Zhou, Y., Cao, L.: Influence analysis in social networks: A survey. Journal of Network and Computer Applications **106**, 17–32 (2018)
22. Popat, K.: Assessing the credibility of claims on the web. In: Proceedings of the 26th International Conference on World Wide Web Companion. pp. 735–739 (2017)
23. Potthast, M., Kiesel, J., Reinartz, K., Bevendorff, J., Stein, B.: A stylometric inquiry into hyperpartisan and fake news. arXiv preprint arXiv:1702.05638 (2017)
24. Riquelme, F., González-Cantergiani, P.: Measuring user influence on twitter: A survey. Information processing & management **52**(5), 949–975 (2016)
25. Rong, Y., Huang, W., Xu, T., Huang, J.: Dropedge: Towards deep graph convolutional networks on node classification. arXiv preprint arXiv:1907.10903 (2019)
26. Sampson, J., Morstatter, F., Wu, L.: Leveraging the implicit structure within social media for emergent rumor detection. In: Proceedings of the 25th ACM international on conference on information and knowledge management. pp. 2377–2382 (2016)
27. Thomas, S.A.: Lies, damn lies, and rumors: an analysis of collective efficacy, rumors, and fear in the wake of katrina. Sociological Spectrum **27**(6), 679–703 (2007)
28. Yang, F., Liu, Y., Yu, X.: Automatic detection of rumor on sina weibo. In: Proceedings of the ACM SIGKDD workshop on mining data semantics. pp. 1–7 (2012)
29. Yu, F., Liu, Q., Wu, S., Wang, L., Tan, T., et al.: A convolutional approach for misinformation identification. In: IJCAI. pp. 3901–3907 (2017)

Efficient Truss Computation for Large Hypergraphs

Xinzhou Wang[1], Yinjia Chen[2], Zhiwei Zhang[1(✉)], PengPeng Qiao[1], and Guoren Wang[1]

[1] Beijing Institute of Technology, Beijing, China
{xzwang,zwzhang,qpp}@bit.edu.cn, wanggrbit@126.com
[2] Beihang University, Beijing, China
chenyinjia2000@gmail.com

Abstract. Cohesive subgraph mining has been applied in many areas, including social networks, cooperation networks, and biological networks. The k-truss of a graph is the maximal subgraph in which each edge is contained in at least k triangles. Existing k-truss models are defined solely in pairwise graphs and are hence unsuitable for hypergraphs. In this paper, we propose a novel problem, named (k, α, β)-truss computation in hypergraphs. We then propose two hypergraph conversions. The first converts a hypergraph into a pairwise graph, while the second converts it into a projected graph. We further propose two algorithms for computing (k, α, β)-truss in hypergraphs based on these two types of conversions. Experiments show that our (k, α, β)-truss model is effective and our algorithms are efficient in large hypergraphs.

Keywords: Cohesive subgraph · Hypergraph · Truss computation

1 Introduction

Graphs are widely used to represent pairwise relationships between entities in many fields, such as social networks [17], collaboration networks [7], and protein networks [5]. Although graphs are effective modeling tools for pairwise relationships, most real-world relationships are groupwise rather than pairwise. For instance, a paper can have multiple authors, and an email can be sent to multiple recipients. In these scenarios, data can be represented as hypergraphs. A hypergraph contains a set of vertices and a set of hyperedges, where a hyperedge is a subset of vertices. Thus, this paper studies the modeling of cohesive subgraphs in hypergraphs.

As a fundamental problem in graph mining, discovering cohesive subgraphs has attracted much attention in recent years. Many cohesive subgraph models are proposed, including k-core [16], k-truss [3], k-clique [14], etc. In these models, k-truss achieves a good balance between cohesiveness and computation cost. The k-truss of a graph is a maximal subgraph where each edge is contained in at least k triangles. However, triangles do not exist naturally in hypergraphs, hence the

© The Author(s), under exclusive license to Springer Nature Switzerland AG 2022
R. Chbeir et al. (Eds.): WISE 2022, LNCS 13724, pp. 290–305, 2022.
https://doi.org/10.1007/978-3-031-20891-1_21

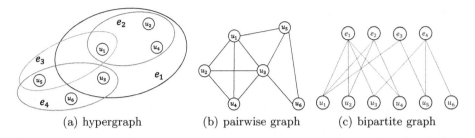

(a) hypergraph   (b) pairwise graph   (c) bipartite graph

Fig. 1. (a) an example of hypergraph (b) the corresponding pairwise graph (c) the corresponding bipartite graph

existing k-truss models are not suitable for hypergraphs. If we convert a hypergraph to a pairwise graph via clique expansion [15] and then compute k-truss in it, we will not obtain a decent result since k-truss considers all triangles as the same. For example, considering a hypergraph shown in Fig. 1(a) and the pairwise graph converted from it shown in Fig. 1(b), (u_1, u_2, u_4) and (u_3, u_5, u_6) are both triangles. However, (u_1, u_2, u_4) is more cohesive than (u_3, u_5, u_6) because three vertices u_1, u_2, u_4 contained in two hyperedges while u_3, u_5, u_6 only contained in one hyperedge.

Converting a hypergraph to a bipartite graph and employing the k-bitruss model [23] or k-Ctruss model [21] is another way to compute k-truss in hypergraphs. However, these two models are not suitable for hypergraphs. For example, considering the hypergraph shown in Fig. 1(a), if we compute k-bitruss on the corresponding bipartite graph shown in Fig. 1(c), we will only find a 2-bitruss induced by u_1, u_2, u_4, e_1 and e_2, while other cohesive subgraphs cannot be discovered. Similarly, if we compute k-Ctruss on it, we will only find a 1-Ctruss formed by u_1, u_3 and u_5.

In this paper, we propose a novel problem, named (k, α, β)-truss computation in hypergraphs. The main idea of the (k, α, β)-truss model is to define triangles in hypergraphs and add the cohesiveness constraint for each triangle. To solve this issue, we introduce two kinds of conversions of hypergraphs, i.e., converting to pairwise graphs and converting to projected graphs. To convert a hypergraph to a pairwise graph, we still follow the concept of clique expansion. However, unlike clique expansion, we retain the information of hyperedges after conversion. Formally, for an edge $e = (u, v)$ in the pairwise graph, we associate it with a set of hyperedges in which each hyperedge contains both vertices u and v. To convert a hypergraph to a projected graph, for any two vertices contained in at least one hyperedge, we record the number of hyperedges containing them. Based on these two conversions, we propose two algorithms to compute (k, α, β)-truss in hypergraphs, including a clique expansion-based algorithm and a projected graph-based algorithm. Our contributions are summarized in the following.

- We propose (k, α, β)-truss in hypergraphs, where α and β are two integers to measure the cohesiveness of a triangle.

- We propose two algorithms to compute (k, α, β)-truss in hypergraphs, including a clique expansion-based algorithm and a projected graph-based algorithm.
- We conduct extensive experiments one five real-world datasets to show the effectiveness and efficiency of our algorithms.

The rest of this paper is organized as follows. In Sect. 2, we introduce some related works. In Sect. 3, we give formally definitions of our work. In Sect. 4, we propose two algorithms to compute (k, α, β)-truss in hypergraphs. In Sect. 5, we report the results of our experiments. We conclude this paper in Sect. 6.

2   Related Works

Community Search. Community search problem is initially introduced in [17], aiming to find a cohesive subgraph containing query vertices. In existing works, a community structure is often defined by a cohesive subgraph model such as k-core [16], k-truss [19], k-clique [14], k-ECC [2], etc. In these models, k-truss has good balance between cohesiveness and computation cost. Huang et al. [7] firstly propose k-truss based community, providing a BFS based online querying algorithm and an index based algorithm. Literatures [12] proposes k-truss based community models with minimum diameter. The community search problem defined in heterogeneous information networks (HINs) and bipartite graphs can be directly used in hypergraphs. The community structure in bipartite graphs has been defined by (α, β)-core [20] and k-bitruss [23]. However, these models aim to find cohesive structure between both two types of vertex instead of one. Literatures [4] and [21] define k-core and k-truss in HINs. While they only consider different meta-path instances between different vertex pairs, ignoring multiple meta-path instances that connect one vertex pair.

Hypergraph. In recent years, several hypergraph problems have been researched, including structure characteristics [8], hypergraph partition [11] and cohesive sub-hypergraph [6,10]. Lee et al. [9] propose 26 hypergraph motifs that can capture local structure patterns from hypergraphs. Hu et al. [6] introduce the densest subset problem in hypergraphs, and provide exact algorithms to compute and maintain densest subset in hypergraphs. Leng et al. [10] firstly extend the concept of k-core to the hypergraph and solves the problem in linear time by the peeling algorithm. Sun et al. [18] study the k-core problem in the dynamic hypergraph and propose approximation algorithms to maintain k-core when hyperedges are inserted or deleted. To maintain k-core in hypergraphs exactly, Luo et al. [13] propose an exact algorithm to update hypercore numbers of vertices and hyperedges.

3   Problem Definition

A hypergraph is modeled as $G = (V, E)$, where V is a set of vertices and E is a set of hyperedges. Each hyperedge $e \in E$ is a subset of V, i.e., $E = \{e | e \subseteq V\}$, and $|e|$ is the degree of e, denoted as $deg(e)$. For any two vertices $u, v \in V$, if they contained in one hyperedge, we call (u, v) is a vertex pair. We define the H-set of two vertices u, v, denoted as $H_G(u, v)$, as the set of hyperedge which contains both u and v, i.e. $\forall e \in H_G(u, v), \{u, v\} \subseteq e$.

We define three vertex pairs $(u, v), (u, w), (v, w)$ as a triangle in a hypergraph, denoted as $\triangle_{u,v,w}$. For one triangle $\triangle_{u,v,w}$, we denote the intersection size of it as $I(u, v, w) = |H_G(u, v) \cap H_G(u, w) \cap H_G(v, w)|$, and denote the union size of it as $U(u, v, w) = |H_G(u, v) \cup H_G(u, w) \cup H_G(v, w)|$. We use $I(u, v, w)$ and $U(u, v, w)$ as a cohesive evaluation of a triangle. We give some definitions in the following.

Definition 1 ((α, β)-triangle). *Given a triangle $\triangle_{u,v,w}$ in a hypergraph G and two integers α, β. $\triangle_{u,v,w}$ is a (α, β)-triangle if and only if $I(u, v, w) \geq \alpha, U(u, v, w) \geq \beta$.*

Definition 2 ((α, β)-support). *Given a hypergraph G, a set of vertex pairs P and two integers α, β. For a vertex pair $(u, v) \in P$, the (α, β)-support of (u, v), denoted as $sup_{\alpha,\beta}(u, v, P)$, is the number of (α, β)-triangles, which are formed by vertex pairs in P, containing (u, v).*

Definition 3 ((k, α, β)-truss). *Given a hypergraph G, three integers k, α, β, the (k, α, β)-truss of G, is a maximal vertex pair set P_k such that each vertex pair $(u, v) \in P_k$, $sup_{\alpha,\beta}(u, v, P_k) \geq k$.*

Example 1. Consider a hypergraph G in Fig. 1(a) with six vertices, four hyperedges and ten vertex pairs. H-sets of three vertex pairs $(u_1, u_3), (u_1, u_5), (u_3, u_5)$ are $\{e_1\}, \{e_3\}$ and $\{e_4\}$, respectively. Thus, $I(u_1, u_3, u_5) = 0, U(u_1, u_3, u_5) = 3$ and $(u_1, u_3), (u_1, u_5), (u_3, u_5)$ form a $(0, 3)$-triangle. Another three vertex pairs $(u_3, u_5), (u_3, u_6), (u_5, u_6)$ form a $(1, 1)$-triangle because all of these vertices are contained in e_4, and of these three vertex pairs' support are 1, so $\{(u_3, u_5), (u_3, u_6), (u_5, u_6)\}$ is a $(1, 1, 1)$-truss.

Then, we formally introduce the problem studied in this paper.

Problem Definition. *Given a hypergraph G and three integers k, α, β, return (k, α, β)-truss of G.*

4   Truss Computation Algorithms

In this section, we first introduce two conversions of hypergraphs, and then propose two algorithms to compute (k, α, β)-truss.

4.1   Conversions of Hypergraphs

Convert to Pairwise Graph. To compute (k, α, β)-truss, we need to enumerate all vertex pairs in the hypergraph and check which of them can form (α, β)-triangles. To do that, we transform a hypergraph to a pairwise graph $G_N = (V_N, E_N)$ by clique expansion [15], i.e., transform each hyperedge to a complete subgraph.

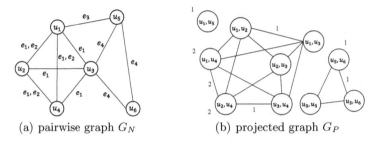

(a) pairwise graph G_N (b) projected graph G_P

Fig. 2. The pairwise graph G_N and the projected graph G_P convert from the hypergraph shown in Fig. 1(a)

Lemma 1. *Given a hypergraph G and a pairwise graph G_N convert from G, an edge in G_N is equivalent to a vertex pair in G, a triangle in G_N is equivalent to a $(0,0)$-triangle in G, and a k-truss in G_N is equivalent to a $(k, 0, 0)$-truss in G.*

Proof. According to the definition of clique expansion, it's obvious that an edge in G_N is equivalent to a vertex pair in G. A triangle in G_N contains three vertex pairs and each two of them have one common vertex, so a triangle in G_N is equivalent to a (0,0)-triangle in G. Thus, the k-truss in G_N is equivalent to the $(k, 0, 0)$-truss in G.   □

Based on the Lemma 1, we can conduct truss decomposition Algorithm [19] in G_N to compute $(k, 0, 0)$-truss of G. However, we cannot find (α, β)-triangles by G_N when $\alpha, \beta \neq 0$, because for a triangle (u, v, w) in G_N, we do not know $H_G(u, v), H_G(u, w)$ or $H_G(v, w)$. To solve this issue, we need to add information of hyperedges into G_N. We model $G_N = (V_N, E_N, H_N)$, where each edge $e = (u, v) \in E_N$ is associated with a set of hyperedges, which is $H_G(u, v)$, denoted as $H_N(e)$. For example, G_N convert from hypergraph in Fig. 1(a) is shown in Fig. 2(a).

Convert to Projected Graph. Inspired by n projected graph proposed in [22], we use the projected graph to keep the size of H-set for every vertex pair, to efficiently compute the size of intersection and union of three H-sets. We give the definitions in the following.

Definition 4 (Projected graph). *Given a hypergraph $G = (V, E)$, the projected graph of G is $G_P = (V_P, E_P, \omega_P, \sigma_P)$, where each node $n \in V_P$ (we use "node" to denote a vertex in G_P) contains a vertex pair $(u_n, v_n) \in V$, i.e., $\forall n \in V_P, n = \{u_n, v_n\} \subseteq V$. Two nodes $n_1, n_2 \in V_P$ is adjacent if and only if $|n_1 \cap n_2| = 1$ and $\exists e \in E, n_1 \cup n_2 \subseteq e$. Each node $n \in V_P$ is associated with a weight, denoted as $\omega_P(n)$, corresponds to the number of hyperedges which contains both u_n and v_n, i.e., $\omega_P(n) = |\{e \in E : \{u_n, v_n\} \subseteq e\}| = H_G(u_n, v_n)$. Each edge $e = (n_1, n_2) \in E_P$ is associated with a weight, denoted as $\sigma_P(e)$, corresponds to the number of hyperedges which contains $n_1 \cup n_2$, i.e., $\sigma_P(e) = |\{e \in E : n_1 \cup n_2 \subseteq e\}|$.*

Algorithm 1. CE-Truss

Input: Hypergraph G, three integers k, α, β
Output: (k, α, β)-truss
1: build $G_N = (V_N, E_N, H_N)$ from G
2: $Q \leftarrow \emptyset$
3: **for each** $e = (u, v) \in E_N$ **do**
4:     compute $sup_{\alpha, \beta}(u, v, E_N)$
5:     **if** $sup_{\alpha, \beta}(u, v, E_N) < k$ **then**
6:        $Q.add(e)$
7: **while** $Q \neq \emptyset$ **do**
8:     $e = (u, v) \leftarrow Q.pop()$
9:     delete e from G_N
10:     assume, w.l.o.g, $deg(u, G_N) \leq deg(v, G_N)$
11:     **for each** vertex $w \in Nbr(u, G_N) \cap Nbr(v, G_N)$ **do**
12:        **if** $I(u, v, w) \geq \alpha$ **and** $U(u, v, w) \geq \beta$ **then**
13:           $sup_{\alpha, \beta}(u, w, E_N) \leftarrow sup_{\alpha, \beta}(u, w, E_N) - 1$
14:           $sup_{\alpha, \beta}(v, w, E_N) \leftarrow sup_{\alpha, \beta}(v, w, E_N) - 1$
15:           **if** $sup_{\alpha, \beta}(u, w, E_N) < k$ **then**
16:              $Q.add((u, w))$
17:           **if** $sup_{\alpha, \beta}(v, w, E_N) < k$ **then**
18:              $Q.add((v, w))$
19: **return** residue edges of G_N

Definition 5 (Triangle node). *Given a projected graph G_P, two adjacent nodes $n_1 = \{u, v_{n_1}\}$, $n_2 = \{u, v_{n_2}\} \in V_P$. The triangle node of n_1 and n_2, denoted as $TN(n_1, n_2, G_P)$, is a node $n_3 \in V_P$ which contains $\{v_{n_1}, v_{n_2}\}$.*

Example 2. Figure 2(b) shows the projected graph build from the hypergraph in Fig. 1(a). For clarity, we only show a part of weight of nodes and edges in this figure. We denote the node contains $\{u_1, u_4\}$ as n_1, the node contains $\{u_2, u_4\}$ as n_2. u_1, u_4 contained in two hyperedges e_1 and e_2, so $\omega_P(n_1) = 2$. n_1 is adjacent to n_2 because $|\{u_1, u_4\} \cap \{u_2, u_4\}| = 1$ and u_1, u_2, u_4 are all contained in e_1 and e_2, thus $\sigma_P((n_1, n_2)) = 2$. The triangle node of n_1 and n_2 is the node $n_3 \in V_P$ contains $\{u_1, u_2\}$.

4.2 Clique Expansion-Based Algorithm

We use peeling algorithm in G_N to compute (k, α, β)-truss. The procedure of computing (k, α, β)-truss, named as CE-Truss, is shown in Algorithm 1. We first initialize an empty queue Q and build pairwise graph G_N based on hypergraph G (line 1–2). Then we compute $sup_{\alpha, \beta}(u, v, E_N)$ for each $(u, v) \in E_N$. if $sup_{\alpha, \beta}(u, v, E_N) < k$, we add edge (u, v) into Q (line 5–6). We iteratively delete edges from Q. When an edge $e = (u, v) \in E_N$ is deleted, we traverse all common neighbors of u and v, denoted as w (line 11–18). If (u, v, w) can form a (α, β)-triangle, means that $sup_{\alpha, \beta}(u, w, E_N)$ and $sup_{\alpha, \beta}(v, w, E_N)$ will be decreased beacuse of the deletion of (u, v). We update (u, w)'s and (v, w)'s support (line

13–14) and check if it need to be added into Q (line 15–18). Finally, we return the residue edges of G_N as (k, α, β)-truss.

Example 3. Consider the procedure of computing $(2,0,1)$-truss in the pairwise graph G_N shown in Fig. 2(a). First, we compute support of all edges in G_N, regarding to the set of all vertex pairs in G_N. We add edges $(u_1, u_5), (u_3, u_5), (u_5, u_6)$ and (u_3, u_6) into Q since there support are 0, 0, 1, 1, respectively. When we delete (u_1, u_5), we will find $(u_1, u_3), (u_1, u_5), (u_3, u_5)$ form a $(0,1)$-triangle, so support of (u_1, u_3) decrease from 3 to 2. Finally, we get the residue part of G_N as $(2, 0, 1)$-truss.

Lemma 2. *The time complexity of CE-Truss is $O(h_{max}(\sum_{e \in E}(deg(e))^2)^{1.5})$, where $h_{max} = max_{e \in E_N}|H_N(e)|$.*

Proof. To build a normal graph G_N based on hypergraph G, we need to traverse all hyperedges in G. For each hyperedges e, we need to traverse all vertex pair (u, v) and construct an edge in G_N for it. Thus, the time complexity of building G_N is $O(\sum_{e \in E}(deg(e))^2)$ and the number of edges in G_N is $\sum_{e \in E}(deg(e))^2$. For each $\triangle_{u,v,w}$, we need $O(h_{max})$ time to compute $I(u, v, w)$ and $U(u, v, w)$, and we need $O(|E_N|^{1.5})$ time to compute k-truss in G_N [19]. Thus, the time complexity of CE-Truss is $O(h_{max}(\sum_{e \in E}(deg(e))^2)^{1.5})$. □

4.3 Projected Graph-Based Algorithm

We propose another (k, α, β)-truss computation algorithm based on the projected graph G_P. Although we do not record H-set of any vertex pair in G_P, the following lemmas show that the information recorded in G_P is enough to compute (k, α, β)-truss when $\alpha \geq 1$.

Lemma 3. *Given a projected graph G_P convert from a hypergraph G. Two adjacent nodes $n_1, n_2 \in V_P$ and their triangle node n_3 is equivalent to a triangle in G, where the intersection size of the triangle is greater than or equal to 1.*

Proof. According to the Definition 4 and 5, for a node $n_1 = \{u, v\} \in V_P$, (u, v) is a vertex pair. Two adjacent nodes $n_1 = \{u, v\}, n_2 = \{u, w\}$ and their triangle node $n_3 = \{v, w\}$ is equivalent to a triangle $\triangle_{u,v,w}$ in G. Three vertices u, v, w contained in at least one hyperedge, so $I(u, v, w)$ is greater than or equal to 1.

Notice that we cannot compute (k, α, β)-truss by Lemma 3. This is because we find triangles in the hypergraph depending on triangles in the projected graph, while three nodes $n_1 = \{u, v\}, n_2 = \{u, w\}, n_3 = \{v, w\}$ in projected graph will not form a triangle if $I(u, v, w) = 0$.

Lemma 4. *Given a projected graph G_P convert from a hypergraph G, and two adjacent nodes $n_1, n_2 \in V_P$. Assuming that n_1, n_2 and their triangle node $n_3 \in V_P$ form a triangle $\triangle_{u,v,w}$, two equations $I(u, v, w) = \sigma_P((n_1, n_2))$, $U(u, v, w) = \omega_P(n_1) + \omega_P(n_2) + \omega_P(n_3) - 2 \times \sigma_P((n_1, n_2))$ hold.*

Algorithm 2. PG-Truss

Input: Hypergraph G, three integers k, α, β
Output: (k, α, β)-truss
1: **if** $\alpha == 0$ **then**
2:    **return** (k, α, β)-truss computed by CE-Truss
3: build $G_P = (V_P, E_P, \omega_P, \sigma_P)$ from G
4: $Q \leftarrow \emptyset$
5: **for all** $(u, v) \in E_P$: $visit(u, v) \leftarrow$ **false**
6: $G_P \leftarrow$ compute $(2k)$-core of G_P
7: **for each** node $u \in V_P$ **do**
8:    **for each** node $v \in Nbr(u, G_P)$ **and** $visit(u, v) ==$ **false do**
9:        $w \leftarrow TN(u, v, G_P)$
10:       **if** $\sigma_P((u, v)) \geq \alpha$ **and** $\omega_P(u) + \omega_P(v) + \omega_P(w) - 2 \times \sigma_P((u, v)) \geq \beta$ **then**
11:           $sup_{\alpha,\beta}(u, V_P) \leftarrow sup_{\alpha,\beta}(u, V_P) + 1$
12:           $sup_{\alpha,\beta}(v, V_P) \leftarrow sup_{\alpha,\beta}(v, V_P) + 1$
13:           $sup_{\alpha,\beta}(w, V_P) \leftarrow sup_{\alpha,\beta}(w, V_P) + 1$
14:           set $visit(u, v), visit(u, w), visit(v, w)$ as **true**
15: **for each** node $u \in V_P$ **do**
16:    **if** $sup_{\alpha,\beta}(u, V_P) < k$ **then**
17:       $Q.add(u)$
18: **while** $Q \neq \emptyset$ **do**
19:    $u \leftarrow Q.pop()$
20:    **for each** node $v \in Nbr(u, G_P)$ **do**
21:       update $sup_{\alpha,\beta}(v, V_P)$
22:       **if** $sup_{\alpha,\beta}(v, V_P) < k$ **then**
23:          $Q.add(v)$
24:    delete u from G_P
25: **return** residue nodes in G_P

Proof. According to the Definition 4, $I(u, v, w) = \sigma_P((n_1, n_2))$ is obvious, so we only prove the second equation. We denote $H_G(u, v, w)$ as the set of hyperedge s.t. $\forall e \in H_G(u, v, w), \{u, v, w\} \subseteq e$, $H_G(u, v, \neg w)$ as the set of hyperedge s.t. $\forall e \in H_G(u, v, \neg w), \{u, v\} \subseteq e \wedge w \notin e$. $|H_G(u, v, \neg w)| + |H_G(u, w, \neg v)| + |H_G(v, w, \neg u)| + |H_G(u, v, w)|$ is the number of hyperedges which contain more than two vertices of u, v, w, which is equaled to $U(u, v, w)$. Thus, we have

$$U(u, v, w) = |H_G(u, v) \backslash H_G(u, v, w)| + |H_G(u, w) \backslash H_G(u, v, w)| +$$
$$|H_G(v, w) \backslash H_G(u, v, w)| + |H_G(u, v, w)|$$
$$= |H_G(u, v)| - |H_G(u, v, w)| + |H_G(u, w)| - |H_G(u, v, w)| +$$
$$|H_G(v, w)| - |H_G(u, v, w)| + |H_G(u, v, w)|$$
$$= \omega_P(n_1) + \omega_P(n_2) + \omega_P(n_3) - 2 \times \sigma_P((n_1, n_2))$$

Based on the Lemma 3, we can find triangles which the intersection size greater than or equal to 1 in the hypergraph G by the projected graph G_P. Based on the Lemma 4, for a triangle $\triangle_{u,v,w}$ which we find, we can compute the union size of it by G_P. Thus, we can compute (k, α, β)-truss of G by G_P when $\alpha \geq 1$.

To reduce the size of G_P before we computing (k, α, β)-truss on it, we propose a pruning strategy based on the concept of k-core [16], which is a maximal subgraph that each vertex's degree is not less than k.

Lemma 5. *In a projected graph G_P convert from a hypergraph G, if a node n is not contained in the $(2k)$-core of G_P, the vertex pair contained in n cannot be contained in (k, α, β)-truss of G, where $\alpha \geq 1$.*

Proof. Assuming a node $n_1 \in V_P$ contains $\{u, v\}$, if the vertex pair (u, v) contained in a triangle, then n_1 have two different neighbors n_2 and n_3 containing $\{u, w\}$ and $\{v, w\}$, respectively. Thus, if the node n_1 contained in at least k triangles, n_1 should have at least $2k$ neighbors. □

The projected graph-based truss computation algorithm is described in Algorithm 2, denoted as PG-Truss. As we discussed before, all (α, β)-triangles computed by G_P satisfy $\alpha \geq 1$. So we cannot compute $(k, 0, \beta)$-truss by G_P. In this case, we still use CE-Truss (line 1–2). If $\alpha \geq 1$, we first build projected graph G_P from G and initialize an empty queue (line 3–4). We prune G_P to a $(2k)$-core based on Lemma 5 (line 6). Next, we compute the support of each node in G_P in line 7–14. For each pair of adjacent node (u, v) which has not visited, we first find the triangle node of them, denoted as w (line 9). Then we check whether u, v, w represent a (α, β)-triangle based on Lemma 4 (line 10). If the answer is yes, we add support of u, v, w by one (line 11–13). We mark three edges between $(u, v), (u, w), (v, w)$ as visited to avoid duplicate computation (line 14). When we get all support of $u \in V_P$, we add unqualified node into Q (line 15–17). Next, we iteratively delete a node u from Q and update its neighbor v's support which can form a (α, β)-triangle with u (line 18–24). Finally, residue nodes in G_P is the (k, α, β)-truss of G.

Example 4. We compute the $(1, 2, 2)$-truss based on the projected graph shown in Fig. 2(b) as an example. First, we compute 2-core in the projected graph. As a result, one node whose degree equals to 0 is deleted. When we compute support of node $n_1 = \{u_1, u_4\}$, we first visit the node $n_2 = \{u_1, u_2\}$ and find the triangle node $n_3 = \{u_2, u_4\}$. These three nodes form a $(2, 2)$-triangle so supports of them are increased by 1. Other nodes' support are computed in a similar way. When all nodes' support are computed, we find only three nodes n_1, n_2, n_3's support are greater than 1 so other nodes are deleted iteratively. When node $\{u_1, u_3\}$ is deleted, no nodes' support need to be updated since node $\{u_1, u_3\}$ is not contained in any $(2, 2)$-triangle. Finally, only three nodes n_1, n_2, n_3 are left in the projected graph, which means three vertex pairs $\{(u_1, u_4), (u_1, u_2), (u_2, u_4)\}$ is a $(1, 2, 2)$-truss.

Lemma 6. *The time complexity of PG-Truss is $O(\sum_{e \in E} \binom{deg(e)}{3})$.*

Proof. First, we calculate the upper bound of the number of vertices and edges in G_P. In the worst case, each hyperedge do not overlap each other. There will be $\sum_{e \in E} deg^2(e)$ vertices and $3 \times \sum_{e \in E} \binom{deg(e)}{3}$ edges in G_P. So the time complexity of building projected graph in line 3 is $O(\sum_{e\in E}\binom{deg(e)}{3})$. We need $O(|E_P|)$ time to compute the $(2k)$-core of G_P in line 6 [1]. In line 7–14 and line 18–24, we visit each edge in G_P once and only once. So the time complexity of PG-Truss is $O(|E_P|) = O(\sum_{e\in E}\binom{deg(e)}{3})$. $\qquad\square$

4.4   Comparison of CE-Truss and PG-Truss

PG-Truss is more efficient than CE-Truss beacuse it overcomes two limitations of CE-Truss:

1. **Massive Set Operation.** As we discussed in Lemma 2, the time complexity of checking whether a triangle is a (α,β)-triangle in CE-Truss is $O(h_{max})$, which is unefficient for a large H-set. For example, when we visit $\triangle_{u_1,u_2,u_4}$ in CE-Truss, to compute $I(u_1, u_2, u_4)$, we need to check whether u_4 is contained in hyperedge e_1 and e_2. To compute $U(u_1, u_2, u_4)$, we need to add six hyperedges contained in three H-sets into a set. In contrast, we can compute $I(u_1, u_2, u_4)$ and $U(u_1, u_2, u_4)$ by Lemma 4 in line 11 of PG-Truss, which only takes $O(1)$ time.

2. **Duplicate Computation.** Consider a triangle $\triangle_{u,v,w}$ in the hypergraph G, when we compute the support of (u, v) in CE-Truss, we need to visit $\triangle_{u,v,w}$ once. When we compute the support of (u, w) and (v, w), we need to visit $\triangle_{u,v,w}$ again. Thus, we visit each triangle three times in CE-Truss, which makes duplicate computation. For example, when we compute the support of vertex pair (u_1, u_4) in line 4 of CE-Truss, we visit vertex u_2 and compute $I(u_1, u_2, u_4)$ and $U(u_1, u_2, u_4)$. When we compute the support of (u_1, u_2) and (u_2, u_4), we will compute $I(u_1, u_2, u_4)$ and $U(u_1, u_2, u_4)$ again. Although there are 6 triangles in G, we will enumerate 18 triangles. In contrast, when we visit $n_1 = \{u_1, u_2\}$ in line 7 of PG-Truss, we will visit $n_2 = \{u_1, u_4\}$ and $n_3 = \{u_2, u_4\}$ once and mark edges between them as visited in line 14. So when we visit n_2 or n_3 in line 7, we will not visit $\triangle_{u_1,u_2,u_4}$ again.

5   Experiments

In this section, we conduct experiments on five real-world datasets to evaluate the effectiveness of our method and the efficiency of CE-Truss and PG-Truss. All algorithms are implemented in C++ and performed on a Linux Server with 2.1 GHz Intel Xeon Silver 4110 CPU, 256G RAM, running Ubuntu 18.04.

Datasets. We use five real-world datasets of hypergraph in our experiments[1]. Table 1 shows the statistic of these datasets.

Parameters. We set default value of k, α and β as 2, 2 and 3, respectively. For each dataset, we increase k by 10% of k_{max} and increase α, β by 5% of $\alpha_{max}, \beta_{max}$ each time. $k_{max}, \alpha_{max}, \beta_{max}$ are the largest value where a $(k, 0, 0)$-truss, $(1, \alpha, 0)$-truss and $(1, 0, \beta)$-truss exists, respectively.

---

[1] All datasets are obtained from https://www.cs.cornell.edu/~arb/data/.

Table 1. Statistic of datasets

Dataset	$|V|$	$|E|$	k_{max}	α_{max}	β_{max}
tags-ubuntu	3030	271233	70	1075	7049
coauthor-DBLP	1930379	3700067	23	126	493
coauthor-History	1034877	1812511	23	456	652
coauthor-Geology	1261130	1590335	28	74	240
NDC-substances	5557	112405	69	1749	4516

5.1 Effectiveness

We compare our model with k-Btruss [21], k-Ctruss [21], (α, β)-core community [20], k-bitruss [23] and Hypergraph k-core [10]. In k-Btruss and k-Ctruss model, we convert the hypergraph to a heterogeneous information network by considering the vertex and the hyperedge as two types of vertex in the HIN. In (α, β)-core community model and k-bitruss model, we consider the vertex and hyperedge as two layers of a bipartite graph. We adapt these models to community search problem by finding a connected component, including a query vertex q. We only specified queries on two datasets to show the effectiveness of our model due to space limitations.

Querying on DBLP. We set $q=$"Jiawei Han" and $k = 3, \alpha = 1, \beta = 35$ for our model, the same k for k-Btruss, k-Ctruss, k-bitruss and hypergraph k-core model, $\alpha = 6, \beta = 6$ for (α, β)-core community model, which is the largest α and β where the result exist. For the results, we record the number of vertices, the number of induced hyperedges and the density of the induced sub-hypergraph. The results of all models are shown in Table 2. Our (k, α, β)-truss model finds 10 vertex pairs formed by 5 vertices. All of them are researchers in the field of data science. Each two of them have coauthored at least 2 papers and all of them have coauthored one paper. The sub-hypergraph induced by these 5 vertices is shown in Fig. 3(a) (We omit duplicate hyperedges in the figure). (α, β)-core community and k-bitruss aim to find cohesive relationship between vertices and hyperedges, so they do not have good performances when we only focus on the relationship between vertices. Other models find more than one hundred thousand vertices, which is meaningless for a community.

Querying on Tags-ubuntu. In tags-ubuntu dataset, each hyperedge represents a question on askubuntu[2] and each vertex represents a tag applied to the question. We set $q=$"apt" and $k = 5, \alpha = 3, \beta = 300$ for our model, the same k for k-Btruss, k-Ctruss, k-bitruss and Hypergraph k-core model, and $\alpha = 4, \beta = 4$ for (α, β)-core community model, which is the largest α and β where the result exist. The results of all models are shown in Table 3. Our model finds 21 vertex pairs formed by 7 vertices. The induced sub-hypergraph of our model, which is shown in 3(b), has the highest density. We can find that each vertex of our

---

[2] https://askubuntu.com/.

Table 2. Statistic of querying results (DBLP)

Models	$|V|$	$|E|$	density
(k, α, β)-truss	5	93	18.6
k-Btruss	799567	1970915	2.46
k-Ctruss	212416	1020498	4.81
k-bitruss	485543	2126817	4.38
(α, β)-core community	896	3252	3.62
Hypergraph k-core	416282	2316114	5.56

Table 3. Statistic of querying results (tags-ubuntu)

Models	$|V|$	$|E|$	density
(k, α, β)-truss	7	12347	1763.85
k-Btruss	2484	269049	108.31
k-Ctruss	2386	268368	112.47
k-bitruss	2057	264036	128.35
(α, β)-core community	2122	265268	125.01
Hypergraph k-core	2625	270237	102.94

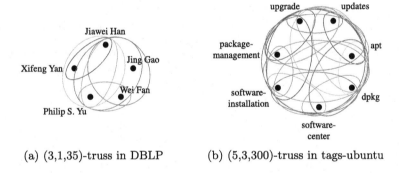

(a) (3,1,35)-truss in DBLP   (b) (5,3,300)-truss in tags-ubuntu

Fig. 3. (k, α, β)-truss querying results

result is closely related to software installation, which indicates our model has good cohesiveness on both structure and semantics. The other five models find thousands of vertices, which is still too large for a community structure.

5.2 Efficiency

Figure 4 shows the time consumption of CE-Truss and PG-Truss. We can find that PG-Truss is much faster than CE-Truss. This is because PG-Truss avoids set operations and duplicate computations. We also record the time consumptions of algorithms without the time of hypergraphs conversions, denoted as CE-

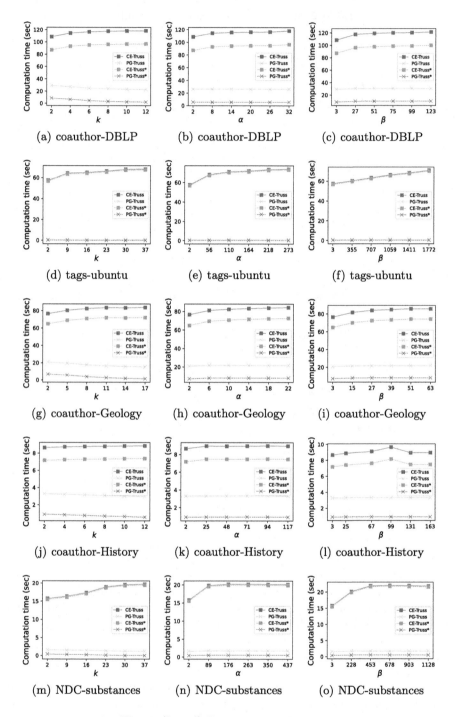

Fig. 4. (k, α, β)-Truss computation time

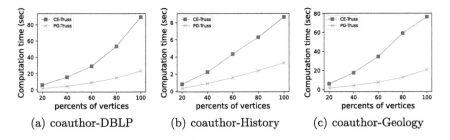

Fig. 5. Varying vertices number of hypergraph

Truss* and PG-Truss*. We can find that the time cost of two conversions is close in coauthor-DBLP, tags-ubuntu and coauthor-Geology datasets. In coauthor-History and NDC-substances, the time cost of converting a hypergraph to a projected graph is significantly higher than converting a hypergraph to a pairwise graph. This is because in these two datasets, there are more overlaps between hyperedges, causing a higher density of the projected graph. Thus we need more time to build the projected graph.

Varying k. We record the time cost of two algorithms by varying k. Results are shown in Fig. 4. When k increased slightly, the computation time of CE-Truss increased because more edges are not satisfied with the constraint of support and needed to be deleted. In contrast, the time cost of PG-Truss decreased slightly when k increased, because our pruning strategy is more powerful when k becomes larger and more nodes can be pruned in line 6 of PG-Truss.

Varying α and β. We record the time cost of two algorithms by varying α and β. Results are shown in Fig. 4. We can find that when α and β increase, the time cost of two algorithms increases slightly because algorithms need to iterate more times to delete unqualified vertex pairs. Compared with CE-Truss, PG-Truss is more stable when α and β increase because PG-Truss needs less time to update the support of a vertex pair.

Varying the Number of Vertices. To evaluate the scalability of our algorithms, we only choose 20%, 40%, 60%, 80% percent of vertices from coauthor-DBLP, coauthor-History, and coauthor-Geology datasets to build a small hypergraph due to space limitations, and record the time cost of CE-Truss and PG-Truss. Results are shown in Fig. 5. We can find that when the size of hypergraph is increased, the time cost of PG-Truss increases much slower than CE-Truss, which indicates that PG-Truss is more scalable than CE-Truss.

6   Conclusions

In this paper, we propose a novel problem, named the (k, α, β)-truss computation in hypergraphs, aiming to find a set of vertex pairs where each vertex is densely connected with others. To compute the (k, α, β)-truss in hypergraphs, we introduce two kinds of conversions of hypergraphs, i.e., converting to pairwise graphs and converting to projected graphs. Based on these two kinds of conversions, we then propose a clique expansion-based algorithm (CE-Truss) and a projected graph-based algorithm (PG-Truss). Our experimental results demonstrate the effectiveness and the efficiency of our solutions.

Acknowledgements. The work was supported by National Key Research and Development Program of China (Grant No. 2020YFB1707900, No. 2021YFB2700700), National Natural Science Foundation of China Grant No. 62072035, Open Research Projects of Zhejiang Lab (Grant No. 2020KE0AB04), CCF-Huawei Database System Innovation Research Plan Grant No. CCF-HuaweiDBIR2021007B.

References

1. Batagelj, V., Zaversnik, M.: An o(m) algorithm for cores decomposition of networks. Comput. Sci. **1**(6), 34–37 (2003)
2. Chang, L., Yu, J.X., Qin, L., Lin, X., Liu, C., Liang, W.: Efficiently computing k-edge connected components via graph decomposition. In: SIGMOD, pp. 205–216. ACM (2013)
3. Cohen, J.: Trusses: cohesive subgraphs for social network analysis. national security agency technical report (2008)
4. Fang, Y., Yang, Y., Zhang, W., Lin, X., Cao, X.: Effective and efficient community search over large heterogeneous information networks. Proc. VLDB Endow. **13**(6), 854–867 (2020)
5. Hu, A.L., Chan, K.C.: Utilizing both topological and attribute information for protein complex identification in PPI networks. IEEE/ACM Trans. Comput. Biol. Bioinf. **10**(3), 780–792 (2013)
6. Hu, S., Wu, X., Chan, T.H.: Maintaining densest subsets efficiently in evolving hypergraphs. In: CIKM, pp. 929–938. ACM (2017)
7. Huang, X., Cheng, H., Qin, L., Tian, W., Yu, J.X.: Querying k-truss community in large and dynamic graphs. In: SIGMOD, pp. 1311–1322. ACM (2014)
8. Lee, G., Choe, M., Shin, K.: How do hyperedges overlap in real-world hypergraphs? - patterns, measures, and generators. In: WWW, pp. 3396–3407 (2021)
9. Lee, G., Ko, J., Shin, K.: Hypergraph motifs: concepts, algorithms, and discoveries. Proc. VLDB Endow. **13**(11), 2256–2269 (2020)
10. Leng, M., Sun, L.Y., Bian, J.N., Yu-Chun, M.A.: An o(m) algorithm for cores decomposition of undirected hypergraph. J. Chin. Comput. Syst. **34**, 2568–2573 (2013)
11. Liu, H., Latecki, L.J., Yan, S.: Dense subgraph partition of positive hypergraphs. IEEE Trans. Pattern Anal. Mach. Intell. **37**(3), 541–554 (2015)
12. Liu, Q., Zhao, M., Huang, X., Xu, J., Gao, Y.: Truss-based community search over large directed graphs. In: SIGMOD, pp. 2183–2197. ACM (2020)
13. Luo, Q., Yu, D., Cai, Z., Lin, X., Cheng, X.: Hypercore maintenance in dynamic hypergraphs. In: ICDE, pp. 2051–2056 (2021)
14. Palla, G., Deranyi, I., Farkas, I., Vicsek, T.: Uncovering the overlapping community structure of complex networks in nature and society. Nature **435**(7043), 814 (2005)

15. Pu, L., Faltings, B.: Hypergraph learning with hyperedge expansion. In: Flach, P.A., De Bie, T., Cristianini, N. (eds.) ECML PKDD 2012. LNCS (LNAI), vol. 7523, pp. 410–425. Springer, Heidelberg (2012). https://doi.org/10.1007/978-3-642-33460-3_32
16. Seidman, S.B.: Network structure and minimum degree. Soc. Netw. **5**(3), 269–287 (1983)
17. Sozio, M., Gionis, A.: The community-search problem and how to plan a successful cocktail party. In: SIGKDD, pp. 939–948 (2010)
18. Sun, B., Chan, T.H., Sozio, M.: Fully dynamic approximate k-core decomposition in hypergraphs. ACM Trans. Knowl. Discov. Data **14**(4), 39:1–39:21 (2020)
19. Wang, J., Cheng, J.: Truss decomposition in massive networks. Proc. VLDB Endow. **5**(9), 812–823 (2012)
20. Wang, K., Zhang, W., Lin, X., Zhang, Y., Qin, L., Zhang, Y.: Efficient and effective community search on large-scale bipartite graphs. In: ICDE, pp. 85–96 (2021)
21. Yang, Y., Fang, Y., Lin, X., Zhang, W.: Effective and efficient truss computation over large heterogeneous information networks. In: ICDE, pp. 901–912. IEEE (2020)
22. Yoon, S., Song, H., Shin, K., Yi, Y.: How much and when do we need higher-order informationin hypergraphs? A case study on hyperedge prediction. In: WWW, pp. 2627–2633 (2020)
23. Zou, Z.: Bitruss decomposition of bipartite graphs. In: Navathe, S.B., Wu, W., Shekhar, S., Du, X., Wang, X.S., Xiong, H. (eds.) DASFAA 2016. LNCS, vol. 9643, pp. 218–233. Springer, Cham (2016). https://doi.org/10.1007/978-3-319-32049-6_14

Security and Privacy

Identifying Privacy Risks Raised by Utility Queries

Hira Asghar$^{(\boxtimes)}$, Christophe Bobineau, and Marie-Christine Rousset

Université Grenoble Alpes, CNRS, Grenoble INP, LIG, Grenoble, France
{hira.asghar,christophe.bobineau,
marie-christine.rousset}@univ-grenoble-alpes.fr

Abstract. Personal data are increasingly disseminated over the Web through mobile devices and smart environments, and are exploited for developing more and more sophisticated services and applications. All these advances come with serious risks for privacy breaches that may reveal private information wanted to remain undisclosed by data producers. It is therefore of utmost importance to help them to identify privacy risks raised by requests of service providers for utility purposes. In this paper, we first formalize privacy risks by *privacy queries* expressed (and kept secret) by each data producer to specify the data they do not want to be disclosed. Then, we develop a formal approach for detecting incompatibility between privacy and utility queries expressed as *temporal aggregate conjunctive queries*. The distinguishing point of our approach is to be data-independent and to come with an *explanation* based on the query expressions only. This explanation is intended to help data producers understand the detected privacy breaches and guide their choice of the appropriate technique to correct it.

Keywords: Temporal aggregated conjunctive queries · Utility queries · Privacy queries

1 Introduction

Personal data are increasingly disseminated over the Internet through mobile devices and smart environments, and are exploited for developing more and more sophisticated services and applications. All these advances come with serious risks for privacy breaches that may reveal private information wanted by users to remain undisclosed. It is therefore of utmost importance to help data producers to keep the control on their data for their privacy protection while preserving the utility of disclosed data for service providers.

In this paper, we approach the problem of utility-aware privacy preservation in the setting of applications where service providers request collecting data from

Partially supported by MIAI@Grenoble Alpes (ANR-19-P3IA-0003), PERSYVAL-Lab (ANR-11-LABX-0025-01) and TAILOR, a project funded by EU Horizon 2020 research and innovation programme under GA No 952215.

data producers in order to perform aggregate data analytics for optimization or recommendation purposes. The approach that we promote to face the privacy versus utility dilemma in this setting can be summarized as follows:

- Data producers specify by a set of *privacy queries* (kept secret) the (possibly aggregated) data that they do not want to disclose.
- Data consumers make explicit by a set of *utility queries* the data that they request from each data producer for offering them services in return.
- The compatibility between privacy and utility queries is automatically verified, and in case of incompatibility data producers get an explanation that can be exploited later to help them find an acceptable privacy-utility trade-off.

Our contribution is twofold. First, we handle the temporal aspect in the definition of privacy and utility by expressing privacy and utility queries as *temporal aggregate queries*. Taking into account the temporal aspect for privacy protection is very important since many applications handle dynamic data (e.g., electrical consumption, time series, mobility data) for which temporal data are considered as sensitive and aggregates on time are important for data analytics. Second, we formally define and *automatically verify incompatibility between privacy and utility queries based on their query expressions only*, and thus independently of the data. Incompatibility proofs come with explanations which can be exploited subsequently for helping data producers choose an appropriate defence strategy while limiting the utility loss. This can be done by applying to their data existing anonymization techniques based on differential privacy [8] or k-anonymity [13]. The paper is organized as follows. Section 2 provides an illustrative scenario of our approach. Section 3 formally defines the queries that we consider. Section 4 is dedicated to checking incompatibility between privacy and utility queries. Section 5 presents related work, and Sect. 6 concludes our paper.

2   Illustrative Scenario

We consider a use-case related to smart power grids, in which the data producers are customers with smart meters in their home. A service provider has a catalog of energy efficiency products (including energy efficient insulation, windows, appliances) and requests collecting data from all the customers to adapt the proposed services to the profile of each of them based on some personal data.

We assume that the service provider and the customers understand each other through a common vocabulary using a a simple ontology such as the one[1] that we have extracted from the ISSDA dataset, a real world power grid dataset provided by the *Irish Social Science Data Archive (ISSDA) Commission for Energy Regulation (CER)*[2]. This shared vocabulary allows service providers to specify their data needs in a precise way through a set of *utility* queries, that

---

[1] Available at https://raw.githubusercontent.com/fr-anonymous/puck/main/issda_schema.ttl.

[2] https://www.ucd.ie/issda/data/commissionforenergyregulationcer/.

can then be compared to a set of *privacy* queries used by each data producer to state the data that they not want to be disclosed directly or indirectly.

Let us suppose that the service provider has the following data needs:

(1) for each identifier of customers that are owners of their home, their yearly income if it is more than 75000;
(2) for each identifier of customers, their smart meter number;
(3) for each smart meter number, the sum of consumptions computed every hour over the meter readings of the previous 3 h.

These needs can be translated into the utility queries shown below by using SPARQL-like query language that will be explained in Sect. 3.

The utility queries into SPARQL-like query language

```
UQ1:  SELECT ?o ?y
      WHERE { ?o issda:yearlyIncome ?y . ?o issda:own ?s.
      FILTER(?y > 75000)}
UQ2:  SELECT ?sm ?o
      WHERE { ?sm issda:associatedOccupier ?o .
      ?o issda:nbOfPersons ?n }
UQ3:  SELECT ?sm   ?timeWindowEnd SUM(?c)
      WHERE {(?sm issda:consumption ?c, ?ts)}
      GROUP BY ?sm ?timeWindowEnd
      TIMEWINDOW (3h, 1h)
```

Now, suppose that a given customer, possibly with the help of privacy officer or tool, states that, among the data they accept to transmit, they want to prevent:

– the association between their smart meter number and their yearly income;
– the disclosure of their energy consumption measurements aggregated over intervals of 6 h.

This can be translated into the following privacy queries for which no answer should be transmitted or inferred by any external data consumer.

The privacy queries of a given customer

```
PQ1:  SELECT ?sm ?y
      WHERE {?sm issda:associatedOccupier ?o .
      ?o issda:yearlyIncome ?y}
PQ2:  SELECT   ?timeWindowEnd SUM(?c)
      WHERE {(?sm issda:consumption ?c , ?ts)}
      GROUP BY   ?timeWindowEnd
      TIMEWINDOW (6h, 6h)
```

With our approach, as it will be explained in Sect. 4, we can automatically detect that the above utility and privacy queries are incompatible, and provide the following privacy diagnosis:

1) The first privacy risk is due to the possible violation of the privacy query PQ1 by the combination of answers to the utility queries UQ1 and UQ2.

2) The second privacy risk is due to the possible violation of the privacy query PQ2 by answers to the utility query UQ3 because:
   a) PQ2 and UQ3 compute the same aggregate under the same conditions;
   b) groups of UQ3 are partitions of groups of PQ2;
   c) and finally, all time windows of PQ2 can be obtained as disjoint unions of some time windows of UQ3.

Based on the above explanations, the data producer could, for example, inform the service provider that:

– they will refuse to answer at least one the utility queries UQ1 or UQ2;
– they could accept to answer UQ3 if the time window is changed, for instance by modifying the step between each consumption computation.

3   Formal Background

We first define *temporal aggregate conjunctive queries* (TACQ) with a SPARQL-like syntax extended with time windows for capturing aggregate on time. Then, we define the compatibility problem between utility and privacy TACQs.

To simplify the exposition, we will only consider aggregate queries with a single aggregation term. In most cases, queries with several aggregate terms are equivalent to the unions of queries with same body and a single aggregate [2]. In particular, AVG can be computed by the union of two queries, one for computing SUM and the other one for computing $COUNT$.

Definition 1 relies on the notion of *temporal graph pattern* that is an extension of the standard notion of graph pattern in SPARQL in which we allow to associate *timestamp variables* to triple patterns involving *dynamic* properties. Through homomorphisms from temporal graph patterns to temporal data graphs, timestamp variables can only be assigned to timestamps appearing in timestamped RDF triples instantiating the dynamic properties.

Definition 1 (Temporal aggregated conjunctive query). *A TACQ is:*

SELECT $\bar{x}$, $agg(y)$
WHERE $\{GP.\ FILTER\}$
GROUP BY $\bar{x}$
TIMEWINDOW (Size, Step)

where:

– *GP is a temporal graph pattern;*
– *FILTER is a conjunction of atomic comparisons of the form $t\ \theta\ t'$ where t and t' are variables of GP or literals (numbers, strings or dates) and $\theta \in \{<>, <, <=, =, >=, >\}$;*
– *$\bar{x}$ is a tuple of variables called the output (or grouping) variables;*

- *when the aggregate term agg(y) is present, y (called the aggregate variable) is not in $\bar{x}$ and agg is an aggregate function that produces a single value when applied to a set of values assigned to y;*
- *Size and Step are time durations (i.e. differences between timestamps).*

The general syntax can be simplified as follows for capturing particular cases:

- when either $\bar{x}$ is empty or there is no aggregate term, we can omit the GROUP BY clause;
- when $Size = \infty$ $(Step = 0)$, the TIMEWINDOW clause can be omitted;
- the $FILTER$ clause can be omitted when the corresponding boolean expression is TRUE (called empty $FILTER$).

Note however, that when TIMEWINDOW is specified, FILTER always contains the implicit following constraints for each timestamp variable $?ts$:

$$?ts \leq ?timeWindowEnd \wedge ?ts > ?timeWindowsEnd - Size.$$

where $?timeWindowEnd$ is a specific timestamp variable that will be mapped successively to the upper bound of each time window computed from the timestamp at which the query is executed.

Given a TACQ defined in Definition 1, its evaluation over a temporal data graph G is defined in terms of filtered homomorphisms (Definition 2) and groups (Definition 3) for obtaining its answer set.

Definition 2 (Filtered homomorphisms). *Let M be the set of homomorphisms from GP to G. The filtered set of homomorphisms is the subset of M of homomorphisms μ such that $\mu(FILTER) = $ TRUE.*

Definition 3 states that there are as many groups as filtered homomorphisms allowing to match the tuple $\bar{x}$ with tuples of values $\bar{v}$ multiplied by the number of time intervals defined by values of k as: $]now - k \times Step - Size, now - k \times Step]$ where *now* denotes the timestamp at which the query is executed.

Definition 3 (Groups). *Let FM be the set of filtered homomorphisms from GP to G. Groups are defined for each tuple $\bar{v}$ and each time interval k as follows: $Group_k(\bar{v}) = \{\mu(y) \mid \mu \in FM, \mu(\bar{x}) = \bar{v}, $ and for each timestamp variable $\mu(?ts) \in]now - k \times Step - Size, now - k \times Step]) $ and $\mu(?timeWindowEnd) = now - k \times Step\}.*$

It is important to note that if there is no aggregate term, there is only one time window (i.e., $] - \infty, now]$) and there are as many groups as distinct tuples $\bar{v}$. For each group $Group_k(\bar{v})$, an answer is either the tuple $\bar{v}$ if there is no aggregate term, or the tuple $(\bar{v}, r)$ obtained by concatenating the tuple $\bar{v}$ with the result r of the aggregation function applied to the values in the group.

The answer set of a query Q_{window}:

SELECT $\bar{x}$ $agg(y)$ WHERE $\{GP.\ FILTER\}$
GROUP BY $\bar{x}$ TIMEWINDOW $(Size, Step)$

is the union of the answer sets resulting of the evaluation over each time window of Q_{window} of the query Q:

SELECT $\bar{x}$ $agg(y)$ WHERE $\{GP.\ FILTER\}$ GROUP BY $\bar{x}$

By interpreting GP as the logical conjunction of atomic formulas, Definition 4 defines the logical signature of an answer to a query as the logical formula characterizing all the (unknown) temporal data graphs leading to this answer for this query.

Definition 4 (Logical signature of answers). *For an answer $(\bar{a}, r)$ to a query Q, let $\mu_{\bar{a}}$ the mapping assigning each grouping variable x in $\bar{x}$ to the corresponding constant a in $\bar{a}$. The logical signature of $(\bar{a}, r)$ and Q, denoted $\sigma((\bar{a}, r), Q)$, is the formula:*

$(\exists y \exists \bar{z}\, \mu_{\bar{a}}(GP) \wedge \mu_{\bar{a}}(FILTER)) \wedge agg(\{y | \exists \bar{z},\, \mu_{\bar{a}}(GP) \wedge \mu_{\bar{a}}(FILTER)\}) = r$

where $\bar{z}$ is the (possibly empty) subset of variables in GP non including the aggregate variable y.

When there is no aggregate variable, the logical signature is reduced to the formula: $(\exists y \exists \bar{z}\, \mu_{\bar{a}}(GP) \wedge \mu_{\bar{a}}(FILTER))$.

The logical signatures of the respective answers (sm1031, 75000) and (sm1031, 2020-07-14T03:30:00, 88) to the (simple conjunctive) privacy query PQ1 and the TACQ utility query UQ3 used in the scenario of Sect. 2, are given below:

Logical signature of the answer (sm1031, 75000) of PQ1

```
∃?o, sm1031 issda:associatedOccupier ?o
∧ ?o issda:yearlyIncome 75000
```

Logical signature of the answer ($sm1031$, 2020-07-14T03:30:00, 88) of UQ3

```
∃?c ∃?ts (sm1031 issda:consumption ?c,?ts)
∧ ?ts ≤ 2020-07-14T03:30:00 ∧ ?ts > 2020-07-14T00:30:00
∧ SUM {?c | ∃?ts (sm1031 issda:consumption ?c, ?ts)
∧ ?ts ≤ 2020-07-14T03:30:00 ∧ ?ts > 2020-07-14T00:30:00 } =
    88
```

Definition 5 formalizes incompatibility as the possibility of inferring answers of a privacy query from answers of utility queries on the same data graph *without necessarily knowing it.*

Definition 5 (Incompatibility between privacy and utility queries). *A privacy query is incompatible with a set of utility queries if the logical signature of an answer to the privacy query is entailed by a conjunction of logical signatures of answers to some utility queries.*

4   Incompatibility Detection

The privacy queries are specific to, and kept secret by, each data producer. Then, the detection of incompatibility is done by algorithms launched by each data producer, given the set of utility queries they receive from a data consumer. In this section, we provide a characterization of incompatibility by distinguishing the cases where privacy queries are without aggregate (Theorem 1) or with aggregate (Theorem 2, Theorem 3 and Theorem 4).

Without loss of generality, by renaming variables within each query, we consider that queries have no variable in common. We will use the following notations:

Privacy query Q_p:
SELECT $\bar{x}_p \ agg_p(y_p)$ WHERE $\{GP_p . \ FILTER_p\}$
GROUP BY $\bar{x}_p$ TIMEWINDOW $(Size_p, \ Step_p)$
Utility query Q_{u_i} :
SELECT $\bar{x}_{u_i} \ agg_{u_i}(y_{u_i})$ WHERE $\{GP_{u_i} . \ FILTER_{u_i}\}$
GROUP BY $\bar{x}_{u_i}$ TIMEWINDOW $(Size_{u_i}, \ Step_{u_i})$

For a TACQ in its general form, we will often rely on its *conjunctive part*, and also on its *plain variant* without aggregate.

Definition 6 (Conjunctive part and plain variant of a query). *Let Q be a TACQ of the form:*

SELECT $\bar{x} \ agg(y)$
WHERE $\{GP . \ FILTER\}$
GROUP BY $\bar{x}$
TIMEWINDOW (Size, Step)

The conjunctive part of Q, noted $Conj(Q)$, is the simple conjunctive query:

$Conj(Q) : SELECT \ \bar{x} \ WHERE \ \{GP\}$

The plain variant of Q, noted $Plain(Q)$, is the query without aggregate that is evaluated before computing the aggregate function:

$Plain(Q) : SELECT \ \bar{x} \ y \ WHERE \ \{GP . \ FILTER\}$

Theorem 1 provides a full characterization of incompatibility of a privacy query Q_p *without aggregate* and a set of n utility queries Q_{u_1}, ..., Q_{u_n}. It relies on evaluating the privacy query on all the (small) data graphs that are representative of the different ways of joining answers of utility queries. Each of these data graph is obtained by *freezing* (Definition 7) the variables in the union of graph patterns in the utility queries, in a way that allows to replace distinct output variables with a same constant (in order to mimic possible joins between output variables coming from different utility queries).

Definition 7 (Freezing of graph patterns). *Let GP a temporal graph pattern and X a subset of its variables. A freezing of X in GP, denoted Frozen(GP, X), is the graph pattern obtained from GP by replacing each occurrence of $x \in X$ by a constant, such that every variable in X that is not an output variable is replaced by a distinct constant.*

Theorem 1 (Incompatibility of privacy queries without aggregate). *A privacy query Q_p without aggregate is* incompatible *with a set of utility queries $Q_{u_1}, ..., Q_{u_n}$ if and only if there exists a freeze of the variables in $\bigcup_{i \in [1..n]} GP_{u_i}$, and an answer $\bar{c} = h(\bar{x})$ of the conjunctive part of Q_p over $freeze(\bigcup_{i \in [1..n]} GP_{u_i})$ and if Q_p has a FILTER condition: $freeze(\bigwedge_{i \in [1..n]} FILTER_{u_i}) \models h(FILTER_p)$*

Proof. If Q_p is incompatible with the utility queries, it means by definition that there exists tuples of constants $\bar{a}, \bar{a}_1, ..., \bar{a}_n$ such that:

$$\exists \bar{z}_1 ... \exists \bar{z}_n\, \mu_{\bar{a}_1}(GP_{u_1}) \wedge \mu_{\bar{a}_1}(FILTER_{u_1}) \wedge ... \wedge \mu_{\bar{a}_n}(GP_{u_n}) \wedge \mu_{\bar{a}_n}(FILTER_{u_n})$$
$$\models \exists \bar{z}\, \mu_{\bar{a}}(GP_p) \wedge \mu_{\bar{a}}(FILTER_p).$$

Since the sets of variables in each query are pairwise disjoint, the entailment is only possible if there exists an homomorphism h from the variables in $\bar{z}$ to the variables or constants in the left hand side so that all the atoms in $h(\mu_{\bar{a}}(GP_p))$ appear in the union of the atoms in $\mu_{\bar{a}_1}(GP_{u_1}) \wedge ... \wedge \mu_{\bar{a}_n}(GP_{u_n})$, and $h(\mu_{\bar{a}}(FILTER_p))$ is entailed by $\mu_{\bar{a}_1}(FILTER_{u_1}) \wedge... \wedge \mu_{\bar{a}_n}(FILTER_{u_n})$. Let *Frozen* be the result on $\bigcup_{i \in [1..n]} GP_{u_i}$ of the freezing *freeze* that replaces each output variable x_{u_i} by $\mu_{\bar{a}_i}(x_{u_i})$. The homomorphism $h \cup \mu_{\bar{a}}$ from the graph pattern GP_p to *Frozen* allows to show that $\bar{a}$ is an answer of the conjunctive part of Q_p when evaluated over *Frozen*, and: $freeze(\bigwedge_{i \in [1..n]} FILTER_{u_i}) \models (h \cup \mu_{\bar{a}})(FILTER_p)$.

For the converse way of the proof, let us consider *Frozen* the result on $\bigcup_{i \in [1..n]} GP_{u_i}$ of a freezing *freeze* of the output variables such that there exists an answer $\bar{c}$ of Q_p when evaluated over *Frozen* with a support homomorphism h such that $h(\bar{x}) = \bar{c}$ and $freeze(\bigwedge_{i \in [1..n]} FILTER_{u_i}) \models h(FILTER_p)$.

The homomorphism h allows to show the entailment between the formulas ϕ_1: $\exists \bar{z}_u$ *Frozen* $\wedge\, freeze(\bigwedge_{i \in [1..n]} FILTER_{u_i})$ and ϕ_2: $\exists \bar{z}\, h_{\bar{c}}(GP_p) \wedge h_{\bar{c}}(FILTER_p)$ where GP_p and *Frozen* are interpreted as the conjunction of their respective triple patterns seen as logical atoms, and $h_{\bar{c}}$ is the restriction of h to the output variables of Q_p. In fact, ϕ_1 and ϕ_2 are respectively the conjunction of logical signatures of the answers $freeze(\bar{x}_{u_i})$ of each Q_{u_i}, and the logical signature of the answer $\bar{c}$ of Q_p. Therefore, the privacy query Q_p is incompatible with the utility queries. ∎

Example 1. Let us consider the following privacy and utility queries PQ_1, UQ_1 and UQ_2, corresponding respectively to the first privacy query and the first two utility queries (up to variable renaming) of the scenario illustrated in Sect. 2:

PQ_1: SELECT ?sm ?y WHERE {?sm issda:associatedOccupier ?o .
　　　　　?o issda:yearlyIncome ?y}
UQ_1: SELECT ?x1 ?y1 WHERE { ?x1 issda:yearlyIncome ?y1 .
　　　　　?x1 issda:owns ?z1 . FILTER (?y1 > 75000)}
UQ_2: SELECT ?x2 ?y2
　　　　　WHERE { ?x2 issda:associatedOccupier ?y2. ?y2 issda:nbOfPersons ?n }

The following *Frozen* and *Frozen'* are different freezing of the variables in the union of the utility graph patterns, where the constants corresponding to the freezing of output variables are denoted by constants oc_i:

$$Frozen = \{oc_1 \text{ issda:yearlyIncome } oc_2 \text{ . } oc_1 \text{ issda:owns } c_3.$$
$$oc_4 \text{ issda:associatedOccupier } oc_5 \text{ . } oc_5 \text{ issda:nbOfPersons } c_6\}$$

obtained by the freezing: $\{$?x1$/oc_1$, ?y1$/oc_2$, ?z1$/c_3$, ?x2$/oc_4$, ?y2$/oc_5$, ?n$/c_6\}$

$$Frozen' = \{oc_1 \text{ issda:yearlyIncome } oc_2 \text{ . } oc_1 \text{ issda:owns } c_3.$$
$$oc_4 \text{ issda:associatedOccupier } oc_1 \text{ . } oc_1 \text{ issda:nbOfPersons } c_6\}$$

obtained by a freezing in which ?x1 and ?y2 that are output variables in each of the utility queries are frozen to the same constant oc_1.

$Ans(PQ_1, Frozen)$ is empty but $Ans(PQ_1, Frozen') = \{(oc_4, oc_2)\}$.
This proves that PQ_1 is incompatible with the utility policy composed by the two utility queries UQ_1 and UQ_2. The corresponding freezing allows to exhibit the encountered privacy risk: an answer (for instance (oc_4, oc_2)) to the privacy query PQ_1 is disclosed each time answering UQ_1 and UQ_2 return answers where the first element of an answer to UQ_1 is equal to the second element of an answer to UQ_2 (for instance (oc_1, oc_2) and (oc_4, oc_1)), thus violating any privacy policy containing PQ_1. It is important to note that PQ_1 is not incompatible with each of the utility queries taken in isolation.

Worst-Case Complexity: In the worst case, checking compatibility using Theorem 1 requires to evaluate the conjunctive part of the privacy query over the frozen graph patterns resulting from all the possible freezing of the output variables of the utility queries. The evaluation of the conjunctive part of privacy query over a frozen graph pattern is polynomial in the size of the utility queries but the number of possible freezing is 2^{OV_u} where OV_u is the number of output variables of the utility queries. Handling privacy queries with FILTER conditions requires to check in addition logical entailment of conjunction of comparison atoms, which can be done using a constraint solver.

In Practice: In fact, a freezing can be obtained from the initial most general freezing, which assigns each output variable to a distinct fresh constant, by equating a subset of these constants. The choice of constants to equate is constrained by the join variables within the privacy query to obtain an answer. We have exploited those constraints in our implementation[3].

We consider now the case of checking incompatibility of a *privacy query with aggregate* with a set of utility queries. In this case, we have to consider separately the utility queries with aggregates from the utility queries without aggregate. First, we check the incompatibility of the privacy query with the set of the *utility queries without aggregate*. For doing so, since groups are computed from the results obtained by evaluating first the query without aggregate, we just

---

[3] Our code is available at https://github.com/fr-anonymous/puck.

have to check incompatibility of the plain variant of Q_p (see Definition 6) with the utility queries without aggregate. This can be done using Theorem 1. Then, we check the incompatibility of the privacy query with the *utility queries with aggregate*.

Theorem 2 establishes the results when aggregates in the privacy query and a given utility query are defined over the same time window.

Theorem 2 (Incompatibility with aggregates). *Let us consider a privacy query Q_p and an utility query Q_u with the same aggregate function on a same time window. Q_p is incompatible with Q_u if there exists a (possibly empty) freezing f_p of output variables in GP_p with constants of GP_u, or a (possibly empty) freezing f_u of output variables in GP_u with constants in GP_p such that $f_p(GP_p)$ and $f_u(GP_u)$ are isomorphic. When Q_p and Q_u have no FILTER conditions, they are incompatible if and only if the above condition is satisfied.*

Proof. Based on Definition 4, an answer $(\bar{a}, r)$ of an aggregate query Q_p can be inferred from a set of answers $\{(\bar{a}_u, r_u)\}$ only if the group $Group_p(\bar{a}) = \{y_p | \exists \bar{z}, \mu_{\bar{a}}(GP_p) \wedge \mu_{\bar{a}}(FILTER_p)\}$ can be obtained as a group, or the union of groups, of Q_u, i.e., unions of $\{y_u | \exists \bar{z}_u, \mu_{\bar{a}_u}(GP_u) \wedge \mu_{\bar{a}_u}(FILTER_u)\}$.

Based on [2], this situation is true only if (if and only if, when there is no FILTER conditions) either $\mu_{\bar{a}}(GP_p)$ and (GP_u) are isomorphic, or if there exists an answer $\bar{a}_u$ of GP_u such that $\mu_{\bar{a}}(GP_p)$ and $\mu_{\bar{a}_u}(GP_u)$ are isomorphic, i.e., GP_p (or one of its freezing of output variables by constants in GP_u) is isomorphic to GP_u (or to one of its freezing of output variables by constants in GP_p). ☐

Example 2. Let us consider the following privacy query Q_p and the following utility query Q_u:

Q_p: SELECT ?building AVG(?nb)
      WHERE {?sm issda:associatedBuilding ?b . ?b rdf:type ?building .
           ?sm issda:associatedOccupier ?o . ?o issda:nbOfPersons ?nb .
           ?o issda:yearlyIncome ?y}
      GROUP BY ?building
Q_u: SELECT ?y' AVG(?nb')
      WHERE {?sm' issda:associatedBuilding ?b' . ?b' rdf:type issda:Apartment.
           ?sm' issda:associatedOccupier ?o' . ?o' issda:nbOfPersons ?nb' .
           ?o' issda:yearlyIncome ?y'}
      GROUP BY ?y'

Freezing the ?building variable of Q_p with the constant issda:Apartment appearing in Q_u results in:

$Frozen = \{$?sm issda:associatedBuilding ?b . ?b rdf:type issda:Apartment.

        ?sm issda:associatedOccupier ?o . ?o issda:nbOfPersons ?nb.

        ?o issda:yearlyIncome ?y}

which is isomorphic with the graph pattern of Q_u. Since, Q_p and Q_u have the same aggregate function, Q_p is incompatible with Q_u.

Let us consider now the case where Q_p and Q_u have *different time windows*: we have to check if time windows of Q_p can be built from time windows of Q_u. Computing an aggregate on a time window I_1 from the results of the same aggregate on different time windows I_2 and I_3 is only possible if I_1 can be built from I_2 and I_3 by *union* or *difference*. As shown in Fig. 1, I_1 can be obtained by union of I_2 and I_3, but I_3 can also be obtained by difference between I_1 and I_2, and I_2 can be built by difference between I_1 and I_3. Therefore, testing if a time window can be built by difference amounts to testing if an union is possible.

From now on, we thus focus, without loss of generality, on checking incompatibility by testing whether time windows of a privacy query can be built as unions of time windows of utility queries.

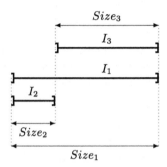

Fig. 1. Building a time window from other ones

Theorem 3 provides a characterization of the incompatibility between a privacy query Q_p and a single utility query Q_u based on the values of $Size_p$, $Step_p$, $Size_u$ and $Step_u$ defining the time windows considered in Q_p and Q_u respectively. It relies on identifying how to build a time window of Q_p as union of some time windows of Q_u, as illustrated in Fig. 2.

Theorem 3 (Incompatibility between a privacy query and a single utility query with aggregates on different time windows). *Let us consider a privacy query Q_p and a utility query Q_u computing the same aggregate Agg on different time windows, and such that Q'_p and Q'_u obtained from Q_p and Q_u by removing their TIMEWINDOW clauses are incompatible. Q_p is incompatible with Q_u using union if and only if the following two conditions are satisfied:*

(1) $\exists m \in \mathbb{N}$ such as $Size_p = Size_u + m \times Step_u$
(2) If Agg is Sum or Count, $\exists n \in \mathbb{N}^+$ and $\exists \alpha \in \mathbb{N}$ such as $Size_u = n \times Step_u$ and $m = \alpha \times n$.

Proof. Computing an aggregate of Q_p from aggregates coming from Q_u is only possible if at least one time window I_p of Q_p can be built by union of m time windows I_{u_x} of Q_u as shown in Fig. 2. The following conditions have thus to be

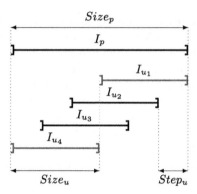

Fig. 2. Union of time windows from a single utility query

satisfied: (a) the union of m time windows of Q_u have the same size than a single time window of Q_p; (b) a time window of Q_u and a time window of Q_p ends at the same time; (c) the union must be disjoint for *Sum* and *Count* (e.g. union of I_{u_1} and I_{u_4} in red in Fig. 2). This is captured by the equations:

$$\begin{cases} Size_p = Size_u + (m-1) \times Step_u & (1) \\ k_p \times Step_p = k_u \times Step_u & (2) \\ Size_u = n \times Step_u \text{ for } Sum \text{ and } Count & (3.1) \\ Size_p = \alpha \times Size_u \text{ for } Sum \text{ and } Count & (3.2) \end{cases}$$

where k_p and k_u are unknown integers, $Size_p$, $Step_p$, $Size_u$ and $Step_u$ are constant integers, and m, n and α are strictly positive constant integers.

Equation (2) has obviously always solutions (e.g. $k_p = k_u = 0$) and can be discarded. Combining Eq. (1) and Eq. (3.2), we obtain:

$$\begin{cases} Size_p = Size_u + (m-1) \times Step_u & (1) \\ Size_u = n \times Step_u \text{ for } Sum \text{ and } Count & (3.1) \\ (\alpha - 1) \times Size_u = (m-1) \times Step_u \text{ for } Sum \text{ and } Count & (3.2) \end{cases}$$

The necessary and sufficient conditions of incompatibility are obtained by combining Eq. (3.1) and Eq. (3.2).   □

This theorem allows to prove the incompatibility between the privacy query PQ2 and the utility UQ3 of the scenario in Sect. 2. Indeed, the size of the time window of PQ2 (equal to 6) is a multiple of the size of the time window of UQ3 (equal to 3), which is also a multiple of its step (equal to 1).

This latter condition would not be satisfied if the step of the time window clause of the utility query is replaced by 2 for instance. In this case, the same theorem would allow to infer that PQ2 is compatible with the modified utility query.

When a privacy query is compatible with all utility queries, it remains to check whether it can be incompatible with *combinations* of utility queries. Based on

Theorem 2, this can only occur by combining utility queries whose graph patterns are isomorphic with the graph pattern of the privacy query.

Theorem 4 checks incompatibility of Q_p with two utility queries Q_{u_1} and Q_{u_2} by testing if it is possible to build a time window of Q_p by the union of time windows of Q_{u_1} and Q_{u_2} as illustrated in Fig. 3.

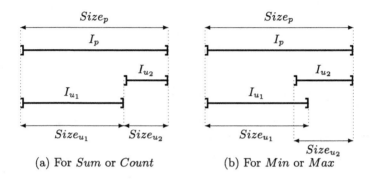

(a) For *Sum* or *Count*   (b) For *Min* or *Max*

Fig. 3. Union of time windows from two utility queries

Theorem 4 (Incompatibility between a privacy query and two utility queries with same aggregates and different time windows). *Let us consider a privacy query Q_p and two utility queries Q_{u_1} and Q_{u_2} computing the same aggregate on different time windows, and such that Q_p without its TIMEWINDOW clause is incompatible with both Q'_{u_1} and Q'_{u_2} obtained from Q_{u_1} and Q_{u_2} by removing their TIMEWINDOW clauses.*

Q_p is incompatible with the pair (Q_{u_1}, Q_{u_2}) using union if and only if the following two conditions are satisfied:

(a) $Size_p = Size_{u_1} + Size_{u_2}$ for SUM or COUNT aggregates
*   or $Size_p \leq Size_{u_1} + Size_{u_2}$ for MIN or MAX aggregates*
(b) $Size_p - Size_{u_1}$ is a multiple of $\gcd(Step_{u_1}, \sigma_p \times Step_{u_2})$
*   where $\sigma_p = \frac{Step_p}{\gcd(Step_p, Step_{u_2})}$*

Proof. Computing an aggregate of Q_p from aggregates coming from a two different utility queries Q_{u_1} and Q_{u_2} is possible if at least one time window I_p of Q_p can be built by union of a time window I_{u_1} of Q_{u_1} and a time window I_{u_2} coming from Q_{u_2} as shown in Fig. 3. *Sum* and *Count* necessitate that I_{u_1} and I_{u_2} are disjoint to avoid double counting of an overlap (a), *Min* and *Max* support overlapping time windows (b).

The following conditions have to be satisfied (Q_{u_1} and Q_{u_2} can be inverted): (a) the union of a time window of Q_{u_1} and a time window of Q_{u_2} have the same size than a single time window of Q_p; (b) a time window of Q_{u_1} starts when a time window of Q_p starts; (c) a time window of Q_{u_2} ends when the same time window of Q_p ends. This is captured by the following equations:

$$\begin{cases} Size_p = Size_{u_1} + Size_{u_2} \text{ (a) or } Size_p \leq Size_{u_1} + Size_{u_2} \text{ (b) (1)} \\ k_1 \times Step_{u_1} + Size_{u_1} = k_p \times Step_p + Size_p \qquad\qquad (2) \\ k_p \times Step_p = k_2 \times Step_{u_2} \qquad\qquad\qquad\qquad\qquad (3) \end{cases}$$

where k_1, k_2 and k_p are unknown integers and $Step_p$, $Size_p$, $Step_{u_1}$, $Size_{u_1}$, $Step_{u_2}$ and $Size_{u_2}$ are constant integers.

The positive integer solutions of Eq. (3) are of the form:

$$\begin{cases} k_p = \kappa \times \sigma_{u_2} \text{ (3.1)} \\ k_2 = \kappa \times \sigma_p \text{ (3.2)} \end{cases} \text{ with } \kappa \in \mathbb{N}^+$$

where $\sigma_p = \frac{Step_p}{\gcd(Step_p, Step_{u_2})}$ and $\sigma_{u_2} = \frac{Step_{u_2}}{\gcd(Step_p, Step_{u_2})}$.

Injecting solutions of Eq. (3) into Eq. (2), we obtain:

$$\begin{cases} Size_p = Size_{u_1} + Size_{u_2} \text{ (a) or } Size_p \leq Size_{u_1} + Size_{u_2} \text{ (b)} \quad (1) \\ k_1 \times Step_{u_1} - \kappa \times \sigma_p \times Step_{u_2} = Size_p - Size_{u_1} \qquad\qquad (2) \\ k_p = \kappa \times \sigma_{u_2} \qquad\qquad\qquad\qquad\qquad\qquad\qquad\qquad (3.1) \\ k_2 = \kappa \times \sigma_p \qquad\qquad\qquad\qquad\qquad\qquad\qquad\qquad\quad (3.2) \end{cases}$$

Equations (3.1) and (3.2) are always satisfied and can be discarded. According to Bachet-Bézout theorem, the Diophantine Eq. (2) has a solution if and only if $Size_p - Size_{u_1}$ is a multiple of $\gcd(Step_{u_1}, \sigma_p \times Step_{u_2})$. □

Example 3. Let us consider the privacy query PQ2 of the scenario in Sect. 2 and the following utility queries:

Q_{u_1}: SELECT ?timeWindowEnd SUM(?cons)
      WHERE {(?sm issda:consumption ?cons, ?ts)}
      GROUP BY ?timeWindowEnd
      TIMEWINDOW (4h, 2h)
Q_{u_2}: SELECT ?timeWindowEnd SUM(?cons')
      WHERE {(?sm' issda:consumption ?cons', ?ts')}
      GROUP BY ?timeWindowEnd
      TIMEWINDOW (2h, 1h)

As $Size_p = 6$ and $Size_{u_1} + Size_{u_2} = 6$, the condition (a) of the theorem is satisfied.

As $Step_p = 6$, $Step_{u_1} = 2$ and $Step_{u_2} = 1$, we get: $\sigma_p = 6$ $\gcd(Step_{u_1}, \sigma_p \times Step_{u_2}) = 2$, and $Size_p - Size_{u_1} = 2$, thus making the condition (b) of the theorem also satisfied. So PQ2 is incompatible with Q_{u_1} and Q_{u_2}.

If we replace the $TIMEWINDOW$ of Q_{u_1} by (3 h, 2 h), the condition (a) of the theorem is not satisfied and PQ_2 is compatible with the new Q_{u_1} and Q_{u_2}.

5   Related Work

A rich variety of privacy models have been proposed, ranging from k-anonymity [13] and l-diversity [11] to t-closeness [10] and ϵ-differential privacy [5]. All these approaches are based on changing the exposed data either by adding noise in the data or by applying generalization operations on sensitive data. Our data-independent approach is complementary and should be used beforehand for detecting privacy breaches. It comes with explanations that can help choose the privacy model to apply to the data concerned by the detected privacy breaches.

Data security is also an important topic for which secure protocols based on encryption has been proposed that enable to do some computations on encrypted outsourced data. In contrast with our work, each protocol may be specific to the target computations to be feasible in practice like in [1].

An alternative approach for protecting against privacy breaches consists in applying access control methods to RDF data [9,12,14]. However, all these works do not handle utility queries.

A query-based logical framework for RDF data has been introduced in [6, 7], where sensitive information is expressed as SPARQL queries whose results must not disclose sensitive information of individual. It has been extended to handling utility queries in [3,4]. These approaches however are restricted to simple conjunctive queries. They do not consider aggregates and they cannot apply to temporal data.

6 Conclusion and Future Work

In this paper we have proposed a data-independent framework for a formal specification and verification of compatibility between privacy and utility policies expressed as temporal aggregate conjunctive queries.

This framework is well suited for helping data producers to keep the control on the protection of their data in many real-world situations where sensitive data are collected by mobile personal devices or smart environments. When a privacy query turns out to be incompatible with utility queries, several solutions can be applied, such as ciphering the exposed data made explicit by the explanation built from the incompatibility proof, anonymize them [3], or use differential privacy [8].

Based on the implementation of this framework, we plan to design and implement a negotiation mechanism that will be triggered in this case. New relaxed utility queries will be automatically computed to restore compatibility with the privacy policy of a given data producer. They will be the formal basis of a dialogue between each data producer and the service provider in order to find a acceptable trade-off in terms of utility while guaranteeing privacy preservation for each data producer.

We also plan to extend our framework to take into account ontological knowledge in the possible inference of answers of privacy queries by answers of utility queries. This will bring stronger constraints on compatibility between privacy and utility policies.

References

1. Ciucanu, R., Lafourcade, P.: Goose: a secure framework for graph outsourcing and SPARQL evaluation. In: IFIP WG 11.3 Conference on Data and Applications Security and Privacy (DBSec), pp. 347–366 (2020)
2. Cohen, S.: Containment of aggregate queries. ACM SIGMOD Rec. **34**(1), 77–85 (2005)
3. Delanaux, R., Bonifati, A., Rousset, M.-C., Thion, R.: Query-based linked data anonymization. In: Vrandečić, D., et al. (eds.) ISWC 2018. LNCS, vol. 11136, pp. 530–546. Springer, Cham (2018). https://doi.org/10.1007/978-3-030-00671-6_31
4. Delanaux, R., Bonifati, A., Rousset, M.-C., Thion, R.: RDF graph anonymization robust to data linkage. In: Cheng, R., Mamoulis, N., Sun, Y., Huang, X. (eds.) WISE 2020. LNCS, vol. 11881, pp. 491–506. Springer, Cham (2019). https://doi.org/10.1007/978-3-030-34223-4_31
5. Dwork, C.: Differential privacy. In: Bugliesi, M., Preneel, B., Sassone, V., Wegener, I. (eds.) ICALP 2006. LNCS, vol. 4052, pp. 1–12. Springer, Heidelberg (2006). https://doi.org/10.1007/11787006_1
6. Grau, B.C., Kostylev, E.V.: Logical foundations of privacy-preserving publishing of linked data. In: Proceedings of the Thirtieth AAAI Conference on Artificial Intelligence, Palo Alto, California, 12–17 February 2016, pp. 943–949. The AAAI Press (2016). https://doi.org/10.5555/3015812.3015953
7. Grau, B.C., Kostylev, E.V.: Logical foundations of linked data anonymisation. J. Artif. Intell. Res. **64**, 253–314 (2019)
8. Hassan, M.U., Rehmani, M.H., Chen, J.: Differential privacy techniques for cyber physical systems: a survey. IEEE Commun. Surv. Tutor. **22**(1), 746–789 (2020). https://doi.org/10.1109/COMST.2019.2944748
9. Kirrane, S., Mileo, A., Decker, S.: Access control and the resource description framework: a survey. Semant. Web **8**(2), 311–352 (2017)
10. Li, N., Li, T., Venkatasubramanian, S.: t-Closeness: privacy beyond k-Anonymity and l-Diversity, In: ICDE, pp. 106–115. IEEE Computer Society (2007)
11. Machanavajjhala, A., Kifer, D., Gehrke, J., Venkitasubramaniam, M.: L-diversity: privacy beyond k-anonymity. TKDD **1**(1), 3 (2007)
12. Oulmakhzoune, S., Cuppens-Boulahia, N., Cuppens, F., Morucci, S.: Privacy policy preferences enforced by SPARQL query rewriting. In: ARES, pp. 335–342. IEEE Computer Society (2012)
13. Sweeney, L.: k-Anonymity: a model for protecting privacy. Int. J. Uncertain. Fuzziness Knowl.-Based Syst. **10**(5), 557–570 (2002)
14. Villata, S., Delaforge, N., Gandon, F., Gyrard, A.: An access control model for linked data. In: Meersman, R., Dillon, T., Herrero, P. (eds.) OTM 2011. LNCS, vol. 7046, pp. 454–463. Springer, Heidelberg (2011). https://doi.org/10.1007/978-3-642-25126-9_57

An Empirical Assessment of Security and Privacy Risks of Web-Based Chatbots

Nazar Waheed[1]([✉]) [ID], Muhammad Ikram[2] [ID], Saad Sajid Hashmi[3,4] [ID],
Xiangjian He[5] [ID], and Priyadarsi Nanda[1] [ID]

[1] University of Technology Sydney, Ultimo, NSW 2007, Australia
nazar.waheed@student.uts.edu.au, priyadarsi.nanda@uts.edu.au
[2] Macquarie University, Macquarie Park, NSW 2109, Australia
muhammad.ikram@mq.edu.au
[3] University of Wollongong, Wollongong, NSW 2522, Australia
shashmi@uow.edu.au
[4] CSIRO's Data61, Sydney, Australia
[5] University of Nottingham Ningbo China, Ningbo, China
sean.he@nottingham.edu.cn

Abstract. Web-based chatbots provide website owners with the benefits of increased sales, immediate response to their customers, and insight into customer behaviour. While Web-based chatbots are getting popular, they have not received much scrutiny from security researchers. The benefits to owners come at the cost of users' privacy and security. Vulnerabilities, such as tracking cookies and third-party domains, can be hidden in the chatbot's iFrame script. This paper presents a large-scale analysis of five Web-based chatbots among the top 1-million Alexa websites. Through our crawler tool, we identify the presence of chatbots in these 1-million websites. We discover that 13,392 out of the top 1- million Alexa websites (1.58%) use one of the five analysed chatbots. Our analysis reveals that the top 300k Alexa ranking websites are dominated by `Intercom` chatbots that embed the least number of third-party domains. `LiveChat` chatbots dominate the remaining websites and embed the highest samples of third-party domains. We also find that 721 (5.38%) web-based chatbots use insecure protocols to transfer users' chats in plain text. Furthermore, some chatbots heavily rely on cookies for tracking and advertisement purposes. More than two-thirds (68.92%) of the identified cookies in chatbot iFrames are used for ads and tracking users. Our results show that, despite the promises for privacy, security, and anonymity given by most websites, millions of users may unknowingly be subject to poor security guarantees by chatbot service providers.

Keywords: Web privacy · Web-based chatbot · Chatbot

This research is supported by the Australian Government Research Training Program Scholarship.

R. Chbeir et al. (Eds.): WISE 2022, LNCS 13724, pp. 325–339, 2022.
https://doi.org/10.1007/978-3-031-20891-1_23

1   Introduction

A Web-based chatbot (or bot) is a computer program interacting with users via a conversational user interface that simulates a conversation with a human user via textual methods [36]. Web-based chatbots offer improved customer services and efficiently manage human resources [31,35]. For example, a website owner performs customer acquisition tasks (such as new customer queries or after-sales services) through customer service (or sales and marketing) personnel. As the business gets bigger and busier, the traditional way of interacting with online customers gets choked up, resulting in an increased waiting queue. Besides, the customer service representative may not be available around the clock. Web-based chatbot provides a website owner with the benefits of increased sales, immediate response to their customers' queries and insights into customers' behaviours. While Web-based chatbots are getting popular, they have not received much scrutiny from security researchers. The benefits of chatbots can come at the cost of privacy and security threats. Third-party domains and cookies inherit these threats, which might be built into the script. These domains and cookies can be used to track users and provide personalised advertisements. There has been a plethora of work done based on the security and privacy issues of a complete website [19,23,34]. However, to our knowledge, no research study focuses explicitly on Web-based chatbots' privacy and security issues.

While Web-based chatbots are getting popular and come with several benefits, as mentioned above, their advantages inherit several disadvantages. *Firstly*, consumers are concerned about their privacy and security [35]. Despite the remarkable improvements in Web-based chatbots being able to mimic a human conversation, they are vulnerable to the Reconnaissance, and Man-in-the-Middle attacks [14]. *Secondly*, since the chatbot is a computer program, it does not have its own identity or emotions like an actual human. Customers often tend to make connections during conversations, which is lacking when engaging with chatbots. The lack of personality in chatbots and their inability to make an emotional connection is a concern for some customers. *Finally*, a Web-based chatbot is still in its infancy since natural language processing is not the core competency in chatbot applications and is still in the development phase [35]. Web-based chatbots are prone to common communication errors; therefore, companies and organisations are cautious in using them to avoid brand damage.

Although several studies have taken place to study chatbots in general, none of them covers their security and privacy comprehensively. There has been extensive research on the security and privacy issues of websites. However, to the best of our knowledge, we did not find any study that focuses on the iFrame component of the Web-based chatbot for the same issues. Despite the assurances for privacy, security, and anonymity given by the websites and privacy policies, users are victims of personally identifiable information (PII) leakages [21]. Similarly, by using chatbot services, users may inadvertently be exposed to privacy and security risks [34].

In summary, the contributions of this paper are as follows.

1. We present the first large-scale study of security and privacy issues in chatbots on Alexa top 1-million popular websites [6]. We detect 13,392 (1.58%) websites leveraging web chatbots for customers' interaction. We release our data and scripts for future research.
2. We analyse the 13,392 (1.58%) websites for the type of chatbots and analyse the coverage of the detected chatbots. We find that 21.78% of the chatbot websites belong to the non-IT business category, while the percentage of Information Technology (IT) chatbot websites is 16.16%, and shopping with 5.89% is the third most dominant category. We also analyse the security and privacy issues of our dataset chatbot websites. We explore the chatbot websites and find that 5.38% of them are still using the insecure HTTP protocol, where an alarming 12.9% of the websites ranking >500k still transfer their visitors' data in plaint-text. This result shows that non-IT business, IT and shopping websites are more vulnerable among the most popular websites than other categories.
3. Our analysis illuminates that chatbots have a disproportionate use of cookies for tracking and *essential* or *useful* functionalities. We discover 5,396 cookies in 2,110 websites leveraging `Drift` chatbot. 5,113 (94.62%) and 283 (5.24%) of the cookies are used for Tracking and essential functionalities, respectively. On the other hand, 2,185 websites rely on `Hubspot` for the provision of chat services via a total number of 15,829 unique cookies with 79.35% (12561) for tracking, while the rest are essential cookies.
4. We identify the top 10 third-party domains embedded in the iFrames of each web-based chatbot. The most common third-parties are well-known operators, for example, googleapis, cloudflare, w3, and facebook. These operators are imported by 39.67% (5361), 15.43% (2085), 6.1% (822), and 3.35% (453) web-based chatbots, respectively.

The rest of this paper is organised as follows: In Sect. 2, we present concepts and terms related to web tracking and services. We present our methodology (Fig. 1) for web-based chatbot detection and data collection in Sect. 3. In Sect. 4, we analyse our chatbots in the top 1-million Alexa websites and present our findings, such as the presence of chatbots on websites, tracking cookies, and third-party domains. Section 5 presents the related work while we conclude our work by presenting the gaps with some future directions in Sect. 6.

2 Concepts and Terms

We begin by introducing the general concepts and terms used in the paper.

Advertising and Tracking Domain: The *advertising and tracking* domain (or tracker) is the URL of an entity embedded in a web page. The purpose of a tracker is to re-identify a user's visit on the web page again for loading custom themes or analytics (*first-party* tracking) or to re-identify a given user across different websites for building the user's browsing profile or providing personalised advertisements (*third-party* tracking).

iFrame: An iFrame or inline Frame is an HTML document embedded within an HTML web page. The purpose of an iFrame is to display embedded HTML contents from a different web page into the current web page. The contents of iFrames can be videos, maps, advertisements, chatbot services, and tracking components like cookies and JavaScript codes. Hence, besides providing utilities and services, iFrames can also be used for third-party tracking.

Cookie: A cookie (or HTTP cookie) is a text file stored on the user's device by the web browser. The content of a cookie is in plain text format. A cookie is generated by the web server (of a web page) and is sent back from the user's device to the web server at each subsequent visit by the user. A cookie can store shopping carts, theme preferences of the user, or the user's authentication status. Cookies generated by third-parties via iFrames can be used for third-party tracking. Section 4.2 discuss different types of cookies in detail.

3   Chatbot Detection Methodology and Dataset

We begin by presenting our methodology, over-viewed in Fig. 1 for detecting chatbots employed in the top 1-million Alexa websites. We then characterise our dataset.

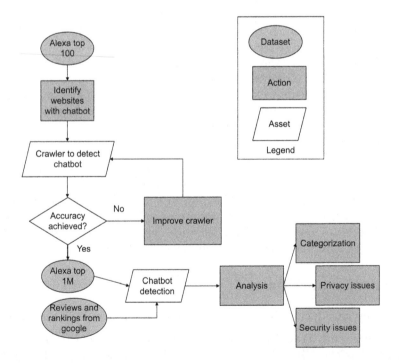

Fig. 1. Overview of our crawling and analysis methodology: We manually inspect the top 100 Alexa websites for chatbots to identify chatbot services and to construct keywords list for automatic detection of chatbots in the top 1-million Alexa websites. We then perform an analysis to categorise websites and analyse security and privacy issues.

3.1 Discovering Chatbots

Using Selenium Web Driver, we develop an automated web crawler to automate analysed websites' visiting and rendering process. We implement a crawler framework to increase our chatbot coverage and maximise the number of detected chatbots. We begin by discovering web-based chatbot services on the Alexa top 1-million websites. To this end, we find the difference between a normal website and the website with a chatbot service. We manually inspect the first Alexa top 100 websites for *potential* web chatbot services. Typically, websites implement chatbot services in iFrames; therefore, we explicitly focused on the iFrame of the chatbot on these 100 websites. The keywords include: '*chat widget*', *let's chat*, *drift-widget*, '*chat now*', and '*chatbot*'. While we acknowledge that our keywords list is not exhaustive to include chatbots on non-English language websites, we do consider our method for chatbots as a *lower-limit* on the number of chatbots on the top 1-million Alexa websites.

Next, we crawl through the chatbot websites and extract their chatbot iFrame cookies only instead of the whole website since we are specifically interested in the security and privacy issues of the web-based chatbots. We then analyse the embedded third-party domains in each of those chatbots. To extract the third-party domains, we only check the contents of the iFrame of a chatbot instead of the complete website's DOM. Overall, we find 13,392 (1.58%) chatbot websites.

Issues and Limitations. For chatbot websites, once a website renders ultimately, the chatbot icon is found at the bottom right corner of the screen. Sometimes, the chatbot is not visible on the respective website mainly due to one of the following reasons: (*i*) the chatbot is only available during specific office hours, and (*ii*) the chatbot is offline/hidden as the developers may be working on it.

3.2 Categorising Chatbot Websites

Next, to analyse the coverage of chatbots on various websites, we aim to categorise the Alexa top websites. There are several databases and tools available and website categories stored. However, due to its popular utility among researchers, we use crawling techniques on *Fortiguard* website classification tool [4] to gather this information. The websites that return errors while rendering in the first phase are manually labelled. This way, we label the category of each chatbot website in our dataset (13,392 websites). The top 10 categories by frequency of occurrence are depicted in Fig. 2. These ten categories comprise 74.9% (10,028 websites) of our dataset. We find that most of the chatbot websites are used by *non-IT Business* and *IT* category websites. Although all five chatbots are prevalent, Intercom chatbot is the preferred choice for these two categories. We also observe that chatbots are not a popular choice among *Games*, and *Government & Legal Organizations* related website owners.

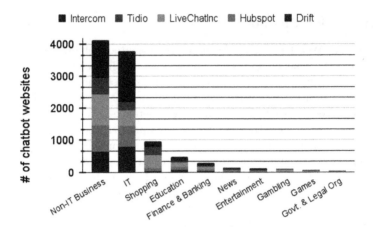

Fig. 2. Categories of chatbot websites in the top 1-million Alexa websites.

3.3 Dataset

We present a comprehensive analysis by breaking the dataset into parts, with each part having 10,000 websites to get an in-depth measurement of our study. Based upon the keywords (cf. Sect. 3), we run our crawler that detects chatbots on 3.5% of the analysed websites. To check the accuracy of our crawler, we manually label the first hundred Alexa ranking websites and perform manual testing on them. We learn that our model is 61% accurate. The reason is that there are several possible ways to write a website script, and using the keywords alone is not an optimum solution.

Finding a common script, or tag among all of them is not possible. However, we find some unique keywords/tags/elements. Figure 3 shows the iFrame of a chatbot website www.synology.com. It has a tag *id='chat-widget-container'*, which can be used to filter the LiveChat chatbot websites. Similarly, we select five chatbots: LiveChat, Drift, Intercom, Tidio and Hubspot based on their frequencies of occurrence in the top 10k Alexa ranking websites. Overall, our crawler identifies 13,392 chatbot websites from Alexa top 1-million websites.

Table 1 summarises our findings. We observe that the Intercom chatbot is the preferred choice for the most popular set of websites (top 300k) followed by LiveChat for the next tier of Alexa ranking websites. Overall, Intercom chatbot is found on 29.88% of them, LiveChat on 26.37%, Drift as well as Hubspot on 15.70%, and Tidio on 12.36% only.

Based on the above findings, in the first round, we crawl the top 10k websites and render their DOMs. After optimising our crawler, we can filter all chatbots with 100% accuracy.

We also search for the top Web-based chatbots by using different keywords over the google search. We find chatbot rankings and reviews on the websites in [5,9,10,18,32,33,39] (accessed in Feb 2022). We choose the top three chatbots. After selecting *MobileMonkey, Aivo,* and *Pandorabots* from the blogs and

Table 1. Frequency (and percentage) of chatbot services amongst the Alexa top 1-million websites. Highlighted trends show `Intercom` chatbot is the preferred choice for the most popular set of websites followed by `LiveChat` which is also the preferred choice for the next tier of popular websites.

Alexa Rank	Chatbots					# Total (%)
	Drift	LiveChat	Hubspot	Tidio	Intercom	
1-100K	613 (0.61%)	433 (0.43%)	205 (0.21%)	81 (0.81%)	933 (0.93%)	2,265 (2.27%)
100K-200K	451 (0.45%)	611 (0.61%)	364 (0.36%)	185 (0.19%)	749 (0.75%)	2,360 (2.36%)
200K-300K	407 (0.41%)	586 (0.59%)	388 (0.39%)	342 (0.34%)	676 (0.68%)	2,399 (2.40%)
300K-400K	295 (0.30%)	573 (0.57%)	409 (0.41%)	364 (0.36%)	527 (0.53%)	2,168 (2.17%)
400K-500K	149 (0.15%)	433 (0.43%)	303 (0.30%)	286 (0.29%)	424 (0.42%)	1,595 (1.60%)
500K-600K	65 (0.07%)	347 (0.35%)	158 (0.16%)	218 (0.29%)	272 (0.27%)	1,060 (1.04%)
600K-700K	51 (0.05%)	337 (0.34%)	138 (0.14%)	125 (0.13%)	180 (0.18%)	831 (0.83%)
700K-800K	45 (0.05%)	142 (0.14%)	70 (0.07%)	4 (0.004%)	149 (0.15%)	410 (0.41%)
≥ 800K	26 (0.05%)	69 (0.15%)	67 (0.14%)	50 (0.11%)	93 (0.20%)	304 (0.64%)
Overall (1-million)	2,102 (0.25%)	3,531 (0.42%)	2,102 (0.25%)	1,655 (0.20%)	4,002 (0.47%)	**13,392 (1.58%)**

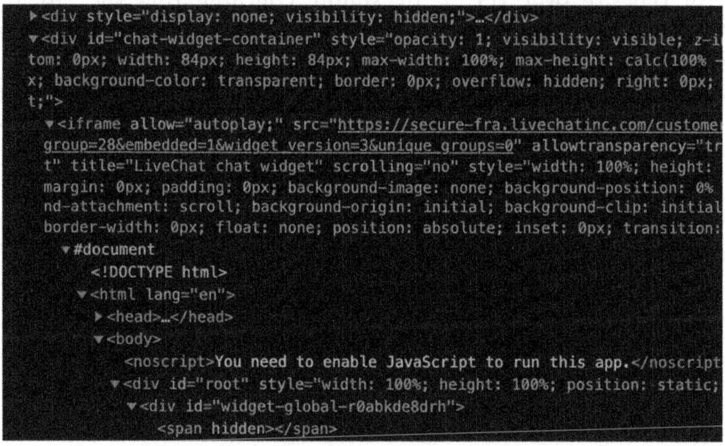

Fig. 3. An example of an iFrame enabling a typical chatbot service on a website.

reviews, we run our automated scraper for the top 200k websites and find only two chatbots belonging to *MobileMonkey*, four chatbots to *Botsify*, and zero for both *Aivo* and *Pandorabots*. Therefore, due to their insignificant presence, we do not consider them in our analysis further.

As a second attempt, we manually re-analyse the top 100 websites and find two relevant chatbots (*SF-chat* and *SnatchBot*) and search for them over the top 10k websites using an automated script. For *Salesforce* chatbot, we only find it to be on their own websites, for example, *cloudforce* and *exactforce*. On all other top 10k websites, we do not find any other websites having either of these chatbots. Seven hundred twenty-nine (729) websites do not render in the first phase, and they are analysed again in the second attempt (we learn that rendering chatbot websites take longer than our previous timeout). We also manually analyse the 100 chatbots from 100,000 to 100,100 range and find three chatbots only, i.e., (i) Drift, (ii) Intercom, and (iii) eLum[1]. Drift is already included in our study, Intercom is found on numerous websites (after initial automated crawler verification), and eLum is not found anywhere else since it is a private custom chatbot. Moreover, please note that social-media related chatbots like Facebook messenger are not valid since they require human interaction and are not automated. Therefore, we do not include them in our analysis. For the rest of the study, we use only five chatbots, which are Drift, Hubspot, LiveChat, Tidio, and Intercom.

4   Exploring Web Chatbots

4.1   Analysis of HTTP Chatbot Websites

To check whether a website uses HTTP, our crawler defaults to communicating with the site over HTTP by simply concatenating the 'http://' or 'http://www.' string with the hostname provided in the Alexa data. Once the crawler receives a final response and does not redirect the client requests from HTTP to HTTPs, it is marked as HTTP. We also check the websites that have errors by manually inspecting each one and discover that such websites are very few. The main reason for the errors is that they do not exist anymore (something that Alexa should take care of as it is not updated). The trend in the Fig. 4b shows that less popular websites are less secure. The percentage of websites that use HTTP version increases for websites ranked >500K. The percentage is calculated from the number of HTTP chatbot websites (Fig. 4b) and the total number of chatbot websites in each of the 100K category (Table 1). Overall, We find that 721 (5.38%) out of 13,392 chatbot websites still use the insecure HTTP version.

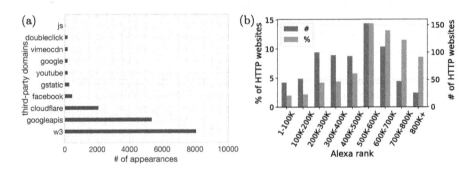

Fig. 4. (a) Breakdown of third-parties found in web-based chatbots. (b) Number (and percentage) of web-based chatbots using insecure HTTP websites in top Alexa websites.

---

[1] https://eluminoustechnologies.com.

4.2   Analysis of Cookies

The online ecosystem is composed of a large number of organizations engaging in tracking user behaviour across the web [15]. This is accomplished by various techniques, including tracking cookies, pixel tags, beacons, and other sophisticated mechanisms. Below, we provide an overview of the most common cookies.

Identification Cookies. These cookies can track visitors' conversations and interactions with a website. The customer service representative uses such information to offer better service. It is challenging to learn about any old chat with the customer without these cookies.

Tracking Cookies. These are the most common cookies used now to track user behaviour, user information and visits to a website.

Performance and Functionality Cookies. These cookies are used to enhance the performance and functionality of a website but are non-essential to their use. However, certain functionalities like videos may become unavailable, or the login details are required every time a user visits the website.

Conditional Cookies. These cookies may be written onto a website since they depend on using a specific feature of a website.

Marketing Cookies. These are account-based marketing cookies used to identify prospects and personalise sales and marketing interactions.

Analytics and Customization Cookies. These cookies are used to determine the effectiveness of marketing campaigns. Website owners use them to collect limited data from end-user browsers to enable them to understand the use of their websites.

Advertising Cookies. These cookies collect information over time about users' online activity on the websites and other online services to customise online advertisements.

The details about all cookies used on every chatbot can be read on their website [2, 22, 27–29].

Drift. According to `Drift`, the primary reason it uses cookies is to track user interactions with the visited website. It also uses cookies to customise products to the need of a customer. `Drift` claims that the data is never sold or sent to third-parties. Instead, it is used in their platform to allow for more personalised and specific messaging [27].

Hubspot. According to `Hubspot`, it uses cookies to track users who visit a `Hubspot` chatbot website. These cookies keep track of visit counts and information about the sessions (such as session start timestamp). When the `Hubspot` software is run on a website, it leaves behind these cookies to help `Hubpost` identify the users on future visits [22].

Table 2. Distribution of cookies across Web-based chatbots.

Chatbots	Categories of cookies			Total
	Essential	Tracking & Analytics	Ads & Marketing	
Drift	283 (5.38%)	5,113 (94.62%)	-	5,396
Hubspot	3,268 (20.65%)	12,561 (79.35%)	-	15,829
Intercom	8,942 (47.08%)	6,620 (34.85%)	3,433 (18.07%)	18,995
Total	12,493 (31.06%)	24,294 (60.4%)	3,433 (8.54%)	40,220

LiveChat. We search for LiveChat cookies manually by inspecting several websites. We do not find any tracking cookie in our manual search. To confirm, we inquire from the LiveChat support team to ensure that none of the cookies is used for tracking purposes. The support team confirmed the same. The LiveChat chatbots automatically save and store two essential cookies on the user's device when a user visits a website with LiveChat widget [28]. The two essential cookies are as follows:

_ _ lc_ cid (customerID). This is a functional cookie that LiveChat account service uses. The purpose of this cookie is to verify the identity of a customer created.

_ _ lc_ cst (customerSecureToken). This is also a functional cookie that LiveChat account service uses to identify a user, for example, *name, IP address,* and *geolocation.*

Tidio. According to Tidio, it uses cookies to maintain, improve and customise the user experience. Additionally, the cookies are used to remember the visitor's choice, such as language preference. Tidio claims to collect information, including PII, and assures that it will be used by them only. We cannot find any evidence of Tidio cookies on any of the websites using their chatbots, nor can we find any information about what cookies are used on their website [29].

Intercom. According to Intercom, its chatbot writes "first-party" cookies only and assures that its cookies are strictly private and confidential. The purpose of these cookies is to identify users and keep track of sessions. Intercom states that it uses two cookies only [2]; however, this claim is contradictory to our findings discussed below

Findings/Discussion. To distinguish between a first-party and a third-party cookie, we consider any cookie with the same name as the respected chatbot as a first-party. We also consider the cookies that chatbot service providers have mentioned on their websites as first-party. We declare any other cookie as a third-party. We present the distribution of cookies across Web-based chatbots in Table 2. We find a total number of 2,110 websites using Drift. From these, a total

Table 3. Distribution of top ten third-parties embedded in the iFrames of Web-based chatbots.

Third-party Domain	Drift	LiveChat	Intercom	Tidio	Hubspot	Total
w3.org	742	5	0	6,501	813	8,061
googleapis.com	28	3,502	0	1,537	282	5,349
cloudflare.com	2,063	1	0	0	10	2,074
facebook.com	0	0	0	0	453	453
gstatic.com	0	0	0	0	268	268
youtube.com	0	0	0	0	174	174
google.com	0	0	0	0	172	172
vimeocdn.com	0	0	0	0	171	171
doubleclick.net	0	0	0	0	166	166
rlets.com	0	0	5	0	0	5
other domains	0	19	0	7	3,872	3,989
Total	2,833	3,527	5	8,045	2,053	**20,791**

of 5,396 cookies are discovered. 5,113 (94.62%) of them are used for Tracking, and 283 (5.24%) are essential cookies. Hubspot is used on 2,185 websites, which have 15,829 cookies. 12,561 (79.35%) are tracking, while the rest are *essential* cookies. `Intercom` chatbot websites are 4,037, generating 18,995 cookies, out of which 52.92% are either tracking, advertisement or marketing cookies, while 47.08% are essential cookies for functionality. No cookies are found on either `LiveChat` or `Tidio` chatbots. More than two-thirds of the discovered cookies are used for tracking or advertisement purposes.

4.3   Analysis of Third-party Domains

We parse the URLs from the chatbot iFrames, extract the second-level domains using *tldextract*[2], and compare them with the respective website. If they match, it is declared a first-party domain; otherwise, it is stated as a third-party domain. For instance, we extract `googleapis.com` and `drift.com` domains from the iFrame of `Drift` chatbot embedded in the landing page of https://www.drift.com. Given that `googleapis.com` does not match with `drift.com`, our method labelled `googleapis.com` as third-party whilst `drift.com` as first-party.

Figure 4a depicts, and Table 3 lists the top 10 third-party domains embedded in the iFrames of chatbots. We observe that all chatbots rely on third-party services such as W3, Google APIs, and Cloudflare for iFrame templates, fonts, and hosting and storing content, respectively. We observe that only one third-party domain (`rlets.com`) is found on the `Intercom` websites. Since `Intercom` dominates the top 300k Alexa websites (52% of total web-based chatbot websites), suggesting that the top websites do not rely much on advertising and analytical

---

[2] https://pypi.org/project/tldextract/.

services revenues funnelled from chatbots. On the other hand, less popular websites generate 99.9% of the top ten third-party domains. Hubspot based websites have the most variety[3] of third-party domains, making it the most vulnerable. One hundred forty-five different third-party domains are present in Hubspot websites.

5   Related Work

To the best of our knowledge, no prior work has been done to address the privacy and security risks of cookies or third-party scripts embedded in web-based chatbots. Previous work has analysed PII leaks via advertisements and third-party scripts on various domains such as Facebook [7,8,16,38], mobile ecosystem [20,24,26], and web forms [37].

There are security and privacy risks associated with chatbots [17,30]. In *financial* chatbots, Bhuiyan et al. proposed a chatbot leveraging a private blockchain platform to conduct secure and confidential financial transactions [11]. Chatbots have also been developed to remove sensitive information from the conversation before passing it to its NLP engine [12]. Meanwhile, threats on the chatbot's client-side (such as unintended activation attacks and access control attacks) and network-side (such as MITM attacks and DDoS attacks) have been studied in the literature [40]. Bozic et al. conducted a preliminary security study on an open-source chatbot to identify XSS and SQLi vulnerabilities [13]. Their work did not find any XSS and SQLi vulnerabilities and was limited to analysing only one chatbot. No prior work has been done to study the iFrames of Web-based chatbots and to determine the types of cookies embedded. In this paper, to fill the gap, we study the prevalence of five chatbots in Alexa top 1-million websites and analyse the chatbot cookies and third-party domains embedded in the iFrames of chatbots.

6   Conclusion and Future Work

In this paper, *firstly*, we have presented the difference between websites with and without chatbots. We have found the keywords to detect chatbots on the analysed websites. We have also manually inspected the top 1,000 websites to validate chatbot detection. *Secondly*, we have designed and implemented a crawler tool that systematically explores and collects DOMs from the top 1-million Alexa websites. We have discovered that a subset of 13,392 (1.58%) of these websites use our five selected chatbots. We have found the frequencies of these chatbots in ten different categories and discovered that non-IT business websites had used 21.78% of them. Our analysis has revealed that the top 300k Alexa ranking websites are dominated by Intercom, while LiveChat dominates the remaining chatbot websites. We have also found that 5.38% of the chatbot use insecure protocols to transfer users' chats in plain-text. Our results show that, despite the

---

[3] Drift = 3, Livechat = 10, Hubspot = 145, Tidio = 4, Intercom = 1.

promises for privacy, security, and anonymity given by the majority of the websites, millions of users may be unknowingly subject to poor security guarantees by chatbot service providers on the same websites.

In our future work, we aim to extend these findings to the distribution of third-party domains and trackers in categories of web-based chatbots websites. This will help analyse and identify the dependence of chatbot websites on advertising and analytical services. Another area to explore is whether any chatbot websites render content that it does not directly load. Informed by the study by Ikram et al. [25], this work can be extended to analyse the dependency web-resources chains of the chatbots. Finally, our work analysed chatbots implemented in iFrames. Chatbots might also be served via new web frameworks such as React [3] and Angular [1], and in such cases, our data collection methodology needs update to capture chatbots implemented via such frameworks.

References

1. Angular - a platform for building mobile and desktop web applications (2022). https://angular.io
2. Intercom cookie policy (2022). https://www.intercom.com/legal/cookie-policy
3. React - a Javascript library for building user interfaces (2022). https://reactjs.org
4. Web filter lookup (2022). https://www.fortiguard.com/webfilter
5. Brooks, A.: 10 best chatbot builders in 2022 (2022). https://www.ventureharbour.com/best-chatbot-builders/
6. Amazon: Alexa top websites (2022). https://www.alexa.com/topsites
7. Andreou, A., Silva, M., Benevenuto, F., Goga, O., Loiseau, P., Mislove, A.: Measuring the Facebook advertising ecosystem. In: Network and Distribution Systems Security Symposium, San Diego (2019)
8. Andreou, A., Venkatadri, G., Goga, O., Gummadi, K.P., Loiseau, P., Mislove, A.: Investigating Ad transparency mechanisms in social media: a case study of Facebook's explanations. In: NDSS, San Diego (2018)
9. Balkhi, S.: 14 best AI chatbots software for your website (compared) (2021). https://www.wpbeginner.com/showcase/best-chatbots-software-ai/
10. Barker, S.: 15 best AI chatbot platforms to boost your conversations in 2022 (2021). https://shanebarker.com/blog/best-ai-chatbot/
11. Bhuiyan, M.S.I., Razzak, A., Ferdous, M.S., Chowdhury, M.J.M., Hoque, M.A., Tarkoma, S.: BONIK: a blockchain empowered chatbot for financial transactions. In: TrustCom (2020)
12. Biswas, D.: Privacy preserving chatbot conversations. In: Proceedings - 2020 IEEE 3rd International Conference on Artificial Intelligence and Knowledge Engineering, AIKE 2020, pp. 179–182 (2020). https://doi.org/10.1109/AIKE48582.2020.00035
13. Bozic, J., Wotawa, F.: Security testing for chatbots. In: Medina-Bulo, I., Merayo, M.G., Hierons, R. (eds.) ICTSS 2018. LNCS, vol. 11146, pp. 33–38. Springer, Cham (2018). https://doi.org/10.1007/978-3-319-99927-2_3
14. Carter, E., Knol, C.: Chatbot - an organisation's friend or foe? Res. Hospitality Manag. 9(2), 113–115 (2019)
15. Cook, J., Nithyanand, R., Shafiq, Z.: Inferring tracker-advertiser relationships in the online advertising ecosystem using header bidding. arXiv preprint arXiv:1907.07275 (2019)

16. Ghosh, A., Venkatadri, G., Mislove, A., Kharagpur, I.: Analyzing political advertisers' use of Facebook's targeting features. In: Workshop on Technology and Consumer Protection (ConPro 2019) (2019). https://facebook-targeting.ccs.neu.edu

17. Gondaliya, K., Butakov, S., Zavarsky, P.: SLA as a mechanism to manage risks related to chatbot services. In: IEEE International Conference on Intelligent Data and Security (2020). https://doi.org/10.1109/BigDataSecurity-HPSC-IDS49724.2020.00050

18. Group, Z.: Top 10 best AI chatbots (2020). https://medium.datadriveninvestor.com/top-10-best-ai-chatbots-f68705a8f559

19. Hashmi, S.S., Ikram, M., Kaafar, M.A.: A longitudinal analysis of online ad-blocking blacklists. In: 2019 IEEE 44th LCN Symposium on Emerging Topics in Networking (LCN Symposium), pp. 158–165. IEEE (2019)

20. Hashmi, S.S., Ikram, M., Smith, S.: On optimization of ad-blocking lists for mobile devices. In: Proceedings of the 16th EAI International Conference on Mobile and Ubiquitous Systems: Computing, Networking and Services, MobiQuitous 2019, pp. 220–227 (2019). https://doi.org/10.1145/3360774.3360830

21. Hashmi, S.S., Waheed, N., Tangari, G., Ikram, M., Smith, S.: Longitudinal compliance analysis of android applications with privacy policies. In: Hara, T., Yamaguchi, H. (eds.) MobiQuitous 2021. LNICST, vol. 419, pp. 280–305. Springer, Cham (2022). https://doi.org/10.1007/978-3-030-94822-1_16

22. HubSpot: Cookies set on HubSpot's websites (2022). https://knowledge.hubspot.com/account/hubspot-cookie-security-and-privacy

23. Ikram, M., Asghar, H.J., Kaafar, M.A., Mahanti, A., Krishnamurthy, B.: Towards seamless tracking-free web: improved detection of trackers via one-class learning. Proc. Priv. Enhancing Technol. **2017**(1), 79–99 (2016). https://doi.org/10.1515/popets-2017-0006

24. Ikram, M., Kaafar, M.A.: A first look at mobile Ad-Blocking apps. In: 2017 IEEE 16th International Symposium on Network Computing and Applications, NCA 2017, pp. 1–8 (2017). https://doi.org/10.1109/NCA.2017.8171376

25. Ikram, M., Masood, R., Tyson, G., Kaafar, M.A., Loizon, N., Ensafi, R.: The chain of implicit trust: an analysis of the web third-party resources loading (2019). https://doi.org/10.1145/3308558.3313521

26. Ikram, M., Vallina-Rodriguez, N., Seneviratne, S., Kaafar, M.A., Paxson, V.: An analysis of the privacy and security risks of Android VPN permission-enabled apps, pp. 349–364 (2016). https://doi.org/10.1145/2987443.2987471

27. Drift Inc.: What is the drift cookie security and privacy policy? (2019). https://gethelp.drift.com/hc/en-us/articles/360019665133-What-is-the-Drift-Cookie-Security-and-Privacy-Policy-

28. Legal Inc.: Privacy policy (2021). https://www.livechat.com/legal/privacy-policy/

29. Tidio Inc.: Privacy policy (2021). https://www.tidio.com/privacy-policy/

30. Ischen, C., Araujo, T., Voorveld, H., van Noort, G., Smit, E.: Privacy concerns in chatbot interactions. In: Følstad, A., et al. (eds.) CONVERSATIONS 2019. LNCS, vol. 11970, pp. 34–48. Springer, Cham (2020). https://doi.org/10.1007/978-3-030-39540-7_3

31. Ivanov, S., Webster, C.: Adoption of robots, artificial intelligence and service automation by travel, tourism and hospitality companies - a cost-benefit analysis. In: International Scientific Conference "Contemporary Tourism - Traditions and Innovations", 19–21 October 2017, Sofia University, pp. 1–9 (2017)

32. Lal, I.: 13 best chatbots to transform your conversation landscape in 2022 (2022). https://surveysparrow.com/blog/best-chatbot-platforms/

33. Leah: The 8 best chatbots of 2022 (2022). https://www.userlike.com/en/blog/best-chatbots
34. Masood, R., Vatsalan, D., Ikram, M., Kaafar, M.A.: Incognito: a method for obfuscating web data, pp. 267–276 (2018)
35. Michiels, E.: Modelling chatbots with a cognitive system allows for a differentiating user experience. In: PoEM Doctoral Consortium (2017)
36. Shawar, B.A., Atwell, E.: Chatbots: are they really useful? LDV Forum **22**, 29–49 (2007)
37. Starov, O., Gill, P., Nikiforakis, N.: Are you sure you want to contact us? Quantifying the leakage of PII via website contact forms. PETS **2016**(1), 20–33 (2015)
38. Venkatadri, G., Lucherini, E., Sapiezynski, P., Mislove, A.: Proceedings on Privacy Enhancing Technologies (2019). https://doi.org/10.2478/popets-2019-0013
39. Geyser, W.: Best AI chatbot platforms for 2022 (2022). https://influencermarketinghub.com/ai-chatbot-platforms/
40. Ye, W., Li, Q.: Chatbot security and privacy in the age of personal assistants. In: Proceedings - 2020 IEEE/ACM Symposium on Edge Computing, SEC 2020, pp. 388–393 (2020). https://doi.org/10.1109/SEC50012.2020.00057

An Information-Driven Genetic Algorithm for Privacy-Preserving Data Publishing

Yong-Feng Ge[1]([✉]), Hua Wang[1], Jinli Cao[2], and Yanchun Zhang[3,4]

[1] Institute for Sustainable Industries and Liveable Cities, Victoria University, Melbourne 3011, Australia
yongfeng.ge@vu.edu.au
[2] Department of Computer Science and Information Technology, La Trobe University, Melbourne 3083, Australia
[3] Peng Cheng Laboratory, Shenzhen 518055, China
[4] Cyberspace Institute of Advanced Technology, Guangzhou University, Guangzhou 510006, China

Abstract. Due to the expanding requirements for data publishing and growing concerns regarding data privacy, the privacy-preserving data publishing (PPDP) problem has received considerable attention from research communities, industries, and governments. However, it is challenging to tackle the trade-off between privacy preservation and data quality maintenance in PPDP. In this paper, an information-driven genetic algorithm (ID-GA) is designed to achieve optimal anonymization based on attribute generalization and record suppression. In ID-GA, an information-driven crossover operator is designed to efficiently exchange information between different anonymization solutions; an information-driven mutation operator is proposed to promote information release during anonymization; a two-dimension selection operator is designed to identify the qualities of different anonymization solutions. Experimental results verify the advantages of ID-GA in terms of solution accuracy and convergence speed. Besides, the impacts of all the proposed components are verified.

Keywords: Data privacy and utility · Genetic algorithm · Data publishing

1 Introduction

Nowadays, data plays a crucial role in people's daily life [19,28,29,33,35,36]. The publication and utilization of data [13–15,31,32,38,39] has created tremendous opportunities for decision making and knowledge discovery [1,3,5,18,25,30,35, 37,40]. For example, in 2006, Netflix released a dataset containing 100 million movie ratings to improve the performance of the recommendation system [2]. Despite these benefits, data privacy is still a concern in data publishing [7,

© The Author(s), under exclusive license to Springer Nature Switzerland AG 2022
R. Chbeir et al. (Eds.): WISE 2022, LNCS 13724, pp. 340–354, 2022.
https://doi.org/10.1007/978-3-031-20891-1_24

8,16,20,22,23,41]. Therefore, privacy-preserving data publishing (PPDP) has received considerable attention. Its goal is to produce an anonymous dataset that can satisfy the privacy requirement while maintaining the data utility as high as possible.

Existing approaches for PPDP can be divided into two categories: decreasing precision of the original dataset and data perturbation [5]. In the first category, one of the most famous approaches was proposed in [26]. In this approach, the anonymization solution is identified by performing a binary search on the generalization lattice. Authors in [17] proposed a generic framework for optimal anonymization. Based on the proposed framework, an algorithm Flash was performed to find the optimal anonymization solution by searching the path in the lattice. In [21], an algorithm was designed to optimize the anonymization solution in an identical generalization hierarchy, which is effective for general Internet of Things (IoT) data privacy protection. Most existing work focuses on a single anonymization operation (e.g., attribute generalization or record suppression). From the perspective of information release, a single anonymization operation may not be effective. It is worthwhile to combine multiple anonymization operations when optimizing the anonymization solution. Besides, most of the existing work utilizes the graph search-based strategy to optimize the anonymization solution. These approaches may lose their effectiveness when the search space of the PPDP problem becomes complex. In the second category, one of the representative approaches is differential privacy [4,43], which guarantees no significant difference in query results when inserting one record. The approaches in this category can effectively tackle the data privacy requirements in query. However, when meeting the scenarios requiring data transparency and truthfulness, these approaches are not applicable.

Genetic algorithm (GA) [24,27] is a population-based stochastic search algorithm [6,10,11] inspired by the theory of natural competition and selection. The population model in GA can effectively maintain search direction diversity and help promote the generation of high-quality solutions. GAs have been utilized in various optimization problems [9,12,34,42] and have shown advantages in high search efficiency and robustness.

In this paper, an information-driven genetic algorithm (ID-GA) is proposed. In ID-GA, anonymization solutions based on attribute generalization and record suppression are optimized. An information-driven crossover operator is designed to exchange information between anonymization solutions and promote information release. An information-driven mutation operator is designed to improve population diversity while enhancing information release. Besides, a two-dimension selection operator is designed to improve individual competitiveness as well as population quality.

The organization of this paper is as follows. Section 2 defines the PPDP problem. In Sect. 3, we describe the proposed ID-GA algorithm. In Sect. 4 and Sect. 5, the experimental setup in this paper is introduced, and the experimental results are analyzed. Finally, in Sect. 6, we conclude this paper.

2 Problem Definition

As the data publisher, the objective of PPDP is to transfer the original dataset D to an anonymous T that can satisfy the given privacy requirement determined by a privacy model and maintain its utility as high as possible.

In D, quasi-identifiers (QIDs) are attributes that could potentially identify the owners of records in the dataset. During the anonymization, various anonymization operations such as generalization and suppression can be utilized on QID and transfer QID to QID' in T.

In our definition, the k-anonymity criterion is set as the privacy model and defined as:

Definition 1 (k-anonymity). *A dataset satisfies the k-anonymity requirement if each combination of QID' attributes exists in at least k records.*

Accordingly, the anonymity degree (AD) value of a k-anonymity T equals k. The objective of PPDP is to identify the optimal anonymization and is defined as:

Definition 2 (Optimal anonymization). *For T, an optimal anonymization solution can satisfy the privacy requirement ($AD(T) \geq k$) and achieves the highest utility degree.*

The utility of T is calculated according to its transparency degree (TD) [5]:

$$TD(T) = \sum_{r \in T} TD(r) \tag{1}$$

$$TD(r) = \sum_{v_g \in r} TD(v_g) \tag{2}$$

where r indicates the record in T; v_g is the generalized value in record r. TD value of v_g is calculated as:

$$TD(v_g) = \frac{1}{|v_g|} \tag{3}$$

where $|v_g|$ is the number of domain values that are descendants of v_g.

3 ID-GA

In this section, the proposed ID-GA is introduced. Firstly, we illustrate the representation of individuals in ID-GA. Afterward, the crossover and mutation strategies in ID-GA are described. We then introduce the two-dimension selection operator in ID-GA. Finally, the entire process of ID-GA is illustrated.

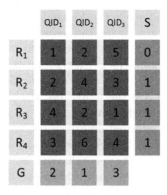

Fig. 1. Illustration of representation in ID-GA, where a sample dataset containing three QID attributes and four records is given.

3.1 Representation

In Fig. 1, a sample dataset and its anonymization solution are given. As shown in the figure, the sample dataset contains three QID attributes and four records. Accordingly, an anonymization solution is given. Such a solution contains a vector for attribute generalization represented by "G" and a vector for record suppression indicated by "S". In vector G, each QID attribute is generalized according to its level. In vector S, each record is suppressed according to the value in the vector. The value "0" indicates the corresponding record is removed, while the value "1" indicates the corresponding record is kept.

In ID-GA, each individual represents an anonymization solution. Therefore, each individual contains two vectors, i.e., vector G and vector S. The length of vector G equals the number of QID attributes. The length of vector S equals the number of records. During the update of individuals in ID-GA, the competitiveness of anonymization solutions is improved.

3.2 Information-Driven Crossover

In this crossover operator, two different strategies are utilized. When exchanging information between two individuals, the information in vectors G and S is exchanged separately. For vector G, on each bit of the offspring, the value is randomly chosen from two values on the corresponding bits in parent individuals. For vector S, the OR gate rules are utilized. More specifically, on each bit of the offspring, its value is one if at least one value on the corresponding bits in parent individuals is one. Otherwise, its value is zero.

An example of the crossover operator is given in Fig. 2. In this example, two individuals contains two G vectors (G_1 and G_2) and two S vectors (S_1 and S_2). The crossover operator is carried out separately, and two offspring vectors ($G_{1\times2}$ and $S_{1\times2}$) are generated. On each bit of vector $G_{1\times2}$, its value is randomly chosen from the values in G_1 and G_2. In this example, on the first bit, the value of $G_{1\times2}$

is chosen from two in G_1 and one in G_2. Value two is then randomly chosen from G_1. In the same manner, the value on the second bit is chosen from G_1 and the value on the third bit is chosen from G_2. On each bit of vector $S_{1 \times 2}$, its value is calculated based on OR gate rules. On the first bit, the value in $S_{1 \times 2}$ is one because the value in S_2 is one. In the same manner, the values on the second bit and third bit are both one. On the fourth bit, the value in $S_{1 \times 2}$ is zero, since two values in S_1 and S_2 are both zero.

Through our proposed information-driven crossover operator, the information in parent individuals is exchanged. For two G vectors, their values are randomly exchanged. Accordingly, the generalization levels in these two anonymization solutions are mixed. If parent individuals can achieve the requirement of privacy preservation, likely, the offspring solution can still achieve the privacy-preserving requirement. For two S vectors, their values are accumulated. As long as one record in one anonymization solution is released, the corresponding record in the offspring anonymization solution is released. Thus, more information is released in the offspring anonymization solution.

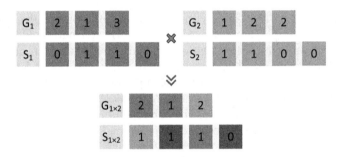

Fig. 2. Illustration of information-driven crossover operator, in which the information in two anonymization solutions is exchanged.

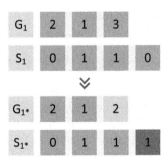

Fig. 3. Illustration of information-driven mutation operator, in which two vectors in the solution are adjusted separately.

3.3   Information-Driven Mutation

Vector G and S are tackled separately in the information-driven mutation operator. For vector G, with the predefined mutation rate MR, one bit is chosen randomly, and its value is randomly initialized in its generalization boundary. For vector S, with the same mutation rate MR, one bit is randomly chosen, and its value is transferred to one. Accordingly, the record is released.

In Fig. 3, an example of the mutation operator is given. The mutant version of vectors G_1 and S_1 are G_1* and S_1*. In G_1, the third bit is chosen by random. Its value is then transferred from three to two, which means the generalization level of the third QID attribute is changed from three to two. In S_1, its fourth bit is randomly chosen. Therefore, its value is changed from zero to one, which means the fourth record in the mutant anonymization solution is released.

After executing the proposed mutation operator, the corresponding anonymization solution is adjusted. The generalization levels in the randomly chosen QID attributes are changed in vector G. It is likely to generate an anonymization solution that can achieve a higher anonymity degree or transparency degree. In vector S, the records in the randomly chosen positions are released. It is likely to generate an anonymization solution that can achieve a higher transparency degree while satisfying the privacy requirement.

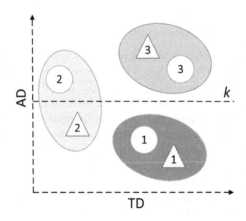

Fig. 4. Illustration of two-dimension operator, where three pairs of solutions are compared according to three defined rules.

3.4   Two-Dimension Selection

Two indicators (AD and TD) are utilized for each anonymization solution to measure its quality. According to the problem definition, the optimal anonymization solution obtains the highest TD while satisfying the requirement in AD. Thus, different priorities should be assigned to these two indicators in different situations. To be specific, three rules are defined as follows:

Algorithm 1. Pseudo-code of ID-GA

1: Set generation index $G = 0$
2: Initialize population P
3: Evaluate population P
4: **while** stopping criterion is not met **do**
5:     **for** each two parent individuals in P **do**
6:         Perform crossover operator on two individuals and generate offpsring
7:         Execute mutation operator on offspring
8:         Evaluate offspring
9:         **if** offspring is more competitive than one parent individual **then**
10:             Replace the parent individual with offspring
11:         **end if**
12:     **end for**
13:     $G = G + 1$
14: **end while**
15: **Output** the best anonymization solution

---

1. If neither of two individuals can reach the requirement in privacy preservation, the individual with a higher AD value is more competitive;
2. If one individual can reach the requirement in privacy preservation while the other one cannot, the former individual is more competitive;
3. If both two individuals can reach privacy preservation requirements, the individual with a higher TD value is better.

In Fig. 4, three pairs of individuals are given according to these three comparison rules. In each pair, the individual represented by a circle is more competitive than the individual indicated by a triangle. In the first pair, the first rule is applied. As shown in this example, although both individuals cannot reach the privacy protection requirement, the circle individual can achieve a higher AD value. In the second pair, the circle individual is better since it can reach the requirement in privacy protection. In the third pair, both two individuals can reach the privacy protection requirement. The circle individual can outperform the triangle individual since the circle individual obtains a higher TD value.

Such a two-dimension selection operator can effectively improve the population quality in ID-GA. When no individual in the population can reach the privacy protection requirement, the individuals with higher privacy degrees are kept in the population. Thus, the entire population can approach the privacy protection requirement during the update. When part of the individuals in the population can reach the privacy protection requirement, these individuals are kept in the population. Finally, when most of the population can reach the privacy protection requirement, the individuals with higher TD values are kept in the population to improve the population quality.

3.5   Overall Process

The entire process of the ID-GA is described in Algorithm 1. At the beginning of the process, the population of ID-GA is initialized, and each individual in the population is evaluated. While the predefined stopping criterion is not met, the evolutionary procedure is carried out. Every two parent individuals in the population are used to generate the offspring. Then the mutation operator is executed on the offspring. Afterward, the offspring is evaluated. If the mutant offspring is better than any parent individual, the parent individual is replaced by the offspring. During this process, the population of ID-GA is updated, and the anonymization solutions in the population are improved. Finally, the best anonymization solution is outputted once the stopping criterion is met.

Table 1. Properties of 16 test instances

Test instances	nA	$nQID$	nR
T_1	16	8	200
T_2	16	8	200
T_3	16	8	400
T_4	16	8	400
T_5	18	10	200
T_6	18	10	200
T_7	18	10	400
T_8	18	10	400
T_9	20	12	200
T_{10}	20	12	200
T_{11}	20	12	400
T_{12}	20	12	400
T_{13}	22	14	200
T_{14}	22	14	200
T_{15}	22	14	400
T_{16}	22	14	400

4 Experimental Setup

This section illustrates the test instances, parameters settings, and algorithm implementation in the following experiments.

4.1 Test Instances

In the subsequent experimental studies, 16 test instances are utilized to investigate the performance of the proposed ID-GA. These test instances are generated based on the public datasets released by the New York State Department of Health[1]. Table 1 outlines the properties of these test instances, including the

---

[1] https://health.data.ny.gov/Health/Hospital-Inpatient-Discharges-SPARCS-De-Identified/82xm-y6g8.

number of attributes nA, the number of QID attributes $nQID$, and the number of records nR. In addition, in each test instance, the privacy requirement of anonymity degree k is set as 2.

4.2   Parameter Settings

In the baseline algorithm GA and proposed ID-GA, population size N is set as 30; mutation rate MR is set as 0.1. For all the algorithms, the maximum fitness evaluation number is set as $nQID \times nR$.

4.3   Algorithm Implementation

ID-GA and all the compared algorithms in this paper are implemented in C++ and performed on a local cluster containing 60 compute nodes (OS: Ubuntu 16.04; CPU: 3.40 GHz 4-Core Intel i5-7500; Memory: 8 GB).

5   Experimental Result

In this section, we verify the advantages of ID-GA by comparing it with the baseline algorithm GA and a competitive optimal anonymization algorithm Flash. Moreover, the effect of all the proposed operators is investigated.

5.1   Comparison with Existing Approaches

To verify the effectiveness of the proposed ID-GA algorithm, two existing algorithms, i.e., genetic algorithm (GA) [24] and Flash [17] are utilized for comparison. These two algorithms are listed as follows:

1. GA [24]: This algorithm acts as a baseline algorithm in the comparison. When compared with the proposed ID-GA, the effect of our designed operators in ID-GA is confirmed.
2. Flash [17]: In this paper, a generic framework for globally-optimal k-anonymity was presented. Furthermore, an algorithm based on a binary search was proposed based on the proposed framework.

In Table 2, the mean and standard deviation values of TD over 25 independent runs are presented, and the best results are highlighted in **boldface**. Overall, our proposed ID-GA can outperform the compared existing algorithms on 15 out of 16 test instances. Compared with GA, the advantage of our proposed operators in ID-GA is verified. With the help of these operators, individuals can effectively identify solutions that can achieve higher TD values while reaching the requirement of privacy preservation. Compared with Flash, the advantage of ID-GA in search efficiency is verified. With the increase of attribute numbers, the complexity of such an optimization problem promptly increases. In this situation, the individuals in ID-GA are more likely to maintain diversity and identify more competitive solutions.

Table 2. Comparison with existing approaches

Test instances	GA		Flash	ID-GA	
	Avg	Std	Result	Avg	Std
T_1	1.12E+02	3.94E+01	3.36E+02	**7.12E+02**†	9.65E+01
T_2	1.01E+02	7.62E+01	3.39E+02	**5.35E+02**†	5.50E+01
T_3	3.39E+02	7.57E+01	8.78E+02	**1.39E+03**†	1.33E+02
T_4	2.91E+02	9.28E+01	8.47E+02	**1.24E+03**†	8.01E+01
T_5	1.23E+02	9.56E+01	5.11E+02	**7.50E+02**†	7.87E+01
T_6	7.94E+01	9.98E+01	5.14E+02	**6.22E+02**†	7.71E+01
T_7	3.78E+02	1.26E+02	1.12E+03	**1.59E+03**†	9.89E+01
T_8	3.36E+02	1.62E+02	1.12E+03	**1.32E+03**†	9.81E+01
T_9	3.74E+01	8.75E+01	4.77E+02	**6.71E+02**†	1.22E+02
T_{10}	1.87E+01	6.39E+01	**5.20E+02**†	5.00E+02	8.30E+01
T_{11}	1.70E+02	2.10E+02	1.21E+03	**1.49E+03**†	1.18E+02
T_{12}	1.76E+02	2.02E+02	1.01E+03	**1.29E+03**†	1.81E+02
T_{13}	1.45E+01	7.12E+01	6.83E+02	**7.33E+02**†	1.02E+02
T_{14}	2.78E+01	9.59E+01	6.80E+02	**6.95E+02**†	1.10E+02
T_{15}	1.25E+02	2.52E+02	1.18E+03	**1.74E+03**†	1.33E+02
T_{16}	1.05E+02	2.42E+02	1.18E+03	**1.65E+03**†	1.81E+02

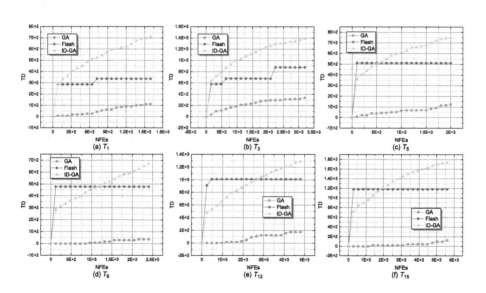

Fig. 5. Convergence curves of ID-GA and compared algorithms on six typical test instances.

Moreover, to investigate the advantage of ID-GA in a statistical sense, the Wilcoxon rank-sum test with a 0.05 level is utilized. In Table 2, the symbol † shows that the corresponding result is significantly better than the compared results. Overall, ID-GA can obtain significantly better results in 15 out of 16 test instances.

In Fig. 5, the convergence curves of ID-GA and two compared existing algorithms are plotted. In this figure, three algorithms are indicated by three symbols with different colors. For each point, the value on the horizontal axis represents the number of fitness evaluations, and the vertical axis represents the value of TD. Compared with GA, the advantage of ID-GA in search efficiency is verified. Due to the proposed crossover and mutation operators, ID-GA can achieve a higher convergence speed during the entire process. Compared with Flash, ID-GA shows its advantage in population diversity and continuous search ability. Although the heuristic strategy in Flash can achieve quick convergence at the beginning of the optimization, it is then trapped by the local optima due to the limitation of population diversity. Overall, our proposed ID-GA can achieve the highest convergence speed during the entire process in all six typical test instances.

Table 3. Impact of the proposed operators

Test instances	ID-GA-no-crossover		ID-GA-no-mutation		ID-GA	
	Avg	Std	Avg	Std	Avg	Std
T_1	2.29E+02	4.09E+01	6.38E+02	9.87E+01	**7.12E+02**†	9.65E+01
T_2	2.17E+02	3.47E+01	4.46E+02	5.13E+01	**5.35E+02**†	5.50E+01
T_3	6.01E+02	6.34E+01	1.26E+03	1.38E+02	**1.39E+03**†	1.33E+02
T_4	4.99E+02	1.29E+02	1.05E+03	1.33E+02	**1.24E+03**†	8.01E+01
T_5	2.83E+02	6.34E+01	6.20E+02	6.30E+01	**7.50E+02**†	7.87E+01
T_6	2.53E+02	5.06E+01	5.52E+02	5.39E+01	**6.22E+02**†	7.71E+01
T_7	7.41E+02	1.56E+02	1.41E+03	1.59E+02	**1.59E+03**†	9.89E+01
T_8	8.54E+02	1.69E+02	1.14E+03	1.53E+02	**1.32E+03**†	9.81E+01
T_9	2.22E+02	6.10E+01	5.24E+02	1.41E+02	**6.71E+02**†	1.22E+02
T_{10}	1.67E+02	6.48E+01	4.12E+02	1.01E+02	**5.00E+02**†	8.30E+01
T_{11}	8.18E+02	1.80E+02	1.17E+03	1.86E+02	**1.49E+03**†	1.18E+02
T_{12}	8.40E+02	1.61E+02	9.07E+02	1.73E+02	**1.29E+03**†	1.81E+02
T_{13}	3.61E+02	8.02E+01	5.74E+02	1.01E+02	**7.33E+02**†	1.02E+02
T_{14}	2.83E+02	7.31E+01	5.09E+02	8.80E+01	**6.95E+02**†	1.10E+02
T_{15}	1.19E+03	1.24E+02	1.32E+03	1.89E+02	**1.74E+03**†	1.33E+02
T_{16}	1.10E+03	1.55E+02	1.14E+03	2.41E+02	**1.65E+03**†	1.81E+02

5.2 Impact of the Proposed Operators

In this section, we investigate the impact of the proposed operators by comparing ID-GA with two variants. These two variants are described as follows:

1. ID-GA-no-crossover: In this variant, the information-driven crossover operator is removed from ID-GA. Accordingly, the traditional crossover operator in GA is used.
2. ID-GA-no-mutation: In this variant, the information-driven mutation operator is replaced by the traditional mutation operator in GA.

In Table 3, the average and standard deviation values of TD over 25 independent runs are calculated and listed. The best results in these test instances are marked in **boldface**. Overall, the original ID-GA can outperform these two variants on 16 test instances. Compared with ID-GA-no-crossover, the advantage of the proposed information-driven crossover operator is confirmed, which can effectively improve the information release while exchanging information between different anonymization solutions. Compared with ID-GA-no-mutation, the advantage of the proposed information-driven mutation operator is verified, improving the information release while enhancing the population diversity. Our proposed ID-GA can outperform two variants since both proposed operators are effective during the optimization.

In addition, the Wilcoxon rank-sum test with a 0.05 level is utilized. The symbol † shows that the corresponding result is significantly better than the compared results. Overall, in all 16 test instances, the advantage of the original ID-GA algorithm is significant.

6 Conclusion

In this paper, an information-driven genetic algorithm has been designed to achieve optimal anonymization based on attribute generalization and record suppression. An information-driven crossover operator has been proposed in the proposed algorithm to exchange information between anonymization solutions. An information-driven mutation operator has been designed to promote information release in the mutant anonymization solutions. A two-dimension selection operator has been designed to identify the competitiveness of different anonymization solutions. Finally, the advantages of the proposed algorithm in solution accuracy and convergence speed have been verified through the experiments. Also, the effectiveness of all the proposed components has been confirmed.

Acknowledgements. This work was supported by The Major Key Project of PCL (Grant No. PCL2022A03, PCL2021A02, PCL2021A09).

References

1. Ayyoubzadeh, S.M., Ayyoubzadeh, S.M., Zahedi, H., Ahmadi, M., Kalhori, S.R.N.: Predicting COVID-19 incidence through analysis of Google trends data in Iran: data mining and deep learning pilot study. JMIR Public Health Surveill. **6**(2), e18828 (2020). https://doi.org/10.2196/18828
2. Bennett, J., Lanning, S.: The Netflix prize. In: Proceedings of KDD Cup and Workshop 2007, pp. 3–6 (2007)
3. Cheng, K., et al.: Secure k-NN query on encrypted cloud data with multiple keys. IEEE Trans. Big Data **7**(4), 689–702 (2017). https://doi.org/10.1109/tbdata.2017.2707552
4. Dwork, C., McSherry, F., Nissim, K., Smith, A.: Calibrating noise to sensitivity in private data analysis. In: Halevi, S., Rabin, T. (eds.) TCC 2006. LNCS, vol. 3876, pp. 265–284. Springer, Heidelberg (2006). https://doi.org/10.1007/11681878_14
5. Fung, B.C.M., Wang, K., Chen, R., Yu, P.S.: Privacy-preserving data publishing: a survey of recent developments. ACM Comput. Surv. **42**(4) (2010). https://doi.org/10.1145/1749603.1749605
6. Ge, Y.-F., Cao, J., Wang, H., Zhang, Y., Chen, Z.: Distributed differential evolution for anonymity-driven vertical fragmentation in outsourced data storage. In: Huang, Z., Beek, W., Wang, H., Zhou, R., Zhang, Y. (eds.) WISE 2020. LNCS, vol. 12343, pp. 213–226. Springer, Cham (2020). https://doi.org/10.1007/978-3-030-62008-0_15
7. Ge, Y.F., Orlowska, M., Cao, J., Wang, H., Zhang, Y.: Knowledge transfer-based distributed differential evolution for dynamic database fragmentation. Knowl.-Based Syst. **229**, 107325 (2021). https://doi.org/10.1016/j.knosys.2021.107325
8. Ge, Y.F., Orlowska, M., Cao, J., Wang, H., Zhang, Y.: MDDE: multitasking distributed differential evolution for privacy-preserving database fragmentation. VLDB J. (2022). https://doi.org/10.1007/s00778-021-00718-w
9. Ge, Y.F., et al.: Distributed memetic algorithm for outsourced database fragmentation. IEEE Trans. Cybern. **51**(10), 4808–4821 (2021). https://doi.org/10.1109/tcyb.2020.3027962
10. Ge, Y.F., et al.: Distributed differential evolution based on adaptive mergence and split for large-scale optimization. IEEE Trans. Cybern. **48**(7), 2166–2180 (2018). https://doi.org/10.1109/tcyb.2017.2728725
11. Ge, Y.F., Yu, W.J., Zhang, J.: Diversity-based multi-population differential evolution for large-scale optimization. In: Proceedings of the 2016 on Genetic and Evolutionary Computation Conference Companion. ACM (2016). https://doi.org/10.1145/2908961.2908995
12. Gong, D., Sun, J., Miao, Z.: A set-based genetic algorithm for interval many-objective optimization problems. IEEE Trans. Evol. Comput. **22**(1), 47–60 (2018). https://doi.org/10.1109/tevc.2016.2634625
13. Kabir, M.E., Mahmood, A.N., Wang, H., Mustafa, A.K.: Microaggregation sorting framework for k-anonymity statistical disclosure control in cloud computing. IEEE Trans. Cloud Comput. **8**(2), 408–417 (2020). https://doi.org/10.1109/tcc.2015.2469649
14. Kabir, M.E., Wang, H.: Conditional purpose based access control model for privacy protection. In: Proceedings of the Twentieth Australasian Conference on Australasian Database, pp. 135–142 (2009)
15. Kabir, M.E., Wang, H., Bertino, E.: A role-involved purpose-based access control model. Inf. Syst. Front. **14**(3), 809–822 (2011). https://doi.org/10.1007/s10796-011-9305-1

16. Kifer, D., Machanavajjhala, A.: No free lunch in data privacy. In: Proceedings of the 2011 International Conference on Management of Data. ACM Press (2011). https://doi.org/10.1145/1989323.1989345
17. Kohlmayer, F., Prasser, F., Eckert, C., Kemper, A., Kuhn, K.A.: Flash: efficient, stable and optimal k-anonymity. In: 2012 International Conference on Privacy, Security, Risk and Trust and 2012 International Conference on Social Computing. IEEE (2012). https://doi.org/10.1109/socialcom-passat.2012.52
18. Lau, B.P.L., et al.: A survey of data fusion in smart city applications. Inf. Fusion **52**, 357–374 (2019). https://doi.org/10.1016/j.inffus.2019.05.004
19. Li, J.Y., Zhan, Z.H., Wang, H., Zhang, J.: Data-driven evolutionary algorithm with perturbation-based ensemble surrogates. IEEE Trans. Cybern. **51**(8), 3925–3937 (2021). https://doi.org/10.1109/tcyb.2020.3008280
20. Liu, C., Chen, S., Zhou, S., Guan, J., Ma, Y.: A novel privacy preserving method for data publication. Inf. Sci. **501**, 421–435 (2019). https://doi.org/10.1016/j.ins.2019.06.022
21. Mahanan, W., Chaovalitwongse, W.A., Natwichai, J.: Data anonymization: a novel optimal k-anonymity algorithm for identical generalization hierarchy data in IoT. SOCA **14**(2), 89–100 (2020). https://doi.org/10.1007/s11761-020-00287-w
22. Martin, K.D., Murphy, P.E.: The role of data privacy in marketing. J. Acad. Mark. Sci. **45**(2), 135–155 (2016). https://doi.org/10.1007/s11747-016-0495-4
23. Mehmood, A., Natgunanathan, I., Xiang, Y., Hua, G., Guo, S.: Protection of big data privacy. IEEE Access **4**, 1821–1834 (2016). https://doi.org/10.1109/access.2016.2558446
24. Mirjalili, S.: Evolutionary Algorithms and Neural Networks. SCI, vol. 780. Springer, Cham (2019). https://doi.org/10.1007/978-3-319-93025-1
25. Romero, C., Ventura, S.: Educational data mining and learning analytics: an updated survey. WIREs Data Min. Knowl. Discov. **10**(3) (2020). https://doi.org/10.1002/widm.1355
26. Samarati, P., Sweeney, L.: Generalizing data to provide anonymity when disclosing information. In: Proceedings of the Seventeenth ACM SIGACT-SIGMOD-SIGART Symposium on Principles of Database Systems. ACM Press (1998). https://doi.org/10.1145/275487.275508
27. Srinivas, M., Patnaik, L.: Genetic algorithms: a survey. Computer **27**(6), 17–26 (1994). https://doi.org/10.1109/2.294849
28. Sun, L., Ma, J., Wang, H., Zhang, Y., Yong, J.: Cloud service description model: an extension of USDL for cloud services. IEEE Trans. Serv. Comput. **11**(2), 354–368 (2018). https://doi.org/10.1109/tsc.2015.2474386
29. Sun, X., Wang, H., Li, J., Zhang, Y.: Satisfying privacy requirements before data anonymization. Comput. J. **55**(4), 422–437 (2011). https://doi.org/10.1093/comjnl/bxr028
30. Sun, X., Li, M., Wang, H.: A family of enhanced (1, α)-diversity models for privacy preserving data publishing. Futur. Gener. Comput. Syst. **27**(3), 348–356 (2011). https://doi.org/10.1016/j.future.2010.07.007
31. Sun, X., Li, M., Wang, H., Plank, A.: An efficient hash-based algorithm for minimal k-anonymity. In: Conferences in Research and Practice in Information Technology, vol. 74, pp. 101–107 (2008)
32. Sun, X., Wang, H., Li, J., Pei, J.: Publishing anonymous survey rating data. Data Min. Knowl. Disc. **23**(3), 379–406 (2010). https://doi.org/10.1007/s10618-010-0208-4

33. Sun, X., Wang, H., Li, J., Zhang, Y.: Injecting purpose and trust into data anonymisation. Comput. Secur. **30**(5), 332–345 (2011). https://doi.org/10.1016/j.cose.2011.05.005

34. Sun, Y., Xue, B., Zhang, M., Yen, G.G., Lv, J.: Automatically designing CNN architectures using the genetic algorithm for image classification. IEEE Trans. Cybern. **50**(9), 3840–3854 (2020). https://doi.org/10.1109/tcyb.2020.2983860

35. Wang, H., Cao, J., Zhang, Y.: Ticket-based service access scheme for mobile users. Austral. Comput. Sci. Commun. **24**(1), 285–292 (2002)

36. Wang, H., Sun, L.: Trust-involved access control in collaborative open social networks. In: 2010 Fourth International Conference on Network and System Security. IEEE (2010). https://doi.org/10.1109/nss.2010.13

37. Wang, H., Sun, L., Bertino, E.: Building access control policy model for privacy preserving and testing policy conflicting problems. J. Comput. Syst. Sci. **80**(8), 1493–1503 (2014). https://doi.org/10.1016/j.jcss.2014.04.017

38. Wang, H., Wang, Y., Taleb, T., Jiang, X.: Editorial: special issue on security and privacy in network computing. World Wide Web **23**(2), 951–957 (2019). https://doi.org/10.1007/s11280-019-00704-x

39. Wang, H., Zhang, Y., Cao, J., Varadharajan, V.: Achieving secure and flexible m-services through tickets. IEEE Trans. Syst. Man Cybern. - Part A: Syst. Hum. **33**(6), 697–708 (2003). https://doi.org/10.1109/tsmca.2003.819917

40. Yang, J., et al.: Brief introduction of medical database and data mining technology in big data era. J. Evid. Based Med. **13**(1), 57–69 (2020). https://doi.org/10.1111/jebm.12373

41. Zheng, X., Luo, G., Cai, Z.: A fair mechanism for private data publication in online social networks. IEEE Trans. Netw. Sci. Eng. **7**(2), 880–891 (2020). https://doi.org/10.1109/tnse.2018.2801798

42. Zhou, M., et al.: Adaptive genetic algorithm-aided neural network with channel state information tensor decomposition for indoor localization. IEEE Trans. Evol. Comput. **25**(5), 913–927 (2021). https://doi.org/10.1109/tevc.2021.3085906

43. Zhu, T., Li, G., Zhou, W., Yu, P.S.: Differentially private data publishing and analysis: a survey. IEEE Trans. Knowl. Data Eng. **29**(8), 1619–1638 (2017). https://doi.org/10.1109/tkde.2017.2697856

Information Retrieval and Text Processing

Enhanced Topic Representation
by Ambiguity Handling

Dakshi Kapugama Geeganage[(✉)], Yue Xu, Darshika Koggalahewa,
and Yuefeng Li

School of Computer Science, Queensland University of Technology,
Brisbane, Australia
{kapugama,yue.xu,darshika.koggalahewa,y2.li}@qut.edu.au

Abstract. Most of the existing semantic-based topic models and topic
generation approaches use external knowledgebases or ontology to interpret the meanings of the words. However, general ontologies do not cover
many ambiguous or specific domain-related words in a text collection.
Hence those ambiguous or domain-specific words are neglected in capturing the meanings in topic generation. In this paper, we introduce an
approach to disambiguate the unmatched words in a text collection based
on related and similar meaning words. Word embeddings are applied to
discover similar or related words. We evaluated the topic generation approach with our ambiguity handling technique with a set of state-of-the-art
systems which uses an external ontology. Our approach outperformed,
and the generated topics were more meaningful. Our ambiguity handling
approach interpreted all the important words and included them in the
topic generation process.

Keywords: Ambiguity · Semantics · Concepts · Topic representation

1 Introduction

Text data is generated in exponential growth. An enormous amount of text
content is available, and it is essential to understand, categorise and explore the
hidden thematic structure in text content. Different topic modelling techniques
are applied to discover the topics in text collections. Most of the existing topic
generation approaches were based on the probabilistic approaches [3,4,9,17].
Semantics were ignored in those probabilistic approaches [3,4,9,17] where topics
were produced based on the frequency and co-occurrences of words. However,
statistical features alone may not adequately represent the text collections if
the text semantics are ignored. Semantic-based topic generation approaches [12,
19,21] were introduced as a result of realising the importance of semantics in
understanding the text contents. Most of the semantic-based approaches were
combined with an ontology, or external taxonomy [7,19,21].

An ontology is considered as a widely used knowledge representation technique that stores the concepts, categories and relationships among concepts.

© The Author(s), under exclusive license to Springer Nature Switzerland AG 2022
R. Chbeir et al. (Eds.): WISE 2022, LNCS 13724, pp. 357–369, 2022.
https://doi.org/10.1007/978-3-031-20891-1_25

Freebase [5], Probase [20], Yago [18], DBPedia [2] are some of the well-known ontology used in text mining and specifically semantic-based topic models. Some of the popular ontology covers specific domain (specialised) knowledge while others cover the general knowledge [2,18,20]. Ontologies have used different knowledge representation structures. However, it is difficult to find an ontology that covers all the concepts of all the words occurring in a text collection.

Ontologies and external knowledgebases are used in most semantic-based topic modelling approaches to capture the semantics of the words in documents, which are described in terms of concepts. However, no ontology can cover universal knowledge, and existing ontology-based approaches have limited capabilities in capturing the meaning of all the words occurring in documents with the concepts in an ontology. So not every valid word in a document collection will find a match with a concept in any specific ontology. A word, phrase or sentence can be considered ambiguous if it was not defined with a clear meaning or could have multiple meanings. Thus, the inability to interpret a word's meaning using the concepts available in the ontology can be defined as a form of ambiguity. We noticed that several words could not be matched with any available concepts in Probase; for example, some popular words related to crime stories such as 'crime', 'kill', 'death', 'rapist', 'pornography', 'paedophilia' etc. These words are valid and important in news, and current affairs but cannot be interpreted. Ignoring those words could significantly change the meaning of a topic. Hence, ignoring unmatched words is a limitation in most semantic-based approaches. Thus, this paper focuses on interpreting and including unmatched words in the topic modelling process.

Interpreting the meaning of a new word is considered as challenging in learning, and linguistic related researches [1,6,11]. Similarly, explaining unfamiliar/new words to a kid is a part of the learning process. It has been found that explaining a new word with the context information, or other related words is a successful mechanism [1,6,11]. We followed a similar technique to explain the new/unmatched words in the ontology. In this paper, we propose to interpret the meanings of unmatched words using related or similar words in the ontology. A vital requirement in handling this ambiguity is to generate relationships between the unmatched words with some related or similar words that can match with concepts in the ontology. We introduced a word embedding-based word similarity mapping approach to achieve this objective. Finally, the unmatched words can be interpreted based on similar or related words and would be included in the topic generation.

As the main contribution of this paper, we enhanced the semantic topic representation introduced in the research work [7]. STRuFSP [7] is a two-phase semantic-based topic representation that incorporates knowledge from Probase ontology [20] in the second phase for the semantic capturing process. Even though the semantics are captured in the topic generation process, the words which cannot be matched with any concepts in Probase were ignored in the topic representation process. The approach to be introduced in this paper can handle the unmatched words using the context information of the words, which is considered as an essential criterion in explaining new words [1,6,11]. The proposed ambiguity handling technique can be applied in any text mining application which uses external ontology.

Research works related to semantic-based topic generation approaches which apply ontology are described in Sect. 2. Our approach is explained in Sect. 3. Section 4 contains the evaluation of the experimental results and discusses the results with state-of-the-art systems. Finally, Sect. 5 concludes the research paper.

2   Related Works

Semantic-based topic generation approaches were introduced after recognising the importance of semantics in understanding the text contents. Various techniques have been applied to capture and interpret the semantics, and among those methods, ontology or external knowledge sources were commonly used to capture the meanings. Wikipedia, Freebase [5], Yago [18], DBPedia [2], Probase [20], Open Directory Project, Library of Congress Subject Headings (LCSH), BabelNet [15] and WordNet [13] are set of widely used external taxonomies and lexical knowledgebases.

OntoLDA [12] is an ontology-based topic model which applied DBPedia [2] to label the topics. They used ontological concepts to label the topics. Yao et al. [21] introduced a semantic-based topic model by incorporating probabilistic knowledge. They incorporated Probase [20] to extract the concepts, and probabilities derived from Probase were used to define the Dirichlet priors. CLDA (conceptualisation topic model) [19] is also a semantic-based topic model which contains a concept layer to capture the meanings of the words. CLDA also used Probase as the ontology, and words were interpreted based on the concept given word probability available in the Probase. In their approach, if the word is not available in the Probase, they did the calculation for those words based on LDA [4] without interpreting the meaning of unmatched words. Similarly, a pattern-based topic representation called STRuFSP [7] was introduced based on Probase. STRuFSP applied two-phase semantic approaches to capture the semantics. In their approach, they constructed semantic patterns based on matching concepts with Probase. However, unmatched words were ignored in the final topic representation.

To this end, ontology-based approaches select the most appropriate ontology for the application domain with a higher word coverage. There is no effective solution proposed to handle the unmatched words while most of the ontology-based semantic topic generation approaches describe the words available in the ontology, and they neglect or do not consider the meaning of the unmatched words in the topic generation process. Hence, we embedded our ambiguity handling approach to STRuFSP [7] and interpreted the unmatched words in our research. We evaluated the results using state-of-the-art topic generation approaches based on Probase ontology.

3   The Proposed Approach

The research focuses on handling the ambiguities in unmatched words with ontology and enhancing the semantic-based topic representation STRuFSP [7] by incorporating an ambiguity handling approach based on related or similar meaning words. The high-level overview of our enhanced topic representation with disambiguation (STRuFSP+Disambiguation) is depicted in Fig. 1. While STRuFSP [7] generated the topic representation only from the matched words, our extended approach (STRuFSP+Disambiguation) incorporated the unmatched words into the topic list. Section 3.1 provides a summary of STRuFSP [7]. As depicted in Fig. 1, semantic clique G_1 is created with a set of similar and related words. Then, the words in G_1 are matched with the concepts in Probase ontology. Semantic patterns are generated based on matching concepts, and unmatched words such as w_4, w_6 are not included in the semantic patterns. Our approach finds the similarity between unmatched and matched words, and unmatched words are included with most similar matched words.

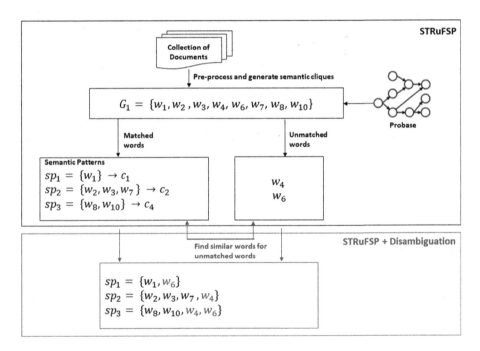

Fig. 1. Overview of STRuFSP+Disambiguation

3.1   STRuFSP - Semantic-Based Topic Representation Using Frequent Semantic Patterns

STRuFSP is a two-phase semantic-based topic representation that captures semantics in two phases. In phase-1, STRuFSP extracts words from the document collection and generates semantic cliques by clustering the words based on the semantic similarity derived from word embeddings. Each word cluster containing similar or related words is called a semantic clique. The GloVe [16] word embeddings were used to discover the semantic similarity of words.

In phase-2, patterns were generated on top of the words in each semantic clique based on the concepts of Proabse [20] ontology. Words in each semantic clique are matched with the concepts in Probase, and a set of patterns called semantic patterns was generated based on commonly shared concepts in Probase. Each semantic pattern consists of a set of words that share some common concepts. In this phase, only the words matched with Probase concepts were included in semantic patterns. The words that were not matched with any concepts in the Probase were automatically abandoned, which could make the pattern-based semantic topic representation miss out important aspects of the document collection. Another issue is that some semantic patterns may not be representative due to low occurring frequency in the text collection. To deal with the low-frequency issue, frequent patterns were generated from each semantic clique by applying a frequent pattern mining technique such as the FP-Growth [8] algorithm. Finally, frequent semantic patterns were generated in each semantic clique.

Let $D = \{d_1, d_2, \ldots, d_m\}$ be a collection of documents with a set of unique words T_D, and $G = \{g_1, g_2, \ldots, g_n\}$ be a set of semantic cliques generated from D. "For a semantic clique g_i, let SP_i be a set of semantic patterns and FP_i be a set of frequent patterns generated for g_i, then a set of frequent semantic patterns for g_i, denoted as FSP_i, $FSP_i = \{FSP_{i1}, FSP_{i2}, \ldots, FSP_{in}\}$" [7].

The frequent semantic patterns generated in semantic cliques and the set of matched concepts are considered as the topic representation to represent the main themes in D.

3.2   Disambiguate the Unmatched Words

As mentioned above, ignoring the unmatched words is one of the main problems in STRuFSP. To address this problem, we propose to capture the meaning of those unmatched words from their similar or related words. As described in Sect. 3.1, the semantic cliques were generated based on similar and related words, and accordingly, the words in each semantic clique can be considered similar or related to each other. As explained in the linguistic research, [1,6,11], the related words and context information are important to interpret the meaning of a new word. We adhered to that concept and identified the words in semantic cliques which have a similar meaning or relate to unmatched words. Those similar or related words will share similar concepts with the unmatched words. In STRuFSP, each semantic pattern is described by one or more concepts. With this idea in mind, we propose identifying a semantic pattern containing similar words to the unmatched word and then interpreting the unmatched word by adding it to the semantic pattern. Finally, the expanded semantic pattern can cover the meaning of the unmatched word. In this paper, the similar semantic patterns of an unmatched word are identified based on the similarity of word embeddings of the unmatched word and the words in semantic patterns.

For a given word w and a pattern p, the similarity between w and p is defined below:

$$sim(w, p) = \frac{1}{|p|} \sum_{t \in p} embedding\_sim(w, t) \tag{1}$$

$embedding\_sim(w, t)$ is the similarity between the embeddings of w and t, $sim(w, p)$ is the average similarity of w with the words in p.

For a given semantic clique $g_i \in G$, a set of patterns can be generated, $P_i = \{p_1, p_2, \ldots, p_m\}$, and the words in $mg_i = \bigcup_{p \in P_i} p$ can be matched with some concepts in Probase. mg_i is a set of matched words for clique g_i. However, if mg_i is a true subset of g_i, there must be some words in g_i which are unmatched words. Let $ug_i = (g_i - mg_i)$ and $ug_i \neq \phi$, for each $w \in ug_i$, the top-k most similar patterns are calculated using the equation below:

$$simPattern(w) = argMax_{p \in P_i}^k sim(w, p) \tag{2}$$

Thus, we have applied Eq. 1 to calculate the similarity between unmatched words and semantic patterns in clique g_i. As per Eq. 2, we selected the most similar semantic patterns for each unmatched word. Algorithm 1 depicts the process of handling ambiguity for one semantic clique.

A set of semantic patterns $SP_i = \{sp_{i1} \ldots, sp_{i|SP_i|}\}$ and the set of unmatched words UW_i of semantic clique $g_i \in G$ will be the input for Algorithm 1. First, we get each unmatched word $uw \in UW_i$ for the semantic clique (line 1). A set of semantic patterns with the highest similarity to the unmatched word, $simPattern(uw)$, is selected (line 2). The unmatched word uw will subsequently be added to the most similar patterns (line 4–6) resulting in modified semantic patterns.

Algorithm 1. The process of handling ambiguity for unmatched words

---

Input: A set of semantic patterns $SP_i = \{sp_{i1}, \ldots, sp_{i|SP_i|}\}$ and a set of unmatched words UW_i in clique g_i.
Output: A set of modified semantic patterns generated for clique g_i.

1: **for** each unmatched word $uw \in UW_i$ **do**
2:     $simPattern(uw) := argMax_{sp \in SP_i}^k sim(uw, sp)$
3:     **for** each pattern $p \in simPattern(uw)$ **do**
4:         $SP_i := SP_i - \{p\}$
5:         $p := p \bigcup \{uw\}$
6:         $SP_i := \{p\} \bigcup SP_i$
7:     **end for**
8: **end for**

After including the unmatched word into a semantic pattern, we can calculate the probability of each related concept c of the pattern given the unmatched word uw, $P(c|uw)$ according to the Eq. 3. Because w is similar to the patterns in $simPattern(w)$, it is considered that w can be semantically interpreted by the concepts of the patterns. Therefore, these patterns are updated by adding the word w, i.e., for each $p \in simPattern(w), p = p \bigcup \{w\}$. Let C_p be a set of concepts that relate to p, for each concept $c \in C_p$, the probability $Pr(c|w)$ is estimated below:

$$Pr(c|w) = \frac{1}{|p|} \sum_{t \in p} Pr(c|t) * embedding\_sim(w, t) \qquad (3)$$

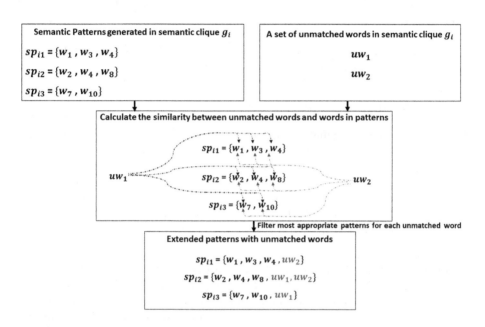

Fig. 2. Example of merging unmatched words into existing semantic patterns

Figure 2 provides an example of how unmatched words are handled. For each semantic clique, there is a set of semantic patterns and a set of unmatched words which did not occur in any of the semantic patterns because they are not covered by the ontology. In this example, in semantic clique g_i, there are three semantic patterns $sp_{i1} : \{w_1, w_3, w_4\}$, $sp_{i2} : \{w_2, w_4, w_8\}$, and $sp_{i3} : \{w_7, w_{10}\}$. We will consider uw_1 and uw_2 as unmatched words in g_i. Pair-wise similarity based on word embeddings is calculated between each word in each pattern with the unmatched words. Pattern similarity is calculated based on the average similarity and the unmatched words are included into their most similar patterns based on the similarity value. Finally the modified patterns with unmatched words are generated. Accordingly for the unmatched word uw_1 the most appropriate patterns are sp_{i2} and sp_{i3}, hence uw_1 is added to the patterns sp_{i2} and sp_{i3}. Similarly, uw_2 is added to sp_{i1} and sp_{i2} because those are the most appropriate patterns for unmatched word uw_2.

Our approach can successfully handle the unmatched words, and we could represent the unmatched words in semantic patterns based on the related or similar meaning words. Hence, unmatched words can be explained interms of one or more concepts associated with the semantic pattern.

4   Evaluation

We construct an enhanced STRuFSP by embedding our ambiguity handling approach to STRuFSP. We have conducted a topic quality evaluation and information filtering evaluation to evaluate our approach, and we selected three state-of-the-art systems; Probase-LDA [21], CLDA [19], and STRuFSP [7] which used the knowledge of Probase ontology. Our approach is an enhancement for STRuFSP and denoted as (STRuFSP+Disambiguation).

4.1   Topic Quality Evaluation

In the topic quality evaluation, we measured the coherence and observed the generated topic list of each model. We have used the collections of three datasets, Reuters Corpus 1- RCV1 [10], 20 Newsgroups and R8 datasets. All three datasets contained news stories. Probase-LDA [21] and CLDA [19] are LDA based topic models and we tuned the parameters as follows; $\alpha = 1, \beta = 0.1$ and number of iterations $= 2000$. STRuFSP [7] is a pattern-based topic representation and top 5 concepts are retrieved from Probase for each word in a clique.

Coherence. Coherence evaluates the semantic similarity among the topic words in the generated topic lists. A higher coherence score indicates the higher similarity and relevance of the topic words within one topic or one semantic clique. The topics generated by good quality topic generation approaches can have a higher coherence score compared to that generated by other approaches. We applied Eq. 4 [14] to calculate the coherence score. Figure 3 shows the coherence scores for varying numbers of topics for the proposed ambiguity handling approach and the state-of-the-art systems run on the RCV1, R8 and 20 Newsgroups datasets.

$$Coherence(t) = \sum_{m=2}^{M} \sum_{l=1}^{m-1} log \frac{D(v_m^{(t)}, v_l^{(t)}) + 1}{D(v_l^{(t)})} \qquad (4)$$

where $v_m^{(t)}$ and $v_l^{(t)}$ are the mth and l^{th} words within topic t, $D(v_m^{(t)}, v_l^{(t)})$ is the co-document frequency of the two words, and $D(v_l^{(t)})$ is the document frequency of the word $v_l^{(t)}$.

STRuFSP+Disambiguation produced the highest coherence score for all the topic variations. It indicates that the topic-words generated by our disambiguation approach are more meaningful and closely related. It is evident that the unmatched words are appropriately included in the topic list.

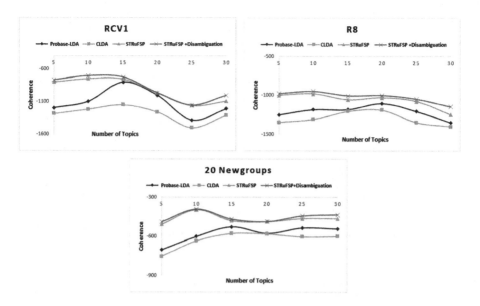

Fig. 3. Coherence score for various numbers of topics

Observations. We observed some of the generated topics of STRuFSP and our enhanced ambiguity handling approach (STRuFSP+Disambiguation). We selected 102 collection from the RCV1 dataset, because it contains words related to crimes. Table 1 shows the topical words in five sample topics/ semantic cliques generated by STRuFSP and STRuFSP+Disambiguation.

According to Table 1, the topical words generated in STRuFSP in each semantic clique are closely related. But many important words are missing due to the unavailability in Probase. Since this collection contains newstories related to crimes, many of the key crime-related words are not included in the topic list. It is not possible to see the crime words such as *kill, paedophilia, rapist, crime* etc. in STRuFSP. Not only the specific words such as crime related words but also the general words such as *european, kid, adult* etc. are also not available in Probase. Our disambiguation approach has appropriately matched the unmatched words, for example, in semantic clique G_1, the unmatched words *porn, pornography, prostitution* with the word *scandal*, the unmatched words *paedophilia, dutroux, rapist* with the word *offender*. In G_3, the unmatched words *rapist, kill, crime* with the word *kidnap* and the semantic pattern can be correctly matched with the concept 'serious event', the unmatched word *crime* with the word *abduction, theft* and the semantic pattern can be appropriately matched with the concept 'offence'. Hence, our ambiguity handling mechanism is more meaningful.

When we observed the sample topic-words generated from each approach, STRuFSP+Disambiguation generates more meaningful topic lists with all the important words where STRuFSP ignores the unmatched words in topic generation. Observations indicate the importance of including the unmatched words into the topic generation process.

Table 1. Topic-words generated from STRuFSP+Disambiguation and STRuFSP

Semantic clique	STRuFSP+Disambiguation	STRuFSP
G_1	$\{offender, scandal\}$, $\{coverup\}$, $\{scandal,$ **porn, pornography, prostitution**$\}$, $\{offender,$ **paedophilia, dutroux, rapist**$\}$	$\{offender, scandal\}$, $\{coverup\}$, $\{scandal\}$, $\{offender\}$
G_2	$\{belgium, austria,$ **european**$\}$, $\{belgian,$ **european**$\}$, $\{brussels, liege, charleroi, ostend\}$, $\{dutch, french\}$, $\{charleroi, ostend\}$	$\{belgium, austria\}$, $\{belgian\}$, $\{brussels, liege, charleroi, ostend\}$, $\{dutch, french\}$, $\{charleroi, ostend\}$
G_3	$\{kidnap,$ **rapist, kill, crime**$\}$, $\{kidnapping, theft\}$, $\{kidnap, abduction,$ **seized, kill**$\}$, $\{abduction, theft,$ **crime**$\}$, $\{stolen,$ **kill**$\}$, $\{murdering,$ **criminal, kill**$\}$	$\{kidnap\}$, $\{kidnapping, theft\}$, $\{kidnap, abduction\}$, $\{abduction, theft\}$, $\{stolen\}$, $\{murdering\}$
G_4	$\{police, interpol,$ **cop, crime**$\}$, $\{police, gendarmerie,$ **cop, crime, criminal**$\}$, $\{gendarme,$ **cop, criminal**$\}$, $\{gendarmerie,$ **crime**$\}$, $\{detective,$ **criminal**$\}$, $\{official, investigator\}$	$\{police, interpol\}$, $\{police, gendarmerie\}$, $\{gendarme\}$, $\{gendarmerie\}$, $\{detective\}$, $\{official, investigator\}$
G_5	$\{child, young, children, aged,$ **kid**$\}$, $\{child, young, teenager, children,$ **adult, kid**$\}$, $\{child, children, aged\}$, $\{child, children,$ **kid**$\}$	$\{child, young, children, aged\}$, $\{child, young, teenager, children\}$, $\{child, children, aged\}$, $\{child, children\}$

4.2   Information Filtering Evaluation

The frequent semantic patterns generated from STRuFSP can be considered as the features to model a user interest for filtering relevant documents for the user. We embedded the unmatched words in frequent semantic patterns (STRuFSP+Disambiguation) and conducted an information filtering based evaluation. We conducted the information filtering evaluation on RCV1 dataset with the same state-of-the art systems we applied in previous evaluation and Table 2 shows the comparison results.

Eventhough there is no considerable improvement in Table 2 for the entire dataset which consists of RCV1 collections, our enhanced approach shows the highest results in the information filtering evaluation. However, our proposed ambiguity handling approach shows notable improvement to some collections which contain words related to crimes, politics, health which are often not available in general ontology. But, those words are important to represent the topics and derive the meaning of the textual content. We have noticed that a considerable number of words are unmatched in news stories which belong to crime, disaster and accidents, politics and international affairs. We have done an information filtering evaluation specifically for those categories and there is a considerable improvement in results due to the importance of the unmatched words. Table 3 depicts the results for different categories.

Table 2. Results of a comparison of all models for information filtering (RCV1 dataset)

Approach	Top 20	F1	MAP
STRuFSP+Disambiguation	**0.566**	**0.479**	**0.486**
STRuFSP [7]	0.563	0.479	0.484
Probase-LDA [21]	0.413	0.327	0.429
CLDA [19]	0.380	0.376	0.401

Table 3. Results of a comparison of all models for different content categories

Approach	Category								
	Crime			Disasters and Accidents			Politics and International affairs		
	Top 20	F1	MAP	Top 20	F1	MAP	Top 20	F1	MAP
STRuFSP+ Disambiguation	**0.391**	**0.403**	**0.398**	**0.515**	**0.522**	**0.519**	**0.533**	**0.548**	**0.544**
STRuFSP [7]	0.372	0.396	0.382	0.487	0.451	0.447	0.491	0.501	0.536
Probase-LDA [21]	0.335	0.349	0.327	0.325	0.347	0.321	0.416	0.425	0.433
CLDA [19]	0.365	0.374	0.372	0.475	0.412	0.439	0.425	0.437	0.454

Our ambiguity handling mechanism is important because the unmatched words are often key words in the collection. For example, crime related words such as *kill, rape, paedophilia, criminal* etc. disaster and accident related words such as *crash, dead, death* etc are not available in a general ontology such as Probase. When STRuFSP generates the final topic representation from these specific collections such as criminal, politics etc., most of the important words are missing in the final topic representation. In some approaches, the meaning of those words have not been considered to generate the topic list. Overall, our enhanced ambiguity handling approach is beneficial by incorporating the unmatched words into the final topic lists. Interpreting all the important words is a vital requirement in generating topics from social media posts, news and digital libraries where our ambiguity handling approach can be easily applied to interpret any unmatched word.

STRuFSP+Disambiguation generated the highest Top 20 and MAP values in information filtering evaluation and F1-Measure is same as STRuFSP. Our disambiguation approach shows a considerable improvement when compared to other two semantic based approaches (CLDA and Probase-LDA) which do not consider the semantics of unmatched words. There is a considerable improvement in the specific categories such as criminals, disasters and accidents, politics and international affairs which indicates the importance of our ambiguity handling in many domains.

Overall, our ambiguity handling approach is beneficial because, generating the topic lists without the unmatched words may damage the meaning of the content and final topic list.

5   Conclusion

Most of the existing semantic-based topic models use external ontologies or knowledgebases to capture the semantics. Nevertheless, finding a knowledge base that can describe and cover all the required words and match them with concepts is challenging. Ignoring the unmatched words and not considering the meaning of the unmatched words are the common methods used to handle the unmatched words. As a result, some important words may be missed or not interpreted correctly in the final topic list due to the unavailability of the words in the ontology. Therefore, we have proposed a word embedding-based approach to handling words that do not match the concepts in ontologies. We used the related or semantically similar meaning words to interpret the unmatched words and handle ambiguities. Our approach handled the unmatched words and interpreted the meaning of those words in the topic generation. In future work, we aim to improve the performance of our approach and apply it to different ontologies.

References

1. Anderson, R.C., Nagy, W.E.: The vocabulary conundrum. Technical report. University of Illinois at Urbana-Champaign (1993)
2. Auer, S., Bizer, C., Kobilarov, G., Lehmann, J., Cyganiak, R., Ives, Z.: DBpedia: a nucleus for a web of open data. In: Aberer, K., et al. (eds.) ASWC/ISWC -2007. LNCS, vol. 4825, pp. 722–735. Springer, Heidelberg (2007). https://doi.org/10.1007/978-3-540-76298-0_52
3. Blei, D.M., Lafferty, J.D.: Correlated topic models. In: Proceedings of the 18th International Conference on Neural Information Processing Systems, NIPS 2005, pp. 147–154. MIT Press, Cambridge (2005). http://dl.acm.org/citation.cfm?id=2976248.2976267
4. Blei, D.M., Ng, A.Y., Jordan, M.I.: Latent Dirichlet allocation. J. Mach. Learn. Res. 3, 993–1022 (2003). http://dl.acm.org/citation.cfm?id=944919.944937
5. Bollacker, K., Evans, C., Paritosh, P., Sturge, T., Taylor, J.: Freebase. In: Proceedings of the 2008 ACM SIGMOD International Conference on Management of Data, SIGMOD 2008. ACM Press (2008). https://doi.org/10.1145/1376616.1376746
6. Carnine, D., Kameenui, E.J., Coyle, G.: Utilization of contextual information in determining the meaning of unfamiliar words. Read. Res. Q. 19(2), 188 (1984). https://doi.org/10.2307/747362
7. Geeganage, D.T.K., Xu, Y., Li, Y.: Semantic-based topic representation using frequent semantic patterns. Knowl.-Based Syst. 216, 106808 (2021). https://doi.org/10.1016/j.knosys.2021.106808
8. Han, J., Pei, J., Yin, Y.: Mining frequent patterns without candidate generation. ACM SIGMOD Rec. 29(2), 1–12 (2000). https://doi.org/10.1145/335191.335372
9. Hofmann, T.: Probabilistic latent semantic indexing. In: Proceedings of the 22nd Annual International ACM SIGIR Conference on Research and Development in Information Retrieval, SIGIR 1999. ACM Press (1999). https://doi.org/10.1145/312624.312649
10. Lewis, D.D., Yang, Y., Rose, T.G., Li, F.: RCV1: a new benchmark collection for text categorization research. J. Mach. Learn. Res. 5, 361–397 (2004). http://dl.acm.org/citation.cfm?id=1005332.1005345

11. McGinnis, D., Zelinski, E.M.: Understanding unfamiliar words: the influence of processing resources, vocabulary knowledge, and age. Psychol. Aging **15**(2), 335–350 (2000). https://doi.org/10.1037/0882-7974.15.2.335
12. Allahyaria, M., Pouriyeha, S., Kochuta, K., Arabniaa, H.R.: OntoLDA: an ontology-based topic model for automatic topic labeling. In: IEEE 14th International Conference on Machine Learning and Applications (2015)
13. Miller, G.A.: WordNet: a lexical database for English. Commun. ACM **38**(11), 39–41 (1995). https://doi.org/10.1145/219717.219748
14. Mimno, D., Wallach, H.M., Talley, E., Leenders, M., McCallum, A.: Optimizing semantic coherence in topic models. In: Proceedings of the Conference on Empirical Methods in Natural Language Processing, EMNLP 2011, Stroudsburg, PA, USA, pp. 262–272 (2011). http://dl.acm.org/citation.cfm?id=2145432.2145462
15. Navigli, R., Ponzetto, S.P.: BabelNet: building a very large multilingual semantic network. In: Proceedings of the 48th Annual Meeting of the Association for Computational Linguistics, ACL 2010, pp. 216–225 (2010)
16. Pennington, J., Socher, R., Manning, C.D.: Glove: global vectors for word representation. In: Empirical Methods in Natural Language Processing (EMNLP), pp. 1532–1543 (2014). http://www.aclweb.org/anthology/D14-1162
17. Steyvers, M., Griffiths, T.: Probabilistic topic models. In: Handbook of Latent Semantic Analysis. Routledge (2013). https://doi.org/10.4324/9780203936399.ch21
18. Suchanek, F.M., Kasneci, G., Weikum, G.: Yago. In: Proceedings of the 16th International Conference on World Wide Web, WWW 2007. ACM Press (2007). https://doi.org/10.1145/1242572.1242667
19. Tang, Y.-K., Mao, X.-L., Huang, H., Shi, X., Wen, G.: Conceptualization topic modeling. Multimed. Tools Appl. **77**(3), 3455–3471 (2017). https://doi.org/10.1007/s11042-017-5145-4
20. Wu, W., Li, H., Wang, H., Zhu, K.Q.: Probase. In: Proceedings of the 2012 International Conference on Management of Data, SIGMOD 2012. ACM Press (2012). https://doi.org/10.1145/2213836.2213891
21. Yao, L., Zhang, Y., Wei, B., Qian, H., Wang, Y.: Incorporating probabilistic knowledge into topic models. In: Cao, T., Lim, E.-P., Zhou, Z.-H., Ho, T.-B., Cheung, D., Motoda, H. (eds.) PAKDD 2015. LNCS (LNAI), vol. 9078, pp. 586–597. Springer, Cham (2015). https://doi.org/10.1007/978-3-319-18032-8_46

Enhancing Seq2seq Math Word Problem Solver with Entity Information and Math Knowledge

Lei Li[1], Dongxiang Zhang[2], Chengyu Wang[3], Cheqing Jin[1], Ming Gao[1(✉)], and Aoying Zhou[1]

[1] School of Data Science and Engineering,
East China Normal University, Shanghai, China
leili@stu.ecnu.edu.cn, {cqjin,mgao,ayzhou}@dase.ecnu.edu.cn
[2] College of Computer Science and Technology,
Zhejiang University, Hangzhou, China
zhangdongxiang@zju.edu.cn
[3] Alibaba Group, Hangzhou, China
chengyu.wcy@alibaba-inc.com

Abstract. Devising an automatic Math Word Problem (MWP) solver has emerged as an important task in recent years. Various applications such as online education and intelligent assistants are expecting better MWP solvers to process complex user queries that involve numerical reasoning. Current seq2seq MWP solvers encounter two critical challenges: ordinal indices without semantics and insufficient training data. In this work, we propose Entity Random Indexing to equip indices with semantics and design diverse representations of math expressions to augment training data. Experimental results show that our approach effectively enhances the seq2seq MWP solver, which outperforms strong baselines.

Keywords: Math word problem · Seq2seq model · Entity information · Math knowledge

1 Introduction

Math Word Problem (MWP) [20], which aims at answering a mathematical question automatically according to the textual content, is an essential language understanding task. A typical MWP is usually organized as sentences containing conditions and a final question about an unknown variable. Various domain-specific applications such as online education, e-commerce websites, and intelligent assistants, are expecting better MWP solvers to process complex queries involving numerical reasoning [3,8,12].

Table 1 shows an MWP example with its problem text, solution expression, and answer. Most solvers replace numeric values in problems with abstract indices since we are interested in modeling relations among operands rather than their specific values. It is a common practice for existing MWP solvers to

© The Author(s), under exclusive license to Springer Nature Switzerland AG 2022
R. Chbeir et al. (Eds.): WISE 2022, LNCS 13724, pp. 370–385, 2022.
https://doi.org/10.1007/978-3-031-20891-1_26

Table 1. An example of MWP.

Original MWP
Problem: Mary has 2 books, Jack's books are 3 times over Mary's. Tom's books are 4 times over Jack's. Mike's books are 6 more than Tom's. How many times Mike's books are compared to Mary's books?
Solution: (2 * 3 * 4 + 6)/2   **Answer:** 15
Indexed MWP
Indices for Numbers:
{$NUM1$: 2, $NUM2$: 3, $NUM3$: 4, $NUM4$: 6}
Indexed Problem: Mary has $NUM1$ books, Jack's books are $NUM2$ times over Mary's. Tom's books are $NUM3$ times over Jack's. Mike's books are $NUM4$ more than Tom's. How many times Mike's books are compared to Mary's books?
Indexed Solution: $(NUM1*NUM2*NUM3+NUM4)/NUM1$
Indexed Answer: 15

index the numeric values according to their occurrence order and process them as regular tokens. For example, the token "NUM1" is used to refer to the first numeric value in the problem text.

Current seq2seq MWP solvers encounter two critical challenges. (1) To capture relations between operands rather than specific numbers, previous works replace numbers with ordinal indices. We suggest that such a way of handling numeric values can cause a drawback. Each frequent numeric token (e.g., "NUM1", "NUM2", etc.) is associated with various semantic contexts in the input problems; hence it is challenging for seq2seq models to learn effective representations that are able to disambiguate different semantic contexts. (2) Domain-specific MWP training data is not sufficient enough to train an MWP solver based on deep neural networks, which leads to model overfitting.

To overcome these two challenges, we enhance seq2seq MWP solvers with entity information and math knowledge. First, we should indexing numeric values according to related entities. Thus, a solver can infer semantics of indices of numeric values to better capture the information MWP. Second, we should utilize math knowledge to augment MWP training data since math knowledge enable us to produce a lot of variants for original math expressions of MWP.

Our contributions are summarized as follows: (1) We propose an algorithm named Entity Random Indexing which can equip indices with rich semantics. (2) We design diverse representations of math expressions to augment training data. (3) Based on the vanilla seq2seq model and our approaches (Entity Random Indexing and diverse representations of math expressions), we provide a new competitive MWP solver that outperforms strong baselines.

2   Related Work

2.1   Seq2seq-Based MWP Solvers

The earliest work to apply the seq2seq model was proposed by Wang et al. [17], where a seq2seq model is combined with a similarity-based retrieval model to generate expressions. Huang et al. [5] propose to incorporate copy and alignment mechanisms to seq2seq models for performance improvement. Wang et al. [16] observe that seq2seq models tend to suffer from equation duplication and propose an equation normalization method to normalize the duplicated equations.

2.2   Tree-Based MWP Solvers

Most state-of-the-art MWP solvers are based on trees since the solution can be naturally represented as an expression tree. GTS [18] develops a tree-structured neural network in a goal-driven manner to generate expression trees. Graph2Tree [21] combines the merits of the graph-based encoder and the tree-based decoder to generate better solution expressions. RODA [11] makes use of mathematical logic to produce new high-quality math problems and augments data for GTS to achieve better results.

2.3   Data Augmentation

Solving MWP is related to common tasks in NLP, such as Natural Language Inference (NLI) and Question Answering (QA), which can benefit from rule-based data augmentation. Kang et al. [6] propose NLI-specific logic-based data augmentation by replacing tokens or changing labels on the original training examples. Asai and Hajishirzi [1] propose a method that leverages logical and linguistic knowledge to augment labeled training data. Liu et al. [11] propose a reverse operation-based data augmentation method that makes use of mathematical logic to produce new high-quality math problems.

3   Methodology

In this section, we elaborate the techniques of the proposed approach for building MWP solvers.

3.1   Problem Statement

An MWP can be formulated as a triple $\{P, I, A\}$. The problem text P is a sequence of word tokens and numeric values. Let $T_p = \{t_1, \cdots, t_a\}$ denote the word tokens in P and $N_p = \{n_1, \cdots, n_b\}$ denote the set of numeric values in P. Thus, we have $P = \{p_1, \cdots, p_c | p_c \in T_p \cup N_p\}$. Given an MWP P, the goal is to map P to several computable intermediate sequences (CIS) which can be used to produce the answer of P. $I = \{i_1, \cdots, i_d\}$ is the set that consists of CIS i_d. i_d only needs to be a parsable sequence for computation (e.g., a math expression, a postfix expression) and describes a computational process including numeric values N_p, the set of math operators $\{+, -, *, /\}$ and constants. Constants include some special values such as 3.14 (π), 1 and 2. Each correct i_d is able to produce the correct answer A to the problem text P. In this paper, we only consider problems whose the answers A are unique values. Furthermore, we convert fractional answers into decimals. Since manipulating floating-point numbers will result in rounding errors, we consider a problem to be "solved" when the absolute value of the difference between the produced and true answers is less than a small acceptable tolerance, i.e., 0.001.

Algorithm 1. Entity Random Indexing (ERI)

Input: $S_P = \{P_1, \cdots, P_h\}$, $P_h = \{P_{h,1}, \cdots, P_{h,c}\}$
    S_P is original training data, P_h is one problem text, $P_{h,c}$ is one token in P_h
Output: D_t (the indexed training data)
 1: Build S_E containing common entities and units.
 2: Variables: *Range* and *Occupied* are hashtables; C_i is the times for indexing; C_j is
    the length of the indexing range; C_n is the number of the indexing range.
 3: **repeat** C_i times
 4:    **for** each element E_g in S_E **do**
 5:        $Random(0, C_n) \in \{0, 1, 2, ..., C_n - 1\}$
 6:        $Range[E_g] \leftarrow C_j * Random(0, C_n)$
 7:    **Let** $S_{P,C}$ be a copy of S_P.
 8:    **for** P_h in $S_{P,C}$ **do**
 9:        **for** $P_{h,c}$ in P_h **do**
10:            **if** $P_{h,c}$ is number **then**
11:                Find the entity or unit E_g that follows $P_{h,c}$.
12:                Start numbering $r_s \leftarrow Range[E_g]$.
13:                **while** $Occupied[r_s] = True$ **do**
14:                    $r_s \leftarrow r_s + 1$ // skip occupied indices.
15:                $Occupied[r_s] \leftarrow True$ // occupy the index.
16:                Replace $P_{h,c}$ with $NUMr_s$.
17:    Append $S_{P,C}$ to D_t.

3.2 Entity Random Indexing

We provide a heuristic algorithm to handle numeric values based on an observation that most numeric values in MWP are followed by entities or units (e.g., "2 books" and "3 h"), which incorporate semantic contexts of the numeric values. Thus, we are motivated to allocate an index interval for each type of entity or unit. For example, the range NUM16-NUM20 is allocated to represent numeric values associated with "books". Furthermore, inspired by multi-headed self-attention [15], where multiple linear transformations are applied to the input data for more effective representation learning, we randomly produce multiple indexing range divisions for the same entity or unit. We name our algorithm as Entity Random Indexing (ERI) and show the details in Algorithm 1. In contrast, the pointer-generator network [13] relies on massive data to learn copying tokens from the source to the target, while ERI is fully zero-shot and requires no training data.

3.3   Diverse Representations of Math Expressions

In this section, we offer a series of equivalent transformations based on math knowledge to augment the MWP training data. Given a solution expression, we propose four types of equivalent transformation, namely expression transformation, equation transformation, matrix transformation, and template transformation, which in total can generate 30 counterparts to the same answer. In the following, we assume that the solution expression in Table 1 is converted by ERI into

$$E : (NUM16 * NUM46 * NUM31 + NUM76)/NUM16$$

and use it to explain the idea of equivalent transformations. Note that transformed sequences may not be human-readable. However, they can be effectively calculable by the programs that we implement.

Expression Transformation. Our first equivalent transformation is to inject spaces to split operands and operators in E. We have:

$$E_1 : (NUM16 * NUM46 * NUM31 + NUM76)/NUM16.$$

The second alternative transformation is to apply postfix expression on E_1, i.e.,

$$E_3 : NUM16\ NUM46 * NUM31 * NUM76 + NUM16/.$$

Note that E_3 can be converted uniquely back to E_1. Besides postfix expression, we can also use reversion as a transformation operator. When this operator is applied on E_1 and E_3, we obtain E_2 and E_4 respectively.

$$E_2 : NUM16/)\ NUM76 + NUM31 * NUM46 * NUM16 ($$

$$E_4 : /NUM16 + NUM76 * NUM31 * NUM46\ NUM16$$

Equation Transformation. The idea of equation transformation is to introduce an additional unknown variable X and convert an arithmetic expression into its equivalent form of an equation. For example, expression E can be naturally converted into

$$E' : (NUM16 * NUM46 * NUM31 + NUM76)/NUM16 = X.$$

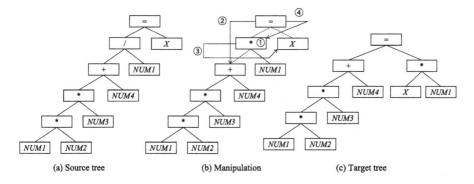

(a) Source tree   (b) Manipulation   (c) Target tree

Fig. 1. Left shift of the equal sign based on tree manipulations.

From E', we can generate multiple equivalent variants of equations by shifting the equal sign leftwards. As shown in Fig. 1, we represent the E' as a binary tree. Left shift of equal sign involves four steps:

1. Replace root.left_child with reverse operator (e.g., / will be replaced by $*$).
2. Move root→left_child and root→left_child→right_child to root→right_child.
3. Put root→left_child→left_child as the new left child of root.
4. Put variable X as the left child of root→right_child

After the manipulation, we can generate the target tree that represents the target equation

$$E'' : NUM16 * NUM46 * NUM31 + NUM76 = X * NUM16.$$

Similarly, we can define the manipulation of the right shift to generate equivalent equations in Fig. 2.

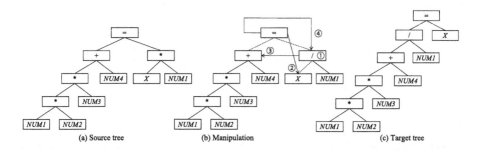

(a) Source tree   (b) Manipulation   (c) Target tree

Fig. 2. Right shift of the equal sign based on tree manipulations.

As shown in Fig. 3, among the various equations generated by the left (or right) shift, we only select two of them based on the following criteria. First, we prefer the equation

$$E''' : NUM16 * NUM46 * NUM31 = X * NUM16 - NUM76$$

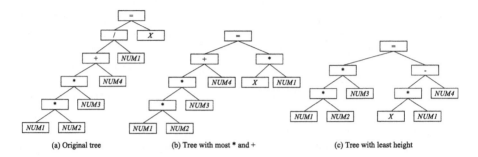

(a) Original tree   (b) Tree with most * and +   (c) Tree with least height

Fig. 3. Among the various equations generated by the left (or right) shift, we prefer equations with the minimal tree height or with most $*$ and $+$.

with the minimal tree height. Second, we prefer the equation

$$E'''' : NUM16 * NUM46 * NUM31 + NUM76 = X * NUM16$$

with most $*$ and $+$ for trying to reduce the operator that a solver need to learn from 4 types $(*, /, +, -)$ to 2 types $(*, +)$. Following the way producing equivalent transformations E_1 to E_4, we produce E_5 to E_8 based on E''' and list them in Table 2. For simplicity, we use N to replace NUM. Similarly, we produce E_9 to E_{12} based on E''''.

Table 2. Equation transformation.

E_5	$N16 * N46 * N31 = X * N16 - N76$
E_6	$N76 - N16 * X = N31 * N46 * N16$
E_7	$N16\ N46 * N31 * X\ N16 * N76\ -\ =$
E_8	$=\ -\ N76 * N16\ X * N31 * N46\ N16$
E_9	$N16 * N46 * N31 + N76 = X * N16$
E_{10}	$N16 * X = N76 + N31 * N46 * N16$
E_{11}	$N16\ N46 * N31 * N76 + X\ N16 * =$
E_{12}	$=\ * N16\ X + N76 * N31 * N46\ N16$

Matrix Transformation. In this part, we propose a strategy that converts binary trees into sequences based on the adjacency matrix. Let m denote the number of operands in an expression and n denote the maximum number of frequencies for an operand to appear in an expression (since it is possible for the same operand to appear multiple times in an expression). We transform a binary tree with m operands into a square matrix M with the maximum size $(m * n) * (m * n)$. Each element $M[i, j]$ with $i \neq j$ stores a binary operator represented by an integer. We assign $\{1, 2, 3, 4\}$ for operators $\{+, -, *, /\}$ respectively. The diagonal elements, i.e., $M[i, j]$ with $i = j$, store unary operators that allow us to build a smaller matrix to capture all the information in the binary tree. Details of unary operators are presented in Fig. 4, where we illustrate an example of matrix transformation.

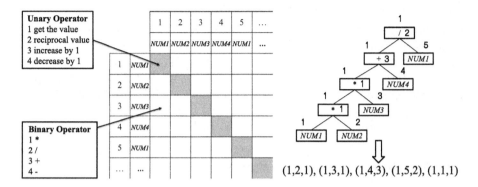

Fig. 4. Encoding a binary tree to a sequence of triples based on the adjacent matrix.

In Fig. 4, each row or column refers to an operand. Rows (and columns) "1, 2, 3, 4" refer to operands *NUM16, NUM46, NUM31, NUM76* respectively. Since *NUM16* appear twice in the expression, rows (and columns) "5, 6, 7, 8" also refer to indexes *NUM16, NUM46, NUM31, NUM76*. For matrix transformation, we perform post-order traversal to the binary tree. Each non-leaf node will output a triple. For example, in $(1, 2, 1)$, the first "1" stands for left operand *NUM16*, "2" stands for right operand *NUM46*, and the last "1" stands for binary operator $*$. It can be decoded as a computation "*NUM16 * NUM46*" and the temporary result will be stored at the first "1". Hence, its subsequent triple $(1, 3, 1)$ represents "$(NUM16 * NUM46) * NUM31$". We can perform recursive visit on the binary tree to generate the complete sequence of triples "$(1, 2, 1), (1, 3, 1), (1, 4, 3), (1, 5, 2), (1, 1, 1)$".

With the derived sequence "$(1, 2, 1), (1, 3, 1), (1, 4, 3), (1, 5, 2), (1, 1, 1)$", we further construct six equivalent variants to include more diversified knowledge and information. The equivalent transformation E_{13} is formatted as "1_2_1 1_3_1 1_4_3 1_5_2 1_1_1". 1) We reverse E_{13} to get E_{14} "1_1_1 1_5_2 1_4_3 1_3_1 1_2_1". 2) We swap the first and second elements of triples in E_{13} to get E_{15} "2_1_1 3_1_1 4_1_3 5_1_2 1_1_1". 3) We reverse E_{15} to get E_{16} "1_1_1 5_1_2 4_1_3 3_1_1 2_1_1". 4) We split triple tokens of E_{13} i.e. "1_2_1" into two sub tokens "1_2" and "1" to get E_{17} "1_2 1 1_3 1 1_4 3 1_5 2 1_1 1". 5) We reverse E_{17} to get E_{18} "1 1_1 2 1_5 3 1_4 1 1_3 1 1_2".

Readers can refer to Fig. 5 for the decoding process. For three numbers in a triple, the first and the second numbers represent a row. We retrieve its *NUM-index* and corresponding value and set the value to the corresponding position in the array. The third number refers to an operator. If the first number is not equal to the second number, it is a binary operator. For a binary operator, we evaluate a temporary expression "first_number binary_operator second_number" i.e. $NUM16 * NUM46$ and update the result to the position of its left operand in the array. For a unary operator, we employ the left operand as the argument and update the result to the position of the left operand in the array. Until all triples are processed, the final result is provided.

Template Transformation. Our template transformation is generated by replacing the numeric tokens with a specific placeholder (e.g., @) and consider the concrete indexes as arguments of the template. For example, the expression in E_1 "$(NUM16 * NUM46 * NUM31 + NUM76)/NUM16$" can be encapsulated as a template "$(@*@*@+@)/@$" with sequence "$NUM16\ NUM46\ NUM31\ NUM76\ NUM16$" as the arguments. In this way, we can produce corresponding template transformations E_{19} to E_{30} for E_1 to E_{12}.

3.4   Architecture of Our MWP Solver

Based on ERI and equivalent transformations aforementioned, we present the architecture of our MWP solver named Solver with Entity and Math (SEM) in Fig. 6. Firstly, SEM uses ERI to preprocess problem texts and solutions in the MWP dataset. SEM repeatedly uses the indexed problem text as the source sequence and 30 equivalent transformations of MWP solutions as different target sequences to train 30 vanilla seq2seq models. After 30 seq2seq models are trained, SEM can solve an MWP by using its indexed problem text as the source sequence and let 30 seq2seq models produce 30 different target sequences. Then, SEM will recover numeric values by indices and compute each target sequence by the corresponding program. Invalid target sequences will be dropped out, while valid target sequences will result in numeric answers. A plurality vote [4,9,19] will be conducted on numeric answers and output the answer which receives the largest number of votes. Ties are broken arbitrarily.

4   Experiments

4.1   Experimental Configuration

Dataset. The dataset **Math23K** [17] is a large and widely-used benchmark[1] for MWP solvers. It contains $23,162$ text problems annotated with solution expressions and answers. Each problem can be solved by one linear algebra expression with four types of operators $\{*, /, +, -\}$. The results reported in this paper are derived from 5-fold cross-validation.

Baselines. We compare our solver to a plenty number of baselines and state-of-the-art models. DNS [17] uses a vanilla seq2seq model to generate solution

---

[1] Zhao et al. [22] build a new large-scale and template-rich math word problem dataset named Ape210K. However, the publication of the dataset has been withdrawn in Arxiv (https://arxiv.org/abs/2009.11506).

Rows (cols) and indexes: {1: *NUM16*, 2: *NUM46*, 3: *NUM31*, 4: *NUM76* , 5: *NUM16*, ...}
Indexes and values: {*NUM16*: 2, *NUM46*: 3, *NUM31*: 4, *NUM76*: 6}

(1,2,1), (1,3,1), (1,4,3), (1,5,2), (1,1,1)

1	2	3	4	5	6
2	3				

(1,2,1), (1,3,1), (1,4,3), (1,5,2), (1,1,1)

1	2	3	4	5	6
6	3				

(1,2,1), (1,3,1), (1,4,3), (1,5,2), (1,1,1)

1	2	3	4	5	6
6	3	4			

(1,2,1), (1,3,1), (1,4,3), (1,5,2), (1,1,1)

1	2	3	4	5	6
24	3	4			

(1,2,1), (1,3,1), (1,4,3), (1,5,2), (1,1,1)

1	2	3	4	5	6
24	3	4	6		

(1,2,1), (1,3,1), (1,4,3), (1,5,2), (1,1,1)

1	2	3	4	5	6
30	3	4	6		

(1,2,1), (1,3,1), (1,4,3), (1,5,2), (1,1,1)

1	2	3	4	5	6
30	3	4	6	2	

(1,2,1), (1,3,1), (1,4,3), (1,5,2), (1,1,1)

1	2	3	4	5	6
15	3	4	6	2	

(1,2,1), (1,3,1), (1,4,3), (1,5,2), (1,1,1)

1	2	3	4	5	6
15	3	4	6	2	

Fig. 5. Calculating a sequence of triples to generate the answer of the MWP.

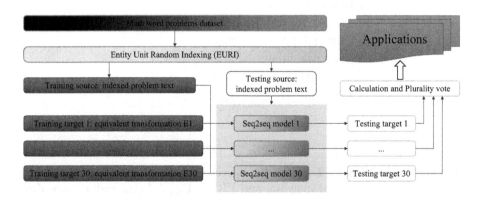

Fig. 6. Overall architecture of the SEM solver.

expressions. S-Aligned [2] designs the decoder with a stack to track the semantic meanings of operands. GROUP-ATT [10] adopts the idea of multi-head attention from the transformer [15]. GTS [18] develops a tree-structured neural network in a goal-driven manner to generate expression trees. Graph2Tree [21] combines the merits of the graph-based encoder and tree-based decoder to generate better solution expressions. RODA [11] makes use of mathematical logic to produce new high-quality math problems. ERNIE 3.0 [14] is a pre-trained language model with 10 billion parameters and is trained on a 4TB corpus consisting of plain texts and a large-scale knowledge graph.

Model Configuration. The vanilla seq2seq model used in our architecture is the 4-layer 16-head transformer [15], with $d_k = 12$, $d_v = 32$, and $d_{model} = 512$, where d_k and d_v are the dimension of keys and values respectively, and d_{model} is the output dimension of each sub-layer. We use the Adam optimizer [7] to train the model with the learning rate $1e^{-3}$, $\beta_1 = 0.9$, $\beta_2 = 0.99$, and the dropout rate of 0.3.

4.2   Results

Overall Performance. Table 3 shows the accuracy of our SEM MWP solver and its competitors. We observe that SEM achieves competitive performance compared to state-of-the-art solvers. It proves that entity information and math knowledge can enhance seq2seq solvers to outperform both tree-based solvers and solvers relying on massive data pre-training.

Table 3. Answer Accuracy of SEM and baselines on **Math23K**.

Method	Answer accuracy (%)
DNS [17]	58.1
S-Aligned [2]	65.8
GROUP-ATT [10]	66.9
GTS [18]	74.3
ERNIE 3.0 [14]	75.0
Graph2Tree [21]	75.5
GTS+RODA [11]	76.0
SEM (Our Approach)	**77.1**

Effectiveness of ERI. To verify the effectiveness of ERI, we show frequency percentages of the ordinal indexing and ERI in Fig. 7. Using ordinal indexing, 46% numeric values are indexed as *NUM1*, 36% numeric values are indexed as *NUM2*, and 12% numeric values are indexed as *NUM3*. *NUM1*, *NUM2*, and *NUM3* are bound to uncertain semantics and are ambiguous to MWP solvers.

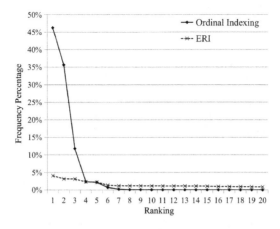

Fig. 7. Frequency percentages of the ordinal indexing and ERI.

However, when ERI is applied, indices are unambiguous since they are bound to certain entities. Furthermore, frequencies of ERI indices are similar and the most frequent indices do not exceed 5%. This is helpful for training a debiased neural network MWP solver.

Ablation Study. We conduct an ablation study to examine the effect of ERI and equivalent transformations, as shown in Table 4. When ERI is removed, there is a significant drop in accuracy (from 77.1% to 74.8%), implying that ERI is indeed effective. For the four types of solution transformations, we first investigate the accuracy when one of them is removed. We can see that matrix transformation is the most effective strategy. As we expected, diversifying the formats of output sequence representation can encourage seq2seq models to master math knowledge. We also conduct experiments to use only one type of solution augmentation, with interesting findings in Table 4. We can see that there is sharp performance degradation since the ensemble model works better if the underlying seq2seq models are more diversified. With only one type of augmentation available, the improvement by the ensemble model is rather limited. At last, the single vanilla seq2seq model that is trained by representation E_1 obtains 62.3% answer accuracy.

Correlation Analysis. As shown in Fig. 6 and Table 4, our SEM MWP solver obtains competitive performance based on plurality voting of solvers trained on diverse data.

Given t classifiers designed for binary classification, plurality voting can derive the correct prediction if at least $\lfloor t/2+1 \rfloor$ classifiers choose the correct class label. Assume that the outputs of the classifiers are independent, and each classifier has an accuracy p, implying that each classifier makes a correct classification at probability p. The probability of the ensemble for making a correct decision

Table 4. Ablation study of SEM.

Model configuration	Answer accuracy (%)
SEM (Full Implementation)	**77.1**
w/o. ERI	74.8, ↓ 2.3
w/o. Expression Transformation	76.8, ↓ 0.3
w/o. Equation Transformation	77.0, ↓ 0.1
w/o. Matrix Transformation	76.3, ↓ 0.8
w/o. Template Transformation	77.0, ↓ 0.1
w/ERI & Expression Transformation	65.3, ↓ 11.8
w/ERI & Equation Transformation	63.5, ↓ 13.6
w/ERI & Matrix Transformation	67.5, ↓ 9.6
w/ERI & Template Transformation	65.8, ↓ 11.3
Single seq2seq model trained on E_1	62.3, ↓ 14.8

Table 5. The Jaccard index between correct answers of two solvers.

	#1	#2	#3	#4	#5	#6	#7	#8	#9	#10	#11	#12	#13	#14	#15	#16
#1	1.00	0.74	0.72	0.74	0.74	0.73	0.74	0.74	0.73	0.73	0.65	0.73	0.74	0.74	0.74	0.74
#2	0.74	1.00	0.70	0.74	0.74	0.73	0.74	0.73	0.72	0.73	0.65	0.72	0.74	0.72	0.73	0.73
#3	0.72	0.70	1.00	0.70	0.69	0.69	0.70	0.70	0.69	0.69	**0.62**	0.69	0.71	0.70	0.70	0.70
#4	0.74	0.74	0.70	1.00	0.74	0.73	0.73	0.74	0.73	0.72	0.65	0.74	0.73	0.73	0.73	0.73
#5	0.74	0.74	0.69	0.74	1.00	0.74	0.75	0.74	0.74	0.73	0.65	0.73	0.73	0.73	0.73	0.73
#6	0.73	0.73	0.69	0.73	0.74	1.00	0.73	0.74	0.72	0.73	0.64	0.73	0.72	0.72	0.72	0.72
#7	0.74	0.74	0.70	0.73	0.75	0.73	1.00	0.74	0.73	0.72	0.66	0.73	0.73	0.73	0.73	0.73
#8	0.74	0.73	0.70	0.74	0.74	0.74	0.74	1.00	0.73	0.73	0.64	0.74	0.73	0.73	0.73	0.73
#9	0.73	0.72	0.69	0.73	0.74	0.72	0.73	0.73	1.00	0.74	0.66	0.75	0.72	0.72	0.72	0.72
#10	0.73	0.73	0.69	0.72	0.73	0.73	0.72	0.73	0.74	1.00	0.66	0.75	0.72	0.71	0.71	0.71
#11	0.65	0.65	**0.62**	0.65	0.65	0.64	0.66	0.64	0.66	0.66	1.00	0.66	0.64	0.64	0.64	0.65
#12	0.73	0.72	0.69	0.74	0.73	0.73	0.73	0.74	0.75	0.75	0.66	1.00	0.72	0.72	0.72	0.72
#13	0.74	0.74	0.71	0.73	0.73	0.72	0.73	0.73	0.72	0.72	0.64	0.72	1.00	0.77	**0.80**	0.78
#14	0.74	0.72	0.70	0.73	0.73	0.72	0.73	0.73	0.72	0.71	0.64	0.72	0.77	1.00	0.77	0.79
#15	0.74	0.73	0.70	0.73	0.73	0.72	0.73	0.73	0.72	0.71	0.64	0.72	**0.80**	0.77	1.00	0.78
#16	0.74	0.73	0.70	0.73	0.73	0.72	0.73	0.73	0.72	0.71	0.65	0.72	0.78	0.79	0.78	1.00

can be calculated using a binomial distribution. Specifically, the probability of obtaining at least $\lfloor t/2 + 1 \rfloor$ correct classifiers out of t is [4]:

$$P_{mv} = \sum_{k=\lfloor t/2+1 \rfloor}^{t} \binom{t}{k} p^k (1-p)^{t-k} \qquad (1)$$

Lam and Suen [9] showed that 1) If $p > 0.5$, then P_{mv} is monotonically increasing in t, and $\lim_{t \to +\infty} P_{mv} = 1$ 2) If $p < 0.5$, then P_{mv} is monotonically decreasing in t, and $\lim_{t \to +\infty} P_{mv} = 0$. 3) If $p = 0.5$, then $P_{mv} = 0.5$ for any t.

Note that plurality voting fails to work well if the underlying models are highly correlated. Thus, our last experiment is to verify the correlation of our solvers. We show the Jaccard index between correct answers of each pair of seq2seq solvers in Table 5 (Limited by space, we only show results between solver #1 to #16). The Jaccard index is computed as

$$J(A_i, A_j) = \frac{|A_i \cap A_j|}{|A_i \cup A_j|} \tag{2}$$

where A_i represents the set of correct answers produced by i-th solver, A_j represents the set of correct answers produced by j-th solver. The #i solver is trained from equivalent representation E_i. The maximal Jaccard index 0.799 is achieved by the pair #13 and #15. The minimal Jaccard index 0.619 is achieved by the pair #3 and #11. E_{13} and E_{15} belong to the same type "Matrix Transformation" while E_3 and E_{11} belong to different types that are "Expression Transformation" and "Equation Transformation" respectively. Such evidence support that there is no highly correlated pair of solvers whose training data should be removed from the training dataset.

4.3 Demonstration

As shown in Fig. 8, we present a potential application of the SEM solver. Assume that we have an electric car with some attributes such as the maximum speed, the endurance mileage, the charging time, and the battery state. Our SEM solver can be trained to answer users' questions such as "I want to go to a place 700 km away, how many hours will it take as fast as possible?". The SEM solver will offer a human-readable math equation according to the answer that receives the most votes in our algorithm. Users can provide feedback on the answers. If "Accept" is clicked by a number of users, the question and the answer will be appended to the training set as the positive sample for iterative model improvement. If the "Reject" button is clicked, another candidate solution will be presented. Administrators of this system will randomly check user-generated data to filter out false positive samples. We are also working on adapting this demonstration to offer shopping recommendations according to the attributes of an item on e-commerce websites.

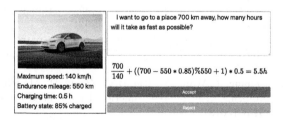

Fig. 8. A demonstration of the SEM solver.

5 Conclusion

In this paper, we propose Entity Random Indexing to equip indices with semantics and propose diverse representations of math expressions to augment training data. Experimental results show that our approaches enhance the seq2seq MWP solver to outperform strong baselines. As for future work, we seek to integrate the proposed approach with pre-trained language models to examine the generalization capability and to further improve the performance of MWP solvers. We are also planning to collect more and diverse MWP data for training and benchmarking. Accelerating the seq2seq model inference is also an interesting topic of making our solver to be a real-time application with low latency.

Acknowledgements. This work has been supported by the National Natural Science Foundation of China under Grant No. U1911203, the National Natural Science Foundation of China under Grant No. 61877018, and Alibaba Group through the Alibaba Innovation Research Program.

References

1. Asai, A., Hajishirzi, H.: Logic-guided data augmentation and regularization for consistent question answering. In: ACL 2020, pp. 5642–5650 (2020)
2. Chiang, T., Chen, Y.: Semantically-aligned equation generation for solving and reasoning math word problems. In: NAACL-HLT 2019, pp. 2656–2668 (2019)
3. Dua, D., Wang, Y., Dasigi, P., Stanovsky, G., Singh, S., Gardner, M.: DROP: a reading comprehension benchmark requiring discrete reasoning over paragraphs. In: NAACL-HLT 2019, pp. 2368–2378 (2019)
4. Hansen, L.K., Salamon, P.: Neural network ensembles. IEEE Trans. Pattern Anal. Mach. Intell. **12**(10), 993–1001 (1990)
5. Huang, D., Liu, J., Lin, C., Yin, J.: Neural math word problem solver with reinforcement learning. In: COLING 2018, pp. 213–223 (2018)
6. Kang, D., Khot, T., Sabharwal, A., Hovy, E.H.: Adventure: adversarial training for textual entailment with knowledge-guided examples. In: ACL 2018, pp. 2418–2428 (2018)
7. Kingma, D.P., Ba, J.: Adam: a method for stochastic optimization. In: ICLR 2015 (2015)
8. Kirkland, P.K., McNeil, N.M.: Question design affects students' sense-making on mathematics word problems. Cogn. Sci. **45**(4) (2021)
9. Lam, L., Suen, C.Y.: Application of majority voting to pattern recognition: an analysis of its behavior and performance. IEEE Trans. Syst. Man Cybern. Part A **27**(5), 553–568 (1997)
10. Li, J., Wang, L., Zhang, J., Wang, Y., Dai, B.T., Zhang, D.: Modeling intra-relation in math word problems with different functional multi-head attentions. In: ACL 2019, pp. 6162–6167 (2019)
11. Liu, Q., Guan, W., Li, S., Cheng, F., Kawahara, D., Kurohashi, S.: RODA: reverse operation based data augmentation for solving math word problems. IEEE ACM Trans. Audio Speech Lang. Process. **30**, 1–11 (2022)
12. Nie, F., Wang, J., Yao, J., Pan, R., Lin, C.: Operation-guided neural networks for high fidelity data-to-text generation. In: EMNLP 2018, pp. 3879–3889 (2018)

13. See, A., Liu, P.J., Manning, C.D.: Get to the point: summarization with pointer-generator networks. In: ACL 2017, pp. 1073–1083 (2017)
14. Sun, Y., et al.: ERNIE 3.0: large-scale knowledge enhanced pre-training for language understanding and generation. CoRR abs/2107.02137 (2021)
15. Vaswani, A., et al.: Attention is all you need. In: NIPS 2017, pp. 5998–6008 (2017)
16. Wang, L., Wang, Y., Cai, D., Zhang, D., Liu, X.: Translating math word problem to expression tree. In: EMNLP 2018, pp. 1064–1069 (2018)
17. Wang, Y., Liu, X., Shi, S.: Deep neural solver for math word problems. In: EMNLP 2017, pp. 845–854 (2017)
18. Xie, Z., Sun, S.: A goal-driven tree-structured neural model for math word problems. In: IJCAI 2019, pp. 5299–5305 (2019)
19. Yue, K., Jin, R., Wong, C., Dai, H.: Federated learning via plurality vote. CoRR abs/2110.02998 (2021)
20. Zhang, D., Wang, L., Zhang, L., Dai, B.T., Shen, H.T.: The gap of semantic parsing: a survey on automatic math word problem solvers. IEEE Trans. Pattern Anal. Mach. Intell. **42**(9), 2287–2305 (2020)
21. Zhang, J., et al.: Graph-to-tree learning for solving math word problems. In: ACL 2020, pp. 3928–3937 (2020)
22. Zhao, W., Shang, M., Liu, Y., Wang, L., Liu, J.: Ape210k: a large-scale and template-rich dataset of math word problems. CoRR abs/2009.11506 (2020)

Mitigating Multi-class Unintended Demographic Bias in Text Classification with Adversarial Learning

Le Pan[1(✉)], Lina Yao[1], Wenjie Zhang[1], and Xianzhi Wang[2]

[1] University of New South Wales, Sydney 2052, Australia
{le.pan,lina.yao,wenjie.zhang}@unsw.edu.au
[2] University of Technology Sydney, Sydney 2007, Australia
XIANZHI.WANG@uts.edu.au

Abstract. Text classification enables higher efficiency on text data queries in information retrieval. However, unintended demographic bias can impair text toxicity classification. Thus, we propose a novel debiasing framework utilizing Adversarial Learning on word embeddings of multi-class sensitive demographic words to alleviate this bias. Slight adjustment over word embeddings with flipped sensitive indices is achieved, and the modified word embeddings are used in the downstream classification task to realize Demographic Parity. The experimental results validate the effectiveness of our proposed method in mitigating multi-class unintended demographic bias without impairing the original classification accuracy.

Keywords: Demographic bias · Word embeddings · Adversarial learning · Text classification

1 Introduction

With the accumulation of online texts, classification over textual data facilitates efficient queries in information retrieval. Text-based mining provides a handy tool for operators of various websites (e.g., shopping, movies) with tremendous data to achieve better management, including abusive language detection, review pooling, question answering, etc. Meanwhile, machine learning algorithms are widely adopted in text classification to automate semantic analysis of textual data to detect toxic comments [7]. Accuracy is no longer the only aim when designing such data-driven detection models. Fairness becomes increasingly essential, which requires recognizing and counteracting biases to avoid prejudice and discrimination.

Unintended demographic bias is highly possible to mislead a text classification model. It concerns demographic attributes such as gender, age, national origins, etc. Whenever this bias exists, text classification results tend to be unfairly associated with relevant demographic identities. For instance, in a toxic comment identification task [1], texts containing specific identity terms are more likely to be classified as toxic. This misclassification in decision-making scenarios can even lead to social discrimination against certain minority groups. Thus, it is crucial to alleviate such bias. To address this issue, we propose a novel debiasing framework based on Adversarial Learning to fine-tune the word embeddings, one of the most popular representations which map words to real-valued numerical word vectors. This process is referred to as debiasing word embeddings of sensitive words in our work, and the contributions are listed as follows:

- We propose a novel debiasing framework in mitigating multi-class unintended bias at the word embedding level using Adversarial Learning, generating artificial non-toxic labels for sensitive words and slightly adjusting word embeddings without impairing their original semantics.
- We conduct sufficient experiments using different debiased word embeddings in text toxicity classification and validate our proposed method, which alleviates unfairness to a great extent.

2   Related Works

The most notable methods in debiasing unfairness in toxicity comments classification are data supplementation [1] and gender-swapping [5]. Both methods aim to balance the training dataset with data manipulation [9], as [1] adds additional 4620 comments with non-toxic labels to the original training dataset and [5] flips the gender-specific identity terms to the semantically opposite ones. Supplementation requires additional labelled data, and the gender-swapping method only takes effect in binary gender-specific unfairness, which cannot tackle multi-class demographic unfairness issues concerning various demographic identity terms. Adversarial learning techniques [2] have recently been proven to be powerful for reducing unintended demographic bias on word embeddings. [8] leverages an adversarial learning framework on word embedding to mitigate the biases concerning minority groups in word analogy tasks. Based on [7,8] calculates a directional sentiment vector to untie toxicity with sensitive attribute identities in toxicity classifications. It leverages Adversarial Learning to pull away the Sentiment Polarity from the word vectors of specific demographic identity terms and obtains re-embedded word embeddings.

3   Methodology

Although the previous work [7] adopted Adversarial Learning in debiasing word embeddings, it has several limitations. The positive and negative word vectors are rather random to form the sentiment word matrices needed in that work, and the projection using the defined Directional Sentiment Vector does not work well with our attempts, as several initially "toxic" demographic identity terms are assigned with positive sentiment after the projection step, which is inconsistent with the fact. Considering the drawbacks of this previous work, we propose a novel adversarial debiasing framework eliminating the previous projection step before adjusting word embeddings. Instead, we make the best use of the sensitive index to realize better debiasing efficacy. Based on prior observations, we select a set of multi-class demographic words with protected attributes as the target words and set a sensitive index for each term before debiasing. Our proposed algorithm generates flipped sensitive index for each selected word and fine-tunes the real value distribution of the word embeddings of these words through Adversarial Learning.

3.1   Problem Definition

Demographic Parity in Text Toxicity Classification. Suppose x is a target word with demographic attribute(s), and w is the corresponding word vector of x. $z_w \in [0, 1]$ is a binary variable that represents the sensitive index of x. If text comments containing x are more easily to be misclassified as toxic based on prior observations, z_w is set as 1; otherwise 0. Demographic Parity is supposed to be achieved after our debiasing procedure, shown as follows:

$$P\left(\hat{Y} \mid w, z_w = 0\right) = P\left(\hat{Y} \mid w, z_w = 1\right) \tag{1}$$

where P is the probability of a sentence containing x to be classified as toxic, and $\hat{Y}$ is the toxicity classification outcome. This indicates the irrelevance of the toxicity classification result of a comment whether containing sensitive words or not.

Adversarial Learning on Word Embeddings. Given a set of sensitive word vectors $\boldsymbol{W}^{(1)} = \left\{\boldsymbol{w}_1^{(1)}, \boldsymbol{w}_2^{(1)}, \ldots, \boldsymbol{w}_n^{(1)}\right\} \in R^{n \times d}$, $\boldsymbol{w}_i^{(1)}$ represents a corresponding word vector, d refers to the dimension of all the word vectors, and n is the number of words in this set. Each word vector $\boldsymbol{w}_i^{(1)}$ is possessed with a sensitive index z_w. $\boldsymbol{W}^{(2)} = \left\{\boldsymbol{w}_1^{(2)}, \boldsymbol{w}_2^{(2)}, \ldots, \boldsymbol{w}_n^{(2)}\right\} \in R^{n \times d}$ represents the word vector set obtained from the adversarial debiasing process, with exactly the same word quantities and dimensions as $\boldsymbol{W}^{(1)}$.

Inspired by the adoption of Adversarial Learning in distribution discrepancy mitigation [3] and balance [10], we employ Adversarial Learning model to learn a new word embedding distribution p_g over $\boldsymbol{w}_i^{(1)}$, compliant with the pre-set learning targets. With sensitive index z_w set for each word, the Adversarial Learning process is formalized in a supervised learning paradigm where z_w is regarded as the label.

3.2   Adversarial Debiasing Framework

The proposed Adversarial Debiasing Framework (shown in Fig. 1) generates new corresponding word vectors with flipped sensitive indices. The whole training process fine-tunes the values of the original word vectors, which are semantically similar to the new ones but with different sensitive indices.

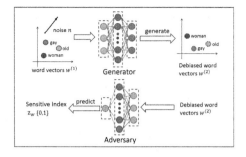

Fig. 1. Adversarial debiasing framework for word embedding of sensitive words

The framework consists of a generator G and an adversary A, which are both multilayer perceptrons. G generates new word vectors $w_i^{(2)}$, while A predicts the sensitive indices z_w of the output word vectors from G. Instead of using random noise samples subject to Gaussian Distribution as the traditional generative adversarial nets did and training from scratch, we concatenate a random noise $v \sim \mathcal{N}(0,1)$ with w_i to obtain a new input vector v' to G, which makes the training process more stable:

$$v' = v \oplus w_i^{(1)} \tag{2}$$

where we obtain a new input vector set $V' = \left\{ v'_1, v'_2, \ldots, v'_n \right\} \in R^{n \times d}$.

In our framework, Adversary A predicts poorly on z_w for the output from G. To achieve this, we employ Binary Cross-Entropy (BCE) loss for A. The objective loss function L_a for A is shown as follows:

$$L_a = \max_A E_{v' \sim W^{(1)}}[-\log A(v')] + E_{w \sim W^{(2)}}[\log A(G(w)) - 1)] \tag{3}$$

If the input word vector to A is originally from $W^{(1)}$, A is supposed to output 0 as z_w during the training process. If the input word vector is a generated word vector from $W^{(2)}$ by G, A is supposed to output 1 conversely. Therefore, we maximize the sum of $E_{v' \sim W^{(1)}}[-\log A(w)]$ and $E_{w \sim W^{(2)}}[\log A(G(v') - 1)]$.

In addition, to preserve the semantic closeness between debiased word vectors $w^{(2)}$ and original word vectors $w^{(1)}$, as well as to remain the sensitive index z_w of each input, we combine Mean Square Error (MSE) loss L_e for G to minimize the distance between two word vectors during training process:

$$L_e = (G(w) - w)^2 \tag{4}$$

and the objective loss function L_g for G is designed as follows:

$$L_g = \min_G E_{w \sim W^{(2)}}[\log A(G(w)) - 1] + (G(w) - w)^2 \tag{5}$$

G and A play a competing min-max game, and the following value function $V(G, A)$ is obtained by combining loss functions L_a and L_g:

$$V(G, A) = \min_G \max_A E_{w \sim W^{(1)}}[-\log A(\boldsymbol{w})] + E_{w \sim W^{(2)}}[1 - \log G(A(\boldsymbol{w}))] \\ +(G(\boldsymbol{w}) - \boldsymbol{w})^2 \tag{6}$$

By training this model until convergence, we obtain debiased word vectors of selected sensitive words with flipped sensitive indices.

4   Experiments and Results

4.1   Downstream Tasks Utility Validation

To validate the efficacy of the proposed debiasing framework, we apply the debiased word embeddings of multi-class demographic identity terms with different types of protected attributes to the downstream toxicity comments classification tasks. We also compare the differences between the original and debiased word embeddings obtained from our framework and gauge their similarity.

We conduct experiments on the two most popular word embeddings, glove 6B (300d) [6] and word2vec [4] respectively. We use the multi-class sensitive word list from [1] to perform our debiasing training, and the post-debiasing word embeddings are adopted in the following three-layer Convolutional Neural Network (CNN) model for text toxicity classification task, with exactly the same settings and hyperparameters of [1]. The generator G and adversary A in our framework are both multilayer perceptrons with two and three hidden layers respectively. And we use Leaky Rectified Linear Unit as the activation functions.

To compare the debiasing effectiveness, we present the performance of three models: the original model without any debiasing techniques, the data supplement model [1] (set as the baseline model), and the existing adversarial learning model on word embeddings [7]. The comparison is conducted on two popular datasets previously used on this problem: **Toxicity Comments** and **Identity Phrase Templates Test Set(IPTTS)** [1]. Each toxicity classification task is repeated for ten runs, and we present the average results of our experiments.

4.2   Data Description

We use the two mostly adopted datasets in text toxicity classification tasks: (1) **Toxicity Comments** is a dataset from Wikipedia Talk Pages, containing 127820 labelled comments as the training data and 31866 labelled comments as test data, where 9.6% of them are toxic (2) **Identity Phrase Templates Test Set (IPTTS)** is a synthetic generated dataset that contains 77,000 examples, 50% of which are toxic and the others are non-toxic examples. A wide range of sensitive identity terms are slotted into every template in this dataset.

4.3 Evaluation Metrics

Cosine Similarity. We leverage cosine similarity to measure the similarity between the original word vector $w_i^{(1)}$ and the debiased word vector $w_i^{(2)}$:

$$\cos(w_i^{(1)}, w_i^{(2)}) = \frac{w_i^{(1)} \cdot w_i^{(2)}}{\left\| w_i^{(1)} \right\| \left\| w_i^{(2)} \right\|} \tag{7}$$

Mean AUC, FNED, and Pinned AUC Equality Difference. An ideal debiasing technique on word embeddings does not impair the original performance on text classification. Thus, mean AUC is leveraged in the measurement to figure out whether the debiased word embeddings undermine the original text classification task performance. False Negative Equality Difference (FNED) and Pinned AUC Equality Difference [1] are common metrics to evaluate how discriminatory the models are in the toxicity classification tasks. The definition of the two metrics are as follows:

$$FNED = \sum_t \mid FNR_t - FNR_{overall} \mid \tag{8}$$

$$pinnedAUCed = \sum_t \mid AUC - pAUC_t \mid \tag{9}$$

In (8), FNR_t represents the False Negative Rates for each comment that contains a specific demographic identity term, and $FNR_{overall}$ is the overall False Negative Rates for each classification task. Fairer models will have similar FNR_t values across all terms, where $FNR_{overall} = FNR_t$ for all sensitive terms. In (9), Pinned AUC ($pAUC_t$) is a metric combining regular AUC with error rate equality difference method and evaluates unintended bias more generally [1], and Pinned AUC Equality Difference indicates the sum of the differences between the per-term pinned AUC and the overall AUC covering all terms with sensitive attributes. **Lower FNED and Pinned AUC Equality Difference signify better model performance on fairness** [9].

4.4 Experimental Results and Analysis

Semantic Maintenance. We conduct validation on the semantic maintenance ability of our proposed adversarial debiasing framework. In order to measure the similarity of word vectors before and after debiasing, we adopt cosine similarity to gauge the changes, as shown in Table 1. As the word list is rather too long, we choose several words with different types of sensitive attributes for demonstration. The word vector similarity maintains well, in accordance with one of the aims of our adversarial debiasing framework.

Text Toxicity Classification. The mean AUC and FNED of all text toxicity classification tasks are presented in Table 2 and Table 3. Table 2 signifies that our debiasing technique on word embedding almost does not decrease the original

Table 1. The cosine similarity of the selected sensitive words between original words and debiased words using glove 6B as word embedding

Word	Cosine similarity	Word	Cosine similarity
Young	0.9977	Homosexual	0.9969
Deaf	0.9981	Gay	0.9973
White	0.9982	African	0.9983
Elderly	0.9978	Male	0.9915
Paralyzed	0.9982	Deaf	0.9981
Straight	0.9984	Trans	0.9983

mean AUC in text classification. For text toxicity classification using glove 6B and word2vec on IPTTS, our method surpasses the other two models and reaches 0.981 and 0.986 respectively. For classification tasks using glove 6B on Toxicity Comments, the mean AUC of our method remains approximately the same where the decrease in AUC compared with the original model is negligible. Table 3 demonstrates that our method significantly reduces FNED using glove 6B and word2vec by 77.7% and 58.0% respectively, compared to the original model on the toxicity classification task on IPTTS. And Compared to the baseline model, our model reduces FNED by 74.5% and 39.6% respectively.

Table 2. Mean AUC on glove 6B and word2vec with IPTTS and toxicity comments

Model	Mean AUC			
	Glove 6B		Word2vec	
	IPTTS	Toxicity comments	IPTTS	Toxicity comments
Original model	0.943	**0.965**	0.958	**0.967**
Baseline model	0.957	0.962	0.973	0.963
Our method	**0.981**	0.962	**0.986**	**0.967**

Table 3. False Negative Equality Difference (FNED) on IPTTS using glove 6B and word2vec

Model	FNED	
	glove 6B	Word2vec
Original model	38.60	26.89
Baseline model	33.77	18.71
Our method	**8.61**	**11.30**

Table 4. Pinned AUC equality difference on glove 6B

Model	Pinned AUC equality difference
Original model	7.73
Debiased Word Embedding [7]	1.77
Our method	**1.15**

As [7] is a recent approach that also leverages Adversarial learning to debias word embedding, we conduct experiments to compare its debiasing performance with ours. Table 4 shows that our model surpasses this method on pinned AUC Equality Difference. Our model is 35.0% lower, indicating a fairer text toxicity classification result.

5 Conclusion

This paper alleviates unintended demographic bias in toxicity text classification tasks by proposing a novel debiasing framework based on Adversarial Learning. Our method slightly adjusts the original word embeddings to gain a new set of debiased word embeddings of sensitive words. Experiments using debiased word embedding show that our proposed method efficiently mitigates unintended demographic bias in toxicity classification on the adopted text datasets. As our method only deals with non-contextual word embeddings (word2vec and glove 6B), it is worthwhile to apply our debiasing algorithm to contextual ones (e.g., BERT) in future work. Moreover, unintended demographic bias not only lies in the comments toxicity classification but also in other fields involving textual classification, where further research is also worth delving into.

References

1. Dixon, L., Li, J., Sorensen, J., Thain, N., Vasserman, L.: Measuring and mitigating unintended bias in text classification. In: Proceedings of the 2018 AAAI/ACM Conference on AI, Ethics, and Society, pp. 67–73 (2018)
2. Goodfellow, I., et al.: Generative adversarial nets. In: Advances in Neural Information Processing Systems, vol. 27 (2014)
3. Kang, Q., Yao, S., Zhou, M., Zhang, K., Abusorrah, A.: Effective visual domain adaptation via generative adversarial distribution matching. IEEE Trans. Neural Netw. Learn. Syst. **32**(9), 3919–3929 (2021). https://doi.org/10.1109/TNNLS.2020.3016180
4. Mikolov, T., Chen, K., Corrado, G., Dean, J.: Efficient estimation of word representations in vector space. arXiv preprint arXiv:1301.3781 (2013)
5. Park, J.H., Shin, J., Fung, P.: Reducing gender bias in abusive language detection. arXiv preprint arXiv:1808.07231 (2018)
6. Pennington, J., Socher, R., Manning, C.D.: Glove: global vectors for word representation. In: Proceedings of the 2014 Conference on Empirical Methods in Natural Language Processing (EMNLP), pp. 1532–1543 (2014)

7. Sweeney, C., Najafian, M.: Reducing sentiment polarity for demographic attributes in word embeddings using adversarial learning. In: Proceedings of the 2020 Conference on Fairness, Accountability, and Transparency, pp. 359–368 (2020)
8. Zhang, B.H., Lemoine, B., Mitchell, M.: Mitigating unwanted biases with adversarial learning. In: Proceedings of the 2018 AAAI/ACM Conference on AI, Ethics, and Society, pp. 335–340 (2018)
9. Zhang, G., Bai, B., Zhang, J., Bai, K., Zhu, C., Zhao, T.: Demographics should not be the reason of toxicity: mitigating discrimination in text classifications with instance weighting. arXiv preprint arXiv:2004.14088 (2020)
10. Zhou, G., Yao, L., Xu, X., Wang, C., Zhu, L.: Cycle-balanced representation learning for counterfactual inference. arXiv preprint arXiv:2110.15484 (2021)

Debias the Black-Box: A Fair Ranking Framework via Knowledge Distillation

Zhitao Zhu[1,2], Shijing Si[1,3], Jianzong Wang[1(✉)], Yaodong Yang[4(✉)],
and Jing Xiao[1]

[1] Ping An Technology (Shenzhen) Co., Ltd., Shenzhen, China
jzwang@188.com, xiaojing661@pingan.com.cn
[2] IAT, University of Science and Technology of China, Hefei, China
andyzzt@mail.ustc.edu.cn
[3] School of Economics and Finance, Shanghai International Studies University,
Shanghai, China
[4] Institute for AI, Peking University, Beijing, China
yaodong.yang@pku.edu.cn

Abstract. Deep neural networks can capture the intricate interaction history information between queries and documents, because of their many complicated nonlinear units, allowing them to provide correct search recommendations. However, service providers frequently face more complex obstacles in real-world circumstances, such as deployment cost constraints and fairness requirements. Knowledge distillation, which transfers the knowledge of a well-trained complex model (teacher) to a simple model (student), has been proposed to alleviate the former concern, but the best current distillation methods focus only on how to make the student model imitate the predictions of the teacher model. To better facilitate the application of deep models, we propose a fair information retrieval framework based on knowledge distillation. This framework can improve the exposure-based fairness of models while considerably decreasing model size. Our extensive experiments on three huge datasets show that our proposed framework can reduce the model size to a minimum of 1% of its original size while maintaining its black-box state. It also improves fairness performance by 15%–46% while keeping a high level of recommendation effectiveness.

Keywords: Information Retrieval · Knowledge distillation · Fairness · Learning to rank · Exposure

1 Introduction

Information Retrieval (IR) systems are nowadays one of the most pervasive techniques in a variety of industries. The sophisticated architectures and growing data scale of application scenarios cause the size of models to increase rapidly. Large models tend to capture complicated interactions between queries and documents, yielding increased performance at the expense of increased computational time and memory phase.

© The Author(s), under exclusive license to Springer Nature Switzerland AG 2022
R. Chbeir et al. (Eds.): WISE 2022, LNCS 13724, pp. 395–405, 2022.
https://doi.org/10.1007/978-3-031-20891-1_28

To tackle the difficulty of applying such large models to web-scale and real-time platforms, a few recent works [8,10,11,23] have applied Knowledge Distillation (KD) [6] to IR. Most ranking distillation approaches, however, focus on the balance of prediction performance and computing speed. Little attention has been paid to the fairness of ranking models during the distillation process [20]. Ranking systems employ deterministic models to assign an individual score to each item, and then sort items in descending order of their assigned scores to obtain rankings. That calculation pattern is succinct and intuitive, yet, leads to unfairness in the distribution of exposure. Exposure represents the expected number of people who will check an item. User behavior is affected by position bias: they are less likely to check items at lower positions. As illustrated in Fig. 1, this results in the allocation of user attention being disproportionate to the rankings on the recommendation list. A small difference in relevance can make a world of difference in exposure as a result of the winner-take-all [20] allocation of exposure. Under this circumstance, the unfairness between candidates is significantly amplified. Furthermore, while the combination of deep learning with ranking models provides a fresh leap forward, its lack of interpretability and increased reliance on data may introduce endogenous biases. The trade-off between model performance and fairness has become a huge issue for ranking models.

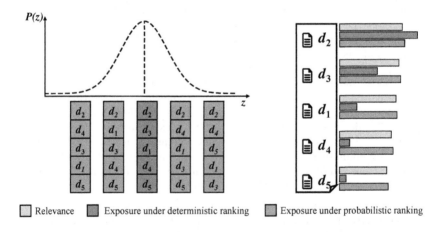

Fig. 1. A simple ranking method that relies only on ordering relevance scores makes the ratio between exposure and relevance disproportionate, magnifying subtle gaps in relevance. In contrast, a probabilistic ranking model maintains a positive relationship between exposure and relevance. z denotes possible permutations.

In this research, we propose a general Fairness-aware Ranking Distillation framework (FRD) for improving the fairness of top-K ranking models. FRD eliminates the average disparity of exposures documents received, and it is a direct approach irrelevant to specific protected attributes. Our framework takes advantage of ranking distillation, so it can build on top of large well-trained ranking models without extra retraining cost. The main contributions of this work can be summarized as follows:

- We adopt a ranking distillation framework with sub-regional treatment that retains the top rankings while penalizing items ranked lower by teachers. Since only the soft label results of the teacher model are used, our framework can be effectively applied to the black-box models.
- We identify the great potential of ranking distillation and propose that implementing a personalized fairness correction in the process of ranking distillation can avoid the vast additional computational costs necessary to achieve fairness purposes directly on complex models.
- By applying the latest optimization method of the Plackett-Luce ranking model, we have further reduced the computational cost of fairness correction significantly.

2   Related Work

2.1   Knowledge Distillation

The initial KD method transfers knowledge through the softmax output of a teacher model. Some subsequent work has extended the scope of statistics used for matching, such as intermediate feature responses [3], gradient [22], and distribution [7], etc. Other work, on the other hand, opted for a more subtle structural design. For example, DE-RRD [8] uses distillation experts to learn the middle layer representation space mapping function of Teacher while additionally using the rank order given by Teacher for rank matching; DCD [12] assigns more training resource to instances that were not correctly predicted by Student; MiniLM [24] proposes an assistant mechanism to distill only the last layer of the self-attentive matrix and the value-value matrix of the pre-trained model. But the potential of KD for other objectives remains largely unexplored.

2.2   Fairness in Rankings

Despite the growing impact of online information systems on our society and economy, the fairness of rankings has been a relatively under-explored area. In the existing work, some consider the equity of groups with respect to a set of categorical sensitive attributes (or features) to be ranked according to the principle of population parity, which can be further divided into group fairness [9] and individual fairness [15]. But there are other works such as [4,20] that argue that the fairness of ranking systems corresponds to how they assign exposure-based on the merits of individual items or item groups. These works specify and enforce fairness constraints that explicitly link relevance to exposure in expectation or amortized over a set of queries [21].

3   Methodology

In this section, we illustrate FRD, our universal fairness-aware ranking distillation framework, which is made up of ranking distillation and a fairness penalty. We elaborate on these two components in this section and present the algorithm for FRD.

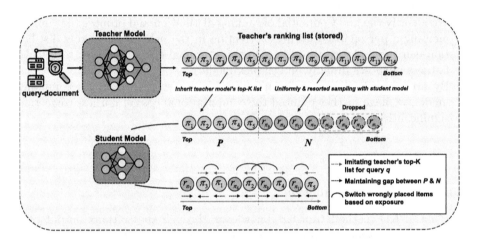

Fig. 2. Illustration of FRD framework. Student studies to rearrange the items into two sets to (a). maintain the same top-K list as the teacher; (b). penalize negative set items that are ranked too high; (c). ensure that items expected to get more exposure are placed higher up the list by pairwise comparison

3.1   Ranking Distillation

Ranking distillation attempts to mimic the teacher ranking model by transferring its knowledge to the student. For we only care about the top performers, considering the scores of all query-document pairs is undoubtedly inefficient and wasteful. A straightforward approach is to use only the information of top-K items and discard items ranked low by the teacher like [23]. But this approach leads to performance degradation because some useful information is discarded. It is undesirable to discard directly or incorporate wholesale into the training for candidate items that are not on the teacher model recommendation list.

1). For items recommended by Teacher, student network learns to match all their orders to get fine-grained scoring results.
2). Candidates not recommended by the teacher model are also internally differentiated: items with very low scores do not help maintain a distinct score boundary, and the model should be allowed to learn more information from candidates close to the boundary.

FRD treats Teacher's top-K candidates as positive set P to help the student imitate top performers' order and samples out negative set N to keep less relevant documents at lower end. Inspired by [19], two categorical ranking losses $\mathcal{L}_P(t, s, P)$ and $\mathcal{L}_N(s, P, N)$ are employed to allocate computing resources rationally according to importance, where t, $s \in \mathbb{R}^A$ represent the score list generated by Teacher and Student respectively. For the top-K list containing more refined sorting information of f^T, we construct a softmax based cross-entropy loss to minimize the difference between student's and teacher's top-p lists (positive set P). It is worth mentioning that here we relax K to p in Algorithm 1 to give more items recommendation opportunities.

$$\mathcal{L}_P(t, s, P) = \sum_{i \in P} \left\{ -\frac{e^{t_i}}{\delta_P^t} \cdot \log \frac{e^{s_i}}{\delta_P^s} \right\} \text{ where} \delta_P^t = \sum_{j \in P} e^{t_j} \tag{1}$$

Later, for the large negative sample set, the binary or pairwise comparison loss functions like Eq. (2) with less complexity can be employed since we only need to discriminate the rest items without considering the precise ranking. A negative sampling strategy is adopted to further reduce the number of negative candidates. A compressed set C is first sampled out with a categorical distribution Q, and then score with the student model to pick the top n documents to form the negative set N. This process brings a huge reduction in the calculation amount but no loss of effect.

$$\begin{aligned} \mathcal{L}_{N_b}(s, N) &= \sum_{i \in N} \log(1 + e^{s_i}) &&\text{(Binary)} \\ \mathcal{L}_{N_p}(s, P, N) &= \sum_{i \in N} \sum_{j \in P} \log(1 + e^{s_i - s_j}) &&\text{(Pairwise)} \end{aligned} \tag{2}$$

This categorical distillation strategy helps us concentrate finite computational power on the most useful retrieved list displayed to users while making good use of the remaining items.

3.2 Exposure-Based Fair Ranking

It is widely accepted that an item's position in the rankings has a critical impact on its exposure and financial success. Yet, surprisingly, the algorithms used to learn these rankings are often blind to their impact on items. The key goal of our amelioration is to promote exposure-based fairness during distillation. Based on the exposure estimating approach proposed below, we can explicitly specify how exposure is allocated such as making exposure proportional to relevance.

In recent years, the popularity of the Plackett-Luce (PL) ranking model [14] has increased. It is more efficient to use the PL ranking model to model the probabilistic distribution over rankings directly. Especially for fair distributions of attention exposure, multiple lines of previous works have found that PL ranking models may transfer the deterministic recommendation pattern into reflecting the relevance by the probability of occurrence [4,20,21], which gives an approximately equal possibility of being the top-item to candidates with slightly lower relevance indicators.

In the meantime, we follow the definition of exposure-based fairness: the items with higher ranking should achieve more exposure in practical environment. Thus we can constraint the difference between existing arrangement and counterfactual arrangement by minimize their exchanged exposure difference. For brevity we denote $\varepsilon_d = \varepsilon(q, d)$ as the exposure an item d receives under a probabilistic model π:

$$\varepsilon_d = \sum_{z \in \pi} \pi(z) \sum_{k=1}^{K} \theta_k \mathbb{I}[z_k = d] \tag{3}$$

where z denotes a possible permutation and rank weight θ_k indicates the probability that a user examines the item at rank k (e.g. $\frac{1}{k}$). For each query, this statistic calculates the averaged disparity between every two items and takes the average disparity across all item pairs:

$$\mathcal{L}_{Fair}(s, P) = \frac{1}{|P|(|P| - 1)} \sum_{d \in P} \sum_{d' \in P} (\varepsilon_{d'} \mathcal{R}_d - \varepsilon_d \mathcal{R}_{d'})^2 \tag{4}$$

Here the relevance of a document $\mathcal{R}_d$ is set as a transformation of its label and the exposures are estimated by d's total possibly gained rank weight [16] calculated through a continued product of following softmax principle:

$$\pi(d|z_{1:k-1,A}) = \frac{e^{s(d)} \cdot \mathbb{I}[d \notin z_{1:k-1}]}{\sum_{d' \in A \setminus z_{1:k-1}} e^{s(d')}} \tag{5}$$

where $s(d)$ denotes the score that the student model assigns to document d.

Calculating the gradient of a PL ranking model, on the other hand, necessitates iterating through every conceivable ranking that the model may generate, i.e., every possible permutation. In reality, this computational impossibility is overcome by estimating the gradient using model rankings as samples [17]. Employing the estimator to the gradient of PL model proposed in [16], we can optimize the exposure-based unfairness metrics simultaneously during knowledge distillation. This Metric (4) is designed to measure the difference in reward if the exposures of two items were swapped. Substituting the derivative of this metric with respect to ε_d, we can employ the below-mentioned estimator [16] to estimate its gradient and then update the PL model by back propagation, m denotes the ranking merit and an entire ranking is sampled with Gumble Softmax [5] trick rather than calculating any of the actual probabilities [1].

$$\frac{\delta}{\delta m} \mathcal{M}etric(q) = \sum_{d \in P} \left[\frac{\delta}{\delta m} m(d) \right] \mathbb{E}_z [(\sum_{k=rank(d,z)+1}^{K} \theta_k [\frac{\delta \mathcal{M}etric(q)}{\delta \varepsilon_{z_k}}] $$
$$+ \sum_{k=1}^{rank(d,z)} \pi(d|z_{1:k-1})(\theta_k [\frac{\delta \mathcal{M}etric(q)}{\delta \varepsilon_{z_k}}] \tag{6}$$

Algorithm 1: FRD

1: Student model f^S and well-trained Teacher model f^T.
   Hyper-parameters: Positive set size $p \in [K, a]$, Compressed set size
   $c \leq a - p$, Negative set size $n \leq c$, Learning rate η, Epochs R.
2: **for** each $r \in [0, R - 1]$ **do**
3:    Uniformly randomly select an query x, denote its candidate set of a
      documents as A with stored teacher scores t
4:    /* Indices of vector's largest p elements */
      Compute positive set $P = Top_p(t)$
5:    Randomly sample the compressed set C of c items with $Q(A - P)$
6:    Compute negative set $N = Top_n\left(f^S(C)\right)$
7:    Compute student scores $s = f^S(P \bigcup N)$
8:    Update f^S by optimizing the total loss in Eq. (7)
9: **end for**

In total, the loss of FRD is

$$\mathcal{L} = \mathcal{L}_P(t, s, P) + \mathcal{L}_N(s, P, N) + \lambda \mathcal{L}_{Fair}(s, P) \tag{7}$$

where λ is the tuning parameter specific to the dataset. This framework is model-agnostic as it only requires the teacher network's scoring data, making it easy to distill black box models. It is also able to debias ranking models against many attributes as it does not require any side information.

4   Experiments

In this section, we show empirical performance for FRD. We compare our method with the other baselines on two aspects: 1). ranking performance through imitating teacher; 2). unfairness correction level during distillation.

4.1   Datasets and Training Configurations

Datasets. We conduct our experiments on three public datasets: MSLR-WEB30K (fold 1) [18], Yahoo LETOR [2] and Istella LETOR full dataset [13], which are all benchmark datasets for large-scale experiments on the efficiency and scalability of LTR solutions. The basic statistics of these datasets can be found in [19].

Teacher/Student Models. To better control the ratio of distillation, we employ the Multi-Layered Perceptron (MLP) as the architecture for both the teacher and student networks. Specifically, the teacher model is a 3 layer FC-BN-ReLU model with hidden units of sizes 1024, 512, 256 for all three datasets and the student models are chosen by varying the proportion of parameter counts of the teacher and student models.

Evaluation Protocols. Following [19,23], we measure the ranking performance of student models in terms of the normalized discounted cumulative gain (NDCG) at top 5 & 10, which is commonly used for ranking tasks. For the fairness of a ranking model, we utilize the averaged squared disparity in Eq. (4) over all queries as the disparity metric.

4.2   Ranking and Fairness Performance

The distillation and fairness performances of teacher and student models on three datasets are presented in Table 1. The student model is a two-layered FC-BN-ReLU model of hidden units of sizes 28, 28. We utilize two kinds of distillation loss, the pairwise and binary loss, shown in methods ending with 'P' and 'B', respectively.

FRD consistently outperforms RankDistil and the teacher model in fairness. The averaged disparity of FRD methods decreases by 15%–46%, compared with the teacher model. The student models of RankDistil also exhibit a slight improvement in fairness, which is caused by the reduced size of the model. Note that we attribute to the differences unfairness values due to the different composition of the datasets, for example, each query in the Istella test set corresponds to an average of 319 documents, while for the Yahoo dataset, the number is 24. Deeper reasons remain to be explored, but for now, this fairness metric is not applicable to cross-dataset comparisons. With regards to the ranking performance, student models trained with pairwise loss significantly outperform binary loss. Both RankDistil and FRD with pairwise loss yield similar performances to the teacher model on MSLR Web30K and Yahoo LETOR datasets. On Istella dataset, student models perform significantly worse than the teacher model due to their lack of capacity to capture enough patterns from the huge dataset.

Table 1. Performance of various distillation methods on three datasets. Methods ending with 'B' indicate that binary loss is used for distillation, and 'P' denotes pairwise distillation loss. 'Disp.' denotes the averaged disparity over all queries.

Method/data	MSLR Web30K			Yahoo LETOR			Istella		
	N_5 ↑	N_{10} ↑	Disp.↓	N_5 ↑	N_{10} ↑	Disp.↓	N_5 ↑	N_{10} ↑	Disp.↓
Teacher	0.467	0.488	0.080	0.722	0.764	0.647	0.628	0.684	0.013
Ranking distillation [23]	0.428	0.451	0.080	0.684	0.731	0.641	**0.490**	0.525	0.013
RankDistil-B [19]	0.423	0.457	0.075	0.683	0.725	0.621	**0.490**	0.525	0.011
RankDistil-P [19]	**0.457**	**0.479**	0.076	**0.710**	<u>0.750</u>	0.625	0.481	**0.528**	0.012
FRD-B (*ours*)	0.420	0.452	0.063	0.678	0.721	0.551	0.483	0.520	0.008
FRD-P (*ours*)	<u>0.455</u>	<u>0.478</u>	**0.059**	<u>0.706</u>	**0.751**	**0.550**	<u>0.487</u>	<u>0.526</u>	**0.007**

4.3   Performance of Student Models Versus Size

Table 2 displays the performance of pairwise distillation methods on two datasets while varying the size of student models from 50% to 1% of Teacher. We vary the size of student models by adjusting the number of hidden neuron units. Fewer parameters means faster inference.

Table 2. Performance of distillation methods while varying the size of student models. The 'NDCG' is evaluated on top-5 documents, and 'Disp.' is the averaged disparity over all queries.

Models	Size	MSLR Web30K		Yahoo LETOR	
		N_5 ↑	Disp. ↓	N_5 ↑	Disp. ↓
Teacher	100%	0.467	0.080	0.722	0.647
RankDistil-P	50%	0.435	0.079	0.721	0.635
FRD-P	50%	0.433	0.069	0.720	0.578
RankDistil-P	10%	0.431	0.078	0.721	0.612
FRD-P	10%	0.428	0.064	0.719	0.563
RankDistil-P	1%	0.422	0.074	0.715	0.589
FRD-P	1%	0.421	**0.059**	0.714	**0.550**

Both RankDistil and FRD methods with pairwise loss are robust to the size of student models, as the $NDCG_5$ scores of the 1% student models are comparable to the teachers. FRD can reduce the average squared disparity significantly faster than RankDistil, which indicates that the fairness penalty plays an essential role in alleviating the disparity in ranking. The distillation performance of FRD has some decrease compared to RankDistil, but not more than 0.06%, which is negligible considering the improvement in fair performance.

5 Conclusion

In this paper, we propose FRD, a fairness-aware ranking distillation framework that leverages the potential of knowledge distillation. It can inherit the excellent ranking retrieval capabilities of the teacher model in the black-box state, while reducing the model size to a minimum of one percent. We pioneer the use of KD in achieving the exposure fairness. Our experiments show that the FRD with a bias correction strategy can achieve a significant reduction in model size and a large improvement in the reasonable distribution of exposure.

Acknowledgements. Zhitao Zhu and Shijing Si contributed equally to this work. Co-corresponding authors: Jianzong Wang and Yaodong Yang. This work is supported by the Key Research and Development Program of Guangdong Province under grant No. 2021B0101400003.

References

1. Bruch, S., Han, S., Bendersky, M., Najork, M.: A stochastic treatment of learning to rank scoring functions. In: Proceedings of the 13th International Conference on Web Search and Data Mining, pp. 61–69. ACM (2020)
2. Chapelle, O., Chang, Y.: Yahoo! learning to rank challenge overview. In: Proceedings of the Yahoo! Learning to Rank Challenge, Held at ICML. JMLR Proceedings, vol. 14, pp. 1–24. JMLR.org (2011)
3. Denton, E.L., Zaremba, W., Bruna, J., LeCun, Y., Fergus, R.: Exploiting linear structure within convolutional networks for efficient evaluation. In: NeuIPS, pp. 1269–1277 (2014)
4. Diaz, F., Mitra, B., Ekstrand, M.D., Biega, A.J., Carterette, B.: Evaluating stochastic rankings with expected exposure. In: Proceedings of the 29th ACM International Conference on Information & Knowledge Management, pp. 275–284. ACM (2020)
5. Gumbel, E.J.: Statistical theory of extreme values and some practical applications: a series of lectures, vol. 33. US Government Printing Office (1954)
6. Hinton, G.E., Vinyals, O., Dean, J.: Distilling the knowledge in a neural network. In: NeuIPS, pp. 1–9. MIT Press (2015)
7. Huang, Z., Wang, N.: Like what you like: knowledge distill via neuron selectivity transfer. arXiv preprint arXiv:1707.01219 (2017)
8. Kang, S., Hwang, J., Kweon, W., Yu, H.: DE-RRD: a knowledge distillation framework for recommender system. In: Proceedings of the 29th ACM International Conference on Information & Knowledge Management, pp. 605–614. ACM (2020)
9. Kusner, M.J., Loftus, J.R., Russell, C., Silva, R.: Counterfactual fairness. In: NeurIPS, pp. 4066–4076 (2017)
10. Kweon, W., Kang, S., Yu, H.: Bidirectional distillation for top-K recommender system. In: Proceedings of the Web Conference 2021, pp. 3861–3871. ACM/IW3C2 (2021)
11. Lee, J., Choi, M., Lee, J., Shim, H.: Collaborative distillation for top-N recommendation. In: 2019 IEEE International Conference on Data Mining (ICDM), pp. 369–378. IEEE (2019)
12. Lee, Y., Kim, K.E.: Dual correction strategy for ranking distillation in top-N recommender system. In: Proceedings of the 30th ACM International Conference on Information & Knowledge Management, pp. 3186–3190. ACM (2021)
13. Lucchese, C., Nardini, F.M., Orlando, S., Perego, R., Tonellotto, N., Venturini, R.: Exploiting CPU SIMD extensions to speed-up document scoring with tree ensembles. In: Proceedings of the 39th International ACM SIGIR conference on Research and Development in Information Retrieval, pp. 833–836. ACM (2016)
14. Luce, R.D.: Individual choice behavior: a theoretical analysis. Courier Corporation (2012)
15. Maity, S., Xue, S., Yurochkin, M., Sun, Y.: Statistical inference for individual fairness. In: ICLR, pp. 1–19. OpenReview.net (2021)
16. Oosterhuis, H.: Computationally efficient optimization of Plackett-Luce ranking models for relevance and fairness. In: Proceedings of the 44th International ACM SIGIR Conference on Research and Development in Information Retrieval, pp. 1023–1032. ACM (2021)
17. Oosterhuis, H., de Rijke, M.: Unifying online and counterfactual learning to rank: a novel counterfactual estimator that effectively utilizes online interventions. In: Proceedings of the 14th ACM International Conference on Web Search and Data Mining, pp. 463–471. ACM (2021)

18. Qin, T., Liu, T.: Introducing LETOR 4.0 datasets. arXiv preprint arXiv:1306.2597 (2013)
19. Reddi, S., et al.: RankDistil: knowledge distillation for ranking. In: International Conference on Artificial Intelligence and Statistics, pp. 2368–2376. PMLR, JMLR (2021)
20. Singh, A., Joachims, T.: Fairness of exposure in rankings. In: Proceedings of the 24th ACM SIGKDD International Conference on Knowledge Discovery & Data Mining, pp. 2219–2228. ACM (2018)
21. Singh, A., Joachims, T.: Policy learning for fairness in ranking. In: NeurIPS, pp. 5427–5437. MIT Press (2019)
22. Srinivas, S., Fleuret, F.: Knowledge transfer with Jacobian matching. In: International Conference on Machine Learning. Proceedings of Machine Learning Research, vol. 80, pp. 4730–4738. PMLR (2018)
23. Tang, J., Wang, K.: Ranking distillation: learning compact ranking models with high performance for recommender system. In: Proceedings of the 24th ACM SIGKDD International Conference on Knowledge Discovery & Data Mining, pp. 2289–2298. ACM (2018)
24. Wang, W., Wei, F., Dong, L., Bao, H., Yang, N., Zhou, M.: MiniLM: deep self-attention distillation for task-agnostic compression of pre-trained transformers. Adv. Neural. Inf. Process. Syst. **33**, 5776–5788 (2020)

Reinforcement Learning

Incorporating News Summaries for Stock Predictions via Graphical Learning

Hanlei Jin, Jun Wang, Jinghua Tan$^{(\boxtimes)}$, Junxiao Chen, and Tao Shu

Southwestern University of Finance and Economics, Chengdu, China
595915575@qq.com

Abstract. Financial news shows significant impacts on stock movement. Previous stock movement prediction models mainly incorporated textual information without considering text quality, resulting in irrelevant text misleading prediction. Meanwhile, the models do not provide key news about the stock market to help investors make more rational investment decisions based on textual information. In this paper, we propose a framework for incorporating news summaries into stock predictions (SumSP) via graphical learning. It uses a graph-clustering mechanism to extract financial news closely related to stock price fluctuations as summaries and then predicts stock price movement based on the impact of the summaries. The model ultimately yields meaningful, thematically diverse and economically meaningful summaries, as well as better prediction results. Experiments demonstrate the effectiveness of our model, comparing to state-of-the-art methods (The code will be released at https://github. com/JinHanLei/SumSP).

Keywords: Multi-view · Summarization · Graph clustering

1 Introduction

The influence of texts on stock markets has increased considerably [14]. With a wide range of broad communication channels, such as tweets/blogs and discussion boards, investors can rapidly reach more information and adjust their holdings to obtain maximum return timely. However, financial news grows exponentially on a daily basis. It is impossible for investors to manually analyze this huge amount of textual data [27]. Recently, automatic techniques for observing the influence of texts on stock price fluctuations are investigated and applied.

Statistical models focus on the causal relationship between stocks and information sources without considering the interactions among different information sources [1,18,25], leading to the loss of valuable information. To solve this problem, machine learning-based models concatenate the features of stocks and texts into a super feature vector to predict stock movement [10,21,31]. However, these methods fail to filter out the texts that really affect stock prices, which leads to irrelevant text misleading the model's judgment. One way of extracting the important sentences is the automatic text summarization (ATS).

© The Author(s), under exclusive license to Springer Nature Switzerland AG 2022
R. Chbeir et al. (Eds.): WISE 2022, LNCS 13724, pp. 409–417, 2022.
https://doi.org/10.1007/978-3-031-20891-1_29

Most ATS methods [2,11,17] consider the multiple input documents as a concatenated flat sequence and ignore the cross-sentence dependency. Thus, graph-based methods [4,20,22] are proposed to represent the relations of sentences. Clustering mechanisms are further incorporated to gather information and remove redundant texts [35]. However, the summaries generated above are not economically meaningful and therefore are not suitable for stock forecasting. To extract significant and related sentences to guide stock movement prediction, a fusion method that incorporates summaries and stock fundamentals is needed.

In this paper, we propose a framework for incorporating news summaries into stock predictions (SumSP) via graphical learning. This method extracts key sentences that are closely related to stock price fluctuations, and then predicts stock price fluctuations based on the impact of these sentences. Specifically, the summaries are extracted by a graph clustering mechanism, where the graph structure is built with the relations between sentences as edges and sentence embeddings as nodes. Meanwhile, the stock fundamental is represented by long short-term memory mechanism with time-series characteristics. Through the multi-view attention mechanism, the summaries are combined with the temporal sequence transaction data. The model ultimately yields meaningful, thematically diverse and economically meaningful sentences as summaries, as well as better prediction results. The contributions of this paper are three folds:

- We propose a multi-view attention mechanism to combine key news in stock movement prediction tasks to detect the abrupt change of price caused by important texts, in addition to the long short-term trading data.
- We adopt graph-clustering mechanism and incorporate the economic significance into the summarization, which is able to capture the diverse topics that may affect the stock market and avoid the redundant information.
- Experiment results show that our method can outperform other strong baselines by a large margin. Further analyses testify the effectiveness of the proposed multi-view modeling and correlation learning module.

2   Related Work

Extractive Summarization. The methods for extractive summarization [7,13,30,32] extracts sentences from the original documents and place them into summary. Graph-based methods capture cross-sentence relations [4,19] and select better sentences based on such relations. To learn more expressive sentences representations with less noise, [33] introduced a neural sentence ordering model based on the sentence-entity graphs. [30] proposed a heterogeneous graph neural network for capturing inter-sentence relationships. None of these methods can be applied directly to financial scenarios to obtain a summary of economic sense.

Text Aware Stock Movement Prediction. Statistic models study the statistical relationship between economic phenomena and texts [1,18,25], which lose valuable information. More research is turning to study ML techniques to concatenate features of stocks and texts into a super feature vector [10,21,31]. The weakness of the above methods is that they do not adjust the texts according to the fluctuations of the stock prices, nor provide summaries to help investors make better investment decisions based on the textual information.

3   The Proposed Method

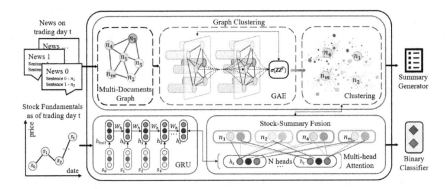

Fig. 1. System framework.

In this section, we first explain the model architecture of our model, which is demonstrated in Fig. 1 The proposed model consists of three main components: (1) graph-clustering summarization mechanism, (2) time series based stock embedding, (3) multi-head attention based stock-summary fusion. For multi-document texts, first split them into sentences and embed them via BERT [26] to get better representations. The graph structure is built with the cosine similarities between sentences as edges and sentence embeddings as nodes. The summaries are then extracted by the graph clustering mechanism [28]. For stock fundamental information, the representation with time-series information is obtained by gated recurrent unit (GRU) [3]. The last layer of GRU is added to each selected summary through the attention mechanism. We further employ a multi-head attention fusion to focus on different dimensions of the stock. The model finally ultimately yields meaningful, topic-diverse and economically significant sentences as summaries, as well as better predictions.

3.1   Graph Clustering Summarization

We use a multi-document graph-clustering mechanism to integrate graph structure and node information for the goal-directed representation learning, which is comprised of a GAE network and a clustering layer.

Specifically, we follow [34] in splitting source documents into multiple sentences. Considering the promising results of the graph-based methods for capturing relations [16,33], we adopt the graph-clustering mechanism in our framework.

Graph $\mathbb{G}$ is constructed to represent the input multiple documents. The nodes N are the set of m sentences, represented by BERT [29]. The edges E are the cosine similarities between sentences. $A \in \mathcal{R}^{m \times m}$ is the adjacent matrix. We adopt the Graph Autoencoder to learn the latent embeddings Z, which is produced by the two-layer Graph Convolutional Networks [9], and expressed as:

$$Z = GCN(N, A) = \tilde{A} ReLU(\tilde{A} N W_0) W_1 \tag{1}$$

where W_0 and W_1 are weight matrices. $X \in \mathcal{R}^{m \times d}$ is the node feature matrix. The outputs representations $Z \in \mathcal{R}^{m \times f}$. $\tilde{A}$ is the symmetrically normalized adjacency matrix obtained by using $D^{-\frac{1}{2}} A D^{-\frac{1}{2}}$. D is the node degree matrix with $D_{ii} = \sum_j A_{ij}$. Then, as suggested by [9], we choose the simple inner product to calculate the reconstructed adjacency matrix $\hat{A}$, with $\hat{A} = \sigma(ZZ^T)$. To learn the node information, we minimize the cross-entropy loss between the adjacency matrix A and the reconstructed $\hat{A}$, defined as:

$$L_g = -\frac{1}{M} \sum_{i=1}^m a log(\hat{a}) + (1 - a) log(1 - \hat{a}) \tag{2}$$

Graph clustering is further utilized to improve node representations. We minimize the Kullback-Leibler divergence [12] between the representations of cluster centers C and summaries N' to update representations, by:

$$L_c = KL(C|N') = \sum_i \sum_j c_{ij} log \frac{c_{ij}}{n'_{ij}} \tag{3}$$

We then follow [28] and jointly optimize the two parts to benefit each component by $L_{gc} = L_g + \gamma L_c$ where γ is a hyper-parameter. The joint Learning of graph and clustering achieves the extraction of non-redundancy sentences with diverse topics. Once obtain the representations Z and the centroids C. The closest node to each centroids can be selected based on the Euclidean distance. We concatenate the result sentences as financial summary.

3.2 Stock-Summary Fusion

We define the initial features S of each stock. The basic daily features s_t of each stock at day j, including opening $open_t$ and closing prices $close_t$, the highest $high_t$ and lowest low_t prices, the pe, pb, $volume$ and $turnoverrate$. We exploit GRU to learn short-term sequential features. The stock representation with time-series information is given by:

$$\hat{S}_t = GRU(\hat{S}_{t-1}, S_t) \tag{4}$$

where $\hat{S}_{t-1}$ is the hidden-state vector of day $t - 1$. The next step is to fuse the news summaries with the stock representations.

We assume stock fundamentals would have certain correlations with news. To characterize these relations, we propose a multi-head attention mechanism.

Specifically, the stock neurons having similar meanings with the word should be assigned with more weights. To achieve this goal, we combine the summary representations into the hidden-state vector of the GRU as guidance. The attention mechanism concatenate stock i in time t $\hat{s}_{ti}$ into each sentence in N', give by:

$$f(N, S_t, S_t) = Concat(head_1, ..., head_h) \tag{5}$$

$$head_i = Attention(N'W_i^N, S_t W_i^{S_t}, S_t W_i^{S_i'}) \tag{6}$$

where W_i^N, $W_i^{S_t}$ are weights in the two fully-connectedly layers, and $W_i^{S_i'}$ is the attention value for the i-th stock neuron. We use the average-pooling operation and softmax to generate the output. The loss function is given by:

$$L_s = -\frac{1}{T} \sum_{i=1}^{t} u\,log(\hat{u}) + (1 - u)log(1 - \hat{u}) \tag{7}$$

where u represents the increase or decrease of the closing price on the forecast day. Finally, our model achieves the generation of meaningful and topic-diverse sentences as summaries, as well as better movement prediction results.

4 Experiments

To the best of our knowledge, this work is the first study on fusing summaries and stock features with neural networks for the stock movement prediction task. We evaluate our model on the CSI-300, and compare it with several methods. The financial news dataset is crawled from the Internet. In addition, a case study is further conducted on the financial news dataset.

Model Setting. The dimension of the word embeddings is 768. The hidden layers sizes of GAE are 32 and 8. The hidden sizes of GRU is 8, and the attention has 4 heads. The optimizer is Adam [8] with learning rate $\alpha = 0.005$, momentum $\beta_1 = 0.9$, $\beta_2 = 0.998$ and weight decay $\epsilon = 10^{-5}$. We apply dropout rate to 0.1 and epochs to 50. The clustering coefficient γ is set to 1.

Baseline. We describe several baselines for comparison, which are widely employed in stock market. The first category is machine learning models that deal only with fundamental information. **Random:** this model predicts the movement to improve or decline randomly. **Support vector machine (SVM)** [24]: directly concatenates trading information and news information into a vector and uses this vector as an input. **Decision tree (DT)** [23]: is an effective modeling method for price analysis. The second category is predictive models that incorporates news. **BP neural network (BPNN)** [6]: we connect trading information and news information into a composite vector and feed it into a BP neural network to generate predictive analysis results. **LSTM** [5]: has excellent performance on time series data. We use an LSTM model to capture the temporal correlation of data, using a tandem composite vector as the input to the LSTM model. **Event-LSTM** [15]: an event-driven gating mechanism to effectively compensate for the imbalanced sampling of data in different dimensions.

4.1 Results

Table 1. Main experimental results.

Model	Accuracy	Rise			Fall		
		Precision	Recall	F1	Precision	Recall	F1
Random	0.4977	0.5000	0.5364	0.5175	0.4950	0.4587	0.4762
SVM	0.4338	0.4239	0.3545	0.3861	0.4409	0.5138	0.4746
DT	0.4795	0.4815	0.4727	0.4771	0.4775	0.4862	0.4818
BPNN	0.4932	0.4928	0.3091	0.3799	0.4933	0.6789	0.5714
LSTM	0.5068	0.5093	0.5000	0.5046	0.5045	0.5138	0.5091
e-LSTM	0.5160	0.5227	0.4182	0.4646	0.5115	0.6147	0.5583
Ours w/o clustering	0.5251	0.5341	0.4273	0.4747	0.5191	**0.6239**	0.5667
Ours	**0.5845**	**0.5922**	**0.5545**	**0.5728**	**0.5776**	0.6147	**0.5956**

The overall performance is shown in Table 1. There are several major observations. First, SVM yields the weakest result which is about 43.38%, and our proposed model outperforms all the baselines by a large margin, exceeding the best Event-LSTM baseline by 6.85% improvement, which confirms the validity of our proposed model. Second, our model surpasses the second class of models trained to treat news as sequential. It may be that the update mechanism of graph structure can characterize sentences more reasonably. And the sentences can focus on the important parts of the fundamentals by the attention mechanism. Third, compared to other models that include all news in the prediction, and our model without clustering, our full model achieves better results. This may be due to the large amount of noise in the source text, which interferes and misleads the prediction results. The inclusion of the summary method is able to filter out sentences with significant impact based on stock fluctuations and guide the prediction better.

4.2 Case Study

We present samples summaries generated by our proposed method. As shown in Fig. 2, our model is able to identify the critical information from the input documents. The financial summary effectively focuses on the influential contents that may cause the stock fluctuations. Moreover, The extractive method tends to generate short sentences that are fluency and linguistic, while uses the original sentences. It can be seen that, our proposed method generates diverse and non-redundant summaries with financial meanings.

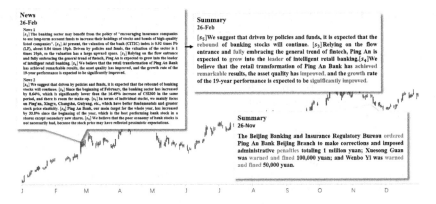

Fig. 2. Case study.

5 Conclusion

We propose a Multi-view Model that generates summaries to guide stock movement prediction. Our method uses a graph-clustering mechanism to extract financial news closely related to stock price fluctuations as summaries and then predicts stock price movement based on the impact of the summaries. Through the multi-view attention layer, the summaries are combined into the temporal sequence of stock data, allowing the model to focus on the impact of text on different levels of the trading data. Our model ultimately yields meaningful, thematically diverse and economically meaningful summaries, as well as better prediction results. Extensive experiments conducted on CSI-300 datasets show that the proposed model can effectively predict the stock movement on multiview content, in comparison with existing featurebased methods and several multimodal fusion methods based on neural networks.

Acknowledgements. This work has been supported by the National Natural Science Foundation of China (NSFC) (71671141, 71873108), Fundamental Research Funds for the Central Universities (JBK 171113, JBK 170505, JBK 1806003), Sichuan Province Science and Technology Department (2019YJ0250), and the Financial Innovation Center of the Southwestern University of Finance and Economics.

References

1. Antweiler, W., Frank, M.Z.: Is all that talk just noise? The information content of internet stock message boards. J. Finance **59**(3), 1259–1294 (2004)
2. Banerjee, S., Mitra, P., Sugiyama, K.: Multi-document abstractive summarization using ILP based multi-sentence compression. In: Proceedings of the 24th International Conference on Artificial Intelligence, pp. 1208–1214 (2015)
3. Cho, K., et al.: Learning phrase representations using RNN encoder-decoder for statistical machine translation. arXiv preprint arXiv:1406.1078 (2014)

4. Erkan, G., Radev, D.R.: LexRank: graph-based lexical centrality as salience in text summarization. J. Artif. Intell. Res. **22**, 457–479 (2004)
5. Hochreiter, S., Schmidhuber, J.: Long short-term memory. Neural Comput. **9**(8), 1735–1780 (1997)
6. Jin, W., Li, Z.J., Wei, L.S., Zhen, H.: The improvements of BP neural network learning algorithm. In: 2000 5th International Conference on Signal Processing Proceedings. 16th World Computer Congress (WCC-ICSP 2000), vol. 3, pp. 1647–1649. IEEE (2000)
7. Kedzie, C., McKeown, K., Diaz, F.: Predicting salient updates for disaster summarization. In: Proceedings of the 53rd Annual Meeting of the Association for Computational Linguistics and the 7th International Joint Conference on Natural Language Processing (Long Papers), vol. 1, pp. 1608–1617 (2015)
8. Kingma, D., Ba, J.: Adam: a method for stochastic optimization. In: Proceedings of the International Conference on Learning Representations (2015)
9. Kipf, T.N., Welling, M.: Variational graph auto-encoders. arXiv preprint arXiv:1611.07308 (2016)
10. Lavrenko, V., Schmill, M., Lawrie, D., Ogilvie, P., Jensen, D., Allan, J.: Language models for financial news recommendation. In: Proceedings of the Ninth International Conference on Information and Knowledge Management, pp. 389–396 (2000)
11. Lebanoff, L., Song, K., Liu, F.: Adapting the neural encoder-decoder framework from single to multi-document summarization. In: Proceedings of the Conference on Empirical Methods in Natural Language Processing, pp. 4131–4141 (2018)
12. Leibler, S.K.A.: On information and sufficiency. Ann. Math. Statist. **22**(1), 79–86 (1951)
13. Li, C., Qian, X., Liu, Y.: Using supervised bigram-based ILP for extractive summarization. In: Proceedings of the 51st Annual Meeting of the Association for Computational Linguistics (Long Papers), vol. 1, pp. 1004–1013 (2013)
14. Li, Q., Chen, Y., Wang, J., Chen, Y., Chen, H.: Web media and stock markets: a survey and future directions from a big data perspective. IEEE Trans. Knowl. Data Eng. **30**(2), 381–399 (2017)
15. Li, Q., Tan, J., Wang, J., Chen, H.: A multimodal event-driven LSTM model for stock prediction using online news. IEEE Trans. Knowl. Data Eng. **33**(10), 3323–3337 (2020)
16. Li, W., Xiao, X., Liu, J., Wu, H., Wang, H., Du, J.: Leveraging graph to improve abstractive multi-document summarization. In: Proceedings of the 58th Annual Meeting of the Association for Computational Linguistics, pp. 6232–6243 (2020)
17. Liu, P.J., Saleh, M., Pot, E., Goodrich, B., Sepassi, R., Kaiser, L., Shazeer, N.: Generating Wikipedia by summarizing long sequences. In: Proceedings of the International Conference on Learning Representations (2018)
18. Luo, X., Zhang, J., Duan, W.: Social media and firm equity value. Inf. Syst. Res. **24**(1), 146–163 (2013)
19. Mei, Q., Guo, J., Radev, D.R.: DivRank: the interplay of prestige and diversity in information networks. In: Proceedings of the International Conference on Knowledge Discovery and Data Mining, pp. 1009–1018 (2010)
20. Mihalcea, R., Tarau, P.: TextRank: bringing order into text. In: Proceedings of the 2004 Conference on Empirical Methods in Natural Language Processing, pp. 404–411 (2004)
21. Mittermayer, M.A., Knolmayer, G.F.: NewsCATS: a news categorization and trading system. In: Sixth International Conference on Data Mining (ICDM 2006), pp. 1002–1007. IEEE (2006)

22. Moratanch, N., Chitrakala, S.: A survey on extractive text summarization. In: 2017 International Conference on Computer, Communication and Signal Processing (ICCCSP), pp. 1–6. IEEE (2017)
23. Myles, A.J., Feudale, R.N., Liu, Y., Woody, N.A., Brown, S.D.: An introduction to decision tree modeling. J. Chemom. **18**(6), 275–285 (2004)
24. Noble, W.S.: What is a support vector machine? Nat. Biotechnol. **24**(12), 1565–1567 (2006)
25. Si, J., Mukherjee, A., Liu, B., Pan, S.J., Li, Q., Li, H.: Exploiting social relations and sentiment for stock prediction. In: Proceedings of the 2014 Conference on Empirical Methods in Natural Language Processing (EMNLP), pp. 1139–1145 (2014)
26. Vaswani, A., et al.: Attention is all you need. Adv. Neural Inf. Process. Syst. **30**, 5998–6008 (2017)
27. Vilca, G.C.V., Cabezudo, M.A.S.: A study of abstractive summarization using semantic representations and discourse level information. In: Ekštein, K., Matoušek, V. (eds.) TSD 2017. LNCS (LNAI), vol. 10415, pp. 482–490. Springer, Cham (2017). https://doi.org/10.1007/978-3-319-64206-2_54
28. Wang, C., Pan, S., Hu, R., Long, G., Jiang, J., Zhang, C.: Attributed graph clustering: a deep attentional embedding approach. In: Proceedings of the Twenty-Eighth International Joint Conference on Artificial Intelligence, pp. 3670–3676 (2019)
29. Wang, D., Liu, P., Zheng, Y., Qiu, X., Huang, X.: BERT: pre-training of deep bidirectional transformers for language understanding. In: Proceedings of the Meeting of the Association for Computational Linguistics, vol. 1, pp. 4171–4186 (2019)
30. Wang, D., Liu, P., Zheng, Y., Qiu, X., Huang, X.: Heterogeneous graph neural networks for extractive document summarization. In: Proceedings of the Meeting of the Association for Computational Linguistics, pp. 6209–6219 (2020)
31. Wuthrich, B., Cho, V., Leung, S., Permunetilleke, D., Sankaran, K., Zhang, J.: Daily stock market forecast from textual web data. In: SMC 1998 Conference Proceedings. 1998 IEEE International Conference on Systems, Man, and Cybernetics (Cat. No. 98CH36218), vol. 3, pp. 2720–2725. IEEE (1998)
32. Yasunaga, M., Zhang, R., Meelu, K., Pareek, A., Srinivasan, K., Radev, D.: Graph-based neural multi-document summarization. In: Proceedings of the Conference on Computational Natural Language Learning, pp. 452–462 (2017)
33. Yin, Y., Song, L., Su, J., Zeng, J., Zhou, C., Luo, J.: Graph-based neural sentence ordering. arXiv preprint arXiv:1912.07225 (2019)
34. Zheng, H., Lapata, M.: Sentence centrality revisited for unsupervised summarization. arXiv preprint arXiv:1906.0350 (2019)
35. Zheng, X., Sun, A., Li, J., Muthuswamy, K.: Subtopic-driven multi-document summarization. In: Proceedings of the 2019 Conference on Empirical Methods in Natural Language Processing and the 9th International Joint Conference on Natural Language Processing, pp. 3153–3162 (2019)

Bootstrapping Joint Entity and Relation Extraction with Reinforcement Learning

Min Xia[1], Xiang Cheng[1(✉)], Sen Su[1], Ming Kuang[2], and Gang Li[2]

[1] State Key Laboratory of Networking and Switching Technology, Beijing University of Posts and Telecommunications, Beijing, China
{min.xia,chengxiang,susen}@bupt.edu.cn
[2] Hangzhou Kangsheng Health Management Consultant Co., Ltd., Hangzhou, China
{mkuang2,gli}@91jkys.com

Abstract. Extracting entities and relations for types of interest from text is important for knowledge graph construction. Previous methods of entity and relation extraction rely on human-annotated corpora and adopt an incremental pipeline, which require abundant human expertise and are vulnerable to errors cascading. In this paper, we present ROTATE, a novel approach for jointly bootstrapping entity and relation extraction with reinforcement learning. The bootstrapping process of ROTATE consists of three bootstrapping sub-processes, which extract head entity, tail entity, and relation, respectively. Each sub-process starts with a few seed instances, then generates patterns and expands the seed set to start the next iteration. In particular, we propose a joint pattern scoring strategy in which the scores of patterns in each bootstrapping sub-process also take the seed information of the other two sub-processes into account. Moreover, we introduce reinforcement learning to solve the semantic drift problem in the bootstrapping process by formulating the seed expansion problem as a sequential decision making problem, and design a reward function that considers both seed quality and quantity. Experimental results on a collection of sentences from news articles confirm the effectiveness of our approach.

Keywords: Information extraction · Knowledge graph · Reinforcement learning

1 Introduction

Large-scale knowledge graphs such as Freebase, DBpedia, and Wikidata store real-world facts in the form of triples (head entity, relation, tail entity), abbreviated as (h, r, t), where relation represents the relationship between the head entity and tail entity. They are important resources for many intelligence applications like web search and question answering. Therefore, knowledge graph construction has been a widely concerned topic in both academia and industry.

Entity and relation extraction is the central step in knowledge graph construction. The problem is traditionally approached as two separate subtasks,

© The Author(s), under exclusive license to Springer Nature Switzerland AG 2022
R. Chbeir et al. (Eds.): WISE 2022, LNCS 13724, pp. 418–432, 2022.
https://doi.org/10.1007/978-3-031-20891-1_30

namely (i) named entity recognition (NER) and (ii) relation extraction (RE). The main limitations of the pipeline models are: (i) error propagation between the components (i.e., NER and RE) and (ii) possible useful information from one task is not exploited by the other (e.g., identifying a "founded" relation might be helpful for the NER module in detecting the type of the two entities, i.e., PERSON, ORGANIZATION, and vice versa).

Different from the pipelined methods, joint extraction is to detect entities together with their relations using a joint model. Previous studies [5, 25] show that joint learning approaches can effectively integrate the information of entity and relation, and therefore achieve better performance in both sub-tasks. Recently, several neural architectures have been applied, most of which utilize parameter sharing for joint modeling [8, 13, 17]. Zheng et al. [31] propose a special tagging scheme to convert joint extraction to a sequence labeling problem. Zeng et al. [29] propose an encoder-decoder model with copy mechanism to extract relation tuples with overlapping entities. However, these methods require manually labeling a training set with a large number of entity and relation types, which is too expensive. To solve this problem, distant supervised methods [19, 22] generate training data automatically by possessing an ideal hypothesis that all instances containing the same entity pairs express the same relation. But this is far from reality, because there may exist multiple relations between a specific entity pair.

In this paper, we propose a novel approach for bootstrapping joint entity and relation extraction with reinforcement learning, called ROTATE. The bootstrapping process of ROTATE consists of three bootstrapping sub-processes, which extract head entity (BHE), tail entity (BTE), and their relation (BRE), respectively. Each sub-process works as follows. It starts with a few seed instances and scans the text to collect occurrence contexts for the seed instances. Based on these contexts, it then generates extraction patterns and scans the text again to match candidate instances by using these extraction patterns. In particular, to improve the quality of the new extracted instances in all the sub-processes, we propose a joint pattern scoring strategy in which the scores of patterns in each bootstrapping sub-process also consider the seed information of the other two sub-processes. Moreover, we introduce reinforcement learning (RL) to solve the semantic drift problem in the bootstrapping process. We formulate the seed expansion problem in the bootstrapping process as a sequential decision making problem. The candidate instances found by BHE, BTE, and BRE in the current iteration are considered as the state of the external environment. The RL agent chooses which instances to expand the seed sets for the next iteration according to the state and the learned policy. The iterative process is repeated until the agent chooses no new seeds to add or reaches the maximum iteration number. In particular, to better guide the RL agent, we design a novel reward function that jointly encourages seed quality and seed quantity to add semantically correct and rich seeds.

In summary, our contributions are fourfold:

- We propose a bootstrapping approach with reinforcement learning for joint entity and relation extraction. To our best knowledge, this is the first semi-supervised joint entity and relation extraction approach.

- We propose a joint pattern scoring strategy to improve the quality of the extracted new instances. The scores of patterns in each bootstrapping sub-process consider the seed information of all the sub-processes.
- We introduce reinforcement learning to solve the semantic drift problem in the bootstrapping joint extraction by formulating the seed expansion problem as a sequential decision making problem, and design a reward function that takes both seed quality and seed quantity into consideration.
- We conduct experiments on a collection of news sentences from AFP and APW [18]. Experimental results confirm the effectiveness of our approach.

2   Related Work

Entity and Relation Extraction. Entity and relation extraction is an important task that has been extensively studied. Existing studies can be broadly categorized into two classes. The first class of studies [6,28] uses a pipelined approach where relations are extracted after all entities are detected. The second class of studies tries to detect entities together with their relations using a joint model. Some of them utilize parameter sharing for joint modeling [8,17]. Zheng et al. [31] propose a special tagging scheme to convert joint extraction to a sequence labeling problem. Zeng et al. [29] propose an encoder-decoder model with copy mechanism to extract relation tuples with overlapping entities. Li et al. [15] tackle the joint entity and relation extraction problem under the framework of multi-turn QA. Recently, multi-task learning [23], reinforcement learning [24,27] and GCN [21] are also introduced to enhance the interaction between entity extraction and relation extraction. However, all the above works rely on a large amount of manually annotated corpus which is too expensive. To solve this problem, Ren et al. [19] and Sun et al. [22] introduce distant supervision to generate training data automatically, which needs an existing knowledge base and suffers from noisy samples.

Bootstrapping. Bootstrapping is a widely studied technique in NER. Riloff et al. [20] use a set of seed entities to learn rules for entity extraction from unlabeled text. To further improve NER performance, many studies exploit pattern [9,10] and contextual features [11,12] in the bootstrapping process.

Bootstrapping technique is also widely used for RE. Brin et al. [4] develop the bootstrapping relation extraction system DIPRE that generates extractors by clustering contexts based on string matching. Snowball [1] is inspired by DIPRE but computes a TF-IDF representation of each context. BREDS [2] follows the framework of Snowball but uses word embedding to find new relations. BREX [7] uses entity and template seeds jointly to bootstrap relation.

3   Preliminaries

3.1   Problem Statement

In this paper, we focus on the semi-supervised entity and relation extraction problem, which aims to find all correct entities and relations for types of interest from unstructured text according to a small amount of annotated entities and relations.

3.2 Reinforcement Learning

Reinforcement Learning (RL) is a type of machine learning technique that enables an agent to learn in an interactive environment by trial and error using feedback from its own actions and experiences. By interacting with the environment, the RL agent can be applied to a sequential decision-making task. Considering a discounted episodic Markov Decision Process (MDP) $< \mathcal{S}, \mathcal{A}, \gamma, \mathcal{P}, \mathcal{R} >$, the agent chooses an action a_t according to the policy $\pi(a_t \mid s_t)$ at the state s_t. The environment receives the action, produces a reward r_{t+1}, and transfers it to the next state s_{t+1} according to the transition probability $P(s_{t+1} \mid s_t, a_t)$. Let R_t denote a γ-discounted cumulative return from t for an infinite horizon problem, i.e. $R_t = \sum_{t'=t}^{\infty} \gamma^{t'-t} r(s_{t'}, a_{t'})$. The process continues until the agent reaches a terminal state or a maximum time step. The objective is to maximize the expected discounted cumulative rewards:

$$\mathbb{E}_\pi [R_0] = \mathbb{E}_\pi \left[\sum_{i=0}^{\infty} \gamma^i r_{t+i} \right], \tag{1}$$

where $\gamma \in (0, 1]$ is the discount factor.

In this paper, we mainly focus on the policy-based method Monte-Carlo Policy Gradient [26]. There is a policy $\pi(a \mid s)$ as the probability of taking action a given state s such that $\sum_{a \in \mathcal{A}} \pi(a \mid s) = 1$. The policy $\pi(\cdot \mid s)$ models the agent's behavior after experiencing the environment's state s. The objective function is defined as

$$J(\theta) = \mathbb{E}_\pi \left[\sum_{t=0}^{\infty} \log \pi_\theta (a_t \mid s_t) R \right], \tag{2}$$

where R is the total accumulated reward and θ are the parameters that Policy Gradient parameterizes the policy.

4 Methodology

4.1 Overview

As shown in Fig. 1, ROTATE consists of two parts, namely a bootstrapping joint extraction and a reinforcement learning (RL) framework. The bootstrapping joint extraction is achieved by using three bootstrapping sub-processes, which extract head entity (BHE), tail entity (BTE), and relation (BRE), respectively. BHE, BTE, and BRE are initially given three seed sets $SEED_h$, $SEED_t$, and $SEED_r$, respectively. Then they iteratively go through five processing phases: finding seed matches, generating extraction patterns, finding candidate

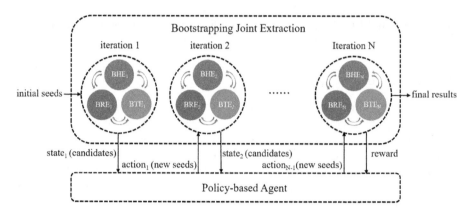

Fig. 1. Overview of our approach. **Above:** Bootstrapping joint extraction includes three bootstrapping sub-processes to extract head entity (BHE), tail entity (BTE), and their relation (BRE), respectively. **Below:** A Reinforcement learning framework for controlling semantic drift in the bootstrapping joint extraction. In each iteration, by interacting with the joint extraction process, the policy-based agent learns to pick promising new seeds for the following iteration.

instances, calculating pattern confidences, and calculating candidate confidences. In particular, we adopt a joint pattern scoring strategy in which scores of patterns in each sub-process also consider the seed information of the other two sub-processes to improve the quality of the extracted new instances in all the sub-processes.

The RL framework is introduced to solve the semantic drift problem in the joint extraction process. The problem of seed expansion in the bootstrapping joint extraction is formulated as a sequential decision making problem. By interacting with the bootstrapping joint extraction, a policy-based agent learns to pick the promising new seeds. In particular, we design a reward function that takes both the seed quality and seed quantity into consideration to encourage the agent to add semantically correct and rich seeds.

4.2   Bootstrapping Joint Extraction

The bootstrapping joint extraction consists of three bootstrapping sub-processes to extraction head entity (BHE), tail entity (BTE), and their relation (BRE), respectively. The three sub-processes are respectively given the initial seed sets $SEED_h$, $SEED_t$, and $SEED_r$. Each sub-process works in the following manner: scans the text to find seed matches according to the seed set, generates extraction patterns based on the seed matches, scans text again to match candidate instances using the extraction patterns, calculates the confidence of each pattern by the extracted candidate instances, and calculates the confidence of each candidate instance by the scores of patterns. Finally, the agent selects which candidate instances are to be added to the seed sets for the following iteration.

Find Seed Matches. BHE, BTE, and BRE scan the text to find the text segments where instances in seed sets appear and use the context vectors of the text segments to represent the seed matches. Specifically, for BHE and BTE, a seed match is represented by a three-tuple $< BEF, e, AFT >$. For BRE, a seed match is represented by a five-tuple $< BEF, e_1, BET, e_2, AFT >$. BEF, BET, and AFT are the context before, between, and after the matched text segment transformed into a single vector. The vector is generated by a simple compositional function that starts by removing stopwords and then sums the word embedding vectors of each individual word [16].

Generate Extraction Patterns. BHE, BTE, and BRE respectively generate patterns by using their seed matches with a single-pass algorithm [2] based on the cosine similarities between context vectors. In particular, each pattern p is represented by a set of seed matches.

For BHE, the cosine similarity is calculated as:

$$
\begin{aligned}
\mathrm{Sim}\,(t_1, t_2) =&\alpha_h \cdot \cos\,(BEF_1, BEF_2) \\
&+ \beta_h \cdot \cos\,(AFT_1, AFT_2),
\end{aligned}
\tag{3}
$$

where the parameters α_h and β_h weight each vector and $\alpha_h + \beta_h = 1$.

For BTE:

$$
\begin{aligned}
\mathrm{Sim}\,(t_1, t_2) =&\alpha_t \cdot \cos\,(BEF_1, BEF_2) \\
&+ \beta_t \cdot \cos\,(AFT_1, AFT_2),
\end{aligned}
\tag{4}
$$

where the parameters α_t and β_t weight each vector and $\alpha_t + \beta_t = 1$.

For BRE:

$$
\begin{aligned}
\mathrm{Sim}\,(t_1, t_2) =&\alpha_r \cdot \cos\,(BEF_1, BEF_2) \\
&+ \beta_r \cdot \cos\,(BET_1, BET_2) \\
&+ \gamma_r \cdot \cos\,(AFT_1, AFT_2),
\end{aligned}
\tag{5}
$$

where the parameters α_r, β_r, and γ_r weight each vector and $\alpha_r + \beta_r + \gamma_r = 1$.

Find Candidate Instances. The patterns generated from the previous step are used to scan the text again. For each text segment, a three-tuple is generated and similarities between the tuple and all previously generated extraction patterns in BHE and BTE are computed. For each pair of text segments, a five-tuple is generated and similarities between the tuple and all previously generated extraction patterns in BRE are computed. If more than half of the similarities between the tuple and the seed matches in pattern p is equal or above τ_{sim}, the tuple is considered to be a candidate instance i extracted by p [2].

Calculate Pattern Confidences. In BHE, BTE, and BRE, a pattern p is scored based on the candidate instances, which is extracted by p.

For BHE, a candidate instance, which is a three-tuple $< BEF, e, AFT >$, can be added to one of three sets: positive set P, negative set N, and unknown set U. If e is in $SEED_h$, the instance is added to P. If e is in $SEED_t$ and the types of head entity and tail entity are different, the instance is added to N. If e is in $SEED_t$ but the types of head entity and tail entity are the same, the instance is added to P. Otherwise, the instance is added to U.

For BTE, a candidate instance, which is a three-tuple $< BEF, e, AFT >$, can also be added to one of three sets: positive set P, negative set N, and unknown set U. If e is in $SEED_t$, the instance is added to P. If e is in $SEED_h$ and the types of head entity and tail entity are different, the instance is added to N. If e is in $SEED_h$ but the types of head entity and tail entity are the same, the instance is added to P. Otherwise, the instance is added to U. A score is assigned to each pattern p in BHE and BTE according to:

$$\text{Conf}_e(p) = \frac{|P|}{|P| + W_n \cdot |N| + W_u \cdot |U|}, \tag{6}$$

where W_n and W_u are weights associated with N and U, respectively.

For BRE, a candidate instance, which is a five-tuple $< BEF, e_1, BET, e_2, AFT >$, can be added to one of five sets: positive set P, negative set N, positive unknown set PU, negative unknown set NU, and unknown set U. Specifically, if the candidate instance contains e_1, which is the head entity of a seed in $SEED_r$, and if e_2 matches the tail entity of the seed, the instance is added to P. If e_1 matches the head entity of a seed in $SEED_r$ but e_2 does not match the tail entity of the seed, the instance is added to N. If e_2 matches the tail entity of a seed in $SEED_r$ but e does not match the head entity of the seed, the instance is added to N. If e_1 and e_2 are not in $SEED_r$, and e_1 is in $SEED_h$ and e_2 is in $SEED_t$, the instance is added to PU. If e_1 and e_2 are not in $SEED_r$, and e_1 is in $SEED_t$ and e_2 is in $SEED_h$, the instance is added to NU. Otherwise, the instance is added to U. A score is assigned to each pattern p in BRE according to:

$$\text{Conf}_r(p) = \frac{|P| + W_{pu} \cdot |PU|}{\begin{array}{c} |P| + W_{pu} \cdot |PU| + W_{nu} \cdot |NU| \\ + W_u \cdot |U| + W_n \cdot |N| \end{array}}, \tag{7}$$

where W_{pu}, W_{nu}, W_u, and W_n are weights associated with PU, NU, U, and N, respectively.

Calculate Candidate Confidences. The confidence of a candidate instance i is calculated according to the scores of patterns that extract the candidate instance i:

$$\text{Conf}_\iota(i) = 1 - \prod_{p \in \xi} (1 - \text{Conf}_\rho(p) \times \text{Sim}_p(i, p)), \tag{8}$$

where ξ is the set of patterns that are used to extract candidate instance i, and $\text{Sim}_p(i, p)$ is the maximum similarity between i and tuples in p:

$$\text{Sim}_p(i, p) = \max \{ \text{Sim}(i, t) \, | t \in p \}. \tag{9}$$

4.3   RL-Based Semantic Drift Control

The bootstrapping process suffers from a "semantic drift" problem, i.e., the semantic of the extraction drifts away from the given seed. The key to control the semantic drift in the bootstrapping process is to expand the seed set with reliable new seeds. Therefore, we introduce reinforcement learning to solve the problem by formulating the seed expansion problem as a sequential decision making problem. The policy-based agent learns to pick the promising new seeds by interacting with the bootstrapping joint extraction. The interaction between the agent and the bootstrapping joint extraction is modeled as a Markov Decision Process (MDP). A tuple $< \mathcal{S}, \mathcal{A}, \gamma, \mathcal{P}, \mathcal{R} >$ is defined to represent the MDP, where $\mathcal{S}$ is the continuous state space, $\mathcal{A} = \{a_1, a_2, \ldots, a_n\}$ is the set of all available actions, $\mathcal{P}(S_{t+1} = s' \mid S_t = s, A_t = a)$ is the transition probability matrix, and $\mathcal{R}(s, a)$ is the reward function of every (s, a) pair. We first describe the fundamental elements (i.e., states, actions, rewards) of the interaction between the policy-based agent and the bootstrapping joint extraction, then we show the network structure of the agent.

States. The state of the external environment is made up of the candidate instances found by the joint extraction in the current iteration. The size of state space is the maximum number of candidate instances $max\_candidates$, and the state vector is composed of the confidence score of each candidate instance.

Actions. Given all candidate instances, the agent chooses which candidate instances should be added into the seed sets. The size of the action space is the maximum number of candidate instances $max\_candidates$. Each dimension corresponds to a candidate instance and has a single value of either 1 or 0. 1 means to add the candidate instance to seed sets and 0 means not.

Rewards. There are a few factors that contribute to the seed addition policy by the RL agent. To encourage the agent not to drift to other semantic and introduce diverse semantic information, our reward function consists of the following scoring criteria:

Seeds Quality: For the joint extraction task, the semantic of the seeds guide the entire extraction process. So the quality reward is defined as follows:

$$r_{\text{QUALITY}} = \frac{1}{|S|} \sum_{i \in S} \text{Conf}_\iota(i), \tag{10}$$

where S is the set of instances that the agent decides to add to the seed sets.

Seeds Quantity: Since more seeds will provide more comprehensive and diverse semantic information, the quantity reward is defined as follows:

$$r_{\text{QUANTITY}} = \frac{|S|}{|C|}, \tag{11}$$

Algorithm 1: Training Procedure

---

for *episode* ← 1 **to** N **do**
    Initialize $S \leftarrow \emptyset$, $C \leftarrow \emptyset$
    Initialize $SEED_h$, $SEED_t$, and $SEED_r$
    Initialize *iterations* ← 1
    while *iterations* < *max_iterations* **do**
        Bootstrapping joint extraction finds candiate instances set C'
        $C \leftarrow C \cup C'$
        Observe state s_t accroding to C'
        Randomly sample action $a \sim \pi (a \mid s_t)$
        if $a_i == 1$ **then**
            $S \leftarrow S \cup i$
            Add i to $SEED_h$ or $SEED_t$ or $SEED_r$
        end
        if *the agent chooses no seeds* **then**
            break
        end
        Increament *iterations*
    end
    $R_{total} \leftarrow \lambda_1 r_{QUALITY} + \lambda_2 r_{QUANTITY}$
    Update θ using $g \propto \nabla_\theta \sum_t \log \pi_\theta (a_t, s_t) R_{total}$
end

---

where S is the set of instances that the agent decides to add to the seed sets, and C is the set of all candidate instances.

The reward function is the linear combination of the defined scoring criteria:

$$R_{\text{total}} = \lambda_1 r_{\text{QUALITY}} + \lambda_2 r_{\text{QUANTITY}}, \qquad (12)$$

where the parameters λ_1 and λ_2 weight each criterion.

Policy Network. We use a fully connected neural network to parameterize the policy function $\pi(s; \theta)$ that maps the state vector s to a probability distribution over all possible actions. The neural network consists of two hidden layers, each of which is followed by a rectifier nonlinearity layer (ReLU). The output layer is normalized using a softmax function.

4.4 Training

In the training phase, given $SEED_h$, $SEED_t$, $SEED_r$, a whole joint extraction process is one episode. Candidate instances extracted by the joint extraction in each iteration constitute the current state s_t. The agent selects new seeds from the candidate instances to expand the seed sets according to the stochastic strategy $\pi(a|s)$, so as to start the next iteration until no new seeds need to be added. To improve the training efficiency, we limit the episode length with an upper bound *max_iterations*. We update parameters θ to maximize the expected cumulative reward using Monte-Carlo Policy Gradient (REINFORCE) [26]. The approximated gradient used to update the policy network is shown as follows:

$$\nabla_\theta J(\theta) = \nabla_\theta \sum_t \log \pi_\theta (a_t, s_t) R_{\text{total}} . \tag{13}$$

The details of the training process are shown in Algorithm 1. In practice, the neural network parameters θ are updated using the Adam Optimizer [14].

5 Experiments

5.1 Datasets

The dataset used in our experiment consists of 8534 sentences sampled from AFP and APW [18], similar to [19]. In this experiment, we evaluate our proposed approach in three types of entities: person (PER), organization (ORG), and location (LOC), and four types of relations: PER-founded-ORG, PER-affiliation-ORG, ORG-headquarter-LOC, and ORG-acquire-ORG. Statistics of the dataset are shown in Table 1. Initial seeds are shown in Table 2.

Table 1. Statistics of the dataset used in our experiments. Sents denotes the number of sentences in the dataset. Foun., Affi., Acq. and Head. denote the number of ground truth relations of founded, affiliation, acquire, and headquarter, respectively.

Dataset	Sents	PER	ORG	LOC	Foun.	Affi.	Acq.	Head.
AFP_APW	8534	1626	1588	197	818	1147	104	388

5.2 Evaluation Metrics

Similar to the existing work [30], we consider Precision (P), Recall (R), and F1 score as the performance metrics. In particular, the F1 score measures the average overlap between the predictions and ground truth answers.

5.3 Baselines

In our experiments, we use a bootstrapping entity extraction method Stanford-NER [10] and two bootstrapping relation extraction methods Snowball [1] and BREDS [2] to design two pipelined joint extraction as baselines:

Pipeline1. A pipelined entity and relation extraction method, which uses StanfordNER to extract entities and then uses Snowball to extract relations based on the results of entity extraction.

Table 2. Entity and relation types and used seeds.

Entity/Relation type	Seeds
PER	{Kofi Annan} {Jack Valenti} {Nelson Mandela}
ORG	{NATO} {Viacom} {AOL}
LOC	{Brussels} {Belgium} {Israel}
founded	{Sergey Brin, Google} {Julian Assange, WikiLeaks} {Calisto Tanzi, Parmalat}
affiliation	{Kofi Annan, United Nations} {Kobe Bryant, Los Angeles Lakers} {Larry Sabato, University of Virginia}
acquire	{Viacom, CBS} {AOL, Time Warner} {Viacom, MTV}
headquarter	{NATO, Brussels} {UNITA, Angola} {Likud, Israel}

Pipeline2. A pipelined entity and relation extraction method, which uses StanfordNER to extract entities and then uses BREDS to extract relations based on the results of entity extraction.

We also compare ROTATE with two internal baselines:

ROTATE*. To evaluate the effectiveness of our proposed joint pattern scoring strategy, we introduce ROTATE*, whose scores of patterns in each bootstrapping sub-process only consider the seed information of its own without adopting the joint pattern scoring strategy. Thus for BHE and BTE, Eq. (6) is rewritten as follows:

$$\text{Conf}_\rho(p) = \frac{|P|}{|P| + W_u \cdot |U|}, \tag{14}$$

where P and U are positive and unknown sets of p, respectively. If the entity of a candidate instance extracted by p occurs in the seed set, the instance is added to P, otherwise it is added to U.

For BRE, Eq. (7) is rewritten as follows:

$$\text{Conf}_\rho(p) = \frac{|P|}{|P| + W_u \cdot |U| + W_n \cdot |N|}. \tag{15}$$

ROTATE#. To evaluate the effectiveness of the reinforcement learning framework for semantic drift control, we introduce ROTATE#, whose candidate instances with a score equal or above the threshold τ are added to the seed sets instead of choosing by the RL agent.

Table 3. Results of entity extraction. Larger scores indicate better performances.

Model	Relation	PER			ORG			LOC		
		P	R	F1	P	R	F1	P	R	F1
Pipeline1	–	47.7	**81.4**	60.4	43.3	63.5	51.5	37.3	10.1	15.9
Pipeline2										
ROTATE*	–	60.1	68.7	64.1	50.0	**93.5**	65.2	65.1	**62.2**	63.6
ROTATE#	founded	72.6	58.8	65.0	52.3	92.3	66.7	–	–	–
	affiliation	73.2	56.9	64.0	60.0	81.5	69.1	–	–	–
	acquire	–	–	–	51.5	92.3	66.1	–	–	–
	headquarter	–	–	–	51.2	91.9	65.7	**78.7**	39.9	62.6
ROTATE	founded	**75.4**	61.0	**67.5**	60.8	86.4	**71.4**	–	–	–
	affiliation	**80.4**	61.1	**69.4**	64.9	81.0	**72.1**	–	–	–
	acquire	–	–	–	**55.8**	87.4	**68.1**	–	–	–
	headquarter	–	–	–	**61.2**	82.1	**70.1**	70.0	60.3	**64.8**

5.4 Implementation Details

Our pre-processing pipeline is based on the models provided by the NLTK toolkit [3]: sentence segmentation[1], tokenization[2], and PoS-tagging[3].

With the full sentences set, we compute word embeddings with the skip-gram model[4] using the word2vec[5] implementation from [16].

For BHE and BTE, we consider a window of 3 tokens for the BEF and AFT contexts, ignoring the remaining of sentence. We discard the patterns with only one seed match. The parameters W_u and W_n are set to 0 and 2, respectively.

For RE, we consider BEF and AFT no further away than 12 tokens and a window of 2 tokens for the BEF and AFT contexts. The parameters W_u, W_{pu}, W_{nu}, and W_n are set to 0, 0.5, 1, and 2, respectively.

5.5 Overall Results

The main results of the entity and relation extraction are shown in Table 3 and Table 4, respectively. We can clearly observe that the full approach of ROTATE reaches the state-of-the-art F1 results on the entity and relation extraction. These results demonstrate the effectiveness of the bootstrapping joint extraction with reinforcement learning.

As shown in Table 3, when entity ORG jointly extracts with relation "acquire", we can see ROTATE achieves better performance on ORG than

---

[1] nltk.tokenize.punkt.PunktSentenceTokenizer.
[2] nltk.tokenize.treebank.TreebankWordTokenizer.
[3] taggers/maxent treebank pos tagger/english.pickle.
[4] skip length of 5 tokens and vectors of 200 dimensions.
[5] https://code.google.com/p/word2vec/.

Table 4. Results of relation extraction. Larger scores indicate better performances.

Model	founded			affiliation			acquire			headquarter		
	P	R	F1	P	R	F1	P	R	F1	P	R	F1
Pipeline1	40.0	28.0	32.9	44.1	31.9	37.0	35.7	36.2	35.9	60.1	09.3	16.1
Pipeline2	34.8	34.3	34.5	44.8	21.5	29.0	29.5	33.3	31.3	65.7	10.1	17.5
ROTATE*	51.8	60.3	55.7	45.8	**83.1**	63.0	59.5	52.2	55.4	45.8	**54.6**	49.8
ROTATE#	58.1	58.7	58.4	52.3	80.2	63.3	**63.9**	51.0	56.7	**74.0**	39.9	51.8
ROTATE	**60.3**	**64.5**	**62.3**	**61.2**	75.1	**67.4**	60.9	**60.6**	**60.7**	67.3	54.1	**60.0**

Pipeline1 and Pipeline2. Since both the head entity and tail entity of "acquire" are ORG, there is no additional entity information in the joint extraction process, which means it's helpful to introduce the information of relation for entity extraction. As shown in Table 3, We can clearly observe that the full approach of ROTATE reaches the state-of-the-art results on the relation extraction.

From Table 3, ROTATE achieves better performance on entity PER than Pipeline1 and Pipeline2. But the results are different when PER is extracted jointly with different relations (e.g., "founded" and "affiliation"). This means that our approach has the ability to deal with the multi-relation problem, but different relations have different promoting effects on the same type of entity extraction.

From Table 3 and Table 4, we can also find that Pipeline1 and Pipeline2 achieve worse performance on entity LOC than other types of entities and on relation "headquarter" whose tail entity is LOC than other relations. This is because entities of LOC make up a smaller percentage of the dataset leading to greater interference from other types of entities in the extraction process. ROTATE reliefs this problem to some extent by adopting the joint extraction. It indicates that our proposed approach can improve the performance for extracting the entities that do not appear frequently and the relations associated with such entities.

5.6   Further Analysis

To analyze the effectiveness of the proposed joint pattern scoring strategy, we compare ROTATE with ROTATE*, whose scores of patterns in each bootstrapping sub-process only utilize the seed information of its own. As shown in Table 3 and Table 4, ROTATE achieves better F1 scores than ROTATE*, mainly as a consequence of much higher precision scores, which is due to the stricter pattern scoring strategy caused by using the seed information of the three bootstrapping sub-processes. The recall scores of ROTATE drop, but without affecting the F1 scores, since the higher precision compensates for the small loss in the recall.

To analyze the effectiveness of the introduced reinforcement learning for semantic drift control, we compare ROTATE with ROTATE#, which adds candidate instances with scores equal or above the threshold τ to the seed sets without using reinforcement learning. From Table 3 and Table 4, we can see that

ROTATE achieves better F1 scores than ROTATE$^{\#}$ mainly as the precision and recall of ROTATE are more balanced than that of ROTATE$^{\#}$. This is because ROTATE$^{\#}$ adds seeds only according to the quality of seeds in the current iteration. The RL-based framework in ROTATE optimizes the seed expansion strategy by maximizing the ultimate expected reward that considers both seed quality and quantity.

6 Conclusion

In this paper, we propose a novel bootstrapping approach with reinforcement learning for joint entity and relation extraction. In particular, we propose a joint pattern scoring strategy in the bootstrapping joint extraction to improve the quality of the extracted instances. Moreover, we introduce reinforcement learning to solve the problem of semantic drift in the bootstrapping joint extraction. The experimental results confirm the effectiveness of our approach. In the future, we plan to use some extra information, such as seed patterns, to improve the performance of the joint entity and relation extraction.

References

1. Agichtein, E., Gravano, L.: Snowball: extracting relations from large plain-text collections. In: Proceedings of ACM, pp. 85–94 (2000)
2. Batista, D.S., Martins, B., Silva, M.J.: Semi-supervised bootstrapping of relationship extractors with distributional semantics. In: Proceedings of EMNLP, pp. 499–504 (2015)
3. Bird, S., Klein, E., Loper, E.: Natural Language Processing with Python: Analyzing Text with the Natural Language Toolkit. O'Reilly Media Inc, Sebastopol (2009)
4. Brin, S.: Extracting patterns and relations from the world wide web. In: Atzeni, P., Mendelzon, A., Mecca, G. (eds.) WebDB 1998. LNCS, vol. 1590, pp. 172–183. Springer, Heidelberg (1999). https://doi.org/10.1007/10704656_11
5. Dai, D., Xiao, X., Lyu, Y., Dou, S., She, Q., Wang, H.: Joint extraction of entities and overlapping relations using position-attentive sequence labeling. In: Proceedings of AAAI, vol. 33, pp. 6300–6308 (2019)
6. Guo, Z., Zhang, Y., Lu, W.: Attention guided graph convolutional networks for relation extraction. arXiv preprint arXiv:1906.07510 (2019)
7. Gupta, P., Roth, B., Schütze, H.: Joint bootstrapping machines for high confidence relation extraction. arXiv preprint arXiv:1805.00254 (2018)
8. Gupta, P., Schütze, H., Andrassy, B.: Table filling multi-task recurrent neural network for joint entity and relation extraction. In: Proceedings of COLING, pp. 2537–2547 (2016)
9. Gupta, S., MacLean, D.L., Heer, J., Manning, C.D.: Induced lexico-syntactic patterns improve information extraction from online medical forums. J. AMIA **21**(5), 902–909 (2014)
10. Gupta, S., Manning, C.D.: Improved pattern learning for bootstrapped entity extraction. In: Proceedings of CoNLL, pp. 98–108 (2014)
11. Gupta, S., Manning, C.D.: Distributed representations of words to guide bootstrapped entity classifiers. In: Proceedings of NAACL, pp. 1215–1220 (2015)

12. He, Y., Grishman, R.: ICE: rapid information extraction customization for NLP novices. In: Proceedings of NAACL, pp. 31–35 (2015)
13. Katiyar, A., Cardie, C.: Going out on a limb: joint extraction of entity mentions and relations without dependency trees. In: Proceedings of ACL, pp. 917–928 (2017)
14. Kingma, D.P., Ba, J.: Adam: a method for stochastic optimization. arXiv preprint arXiv:1412.6980 (2014)
15. Li, X., et al.: Entity-relation extraction as multi-turn question answering. arXiv preprint arXiv:1905.05529 (2019)
16. Mikolov, T., Chen, K., Corrado, G., Dean, J.: Efficient estimation of word representations in vector space. arXiv preprint arXiv:1301.3781 (2013)
17. Miwa, M., Bansal, M.: End-to-end relation extraction using LSTMs on sequences and tree structures. arXiv preprint arXiv:1601.00770 (2016)
18. Parker, R., Graff, D., Kong, J., Chen, K., Maeda, K.: English gigaword fifth edition ldc2011t07, Technical Report. Linguistic Data Consortium, Philadelphia (2011)
19. Ren, X., et al.: CoType: joint extraction of typed entities and relations with knowledge bases. In: Proceedings of WWW, pp. 1015–1024 (2017)
20. Riloff, E.: Automatically generating extraction patterns from untagged text. In: Proceedings of AAAI, pp. 1044–1049 (1996)
21. Sun, C., et al.: Joint type inference on entities and relations via graph convolutional networks. In: Proceedings of ACL, pp. 1361–1370 (2019)
22. Sun, C., Wu, Y.: Distantly supervised entity relation extraction with adapted manual annotations. In: Proceedings of AAAI, vol. 33, pp. 7039–7046 (2019)
23. Sun, K., Zhang, R., Mensah, S., Mao, Y., Liu, X.: Progressive multi-task learning with controlled information flow for joint entity and relation extraction. In: Proceedings of AAAI, vol. 35, pp. 13851–13859 (2021)
24. Takanobu, R., Zhang, T., Liu, J., Huang, M.: A hierarchical framework for relation extraction with reinforcement learning. In: Proceedings of AAAI, vol. 33, pp. 7072–7079 (2019)
25. Tan, Z., Zhao, X., Wang, W., Xiao, W.: Jointly extracting multiple triplets with multilayer translation constraints. In: Proceedings of AAAI, vol. 33, pp. 7080–7087 (2019)
26. Williams, R.J.: Simple statistical gradient-following algorithms for connectionist reinforcement learning. Mach. Learn. 8(3), 229–256 (1992). https://doi.org/10.1007/BF00992696
27. Xiao, Y., Tan, C., Fan, Z., Xu, Q., Zhu, W.: Joint entity and relation extraction with a hybrid transformer and reinforcement learning based model. In: Proceedings of AAAI, vol. 34, pp. 9314–9321 (2020)
28. Zeng, D., Liu, K., Lai, S., Zhou, G., Zhao, J.: Relation classification via convolutional deep neural network. In: Proceedings of COLING, pp. 2335–2344 (2014)
29. Zeng, X., Zeng, D., He, S., Liu, K., Zhao, J.: Extracting relational facts by an end-to-end neural model with copy mechanism. In: Proceedings of ACL, pp. 506–514 (2018)
30. Zhang, M., Zhang, Y., Fu, G.: End-to-end neural relation extraction with global optimization. In: Proceedings of EMNLP, pp. 1730–1740 (2017)
31. Zheng, S., Wang, F., Bao, H., Hao, Y., Zhou, P., Xu, B.: Joint extraction of entities and relations based on a novel tagging scheme. arXiv preprint arXiv:1706.05075 (2017)

EEML: Ensemble Embedded Meta-Learning

Geng Li⬤, Boyuan Ren⬤, and Hongzhi Wang(✉)⬤

Harbin Institute of Technology, Harbin, China
{21S003022,1180300207}@stu.hit.edu.cn, wangzh@hit.edu.cn

Abstract. To accelerate learning process with few samples, meta-learning resorts to prior knowledge from previous tasks. However, the inconsistent task distribution and heterogeneity is hard to be handled through a global sharing model initialization. In this paper, based on gradient-based meta-learning, we propose an ensemble embedded meta-learning algorithm (EEML) that explicitly utilizes multi-model-ensemble to organize prior knowledge into diverse specific experts. We rely on a task embedding cluster mechanism to deliver diverse tasks to matching experts in training process and instruct how experts collaborate in test phase. As a result, the multi experts can focus on their own area of expertise and cooperate in upcoming task to solve the task heterogeneity. The experimental results show that the proposed method outperforms recent state-of-the-arts easily in few-shot learning problem, which validates the importance of differentiation and cooperation.

Keywords: Meta-learning · Ensemble-learning · Few-shot learning

1 Introduction

One of the Intelligent advantages of human being is acquiring new skill for unseen task from few samples. To achieve the fast learning capability, meta-learning also known as learning to learn, leverages what we learned from past tasks to improve learning in a new task. As a common practice for few-shot learning problem, meta-learning contains several series which differ in the way of employing prior knowledge [12]: metric-based [13,29], model-based [19], gradient-based (a.k.a. optimization-based) meta-learning [8].

Though these methods earn relative improvement comparing with past methods, most of them hypothesize the prior knowledge learned from past should be shared indifferently for all tasks. As a consequence, they suffer from the tasks heterogeneity. On the other hand, a few research works try to fix the problem by customizing the prior knowledge to each task [1,25,35]. However, the defect of such methods lie in resorting to only a single expert who may not be sufficient for achieving the best result. In other words, instead of reasonably utilizing overall intelligence, these methods prefer to choose an expert as dictator.

Supported by Harbin Institute of Technology.

R. Chbeir et al. (Eds.): WISE 2022, LNCS 13724, pp. 433–442, 2022.
https://doi.org/10.1007/978-3-031-20891-1_31

Hence, we are motivated to pursue a meta-learning framework both effectively diverge knowledge into multi experts and comprehensively utilizing overall experts to aggregate an stable answer for new task to enhance the final performance. The inspiration comes from classical ensemble learning, bagging [4] or random forest [5]. In ensemble learning, though single learner may perform trivially or sometimes blindly on the whole task distribution, but the ensemble mechanism can help each expert reach a relatively good cooperative result through counteracting mutual bias.

Inspired by this, we propose a novel meta-learning algorithm named Ensemble Embedded Meta-learning (EEML). The key idea of EEML is to organize heterogeneous training tasks into matching experts and collecting all experts opinions to form a comprehensive answer for a new task. In this paper, we resorts to gradient-based meta-learning as the backbone which instantiates knowledge as parameter initialization. Specifically, we employ a task embedding cluster to cover the domain of each expert. The gradient of task would be considered as a strong embedding and we assign training task to the matching expert according to the similarity between the gradient and the expert domain. In predicting phase, all experts can utilize few samples to contribute its opinions, and the final result is composed as a weighted voting answer from all experts.

We would highlight the contributions of EEML as two points: 1) it employs multi-experts cooperation framework instead of single expert for uncertain tasks, so that it outperforms recent state-of-the-art meta-learning algorithms in few-shot learning. 2) as we know, EEML is the first generic meta-learning algorithm combined with ensemble learning, whose experiment results show great confidence in exploring further in composing meta-learning and ensemble learning for future work.

2 Related Work

2.1 Meta-Learning

Meta-learning is understood as "learning to learn" [17,28,31–33], it starts with the form of learning to optimize model [2,11] and now are mainly divided into three series, metric-based meta-learning [13,16,29,30,34], network-based meta-learning [19–21,23,26] and gradient-based meta-learning [6,9,10,15,18,36]. The goal of metric-based algorithms is to measure the similarity between support samples and query samples with elaborate metric methodology. Network-based approaches emphasize finding structures effective in capturing the prior knowledge in training data. Gradient-based meta-learning aims to use different task gradients to optimize a base model with a batch form.

In this work, we focus on the discuss about gradient-based meta-learning. The most powerful representation should be MAML [8], which presents the "inner-loop and outer-loop" framework commonly used by plenty of followers. Reptile [22] uses accumulated first gradient replace the second derivative and earns speeding up but instability. MetaOptNet [3,14,29] reset the inner optimization by dividing the model into feature extractor and head classifier and apply on complex base learner like ResNet-12 without overfitting. LEO [25] introduces lower-dimensional latent space to consider task-conditioned initialization. L2F [1] uses extra MLP network to help attenuate the base learner parameters to gain a task-conditioned initialization.

2.2   Ensemble Learning

Ensemble learning exploits multiple base machine learning algorithms to obtain weak predictive results and fuse results with voting mechanism to achieve better performance than that obtained from any constituent algorithm alone [7]. The main classical ensemble learning algorithms are AdaBoost [27], Random Forest [5] and Bagging [4]. In this paper, to start with clarity we mainly rely on the bagging mechanism which is simple and efficient, besides, it's naturally adaptive to parallel training paradigm, which can effectively speedup our training process. However, with the precisely designed coefficients adopted during training and test phase, our method has inherent difference with original bagging.

3   Preliminaries

3.1   The Problem Definition

Supposed that a sequence of tasks $\{\mathcal{T}_1, \mathcal{T}_2, ..., \mathcal{T}_N\}$ are sampled from a probability $p(\mathcal{T})$. Each task sampled from $p(\mathcal{T})$ is defined as $\{x_i, y_i\}_{i=1}^m$. Dividing parts samples into training set $\mathcal{D}^{tr} = \{x_i, y_i\}_{i=1}^{n^{tr}}$ and the rest as test set $\mathcal{D}^{te} = \{x_i, y_i\}_{i=n^{tr}+1}^m$, we then can also describe a task $\mathcal{T}$ as $\{\mathcal{D}^{tr}, \mathcal{D}^{te}\}$. Given a model f_θ, the training aim is to obtain the optimal parameters θ to minimize the loss function:

$$Loss(f_\theta(D^{tr}, \{x_i\}_{i=n^{tr}+1}^m), \{y_i\}_{i=n^{tr}+1}^m))$$

which can be simply noted as $\mathcal{L}_{\mathcal{T}}^{\mathcal{D}^{te}}(f_\theta)$.

Based on this, the meta-learning considers model f as a learning process, which earn θ' from θ and give final prediction based on θ'. To find a globally shared parameters θ_g, we follow:

$$\min_{\theta_g} \Sigma_{k=1}^N Loss(f_{\theta_g}(\mathcal{D}_k^{tr}, \{x_{k,i}\}_{i=n^{tr}+1}^m), \{y_{k,i}\}_{i=n^{tr}+1}^m)) \tag{1}$$

Different meta-learning algorithms mainly diverge in f, which is also utilized in test phase to map θ_g to θ'_g for new task t_i and gain predictions corresponding.

3.2   The Gradient-Based Meta-Learning

Here, we compactly give an overview of the representative algorithm of gradient-based meta-learning, i.e. model-agnostic meta-learning. With the aim of searching for a globally sharing parameters initialization for unseen tasks, MAML

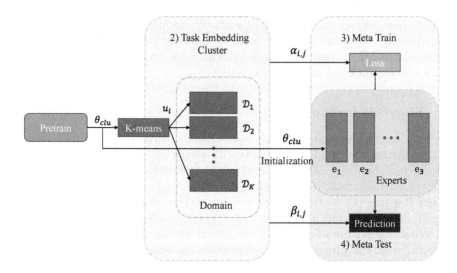

Fig. 1. The framework of EEML mainly concerns three stages: a) Task Embedding Cluster: We employ the $\theta_c lu$ to gain task gradient embedding u_i, then leverage K-means to get Domains. b) Meta Train: via calculating coefficients $\alpha_{i,j}$, we train experts towards costumed loss function. c) Meta Test: Given coefficients $\beta_{i,j}$, we gain cooperative results through weighted voting mechanism.

define learning process f like below. Formally, given the task distribution $p(\mathcal{T})$, we sample a task $\mathcal{T}_i$ from it and define the base learner as g_θ then we can get:

$$\theta'_i = \theta - \nabla_\theta \mathcal{L}_{\mathcal{T}_i}^{\mathcal{D}_i^{tr}} (g_\theta) \tag{2}$$

$$f_\theta(\mathcal{D}_i^{tr}, \{x_i\}_{i=n^{tr}+1}^m) = g_{\theta'_i}(\{x_i\}_{i=n^{tr}+1}^m) \tag{3}$$

To update θ, MAML then follows:

$$\theta \leftarrow \theta - \nabla_\theta \sum_{\mathcal{T}_i \sim p(\mathcal{T})} \mathcal{L}_{\mathcal{T}_i}^{\mathcal{D}_i^{te}} (f_{\theta_i}) \tag{4}$$

For simplicity of description, We define gradient of task $\mathcal{T}_i$, $\nabla_\theta \mathcal{L}_{\mathcal{T}_i}^{\mathcal{D}_i^{te}} (f_{\theta_i})$, as u_i in following sections.

4   Methodology

In this section, we detail the proposed EEML algorithm like the Fig. 1. The EEML aims to raise a group of experts covering heterogeneous knowledge domains in meta-training, then collect all experts opinions in a weighted voting schema to achieve better results in test phase. The following parts of this section are organized in task embedding cluster, meta-training and meta-test.

4.1   Task Embedding Cluster

Instead of abstracting task embedding from only labeled data, we argue that gradient u_i calculated in Eq. (4) can consider dynamical training process which implies optimization direction information ignored by static task embedding mechanism like auto-encoder or rnn-based encoder. With gradient u_i considered as task $\mathcal{T}_i$ embedding, we resorts to a classical cluster algorithm, K-means to divide sampled tasks into different groups. The distance function leveraged in K-means is cosine distance which focuses on the difference in direction instead of embedding norm. Given hyperparameter K, we then obtain K clusters which correspond to different optimization direction for specific model parameters θ_{clu}. We collect the centers of different clusters as $\{c_1, c_2, ..., c_K\}$. To measure the distance between future coming task and existing clusters, we follow the cosine distance as the standard metric.

4.2   Meta Train

Unlike training single dictator model, raising a group of experts should carefully maintain the balance between diversity and generalization. To start with a generic initialization, we initialize the experts $\{g_{e_1}, g_{e_2}, .., g_{e_K}\}$ as K copies from $g_{\theta_{clu}}$, whose generalization then can be controlled through parameter initialization θ_{clu}. To get an effective initialization without introducing too many operations, we simply exploit MAML to earn a relatively proper θ_{clu} as the initialization parameters for clustering and experts. We can adjust the pretraining via limiting the total training epochs.

In training stage, to strengthen the diversity of experts in training paradigm, we utilize the loss function below as the target training loss.

$$\mathcal{L}oss = \Sigma_{i=1}^{N} \Sigma_{j=1}^{K} \alpha_{i,j} \mathcal{L}_{\mathcal{T}_i}^{\mathcal{D}_i^{te}} (g_{e_j}) \tag{5}$$

The coefficient $\alpha_{i,j}$ would induce the final tendency of expert e_i towards specific tasks. In our assumption, a qualified expert e_i should be familiar with a task from a specific domain D_i while has no strict demanding about the competence for other tasks outside. We define the D_i as $\{\mathcal{T}_j | Dist(\mathcal{T}_j, c_i) = \min_{p=1:K} Dist(\mathcal{T}_j, c_p)\}$, which indicates a task $\mathcal{T}_j$ belonging to D_i should be nearest to the domain center c_i comparing with other domain centers. To expand the generalization, we do not assign coefficient $\alpha_{i,j}$ from the indicator of whether task $\mathcal{T}_i$ is in D_j, instead, we choose the cosine similarity metric after softmax layer as final $\alpha_{i,j}$ to ensure the probability sum as one.

In this paper, instead of considering static task embedding without any information from model, we decide to leverage the gradient u_i as the embedding of task $\mathcal{T}_i$. With both model optimization information and labelled data contained, the u_i help EEML achieve better performance.

$$\begin{aligned}
\alpha &= Softmax(Sim(\mathcal{T}_j, \mathbf{c})) \\
&= Softmax(\frac{u_i \cdot \mathbf{c}}{\|u_i\| \|\mathbf{c}\|})
\end{aligned} \tag{6}$$

4.3   Meta Test

Facing unseen task from heterogeneity distribution, single dictator model is insufficient and easy to be blind. In our paradigm, all experts are able to join the test phase through two steps. First, the experts fine-tune the parameters with training set $\mathcal{D}_i^{tr}$ from $\mathcal{T}_{test}$.

$$e_i' = e_i - \nabla_\theta \mathcal{L}_{\mathcal{T}_{test}}^{\mathcal{D}_{test}^{tr}}(e_i) \qquad (7)$$

With fine-tuned experts $\mathbf{e}' = e_1', e_2', ..., e_n'$. We leverage a weighted voting mechanism inspired by Bagging like:

$$p_j = \Sigma_{i=1}^K \beta_{i,j} g_{e_i'}(\mathcal{T}_j) \qquad (8)$$

The coefficient $\beta_{i,j}$ is designed as:

$$\beta_{i,j} = \frac{Sim(\mathcal{T}_j, c_i)}{err_{i,j}} \qquad (9)$$

The $err_{i,j}$ is the error value of training set $\mathcal{D}_j^{tr}$ with model g_{e_i}, which implies the adaptation level of expert e_i. Like $\alpha_{i,j}$ we also take the softmax function as filter to maintain probability property.

$$err_j = Softmax(\mathcal{L}_{\mathcal{T}_j}^{\mathcal{D}^{tr}}(g_{\mathbf{e}})) \qquad (10)$$

$\mathcal{L}_{\mathcal{T}_j}^{\mathcal{D}^{tr}}(g_{\mathbf{e}})$ is a vector composed of $\{\mathcal{L}_{\mathcal{T}_j}^{\mathcal{D}^{tr}}(g_{e_1}), \mathcal{L}_{\mathcal{T}_j}^{\mathcal{D}^{tr}}(g_{e_2}), ..., \mathcal{L}_{\mathcal{T}_j}^{\mathcal{D}^{tr}}(g_{e_K})\}$. In our paradigm, the final prediction of all experts would be considered based on the expert similarity with the task and the final performance. And the dictator mechanism which consists of only one final model can be considered as a specific instance when $K = 1$.

5   Experiments

In this section, we evaluate the effectiveness of our proposed EEML on both toy regression and complex image few-shot classification cases. This section is organized as Datasets and Implementation Details, Toy Regression, and Image Few-shot Classification.

Table 1. Toy regression function family definition details.

Function family	Formulation $(y(x))$	Parameters range			
		p_1	p_2	p_3	p_4
Sinusoids	$p_1 \sin(p_2 x + p_3)$	$[0.1, 5.0]$	$[0.8, 1.2]$	$[0, 2\pi]$	–
Line	$p_1 x + p_2$	$[-3.0, 3.0]$	$[-3.0, 3.0]$	–	–
Quadratic	$p_1 x^2 + p_2 x + p_3$	$[-0.2, 0.2]$	$[-2.0, 2.0]$	$[-3.0, 3.0]$	–
Cubic	$p_1 x^3 + p_2 x^2 + p_3 x + p_4$	$[-0.1, 0.1]$	$[-0.2, 0.2]$	$[-2.0, 2.0]$	$[-3.0, 3.0]$

5.1   Datasets and Implementation Details

Datasets for Regression and Classification. For toy regression, to compare with [8,35]. We follow the task design from four function families. They are (1) Sinusoids (2) Line (3) Cubic (4) Quadratic. See Table 1 for details of function definition. We also take MSE as the final evaluation metric. As for image few-shot classification, we use the widely accepted dataset, i.e. MiniImageNet, as benchmark to validate the effectiveness. MiniImageNt is a larger benchmark containing 100 classes randomly chosen from ImageNet ILSVRC-2012 challenge [24] with 600 images of size 84×84 pixels per class. It is split into 64 base classes, 16 validation classes and 20 novel classes.

Models for Regression and Classification. Following [8,35], we take 2 hidden layer mlp and 4-conv network as backbones for toy regression and image classification respectively. The related hyperparameters are listed in Table 2.

Table 2. Hyperparameters of the experiments.

Hyperparameter	Toy regression	MiniImageNet
Task batch size	32	32
Inner loop learning rate	0.001	0.03
Outer loop learning rate	0.001	0.001
Inner loop adaptation steps	5	5
Epoch for pretraining	15000	20000
Epoch for meta-train	5000	10000
K selected for k-means	4	3

Table 3. Performance of MSE ± 95% confidence intervals on toy regression tasks, averaged over 4,000 tasks. Both 5-shot and 10-shot results are reported.

Model	5-shot	10-shot
MAML	2.205 ± 0.121	0.761 ± 0.068
Meta-SGD	2.053 ± 0.117	0.836 ± 0.065
MT-net	2.435 ± 0.130	0.967 ± 0.056
HSML	0.856 ± 0.073	0.161 ± 0.021
EEML	$\mathbf{0.765 \pm 0.140}$	$\mathbf{0.151 \pm 0.032}$

5.2 Toy Regression

We compare our methods with recent state-of-the-art works in meta-learning, such as MAML, Meta-SGD, HSML. We can see from Table 3 that our method achieves better results which indicates the effectiveness of our ensemble mechanism.

Table 4. Accuracy of image few-shot classification problem on MiniImageNet. Comparing with gradient-based meta-learning on 1-shot and 5-shot cases with 4-conv model as backbone. The results are with $\pm 95\%$ confidence intervals.

Model	MiniImageNet	
	1-shot	5-shot
MAML	48.07 ± 1.75	63.15 ± 0.91
Meta-SGD	50.47 ± 1.87	64.03 ± 0.94
ANIL	46.70 ± 0.40	61.50 ± 0.50
BOIL	49.61 ± 0.16	66.45 ± 0.37
MT-net	51.70 ± 1.84	–
Sparse-MAML	50.35 ± 0.39	67.03 ± 0.74
HSML	50.38 ± 1.85	–
EEML	$\mathbf{52.42 \pm 1.75}$	$\mathbf{68.40 \pm 0.95}$

5.3 Image Few-Shot Classification

We keep comparing with recent SOTA methods in much more complex images classification problem. As the Table 4 show, our method improves at least %4 for original MAML, which easily outperform recent SOTA like Meta-SGD, MT-net, HSML. Both 1-shot and 5-shot cases earn stable improvement which validates the effectiveness of our method.

6 Conclusion

In this paper, we propose a novel ensemble embedded meta-learning (EEML) algorithm, and comparing with recent meta-learning on both toy regression and image few-shot classification tasks. The experiment results show that our method possesses great potential not only for simple task like function regression, but also complex task like image classification. Through replacing the single dictatorial expert with an cluster based ensemble voting mechanism, our method earn easily improvement comparing with recent state-of-the-arts.

Although our method already earns explicit effects on two benchmarks, the potential of combining ensemble learning with meta-learning still calls for more exploration. And in reality employment case, the hyperparameters should be searched carefully to gain better performance.

References

1. Baik, S., Hong, S., Lee, K.M.: Learning to forget for meta-learning. arXiv preprint arXiv:1906.05895 (2020)
2. Bengio, S., Bengio, Y., Cloutier, J., Gecsei, J.: On the optimization of a synaptic learning rule. In: Optimality in Biological and Artificial Networks? vol. 2, pp. 281–303. Routledge (1992)
3. Bertinetto, L., Henriques, J.F., Torr, P.H., Vedaldi, A.: Meta-learning with differentiable closed-form solvers. arXiv preprint arXiv:1805.08136 (2018)
4. Breiman, L.: Bagging predictors. Mach. Learn. **24**(2), 123–140 (1996). https://doi.org/10.1007/BF00058655
5. Breiman, L.: Random forests. Mach. Learn. **45**(1), 5–32 (2001). https://doi.org/10.1023/A:1010933404324
6. Denevi, G., Ciliberto, C., Grazzi, R., Pontil, M.: Learning-to-learn stochastic gradient descent with biased regularization. In: International Conference on Machine Learning, pp. 1566–1575. PMLR (2019)
7. Dong, X., Yu, Z., Cao, W., Shi, Y., Ma, Q.: A survey on ensemble learning. Front. Comput. Sci. **14**(2), 241–258 (2019). https://doi.org/10.1007/s11704-019-8208-z
8. Finn, C., Abbeel, P., Levine, S.: Model-agnostic meta-learning for fast adaptation of deep networks. arXiv preprint arXiv:1703.03400 (2017)
9. Finn, C., Xu, K., Levine, S.: Probabilistic model-agnostic meta-learning. arXiv preprint arXiv:1806.02817 (2018)
10. Grant, E., Finn, C., Levine, S., Darrell, T., Griffiths, T.: Recasting gradient-based meta-learning as hierarchical bayes. arXiv preprint arXiv:1801.08930 (2018)
11. Hochreiter, S., Younger, A.S., Conwell, P.R.: Learning to learn using gradient descent. In: Dorffner, G., Bischof, H., Hornik, K. (eds.) ICANN 2001. LNCS, vol. 2130, pp. 87–94. Springer, Heidelberg (2001). https://doi.org/10.1007/3-540-44668-0_13
12. Hospedales, T., Antoniou, A., Micaelli, P., Storkey, A.: Meta-learning in neural networks: a survey. IEEE Trans. Pattern Anal. Mach. Intell. **44**(9), 5149–5169 (2021). https://doi.org/10.48550/ARXIV.2004.05439
13. Koch, G., Zemel, R., Salakhutdinov, R.: Siamese neural networks for one-shot image recognition. In: ICML Deep Learning Workshop, vol. 2. Lille (2015)
14. Lee, K., Maji, S., Ravichandran, A., Soatto, S.: Meta-learning with differentiable convex optimization. In: Proceedings of the IEEE/CVF Conference on Computer Vision and Pattern Recognition, pp. 10657–10665 (2019)
15. Lee, Y., Choi, S.: Gradient-based meta-learning with learned layerwise metric and subspace. In: International Conference on Machine Learning, pp. 2927–2936. PMLR (2018)
16. Li, H., Eigen, D., Dodge, S., Zeiler, M., Wang, X.: Finding task-relevant features for few-shot learning by category traversal. In: Proceedings of the IEEE/CVF Conference on Computer Vision and Pattern Recognition, pp. 1–10 (2019)
17. Li, S., Xue, L., Feng, L., Wang, Y., Wang, D.: Object detection network pruning with multi-task information fusion. World Wide Web **25**(4), 1667–1683 (2022). https://doi.org/10.1007/s11280-021-00991-3
18. Li, Z., Zhou, F., Chen, F., Li, H.: Meta-SGD: learning to learn quickly for few-shot learning. arXiv preprint arXiv:1707.09835 (2017)
19. Munkhdalai, T., Yu, H.: Meta networks. In: International Conference on Machine Learning, pp. 2554–2563. PMLR (2017)

20. Munkhdalai, T., Yuan, X., Mehri, S., Trischler, A.: Rapid adaptation with conditionally shifted neurons. In: International Conference on Machine Learning, pp. 3664–3673. PMLR (2018)
21. Munkhdalai, T., Yuan, X., Mehri, S., Wang, T., Trischler, A.: Learning rapid-temporal adaptations. CoRR abs/1712.09926 (2017). http://arxiv.org/abs/1712.09926
22. Nichol, A., Achiam, J., Schulman, J.: On first-order meta-learning algorithms. arXiv preprint arXiv:1803.02999 (2018)
23. Oreshkin, B.N., Rodriguez, P., Lacoste, A.: TADAM: task dependent adaptive metric for improved few-shot learning. arXiv preprint arXiv:1805.10123 (2018)
24. Russakovsky, O., et al.: ImageNet large scale visual recognition challenge. Int. J. Comput. Vis. **115**(3), 211–252 (2015). https://doi.org/10.1007/s11263-015-0816-y
25. Rusu, A.A., Rao, D., Sygnowski, J., Vinyals, O., Pascanu, R., Osindero, S., Hadsell, R.: Meta-learning with latent embedding optimization. arXiv preprint arXiv:1807.05960 (2019)
26. Santoro, A., Bartunov, S., Botvinick, M., Wierstra, D., Lillicrap, T.: Meta-learning with memory-augmented neural networks. In: International Conference on Machine Learning, pp. 1842–1850. PMLR (2016)
27. Schapire, R.E.: Explaining AdaBoost. In: Schölkopf, B., Luo, Z., Vovk, V. (eds.) Empirical Inference, pp. 37–52. Springer, Heidelberg (2013). https://doi.org/10.1007/978-3-642-41136-6_5
28. Schmidhuber, J.: Learning to control fast-weight memories: an alternative to dynamic recurrent networks. Neural Comput. **4**(1), 131–139 (1992). https://doi.org/10.1162/neco.1992.4.1.131
29. Snell, J., Swersky, K., Zemel, R.S.: Prototypical networks for few-shot learning. arXiv preprint arXiv:1703.05175 (2017)
30. Sung, F., Yang, Y., Zhang, L., Xiang, T., Torr, P.H., Hospedales, T.M.: Learning to compare: relation network for few-shot learning. In: Proceedings of the IEEE Conference on Computer Vision and Pattern Recognition, pp. 1199–1208 (2018)
31. Thrun, S.: Lifelong Learning Algorithms. In: Thrun, S., Pratt, L. (eds) Learning to Learn, pp. 181–209. Springer, Boston (1998). https://doi.org/10.1007/978-1-4615-5529-2_8
32. Thrun, S., Pratt, L.: Learning to learn: introduction and overview. In: Thrun, S., Pratt, L. (eds) Learning to Learn, pp. 3–17. Springer, Boston (1998). https://doi.org/10.1007/978-1-4615-5529-2_1
33. Vilalta, R., Drissi, Y.: A perspective view and survey of meta-learning. Artif. Intell. Rev. **18**(2), 77–95 (2002)
34. Vinyals, O., Blundell, C., Lillicrap, T., Kavukcuoglu, K., Wierstra, D.: Matching networks for one shot learning. arXiv preprint arXiv:1606.04080 (2016)
35. Yao, H., Wei, Y., Huang, J., Li, Z.: Hierarchically structured meta-learning. In: International Conference on Machine Learning, pp. 7045–7054. PMLR (2019)
36. Yoon, J., Kim, T., Dia, O., Kim, S., Bengio, Y., Ahn, S.: Bayesian model-agnostic meta-learning. In: Proceedings of the 32nd International Conference on Neural Information Processing Systems, pp. 7343–7353 (2018)

Click is Not Equal to Purchase: Multi-task Reinforcement Learning for Multi-behavior Recommendation

Huiwang Zhang[1], Pengpeng Zhao[1(✉)], Xuefeng Xian[2(✉)], Victor S. Sheng[3], Yongjing Hao[1], and Zhiming Cui[4]

[1] School of Computer Science and Technology, Soochow University, Suzhou, China
{hwzhangcs,yjhaozb}@stu.suda.edu.cn, ppzhao@suda.edu.cn
[2] Suzhou Vocational University, Suzhou, China
xianxuefeng@jssvc.edu.cn
[3] Texas Tech University, Texas, USA
Victor.Sheng@ttu.edu
[4] SuZhou University of Science and Technology, Suzhou, China
zmcui@mail.usts.edu.cn

Abstract. Reinforcement learning (RL) has achieved ideal performance in recommendation systems (RS) by taking care of both immediate and future rewards from users. However, the existing RL-based recommendation methods assume that only a single type of interaction behavior (e.g., clicking) exists between user and item, whereas practical recommendation scenarios involve multiple types of user interaction behaviors (e.g., adding to cart, purchasing). In this paper, we propose a Multi-Task Reinforcement Learning model for multi-behavior Recommendation (MTRL4Rec), which gives different actions for users' different behaviors with a single agent. Specifically, we first introduce a modular network in which modules can be reused or isolated from each other to model the commonalities and differences between users' behaviors. Then a task routing network is used to generate routes in the modular network for each behavior task. Finally, we adopt a hierarchical reinforcement learning architecture to improve the efficiency of MTRL4Rec. Experiments on two public datasets validated the effectiveness of MTRL4Rec.

Keywords: Recommendation system · Multi-behavior · Reinforcement learning · Multi-task

1 Introduction

Recommendation systems assist users by suggesting personalized items that best fit their needs and preferences. The methods of RS can be summarized into three categories: traditional methods, deep learning (DL) based methods, and reinforcement learning (RL) based methods. Traditional recommendation methods, whose main idea is to recommend items with similar attributes to people with

R. Chbeir et al. (Eds.): WISE 2022, LNCS 13724, pp. 443–459, 2022.
https://doi.org/10.1007/978-3-031-20891-1_32

similar interests, mainly include collaborative filtering [3], content-based filtering [10], etc. The DL-based methods have become the current mainstream due to their capability of modeling complex user-item interactions [7,18,20,23].

Since the traditional methods and DL-based methods cannot continuously update the strategies during the interactions and maximize the expected long-term cumulative reward from users, RL-based methods were proposed. For example, Shani et al. [13] modeled recommendation systems as a Markov Decision Process (MDP) and estimated the transition probability and the Q-value table. Zheng et al. [25] proposed a Deep Q-Network (DQN) based method which can take care of both immediate and future rewards. Zhao et al. [24] argued that some recommended items that users skipped can influence the recommendation performance and proposed a model considering both positive feedback and negative feedback. Per et al. [11] proposed an RL-based value-aware recommendation to maximize the profit in an E-commerce scenario. Wang et al. [16] built a Knowledge-guided Reinforcement Learning model (KERL) for fusing knowledge graph information into an RL-based sequential recommendation system. Zhao et al. [22] designed a deep hierarchical reinforcement learning model to overcome the problem of sparse feedback signals in recommendation systems.

However, existing RL-based recommendation methods ignore the interest gap in the different behaviors of users. The interest gap means that users have different preferences on different behaviors. In simple terms, a person may be interested in an item and click on it, but never buy it. It pays off to value this difference and use several recommendation strategies. For example, the recommendation on the homepage should use a click-targeted strategy, and when placing an order, it should be a purchase-targeted strategy. Suppose we treat each behavior as an individual task, and build several independent models with existing methods for multi-behavior recommendation. It costs too much and ignores the commonality between tasks since the models are independent.

To this end, we propose a **Multi-Task Reinforcement Learning for** multi-behavior **Rec**ommendation (MTRL4Rec), which gives different actions for users' different behaviors with a single policy. We use a modular network to model the commonalities and differences between behavior tasks. The modular network consists of several Modular Units (MoUs). A task routing network is used to select routes automatically for different behavior tasks in the modular network. It reweighs the outputs of each MoU in the modular network for different behavior tasks. In this way, the MoUs that model commonalities of tasks can be reused, and the MoUs that model differences of tasks can be isolated. To improve the model's efficiency, we adopt a hierarchical reinforcement learning structure that consists of a high-level agent and a low-level agent. The high-level agent is a category selector which generates the category that should be recommended. In contrast, the low-level agent recommends a specific item to users in the category selected by the high-level agent. Finally, we evaluated our method on pre-trained environment simulators, as [24]. Experiments on two datasets validate the effectiveness of our model. Our model outperforms the state-of-the-art models in both offline test and online test. Moreover, we further give sufficient ablation test and parameter analyses to better understand our model. We summarize our major contributions as follows:

- To the best of our knowledge, this is the first work to treat the multi-behaviors as multi-tasks in a RL-based recommendation.
- We propose the MTRL4Rec model which uses a modular network and a task routing network to solve the multi-task problem in multi-behavior recommendation with reinforcement learning.
- Experimental results demonstrate that users do have different preferences in different behaviors, and our MTRL4Rec model outperforms state-of-the-art models in multi-behavior recommendation.

2   Related Work

In this section, we briefly review related work, including RL in recommendation and multi-task learning.

2.1   Reinforcement Learning in Recommendation

Some works use reinforcement learning to continuously update the strategy during the interaction and maximize the expected long-term cumulative reward from users [25]. Shani et al. [13] modeled the recommender system as an MDP process and estimated the transition probability and the Q-value table. Zheng et al. [25] proposed a DQN based method that can take care of both immediate and future reward. Zhao et al. [24] argued that some recommended items that users skipped can influence the recommendation performance and proposed a model considering both positive feedback and negative feedback. Per et al. [11] built an RL-based value-aware recommendation to maximize the profit of a RS directly. Bai et al. [1] proposed a solution to more effectively utilize log data with model-based RL algorithms to avoid the high interaction cost. Wang et al. [16] proposed a KERL model for fusing knowledge graph information into an RL-based sequential recommendation system. Hierarchical reinforcement learning (HRL) was proposed to solve more complex and difficult problems in the work of Barto and Mahadevan [2]. Zhao et al. [22] designed a multi-goals abstraction based HRL algorithm to overcome the problem of sparse feedback signals in recommendation systems. However, these are all single-task methods and cannot perform well in multi-behavior recommendation systems.

2.2   Multi-task Learning

Multi-task learning (MTL) is one of the core topics of machine learning [4]. Many researches [12] have shown that multiple objectives make different tasks benefit each other. Some works adopt MTL to improve the recommendation performance. MOE [5] is proposed to share some experts at the bottom and combine experts through a gating network. Ma et al. [8] extended MOE to utilize different gates for each task to obtain different fusing weights in MTL. Tang et al. [15] found seesaw phenomena in MTL and proposed a progressive layered extraction method. Multi-task Learning is also a challenging problem in RL. Singh [14] proposed a method of selecting different Q functions for different tasks using a gate mechanism. Wilson et al. [17] proposed a hierarchical Bayesian-based multi-task RL framework. Instead of directly selecting routes for each task, a soft modularization method is proposed in the work of Yang et al. [21] to softly combine possible routes. However, no previous work has attempted to improve multi-behavior recommendation using multi-task reinforcement learning. In this work, we use a multi-task reinforcement learning framework with modular networks and task routing networks to implement the multi-behavior recommendation.

3 Method

We model recommendation tasks on different behaviors as several Markov Decision Processes (MDPs) and leverage reinforcement learning to automatically learn the optimal recommendation strategy. The user is the environment, while the recommender system that recommends items to users is the agent. The user's information and interaction history is the state of the environment. According to the current state, the agent selects an action (recommends an item to the user). The feedback from the users is seen as a reward to the agent. Then the agent is updated according to the reward, and the following interaction starts.

We Define Our Problem as Follows: When a user u interacts with the agent (i.e., the recommendation system) and has a request on task (behavior) t, the agent is going to select an action a from the item set for this user. Then, the agent observes the user's feedback r and adjusts the policy for the next time recommendation.

3.1 Basic RL Model for Multi-behavior Recommendation

In this subsection, we discuss two methods to implement multi-behavior recommendation using existing RL-based recommendation methods. As shown in Fig. 1(a), each task has its corresponding agent. Recommendation agents for different behaviors are completely independent of each other. Figure 1(b) depicts another method. In this method, we allow the agent to observe the state, action, and reward of other tasks to improve its performance.

Algorithm 1 describes this method formally. The agents and replay memories are initialized in Line 1–2. At the beginning of each session, we use the previous session as the current state (Line 4). Before each interaction step, we call all single-task agents to generate recommended items for each task (Line 6–7). When a user requests, we give a corresponding recommendation a_i^t based on the user's behavior task t, observe the reward r_i from the user, and store this transition to the replay memory D_t (Line 8–11). Then we sample some transitions from D_t and update the current agent A_t as defined in each RL method (Line 12–13).

MTRL4Rec

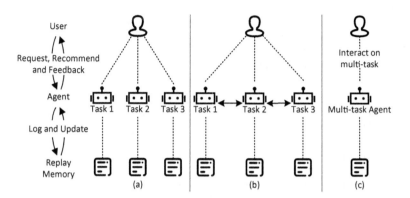

(a)   (b)   (c)

Fig. 1. The RL Model for Multi-behavior Recommendation. (a) Recommendation agents for different behavior tasks are completely independent of each other. Each task has its corresponding agent. (b) The tasks are still independent of each other, but agents can observe each other. (c) One agent is responsible for all tasks. An MTRL4Rec model, which is in this framework, is proposed in Subsect. 3.2.

3.2   The Proposed MTRL4Rec Model

We have proposed two methods to implement multi-behavior recommendation using existing RL based methods in the previous subsection. However, as we mentioned in the introduction, existing RL based methods cannot capture the commonalities between tasks, and tasks cannot benefit from each other. To overcome these problems, we propose a Multi-Task Reinforcement Learning for multi-behavior Recommendation (MTRL4Rec). In our method, a single agent serves multi-behavior recommendation as shown in Fig. 1(c). Next, we will describe our MTRL4Rec in detail.

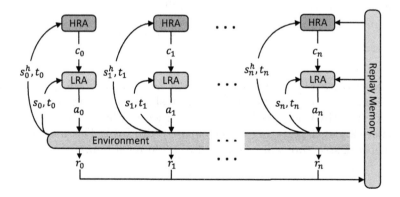

Fig. 2. The hierarchical RL framework of our model. In each step of the interaction, the high-level agent (HRA) chooses a category, and the low-level agent (LRA) recommends an item in the category HRA selected.

Algorithm 1. Off-policy Training of Single-task RL Model for Multi-behavior Recommendation

1: Initialize the parameters of single-task agents $A = \{A_1, A_2, \ldots\}$ for each tasks
2: Initialize the replay memories $D = \{D_1, D_2, \ldots\}$ for each tasks
3: **for** session $= 1, M$ **do**
4:     Initialize state s_0 from previous sessions
5:     **for** step $i = 1, T$ **do**
6:         **for** task t in $task\_list$ **do**
7:             generate a_i^t with A_t
8:         Observe user's behavior as t
9:         Execute action a_i^t
10:        Observe reward r_i and next state s_{t+1} from user
11:        Store transition $(s_i, a_i^t, r_i, s_{i+1})$ in D_t
12:        Sample minibatch of transitions from D_t
13:        Update parameters of current task agent A_t
14:        **if** s_{i+1} is terminal state **then**
15:            break

Hierarchical RL Structure. For higher exploration and exploitation efficiency in RL, a hierarchical structure is adopted in our model, which consists of a high-level agent (HRA) and a low-level agent (LRA), as shown in Fig. 2.

The high-level agent is a category selector. The input of the HRA network is a state-category-task tuple (s^h, c, t). And it outputs a score of the category $Q_H(s^h, c, t; \theta^H)$. Then HRA generates the category that should be recommended following an ε-greedy strategy according to:

$$c_i^t = \arg\max_c Q_H(s_i^h, c, t; \theta^H). \tag{1}$$

In other words, the agent chooses the category with the highest score with a probability of $1 - \varepsilon$, or randomly chooses a category with the probability ε to explore. Similarly, the low-level agent recommends specific items to users based on the output of the high-level agent according to:

$$a_i^t = \arg\max_{cate(a)=c_i^t} Q_L(s_i, a, t; \theta^L). \tag{2}$$

LRA Network. The structure of the LRA network is shown in Fig. 3. It has three important components (embedding, task routing network, and modular network). The HRA network has a similar structure whose action space and the state space are at the category level compared with LRA. The illustration of the HRA network structure will be omitted to avoid repetition.

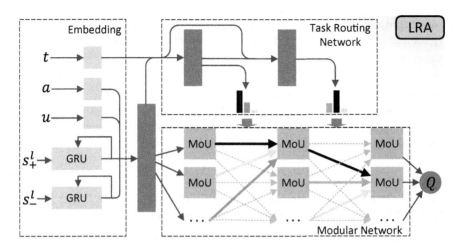

Fig. 3. LRA network. It has three critical components (embedding, modular network, and task routing network). The modular network captures the commonalities and differences of tasks, and the task routing network selects a route for each task.

Embedding. The role of this component is to process the input of the network. The one-hot inputs (action, user, and task tag) are mapped as vectors. Two RNN models with GRU are utilized. One RNN receives the user's latest interacted item sequence s_+ as inputs and outputs the final hidden state of GRU cells. And another receives the negative item sequence s_- (items that the user skipped) as inputs and outputs the final hidden state of GRU cells. Finally, a fully connected layer merges the action, user, and item sequences (positive and negative) information. Task information is only used as a part of the input of the Task Routing Network.

Modular Network. To improve the performance of the model on multiple tasks, we build a Modular Network to capture the commonalities and differences of tasks. The Modular Network has multiple layers, and each layer has M Modular Units (MoUs), as shown in Fig. 3. In this way, MoUs that model commonalities can be reused, and MoUs that model differences can be isolated from each other in different tasks. Each MoU has the same multi-layer fully connected structure, as shown in Fig. 4.

Task Routing Network. The role of the task routing network is to control the route of different tasks in the modular network. In addition to the current state, the input of the task routing network also contains the current task, which is not considered in the modular network. It is also a multi-layer structure with one fewer layers than the modular network. Figure 4 depicts how the task routing network controls the weight of each MoU. Each layer of the task routing network outputs a weight matrix W_l and a hidden state H_l, according to

$$(W_l, H_l) = TR_l(s, t, H_{l-1}) \tag{3}$$

where s is the current state embedding, t is the current task embedding, and H_{l-1} is the hidden state of the last layer. We set H_0 as a zero vector. The weight matrix reweighs the outputs of each MoU in the modular network for different tasks. The input of an MoU in the the modular network can be calculated by

$$X_{l+1,k} = softmax(W_{l,k})Y_l, 1 \leq k \leq M, \tag{4}$$

where $W_{l,k}$ is a column vector in W_l for the k-th MoU in layer l, and Y_l is the output of MoUs in the l-th layer of the modular network.

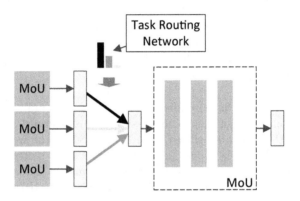

Fig. 4. The structure of Modular Unit (MoU). Each MoU has the same multi-layer fully connected structure. The weight of MoU is controlled by the task routing network.

Off-Policy Training Algorithm. In the MTRL4Rec method, both HRA and LRA adopt the DQN architecture. Here we will illustrate how to utilize the DQN based algorithm to train our MTRL4Rec model.

First, we randomly initialize the HRA network parameters θ^H and the LRA network parameters θ^L and create an empty replay memory D. At the beginning of a session, we set the initial state s_0 as the user's information and previous session. Before each interaction step i , we call the HRA to generate different item categories $\{c_i^{t_1}, c_i^{t_2}, \ldots\}$ according Eq. (1) for different behavior tasks $\{t_1, t_2, \ldots\}$. Then we call the LRA to generate different items $\{a_i^{t_1}, a_i^{t_2}, \ldots\}$ for each task according Eq. (2). When the user requests on behavior t, we give the corresponding recommendation a_i^t and observe the feedback from the user. If the user interacted with the item, we set the current reward $r_i = 1$, add a_i^t to the positive item sequence s_+ and generate next state s_{i+1}. Otherwise, we set current reward $r_i = 0$ and add a_i^t to the negative item sequence s_-. Then the transition $< s_i, t, a_i^t, r_i, s_{i+1} >$ will be stored to the replay memory D. We sample a mini-batch of transitions $< s, t, a, r, s' >$ from D and update HRA network parameters θ^H and the LRA network parameters θ^L. The LRA network has the loss function:

$$Loss^L(\theta^L) = \mathbb{E}_{s,a,r,s',t}(y_L - Q_L(s,a,t;\theta^L))^2, \tag{5}$$

where y_L is the target for the current iteration, as in Eq. (6).

$$y_L = \begin{cases} r & \text{terminal } s' \\ r + \gamma \max_{a'} Q_L(s', a', t; \theta^L) & \text{otherwise} \end{cases} \tag{6}$$

Algorithm 2. Off-policy Training of Multi-task Reinforcement Learning Model for Multi-behavior Recommendation

---

1: Initialize the HRA network parameters θ^H and the LRA network parameters θ^L
2: Initialize the replay memory D
3: **for** session $= 1, M$ **do**
4:     Initialize state s_0 from previous sessions
5:     **for** step $i = 1, T$ **do**
6:         **for** task t in $task\_list$ **do**
7:             generate c_i^t according to Eq. (1)
8:             generate item a_i^t according to Eq. (2)
9:         Observe user's behavior as t
10:         Execute action a_i^t
11:         Observe reward r_i and next state s_{i+1} from user
12:         Store transition $< s_i, t, a_i^t, r_i, s_{i+1} >$ in D
13:         Sample minibatch of transitions $< s, t, a, r, s' >$ from D
14:         Update the LRA network parameters θ^L based of Eq. (7)
15:         Update the HRA network parameters θ^H based of Eq. (10)
16:         **if** s_{i+1} is terminal state **then**
17:             break

The hyper-parameter γ is a discount factor that controls the weight of future reward. Equation (5) can be minimized according to:

$$\nabla_{\theta^L} Loss^L(\theta^L) = \mathbb{E}_{s,a,r,s',t}[(y_L - Q_L(s,a,t;\theta^L)) \\ \nabla_{\theta^L} Q_L(s,a,t;\theta^L)]. \tag{7}$$

Similarly, the HRA ignores specific items and generates candidate categories for each behavior task. The state of HRA, s^h, is generated from s. It ignores the specific item information and keeps the category information. The HRA network has the loss function:

$$Loss^H(\theta^H) = \mathbb{E}_{s^h,cate(a),r,s^{h'},t}(y_H - Q_H(s^h, cate(a), t; \theta^H))^2, \tag{8}$$

where $cate(x)$ is the category of item x and y_H is calculated from Eq. (9).

$$y_H = \begin{cases} r & \text{terminal } s^{h'} \\ r + \gamma \max_c Q_L(s^{h'}, c, t; \theta^H) & \text{otherwise} \end{cases} \tag{9}$$

The HRA network parameters θ^H can be updated according to:

$$\nabla_{\theta^H} Loss^H(\theta^H) = \mathbb{E}_{s^h,cate(a),r,s^{h'},t}[(y_H - Q_H(s^h, cate(a), t; \theta^H)) \\ \nabla_{\theta^H} Q_H(s^h, cate(a), t; \theta^H)]. \tag{10}$$

Formally, Algorithm 2 describes the process of off-policy training for our MTRL4Rec model.

4   Experiment

In this section, we conduct a series of experiments with the two public datasets to evaluate the effectiveness of our proposed MTRL4Rec. We mainly focus on four research questions (RQs): **RQ1:** How does the proposed MTRL4Rec perform compared to baselines? **RQ2:** How do the components in MTRL4Rec contribute to performance? **RQ3:** Can MTRL4Rec achieve better performance in the interaction with the online environment? **RQ4:** How do the key hyper-parameters affect the model performance?

4.1   Datasets

We evaluate our model on two public datasets.

Tmall[1] is a dataset of user behaviors from Tmall for recommendation problems with implicit feedback offered by Alibaba. This dataset randomly selects users' behavior logs, including clicking, purchasing, adding items to shopping cart and item favouring, during November 25 to December 03, 2017. The dataset is organized in a very similar form to MovieLens-20M.

Another dataset is **Tianchi**[2] from the Tianchi competition. It is sampled from Taobao mobile application and has a similar structure to the Tmall dataset. Compared with Tmall, Tianchi contains side information of users and items.

---

[1] https://tianchi.aliyun.com/dataset/dataDetail?dataId=649.
[2] https://tianchi.aliyun.com/dataset/dataDetail?dataId=46.

Since the data on item favoring is too sparse, in the following experiment, we choose clicking, purchasing, and adding items to shopping cart as three different behavior tasks and discard the data on item favoring.

4.2   Baselines

We compare our MTRL4Rec model with two types of baselines. The first is the state-of-the-art RL-based recommendation methods to demonstrate the overall performance of our MTRL4Rec. We use the method in Algorithm 1 to implement the multi-behavior recommendation for comparison. The second type is the variants of our MTRL4Rec model to show its ablation performance. In detail, we compare our MTRL4Rec method with the following baselines: **DQN** [9]: This is a single task method with a deep Q-network. We use an independent deep Q-network for each task. **DEERS** [24]: This baseline adopts a classical DQN framework and considers both positive feedback and negative feedback. And a pairwise regularization term is used to maximize the difference of Q-values between positive items and negative items. **HRL**: This is a baseline with a hierarchical RL structure like [19,22]. For fairness, both the high-level agent and the low-level agent adopt the DQN framework. **X+MT**: We add task tags to the state to adapt existing methods to the multi-behavior recommendation. The baseline HRL+MT(MTRL4Rec w/o M) is also a variant of our model whose modular network is replaced by fully connected layers. **MTRL4Rec w/o R**: To verify the influence of the routing network, we removed it and set the weights of the MoUs in the modular network to be equal. **MTRL4Rec w/o H**: This variant is to evaluate the performance of the hierarchical RL structure. So the users interact with the LRA directly.

4.3   Simulator

Due to the difficulty and huge cost of A/B tests, we train our method and RL based baselines on a simulated environment as [22,24]. The simulated environment is trained on users' logs. The simulator is a deep neural network. It outputs a one-hot vector that predicts the immediate feedback for a state-action pair $< s, a >$ for every behavior task t. We tested the simulator on users' logs (not the data for training), and experimental results suggest that the simulated online environment can predict immediate feedback accurately and simulate the real online environment. This enables us to train and test our model on it. To get closer to reality, the simulator randomly requests on different behavior tasks according to the distribution of different behaviors in the dataset.

Moreover, the user randomly terminates the session with a probability of $1 - p_i$ in each step. If the user interacted with the last recommended item a_{i-1}, we set p_i as 1. Otherwise, we set p_i as $p_{i-1}d_p$, where d_p is a patient discount factor, a hyper-parameter between $0 - 1$. This means that if the agent cannot recommend satisfactory items to users, the users may terminate the session earlier.

4.4 Offline Test (RQ1 and RQ2)

In the offline test, we re-rank the items from users' log in a testing set according to items' Q-values output by the models. The interacted items will be ranked at the top of the ranked new list if a method works well. For the hierarchical RL algorithm, we use their LRA to re-rank these items. We select Hit Ratio @K (HR@K) and Normalized Discounted Cumulative Gain @K (NDCG@K) [6] as metrics to measure the performance of methods, where $K \in \{5, 10\}$. The modular network has 6 layers, and each layer has 4 MoUs ($M = 4$). The learning rate in RL is 0.01. We set the patient discount p_d of the simulator as 0.98.

The experimental results are shown in Table 1.

Table 1. Performance comparisons among different models. We evaluate our model and baselines on two public datasets. There are 3 lines for each method, corresponding to performance on 3 behavior tasks (clicking, purchasing, and adding items to shopping cart). Our experimental results show that our model outperforms most baseline methods on different tasks.

Methods	Tmall				Tianchi			
	HR	NDCG	HR	NDCG	HR	NDCG	HR	NDCG
	@5		@10		@5		@10	
DQN	0.2718	0.1630	0.5363	0.2448	0.3150	0.1863	0.5965	0.2706
	0.2812	0.1666	0.5286	0.2458	0.3279	0.1990	0.6257	0.2830
	0.2947	0.1783	0.5376	0.2549	0.3302	0.2026	0.6032	0.2822
DQN+MT	0.2718	0.1609	0.5238	0.2384	0.3268	0.1940	0.5787	0.2711
	0.2746	0.1642	0.5286	0.2460	0.3279	0.1954	0.6175	0.2808
	0.2871	0.1740	0.5384	0.2463	0.3333	0.2070	0.6063	0.2887
DEERS	0.2714	0.1623	0.5318	0.2419	0.3248	0.1913	0.5768	0.2667
	0.2840	0.1692	0.5239	0.2447	0.3251	0.2044	0.5929	0.2937
	0.2796	0.1646	0.5225	0.2416	0.3238	0.1971	0.6063	0.2856
HRL	0.2784	0.1648	0.5290	0.2428	0.3248	0.2025	0.5906	0.2859
	0.2812	0.1663	0.5361	0.2458	0.3497	0.2118	0.6093	0.2925
	0.2913	0.1763	0.5451	0.2565	0.3556	0.2067	0.6222	0.2909
HRL+MT (MTRL4Rec w/o M)	0.2746	0.1629	0.5297	0.2436	0.3287	0.2036	0.6004	0.2813
	0.2826	0.1690	0.5380	0.2464	0.3361	0.2077	0.6230	0.2909
	0.2963	0.1768	0.5668	0.2625	0.3492	0.2183	0.6349	0.2923
MTRL4Rec w/o R	0.2812	0.1699	0.5349	0.2510	0.3425	0.2052	0.6201	0.2896
	0.2793	0.1678	0.5239	0.2450	0.3770	0.2270	0.6230	0.3015
	0.2796	0.1682	0.5384	0.2496	0.4000	0.2518	0.6667	0.3240
MTRL4Rec w/o H	0.2714	0.1590	0.5189	0.2372	0.3150	0.1870	0.5965	0.2670
	0.2666	0.1546	0.5206	0.2352	0.3087	0.1850	0.5656	0.2630
	0.3097	0.1859	0.5434	0.2603	0.3111	0.1907	0.5810	0.2740
MTRL4Rec	**0.3034**	**0.1824**	**0.5554**	**0.2623**	**0.3543**	**0.2230**	**0.6201**	**0.3011**
	0.3079	**0.1886**	**0.5515**	**0.2659**	**0.4153**	**0.2622**	**0.6803**	**0.3466**
	0.3222	**0.2028**	**0.5701**	**0.2811**	**0.4159**	**0.2559**	**0.6857**	**0.3331**

We can find the following four points:

- Comparing the performance difference between X and X+MT, we find that X+MT has better performances on some behaviors. This proves that recommendation tasks with different behaviors can benefit each other. However, the improvement is not significant since the X+MTs cannot well model the commonalities and differences of different behavior tasks of users.
- Our MTRL4Rec method outperforms baselines on all tasks. It can better capture the similarities and differences of users' different behaviors. It has greater capability in a multi-behavior recommendation scenario.
- The ablation tests (experiment on variants of MTRL4Rec) demonstrate that our model's hierarchical structure, modular network, and routing network are all meaningful for multi-behavior recommendation.
- On sparse behaviors, our MTRL4Rec method achieves larger performance gains. The reason is that the task on sparse behavior can benefit from other tasks, and our MTRL4Rec, with a modular network and a task routing network, has a better ability to capture the features of sparse behaviors.

4.5 Online Test (RQ3)

We do the online test in the simulated online environment. Due to limited space, we compare our method with the best baseline in the offline test.

In the online test, we choose Session Length and Average Reward as metrics to measure the performance of methods. Longer Session Length proves that the model works better. Because when the agent cannot recommend satisfactory items to the user, the user may have a greater probability of terminating the current session. The second metric, Average Reward, describes the average reward per step in a session.

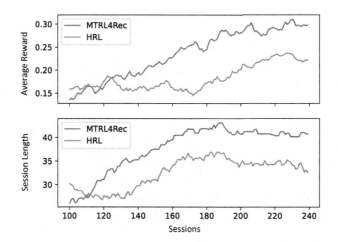

Fig. 5. Online test performance comparison. Data is smoothed by a sliding window.

Figure 5 shows the online test result. Due to the instability of reinforcement learning at the beginning of a training, we make comparisons starting from session 100. To ignore the noise, the data in Fig. 5 is smoothed by a sliding window as

$$data'_i = avg([data_{i-k+1}, \ldots, data_i]). \tag{11}$$

Here we set $k = 30$. We can find that the average reward obtained by MTRL4Rec is greater than the baselines. And it increases faster in training. The number of steps in sessions of MTRL4Rec is also greater than baselines, which indirectly shows that it brings better customer satisfaction.

4.6   Parameter Analysis (RQ4)

Our method has two key parameters: the discount factor γ controls the weight of future reward, and M is the number of MoU in a layer of modular networks. To study the impact of these parameters, we investigate how the proposed framework works with the changes of one parameter while fixing other parameters.

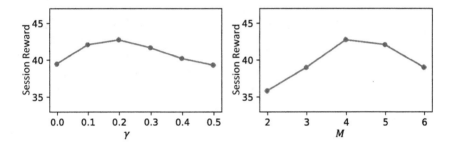

Fig. 6. Results of parameter analysis.

Figure 6 shows the parameter sensitivity of our model to γ and M. The metric to measure the performance is the average cumulative reward in a number of consecutive sessions. The performance of MTRL4Rec achieves the peak when $\gamma = 0.2$. In other words, considering future reward indeed improves the performance of the model. However, it is less important than the current reward. A small γ also appears in other RL-based recommendation researches [19,25].

In terms of the parametric analysis of M, MTRL4Rec has the best performance when $M = 4$. We analyze that the modular network with a small M does not have enough MoUs to capture the commonalities and differences between users' behaviors. When M is too large, there may be redundant and similar

MoUs, which reduce the model performance. In future work, we may build a mechanism to force MoUs in the modular network to have low similarity to further improve the performance.

5 Conclusion

In this paper, we proposed a Multi-Task Reinforcement Learning model for multi-behavior Recommendation (MTRL4Rec), which gives different actions for users' different behaviors with a single policy. We treated the recommendation for different behaviors to users as different tasks and built a multi-task reinforcement learning based recommendation model. We use a modular network to capture the commonalities and differences between users' behaviors, and use a task routing network to generate routes in the modular network for each behavior task. Our MTRL4Rec model adopts a hierarchical structure for higher exploration and exploitation efficiency. We demonstrate the effectiveness of the proposed MTRL4Rec in real-world e-commerce datasets and validate the importance of multi-task reinforcement learning for multi-behaviors recommendation.

Acknowledgements. This research was partially supported by the NSFC (61876117, 61876217, 62176175), the major project of natural science research in Universities of Jiangsu Province (21KJA520004) and Project Funded by the Priority Academic Program Development of Jiangsu Higher Education Institutions.

References

1. Bai, X., Guan, J., Wang, H.: A model-based reinforcement learning with adversarial training for online recommendation. Adv. Neural. Inf. Process. Syst. **32**, 10734–10745 (2019)
2. Barto, A.G., Mahadevan, S.: Recent advances in hierarchical reinforcement learning. Discret. Event Dyn. Syst. **13**(1–2), 41–77 (2003)
3. Breese, J.S., Heckerman, D., Kadie, C.M.: Empirical analysis of predictive algorithms for collaborative filtering. arXiv preprint arXiv:1301.7363 (2013)
4. Caruana, R.: Multitask learning. Mach. Learn. **28**(1), 41–75 (1997). https://doi.org/10.1023/A:1007379606734
5. Jacobs, R.A., Jordan, M.I., Nowlan, S.J., Hinton, G.E.: Adaptive mixtures of local experts. Neural Comput. **3**(1), 79–87 (1991)
6. Järvelin, K., Kekäläinen, J.: Cumulated gain-based evaluation of IR techniques. ACM Trans. Inf. Syst. **20**(4), 422–446 (2002)
7. Liu, J., et al.: Exploiting aesthetic preference in deep cross networks for cross-domain recommendation. In: Proceedings of the Web Conference, pp. 2768–2774 (2020)

8. Ma, J., Zhao, Z., Yi, X., Chen, J., Hong, L., Chi, E.H.: Modeling task relationships in multi-task learning with multi-gate mixture-of-experts. In: Proceedings of the 24th ACM SIGKDD International Conference on Knowledge Discovery & Data Mining, pp. 1930–1939 (2018)

9. Mnih, V., et al.: Playing Atari with deep reinforcement learning. arXiv preprint arXiv:1312.5602 (2013)

10. Mooney, R.J., Roy, L.: Content-based book recommending using learning for text categorization. In: Proceedings of the Fifth ACM Conference on Digital Libraries, pp. 195–204 (2000)

11. Pei, C., et al.: Value-aware recommendation based on reinforcement profit maximization. In: The World Wide Web Conference, pp. 3123–3129 (2019)

12. Pinto, L., Gupta, A.: Learning to push by grasping: using multiple tasks for effective learning. In: IEEE International Conference on Robotics and Automation, pp. 2161–2168 (2017)

13. Shani, G., Heckerman, D., Brafman, R.I.: An MDP-based recommender system. J. Mach. Learn. Res. **6**, 1265–1295 (2005)

14. Singh, S.P.: Transfer of learning by composing solutions of elemental sequential tasks. Mach. Learn. **8**, 323–339 (1992)

15. Tang, H., Liu, J., Zhao, M., Gong, X.: Progressive layered extraction (PLE): a novel multi-task learning (MTL) model for personalized recommendations. In: Fourteenth ACM Conference on Recommender Systems, pp. 269–278 (2020)

16. Wang, P., Fan, Y., Xia, L., Zhao, W.X., Niu, S., Huang, J.: KERL: a knowledge-guided reinforcement learning model for sequential recommendation. In: Proceedings of the 43rd International ACM SIGIR Conference on Research and Development in Information Retrieval, pp. 209–218 (2020)

17. Wilson, A., Fern, A., Ray, S., Tadepalli, P.: Multi-task reinforcement learning: a hierarchical Bayesian approach. In: Proceedings of the 24th International Conference on Machine Learning, vol. 227, pp. 1015–1022 (2007)

18. Xiao, K., Ye, Z., Zhang, L., Zhou, W., Ge, Y., Deng, Y.: Multi-user mobile sequential recommendation for route optimization. ACM Trans. Knowl. Discov. Data **14**(5), 52:1–52:28 (2020)

19. Xie, R., Zhang, S., Wang, R., Xia, F., Lin, L.: Hierarchical reinforcement learning for integrated recommendation. In: Proceedings of the AAAI Conference on Artificial Intelligence, pp. 4521–4528 (2021)

20. Xu, C., et al.: Long- and short-term self-attention network for sequential recommendation. Neurocomputing **423**, 580–589 (2021)

21. Yang, R., Xu, H., Wu, Y., Wang, X.: Multi-task reinforcement learning with soft modularization. Adv. Neural. Inf. Process. Syst. **33**, 4767–4777 (2020)

22. Zhao, D., Zhang, L., Zhang, B., Zheng, L., Bao, Y., Yan, W.: MaHRL: multi-goals abstraction based deep hierarchical reinforcement learning for recommendations. In: Proceedings of the 43rd International ACM SIGIR Conference on Research and Development in Information Retrieval, pp. 871–880 (2020)

23. Zhao, J., Zhao, P., Zhao, L., Liu, Y., Sheng, V.S., Zhou, X.: Variational self-attention network for sequential recommendation. In: 2021 IEEE 37th International Conference on Data Engineering (ICDE), pp. 1559–1570 (2021)

24. Zhao, X., Zhang, L., Ding, Z., Xia, L., Tang, J., Yin, D.: Recommendations with negative feedback via pairwise deep reinforcement learning. In: Proceedings of the 24th ACM SIGKDD International Conference on Knowledge Discovery & Data Mining, pp. 1040–1048 (2018)
25. Zheng, G., et al.: DRN: a deep reinforcement learning framework for news recommendation. In: Proceedings of the 2018 World Wide Web Conference, pp. 167–176 (2018)

Learning and Optimization

Multi-document Question Answering Powered by External Knowledge

Zhenting Yan and Weiguo Zheng[⊠]

School of Data Science, Fudan University, Shanghai, China
{20210980054dcff,zhengweiguo}@fudan.edu.cn

Abstract. Multi-document question answering is a hot-spot research task that retrieves answers for a natural language question from a set of documents. Although existing models try to enhance the recall ability, the performance of answering short questions is still far from satisfaction. In this paper, we address multi-document question answering by leveraging external knowledge to assist the semantic understanding, improving the overall performance. Specifically, we learn the relationship between questions and candidate paragraphs, and select valuable external knowledge. The machine reading comprehension model is trained to predict the answers in the screened external knowledge, which verifies the role of external knowledge in supplementing the answers. Then keywords are extracted to assist the indexing ability of answering short queries over multiple documents. Gate and Attention components are designed to integrate external knowledge through the deep neural network, assisting the retrieval of answers. We investigate the role of external knowledge in supplementing answers, assisting recall, and automatically assisting of deep neural network in the multi-document question answering system. Experimental results confirm the effectiveness of the proposed method.

Keywords: Multi-document QA · Information fusion · Machine reading comprehension

1 Introduction

Question answering (QA) system is widely used in varieties of applications and thus attracting increasing attentions. Currently, the existing QA systems can be divided into three groups, i.e., open-domain chat systems, task-driven systems, and domain-specific QA systems. The open-domain chat systems, e.g., Microsoft Xiaobing, can have text dialogue with users to interact and chat [5,10,19], to bring certain emotional value to users. Task-driven systems, e.g., Siri, mainly provide users with the retrieval of functional steps, such as querying the weather, setting the alarm clock, etc., which brings convenience to users' life and reduces the complexity of using mobile phones and other electronic products. Taking the left-handed doctor as an example, the domain-specific systems mainly establish

© The Author(s), under exclusive license to Springer Nature Switzerland AG 2022
R. Chbeir et al. (Eds.): WISE 2022, LNCS 13724, pp. 463–477, 2022.
https://doi.org/10.1007/978-3-031-20891-1_33

a QA model to provide users with a function similar to information retrieval and extract the information they want to acquire from the information in a specific field.

Multi-document QA can be used in many downstream tasks and has attracted increasing attention from both academic and industrial communities in recent years. In general, the existing methods for multi-document QA consist of three-stage recalls. In the first stage, rough recall is used to screen out relevant document sets; The second stage is a fine recall to further screen out relevant paragraphs, and the third stage is a fine recall to extract answers. Although multi-document QA originated from search and retrieval systems such as Baidu and Google [1,2,13,15,18], it mostly draws lessons from the idea of machine reading comprehension in the actual training process. The task of machine reading comprehension [6–9,14] mainly experienced three periods of technological changes. The early question-answering model mainly used retrieval technology to find the most relevant sentences in the article as the answers according to the questions. The retrieval technology mainly depended on the matching of keywords; Then, deep learning came into the vision of scholars. With the introduction of the neural network model, the question-answering model can gradually contain more abundant natural language information and build more complex models. Some excellent and complete models even exceeded the average human level in the score; With the maturity of natural language processing technology and the emergence of a classic turning point, attention mechanism, the ranking list of almost all natural language-related tasks was refreshed at that time, and machine reading comprehension tasks were no exception. The attention mechanism takes the correlation between questions and paragraphs as attention and introduces this natural correlation into the coding of article information, to get a better model. Currently, there are two major challenges to be addressed for multi-document QA:

QA Pairs are Not Built Directly from Documents . For the data set construction of the machine reading comprehension task, the question is directly generated by the context, and the answer is directly a fragment of it. It is even said that the question is designed by seeing the answer first and then associating it; The data set construction of multi-document QA is very labor-consuming. For MS Marco data set, it is generated based on user search logs, and its problem essence is generated according to human needs.

Short Text Features of the Problem. The bottleneck of document recall is to extract relevant information through a short question and answer sentence or even multiple paragraphs.

Obviously, the traditional model can not solve the above two challenges according to the limited candidate documents. Therefore, we propose to introduce external knowledge to break this limitation. External knowledge contains professional information other than questions and candidate documents, which can effectively supplement information for questions with short text features.

To summarize, we make the following contributions in this paper.

- We propose to use external knowledge to facilitate multi-document question answering;
- We design a novel framework consisting of four steps to integrate external knowledge;
- Extensive experimental results show that the proposed method achieves significant improvement compared to the existing methods.

2   Related Work

As a key research direction in the field of QA, multi-document QA is to extract the answers from multiple documents, which is highly related to text matching and semantic understanding. The traditional multi-document question answering system usually adopts a three-stage method. Firstly, the document is screened to exclude the candidate documents that are not related to the question, secondly, the paragraph is cut to exclude the paragraph information that is not related to the question. Finally, starting from the screened paragraphs, the answer phrases related to the question are extracted through a neural network and other structures to form a complete sentence.

2.1   Machine Reading Comprehension

Many studies have improved the above process and achieved certain results. Xiong et al. [20] adopted the dynamic iteration method. Instead of directly using the output probability in the output layer of the answer, they used the output result of the last time as the reference input model, iterated to specific conditions, and took the output of the last iteration as the answer range. Zhang et al. [22] made some improvements in the understanding of problems, distinguished different problem types, defined cluster centers for each type of problem, updated and added cluster centers in the process of collecting new problems, fused the representation of problem types with the problem text representation, added a soft filter composed of document vector and problem vector interaction layer, and removed words with low attention scores. This method can focus different levels of information according to different problem types and has a certain reference significance. With the maturity of the pretraining language model, glass et al. [4] designed a pretraining task based on BERT for the question-and-answering task, processed the data from Wikipedia, determined the answer words in the question sentence through heuristic rules, and found the most relevant paragraphs of the question as the background document through BM25 algorithm. In the pretraining stage, the pointer network was used to predict the answer words according to the question sentence and background document, In the case of small samples, the performance of the pretraining language model in the question-and-answering task is improved. In addition, graph neural network has outstanding performance in the modeling of different granularity dependencies such as words and sentences. Zheng et al. [23] expressed the document as a tree structure composed of document nodes, paragraph nodes, sentence nodes, and word nodes. Using graph attention network to process different granularity representations obtained based on BERT, we can mine long answers from texts with equal lengths of paragraphs and short answers from short texts such as words, At the same time, the dependence between long and short texts is considered.

Supervised learning requires a large number of high-quality labeled samples, and the samples that QA can provide are limited in quality and quantity. For example, Qu et al. [12] found that there are a large number of unmarked correct answers in the QA data set, which affects the quality of negative samples. In the process of negative sample construction, the interactive model was introduced to eliminate the samples with high confidence, and these samples were used as weakly supervised data as data enhancement, which further improved the effectiveness of the model. In recent years, the transfer learning paradigm has been gradually sought after by the industry. It can not only make use of a large number of existing annotation resources but also make the small model comparable to the accuracy of the large model. For example, Yu et al. [21] introduced the transfer learning framework into the question and answer system, introduced the semi-positive definite covariance matrix to build the feature information and weight information in the modeling domain, and enhanced the robustness of the model by resisting loss, which has achieved certain benefits in terms of accuracy and efficiency.

2.2   Multi-documnet QA

For multi-document QA, Wang et al. [17] proposed the skills of joint training and mutual verification between candidate answers in different documents to assist in answer generation; The research and development team of Ape counseling company uses the cascading attention mechanism to sample multiple candidate answer regions in multiple candidate documents, and on this basis, uses the cross-voting model to optimize the final answer. Given the impact of negative sample selection on the effect of the retrieval stage in the process of model training, Lu et al. [11] proposed a fusion negative sampling strategy as a supplement to negative sampling within the batch, including random sampling, context sampling, BM25 sampling, and model retrieval result sampling, and proved that difficult samples can improve the effectiveness of the model.

3   Problem Definition and Framework

3.1   Task Definition

Given a set of documents D $=\{D_1, D_2, D_3, ..., D_n\}$ and a query $Query$ with a limited length, the task is to find the document most likely to contain the answer and then extract the answer span as the result. As shown in the following formula, pos and j both mean a certain position in the found document, while

StartPos and *EndPos* are expressed as the start and the end position of the extracted span.

$$Document\ Index = \arg\max_i P_{D_i} \tag{1}$$

$$StartPos = \arg\max_{pos} P_{pos}\ for\ pos\ in\ D_{Document\ Index} \tag{2}$$

$$EndPos = \arg\max_{j>StartPos} P_j\ for\ j\ in\ D_{Document\ Index} \tag{3}$$

3.2 Framework of Our Approach

In this paper, we design rich steps to complete the auxiliary verification of external knowledge. The entity external knowledge related to the problem is extracted through the entity link tool; Then, four steps are used to improve the multi-doc enriched BERT, which is the first in the ranking list. The model is designed and tested from the perspectives of supplementary answer, auxiliary understanding and automatic noise reduction and assistance of depth model.

- The first step mainly uses the fine-tuning technology of the pretraining language model to obtain a high-precision model, and then screens the external knowledge;
- The second step extracts the possible answers in the external knowledge by training the answer extraction models of BERT, BiDAF, R-net and FusionNet (only for the questions without answers, verify the function of the supplementary answers of the external knowledge), and annotate them manually;
- The third step directly extracts the Top K keyword in the entity information to verify whether adding common sense and professional knowledge directly to the problem can improve the model effect;
- The fourth step uses the depth model, adds the gate component and attention component, makes the model automatically screen and fuse information, and assists the question and answer system.

4 Methods

The principle is to verify and explain the auxiliary effect of external information on multi-document QA, and explain the reasons for the auxiliary effect.

4.1 Verify the Possibility of Supplementary Answers from External Information

For example, for a model like BERT, the corpus information used when training the model in a self-monitoring way is called General Corpus, and the vector information of sentences or words obtained by the language model trained in this way actually has domain restrictions (general domain). For example, for the financial field, such a model can not be used directly, or the use effect is not good. Therefore, FinBERT achieves better vector representation by retraining the whole BERT with financial corpus information.

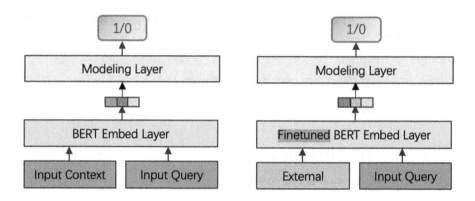

Fig. 1. Step 1 to extract useful external knowledge.

However, for the multi-document question and answer data set, although it is generated by the user search log, the gap between it and the field of general corpus is not so large. Therefore, we can use finetune technology [3,16] to fine tune the parameters of some layers of the model, which can achieve better results under the condition of limited equipment resources. We use this idea for reference. First, use candidate passes to model the semantic vector, and then extract the external knowledge that may be used as the answer to facilitate manual judgment in the next step.

In this paper, the following parts are proposed to refer to the finetune scheme of BERT or other language models that support fine-tuning. Record the passages with answers in the training set as sentence_1. Record the excluded passages and external knowledge as sentence_0, the finetune process is divided into three parts (see Fig. 1):

(1) The first part, concatenate query and context to construct positive and negative samples. Since the maximum length that the BERT model can support for input is 512, and there is no limit on the length of the introduced external knowledge, we use the officially recommended truncation method to train the model and then use the hierarchical method to verify the external knowledge. Truncation refers to throwing away the part exceeding the fixed length directly, and layering refers to entering the redundant sentence into the model as a new sentence. Note that the length of external knowledge or passages is L1, and the maximum length supported by the model is max_L;

(2) The second part, select the appropriate number of layers and fine tune the weight. According to the experimental results of many authors, we directly select the parameters of the last four layers of BERT model to fine tune.

(3) The third part, select the appropriate learning rate and attenuation ratio, etc. Through the above three parts, we train the vectors required by the model and predict the external knowledge that can assist from the perspective of semantics.

4.2   Verify the Supplementary Answer Function of External Information

To complete the design of this step, we first make a preliminary statistics on the relationship between external knowledge and answers: We classify and label the obtained external information according to whether it contains the meaningful fields in the answer, and records it as 1 (including the answer) or 0 (excluding the answer). Because the external knowledge itself has nothing to do with the data set construction, according to the statistical results, the proportion of all answer fields contained in the external knowledge in the training set and verification set is 0%; Without removing the stop words, the recall percentages in the training set and the verification set were 0.2380 and 0.2449 respectively; After removing the stop words, the proportion decreased to 0.2227 and 0.2299.

Since almost all external knowledge can not meet the needs of directly including all answer fields, this one is reasonably difficult to achieve. However, it can be seen that there are many questions in the data set, and the corresponding answers are displayed as "no answer present.", Whether these unanswerable questions in the original data set can be solved through external information is worth exploring.

Through the design of step 1, we splice query and reference document vectors for training, and locks the external information paragraphs that can best answer the questions through the model. Usually, it is necessary to manually mark the data without standard answers and manually judge whether they constitute the answers. Compared with ordinary text, external information can often get more convincing answers because of its professional construction. Therefore, it can be predicted that the model will have a better effect of answer assistance.

The model of step 2 is mainly to model the question and answer relationship between the query field and the candidate answer set. The optional network structure is relatively rich. You can try all the commonly used models of the question and answer data set. in this paper, four common network structures, BERT, BiDAF, FusionNet, and R-net, are used for training (see Fig. 2).

The implementation of the model relies on the Sogou open source framework SMRC toolkit, uses the above four models for training, and manually judges the generated answers. Step 2 uses four models BERT, BiDAF, FusionNet and R-net to verify the auxiliary role of external information. The complicated procedure is the auxiliary function of manual standard answer. Firstly, the model is used to predict whether the external information can be used as a candidate reference answer, and then the external information marked as "useful" is used to predict the answer field. To save labor cost, we only forecast the external knowledge of the verification set (Fig. 2).

There are 101093 question and answer data in the verification set, including 45457 without answers, 26044 without answers that can introduce external knowledge, and 3415 short text external knowledge screened by step 1. Although the number of results to be observed has been limited to 3415, it is still a little huge for this article. To save the workload, we make a threshold limit on the joint probability. We will judge the joint probability only when the possibility of 1

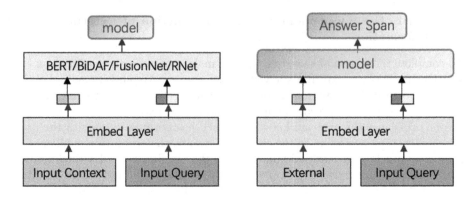

Fig. 2. Step 2 to extract answer span from filtered external knowledge.

tail position being predicted as the answer interval is greater than 0.25. Because this article is only an observation on whether the external information can supplement the answer, this treatment is reasonable. The reason why we only judge the supplementary answers to the unanswered questions is that the questions that can be answered are relatively easy to recall, while the unanswered answers often need to be answered with the help of external knowledge, which reflects the professionalism of external knowledge.

When the model is trained, it uses the query and passes of the original data set. When predicting, it uses query and step 1 to predict the relevant external knowledge. At the same time, the models of BERT, BiDAF, FusionNet and R-net reproduced in this paper refer to the framework SMRC toolkit released by Sogou, which is convenient for us to edit the reading step and model step directly.

4.3   Verify the Function of External Information Auxiliary Index

The essential difference between multi-document QA and machine reading comprehension lies in the ability to index information. For machine reading comprehension, the question is directly generated by the text object of reading comprehension, while for multi-document QA, the question is directly used to filter and match a large number of documents, which shows the importance of the amount of question information in multi-document QA. Because the query field corresponds to short text, there is too little information that can be indexed by short text, which is also the main reason for introducing external information in this paper. Introduce external information to enhance the amount of information of the problem, so as to index more relevant documents. However, the amount of text information of external information is too much. We aim to screen out the external information that can assist in screening the answers.

To reduce the noise in the external information as much as possible and include enough information, we initially use TF-IDF to exclude the words with a low amount of information, and finally retain the TOP-K with the highest amount of information as the auxiliary information of the query. For the case of

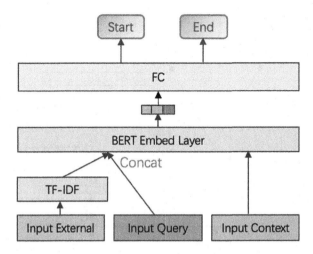

Fig. 3. Step3 to verify the auxiliary understanding function of external information.

polysemy of one word, assuming that there are n word meanings, we process all word meaning texts uniformly and take K words as information extraction. The advantage of screening words in this way is that the supplementary information corresponding to each question will not be so redundant and meet the text size required by the training model.

In the model part, the external information TOP-K information vocabulary is spliced directly behind the problem, and then trained. We select five values of K as 3, 5, 10, 15, and 20 to verify the auxiliary understanding function of external information. It should be noted that the selected K values are limited to non-query words in advance, and the Jaccard similarity between words cannot exceed 80%. At the same time, based on the experimental results of step 2, we only compare the best-performing BERT model (see Fig. 3).

4.4 Verify the Role of Independent Assistance of External Information

The above three steps are some skills constructed in this paper. Whether deep learning can automatically extract features needs to be verified. To verify this, we propose a deep learning framework, which can easily integrate external information (see Fig. 4).

(1) First, embedding the query + context and query + external information to get X_{QC} and $X_{QE} \in R^{n \times d}$;

(2) x_{QC} first enters the leftmost process of the model to maintain the consistent performance with the BERT model, and then makes a residual connection with the new model to avoid spreading negative knowledge;

(3) x_{QE} obtains a score weight matrix through a layer of FC, which is used to measure the importance of external information, which is called as the vector

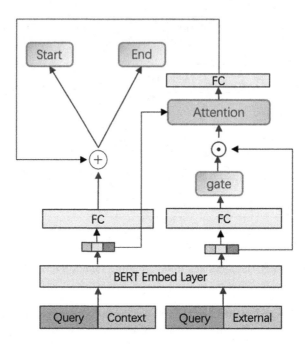

Fig. 4. Step4 to verify the role of independent assistance of external information.

gate. Then vector gate and x_{QE} carry out Hadamard product to obtain the vector added with weight information after fusion, and then it is combined with x_{QC} enters the attention layer code together. The design of attention here refers to the transformer. The specific formula is as follows:

$$gate = x_{QE} \cdot W_{FC} \tag{4}$$

$$\widehat{x_{QE}} = x_{QE} \odot gate \tag{5}$$

$$Q = \widehat{x_{QE}} \cdot W_Q \tag{6}$$

$$K = x_{QC} \cdot W_K \tag{7}$$

$$V = x_{QC} \cdot W_V \tag{8}$$

$$Attention(Q, K, V) = softmax(\frac{QK^T}{\sqrt{d_k}})V \tag{9}$$

(4) On the basis of the original model layer on the left, a residual connection layer introduced by external information is added. Adding residual connection layer is to prevent regression of model results:

$$out = FC(x_{QC}) + FC(Attention(Q, K, V)) \tag{10}$$

$$StartPos = \arg\max_i softmax(out_{dim=1}) \tag{11}$$

Table 1. Model hyperparameter.

Model	Batch$_{Size}$	Epoch	Dropout proba	Learning rate	Optimizer
BERT	8	2	0.1	3×10^{-5}	AdamW
R-net	12	10	0.2	1	Adam
FusionNet	12	10	0.4	0.001	Adam
BiDAF	60	10	0.2	0.001	Adam

$$EndPos = \arg \max_{j>StartPos} softmax(out_{dim=2}) \qquad (12)$$

The model in this paper is implemented based on Tensorflow. In addition to introducing external information into the model, the dropout in the hidden layer and attention layer is set to 0.1, and the learning rate and optimizer are also set to 3 with reference to the original BERT model as 3^{-5} and AdamW, which can be convenient to compare the model effect.

5 Experiments

5.1 Experimental Settings

For step 1, we adopt the gradient descent method of adamW, β_1 and β_2 default to 0.9 and 0.999, learning rate set as 2×10^{-5}, attenuation weight set to 1×10^{-2}, ε set to 1×10^{-8}, one batch_Size is set to 16, epoch is set to 2, the maximum length of the input model is set to 256, and dropout rate is set to 0.1 (Table 1).

For step 2, the hyperparametric settings of several models are shown in the following table:

From step 3 to step 4, we use the BERT model as a baseline and add our components to the experiment, most parameters remain unchanged.

5.2 Experimental Results

Step 1 result analysis: After setting the model parameters, when the loss does not decrease a certain number of times, the prediction accuracy index of the model can be obtained as 0.9325. The external knowledge of the verification set was recalled, and the cumulative number of effective external knowledge recalled was 5828 (counted in the unit of nonduplicate query). It is verified that there may be fragments that can be answered directly in external knowledge.

Step 2 result analysis: After the fine-tuning model of step 1, we not only obtain the semantic vector information more suitable for the multi-document question and answer datasets, but also obtains the external knowledge fragments that the model thinks can directly extract the answers. To verify whether these external knowledge fragments can play the role of auxiliary answers, we design a model to train the model of extracting answers by using the questions and candidate paragraphs of the training set for queries with no answers but external

Table 2. Model performance.

Model	EM	F1	Rouge-L	Blue-1
BERT	53.27	71.17	70.65	63.90
R-net	36.71	57.23	56.31	47.36
FusionNet	39.10	61.64	60.70	51.43
BiDAF	33.46	56.05	54.94	44.18

knowledge in the verification set (about 3415), and then test and generate them in these unanswered verification sets.

We use several models in the model training part, including BERT, BiDAF, FusionNet, and R-net. The experimental results in the training stage are as follows. It is observed that the performance of each model is monotonous with the final evaluation index. At the same time, BERT's performance is unparalleled, far better than other models in each index (Table 2).

After completing the model training, we use the best performing BERT model to predict and label the answers that were originally marked as unanswerable. Among them, 1672 of the 3415 external information predicted that the probability of span is greater than 0.25, and 170 of them play the role of supplementary answers after manual labeling. For example, one of the unanswered questions is "different types of Alocasia plants", and the answer given by the external knowledge through the model is "there are 97 accepted species native to tropical and subtropical Asia and eastern Australia." Thus, the role of external knowledge in assisting answers has been verified.

It should be noted that we limit the use of external knowledge to a certain extent (the number of sentences). At the same time, the proportion of unanswerable data sets in the data set is also relatively small. It can be seen that although the number of 170 answers is small, it is enough to explain the auxiliary answer function of external knowledge.

Step 3 result analysis: Based on the model design of step 2, step 3 can be easily compared. In order to more clearly show the differences between various models, we adopt the form of a broken line diagram (see Fig. 5).

In the multi-document problem, the defect of the short text problem can be made up to a certain extent on the premise of introducing external knowledge. At the same time, when the number of keywords introduced is 5, it reaches the peak of several evaluation indexes. After that, with the increase of the K value, more noise is introduced into the model, which reduces the effect of the model.

Step 4 result analysis: The evaluation index values of the model results of step 4 are: EM value of 54.26, F1 value of 72.20, the rouge-l value of 71.65, and Blue-1 value of 65.80. All indicators are slightly better than the BERT model of step 2 and the keyword model of top-N of step 3. In addition, the convergence speed of the model is much better than the original BERT model. The original BERT model reaches the loss of training set 1.218 and verification set 1.199 after two epochs, while the new model has reached the loss of training set 1.060 and

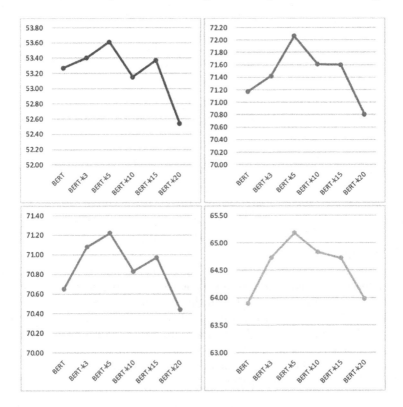

Fig. 5. The upper left subfigure is EM indicator, the upper right subfigure is F1 indicator, the lower left subfigure is Rouge-1 indicator, and the lower right subfigure is Blue-1 indicator. (Color figure online)

verification set 1.187 in the first epoch, as shown in the figure below. The top is the loss decline curve of the BERT model and the bottom is the decline curve of this model. This model can achieve the effect on earlier steps (see Fig. 6).

5.3   Ablation Experiment

To verify the effectiveness of the model components, we removed the gate step and conducted a version of the experiment, that is, directly embedding the words of problems and external knowledge into the attention mechanism. The results show that the values of each evaluation index are 53.25 EM value, 72.19 F1 value, 70.21 rouge-1 value, and 63.75 Blue-1 value. Except that F1 index is slightly improved, other indexes are lower than the BERT baseline to varying degrees, Thus, the effectiveness of the gate step is verified.

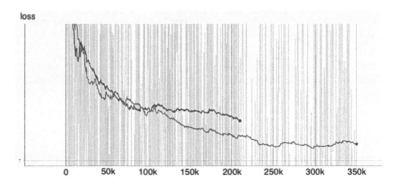

Fig. 6. The loss curve.

6   Conclusion

The principle of introducing external knowledge in this paper is people's expectation of information interaction between the question answering system and open source knowledge base. To bridge the gap between the external knowledge and the target documents, we propose to learn its information first through attention mechanism, and then use these screened and linked knowledge to guide answer selection. Extensive experiments over benchmark datasets confirm the effectiveness of the proposed method.

Acknowledgement. This work was supported by National Natural Science Foundation of China (Grant No. 61902074) and Science and Technology Committee Shanghai Municipality (Grant No. 19ZR1404900).

References

1. Asakiewicz, C., Stohr, E.A., Mahajan, S., Pandey, L.: Building a cognitive application using watson deepqa. IT Prof. **19**(4), 36–44 (2017)
2. Broens, T.H.F., Pokraev, S., van Sinderen, M., Koolwaaij, J., Costa, P.D.: Context-aware, ontology-based service discovery. In: EUSAI, vol. 3295, pp. 72–83 (2004)
3. Devlin, J., Chang, M., Lee, K., Toutanova, K.: BERT: pre-training of deep bidirectional transformers for language understanding. In: NAACL-HLT, pp. 4171–4186 (2019)
4. Glass, M.R., et al.: Span selection pre-training for question answering. In: ACL, pp. 2773–2782 (2020)
5. Goddeau, D., Meng, H.M., Polifroni, J., Seneff, S., Busayapongchai, S.: A form-based dialogue manager for spoken language applications. In: The 4th International Conference on Spoken Language Processing (1996)
6. Group, N.: R-net: machine reading comprehension with self-matching networks (2017)
7. Hao, X., Chang, X., Liu, K.: A rule-based Chinese question answering system for reading comprehension tests. In: IIH-MSP, pp. 325–329 (2007)

8. Huang, H., Zhu, C., Shen, Y., Chen, W.: Fusionnet: fusing via fully-aware attention with application to machine comprehension. In: ICLR (2018)
9. Kruth, J., Ginderachter, T.V., Tanaya, P.I., Valckenaers, P.: The use of finite state machines for task-based machine tool control. Comput. Ind. **46**(3), 247–258 (2001)
10. Lee, C., Cha, Y.S., Kuc, T.Y.: Implementation of dialogue system for intelligent service robots. In: 2008 International Conference on Control, Automation and Systems (2008)
11. Lu, J., Ábrego, G.H., Ma, J., Ni, J., Yang, Y.: Multi-stage training with improved negative contrast for neural passage retrieval. In: EMNLP, pp. 6091–6103 (2021)
12. Qu, Y., et al.: Rocketqa: an optimized training approach to dense passage retrieval for open-domain question answering. In: NAACL-HLT, pp. 5835–5847
13. Sales, J.E., Freitas, A., Handschuh, S.: An open vocabulary semantic parser for end-user programming using natural language. In: ICSC, pp. 77–84 (2018)
14. Seo, M.J., Kembhavi, A., Farhadi, A., Hajishirzi, H.: Bidirectional attention flow for machine comprehension. In: ICLR (2017)
15. Shen, Y., He, X., Gao, J., Deng, L., Mesnil, G.: Learning semantic representations using convolutional neural networks for web search. In: WWW, pp. 373–374 (2014)
16. Sun, C., Qiu, X., Xu, Y., Huang, X.: How to fine-tune BERT for text classification? In: CCL, pp. 194–206 (2019)
17. Wang, Y., et al.: Multi-passage machine reading comprehension with cross-passage answer verification. In: ACL, pp. 1918–1927 (2018)
18. Wei, Z., Xuan, Z., Chen, J.: Design and implementation of influenza question answering system based on multi-strategies. In: CSAE (2012)
19. Wu, Y., Nong, G., Chan, W.H., Han, L.B.: Checking big suffix and LCP arrays by probabilistic methods. IEEE Trans. Comput. **66**(10), 1667–1675 (2017)
20. Xiong, C., Zhong, V., Socher, R.: Dynamic coattention networks for question answering. In: ICLR (2017)
21. Yu, J., et al.: Modelling domain relationships for transfer learning on retrieval-based question answering systems in e-commerce. In: WSDM, pp. 682–690 (2018)
22. Zhang, J., Zhu, X., Chen, Q., Dai, L., Wei, S., Jiang, H.: Exploring question understanding and adaptation in neural-network-based question answering. CoRR (2017)
23. Zheng, B., et al.: Document modeling with graph attention networks for multi-grained machine reading comprehension. In: ACL, pp. 6708–6718 (2020)

A Learning-Based Approach
for Multi-scenario Trajectory Similarity
Search

Chunhui Feng, Zhicheng Pan, Junhua Fang[(✉)], Pingfu Chao, An Liu,
and Lei Zhao

School of Computer Science and Technology, Soochow University, Suzhou, China
chfeng99@stu.suda.edu.cn, {jhfang,pfchao,anliu,zhaol}@suda.edu.cn

Abstract. The ubiquity of positioning devices and wireless networks
has been significantly boosting the development of LBS (location-based
service) technology and applications. As is widely used in LBS, trajectory
top-k query serves as the key operation in a variety of large-scale web
services, such as route recommendation, user behavior pattern analysis,
etc. Unfortunately, existing top-k methods usually measure the trajectory similarity from a certain perspective, which leads to niche applications, not to mention the high computation complexity causing performance bottlenecks. To enable more types of data mining and analysis
for web services, we propose a learning-based approach for multi-scenario
trajectory similarity search with the generic metric, named TrajGS. Different from existing trajectory similarity measurements that are calculated by a single principle, TrajGS aims at proposing a generic rule that
considers the trajectory correlation from multiple aspects and improves
the accuracy of search in any circumstances. Specifically, TrajGS has
two innovative modules: 1) a new trajectory representation enabled by a
bidirectional LSTM model that can better capture the contextual information of trajectory and overcome the position error caused by outliers.
2) A generic trajectory similarity metric combining multiple distance
measures obtains more versatile and accurate top-k results in various
scenarios. Extensive experiments conducted on real datasets show that
TrajGS achieves both impressive accuracy and adequate training time
on trajectory similarity search compared with single-metric solutions. In
particular, it achieves 5x–10x speedup and 20%–30% accuracy improvement over Euclidean, Hausdorff, DTW, and EDR measurements.

Keywords: Bidirectional LSTM · Deep metric learning ·
Multi-scenario trajectory similarity search · Metric-free

1 Introduction

Nowadays, the pervasive use and rapid development of mobile web empowers
various Location-Based Services (LBS) applications that are built based on rich
spatial-temporal information. Specifically, many web services requires the process of massive trajectory data, such as POI (Point of Interest) recommendation,

R. Chbeir et al. (Eds.): WISE 2022, LNCS 13724, pp. 478–492, 2022.
https://doi.org/10.1007/978-3-031-20891-1_34

popular route detection. Despite different objectives and applications, the fundamental operation in those services is the trajectory **top-k similarity query**, which finds k most similar objects ($k \geq 1$) to the given query trajectory [1]. For instance, the route recommendation system usually provides users with a group of route options to maximize the result coverage.

However, two issues remain in existing trajectory top-k search methods. First, some distance measures, such as LCSS, DTW and Hausdorff distance, have high requirements on trajectory sampling rate and positioning accuracy [2], but in the meantime incur performance bottlenecks due to high complexity, which is especially true for long trajectories or trajectory pairs whose points are not aligned [3]. Secondly, different similarity functions are only applicable to corresponding application scenarios. Figure 1 shows an instance of similarity computation between trajectories under different distance measures. Different from finding the most similar trajectory, in top-k query, measuring the similarity by only one dimension may lead to a huge result bias, causing only the top one or a few being relevant, and the rest are close to random and not similar visually. Moreover, in many real-world applications, user may view the similarity from multiple aspects, leading to a strong demand on a generic similarity metric that can accommodate various circumstances, rather than one metric under some specific pattern. Considering that the high complexity of similarity computation is usually a bottleneck for large-scale trajectory data analysis, there are many research efforts for reducing the complexity such as the approximate algorithms. However, most of them are proposed for only one or two specific similarity measures, and thus cannot be extended to other measures. We propose a novel framework named TrajGS (**Traj**ectory top-k query with **G**eneric **S**imilarity) which is an improved approach based on deep metric learning, amending the precision of top-k similarity search.

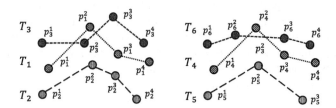

Fig. 1. Example of different measures. T_i represents the i-th trajectory, and p_i^j represents the j-th point of the i-th trajectory.

The core design of TrajGS lies on a deep neural network with bidirectional LSTM encoder and a distance-sensitive loss function under different measures in metric learning approach. TrajGS has two creative modules to make trajectory top-k query more efficient and valid for varieties of applications.

- **Bidirectional LSTM Encoder.** Due to the uncertainty of trajectory quality, sampling rate and length, the position of moving objects at some certain time t is not only related to the previous information, but also related to the afterwards. The traditional recurrent neural networks (RNNs) encoder [4] only considers the states before time t. We develop a trajectory-specific bidirectional LSTM model to capture the features of the entire trajectory better.

- **A Metric-free Paradigm.** The ultimate goal of trajectory top-k search is to obtain the most similar objects by calculating the pairwise distance in any circumstance. Based on this, we design a metric-free learning indicator that integrates multiple distance measures, weighing higher if trajectories keep close spatial distances under several different measures, and correct the trajectory embedding by backward updating network parameters.

To sum up, our contributions can be summarized as follows:

1. We propose a deep metric learning method based on a generic similarity criterion to work out the top-k query problem in any circumstance. To the best of our knowledge, TrajGS is the first framework to verify the correlation between similarity criteria and creatively design a comprehensive metric approach to generalize the learning-based model to approximate trajectory similarities under different measures for top-k query.
2. We employ the bidirectional LSTM model for trajectory embedding and develop the triplet network with a distance-sensitive loss function, overcoming disadvantages of low sampling rate and quality. Finally the trajectory representation can be more reflective of the spatial relationship between pair-wise trajectories precisely.
3. Experimental results on real dataset for top-k query with different k and distance measures demonstrate that TrajGS outperforms state-of-the-art baselines in terms of both efficiency and accuracy.

The rest of this paper is organized as follows. Section 2 reviews the related work. Section 3 formulates the problem of TrajGS. The bidirectional LSTM Encoder is introduced in Sect. 4. The metric learning network with a distance-sensitive loss function is demonstrated in Sect. 5. We conduct experiments, compare TrajGS with three baselines and analyze results in Sect. 6. Finally, the conclusion of TrajGS is shown in Sect. 7.

2   Related Work

In this section we overview existing work related to TrajGS from three perspectives: 1) Trajectory similarity oriented to top-k query; 2) Trajectory representation learning based on neural network; 3) Deep metric learning.

Trajectory Similarity Search. As trajectory similarity computation is the building brick in diverse trajectory analytic tasks, there are various techniques proposed to metric trajectory similarity and accelerate computing progress, which can be divided into the following two categories:

Complete Match Measures. These measures accumulate the distances for all matched pairs such as Euclidean and DTW. Studies on pruning computation have been brought up to improve the efficiency of measurements. For instance, Yi *et al.* [5] extend the piece-wise dynamic time warping operating on higher-level trajectory data. Sakurai *et al.* [6] conduct FastMap algorithm reducing the dimension of trajectory data. Thanawin *et al.* [7] proposed a method which uses combination strategy to accelerate calculation.

Partial Match Measures. These measures compare similarity trajectories using some partial strings such as LCSS and EDR. Both of them [8] support the mean value Q-gram pruning strategy and triangle inequality pruning strategy when performing top-k query.

Although these algorithms have achieved improvement on similarity calculation, they still suffer two shortcomings when answering top-k query. First, the matching strategy is based on trajectory quality which might be unsatisfied and leading to poor accuracy. Second, all approximations are designed for some specific distance measurement. So it is challenging to extend them to accommodate different similarity measures.

Trajectory Representation Based on Neural Network. Li *et al.* takes the lead in proposing a model t2vec that represents trajectories as vectors [9]. By continuously strengthening the characteristics of the trajectory itself (including geographic location, trends, *etc.*), each trajectory can be distinguished from other trajectories. Later, Zhang *et al.* further adds other features such as time and semantic information to represent the trajectory more comprehensively [10]. Unfortunately, they are all designed for modeling one trajectory independently without consideration of the spatial distance between trajectories, which could suffer from overfitting problem. Trajectory representation requires not only the extraction of its intrinsic properties, but also the feature learning of the pairwise relationship between similar trajectories.

Deep Metric Learning. TrajGS modifies the trajectory embedding in virtue of deep metric learning. Yao *et al.* proposes a weighted sampling method Neutraj, which can make use of similar and dissimilar relations more significantly than traditional random sampling, improving the learning effect, which can be regarded as the state-of-the-art model in metric learning [11]. What's more, it is expanded to the time series [12] and region search [13]. Nevertheless, the model is still based on a determined similarity calculation function as the learning target. Although it can be generalized to various methods, those methods are not integrated together.

3   Preliminaries

3.1   Interpretation of Generic Measurement

At present, the mainstream of trajectory top-k query solutions primarily adopts the *filter-and-refinement* framework. The query range is pruned through spatial indices to obtain probable candidates. Then the pairwise distance between each candidate and query trajectory is calculated, and the results are sorted and filtered into the top-k list. The major difference between solutions is the choice of distance functions, which is determined by the application scenario. However, since many real-world applications view the trajectory similarity from multiple perspectives, there is a strong need for a generic trajectory similarity measurement. Related details are shown in V-A.

Therefore, we take the intersection of the four methods as the final result of top-k query, and use this as the ground-truth in the validation experiment for result comparison.

3.2   Problem Definition

Trajectory is kind of structured data in chronological order with abundant spatial information. We signify the set of all trajectories as $\mathcal{T}$, and trajectory $T \in \mathcal{T}$ is initially coordinates (longitude, latitude) tuples of moving objects. Following are formal definitions related (Table 1).

Table 1. Notations used in this paper

Notations	Description
$\mathcal{T}, S$	A Trajectory database and a set of trajectories which are sampled randomly from the database
T	A trajectory in $\mathcal{T}$ which includes a sequence of coordinates tuples
E	d-dimensional embedding of trajectory T learnt by BiLSTM and metric learning in TrajGS
$\mathbf{W}, \mathbf{b}$	The linear weights and bias in bidirectional LSTM module
$\mathbf{f_t}, \mathbf{i_t}, \mathbf{o_t}$	The forget, input and output gates in bidirectional LSTM unit
$\mathbf{c_t}, \mathbf{h_t}, \widetilde{\mathbf{c_t}}$	The cell state, hidden state and internal memory cell state in bidirectional LSTM module at t-time step
$f(T_1, T_2)$	Similarity function between two trajectories
$g(\mathbf{E_i}, \mathbf{E_j})$	Similarity function between two trajectory embeddings

DEFINITION 1. (**Trajectory**). *A trajectory T is denoted by a series of positions which is $T = [X_1, ..., X_t, ...]$ where X_t is the $t - th$ information of the whole trajectory.*

DEFINITION 2. (**Trajectory Distance**). *Given two trajectories T_i and T_j, a distance calculation function $f(T_i, T_j)$ is able to measure the similarity between T_i and T_j, which means how similar they are.*

DEFINITION 3. (**Top-k Trajectories Similarity Search**). *We define the problem as obtaining the most similar trajectories of a query trajectory T in dataset $\mathcal{T}$ satisfying generic similarity, which appears in all top-k results under different distance measures. Therefore, the top-k trajectories' similarity integrates several similarity functions.*

Details will be reported in Section V-A and Section V-C.

3.3 Overview of TrajGS

At the high level, TrajGS conceives an innovative learning metric that integrates multiple trajectory similarity criteria, and develops the triplet mechanism in neural network framework of deep metric learning. At first, we randomly select 10,000 trajectories as the training set, compute the pairwise similarity between all trajectories under different metric functions, and normalize them. After that, we calculate the weighted mean of all similarity distributions, which is the ground-truth of the metric learning process. TrajGS firstly obtains the trajectory embedding of the sampled trajectory data through the bidirectional LSTM model, then uses a deep neural network with a distance-sensitive loss function to perform metric learning on the similarity value between any two trajectories, and captures the different distance relationship between them (Fig. 2).

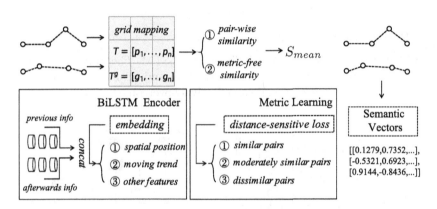

Fig. 2. Framework of TrajGS. Use the preceding and subsequent information to model trajectory embedding. TrajGS calculates similarity matrix under four similarity criteria whose integration is ground-truth to guide TrajGS training.

Encoder Architecture. TrajGS models the trajectory based on the bidirectional LSTM model, using the hidden layer states at the last moment as the trajectory embedding. The bidirectional LSTM can effectively notice the position information from two directions, solving the problems of gradient disappearance and gradient explosion occurring in long trajectories.

A Distance-Sensitive Metric Learning. After using the bidirectional LSTM module to encode trajectories, we design a metric-free learning framework in TrajGS with a specific distance-sensitive loss function. By the means of metric learning network, TrajGS learns the similarity distribution $\mathbf{S}$ between each two trajectory under different distance measures. Finally it achieves better trajectory representation and obtains the most similar trajectories so that is able to achieve higher accuracy and efficiency of top-k query.

4   Encoder Architecture

In this section we introduce how bidirectional LSTM Encoder module to project trajectories into embeddings. Next, we sequentially illustrate the bidirectional LSTM structure, including the feature extraction method and training method, which makes the embedding of trajectories more accurate.

4.1   Grid-Based Preparation

In the preprocessing step, inspired by [9,14], we partition the entire map into some small grids for capturing the shape feature of trajectories better according to [15], and each trajectory point fall into the corresponding grid, so that the shape representation of the entire trajectory consist of $[X_1^g, ..., X_t^g, ...]$ and $[X_1^p, ..., X_t^p, ...]$ which is finally $[X_1, ..., X_t, ..., X_n]$.

4.2   BiLSTM Unit

Figure 3 shows the structure of a bidirectional LSTM. The bidirectional LSTM structure can utilize both historical information and future information in the sequence [16]. For trajectories, it can effectively overcome the negative influence

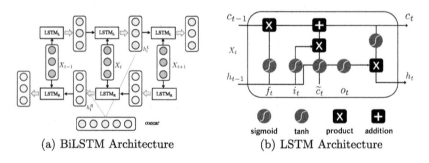

(a) BiLSTM Architecture   (b) LSTM Architecture

Fig. 3. The bidirectional LSTM encoder diagram.

of outliers on trajectory representation, which is more obvious for trajectories with lower sampling rates. The sequence information is input into the model in two directions, two hidden layers are used to save the input information of the two directions, and the corresponding outputs of the hidden layers are connected to the same output layer. In the bidirectional LSTM structure, taking the forward direction as an example, the sequence information is controlled by three gates, the mathematical expression of each gate state is as follows:

$$\mathbf{f_t} = \sigma(\mathbf{W_f} \cdot [\mathbf{h_{t-1}}, X_t] + \mathbf{b_f}) \tag{1}$$

$$\mathbf{i_t} = \sigma(\mathbf{W_i} \cdot [\mathbf{h_{t-1}}, X_t] + \mathbf{b_i}) \tag{2}$$

$$\mathbf{o_t} = \sigma(\mathbf{W_o} \cdot [\mathbf{h_{t-1}}, X_t] + \mathbf{b_o}) \tag{3}$$

$$\widetilde{\mathbf{c}}_\mathbf{t} = \tanh(\mathbf{W_c} \cdot [\mathbf{h_{t-1}}, X_t] + \mathbf{b_c}) \tag{4}$$

$$\mathbf{c_t} = \mathbf{f_t} \cdot \mathbf{c_{t-1}} + \mathbf{i_t} \cdot \widetilde{\mathbf{c}}_\mathbf{t} \tag{5}$$

$$\mathbf{h_t} = \mathbf{o_t} \cdot \tanh(\mathbf{c_t}) \tag{6}$$

$$\mathbf{h_t} = \overrightarrow{\mathbf{h_t}} \oplus \overleftarrow{\mathbf{h_t}} \tag{7}$$

where all of the gates have the same shape: $\mathbb{R}^{d \times 1}$.

To obtain the hidden state $\mathbf{h_t}$, each unit updates by following steps:(1) Forget gate: By Eq. 1, the unit gets the previous hidden state $\mathbf{h_{t-1}}$ and the current input X_t, then applies a sigmoid function σ on the linear transformation. (2) Input gate and output gate: By Eq. 2 and Eq. 3, the unit calculates the state of input gate and output gate. (3) Cell state: By Eq. 4~5, the unit applies a tanh function on the candidate unit and produces the current cell state $\mathbf{c_t}$. (4) Hidden state: By Eq. 6, the unit generates hidden state $\mathbf{h_t}$ and continues let it as the input to next step. Finally, by Eq. 7, $\overrightarrow{\mathbf{h_t}}$ and $\overleftarrow{\mathbf{h_t}}$ are respectively the forward and backward hidden states in the LSTM model, and $\oplus$ represents the integration operation.

5 Distance-Sensitive Metric Learning

In this section, we introduce the metric learning process of TrajGS. Firstly, we evaluate a set of general distance criteria and their reliability; then we describe the design of distance-sensitive loss function and the method of updating network parameters through weighted sampling in detail.

We calculate four methods Euclidean distance, Hausdorff distance, DTW distance and EDR distance during the training process to obtain a new set of general distance criteria, then randomly sample N trajectories in the database and use different similarity functions to obtain the distance matrix D_{func}, and normalize D_{func} to obtain the similarity matrix S_{func} by Eq. 8 where δ is an adjustable parameter for regulating the similarity distributions of different measures. Finally we compare the similarity of these four methods. S_{func} matrix is weighted and averaged to become final similarity distribution $\mathbf{S}$ is obtained as the training guidance. Formally, the loss function is the weighted sum of all pairwise groups: $min \sum_{u=1}^{U} w_u \cdot (f(T_i, T_j) - g(T_i, T_j))^2$ where U is the number of discriminational groups and w_u is the weight of pairwise group u.

$$\mathbf{S_{i,j}} = exp(\delta \cdot \mathbf{D_{i,j}}) / \sum_{n=1}^{N} exp(\delta \cdot \mathbf{D_{i,n}}) \tag{8}$$

For any two input trajectories T_i and T_j, we project them into two d-dimensional vectors $\mathbf{E_i}$ and $\mathbf{E_j}$ with the help of BiLSTM module. Our goal is to learn the set of network parameters so that the similarity distribution of the two embeddings can be consistent with the guidance, and modify embedding representation during this process. The specific training process and distance-sensitive loss function will be described in detail below.

5.1 Loss Function

The deep metric learning module of TrajGS aims to automatically construct task-specific distance metrics from weakly supervised data in a machine learning fashion. Inspired by the previous top-k results using traditional methods [1], we assign a higher weight w_1 to the intersection trajectories in multiple results, and a moderate weight w_2 to the trajectories that only appear once or twice, while do not appear at all in the top-k results. The remaining trajectories are given the lowest weight (because this part of trajectories basically cannot reflect the correlation).

After obtaining the representations $\mathbf{E_i}$ and $\mathbf{E_j}$ of any two input trajectories, we calculate the cosine similarity between the two embeddings, forming the similarity distribution matrix $\mathbf{S}$ between N sample trajectories which is $g(\mathbf{E_i}, \mathbf{E_j}) = exp(-cos(\mathbf{E_i}, \mathbf{E_j}))$. For similar trajectory pairs which belong to all similarity methods, the loss function is defined as

$$L_s = \sum_{i=1}^{n} w_1 \cdot (g(\mathbf{E_i}, \mathbf{E_j}) - f(T_i, T_j))^2 \tag{9}$$

For those similar trajectory pairs satisfying a certain degree(the appearance times r in four top-k query results), the loss function is defined as

$$L_m = \sum_{i=1}^{n} w_2 \cdot [r \cdot (g(\mathbf{E_i}, \mathbf{E_j}) - f(T_i, T_j))^2] \tag{10}$$

The value of r is the appearance times used to adjust trajectories with different degrees of similarity which is $r \in \{1, 2, 3\}$. For the trajectory pairs that are not enough to satisfy the similarity condition, the loss function is defined as

$$L_d = \sum_{i=1}^{n} w_3 \cdot [\mathbf{ReLU}(g(\mathbf{E_i}, \mathbf{E_j}) - f(T_i, T_j))]^2 \tag{11}$$

Finally, the loss function for the training set consisting of three kinds.

$$L_{\mathscr{I}} = \sum_{i=1}^{N} (L_s + L_m + L_d) \tag{12}$$

We modify the trajectory embedding representation in the training process of updating the parameters in neural metric learning and employ dropout strategy and Adam optimizer for probable optimization.

6 Experiment

6.1 Experimental Settings

Dataset. Our experiments are based on realistic and public trajectory dataset in Porto [17]. There are 1.7 millions of taxi trajectories from 2013 to 2014. We select a relatively centered set of trajectories based on their positions with the amount of 500k. Then we remove the records less than 50 points and partition the whole area into 30 m × 30 m grids. After preprocessing, we obtain 475,208 trajectories in Porto.

Experimental Description. For the top-k query problem, we use Euclidean distance, Hausdorff distance, DTW and EDR for testing. The first two functions are metric, which satisfy the triangle inequality. While others are not metric but robust to noisy points in trajectories. We randomly select 10k trajectories as training set. The ground-truth of the exact and correct top-k query consists of the intersection of four results used four different distance function. During training step, the ground-truth is matrix **S** consisting of the weighted average of four kinds of similarity value. We firstly employ R-tree index to prune and obtain candidates, then calculate the accurate distance of every two trajectories. Table 2 shows the overlap percentage of four exact distance function and TrajGS.

Table 2. Percentage of different metrics in top-15 query

Method	500	1k	5k	10k
Euclidean	35.41%	30.82%	31.14%	29.87%
Hausdorff	32.78%	36.76%	40.42%	39.92%
DTW	41.62%	38.97%	40.61%	43.32%
EDR	52.73%	57.21%	55.97%	57.72%
TrajGS	**72.48%**	**69.98%**	**70.15%**	**67.23%**

Compared Methods. For current study related to TrajGS, we compare our model with four baselines grouping roughly into three categories:

- Traditional algorithms: Generally speaking, the framework of top-k query is pruning-refinement structure and compute the exact similarity values under some distance calculation function when refining, denoted as **NO-NN**.
- Neural network algorithms: Different from the above methods, algorithms which use neural networks have also developed rapidly in recent years. We choose *t2vec* and *Neutraj* model as the state-of-the-art study and design top-k query experiment on them denoted as **other-NN**.
- Comparative algorithms: Obviously, the spotlights about TrajGS are including following aspects: the BiLSTM Encoder and a general learning metric. We use the ordinary RNN Encoder and exact metric for comparison demoted as **NOT-bidirectional** and **NOT-general**.

Evaluation Metrics. Focusing on the performance of the model and compared methods, we use the following two metrics to evaluate. Our experiments are organized in top-10 and top-20 query. The first metric is the time performance, which can reflect great advantages of TrajGS in practical application scenarios and the stability of trajectory length, denoted as TP@10 and TP@20 respectively. The second metric is the hitting ratio, which quantifies the difference (calculating the overlapping percentage of top-k query) between TrajGS and ground-truth, denoted as HR@10 and HR@20 respectively. The hitting ratio examines the reliability of TrajGS when top-k query.

6.2   Performance Comparison

Table 3 demonstrates the efficiency of different methods when top-k query in 1k and 5k dataset. TrajGS is verified outperforming in terms of time complexity and accuracy based on the bidirectional embedding and the generic similarity metric learning.

Table 3. Identification of performance indicators of six models

Amount	Method	Euclidean		Hausdorff		DTW		EDR	
		TP@10	HR@10	TP@10	HR@10	TP@10	HR@10	TP@10	HR@10
1000	NO-NN	0.982s	0.150	1.492s	0.203	1.021s	0.192	0.897s	0.253
	t2vec	0.002s	0.105	0.002s	0.108	0.004s	0.057	0.003s	0.086
	NeuTraj	0.002s	0.205	0.004s	0.194	0.004s	0.272	0.003s	0.305
	NOT-bidirectional	0.002s	0.398	0.002s	0.401	0.004s	0.275	0.003s	0.382
	NOT-general	0.004s	0.304	0.003s	0.279	0.003s	0.245	0.005s	0.372
	TrajGS	**0.002s**	**0.619**	**0.002s**	**0.625**	**0.004s**	**0.613**	**0.005s**	**0.637**
5000	NO-NN	4.013s	0.204	3.792s	0.210	3.208s	0.274	2.989s	0.300
	t2vec	0.017s	0.102	0.015s	0.098	0.009s	0.114	0.012s	0.115
	NeuTraj	0.014s	0.302	0.012s	0.277	0.020s	0.320	0.010s	0.226
	NOT-bidirectional	0.017s	0.375	0.015s	0.387	0.021s	0.453	0.019s	0.273
	NOT-general	0.016s	0.189	0.014s	0.204	0.015s	0.214	0.020s	0.198
	TrajGS	**0.015s**	**0.572**	**0.017s**	**0.558**	**0.014s**	**0.593**	**0.013s**	**0.625**

It can be seen from the Table 3 that no matter which distance function is used, the time performance of the traditional method in the top-k query is not as good as that of the neural network method because most of the traditional methods are based on real trajectory points and need to combine geographic features for distance calculation. The hitting ratio of t2vec is very low compared to the others because it does not apply metric learning neural network in the training process, so that the trajectory representation pays more attention to its own features, and the correlation between similar trajectories and dissimilar trajectories is not fully utilized [18]. In the top-k query problem, the larger the value of k, the more obvious the disadvantage. Compared with t2vec, Neutraj is much more accurate, but under different distance measurement standards, it is difficult to guarantee the superiority in a general situation. Similarly, the two ablation experiments also demonstrate the necessity and importance of the bidirectional LSTM model and general metrics for TrajGS.

6.3 Parameter Sensitivity Study

In this part we evaluate the parameters sensitivity of TrajGS on four aspects: the number of top similar trajectories k, the range of top-k query N, the embedding dimension d and the batch size m. Table 4 denotes parameter settings and the best case. Figure 4 illustrates the hitting ratio when perform top-10 query in 1000 trajectories with different parameters.

Table 4. Parameter setting

Parameter	Range	Default	Best case
d	16, 32, 64, 96, 128, 192, 256	32	128
m	1, 3,..., 55, 57	20	50
Search range	100, 300,..., 1000	1000	Around 500
k	1, 5, 10, 15, 20, 25	5	Around 10

The Number of Top Similar Trajectories k. We use random 1000 trajectories in Porto to perform the accuracy, intuitively examining the top-k results of our model with different k where $k \in \{1, 3, 5, ..., 15, 17, 19\}$. The comparison result is shown as Fig. 4(a). The hitting ratio increases by the value of k and reaches the highest when k is about 10. And it is up to 50% in all situations which demonstrates that TrajGS is probably able to retrieve the most similarity trajectories. When the value of k is small, the reason of reduced hitting ratio is mainly the selection of ground-truth has a certain randomness, which is not enough to reflect the common characteristics of multiple similarity measures. Once the k is around 10, the performance advantage shows obviously. This is because the integration of multiple similarity is more appropriate for our metric learning module when k reaches 10 and above.

The Range of Top-10 Query N. We conduct experiments on top-k query in different ranges to evaluate the robustness performance of our model. First, we select 1000 trajectories from the dataset as the total test set, and randomly selected 100 of them for the first top-k query. Each subsequent experiment similarly adds 100 trajectories to the query range. From the results of parameter N sensitivity comparison shown as Fig. 4(b), it is concluded that the hitting ratio@10 in different ranges of dataset keeps stable and achieves up to 60% in all of situations.

The Embedding Dimension d. We tune the embedding dimension d in range {16, 32, 64, 96, 128, 192, 256}. As shown, for 1k trajectories, when the embedding dimension reaches around 100, the increase in hitting ratio slows down significantly while it is obvious when the dimension is less than 100. Moreover, when d value is too large to be suitable for embedding, the model probably has the risk

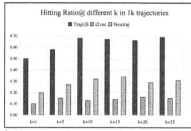

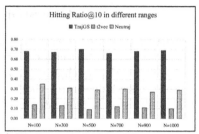

(a) Hitting ratio with different **k** in 1k (b) Hitting ratio@10 in different **ranges**
trajectories

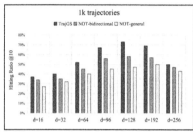

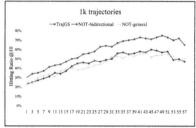

(c) Hitting ratio@10 with different **em-** (d) Hitting ratio@10 with different
bedding dimension   **batch size**

Fig. 4. Parameter sensitivity study

of over-fitting especially for the model without generic metric. Thus we finally decide to set the dimension d is 128 which can balance the complexity of training and the performance of our model. In addition, it is clearly observed that TrajGS model is superior to trajectory embedding than model without BiLSTM or generic metric. Due to the room limitation, we only show the experimental result when the amount of training set is 1000.

The Batch Size m. We also test the top-10 query hitting ratio with different training batch size in range of $\{1, 3, 5, ..., 49, 51, 53, 55, 57\}$. As shown, the efficiency of three kinds of models improves in pace with the increase of batch size m until the value is up to 50. It is reasonable because as the batch size enlarges, the model can better overcome the negative effects of uneven trajectory quality and different lengths during the training process. While if the batch size increases up to a certain extent, it is easy to fall into the state of local extreme value, debasing the performance of final model. We also observe that TrajGS surpasses the ablation models without BiLSTM or generic metric.

7   Conclusion

In this paper, we propose a learning-based approach for multi-scenario trajectory similarity search based on a distance-sensitive metric learning named TrajGS, integrating various distance measures, achieving more general and accurate results. The originality of TrajGS lies on two aspects: a fixed-dimensional embedding representation with the help of a bidirectional LSTM model; and a general-purpose metric according to trajectory top-k results to approximate the similarity measures. Experimental results and analysis on real mobile-based trajectory dataset can verify the accuracy and efficiency of TrajGS.

Certainly there are several interesting studies existing for future consideration. It would be worthy to explore broader queries (*e.g.* range, statistic) or extension to other data structures (*e.g.* network streams) for more powerful and prevailing web services.

Acknowledgment. This work was supported by National Natural Science Foundation of China under grant (No. 61802273, 62102277), Postdoctoral Science Foundation of China (No. 2020M681529), Natural Science Foundation of Jiangsu Province (BK20210703), China Science and Technology Plan Project of Suzhou (No. SYG202139), Postgraduate Research & Practice Innovation Program of Jiangsu Province (SJCX2_11342), Extracurricular Academic Research Foundation of Jiangsu Province (KY20220079A), Project Funded by the Priority Academic Program Development of Jiangsu Higher Education Institutions.

References

1. Ma, C., Hua, L., Shou, L., Chen, G.: Ksq: Top-k similarity query on uncertain trajectories. IEEE Trans. Knowl. Data Eng. **25**(9), 2049–2062 (2012)
2. Toohey, K., Duckham, M.: Trajectory similarity measures. Sigspatial Spec. **7**(1), 43–50 (2015)
3. Fang, Z., Du, Y., Chen, L., Hu, Y., Gao, Y., Chen, G.: E2 dtc: an end to end deep trajectory clustering framework via self-training. In: 2021 IEEE 37th International Conference on Data Engineering (ICDE), pp. 696–707. IEEE (2021)
4. Schuster, M., Paliwal, K.K.: Bidirectional recurrent neural networks. IEEE Trans. Signal Process. **45**(11), 2673–2681 (1997)
5. Yi, B.-K., Jagadish, H.V., Faloutsos, C.: Efficient retrieval of similar time sequences under time warping. In: Proceedings 14th International Conference on Data Engineering, pp. 201–208. IEEE (1998)
6. Sakurai, Y., Yoshikawa, M., Faloutsos, C.: Ftw: fast similarity search under the time warping distance. In: Proceedings of the twenty-fourth ACM SIGMOD-SIGACT-SIGART Symposium on Principles of Database Systems, pp. 326–337 (2005)
7. Rakthanmanon, T., et al. Searching and mining trillions of time series subsequences under dynamic time warping. In: Proceedings of the 18th ACM SIGKDD International Conference on Knowledge Discovery and Data Mining, pp. 262–270 (2012)
8. Chen, L., Tamer Özsu, M., Oria, V.: Robust and fast similarity search for moving object trajectories. In: Proceedings of the 2005 ACM SIGMOD International Conference on Management of Data, pp. 491–502 (2005)
9. Li, X., Zhao, K., Cong, G., Jensen, C.S., Wei, W.: Deep representation learning for trajectory similarity computation. In: 2018 IEEE 34th International Conference on Data Engineering (ICDE), pp. 617–628. IEEE (2018)

10. Zhang, Y., Liu, A., Liu, G., Li, Z., Li, Q.: Deep representation learning of activity trajectory similarity computation. In: 2019 IEEE International Conference on Web Services (ICWS), pp. 312–319. IEEE (2019)
11. Yao, D., Cong, G., Zhang, C., Bi, J.: Computing trajectory similarity in linear time: a generic seed-guided neural metric learning approach. In: 2019 IEEE 35th International Conference on Data Engineering (ICDE), pp. 1358–1369. IEEE (2019)
12. Yao, D., Cong, G., Zhang, C., Meng, X., Duan, R., Bi, J.: A linear time approach to computing time series similarity based on deep metric learning. IEEE Trans. Knowl. Data Eng. (2020)
13. Liu, Y., Zhao, K., Cong, G.: Efficient similar region search with deep metric learning. In: Proceedings of the 24th ACM SIGKDD International Conference on Knowledge Discovery & Data Mining, pp. 1850–1859 (2018)
14. Zhang, D., Li, N., Zhou, Z.H., Chen, C., Sun, L., Li, S.: ibat: detecting anomalous taxi trajectories from gps traces. In: Proceedings of the 13th International Conference on Ubiquitous Computing, pp. 99–108 (2011)
15. Yang, P., Wang, H., Zhang, Y., Qin, L., Zhang, W., Lin, X.: T3s: effective representation learning for trajectory similarity computation. In: 2021 IEEE 37th International Conference on Data Engineering (ICDE), pp. 2183–2188. IEEE (2021)
16. Siami-Namini, S., Tavakoli, N., Namin, A.S.: The performance of LSTM and BILSTM in forecasting time series. In: 2019 IEEE International Conference on Big Data (Big Data), pp. 3285–3292. IEEE (2019)
17. Moreira-Matias, L., Gama, J., Ferreira, M., Mendes-Moreira, J., Damas, L.: Time-evolving OD matrix estimation using high-speed GPS data streams. Expert Syst. Appl. **44**, 275–288 (2016)
18. Taghizadeh, S., Elekes, A., Schäler, M., Böhm, K.: How meaningful are similarities in deep trajectory representations? Inf. Syst. **98**, 101452 (2021)

Transformer-Based Cache Replacement Policy Learning

Meng Yang[1], Chenxu Yang[1,2], and Jie Shao[1,2,3(✉)]

[1] University of Electronic Science and Technology of China, Chengdu 611731, China
{yangm,yangchenxu}@std.uestc.edu.cn
[2] Shenzhen Institute for Advanced Study, UESTC, Shenzhen 518110, China
[3] Sichuan Artificial Intelligence Research Institute, Yibin 644000, China
shaojie@uestc.edu.cn

Abstract. Cache replacement policy is critical in computer system. It determines which data to be evicted from the cache when new data is coming. A good cache replacement policy increases the cache hit rate and decreases system delay significantly. There are a few heuristic methods designed for specific access patterns, but they perform poorly on diverse and complex access patterns. In order to deal with complicated access patterns, we formulate the cache replacement problem as matching question answering and design a Transformer-based cache replacement (TBCR) model. TBCR learns access patterns based on a Transformer encoder, and this architecture performs well even on complex access patterns. We evaluated on six memory-intensive Standard Performance Evaluation Corporation (SPEC) applications. TBCR increases cache hit rates by 3% over the state-of-the-art.

Keywords: Cache · Cache replacement · Deep learning · Transformer

1 Introduction

Modern applications spend over 50% of all computing cycles waiting for data to arrive from memory [4]. Caching is used to moderate performance differences among different levels of data storage system [5,8,19]. When the data to be accessed exist in the cache, there is no need to access the next storage level. On the contrary, the system needs to spend extra time searching for data at a slower storage level. The study of [5] shows 1% improvement in the cache hit rate results in a 35% reduction in system latency.

This paper aims to solve the single-level cache replacement problem in complex access patterns. It is challenging because it requires planning far ahead. In this work, we apply the deep learning method to computer storage to solve the problem of cache replacement when dealing with complex access patterns. As we collate the knowledge that can be used as input to the model, we find similarities between the cache replacement problem and matching question answering. Based on the discovery, we represent a novel way of designing models for cache

© The Author(s), under exclusive license to Springer Nature Switzerland AG 2022
R. Chbeir et al. (Eds.): WISE 2022, LNCS 13724, pp. 493–500, 2022.
https://doi.org/10.1007/978-3-031-20891-1_35

replacement. Consequently, we propose a Transformer-base cache replacement (TBCR) model. Our model is mainly composed of a Transformer encoder [17] and a general attention [13]. It tries to discover implicit access patterns specific to individual applications, which are likely to occur in future access sequences, and uses this knowledge to make more precise eviction decisions.

Our contributions can be summarized as follows:

1. We propose TBCR, an approach to improve cache hit rate in complex and various access patterns settings.
2. We formulate the cache replacement problem as a matching question answering problem and a well-designed Transformer encoder network can easily learn from the complex and diverse access patterns.
3. The experiments over a set of SPEC applications demonstrate that our approach increases raw cache hit rates by 24.5% over LRU and increases normalized cache hit rate by 3% over Parrot.

The remainder of this paper is organized as follows. Section 2 introduces related studies. In Sect. 3, our method to improve the cache hit rate is presented. Section 4 discusses the evaluation result, and finally, Sect. 5 concludes this work.

2   Related Work

Most traditional cache replacement policies are designed based on a specific access pattern observed, such as least recently used (LRU), least frequently used (LFU) and most recently used (MRU). These policies have significant limitations, and they all perform poorly on diverse and complex access patterns [2].

With the development of machine learning in recent years [10,11,14], many researches note its great potential in optimizing computer architecture, and apply machine learning to optimize the design of cache replacement policies. Glider [16] is the first use of deep learning methods to improve the design of cache replacement policy. It designs a long short-term memory (LSTM)-based neural network using access history to label the data that the CPU is accessing as cache-friendly or cache-averse. Nevertheless, after labelling, it still relies on traditional heuristics to determine which cache-averse one to evict. This method means Glider inherits the shortcoming of traditional heuristics and will cause a high cache miss rate on some access patterns. To solve the disadvantage of Glider, Parrot [12] directly trains a replacement policy end-to-end by imitating Belady's. Parrot casts cache replacement as learning a policy on an episode Markov decision process. It takes as inputs currently accessed line and the lines in the cache then outputs the final decision. Phoebe [18] also models the cache replacement problem as a Markov decision process. Still, the agent observes the considered length of the history information as of the current access. The state s_t encodes the locality information from a past fixed-length sequence of accesses. The agent takes as input a two-dimensional matrix, just like an image. Nonetheless, Phoebe uses reinforcement learning, which needs an appropriate environment, so it takes a lot of effort to train for different caches. In contrast, our model can be trained only relying on offline access traces.

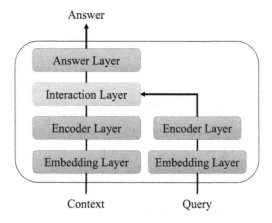

Fig. 1. Reading comprehension question answering framework.

3   Methodology

3.1   Problem Formulation

We treat the cache replacement problem as a matching question answering based on reading comprehension [7,9]. In our problem setting, each input can be divided into two parts: $input = (A, L)$, where

- $A = \{access_{t-H+1}, ..., access_t\}$ is access history of length H, consisting H most recent cache accesses. $access_k$ is defined as $access_k = \{addr_k, pc_k\}$ where $addr$ presents cache line address and pc presents the unique program counter of the access.
- $L = \{line_1, line_2, ..., line_N\}$ is the lines in the cache set currently.

The output means to choose an optimal line from L to evict. We map the cache replacement problem to matching question answering, as shown in Eq. 1 and Eq. 2, and attempt to design a model similar to it.

$$A = \{access_{t-H+1}, ..., access_t\} \rightarrow C = \{token_1, ..., token_H\}, \qquad (1)$$

$$L = \{line_1, line_2, ..., line_N\} \rightarrow Q = \{option_1, option_2, ..., option_N\}. \quad (2)$$

Generally, reading comprehension question answering is summarized in a similar framework as shown in Fig. 1 [6,15]. Our Transformer-based cache replacement (TBCR) model is also constructed based on these four layers.

3.2   Our Model

Overview of Our Model. Although the pre-trained models have made great progress in natural language processing in recent years, we cannot apply them to the cache replacement policy learning because these powerful learning models are

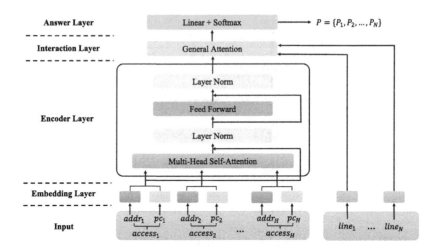

Fig. 2. The architecture of our model.

too large. Thus, we design a relatively small model based on the basic framework, as illustrated in Fig. 2.

Embedding Addresses and PCs. As the memory size is too large to model, we use embedding to map data addresses and program counters to another vector representation, which transforms high-dimensional sparse feature vector to low-dimensional dense feature vector. Our model uses dynamic vocal embedding in the embedding layer, similar to word vector processing in natural language processing. It dynamically constructs a vocabulary, assigning embeddings to new inputs. After embedding respectively, address embeddings and PC embeddings are concatenated into new vectors.

Transformer for Sequential Encoding. We use a Transformer encoder instead of LSTM to extract the sequence feature. Our input is a complete access history, and we hope the model focuses more on the connections between each access rather than just reading each access sequentially. The Transformer encoder makes use of the self-attention mechanism, which concentrates on the essential information in the sequence.

Interaction with Attention. Attention in the interaction layer is different from the encoder layer. We want to capture the relationship between the lines in the cache set and accesses in the access sequence. Therefore, input of this layer are lines after embedding ($L_{embed} = \{e(l_1), e(l_2), ..., e(l_N)\}$) and the hidden state output by the encoder layer ($A_{hidden} = \{a_1, a_2, ...a_H\}$). Since we use a Transformer encoder in the encoder layer, it is necessary to add positional embedding to the hidden state, and we use the positional embedding the same with Transformer. In this layer, we apply general attention [13], and we treat lines in the cache set (L_{embed}) as queries and hidden states as keys. First, we calculate the similarity between the embedded lines and each hidden state to get weights. Then, we use a softmax function to normalize these weights. Finally, we get attention by summing the weights with the corresponding value.

Answering with Normalization. At last, we send attention scores obtained from the interaction layer to a linear layer and a softmax layer to get the possibility for each line in the cache set. In practice, when the number of lines in the cache set is less than N, no line will be evicted. However, when training the model, we also calculate the probability of each line being evicted even if there is no eviction. In this case, we normalize the results in the following way:

$$P_i = \begin{cases} S_i/(S \cdot mask), mask_i = 1, \\ 0, mask_i = 0, \end{cases} \tag{3}$$

where $mask[i]$ equals 1 when the ith line exists in the cache set, otherwise $mask[i]$ equals 0, and S means score vector of the lines in the cache set.

4   Experiments

4.1   Experiment Settings

In our experiments, we are required to simulate a last-level cache. We use the cache simulation provided by Parrot [12] and set the cache size to 2GB. Following [12], we apply a 16-way set associative in the cache, and set cache line size to 64B. The cache set size is 1 KB. There are 2048 sets in the cache.

We use similar datasets with Parrot in our experiments. We download the programs provided by the 2nd Cache Replacement Championship [1] and then follow the procedure from the authors of Parrot to get six available datasets. Since the raw access sequences are too long and each access corresponds to a unique cache set, we select 64 cache sets and filter accesses by these cache sets. Finally, we get relatively short but expressive datasets.

Specifically, the datasets we get are long sequences, and each piece of data in the sequence consists of an address of a memory block and an instruction address (program counter). We split each sequence into a training set, a validation set and a test set according to the ratio of 80%/10%/10%, as shown in Table 1.

Since our goal is to learn a cache replacement policy end-to-end, there are two important metrics. First, the most intuitive measure of a cache replacement policy is the cache hit rate (HR), which means the percentage of access hits by the total accesses as shown in Eq. 4. Second, we treat Belady's as the ceiling of the cache replacement policies, as the entire access sequence is unknown, and treat LRU as the floor of learning based policies, as LRU is the most widely used nowadays. The second metric is normalized hit rate (NHR), which is defined as Eq. 5,

$$HR = \frac{cache\_hits}{total\_access}, \tag{4}$$

$$NHR = \frac{r - r_{LRU}}{r_{opt} - r_{LRU}}, \tag{5}$$

Table 1. Datasets details used in experiments.

Program	Total step	Train data		Test data	
		Addresses	PCs	Addresses	PCs
astar	1442560	5132	48	4792	25
bzip	209292	31101	274	8120	232
cactusadm	277186	108752	142	15133	117
mcf	3706880	860994	64	191809	44
sphinx3	410880	5929	184	3427	136
xalanc	86406	21950	413	5159	275

Table 2. Performance comparison in hit rates.

	astar	bzip	cactusadm	mcf	sphinx3	xalanc
LRU [12]	3.64%	56.23%	0.00%	25.72%	6.01%	15.42%
Belady's [3]	36.79%	71.51%	33.93%	43.90%	64.96%	35.31%
TBCR (ours)	31.28%	61.31%	33.65%	42.47%	57.07%	28.69%

where r_{LRU} means hit rate of LRU and r_{opt} means hit rates of Belady's. This metric reflects the improvement to LRU and the gap with Belady's of our learning-based approach.

4.2   Main Results

We compare the hit rate of LRU, Belady's, and our TBCR method in Table 2. As is shown in the table, TBCR gets great improvement over LRU. On astar, bzip and sphinx3, LRU almost plays no role, but learning-based policies work well. On other datasets, our method also performs better than LRU, ranging from 5% to 51%. On average, TBCR increases cache hit rates by 24.5% over LRU. The results show that some specific applications contain diverse access patterns. In such cases, the heuristic works partially or not at all. In contrast, methods based on learning have a huge advantage. Besides, the basic structure of matching question answering is suitable for the cache replacement learning problem.

We compare the normalized hit rate of the proposed TBCR method with Parrot in Table 3. The normalized hit rate of LRU is 0, and Belady's normalized hit rate is 1. As we can see in the table, on cactusadm and mcf, our method appears to be very close to the optimal replacement policy. The model learns the access patterns of the two datasets better. In the access patterns represented by other datasets, learning-based policies have a lot of room for improvement, but even on these datasets, TBCR gets better performance than Parrot, achieving a 3% higher normalized cache hit rate on average. The main difference between our TBCR method and Parrot is that we use a Transformer encoder to extract

Table 3. Performance comparison in normalized hit rates.

	astar	bzip	cactusadm	mcf	sphinx3	xalanc
Parrot [12]	78.31%	27.33%	98.85%	**94.00%**	84.56%	**67.72%**
TBCR (ours)	**83.47%**	**33.23%**	**99.21%**	92.12%	**88.00%**	66.78%

access sequences features instead of RNNs. The results prove that Transformer performs better than RNNs when processing access sequences.

5 Conclusion

In this paper, we aim to solve the cache replacement problem in the complex access patterns. We formulate the cache replacement problem as matching question answering and built a new model based on Transformer. Instead of using RNN, the proposed TBCR utilizes a Transformer encoder to extract features from sequences, which can get more information. After that, general attention gets the relationship between sequence and lines in the cache set. Experiments on the datasets of SPEC applications show that our approach increases cache hit rates by 24.5% over LRU and increases normalized hit rates by 3% over the current state-of-the-art.

While our approach performs well in the complex access patterns, deep neural network is still too large to be applied in the computer system structure. We will focus on reducing model size by distillation or pruning in the future.

Acknowledgements. This work is supported by the National Natural Science Foundation of China (No. 61832001) and Shenzhen Science and Technology Program (No. JCYJ20210324121213037).

References

1. The 2nd cache replacement championship. https://crc2.ece.tamu.edu/
2. Ali, W., Shamsuddin, S.M., Ismail, A.S.: A survey of web caching and prefetching. Int. J. Adv. Soft Comput. Appl. **3**(1), 18–44 (2011)
3. Belady, L.A.: A study of replacement algorithms for virtual-storage computer. IBM Syst. J. **5**(2), 78–101 (1966)
4. Bryant, R.E., O'Hallaron, D.R.: Computer System: A Programmer's Perspective, 3rd edn. Pearson, Boston (2011)
5. Cidon, A., Eisenman, A., Alizadeh, M., Katti, S.: Cliffhanger: scaling performance cliffs in web memory caches. In: 13th USENIX Symposium on Networked Systems Design and Implementation, NSDI 2016, Santa Clara, CA, USA, 16–18 March 2016, pp. 379–392 (2016)
6. Dhingra, B., Liu, H., Yang, Z., Cohen, W.W., Salakhutdinov, R.: Gated-attention readers for text comprehension. In: Proceedings of the 55th Annual Meeting of the Association for Computational Linguistics, ACL 2017, Vancouver, Canada, 30 July–4 August, vol. 1: Long Papers, pp. 1832–1846 (2017)

7. Jin, Q., et al.: Biomedical question answering: a survey of approaches and challenges. ACM Comput. Surv. **55**(2), 35:1–35:36 (2023)

8. Jouppi, N.P.: Improving direct-mapped cache performance by the addition of a small fully-associative cache and prefetch buffers. In: Proceedings of the 17th Annual International Symposium on Computer Architecture, Seattle, WA, USA, June 1990, pp. 364–373 (1990)

9. Li, L., Zhang, M., Chao, Z., Xiang, J.: Using context information to enhance simple question answering. World Wide Web **24**(1), 249–277 (2021)

10. Li, X., Cao, Y., Li, Q., Shang, Y., Li, Y., Liu, Y., Xu, G.: RLINK: deep reinforcement learning for user identity linkage. World Wide Web **24**(1), 85–103 (2021)

11. Liang, Y., Guo, B., Yu, Z., Zheng, X., Wang, Z., Tang, L.: A multi-view attention-based deep learning system for online deviant content detection. World Wide Web **24**(1), 205–228 (2021)

12. Liu, E.Z., Hashemi, M., Swersky, K., Ranganathan, P., Ahn, J.: An imitation learning approach for cache replacement. In: Proceedings of the 37th International Conference on Machine Learning, ICML 2020, 13–18 July 2020, Virtual Event, vol. 119, pp. 6237–6247 (2020)

13. Luong, T., Pham, H., Manning, C.D.: Effective approaches to attention-based neural machine translation. In: Proceedings of the 2015 Conference on Empirical Methods in Natural Language Processing, EMNLP 2015, Lisbon, Portugal, 17–21 September 2015, pp. 1412–1421 (2015)

14. Man, X., Ouyang, D., Li, X., Song, J., Shao, J.: Scenario-aware recurrent transformer for goal-directed video captioning. ACM Trans. Multim. Comput. Commun. Appl. **18**(4), 104:1–104:17 (2022)

15. Seo, M.J., Kembhavi, A., Farhadi, A., Hajishirzi, H.: Bidirectional attention flow for machine comprehension. In: 5th International Conference on Learning Representations, ICLR 2017, Toulon, France, 24–26 April 2017, Conference Track Proceedings (2017)

16. Shi, Z., Huang, X., Jain, A., Lin, C.: Applying deep learning to the cache replacement problem. In: Proceedings of the 52nd Annual IEEE/ACM International Symposium on Microarchitecture, MICRO 2019, Columbus, OH, USA, 12–16 October 2019, pp. 413–425 (2019)

17. Vaswani, A., et al.: Attention is all you need. In: Advances in Neural Information Processing Systems 30: Annual Conference on Neural Information Processing Systems 2017, Long Beach, CA, USA, 4–9 December 2017, pp. 5998–6008 (2017)

18. Wu, N., Li, P.: Phoebe: reuse-aware online caching with reinforcement learning for emerging storage models. CoRR abs/2011.07160 (2020)

19. Xu, Y., Frachtenberg, E., Jiang, S., Paleczny, M.: Characterizing facebook's memcached workload. IEEE Internet Comput. **18**(2), 41–49 (2014)

Spatial Data Processing

Conats: A Novel Framework for Cross-Modal Map Extraction

Zheng Chen, Junhua Fang$^{(\boxtimes)}$, Pingfu Chao, Jianfeng Qu, Pengpeng Zhao, and Jiajie Xu

Department of Computer Science and Technology, Soochow University, Suzhou, China
zchen6638@stu.suda.edu.cn, {jhfang,pfchao,jfqu,ppzhao,xujj}@suda.edu.cn

Abstract. Nowadays, the quality of digital maps is vital to various road-based applications, like autonomous driving, route recommendation, etc. The traditional way of map extraction/update through land surveying is expensive and usually fails to meet map recency requirements. The recent surge of automatic map extraction from GPS trajectory and/or aerial image data provides a cost-efficient way to update maps timely. However, extracting maps from solely GPS trajectories or aerial images can cause various map quality issues, and the latest neural network-based methods that fuse these two modalities do not consider their characteristics separately, so they suffer from the mutual perturbation of features. To address this issue, we propose a Cross-modal consistent enhancement and joint supervision framework (Conats) using both GPS trajectories and aerial images. It comprehensively extracts the local features and global features of each modality, then features of the same layer from different modalities are first fused to generate a modal consistent information gain which is used to enhance each modality's features afterward. Moreover, we propose a new joint supervision prediction module that uses a combined loss function set consisting of Dice loss, focal loss, and BCE loss to better model the distinct features of different modalities. Extensive experiments are conducted on the Beijing and Porto datasets that show superior performance over existing works in terms of the accuracy of generated maps.

Keywords: Map extraction · Aerial images · GPS trajectories

1 Introduction

As the foundation of the transportation system and Location Based Services (LBS), the quality of digital maps is crucial for various applications such as autonomous driving, navigation, and car-hailing [18]. Currently, major map service providers, like Google, Amap, and Baidu, are spending considerable amount of effort to collect data by mapping fleets equipped with special positioning devices and manually generating maps from the collected data [4]. However, as the road network evolves with time continuously, the time-consuming process of

© The Author(s), under exclusive license to Springer Nature Switzerland AG 2022
R. Chbeir et al. (Eds.): WISE 2022, LNCS 13724, pp. 503–518, 2022.
https://doi.org/10.1007/978-3-031-20891-1_36

manual map generation is unable to meet the demands of timely map construction and update. Therefore, there is a strong need for automatic map creation.

Numerous approaches have been proposed to extract maps from various data sources, such as aerial images and GPS trajectories, but they face different challenges due to respective data features. For example, maps extracted from aerial images [2,19,22,23] usually fail to maintain the road topology as roads in the images are occluded by trees, buildings, and their shadows, while extracting maps from GPS trajectories [5,6,8,14,21] always suffer from excessive noise (e.g., positioning drift) and uneven distribution of trajectories.

Although aerial images and GPS trajectories face respective dilemmas, they capture information from different modalities, so the information lost in one modality could be obtainable from the other one. In other words, different modalities may supplement each other to capture more information. As a result, several recent works [11,15,16] combine the features of aerial images and GPS trajectories to extract maps and achieve some progress. However, problems persist in this approach that noisy features from one modal may perturb the other. Specifically, initial map features extracted from trajectories are usually noisy, but they are directly misjudged as road parts in this model. Using the features with misjudged information to enhance aerial images will introduce new noise to the aerial images. Similarly, extracting information from aerial images has the problem of trees, shadows, and buildings occluding the road. This part of the road will be recognized as the background. The use of inaccurate features containing this situation to enhance trajectories will weaken the characteristics of the trajectories themselves. Although global features are introduced in trajectories and aerial images to mitigate the perturbation of such features, we argue that there is still room for improvement.

In addition, the previous works [11,15,16] all use binary cross entropy or cross entropy as the supervised loss function blindly, which do not consider the respective feature of trajectories and aerial images in such a composite scenario. Specifically, for aerial images, since the road areas only account for a tiny portion of the image, it usually has an unbalanced foreground (road areas) and background (semantic elements other than road areas). Using cross entropy or binary cross entropy as the loss function may cause the predicted results to be biased towards the background. Meanwhile, for the GPS trajectories, after being converted into grayscale trajectory maps, there is an obvious imbalance of positive and negative samples (e.g., negative samples are black areas with no GPS trajectory), and thus affects the classification difficulty. Therefore, a redesign of the supervised loss function is also necessary.

To avoid the mutual perturbation of different modal features, we design a novel cross-modal consistent enhancement module that captures both the local and global information of aerial images and GPS trajectories. The respective features are then combined through a learned weighting framework to finally generate a modal consistent information gain. In addition, to make up for the lack of BCE loss, we propose a new joint supervision prediction module based on the combination of Dice loss [12], focal loss [10] and BCE loss to instruct the network model to learn the features of each modality more effectively during the training process and guide the features to fuse more validly.

In summary, this paper makes three major contributions.

- We design a novel cross-modal consistent enhancement module that adaptively captures a modal consistent information gain from aerial images and GPS trajectories.
- We propose a new joint supervision prediction module based on Dice loss, focal loss, and BCE loss to better extract features of different modalities and guide the fusion of features.
- We conduct extensive experiments on two real-world datasets that compare our proposed method with multiple baselines, and the results clearly demonstrate the effectiveness of our method.

The rest of this paper is organized as follows. We first elaborate major related work of map extraction in Sect. 2. The proposed cross-modal consistent enhancement and joint supervision framework is then detailed in Sect. 3, and experiments and evaluations are conducted in Sect. 4. Finally, we conclude this article in Sect. 5.

2   Related Work

2.1   Extracting Map from Aerial Images

Due to the excellent performance in feature extraction, deep learning is increasingly used to extract maps from aerial images. For instance, Bastani et al. [2] use an iterative search process guided by a CNN-based decision function to derive the road network graph directly from the output of the CNN. Zhang et al. [19] build a network model with residual units, which is similar to U-Net for extracting maps. Zhou et al. [22] adopt encoder-decoder structure, dilated convolution, and pretrained encoder to construct a semantic segmentation neural network for map extraction. Zhu et al. [23] propose a Global Context-aware and Batch-independent Network, which adds the Global Context-Aware (GCA) block to the encoder-decoder structure to effectively integrate global context features to predict maps. The above studies directly extract roads from aerial images through deep convolutional neural networks, which has inherent limitations. Specifically, these methods perform poorly when the road is occluded by trees, buildings, and their shadows in aerial images. Therefore, it is necessary to explore complementary information from other modalities to assist map extraction.

2.2   Extracting Map from GPS Trajectories

With the widespread availability of wireless networks and smartphones, GPS data have become easy to obtain [1]. Consequently, some scholars also explore map extraction based on the distribution of GPS trajectory data. According to the survey [3], existing traditional works are categorized into three classes:

1) road abstraction [5,9], which mainly finds the densest areas on the map by clustering technology and extracts the road network from them. 2) incremental branching [6,21], the idea of which is to insert new roads incrementally on the empty map through trace merging or map expanding until all trajectories have been checked. 3) intersection linking [8,17], which emphasizes the correct detection of intersections, and once the intersections are inferred, the remaining steps are to use the trajectory information to connect the intersections. In recent years, Ruan *et al.* [14] proposed a map generation framework based on deep learning that extracts features from spatial view and transition view of trajectories to infer road centerlines. Overall, despite the variety of trajectory-based methods, the quality of current extracted maps is still unsatisfactory due to the noise and uneven distribution of trajectories.

2.3   Extracting Map from Multi-modal Data

Some recent works attempt to combine aerial images with different modal information for better map extraction performance. For instance, Parajuli *et al.* [13] propose a low-cost and modular deep convolutional neural network named TriSeg, which extracts features from the transformed lidar data and fuses them with the image features to generate final maps via SegNet. In addition to lidar, some works also combine aerial images with GPS trajectories. To be specific, Sun *et al.* [15] concatenate the features of aerial images and trajectory maps and feed them to different segment networks (e.g., UNet and its variant Res-UNet, LinkNet and its variant D-LinkNet) to generate final maps. Wu *et al.* [16] extract the features of the aerial images and trajectory maps at different layers of the U-Net network, each of which is fed to the gated module to form fusion features, and then these fusion features are sent to an independent prediction network to estimate the final road maps. Liu *et al.* [11] feed trajectory maps and aerial images into two D-LinkNet, respectively, to extract features and then use dual augmentation modules to mutually augment the features of different modalities to predict the final maps. Although the above methods have made some progress, these fusion methods do not take into account the perturbation of features between different modalities, so more effective strategies are needed to deal with the fusion of features.

3   Methodology

3.1   Framework Overview

As mentioned above, although aerial images and GPS trajectories have complementary effects in map extraction, while using different modal features to enhance each other, there is also a high chance that the noise from different modals perturbs each other. In order to effectively suppress the perturbation of features, we propose a cross-modal consistent enhancement and joint supervision framework (Conats), as shown in Fig. 1, which can enhance the features of different modalities while suppressing the perturbation of features so as to better

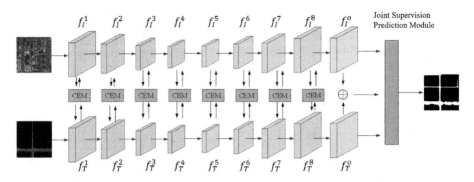

Fig. 1. The architecture of the proposed Conats, which is composed of two AutoEncoders that capture the features of aerial images and GPS trajectories, respectively, and cross-modal consistent enhancement modules that produce a modal consistent information gain for different modalities, and a joint supervision prediction module that is used to optimize the predicted maps.

capture their complementary information.specifically, our model is comprised of three modules: 1) D-LinkNet [22]-based AutoEncoders, which are used to learn the features of each modality; 2) cross-modal consistent enhancement modules (CEM) aiming to capture a modal consistent information gain for enhancing features of each modality; 3) a joint supervision prediction module based on combination loss, which is used to instruct the network model to learn the features of each modality more effectively during the training process and fuse the features properly.

3.2   Modal Feature Learning

We use two D-LinkNet-based backbone networks as AutoEncoders, each of which is composed of four encoders, four decoders, and a transformation map. For a given aerial image I and trajectory map T, we capture features of each modality via different AutoEncoders. As shown in Fig. 1, we capture the features of I through the first AutoEncoder, noted as:

$$F_I = \{F_I^1, F_I^2, F_I^3, F_I^4, F_I^5, F_I^6, F_I^7, F_I^8, F_I^o\} \tag{1}$$

The first four features are generated by encoders, and decoders produce the following four features, and the last is generated by the transformation map. Similarly, features of T generated by the second AutoEncoder are noted as:

$$F_T = \{F_T^1, F_T^2, F_T^3, F_T^4, F_T^5, F_T^6, F_T^7, F_T^8, F_T^o\} \tag{2}$$

The AutoEncoder of the aerial images I is shown in Fig. 2. We use a 7×7 standard convolution with stride $= 2$ to extract preliminary features. Then 2×2 max-pooling, Res-blocks and 3×3 convolutions are used to extract further features. After getting feature f_4, four different dilated convolutions are applied

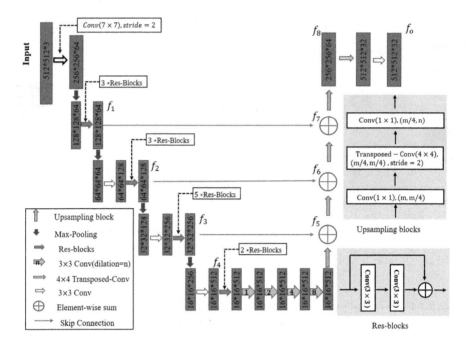

Fig. 2. The structure of AutoEncoder, in which $\text{Conv}(k \times k), (m, n)$ denotes a $k \times k$ standard convolution, whose input channel is m and output channel is n.

to capture more spatial information by broadening the convolution's receptive field. To avoid information loss, we adapt skipping connection after upsampling blocks. Finally, in the transformation map process, we use a 4×4 transposed convolution to recover the resolution of the image, and a 3×3 convolution is applied to reduce the dimension of features for the joint supervision prediction module. The same applies to AutoEncoder of trajectory map extraction module, where the only difference is that the input picture has one channel.

3.3 Cross-Modal Consistent Enhancement

After capturing each modal features, we enhance them by cross-modal consistent enhancement modules, which consist of an information extraction module and a gated fusion module. The former extracts local and global information of each modal feature, and the latter is used to fuse local information and global information of different modalities.

Information Extraction Module: As shown in Fig. 3(a), given an aerial image feature F_I and a GPS trajectory feature F_T, we first capture their corresponding local information $L_I \in R^{h \times w \times c}$ and $L_T \in R^{h \times w \times c}$ with a 3×3 convolution, and the local information is then collected to produce the global information G_I and G_T, respectively. Similar to the previous work [11], we adopt a 3-level Spatial Pyramid Pooling (SPP [7]) and a fully connected layer to generate global information. To be specific, taking L_T as an example, at level i, ($i = 1,2,3$), L_T is divided into $2^{i-1} \times 2^{i-1}$ regions, each of which is fed to a $\frac{h}{2^{i-1}} \times \frac{w}{2^{i-1}}$ max-pooling layer to generate $1 \times 1 \times c$ features. These features at all levels are concatenated and fed to a fully connected layer with c output neurons to obtain a global feature, which is later copied $h \times w$ times and reshaped to form the global information $G_T \in R^{h \times w \times c}$.

Gate Fusion Module: Unlike previous work [11] which uses one modality's local and global information to enhance the other modality's features, we employ a gated fusion strategy to dynamically fuse local and global information of different modalities to mitigate the feature perturbation between modals. Specifically, taking L_I as an example, we use two 1×1 convolutional layers to learn the locally and globally gated weights θ_{L_I} and θ_{G_I}, respectively. And the same operation is applied to L_T as well. After getting four gated weights, namely θ_{L_I}, θ_{G_I}, θ_{L_T}, and θ_{G_T}, to generate a unified information gain, we adopt the softmax function to normalize the gated weights so as to meet the complementary constraints $\tilde{\theta}_{L_I} + \tilde{\theta}_{L_T} = 1$ and $\tilde{\theta}_{G_I} + \tilde{\theta}_{G_T} = 1$. (The calculation process is shown in Eq. 3 and Eq. 4).

$$\tilde{\theta}_{L_I} = \frac{\exp \theta_{L_I}}{\exp \theta_{L_I} + \exp \theta_{L_T}}, \tilde{\theta}_{L_T} = \frac{\exp \theta_{L_T}}{\exp \theta_{L_I} + \exp \theta_{L_T}} \tag{3}$$

$$\tilde{\theta}_{G_I} = \frac{\exp \theta_{G_I}}{\exp \theta_{G_I} + \exp \theta_{G_T}}, \tilde{\theta}_{G_T} = \frac{\exp \theta_{G_T}}{\exp \theta_{G_I} + \exp \theta_{G_T}} \tag{4}$$

The complementary constraints play a role that when one modal features are not credible enough (e.g., the shadows in aerial images and positioning drift in GPS trajectories), a lower weight value will be assigned to the modal, whereas the weight value of the other modal feature increases correspondingly. We weight the local and global information L_I, L_T, G_I, and G_T with normalized gate values $\tilde{\theta}_{L_I}$, $\tilde{\theta}_{L_T}$, $\tilde{\theta}_{G_I}$, and $\tilde{\theta}_{G_T}$ to acquire a locally consistent information gain F_{C_L} and a globally consistent information gain F_{C_G}, which can better extract consistent information and reduce the disturbance of features between different modal information (The calculation process is shown in Eq. 5 and Eq. 6, where $\otimes$ denotes element-wise product.) Then, the locally consistent information gain F_{C_L} and the globally consistent information gain F_{C_G} are added to form a modal consistent information gain F_O.

$$F_{C_L} = \tilde{\theta}_{L_I} \otimes L_I + \tilde{\theta}_{L_T} \otimes L_T \tag{5}$$

$$F_{C_G} = \tilde{\theta}_{G_I} \otimes G_I + \tilde{\theta}_{G_T} \otimes G_T \tag{6}$$

$$F_O = F_{C_L} + F_{C_G} \tag{7}$$

Next step, F_O is used to enhance F_I and F_T with the following equation:

$$F_I = F_O + F_I, F_T = F_O + F_T \tag{8}$$

Specifically, at the i-th level of Conats (i=1, 2...,7), the CEM module generates a modal consistent information gain F_O^i which is used to enhance F_I^i and F_T^i. Then, the enhanced F_I^i and F_T^i are fed to the next encoder or decoder, respectively, to produce F_I^{i+1} and F_T^{i+1}. Finally, the generated F_I^8 and F_T^8 are enhanced and provided to the transformation maps to get F_I^o and F_T^o, and their concatenation will be fed to the joint supervision prediction module to generate predicted maps.

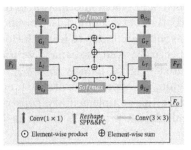 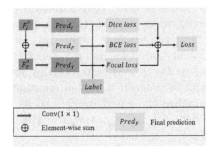

(a) Consistent Enhancement Module   (b) Joint Supervision Prediction Module

Fig. 3. (a) Consistent Enhancement Module (CEM), which explains how to get a modal consistent information gain F_o with the features F_I and F_T captured from aerial images and GPS trajectories, respectively. G_I and G_T are global information obtained by local information L_I and L_T through Spatial Pyramid Pooling [7] and Fully-Connected layer. θ_{G_I}, θ_{G_T}, θ_{L_I}, and θ_{L_T} are the learnable gate values. (b) Joint Supervision Prediction Module, which is composed of 1×1 convolutions that use sigmoid functions as activation functions to generate prediction maps and a combined loss based on Dice loss [12], focal loss [10], and BCE loss.

3.4 Joint Supervision Prediction

Currently, the state-of-the-art method [11] directly concatenates F_I^o and F_T^o to produce predicted maps and minimizes the BCE loss as the only learning objective, which is not optimal since complementary strengths of each modality may be insufficiently utilized. Hence, as depicted in Fig. 3(b), we propose a new joint supervision prediction module. Specifically, we employ the Dice loss [12] to supervise the prediction of aerial images, focal loss [10] to supervise the prediction of GPS trajectories, and the BCE loss to supervise their fusion prediction.

It is common for roads to occupy only a tiny area in aerial images, which often causes the learning process to get stuck in a local minima of the loss function, resulting in a network whose predictions are strongly biased towards the background [12]. Therefore, road areas are often missing or only partially detected. In this situation, Dice loss is used to solve the imbalance of foreground (road area) and background, which is defined by the following equation:

$$L_{Dice} = 1 - \frac{2 \times TP}{(TP + FN) + (TP + FP)} \qquad (9)$$

Here, we denote correctly predicted road pixels, i.e., true positive, as TP, road pixels that are wrongly predicted as non-roads, i.e., false negative, as FN, and non-road pixels which are wrongly predicted as roads, i.e., false positive, as FP.

For GPS trajectories, except above imbalance of foreground (road area) and background, the trajectory maps also have differences in classification difficulty. Specifically, when GPS points in a particular area are dense, it is easier to be identified as a road. On the contrary, when the GPS points in a specific area are sparse, it is more difficult to be identified. Therefore, the very naive idea is to reduce the weight of easy-to-discriminate samples so that the network can focus more on hard-to-classify samples during training. Fortunately, focal loss can exactly deal with this situation, the definition of which is as follow:

$$L_{focal} = -\alpha_t (1 - p_t)^\gamma log(p_t) \qquad (10)$$

$$p_t = \begin{cases} p & \text{if } y = 1 \\ 1 - p & \text{otherwise} \end{cases} \qquad (11)$$

where α_t is applied to control the shared weight of positive and negative samples to the total loss and γ is used to manage the weights of complex and easy-to-classify samples.

Following the previous work [11], for the fusion of aerial image features and GPS trajectory features, BCE loss is adopted to supervise prediction, depicted as follows:

$$L_{BCE} = -\sum_{i=1}^{N} [y_i \ln(\sigma(x_i)) + (1 - y_i) \ln(1 - \sigma(x_i))] \qquad (12)$$

$$\sigma(x) = \frac{1}{1 + \exp^{-x}} \qquad (13)$$

where we denote the ground-truth of a pixel as y_i, the prediction of a pixel as x_i, and the total pixel number as N. In fact, using BCE loss as the loss function for fusion supervision can alleviate the adverse effect of Dice loss on gradient backpropagation and make the training process more stable. Then, the above three loss functions are added to form the final loss function, denoted as:

$$Loss = L_{Dice} + L_{focal} + L_{BCE} \qquad (14)$$

Using a joint loss function for supervision can instruct the network model to learn the features of each modality more effectively during the training process and guide the features to fuse more validly, which in turn makes the map produced by the prediction process more accurate.

4   Experimental Evaluation

4.1   Experimental Setup

Datasets: We conduct our experiments on two real-world datasets, i.e., the Beijing dataset [15] and the Porto dataset [16]. The Beijing dataset contains 348 aerial images, the dimensions of which are 1024×1024, and the corresponding ground-truth label is manually created by the authors [15]. For the convenience of comparison, we resize the resolution to 512×512. The GPS data of the Beijing dataset comes from 8.1 million samples collected from 28,000 taxis over a week. On the basis of the spatial position coordinates, the GPS data is converted into binary image format according to the corresponding relationship between the original aerial images and the GPS latitude and longitude. The Porto dataset includes 6,048 aerial images with a resolution of 512×512, covering an area of about 209 square kilometers in Porto, Portugal. The GPS trajectories of this dataset are generated by 442 taxis from 2013 to 2014. Each dataset is randomly divided into the training, verification, and test dataset, occupying the proportion of 70%, 10%, and 20%, respectively.

Baselines: We compare our Conats with two state-of-the-art fusion-based approaches, i.e., DeepDualMapper [16] and CMMPNet [11]. DeepDualMapper extracts the features of aerial images and trajectory maps at different network layers through U-net and then fuses these features through a gated fusion module. The fused features of different levels are fed to the joint supervision prediction module to generate the finally predicted maps. CMMPNet feeds aerial images and trajectory maps into different AutoEncoders and then strengthens features of each modality via a dual enhancement module. Finally, the predicted maps are produced through the concatenation of different modal features. Since no source code is provided for these methods, we reproduce them according to the corresponding papers.

Metric: We adopt intersection of union (IoU) as the metric to evaluate the performance of map extraction. The IoU score is calculated as follows:

$$IoU = \frac{TP}{TP + FP + FN} \tag{15}$$

where the definition of TP, FP, and FN is the same as that in Dice loss.

Implementation Details: We implement Conats using the PyTorch framework. In addition, we use Adam optimization and set the batch size to 4 and the learning rate to 0.0002. Finally, the model is trained for 110 epochs with combined loss as the final loss function.

4.2   Quantitative Evaluation

We report the IoU score for the two baseline solutions and our approach Conats in Table 1. Note that all approaches achieve better results on the Porto dataset because the Porto aerial images are clear and have less trajectory noise [16].

Table 1. The performance of all approaches on the Beijing dataset and the Porto dataset.

Dateset	Approach	IoU
Beijing	DeepDualMapper	61.73%
	CMMPNet	62.48%
	Conats	63.86%
Porto	DeepDualMapper	73.74%
	CMMPNet	76.23%
	Conats	77.05%

Table 2. The IoU score of the state-of-the-art approach CMMPNet, our approach Conats and three variants Conats-NJ, Conats-NF, and Conats-AD.

Dateset	Approach	IoU
Beijing	CMMPNet	62.48%
	Conats-NJ	62.77%
	Conats-NF	63.22%
	Conats-AD	63.55%
	Conats	63.86%
Porto	CMMPNet	76.23%
	Conats-NJ	76.72%
	Conats-NF	76.89%
	Conats-AD	74.15%
	Conats	77.05%

Compared with the state-of-the-art method CMMPNet, our Conats has a relative improvement of 2.2% and 1.1%, respectively, on the two datasets. DeepDualMapper only uses the fusion idea and does not enhance the features of each modality, so it cannot perform very well. CMMPNet mutually enhances the features of different modalities and thus achieves relatively good performance, but it does not perform well in suppressing the feature perturbation of different modalities. Our method Conats enhances features of different modalities and suppresses perturbation between them by generating a modal consistent information gain from global information and local information and guides features to fuse accurately and efficiently through a joint supervision prediction module.

Evaluation of Consistent Enhancement Module: In previous work [11], feature perturbation is not well resolved. So, we implement a variant of Conats named Conats-NJ to solely verify the effectiveness of our CEM module. Specifically, we remove the joint supervision prediction module and only use the concatenation of F_I^o and F_T^o to generate prediction with BCE loss. As shown in

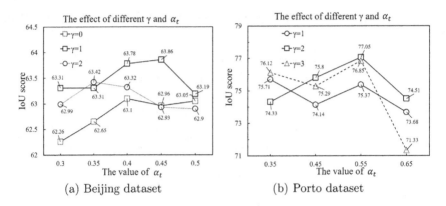

Fig. 4. The performance of focal loss on the Beijing dataset and Porto dataset.

Table 2, when only using the CEM module, Conats-NJ also achieves a relative improvement of about 0.46% and 0.64% on the two datasets, respectively, compared to CMMPNet. This fully demonstrates the effectiveness of our CEM module. Compared with the Beijing dataset, the Porto dataset has more explicit aerial images and better trajectory quality, so more modal consistent information gains can be extracted, resulting in an even better performance.

Evaluation of Joint Supervision Prediction Module: In this section, we will demonstrate the performance improvement brought by Dice loss and focal loss, respectively. Same as above, we also implement two variants of the joint supervision prediction module called Conats-NF and Conats-AD. Conats-NF uses Dice loss, BCE loss, and BCE loss for aerial images, trajectory maps, and the fusion of them, respectively while Conats-AD all uses Dice loss. Compared with Conats-NJ, Conats-NF achieves a 0.45% massive improvement on the Beijing dataset in Table 2, which we deem this is mainly due to the fact that Dice loss is easier to get out of the local minima of the loss function than BCE loss. However, on the Porto dataset, the improvement of Conats-NF compared to Conats-NJ is not significant because the sample size of the Porto dataset is larger, reaching 6048 copies. So even if the loss function cannot get the minimum, a local minimum that is relatively close to the minimum can be obtained. In comparison to Conats-NF, Conats-AD achieve better performance on the Beijing dataset while worse performance on the Porto dataset. We deem the reason is the scale of the Beijing dataset is much smaller than Porto dataset, so the disadvantage of Dice loss with drastic gradient changes and unstable training process are not easy to reflect. Regardless of the datasets, compared with different variants, Conats both achieves more than 0.2% improvement, which is contributed to the focal loss for its excellent performance in dealing with samples with the imbalance in difficulty and samples with the imbalance in positive and negative ratios.

For focal loss, it has two hyperparameters: γ is used to control the weights of complex and easy-to-classify samples, and α_t is used to manage the shared weight of positive and negative samples. On the Beijing dataset, we can draw the

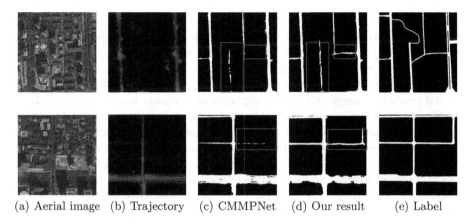

(a) Aerial image (b) Trajectory (c) CMMPNet (d) Our result (e) Label

Fig. 5. The visual comparison of results generated by our method (Conats) and the state-of-the-art method (CMMPNet) on the Beijing dataset.

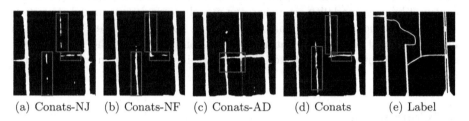

(a) Conats-NJ (b) Conats-NF (c) Conats-AD (d) Conats (e) Label

Fig. 6. The visual comparison of results generated by Conats and variants Conats-NJ, Conats-NF, Conats-AD, respectively, on the Beijing dataset.

conclusion from Fig. 4 that when γ is set to 1, the overall performance of focal loss is the best, and when α_t is assigned to 0.45, Conats achieves a relatively optimal performance of 63.86% IoU score. For the Porto dataset, we know that when α_t is set to 0.55, the overall performance of focal loss is the best, and when γ is assigned to 2, Conats achieves the relatively optimal performance of 77.05% IoU score. Since the GPS data of the Beijing dataset and the Porto dataset are collected by different devices, the sampling time interval and GPS positioning accuracy are different, so the distribution of the converted trajectory map data is dissimilar, which leads to different hyperparameter settings.

4.3 Qualitative Evaluation

When the small road sections of the aerial images are full of shadows and occlusions, there will be apparent noise (shadows and occlusions) in the aerial image features extracted by the AutoEncoder of CMMPNet. Although CMMPNet introduces global information to mitigate the perturbation of such noisy features (shadows and occlusions), we argue that the global information of a single modality is not enough to suppress the noisy features of the modality well. In addition, since the trajectories of the small road segments are sparse, the features of the trajectory maps are not obvious and sufficiently credible, so using the aerial image features with noise to enhance the trajectory map features will suppress the features of the trajectory maps themselves which causes the model makes wrong judgments. The missing and interrupted phenomenon of the generated prediction maps in Fig. 5(c) supports our opinion to a certain extent.

Since our method uses Dice loss as a supervised loss function for aerial images, it is more confident in avoiding background (e.g., shadows and occlusions) and extracting features of foreground (road) regions. As shown in Fig. 6(a) and Fig. 6(b), compared with Conats-NJ, Conats-NF uses Dice loss to improve the supervision module, so the obtained result is more accurate. Compared with Conats-NF, Conats-AD all used Dice loss introduces some untrue road which proves all using Dice loss is not suitable for our tasks. As shown in Fig. 6(b) and Fig. 6(d), Conats employs focal loss to supervise the trajectory map prediction, resulting in a higher quality of the extracted maps compared to Conats-NF which further proves that focal loss can facilitate map extraction. Since the features captured by each modality are noisy, our model requires cross-modal consistent enhancement modules that dynamically assign normalized gate values to each modality's local and global features to sufficiently suppress the noise of each modality and thus generate a modal consistent information gain to enhance the features of each modality.

5   Conclusion

In this paper, we investigate an essential topic, i.e., how to use aerial images and GPS trajectories to improve the performance of map extraction tasks. The innovations of this paper are as follows: We proposed a framework called Conats that fuses the feature of aerial images and GPS trajectories. This framework uses a cross-modal consistent enhancement module to enhance each modality's features and uses a new joint loss function to supervise the network model to learn the features of each modality more effectively. We compared our method with two state-of-the-art methods and found a more than 1% relative performance improvement, respectively.

Acknowledgements. This work was supported by National Natural Science Foundation of China under grant (No. 1802273, 62102277), Postdoctoral Science Foundation of China (No. 020M681529), Natural Science Foundation of Jiangsu Province (BK20210703), China Science and Technology Plan Project of Suzhou (No. SYG202139), Postgraduate Research & Practice Innovation Program of Jiangsu Province (SJCX2_11342), Project Funded by the Priority Academic Program Development of Jiangsu Higher Education Institutions.

References

1. Allheeib, N., Adhinugraha, K., Taniar, D., Islam, M., et al.: Computing reverse nearest neighbourhood on road maps. World Wide Web **25**(1), 99–130 (2022)
2. Bastani, F., He, S., Abbar, S., Alizadeh, M., Balakrishnan, H.: Roadtracer: automatic extraction of road networks from aerial images. IEEE (2018)
3. Chao, P., Hua, W., Mao, R., Xu, J., Zhou, X.: A survey and quantitative study on map inference algorithms from gps trajectories. IEEE Trans. Knowl. Data Eng. **34**, 15–28 (2020)
4. Chen, C., Lu, C., Huang, Q., Yang, Q., Gunopulos, D., Guibas, L.: City-scale map creation and updating using GPS collections. In: Proceedings of the 22nd ACM SIGKDD International Conference on Knowledge Discovery and Data Mining, pp. 1465–1474 (2016)
5. Dørum, O.H.: Deriving double-digitized road network geometry from probe data. In: Proceedings of the 25th ACM SIGSPATIAL International Conference on Advances in Geographic Information Systems, pp. 1–10 (2017)
6. He, S., Bastani, F., Abbar, S., Alizadeh, M., Balakrishnan, H., Chawla, S., Madden, S.: Roadrunner: improving the precision of road network inference from gps trajectories. In: Proceedings of the 26th ACM SIGSPATIAL International Conference on Advances in Geographic Information Systems, pp. 3–12 (2018)
7. He, K., Zhang, X., Ren, S., Sun, J.: Spatial pyramid pooling in deep convolutional networks for visual recognition. IEEE Trans. Pattern Anal. Mach. Intell. **37**, 1904–1916 (2015)
8. Karagiorgou, S., Pfoser, D., Skoutas, D.: A layered approach for more robust generation of road network maps from vehicle tracking data. ACM Trans. Spatial Algor. Syst. (TSAS) **3**(1), 1–21 (2017)
9. Li, H., Kulik, L., Ramamohanarao, K.: Automatic generation and validation of road maps from gps trajectory data sets. In: Proceedings of the 25th ACM International on Conference on Information and Knowledge Management, pp. 1523–1532 (2016)
10. Lin, T.Y., Goyal, P., Girshick, R., He, K., Dollár, P.: Focal loss for dense object detection. In: Proceedings of the IEEE International Conference on Computer Vision, pp. 2980–2988 (2017)
11. Liu, L., Yang, Z., Li, G., Wang, K., Chen, T., Lin, L.: Aerial images meet crowdsourced trajectories: a new approach to robust road extraction. IEEE Trans. Neural Netw. Learn. Syst. (2022)
12. Milletari, F., Navab, N., Ahmadi, S.A.: V-net: Fully convolutional neural networks for volumetric medical image segmentation. In: 2016 Fourth International Conference on 3D Vision (3DV), pp. 565–571. IEEE (2016)
13. Parajuli, B., Kumar, P., Mukherjee, T., Pasiliao, E., Jambawalikar, S.: Fusion of aerial lidar and images for road segmentation with deep cnn. In: Proceedings of the 26th ACM SIGSPATIAL International Conference on Advances in Geographic Information Systems, pp. 548–551 (2018)
14. Ruan, S., Long, C., Bao, J., Li, C., Zheng, Y.: Learning to generate maps from trajectories. In: Proceedings of the AAAI Conference on Artificial Intelligence, vol. 34, no. 1, pp. 890–897 (2020)
15. Sun, T., Di, Z., Che, P., Liu, C., Wang, Y.: Leveraging crowdsourced gps data for road extraction from aerial imagery. In: Proceedings of the IEEE/CVF Conference on Computer Vision and Pattern Recognition, pp. 7509–7518 (2019)

16. Wu, H., Zhang, H., Zhang, X., Sun, W., Zheng, B., Jiang, Y.: Deepdualmapper: a gated fusion network for automatic map extraction using aerial images and trajectories. In: Proceedings of the AAAI Conference on Artificial Intelligence, vol. 34, pp. 1037–1045 (2020)
17. Xie, X., Wong, K.B.Y., Aghajan, H., Veelaert, P., Philips, W.: Road network inference through multiple track alignment. Transp. Res. Part C: Emerg. Technol. **72**, 93–108 (2016)
18. Xu, J., Zhao, J., Zhou, R., Liu, C., Zhao, P., Zhao, L.: Predicting destinations by a deep learning based approach. IEEE Trans. Knowl. Data Eng. **33**(2), 651–666 (2019)
19. Zhang, Z., Liu, Q., Wang, Y.: Road extraction by deep residual u-net. IEEE Geosci. Remote Sens. Lett. **15**, 1–5 (2017)
20. Zhang, Z., Liu, Q., Wang, Y.: Road extraction by deep residual u-net. IEEE Geosci. Remote Sens. Lett. **15**(5), 749–753 (2018)
21. Zheng, K., Zhu, D.: A novel clustering algorithm of extracting road network from low-frequency floating car data. Cluster Comput. **22**(5), 12659–12668 (2019)
22. Zhou, L., Zhang, C., Ming, W.: D-linknet: linknet with pretrained encoder and dilated convolution for high resolution satellite imagery road extraction. In: 2018 IEEE/CVF Conference on Computer Vision and Pattern Recognition Workshops (CVPRW) (2018)
23. Zhu, Q., et al.: A global context-aware and batch-independent network for road extraction from VHR satellite imagery. ISPRS J. Photogram. Remote Sens. **175**, 353–365 (2021)

Attentive Knowledge-Aware Path Network for Explainable Travel Mashup

Marwa Boulakbech$^{(\boxtimes)}$, Nizar Messai, Yacine Sam, and Thomas Devogele

LIFAT, University of Tours, Tours, France
{marwa.boulakbech,nizar.messai,yacine.sam,thomas.devogele}@univ-tours.fr

Abstract. Personalized travel mashups aim to assist users in making decision i.e what places to visit. To facilitate human decisions with credible suggestions, these systems should have the ability to generate corresponding explanations while making recommendations. Knowledge graphs (KG), which contain rich and comprehensive information among items are widely used to enable this. By reasoning over a KG in a node-by-node manner, the connectivity between items can be discovered as paths that serve as an explanation to enhance the interpretability of recommendations. However, existing methods failed to utilize the information of collective-level POI sequences. The individual-level cannot represent more holistic semantic features and cannot express complete transition patterns. To this end, we propose knowledge-aware approach for explainable travel mashup that joints the multi-granularity representation and the attention mechanism to capture the sequential dependencies at collective-level POI on different granularities. Specifically, we encode a diversity of semantic relations and connectivity patterns into a travel knowledge graph. Then, we employ a recurrent network architecture to exploit the semantics of paths entities pair, which are fused into explainable recommendation using attentive graph. Extensive validation on a real-world datasets shows the effectiveness of the proposed approach.

Keywords: Mashups · Knowledge graph · Recurrent neural network · Attention mechanism

1 Introduction

Travel Web APIs such as Google places, Sygic travel[1], Foursquare[2], Tourinsoft[3], etc. provide easy access to travel information. While each of these services provides a fragmented view of the travel information, a simple way, in which they are easily connected, is through the composition of relevant services that cover a particular travel information need. Thus, Travel Mashup may be defined as the combination of a set of travel services that do not only retrieve relevant information from multiple sources but also merge it in order to present them

---

[1] https://travel.sygic.com/fr.

[2] https://developer.foursquare.com/docs.

[3] http://api-doc.tourinsoft.com/#/home.

to the end-user as directly usable information [1]. To enhance user satisfaction, we believe that personalized travel mashup should have the ability to generate corresponding explanations while making recommendations.

Recently, knowledge graphs (KGs) have been widely used due to their rich structured knowledge. They are considered as efficient form of knowledge representation that captures the semantics of web objects based on different entities and their relationships making recommendations interpretable.

By exploring the interlinks within a KG, the connectivity between entities can be discovered as paths. This offers a rich and **complementary information**. Such connectivity not only reveals the semantics of entities and relations, but also serves as an explanation and reflects a simulated decision-making process which provides explicit semantics for the explanations. However, existing efforts have not fully explored this **connectivity** to infer user interest regarding the sequential dependencies modeling with a holistic semantics. In fact, they usually exploit the individual-level sequences but fail to utilize the information of collective-level sequences that is common in the real world. Explaining sequential recommendation is a challenging task, as it requires the ability to effectively encoding a diversity of semantic relations and sequential dependencies at collective-level to express complete transition patterns. Furthermore, these knowledge-aware paths derived from KG help to reason about **explanation** of recommendations by synthesizing information, so as to increase users' satisfaction and trust.

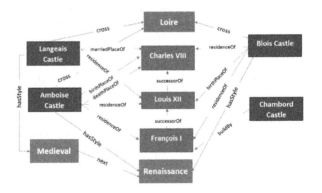

Fig. 1. Illustration of KG-aware mashup in the travel domain

Running Example: Synthesizing the heterogeneous information encoded in KGs shown in Fig. 1 provides personalised travel paths.

$(AmboiseCastle, birthPlaceOf, CharlesVIII) \wedge (BloisCastle, residenceOf,$

$CharlesVIII) \wedge (LangeaisCastle, marriedPlaceOf, CharlesVIII) \wedge$

$(BloisCastle, birthPlaceOf, LouisXII) \wedge (LouisXII, successorOf, CharlesVIII)$

$\rightarrow$ Amboise Castle , Langeais Castle and Blois Castle are **complementary** POIs

as they tell the story of Charles VIII and Louis XII.

Thus, the travel mashup recommendation *(Amboise Castle, Langeais Castle, Blois Castle)* is explained by this connection. We consider that the user demand constitutes a practical user-centric guidance during the reasoning process and can reveal items of potential interest for a given user.

Our goal is to fully exploit entity relations in KG to extract qualified paths with different semantics of individual-level and collective-level POI sequences. This provides **sequence-aware travel mashup** that reflects **explainable recommendations** over path reasoning based on a user-centric view.

To achieve this goal, we propose an Attentive Knowledge-aware Path Recurrent Network approach, which not only generates representations for paths by accounting for both entities and relations, but also performs reasoning based on paths to infer explainable recommendations.

Specifically, we construct first a travel-domain specific knowledge graph gathering fine-granular attraction types that allows a deep convergence of all the data and full considerations of such semantic relations. Then, we model it using a recurrent network based on Gated Recurrent Unit (GRU) technique. The user-centric path reasoning utilizes the multi-granularity representation and the attention mechanism to capture the contribution of paths on different levels of granularities for the travel mashup explanation.

The contributions of this work are summarized as follows:

– We propose a travel knowledge graph which models mashup data as a knowledge graph (called TKG), to represent the relationships between travel related data. The TKG is built by mining several data sources, in order to extract relevant entities, as well as the relationships between them in a multi-granularity representation.
– We propose an attentive neural network to model entities' sequential dependencies and adopt user-guided path reasoning to infer useful explanations.
– We conduct experiments with real-world datasets to demonstrate the effectiveness of our approach.

The rest of this article is organised as follows. First, Sect. 2 presents Attentive Knowledge-aware Path Network for Explainable Travel Mashup approach. In Sect. 3 we describe the conducted evaluation. Related works are discussed in Sect. 4 while the last section sums up our approach and suggests future perspectives.

2 Attentive Knowledge-Aware Path Network

To provide explainable recommendation, it is compulsory to take side information into account. We investigate the utility of knowledge graph which breaks down the independent interaction assumption by linking items with their attributes. We propose an attentive knowledge-aware approach to encode a diversity of semantic relations and discover personalized connectivity patterns in order to explain travel mashup. Figure 2 shows an overview of our proposed approach which is structured into two steps: *TKG Construction* and *Attentive Path Network Modeling*.

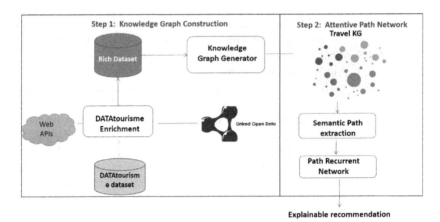

Fig. 2. Attentive knowledge-aware path network for explainable travel mashup approach overview

2.1   Travel Knowledge Graph Construction

The Knowledge Graph Construction step is used to build the TKG in order to capture more complex relationships among objects at a deeper semantic level. We generate KG triples using the DATAtourism[4] model which is augmented to create a rich set of linked data through a light integration process. This process is out of scope of this paper.

Formally, a knowledge graph is a directed graph connecting entities, E, using the relationship that exists among those entities, R. The nodes are the entities and the edges are the relations. These are popularly referred to as triples. For each triple, the edge and the 2 nodes it connects can be expressed as:

$$(h, r, t) \mid h,\ t \in E,\ r \in R$$

Here, h and t are the head and tail entities respectively and r is the relation that links them.

In the Knowledge graph, there may be multiple types of relations between each pair of entities (Place, POI, Period and Person). Figure 3 describes the TKG global schema.

To create the travel knowledge graph, the knowledge graph generator is structured into 2 modules: (i) *Entity Extraction Module* and (ii) *Relation Extraction Module*

For entity extraction, it is easy to identify the POI entity from the DATA-tourisme dataset. For the other entities, the entity extraction module extracts an entity from the POI description attribute and links it to corresponding entity in the KG. The aim of this module is to map an entity in unstructured text to a uniform resource identifier (URI) from the LOD cloud such us DBpedia. Entities

---

[4] http://www.datatourisme.fr/fonctionnement/ontologie/.

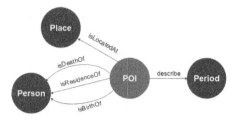

Fig. 3. Travel Knowledge Graph Schema

are recognized from natural language text to create a set of extracted entities. If an extracted entity can be mapped to an identified resource in the dataset, the URI of such resource can be used as a representative for the extracted entity. Otherwise, a new URI is assigned to the entity through DBpedia research query. As natural language text usually contains abbreviations, pronouns, and different expressions that refer to the same entities, the mapping process detects coreferring chains of entities in the description. To further illustrate the flow of the knowledge graph generator, an example is given in Fig. 4. The extraction module extracts 3 entities *{ Château d'Amboise= { datatourisme: Chateau_Amboise }; Renaissance= {datatourisme: Renaissance}; Loire Valley= {datatourisme: Loire_Valley}}* from the semantic dataset and connects 2 others Person entities from dbpedia *{ Charles VIII= { dbpedia: Charles_VIII_de_France}; François I = {dbpedia: François_Ier}}*. We used DBpedia Spotlight tool[5] for dbpedia resource linking and a coreference resolver [2] to discover chains of coreferring entities.

The relation extraction module aims to extract a relation triple from the description attribute then integrates the results of the entity extraction module for triple mapping using a rule-based method.

In our scenario, the relation is a predicate of a triple and its associated arguments are the subject of a triple and the object of a triple. Open information extraction techniques are used to extract information from an arbitrary sentence using pattern templates, and then to convert such information into a relation triple. In particular, as depicted in Fig. 4, the example of the relation triple from the triple extraction component is *{ Château d'Amboise, in, Loire Valley}* , where "in" is a relation, which is the predicate of the triple, and *"Château d'Amboise"* and *"Loire Valley"* are its arguments, which are the subject and the object of the triple, respectively.

For triple mapping, we enrich first generated text triples using outputs from the entity extraction module to create the bootstrapping triples. As shown in Fig. 4, the triple *{ Château d'Amboise, becames royal residence, Charles VIII}* is enriched as follow *{datatourisme: Chateau_Amboise, ex: becames_royal_residence:, dbpedia: Charles_VIII}*. Then, a rule-based method is used to generate predicate candidate pairs for the text predicate from the bootstrapping triples. For example, *ex: becames_royal_residence* is mapped to *dbpe-*

---

[5] https://www.dbpedia-spotlight.org/.

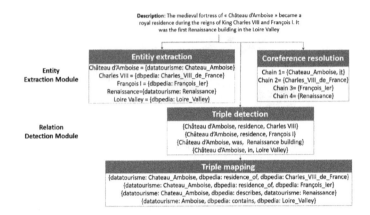

Fig. 4. Graph Generation Flow Example

dia: residence_of. Since we build a domain-specific knowledge graph, a rule-based method for triple mapping is adequate. For instance, triple in the form {*POI, ex: $reside$, Person*} is mapped to *dbpedia: residence_of*, the form {*POI, ex: in, Place*} is mapped to *dbpedia: isLocatedAt*.

2.2 Attentive Path Recurrent Network

Given the heterogeneous information encoded in the TKG, our goal is to capture more complex relationships among entities at a deeper semantic level to be used in recommendation explanation for personalised travel mashup. We take the advantages of path connectivity and leverage the sequential dependencies of entities and sophisticated relations using a path recurrent network. We first mine semantic paths, then encode them using a GRU network architecture and discriminate the contributions of different paths to compute paths scores as shown in Fig. 5.

A.Path Extraction: in this study, the TKG investigated can be considered as a heterogeneous information network, since it includes more than one type of entities (POI, person, period, ...) and entity relations (residence, hasTheme, building, ...). The connectivity between entities can be discovered as paths, which provides rich and complementary information.

Definition 1. *Mashup: a mashup M can be represented as a set of items i_k (service instance) invoked in the mashup: $M = (i_1, i_2, ...i_n)$*

Definition 2. *Path: a knowledge-aware path relating items can be defined as a sequence of entities and relations:*
$p_L = [e_1 \xrightarrow{r_1} e_2 \xrightarrow{r_2} ... \xrightarrow{r_{L-1}} e_L]$*, where $L - 1$ denotes the number of triples in the path. $P(M) = (p_1, p_2, ...p_k)$ represents the paths between entities e_i contained in the mashup M.*

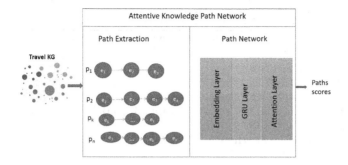

Fig. 5. Path-based Reasoning Framework

Due to the large volume and complexity of KGs, there are a large number of paths connecting entity pairs that may contain different entity types and relation types in different orders and with various lengths. To increase model efficiency, we thus devise two strategies to help the selection of relevant paths:

Strategy 1: we only consider paths where e_1 and e_L are POI entity type. These paths are most helpful for travel mashup explanation.

Strategy 2: we only consider paths with length up to six. As discussed in [3], paths with relatively short length are good enough to model entity relations, whereas longer paths may bring in remote neighbors and lose semantic meanings, thus introducing much noise. Thus, we consider paths that are longer than six hops as noise.

Guided by the two strategies, we propose a path extraction Algorithm to retrieve all qualified paths as described in Algorithm 1. First, we abstract the TKG to its schema graph KGS by changing the entities in the triples to entity types. It can be displayed via a matrix where every dimension has a list of all entity types. Thus we can store the types of relations between the entity types. Given a knowledge graph TKG and a mashup M, Algorithm 1 finds a path set P connecting the included entities with different semantics guided with the knowledge schema KGS. For each item i_k in M, we adopt the depth-first-search (DFS) idea to retrieve candidate paths C then we choose target path . In fact, candidate paths set C can be generated in parallel which significantly enhances the efficiency of path extraction by designing a multi-threaded program. These paths will be further processed by the recurrent network to automatically learn their semantic representations.

B. Path Recurrent Network: by considering paths between entities as a sequence, where elements in the sequence are the entities in the path, we are naturally guided to adopt recurrent networks to encode the path. Moreover, we are motivating by their capability in modeling sequences with various lengths and in capturing the semantics of both entities and the entire path between entity pairs. The Path Recurrent Network (PRN) takes as input a set of paths and leverages the sequential dependencies of entities and sophisticated relations of a

---

Algorithm 1: Path Extraction Algorithm

Data: Knowledge graph schema KGS, knowledge graph KG, mashup M
Result: path set P
1   $P= \emptyset$
2   **for each** $i_k \in M$ **do**
3          $C = traverse(KG, e_k)$ {retrieve paths starting from e_k (entity corresponding to the instance i_k) within 6 hop}
4   **for each** $p \in C$ **do**
5   **if** p satisfies M **then**
6   add p to P
7   **Return** P

---

path in order to infer explanations. There are 3 key components: (1) embedding layer to project information about the entity, entity type, and the relation into a latent space, (2) GRU layer that encodes the elements sequentially with the goal of capturing the compositional semantics of entities conditioned on relations, and (3) pooling layer to combine multiple paths (Fig. 5).

Embedding Layer: The embedding layer focuses on learning representations for paths in the KG. It uses a set of paths $P(M) = (p_1, p_2, ..., p_k)$ as input to generate a set of path representations $P_l = (p_{l1}, p_{l2}, ..., p_{lk})$.

For each entity p_i, the embedding layer learns a distributed representation $p_{li} = [x_1, x_2, ..., x_L]$. As it is common in real-world scenarios that the same entity pair can have different semantics since different relations connecting them, diverse intents can be inferred. For example, let (Chambord castle, buildBy, François I) and (Chambord castle, residenceOf, François I) be the triples in two paths. Without specifying the relations, these paths will be represented as the same embeddings, regardless of the possibility that the user only interested in achievements of François I, rather than that his history. Thus, it is important to explicitly incorporate the semantics of relations into path representation learning. The l-th vector in the path can be defined as:

$$x_l = e_l \oplus e_l' \oplus r_l$$

where $\oplus$ is the concatenation operation, $e_l \in R^d$ and $e_l' \in R^d$ are embedding vectors representing the entity in the path and the entity type respectively, $r_l \in R^d$ is the relationship representation, d is the embedding size. We add to the end of path a null relation. Hence, the input vector contains not only the sequential information, but also the semantic information of the entity and its relation to the next entity.

GRU Layer: This layer aims to learn a single representation that encodes the entire path. We employ RNN models to explore the sequential information. Among various RNN methods, we adopt GRU since it is capable of memorizing long-term dependency in a sequence and can be trained faster and performs better than LSTM in the sequence-based recommendation. It uses only two gates, i.e., reset and forget gates to control the flow of information. Long-term sequential pattern is crucial to reason on paths connecting entities to infer explainable recommendations. The GRU layer takes a flow-based approach to learn a hidden state h_i that encodes the sub-sequence $[e_1, r_1, \ldots, e_i, r_i]$. Considering the memory state, the final state h_t will encode the whole path p_k. The GRU cell is computed as follows:

$$z_i = sigmoid\ (W_{xz}.x_i + W_{hz}.h_{i-1} + b_z)$$

$$r_i = sigmoid\ (W_{xr}.x_i + W_{hr}.h_{i-1} + b_r)$$

$$\tilde{h}_i = tanh\ (W_{xh}.x_t + W_h(r_i \times h_{i-1}) + b_h)$$

$$h_i = (1 - z_i) \times h_{i-1} + z_i \times \tilde{h}_i$$

where $W_{x*} = \{W_{xz}, W_{xr}, W_{xh}\}$; $W_{h*} = \{W_{hz}, W_{hr}, W_h\}$ are weights matrices of the corresponding gates, and $b_* = \{b_z, b_r, b_h\}$ are bias vectors. The reset gate r_t regulates the flow of new input to the previous memory, and the update gate z_t defines how much of the memory to keep around. Thus, this technique combines the forget and input gates into a single update gate and merges the cell state and hidden state h_i. Therefore, we can use hidden states h as input to obtain P^h a set of vectors for paths as follows: $P^h = (p_1^h, \ldots, p_n^h)$.

To calculate the path importance, we use an attention layer to identify the importance of each path.

Attention Layer: This layer aims to distinguish the different contributions of different paths based on paths representations and user representation as shown in Fig. 6. It relies on the user-centric level information as an activation gate mechanism to learn the correlation between relation's paths and user's demand. Since, it is interesting to pay more attention to relations like residenceOf, bithPlaceOf and deathPlaceOf rather than others for user interested in celebrity person. To explore the relation between paths, we use P^h as the input to attention layer and obtain a score s_i. For each path representation P_i^h, the activation gate computes the corresponding weight w_i that measures how the ith path matches with user's preferences. More specifically, it can be formulated as:

$$w_i = \frac{exp(f(P_i^h, u))}{\sum_{i=1}^n exp(f(P_i^h, u))}$$

where $f(P_i^h, u)$ describes the attention function. in this work, we use the dot-product attention as the attention function that can be defined as:

$$f(P_i^h, u) = \frac{P_i^h\ u^\top}{\sqrt{d}}$$

where d is the dimension of hidden vectors and u indicates the user's preferences vector.

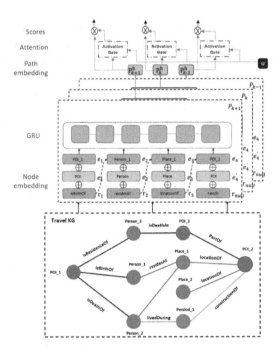

Fig. 6. Illustration of the path network components. The embedding layer consists of three separate layers for entity, entity type and relation type.

Based on the activation score set $W = \{w_1, w_2, ..., w_n\}$, we can lean a correlation score between the candidate paths and the user's preferences. Towards this end, we use a sum pooling and two fully connected layers.

$$v = w_i P_i^h$$

$$s_i = sigmoid(W_{out}(v \oplus u) + b)$$

where W_{out} is a parameter matrice and b is a parameter vector.

Thus, we can learn the path score from different perspectives which provides a more powerful representation.

3 Experiments

In this section, we conduct experiments on a real dataset in tourism domain to evaluate our approach and compare the state-of the-art baselines with our proposed method. We also present a case study to demonstrate the effectiveness of our approach.

3.1   Experimental Setup

We use DATAtourisme dataset which is enriched with auxiliary information such as person, period, etc. to construct a travel domain KG. Table 1 describes the dataset details.

Table 1. Dataset statistics

	Items	Knowledge graph				Path	
	Items	Entities	Relations	Entity types	Relation types	Paths	Avg. Path length
Number	6290	20439	302937	12	8	543344	5.11

In the main experiments, we set the dimension of each input vector of the GRU to 64 and the batch size to 256. We adopt stochastic gradient descent (SGD) in the optimization step with a learning rate in the range $\{0.001, 0.01, 0.1\}$, while the L2 regularization coefficients are tuned in the range $\{10^{-5}, 10^{-4}, 10^{-3}, 10^{-2}\}$.

3.2   Performance Evaluation

We use the normalized discounted cumulative gain (NDCG) that is widely used to evaluate the performance of recommendations. The NDCG@k measures the position influence of items in the ranking list. We compare our proposed method with the existing models:

- FM [4] : a basic model that considers the combination of features and solves the problem.
- CKE [5]: a representative embedding-based method that uses TransR to capture semantic information in KG.
- KGAT [6]: an embedding-based method that uses GCN to explore the high-order connectivities in KG.
- KPRN [7] : a path-based model that learns the user's interest preferences by extracting paths and uses LSTM to model the paths automatically.
- MEIREC [8] : a metapath-guided method based on rich user-item information using HIN.
- EKPN [9] : a knowledge aware-path network that exploits implicit and explicit features between items.
- PeRN [10] : a path based method that uses metapath information to differentiate paths.

Figure 7 and Table 2 show that our model achieves the best performance and outperforms the previous results. The performance of CKE is lower than others methods which indicates that the methods based on knowledge graph embedding may not be able to make full use of the knowledge graph. KPRN and EKPN use a RNN network to capture the semantic features in the knowledge graph, are better than first methods. However, they lack effective reasoning guidance, thus the performance is weaker than our method.

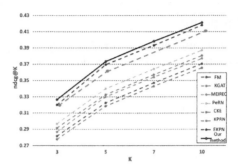

Fig. 7. Methods performance NDCG@K when K is {3, 5, 7, 10}

Table 2. Performance comparison

Method	NDCG@10	Improvement
FM	0.3706	5.19%
KGAT	0.3852	3.73%
MEIREC	0.3770	4.55%
PeRN	0.3867	3.58%
CKE	0.3686	5.39%
KPRN	0.4181	0.44%
EKPN	0.4213	0.12%
Our method	0.4225	

3.3   Case Study

We use a realistic scenario from the running example to demonstrate the effectiveness in terms of explainability of travel mashups. Figure 8 visualizes three paths using our model and provides informative explanations. These paths describe item connectivity from dissimilar angles which can be used as possible explanations of the travel mashup recommended.

In particular, p_1 tells us the story of Charles VIII while p_2 infers that user is a nature lover. p_3 expresses architecture evolution over time for architecture fans. Therefore, we provide some reasonable explanations where s_i represents the importance of path i and w_j the user preference weight.

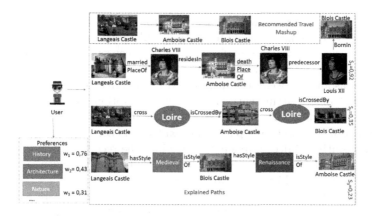

Fig. 8. Visualization of the paths to illustrate the interpretability of our model

4   Related Work

There are generally two forms of incorporating KG into recommender system, namely knowledge graph embedding (KGE) based methods and path-based methods.

KGE methods learn better item latent representations by capturing entity semantics from KG. They usually combine content representations of the items themselves with knowledge-aware embeddings to generate a better representation for items. For instance, KGAT [6] models the high-order connectivities in KG in an end-to-end fashion. However, this regularization of knowledge graph embedding has not fully exploited the connectivity characterization between items. Authors use the knowledge graph structure indirectly which prevents them from effectively modelling the sequential dependencies. They cannot explain their recommendation by providing a path in the KG connecting recommended items.

Despite unifying various types of side information in the recommender system, KGE methods lack the reasoning ability since they only consider direct relations between entities, rather than the multi-hop relation. Hence, they are more suitable for link prediction and inference tasks rather than recommendation.

The second form of methods utilizing KG is path-based methods, which predefine the specific format and length of the paths to capture different semantics carried by KGs. They introduce the connectivity patterns, termed as meta-paths, to explicitly guide the recommender system. For instance, [11] models rich objects and relations in knowledge graph and extracts different aspect-level similarity matrices thanks to meta-paths for the top-N recommendation. However, authors only capture the individual-level, which cannot represent holistic semantic features and limits the explainability of recommendation.

[12] proposes a Meta-Path-based Explainable Recommendation System which can infer users' preferences by reasoning about the Meta-path. The performance of these methods heavily relies on the quality of meta-paths, which requires

domain knowledge. Furthermore, they failed to utilize the information of KG at collective-level to enhance recommendation explainability.

In recent works [10,13], the qualified paths between entity pairs from KG are mined automatically and then are encoded using recurrent networks in order to guide the reasoning process. For instance, [14] uses GRU to model the sequential dependencies among items with rigid order assumption within each session to predict recommendations. In KPRN [10], a long short-term memory (LSTM) network is utilized to encode paths and explore the connectivity between users and items. Authors inject implicit features into the recommendation process to increase interpretability of recommendations. But they deal with static preferences based on user's historical interactions.

To capture user dynamic preferences, [15] proposes a time-aware gated recurrent unit to model user dynamic preferences and profile an item by user's review information. It provides adaptive recommendation explanations tailored for the users' current preferences. Nevertheless, the goals of the method is to capture long-term user demand which is then used as an input feature for precise recommendation. [16] proposes a Strategy Guided Path Reasoning (PGPR) method which generates a recommendation list and finds an explanation path in the constructed knowledge graph. Authors utilize REINFORCE for explicit reasoning in the decision-making process over KG. However, effective guidance is lacking in the reasoning process. Our approach provides explainable recommendations based on path reasoning between items in KG at collective-level which is guided by user's demand.

5   Conclusion

In this paper, we propose a knowledge-aware path recurrent network approach to generate a path by composing semantics of entities and relations among KG. Using GRU and attention mechanism on paths, we can learn the sequential dependencies of elements and reason on paths to infer explainable recommendation. We capture not only the semantics of different paths but also their distinctive saliency based on a user context guided reasoning. Extensive experiments and case study show the well-developed explanations and effectiveness of our method. In the future, we plan to improve the path selection method which is dependent to the topology of the KG in order to optimize the reasoning procedure.

References

1. Cano, A.-E., Dadzie, A.-S., Ciravegna, F.: Travel mashups. In: Semantic Mashups. Springer, pp. 321–347 (2013). https://doi.org/10.1007/978-3-642-36403-7_11
2. Raghunathan, K., et al.: A multi-pass sieve for coreference resolution. In: Conference on Empirical Methods in Natural Language Processing, pp. 492–501 (2010)
3. Sun, Y., Han, J., Yan, X., Yu, P.S., Wu, T.: Pathsim: meta path-based top-k similarity search in heterogeneous information networks. Proc. VLDB Endowment 4(11), 992–1003 (2011)

4. Rendle, S., Gantner, Z., Freudenthaler, C., Schmidt-Thieme, L.: Fast context-aware recommendations with factorization machines. In: Proceedings of the 34th international ACM SIGIR Conference on Research and Development in Information Retrieval, pp. 635–644 (2011)
5. Zhang, F., Yuan, N. J., Lian, D., Xie, X., Ma, W.-Y.: Collaborative knowledge base embedding for recommender systems. In: Proceedings of the 22nd ACM SIGKDD International Conference on Knowledge Discovery and Data Mining (2016)
6. Wang, X., He, X., Cao, Y., Liu, M., Chua, T.-S.: Kgat: knowledge graph attention network for recommendation. In: Proceedings of ACM SIGKDD International Conference on Knowledge Discovery & Data Mining, pp. 950–958 (2019)
7. Wang, X., Wang, D., Xu, C., He, X., Cao, Y., Chua, T.-S.: Explainable reasoning over knowledge graphs for recommendation. In: Proceedings of the AAAI Conference on Artificial Intelligence, vol. 33, no. 01, pp. 5329–5336 (2019)
8. Fan, S., et al.: Metapath-guided heterogeneous graph neural network for intent recommendation. In: Proceedings of the 25th ACM SIGKDD International Conference on Knowledge Discovery & Data Mining, pp. 2478–2486 (2019)
9. Yang, P., Ai, C., Yao, Yu., Li, B.: EKPN: enhanced knowledge-aware path network for recommendation. Appl. Intell. **52**, 1–12 (2021). https://doi.org/10.1007/s10489-021-02758-9
10. Huang, Y., Zhao, F., Gui, X., Jin, H.: Path-enhanced explainable recommendation with knowledge graphs. World Wide Web **24**(5), 1769–1789 (2021). https://doi.org/10.1007/s11280-021-00912-4
11. Han, X., Shi, C., Wang, S., Philip, S.Y., Song, L.: Aspect-level deep collaborative filtering via heterogeneous information networks. In: IJCAI, pp. 3393–3399 (2018)
12. Wang, T., Zheng, X., He, S., Zhang, Z., Wu, D.D.: Learning user-item paths for explainable recommendation. IFAC-PapersOnLine **53**(5), 436–440 (2020)
13. Xie, L., Hu, Z., Cai, X., Zhang, W., Chen, J.: Explainable recommendation based on knowledge graph and multi-objective optimization. Complex Intell. Syst. **7**(3), 1241–1252 (2021). https://doi.org/10.1007/s40747-021-00315-y
14. Wang, N., Wang, S., Wang, Y., Sheng, Q.Z., Orgun, M.: Modelling local and global dependencies for next-item recommendations. In: Huang, Z., Beek, W., Wang, H., Zhou, R., Zhang, Y. (eds.) WISE 2020. LNCS, vol. 12343, pp. 285–300. Springer, Cham (2020). https://doi.org/10.1007/978-3-030-62008-0_20
15. Chen, X., Zhang, Y., Qin, Z.: Dynamic explainable recommendation based on neural attentive models. In: Proceedings of the AAAI Conference on Artificial Intelligence, vol. 33, no. 01, pp. 53–60 (2019)
16. Xian, Y., Fu, Z., Muthukrishnan, S., De Melo, G., Zhang, Y.: Reinforcement knowledge graph reasoning for explainable recommendation. In: Proceedings of the 42nd International ACM SIGIR Conference on Research and Development in Information Retrieval, pp. 285–294 (2019)

Extra Budget-Aware Online Task Assignment in Spatial Crowdsourcing

Lun Jin[1], Shuhan Wan[1], Detian Zhang[1(✉)], and Ying Tang[2]

[1] Institute of Artificial Intelligence, School of Computer Science and Technology,
Soochow University, Suzhou, China
{ljin,20195227042}@stu.suda.edu.cn, detian@suda.edu.cn
[2] Yibin Cowin Automobile Co., Ltd., Yibin, China
tangying@mychery.com

Abstract. With the proliferation of mobile devices, wireless networks and sharing economy, spatial crowdsourcing (e.g., ride hailing, food delivery, citizen sensing services) is becoming popular recently. In spatial crowdsourcing (SC), workers need to physically move to specific locations to conduct the assigned tasks which incurs travel cost. In this paper, we propose a novel SC problem, namely extra budget-aware online task assignment (EBOTA), where tasks have extra budget to subsidize the extra travel cost of workers. EBOTA concerns the strategy of assigning each task to proper worker such that the total satisfaction of completed tasks can be maximized. To address the EBOTA problem, we first propose an efficient algorithm called Deadline-exact algorithm which always computes the optimal assignment for the newly appearing object. Because of Deadline-exact's high time complexity which may limit its feasibility in real world, we propose another two practical algorithms, i.e., Threshold-based algorithm and Priority-based algorithm. Finally, we verify the effectiveness and efficiency of the proposed methods through extensive experiments on real dataset.

Keywords: Spatial crowdsourcing · Online task assignment · Extra budget

1 Introduction

With the popularization of GPS-equipped smart devices and the development of high-speed wireless networks (e.g. 5G), spatial crowdsourcing has drawn increasing attention in recent years. Typical spatial crowdsourcing services include ride hailing(e.g. Uber and Didi), food delivery(e.g. Ele.me and GrubHub) and citizen sensing services(e.g. OpenStreetMap).

As there are massive tasks and workers in spatial crowdsourcing platforms, one of the main problems is how to assign these tasks to workers properly. Existing works focus on assigning tasks to workers according to different goals, such as maximizing the total number of completed tasks [1,22], maximizing expected

R. Chbeir et al. (Eds.): WISE 2022, LNCS 13724, pp. 534–549, 2022.
https://doi.org/10.1007/978-3-031-20891-1_38

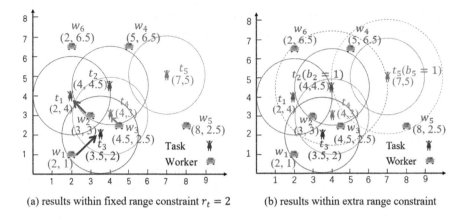

(a) results within fixed range constraint $r_t = 2$ (b) results within extra range constraint

Fig. 1. Tasks without vs with extra budget

total payoff [20,23], minimizing maximum delay [5]. An implicit assumption shared by these works is that a worker is only willing to perform tasks within his spatial vicinity because the worker needs to move to the location of these tasks, which may lead some remote tasks cannot be assigned. For example, Fig. 1(a) shows the locations of 5 tasks and 6 workers. Each circle centered by a task indicates that task can only be assigned to workers within the circle. If all of tasks only have such fixed range constraint, only 3 pairs can be matched, i.e., (t_1, w_2), (t_3, w_1) and (t_4, w_3), while t_2 and t_5 cannot be assigned to any workers.

Unfortunately, most of existing studies only consider that task requesters have such fixed range constraint or budget [6,11,17], which cannot solve this problem. The most closest work is incentive mechanism [2,19,21,25], which formulates the pricing strategy to attract workers to participate. However, not every task requester is willing to accept raising price, and some remote tasks still may be not assigned if the newly attracted workers are far from them.

To overcome this challenge, we propose Extra-Budget Aware Online Task Assignment (EBOTA) problem. In our problem: (1) different tasks have different extra budget to subsidize and attract remote workers, and the SC platform will conduct task assignment not only based on the fixed but also the extra budget of tasks. A task requester can raising his extra budget to increase the accomplishment probability of the task. In the above example, if t_2 and t_5 have extra budget to subsidize workers (i.e., $b_2 = b_5 = 1$), the platform will increase their range constraint, i.e., the dash circles as shown in Fig. 1b, which makes w_4 and w_5 can serve them, respectively. (2) online dynamic task assignment is considered. Since in some real-time spatial crowdsourcing services, tasks and workers arrive dynamically and their temporal and spatial information are only known when they are arrived. Task assignment needs to be performed before the tasks and workers leave to maximize the total satisfaction.

In general, we make the following contributions in this paper:

– We formally define the Extra-Budget Aware Online Task Assignment
  (EBOTA) problem. As far as we know, we are the first one to propose this
  problem.
– We propose three effective algorithms to solve the problem, i.e., Deadline-
  exact algorithm, Threshold-based algorithm, and Priority-based algorithm.
– We conduct extensive experiments to prove the effectiveness and efficiency of
  our algorithms.

The rest of this paper is organized as follows. Section 2 formally defines the
EBOTA problem. The optimal algorithm is proposed in Sect. 3 and online algorithms are proposed in Sect. 4. Extensive experiments on real dataset are presented in Sect. 5. Section 6 reviews some related work. Finally, Sect. 7 concludes
this work.

2   Problem Definitions

Definition 1. *(Task) A task, denoted by $t = <l_t, a_t, d_t, r_t, b_t>$, appears on the
platform with location l_t in the 2D space at time a_t and its required deadline is
d_t. r_t is the radius of t centered in l_t which is the fixed range constraint of t, and
b_t is its provided extra budget.*

The fixed range constraint r_t is the default range for all tasks given by the SC
platform. The extra budget is used for subsiding the extra travel cost of workers,
so b_t is proportion to the extra range constraint. In this paper, we assume the
proportion is at the ratio of 1. For simplicity, we directly take b_t as the extra
range constraint in the rest of the paper. Therefore, a task can only be conducted
by the workers within the range $r_t + b_t$.

Definition 2. *(Worker) A worker, denoted by $w = <l_w, a_w, d_w, u_w>$, is released
on the platform at time a_w and at location l_w in the 2D space, and its service
deadline is d_w. His service score is u_w which is graded by the task requester after
completing the task.*

Definition 3. *(Travel cost) The travel cost, denoted by $cost(t, w)$, is determined
by the travel distance from l_w to l_t.*

Travel distance, which can be measured by any types of distance such as
Euclidean distance or road network distance. In this paper, we use Euclidean
distance as the travel distance and take it as the travel cost directly for simplicity.

Definition 4. *(Extra travel cost) Extra travel cost, denoted by e_t, is the actual
travel cost exceeding the fixed range constraint provided by the task requester,
i.e., $e_t = cost(t, w) - r_t$.*

Since each task has an extra budget b_t, the extra travel cost e_t should be
no more than it, i.e., $e_t \leq b_t$. In this paper, as the travel cost is measured by
the Euclidean distance, we have $e_t = cost(t, w) - r_t = EDist(t, w) - r_t$. After

the worker completing the task, the task requester will score him according to the satisfaction with his service. Since the extra travel cost of the task needs to be paid by the task requester, the satisfaction function considers not only the service score of workers, but also the extra travel cost of the task. With the increase of extra travel cost, the satisfaction becomes smaller. Therefore, we define the satisfaction based on the worker service score u_w and the extra travel cost e_t as below:

Definition 5. *(Satisfaction) Satisfaction is the satisfaction of the task requester who releases the task t to his matched worker w. It is denoted by:*

$$S(t,w) = \begin{cases} u_w, & b_t = 0, \\ u_w \times (1 - \dfrac{e_t}{b_t}), & b_t > 0. \end{cases} \tag{1}$$

In addition, we can add other factors to the satisfaction according to other needs.

Definition 6. *(Extra-Budget Aware Online Task Assignment (EBOTA) problem) Given a set of tasks T and a set workers W, each task or worker arrives sequentially. EBOTA calculates a feasible matching result M whose total satisfaction is maximized, i.e., $Maxsum(M) = \sum_{t \in T, w \in W} S(t,w)$, and is subjected to the following constraints:*

1. *Extra budget constraint, i.e., $e_t \leq b_t$.*
2. *Deadline constraint, i.e., $a_t < d_w$ and $a_w < d_t$.*
3. *Range constraint, i.e., $cost(t,w) \leq r_t + b_t$.*

3 The Optimal Algorithm

In this section, we introduce the optimal solution for the EBOTA problem, where the platform has acquired the entire spatial and temporal information of workers and tasks before matching. Therefore, the optimal solution can not be applied to the online scenario. We take the optimal solution as one of the compared algorithms to show the efficiency of our proposed algorithms.

Given a set of tasks $T = \{t_1, t_2, ...\}$ and a set of workers $W = \{w_1, w_2, ...\}$, we construct a bipartite graph $G = (V, E)$ with V as the set of vertices, and E as the set of edges. The set V contains $|T| + |W|$ vertices including task vertices and worker vertices. The set E contains all possible edges from task vertices to worker verteices, i.e., if all three constraints in Definition 6 are satisfied between task t and worker w, there is an edge (t, w) from t to w, and its weight is $S(t, w)$ defined in Definition 5. Then, we can use an existing flow algorithm (e.g., Kuhn-Munkres (KM) algorithm [12]) to obtain the optimal result. The total amount of pairs is $min(|T|, |W|)$ and only the weight of which greater than 0 are the final matched pairs. The whole procedure of Optimal algorithm is illustrated in Algorithm 1.

Take Fig. 1(b) for example, we first construct a bipartite graph for all possible workers and tasks based constraints in Definition 6. Table 1 presents the arrival

---

Algorithm 1 Optimal algorithm

Input: T, W, $S(.,.)$
Output: the matched pair set M
1: $M \leftarrow \emptyset$
2: **for** each task node $t_i \in T$ **do**
3:     **for** each worker node $w_j \in W$ **do**
4:         **if** (t_i, w_j) satisfies all constraints **then**
5:             add an edge between t_i and w_j, $weight(t_i, w_j) \leftarrow S(t_i, w_j)$
6:         **else**
7:             add an edge between t_i and w_j, $weight(t_i, w_j) \leftarrow 0$
8: $M \leftarrow KM(T, W)$
9: **return** M

Table 1. Arrival order

Arrival order	t_3	w_2	t_1	t_4	w_1	t_2	w_3	w_6	t_5	w_5	w_4
Arrival time	8:01	8:02	8:03	8:05	8:06	8:08	8:10	8:11	8:12	8:14	8:15
Leaving time	8:08	8:09	8:10	8:12	8:13	8:15	8:17	8:18	8:19	8:21	8:22

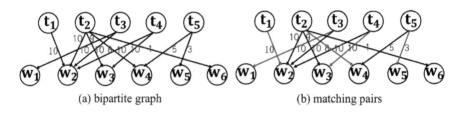

(a) bipartite graph   (b) matching pairs

Fig. 2. The key steps of solving optimal algorithm

and leaving time of tasks and workers, and we assume the service score of each worker is 10, i.e., $u_w = 10$. Since only three workers, i.e., w_1, w_2 and w_3, are online during t_1's active time period. However, w_1 and w_3 are out of the range of t_1, while w_2 is in the range, so there is only one edge connected, i.e., (t_1, w_2). The weight of (t_1, w_2) is the satisfaction between this pair, i.e., $S(t_1, w_2) = u_2 = 10$ (as $b_1 = 0$). From Table 1, we can see all six workers are online during t_2's active time period. With the help of extra budget $b_2 = 1$, the range constraint of t_2 is increased from $r_t = 2$ to $r_t + b_2 = 3$, which makes w_2, w_3, w_4 and w_6 are in the range. Therefore, four edges are connected, i.e., (t_2, w_2), (t_2, w_3), (t_2, w_4) and (t_2, w_6). Since $cost(t_2, w_2) < r_t$, i.e., $e_t = 0$, we have $S(t_2, w_2) = u_2 = 10$. While $cost(t_2, w_3) > r_t$, we have $S(t_2, w_3) = u_5 \times (1 - \frac{cost(t_2, w_3) - r_t}{b_3}) = 9$. Similarly, we can compute $S(t_2, w_4) = 8$ and $S(t_2, w_6) = u_2 = 1$. By the same way, the edges for t_3, t_4 and t_5 can be can be constructed as shown in Fig. 2(a).

After the whole bipartite graph have been built, the KM algorithm is run to get the assignment. The allocation result is shown by the red line in Fig. 2(b), i.e., $\{(t_1, w_2), (t_2, w_4), (t_3, w_1), (t_4, w_3), (t_5, w_5)\}$. Therefore, the total satisfaction is $S = S(t_1, w_2) + S(t_2, w_4) + S(t_3, w_1) + S(t_4, w_3) + S(t_5, w_2) = 10 + 8 + 10 + 10 + 3 = 41$.

Complexity Analysis. The time and space complexity of the Optimal algorithm are $O(max(|T|^3, |W|^3))$ and $O(|T||W|)$ respectively.

4 Online Algorithms

4.1 Greedy Algorithm

Greedy is a straightforward solution for EBOTA. It always chooses a pair with the highest satisfaction when a new object arrives, so the result of Greedy is local optimal. The performance of Greedy is susceptible to the order of tasks' and workers' appearance.

In our running example, when t_3 arrives, there are no workers (see Table 1). When w_2 arrives, there is only a task t_3 online and w_2 is in the range of it (see Fig. 1b). Therefore, t_3 is assigned to w_2. When t_1 and t_4 arrive, there are no workers until w_1 arrives, but it is not in their range. Similarly, there is no worker in t_2's range. When w_3 arrives, as the current task set is $T = \{t_1, t_2, t_4\}$ and it is in the range of t_2 and t_4, so w_3 can be assigned to t_2 or t_4. Since $S(t_2, w_3) = 9 < S(t_4, w_3) = 10$, (t_4, w_3) is selected by the Greedy. Using the same way, we can get the other matched pairs $(t_2, w_6), (t_5, w_5)$. Therefore, the total satisfaction of Greedy is $S = 10 + 10 + 1 + 3 = 24$.

Complexity Analysis. For each new arrival object, the time and space complexity of the Greedy algorithm are $O(max(|T|, |W|))$ and $O(max(|T|, |W|))$.

4.2 Deadline-Exact Algorithm

Since Greedy is local optimal, we propose Deadline-exact algorithm to try to obtain the global optimal matching. The main idea is to determine the assignment between tasks and workers only at their deadline. When a task or worker reaches its deadline, we try to get the global optimal assignment for it.

Algorithm 2 presents the detailed steps of Deadline-exact algorithm. In line 1, the result set M, the unassigned tasks set T' and the unassigned workers set W' are set empty. In line 2, when an object o reaches its deadline d, the algorithm finds the assignment for it. In lines 3–7, the algorithm finds each unassigned object o' who arrives before time d. If the object o' is a task, the algorithm adds it to T'. If the object o' is a worker, the algorithm adds it to W'. In line 8, the KM algorithm is run based on current T' and W' to match tasks and workers. If o is a task and matched in M', we assign it to the worker who is matched with it in M' as shown in lines 9–14. If o is a worker and matched in M', we assign it to the task who is matched with it in M' as shown in lines 15–20. In line 21, the algorithm returns the final matched pair set M.

Back to our running example, t_3 is the first one to reach the deadline (i.e., 8:08, see Table 1). Currently, the unassigned task and worker sets are $T' = \{t_1, t_2, t_3, t_4\}$ and $W' = \{w_1, w_2\}$, respectively. After running KM algorithm, t_3 is assigned to w_1. By the same way, t_1 is assigned to w_2, t_4 is assigned to w_3, t_2 is assigned to w_4 and t_5 is assigned to w_5. The total satisfaction is $S = 10 + 10 + 10 + 8 + 3 = 41$.

Algorithm 2 Deadline-exact algorithm

Input: T, W, $S(.,.)$
Output: the matched pair set M
1: $M \leftarrow \emptyset$, the unassigned tasks set $T' \leftarrow \emptyset$, the unassigned workers set $W' \leftarrow \emptyset$
2: **for** each object o reaches its the deadline d **do**
3:      **for** each object o' arrives before time d **do**
4:          **if** o' is a task **then**
5:              add o' into T'
6:          **else**
7:              add o' into W'
8:      $M' \leftarrow \text{KM}(T', W')$
9:      **if** o is a task **then**
10:         **if** o is matched in M' **then**
11:             $w \leftarrow$ the worker assigned to o in M'
12:             $M \leftarrow M \cup (o, w)$
13:             remove w from W'
14:         remove o from T'
15:     **if** o is a worker **then**
16:         **if** o is matched in M' **then**
17:             $t \leftarrow$ the task assigned to o in M'
18:             $M \leftarrow M \cup (t, o)$
19:             remove t from T'
20:         remove o from W'
21: **return** M

Complexity Analysis. For each new arrival object, the time and space complexity of the Deadline-exact algorithm are $O(max(|T|^3, |W|^3))$ and $O(|T||W|)$.

4.3 Threshold-Based Algorithm

Deadline-exact algorithm takes high time complexity. Random-threshold greedy (Greedy-RT) [16] can alleviate the impact of the order of Greedy algorithm and improve the efficiency of Deadline-exact algorithm. Inspired by this algorithm, we devise Threshold-based algorithm. Threshold-based algorithm first produces a random threshold τ, then the pair whose satisfaction is lower than τ is denied.

The details of Threshold-based algorithm is shown in Algorithm 3. In line 1, the result set M, the unassigned tasks set T' and the unassigned workers set W' are set empty. In lines 2–4, the algorithm randomly chooses a threshold according to the maximum satisfaction S_{max} [16], which can be got from historical data. In line 5, we iteratively process each new arrival object. If the object is a task (lines 6–13), the algorithm filters a worker subset W^* where each worker w satisfies all constraints and the satisfaction of the pair (o, w) exceeds the threshold. If W^* is not empty, the algorithm chooses the worker who has the highest satisfaction with o. If W^* is empty, the algorithm adds the object to the unassigned tasks set. If the object is a worker (lines 14–21), the algorithm filters a task subset T^* where each task t satisfies all constraints and satisfaction of the pair (o, t)

Algorithm 3 Threshold-based algorithm

Input: T, W, $S(.,.)$
Output: the matched pair set M
1: $M \leftarrow \emptyset$; the unassigned tasks set $T' \leftarrow \emptyset$; the unassigned workers set $W' \leftarrow \emptyset$
2: $\theta \leftarrow \lceil ln(S_{max} + 1) \rceil$
3: $k \leftarrow$ randomly choosing an integer from $\{0, 1, ..., \theta - 1\}$ with probability $\frac{1}{\theta}$
4: $\tau \leftarrow e^k$
5: **for** each new arrival object o **do**
6:     **if** o is a task **then**
7:         $t \leftarrow o$
8:         $W^* \leftarrow \{w | S(t, w) \geq \tau, e_t < b_t, a_t < d_w, a_w < d_t, cost(t, w) \leq r_t + b_t\}$
9:         **if** $W^* \neq \emptyset$ **then**
10:            $w \leftarrow \underset{w \in W^*}{argmax} S_{max}$
11:            $M \leftarrow M \cup (o, w)$; remove w from W'
12:        **else**
13:            $T' \leftarrow T' \cup o$
14:    **else**
15:        $w \leftarrow o$
16:        $T^* \leftarrow \{t | S(t, w) \geq \tau, e_t < b_t, a_t < d_w, a_w < d_t, cost(t, w) \leq r_t + b_t\}$
17:        **if** $T^* \neq \emptyset$ **then**
18:            $t \leftarrow \underset{t \in T^*}{argmax} S_{max}$
19:            $M \leftarrow M \cup (t, o)$; remove t from T'
20:        **else**
21:            $W' \leftarrow W' \cup o$
22: **return** M

---

exceeds the threshold. If T^* is not empty, the algorithm chooses the task who has the highest satisfaction with o. If T^* is empty, the algorithm adds the object to the unassigned workers set. The algorithm returns the final matched pair set M in line 22.

In our running example, suppose $S_{max} = 10$, we have $\theta = \lceil ln(10 + 1) \rceil = 3$ and $k = \{0, 1, 2\}$. If $k = 0$, the threshold is $e^0 = 1$. When t_3 arrives, no worker is online until w_2 arrives. Task t_3 is assigned to w_2 because $S(t_3, w_2) > 1$. The algorithm continuously assigns t_4 to w_3, t_2 to w_6 and t_5 to w_5. Finally, we can compute the total satisfaction is $S = 10 + 10 + 1 + 3 = 24$. Similarly, the total satisfaction are 31 and 28 if thresholds are e^1 and e^2, respectively. Threshold-based algorithm randomly chooses one threshold, so the expectation of the total satisfaction is $S = \frac{24+31+28}{3} = 28$.

Complexity Analysis. For each new arrival object, the time and space complexity of Threshold-based algorithm are both $O(max(|T|, |W|))$.

Algorithm 4 Priority-based algorithm with historical threshold

---

Input: T, W, $S(.,.)$
Output: the matched pair set M
1: $M \leftarrow \emptyset$, the unassigned tasks set $T' \leftarrow \emptyset$, the unassigned workers set $W' \leftarrow \emptyset$
2: $\tau \leftarrow \tau^*$
3: **for** each new arrival object o **do**
4:     **if** o is a task **then**
5:         $W^* \leftarrow \{w | S(o,w) \geq \tau, e_t < b_t, a_t < d_w, a_w < d_t, cost(t,w) \leq r_t + b_t\}$
6:         **if** $W^* \neq \emptyset$ **then**
7:             $w \leftarrow \max\limits_{w \in W^*} p_w$
8:             $M \leftarrow M \cup (o,w)$; remove w from W'
9:         **else**
10:             $T' \leftarrow T' \cup o$
11:     **else**
12:         $T^* \leftarrow \{t | S(t,o) \geq \tau, e_t < b_t, a_t < d_w, a_w < d_t, cost(t,w) \leq r_t + b_t\}$
13:         **if** $T^* \neq \emptyset$ **then**
14:             $t \leftarrow \max\limits_{t \in T^*} p_t$
15:             $M \leftarrow M \cup (t,o)$; remove t from T'
16:         **else**
17:             $W' \leftarrow W' \cup o$
18: **return** M

4.4 Priority-Based Algorithm with Historical Threshold

Because the thresholds of Threshold-based algorithm are randomly selected, different thresholds have different impacts on the results, the performance of the algorithm can not be guaranteed. However, the daily actions of people are similar [26], we can utilize the threshold θ^* according to historical data which achieves best result in history. In addition, when a new task/worker o arrives, the oldest unmatched worker/task o' better to be assigned to o first to avoid expiration. Therefore, we bring in the wait time priority as follows:

$$wait = \frac{a_o - a_{o'}}{d_{o'} - a_{o'}},$$

where a_o is the arrival time of the new task/worker o, i.e., the current time of the system, $a_{o'}$ and $d_{o'}$ are the arrival time and deadline of worker/task o', respectively.

Besides, the pair with the high satisfaction is beneficial not only to the worker but also to the task requester. Therefore, both satisfaction and wait time decide the priority of the pair. The priority of the o' is computed as follows:

$$p_{o'} = \alpha \times \frac{S(o,o')}{S_{max}} + (1 - \alpha) \times wait,$$

where α is a system parameter and can be got from historical data that yields the best result.

Based on the above point, we devise Priority-based algorithm with historical threshold, as shown in Algorithm 4. In line 1, the result set M, the unassigned tasks set T' and the unassigned workers set W' are set empty. In line 2, the algorithm sets a threshold according to the historical threshold. In line 3, the algorithm iteratively processes each new arrival object. In lines 4–10, if the object is a task, the algorithm filters a worker subset W^* where each worker w satisfies all constraints and the satisfaction of the pair (o, w) exceeds the threshold. If W^* is not empty, the algorithm chooses the worker who has the highest priority p_w. If W^* is empty, the algorithm adds the object to the unassigned tasks set. In lines 11–17, if the object is a worker, the algorithm filters a task subset T^* where each task t satisfies all constraints and satisfaction of the pair (t, o) exceeds the threshold. If T^* is not empty, the algorithm chooses the task who has the highest priority p_t. If T^* is empty, the algorithm adds the object to the unassigned workers set. The algorithm returns the final matched pair set M in line 18.

Assume that the best threshold is 2 and α is 0.3 based on historical data. We use this threshold in our example. When t_3 arrives, no online worker can serve it. When w_2 arrives, the task t_3 is assigned to w_2 because this pair has the highest priority $p_3 = \alpha \times \frac{S(w_2, t_3)}{S_{max}} + (1 - \alpha) \times \frac{a_{w_2} - a_{t_3}}{d_{t_3} - a_{t_3}} = 0.3 \times \frac{10}{10} + (1 - 0.3) \times \frac{1}{7} = 0.4$. Using the same method, we assign t_4 to w_3, t_5 to w_5 and t_2 to w_4. Thus, we obtain the total satisfaction is $S = 10 + 10 + 3 + 8 = 31$.

Complexity Analysis. For each new arrival object, the time and space complexity of Priority-based algorithm are both $O(max(|T|, |W|))$.

5   Experimental Study

5.1   Experiment Setup

We use the taxi data from Didi Chuxing, which contains order data in Chengdu from November 1 to November 30, 2016. We randomly select the data of orders from 9:00 am to 10:00 am on November 6th, 2016 which has 12753 tasks and 10892 workers. The order data has the information of pick-ups and drop-offs, start and end of billing time. We use the pick-up location and the starting time of billing as the location information and arrival time of the task respectively. Since the worker becomes available again after the passenger gets off the car, the drop off location is used as the location of the worker and the end billing time is used as the arrival time of the worker. We use the dataset of November 5th, 2016 to get the optimal threshold $\tau = 5.5$ and $\alpha = 0.2$ that achieve the best result for Priority-based algorithm. Table 2 depicts our experimental settings, where the default values of parameters are in bold font.

Performance Metrics. We use the following metrics to evaluate the effectiveness and efficiency of the proposed methods:

Table 2. Experiments settings

Factor	Setting
Fixed range constraint r	600, 800, **1000**, 1200, 1400
Extra range constraint b	(400,600), (600,800), **(800,1000)**, (1000,1200), (1200,1400)
Time period p	7:00–8:00, 8:00–9:00, **9:00–10:00**, 10:00–11:00, 11:00–12:00
Service score u	**10**

- **Running Time.** The running time represents the total execution time of an algorithm.
- **Average Response Time of Tasks.** The response time of a task refers to the time it takes to be answered by the platform. If a task is not assigned to any worker eventually, its response time will equal to its deadline.
- **Total satisfaction.** The total satisfaction is the sum of the satisfaction of all the task requesters in the platform. Algorithms achieving higher satisfaction are better.
- **Average Satisfaction.** The average satisfaction represents the satisfaction of each task requester. For each task requester, the high satisfaction means she satisfies this matching.

Compared Algorithms. We evaluate the performance of the representative algorithms, i.e., Optimal algorithm (OPT), Greedy algorithm (Greedy), Deadline-exact algorithm (Exact), Threshold-based algorithm (Threshold) and Priority-based algorithm with historical threshold (Priority). All the algorithms are implemented in Java, run on a machine with Intel(R) Core (TM) i7-7700 CPU @ 3.60 GHz and 16 GB RAM.

5.2 Results on the Real Dataset

Effect of the Fixed Range Constraint. As shown in Fig. 3(a), the running time of Exact is obviously higher than the others due to the high time complexity of KM algorithm. As for average response time of tasks in Fig. 3(b), Greedy, Threshold and Priority outperform Exact as they always try to assign a task or a worker the moment it appears. Average response time of tasks of Exact is the highest since it determines the allocation between the workers and tasks only at their deadlines. In Fig. 3(c), we can observe that the total satisfaction increases reasonably as the fixed range constraint increases. This is because more workers will be located in the fixed range constraint of each task. Also, we can observe that Exact, Threshold and Priority are more effective than Greedy and Exact is only slightly worse than OPT. From Fig. 3(d), we can see that Priority is the most effective, the reason is that Priority filters low satisfaction pairs.

Effect of the Extra Range Constraint. As depicted in Fig. 4(a), Exact takes more time than other algorithms. From Fig. 4(b) we can see that Exact

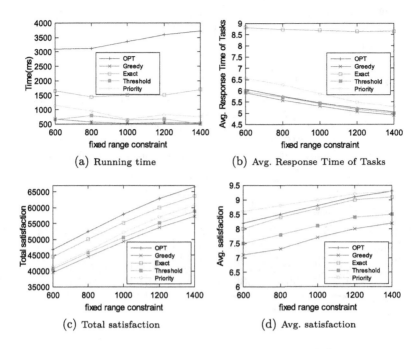

Fig. 3. Effect of the fixed range constraint on real dataset

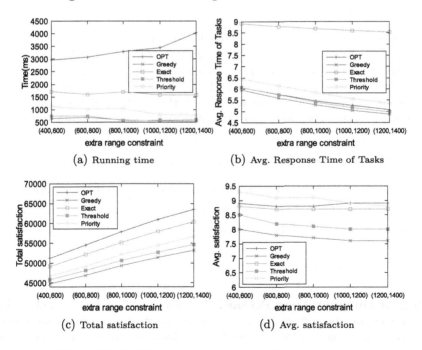

Fig. 4. Effect of the extra range constraint on real dataset

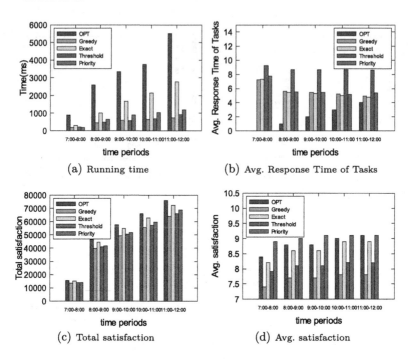

(a) Running time

(b) Avg. Response Time of Tasks

(c) Total satisfaction

(d) Avg. satisfaction

Fig. 5. Effect of different time periods in a day on real dataset

performs worse than others because the decision of assignment is often made at the deadline of tasks or workers. In Fig. 4(c), the total satisfaction increases as the extra range constraint increases which is reasonable as more workers will be in the extra range constraint of tasks. Exact outperforms the other algorithms because it can get global optimal result at the deadline of tasks or workers. Similarly, priority performs better than other algorithms in Fig. 4(d).

Table 3. The number of tasks and workers at different time periods

Time period	7:00–8:00	8:00–9:00	9:00–10:00	10:00–11:00	11:00–12:00
Number of tasks $|T|$	5237	9199	11019	11670	12677
Number of workers $|W|$	3377	8145	9731	11052	12314

Effect of Different Time Periods. To show the effectiveness of algorithms in different time periods of a day, we conduct a set of experiments on different time periods. Table 3 shows the number of tasks and workers in different time periods. As we can see in Fig. 5(a), the number of tasks and workers at 11:00–12:00 is the largest and the running time is the longest. In Fig. 5(b), at 7:00–8:00, the number of tasks and workers is the smallest and average response time of tasks is the longest because more tasks can not be answered before deadlines. In Fig. 5(c), total satisfaction at 11:00–12:00 is the highest, the reason is that the number of tasks and workers are the largest and more pairs can be matched. From Fig. 5(d) we can see that average satisfaction at different time periods is similar because the location distribution at different time is similar.

6   Related Work

6.1   Task Assignment in Spatial Crowdsourcing

Task assignment is one of the most important problems in spatial crowdsourcing [3,14,18]. It is divided into offline task assignment and online task assignment according to the arrival scenario of tasks and workers.

In the offline scenario [10,17], the spatial and temporal information of workers and tasks is pre-known. Kazemi et al. [10] reduce the matching to the maximum flow problem [1], and use Ford-Fulkerson algorithm [9] to calculate the exact solution. In the online scenario, workers and tasks dynamically appear on the platform. The information of requests or workers is not pre-known. Some methods are proposed to maximize the overall utility (i.e., the total number of performed tasks or the total rewards of the assigned tasks) [4,7,14,16,20]. Ting et al. [16] propose Greedy-RT algorithm. They first randomly sample a threshold, and then match the pair whose weight is higher than the threshold. Tong et al. [20] first propose that each task and worker may appear at anytime and anywhere in spatial crowdsourcing. They also extend the Greedy-RT algorithm [16] to solve their problem. A threshold-based randomized framework is proposed to solve the problem. Song et al. [15] first consider that a task requires multiple workers to complete. Chen et al. [4] study the fair assignment of tasks to workers in spatial crowdsourcing. Cheng et al. [7] propose a cross online matching which enables a platform to borrow some unoccupied workers from other platforms. Tong and Liu et al. [11,22] focus on maximizing the total number of completed tasks. Tong et al. [22] set that workers can move to other locations in advance and use the offline-guide-online technique [8] to increase the number of potential matches. Liu et al. [11] first propose that a task requester releases a batch of tasks, requiring workers to complete as many tasks as possible within his fixed budget for rewarding workers. Some methods have been proposed to minimize the waiting time [5,13]. Chen et al. [5] first consider reducing the total waiting time of all tasks. Zhao et al. [13] first consider reducing the average waiting time of users, so as to improve the user experience. However, these studies have not focused on the tasks with extra budget. Wan et al. [24] consider tasks have extra budget but their task assignment is in offline scenario. We design task assignment algorithms assuming that the task has an extra budget in online scenario.

6.2   Incentive Mechanism in Spatial Crowdsourcing

The incentive mechanism problem determines the reward motivating workers to perform the tasks. In reality, supply and demand often change in space and time [19]. The reward should be determined according to the dynamic supply and demand. While the platform determines the reward, the workers decide whether to accept it or not. In Uber, an effective solution is surge pricing. Banerjee et al. [2] use Markov process to determine the reward to workers. Tong et al. [21] define the Global Dynamic Pricing problem in spatial crowdsourcing which is challenging due to unknown demand, limited supply and dependent supply. These above works concentrate on online learning algorithms which determine the reward to workers based on the estimated expectation of workers. There are also many other incentive mechanisms focus on a different scenarios. For example, the auction mechanism determines the reward based on workers' submitted bids. Xiao et al. [25] consider that workers can make detours from their original travel paths to perform tasks and bid for his/her detour cost. However, these methods cannot be directly applied to our EBOTA, since they take the specific pricing strategy into account but did not consider how to allocate tasks. Moreover, the incentive mechanism determines the reward for workers to attract workers before assignment and our problem focuses on task assignment without pricing.

7   Conclusion

In this paper we propose a novel problem, i.e., Extra-Budget Aware Online Task Assignment (EBOTA), to assign the tasks to workers in real time by considering task requesters have extra budget. To solve the problem, we first propose Deadline-Exact algorithm, which always finds a global assignment for the task or worker at its deadline. However, because of the high time complexity of Deadline-Exact, it is not practical in real applications. We next propose Threshold-based algorithm which utilizes a random generated threshold to prune the pairs with small satisfaction, and Priority-based algorithm with historical threshold which learns near optimal threshold from historical data. Extensive experimental results over real dataset verify the effectiveness and efficiency of our approaches.

Acknowledgments. This work was supported by Project Funded by the Priority Academic Program Development of Jiangsu Higher Education Institutions, and by Collaborative Innovation Center of Novel Software Technology and Industrialization.

References

1. Ahuja, R.K., Magnanti, T.L., Orlin, J.B.: Network flows (1988)
2. Banerjee, S., Freund, D., Lykouris, T.: Pricing and optimization in shared vehicle systems: an approximation framework. arXiv preprint arXiv:1608.06819 (2016)
3. Chen, L., Shahabi, C.: Spatial crowdsourcing: challenges and opportunities. Bull. Tech. Committ. Data Eng. **39**(4), 14 (2016)
4. Chen, Z., Cheng, P., Chen, L., Lin, X., Shahabi, C.: Fair task assignment in spatial crowdsourcing. VLDB **13**(12), 2479–2492 (2020)

5. Chen, Z., Cheng, P., Zeng, Y., Chen, L.: Minimizing maximum delay of task assignment in spatial crowdsourcing. In: ICDE, pp. 1454–1465. IEEE (2019)
6. Cheng, P., Lian, X., Chen, L., Han, J., Zhao, J.: Task assignment on multi-skill oriented spatial crowdsourcing. TKDE **28**(8), 2201–2215 (2016)
7. Cheng, Y., Li, B., Zhou, X., Yuan, Y., Wang, G., Chen, L.: Real-time cross online matching in spatial crowdsourcing. In: ICDE, pp. 1–12. IEEE (2020)
8. Feldman, J., Mehta, A., Mirrokni, V., Muthukrishnan, S.: Online stochastic matching: beating 1–1/e. In: FOCS, pp. 117–126. IEEE (2009)
9. Ford, L.R., Fulkerson, D.R.: Maximal flow through a network. Can. J. Math. **8**, 399–404 (1956)
10. Kazemi, L., Shahabi, C.: Geocrowd: enabling query answering with spatial crowdsourcing. In: SIGSPATIAL, pp. 189–198 (2012)
11. Liu, J.X., Xu, K.: Budget-aware online task assignment in spatial crowdsourcing. WWW **23**(1), 289–311 (2020)
12. Munkres, J.: Algorithms for the assignment and transportation problems. J. Soc. Ind. Appl. Math. **5**(1), 32–38 (1957)
13. Peng, W., Liu, A., Li, Z., Liu, G., Li, Q.: User experience-driven secure task assignment in spatial crowdsourcing. World Wide Web **23**(3), 2131–2151 (2020). https://doi.org/10.1007/s11280-019-00728-3
14. Song, T., et al.: Trichromatic online matching in real-time spatial crowdsourcing. In: ICDE, pp. 1009–1020. IEEE (2017)
15. Song, T., Xu, K., Li, J., Li, Y., Tong, Y.: Multi-skill aware task assignment in real-time spatial crowdsourcing. GeoInformatica **24**(1), 153–173 (2020)
16. Ting, H.F., Xiang, X.: Near optimal algorithms for online maximum edge-weighted b-matching and two-sided vertex-weighted b-matching. TCS **607**, 247–256 (2015)
17. To, H., Fan, L., Tran, L., Shahabi, C.: Real-time task assignment in hyperlocal spatial crowdsourcing under budget constraints. In: PerCom, pp. 1–8. IEEE (2016)
18. Tong, Y., Chen, L., Shahabi, C.: Spatial crowdsourcing: challenges, techniques, and applications. VLDB **10**(12), 1988–1991 (2017)
19. Tong, Y., et al.: The simpler the better: a unified approach to predicting original taxi demands based on large-scale online platforms. In: SIGKDD, pp. 1653–1662 (2017)
20. Tong, Y., She, J., Ding, B., Wang, L., Chen, L.: Online mobile micro-task allocation in spatial crowdsourcing. In: ICDE, pp. 49–60. IEEE (2016)
21. Tong, Y., Wang, L., Zhou, Z., Chen, L., Du, B., Ye, J.: Dynamic pricing in spatial crowdsourcing: a matching-based approach. In: SIGMOD, pp. 773–788 (2018)
22. Tong, Y., et al.: Flexible online task assignment in real-time spatial data. VLDB **10**(11), 1334–1345 (2017)
23. Tong, Y., Zeng, Y., Ding, B., Wang, L., Chen, L.: Two-sided online micro-task assignment in spatial crowdsourcing. TKDE **33**, 2295–2309 (2019)
24. Wan, S., Zhang, D., Liu, A., Fang, J.: Extra-budget aware task assignment in spatial crowdsourcing. In: WISE (2021)
25. Xiao, M., et al.: SRA: secure reverse auction for task assignment in spatial crowdsourcing. TKDE **32**(4), 782–796 (2019)
26. Zhao, Y., Zheng, K., Cui, Y., Su, H., Zhu, F., Zhou, X.: Predictive task assignment in spatial crowdsourcing: a data-driven approach. In: ICDE, pp. 13–24. IEEE (2020)

Recommendation

TUR: Utilizing Temporal Information to Make Unexpected E-Commerce Recommendations

Yongxin Ni[1], Ningxia Wang[1(✉)], Li Chen[1], Rui Chen[2], and Lei Li[1]

[1] Hong Kong Baptist University, Hong Kong, China
{csyxni,nxwang,lichen,csleili}@comp.hkbu.edu.hk
[2] Harbin Engineering University, Harbin, China
ruichen@hrbeu.edu.cn

Abstract. *Unexpectedness recommendations* are getting more attention as a solution to the over-specialization of traditional accuracy-oriented recommender systems. However, most of the existing works make limited use of available interaction information to compute distance and neglect the fact that varying time intervals for recommendations would lead to different perceptions of unexpectedness from users. In this work, we propose a novel **Temporal Unexpected Recommendation (TUR)** approach to improve e-commerce recommendations' unexpectedness. Specifically, we consider the complementarity of both implicit and explicit distances, modeling unexpectedness from the latent space (i.e., embedding vectors) and the side information (i.e., item taxonomy) respectively. Meanwhile, we import a module based on the time-aware GRU to leverage the impact of timeliness on recommendation unexpectedness. Experiments on a large-scale e-commerce dataset containing real users' feedback show that TUR significantly outperforms the baselines in enhancing unexpectedness while maintaining a comparable accuracy level.

Keywords: Recommender systems · Unexpectedness · Timeliness · E-commerce

1 Introduction

Over-specialization caused by accuracy-oriented recommendation approaches may isolate users from potential items that may better match their hidden preferences [7]. To counteract such limitations, various beyond-accuracy objectives have been taken into consideration, among which serendipity has been proven to be more effective in affecting user satisfaction [2]. By definition, *serendipity* aims to achieve a desired trade-off between *accuracy* (also call relevance) and *unexpectedness*. The latter usually refers to the degree of items being different from the user's profile and in nature involves the user's emotional response [7]. How to enhance recommendation unexpectedness while still ensuring accuracy comparable to that of classical recommendation algorithms hence becomes a challenging issue.

Either by modifying accuracy-oriented algorithms [1,5,15] or through employing some advanced deep learning techniques (e.g., neural networks) [8–11], existing approaches manage to enhance unexpectedness and alleviate the

© The Author(s), under exclusive license to Springer Nature Switzerland AG 2022
R. Chbeir et al. (Eds.): WISE 2022, LNCS 13724, pp. 553–563, 2022.
https://doi.org/10.1007/978-3-031-20891-1_39

over-specialization, but to a limited extent. For example, most of them capture unexpectedness either by implicit distance (e.g., the difference between item embeddings) [8] or by explicit distance with side information (e.g., co-rated users and/or co-occurrence of items) [6,16]. But few works attempt to leverage their complementarity so as to better model unexpectedness. Moreover, few works consider *timeliness* (i.e., how good the time is to recommend a certain item to the target user) in model design, though its significant relationship with users' perceived unexpectedness was demonstrated in a large-scale user survey [2].

To address the above limitations, we propose a novel Temporal Unexpected Recommendation (TUR) approach for e-commerce recommendations in this work. Specifically, we utilize the complementarity of implicit and explicit distances, as well as capturing recommendation timeliness via a time-aware GRU-based module. As for algorithm evaluation, we employ a user survey dataset containing users' real feedback on recommendation unexpectedness [2,13] to evaluate the performance of our method TUR in comparison with several baselines. Results show that TUR significantly outperforms the baselines in terms of unexpectedness, while still maintaining a comparable level of recommendation accuracy.

2   Related Work

The first type of unexpectedness-oriented recommendation approaches modify conventional accuracy-oriented recommendation algorithms using techniques like pre-filtering [5] or re-ranking [1,15]. However, approaches of this type might be constrained by the prediction ability of the underlying algorithm employed. Therefore, recently, some machine learning methods are proposed. For example, Onuma *et al.* [11] employ the graph-based mining technique to recommend items that are close enough to the target user's preferences but have a high potential to reach other nodes. Li *et al.* [9] identify the target user's short-term preferences for movie genres through a RNN with Gated Recurrent Units (GRU), and calculate the elastic relevance between the target movie's user diversity and the target user's in-profile movie diversity. In their follow-up work [10], they further capture not only users' short-term preferences but also long-term preferences, through Gaussian Mixture Model and Capsule Networks respectively. Li *et al.* [8] define unexpectedness as the distance between the target item and the target user's preference closure in the latent vector space and use Self-Attentive GRU to predict item ratings.

However, those approaches are limited in the following four aspects. *First*, their utilization of available information is limited because they mainly rely on a single type of distance (i.e., either implicit distance or explicit distance) to define item unexpectedness. *Second*, existing approaches for unexpectedness mostly neglect recommendation timeliness. That is, an item would bring the same unexpectedness to the user no matter when it is recommended, which may result in low user satisfaction [2]. *Third*, they mostly evaluate recommendation unexpectedness through self-designed approximation metrics, but lack validation from users' real feedback. *Fourth*, the works purely emphasizing unexpectedness may compromise recommendation accuracy (relevance) to a certain extent [11]. Thus, in this work, we have been engaged in overcoming these limitations.

3   Temporal Unexpected Recommendation (TUR)

Adopting the utility theory that combining relevance and unexpectedness into a hybrid utility function may jointly learn the two for producing the overall utility [1,7,16], we extend the utility function of Personalized Unexpected Recommender System (PURS) [8], which, to the best of our knowledge, is the most recent representative utility-based unexpectedness-oriented work. Formally, given the target user u and the target item i, PURS computes the overall recommendation utility as

$$Utility(u,i) = Rel(u,i) + f(Unexp(u,i)) * Unexp\_factor(u,i) \qquad (1)$$

where $Rel(u,i)$ is the estimated relevance score of the target item i to the target user u; $Unexp(u,i)$ is the predicted unexpectedness of i to u, generalized via the activation function $f(x) = x * e^{-x}$; and $Unexp\_factor(u,i)$ is to measure the user u's propensity to accepting the item i's unexpectedness, which can be learned through a local activation unit.

To overcome the limitations mentioned previously, our proposed method TUR extends the computation of unexpectedness by adding the explicit distance instead of purely computing the implicit distance as in PURS and considering timeliness. The utility function is as follows:

$$Utility^*(u,i,t_r) = Rel(u,i) + f(Unexp^*(u,i,t_r)) * Unexp\_factor(u,i) \qquad (2)$$

where t_r is the time to provide the recommendation, and the unexpectedness score is computed as

$$Unexp^*(u,i,t_r) = \sigma(\alpha \cdot Implicit(u,i) + \beta \cdot Explicit(u,i) + \gamma \cdot Timeliness(u,i,t_r)) \qquad (3)$$

where σ is the sigmoid function that turns the integrated impact into the predicted unexpectedness score, and α, β, and γ are hyperparameters integrating the different scales.

We then predict the user's purchase probability by adding a sigmoid function to the utility, i.e., $Prob(u,i) = \sigma(Utility^*(u,i,t_r))$. With the ground truth labels that indicate whether i is really bought by the target user u, we formally train the framework via a cross-entropy loss function. To be noted, our unexpectedness module can be easily integrated with other accuracy-oriented prediction approaches under this framework, by changing the computation method of $Rel(u,i)$ in Eq. (1).

3.1   Implicit Distance and Explicit Distance

The computation of *implicit distance* is mainly inspired by PURS [8] that calculates the difference between the embedding vector of the target item i and user interest clusters. Concretely, the average Euclidean distance is employed:

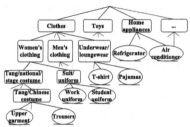

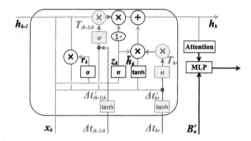

Fig. 1. The item category taxonomy from Mobile Taobao [13].

Fig. 2. The time-aware GRU in our framework.

$$Implicit(u, i) = \frac{\sum_{C_u^j \in C_u} d(\vec{i}, \vec{C_u^j})}{|C_u|} \tag{4}$$

where C_u denotes the set of user interest clusters through an unsupervised clustering algorithm [8] over all the embeddings of items that belong to the user's profile P_u, $\vec{i}$ and $\vec{C_u^j}$ are respectively the embedding vectors of the target item i and one interest cluster C_u^j, and $d(\vec{i}, \vec{C_u^j})$ is the Euclidean distance.

We further consider *explicit distance* based on side information. Because hierarchical item taxonomy (see example in Fig. 1) is typically adopted by popular e-commerce platforms (e.g., Amazon, e-Bay, and Taobao) to categorize products, we calculate **taxonomy-based category distance**. A common approach is to count the least hops between two items' leaf categories (hop-based distance). However, this method cannot well distinguish the category differences between pairs of items when their leaf categories lie at different levels. For example, in Fig. 1, the hop-based distance between an item under the leaf category "Work uniform" and that under "Student uniform" is 2, and that between items under "T-shirt" and "Pajamas" is also 2, but the former two nodes turn different at the 4th-level, while the latter two turn different at the 3rd level, so the distances should be different.

Therefore, we employ a computation method that can identify the level at which two items' category paths start to turn different [13]. Formally, the unexpectedness based on explicit distance is defined as:

$$Explicit(u, i) = \sum_{j \in P_u} \frac{1}{|P_u|}(L + 1 - \mathcal{L}_{ij}) \tag{5}$$

where P_u is the user u's profile, L is the total number of levels in the employed taxonomy (e.g., $L = 5$ in Fig. 1), and $\mathcal{L}_{ij}$ is the category distance of the target item i and an item j as represented by the length of their common category path (e.g., $\mathcal{L}_{ij} = 3$, if i is under "Work uniform" and j is under "Student uniform" in Fig. 1, while it is 2 if i is under "T-shirt" and j is under "Pajamas").

In a short summary, compared to previous works that purely consider either implicit distance or explicit distance, our framework leverages both of them for taking advantage of their complementarity.

3.2   Time-Aware GRU for Unexpectedness

As mentioned before, although the significant effect of timeliness on user perception of unexpectedness has been revealed [2], little algorithm work takes timeliness into consideration when predicting an item's unexpectedness score. To fill this gap, we design a time-aware GRU module (see Fig. 2) to learn the impact of the interaction time of each historical behavior on the unexpectedness degree of a certain item that the target user might perceive.

First, for each item k that belongs to u's profile P_u where all visited items are sorted by their interaction timestamps, we obtain its action embedding $x_k = \mathcal{L}_{ki} \cdot B_u^k$, where $\mathcal{L}_{ki}$ is the length of common category path between k and i, B_u^k is the concatenation of the embedding vectors of the user $\vec{u}$ and the item k's category $\vec{c_k}$, both of which are updated via back-propagation through the utility function optimization. With the dot product, we make x_k a weighted representation of u's historical action at the category level, thus larger category distance $\mathcal{L}_{ki}$ would empower the historical action with greater impact during the learning process since it may imply higher unexpectedness.

Next, we consider the actual temporal distance between the target item and the historical interaction. As users with high-frequency behaviors might be more sensitive to a long time interval from the recent interaction till the current recommendation than those with low-frequency, we encode two kinds of time information as the additional inputs, i.e., the time interval $\Delta t_{(k-1)k} = log(t_{uk} - t_{u(k-1)} + 1) + 1$ between $t_{u(k-1)}$ (when the user u visited the $k-1$-th item) and t_{uk} (when the user visited the k-th item), and the time interval $\Delta t_{kr} = log(t_r - t_{uk} + 1) + 1$ between t_{uk} and the time of providing the current recommendation t_r.

Inspired by the enhancement on LSTM in [14], we introduce two additional time gates for GRU by assigning more trainable dense matrices to the three input variables (i.e., x_k, $\Delta t_{(k-1)k}$, and Δt_{kr}) for linear transformation, so that the historical behaviors and temporal features could be learned in a joint manner (see Eqs. (8) and (9)). To be more specific, we introduce weight matrices W' for $t_{(k-1)k}$ and t_{kr} to integrate the two time features. By adding more matrices W/U and establishing interactions with x_k, the two features are converted into the time gates respectively. The governing equations of the modified part are:

$$\Delta t'_{(k-1)k} = \sigma_h(W'_{(k-1)k}\Delta t_{(k-1)k} + b'_{(k-1)k}) \tag{6}$$

$$\Delta t'_{kr} = \sigma_h(W'_{kr}\Delta t_{kr} + b'_{kr}) \tag{7}$$

$$T_{(k-1)k} = \sigma_g(x_k W_{(k-1)k} + \Delta t'_{(k-1)k}U_{(k-1)k} + b_{(k-1)k}) \tag{8}$$

$$T_{kr} = \sigma_g(x_k W_{kr} + \Delta t'_{kr}U_{kr} + b_{kr}) \tag{9}$$

From Fig. 2 we can see that the current state is controlled not only by the original update gate z_k and the reset gate r_k, but also by the two time gates $T_{(k-1)k}$ and T_{kr}.

To further differentiate the impact of each historical interaction on the item i's unexpectedness to user u, we apply a self-attention block to the output of the

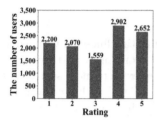

Fig. 3. The distribution of users' ratings on unexpectedness.

Table 1. Statistics of the taobao serendipity dataset

Data	User number	Item number	Interaction number	Sparsity
Historical records	11,383	7,717,420	21,405,555	0.024%
Survey data	11,383	9,985	11,383	0.010%
All	11,383	7,719,403	21,416,938	0.024%

time-aware GRU. The weighted output is subsequently presented to an MLP, incorporated with B_u^r (i.e., the concatenation of user vector $\vec{u}$ and embedding vector of item category $\vec{c_r}$) to forecast how good the time is to surprise the user (i.e., $Timeliness(u, i, t_r)$ in Eq. (3)).

4   Experiment

To measure the performance of our proposed method, we employed *Taobao Serendipity Dataset*[1] that contains users' real feedback on the recommendation's unexpectedness [2,13].

4.1   Taobao Serendipity Dataset

This dataset was collected from *Mobile Taobao*, a popular e-commerce platform in China, from Dec. 21, 2017 to March 17, 2018. Concretely, 11,383 users' feedback on the unexpectedness of recommendation was acquired through an online survey (w.r.t. the question *"The item recommended to me is unexpected"*), as well as their purchase intention (w.r.t. *"I would buy the item recommended, given the opportunity"*), both rated on a 5-point Likert scale from 1 - "strongly disagree" to 5 - "strongly agree". From Fig. 3 we can see that users' unexpectedness ratings are distributed over all the five points. In addition, we have every user's historical records (clicks/purchases) in the past three months before s/he took part in the survey. Each record can be denoted as (u, i, c_i, t_{ui}, p), indicating that the user u clicked ($p = 0$) or purchased ($p = 1$) the item i at the timestamp t_{ui}, the category of which is c_i. In total, there are 21,405,555 historical records, 4.21% of which are purchasing records (see statistics in Table 1). What's more, the category c_i of each item i denotes its leaf category along the path over the hierarchical item taxonomy (see Fig. 1).

To train the time-aware GRU, we followed the idea of session-based recommendation by extracting items during a session window of length $K = 10$ as one input sample. For example, if a user u has an interaction sequence $P_u = [i_{u1}, i_{u2}, i_{u3}, ...i_{u11}]$, there will be 2 data samples $(u, i_{u10}, [i_{u1}, i_{u2}, i_{u3}, ...i_{u9}])$ and

---

$(u, i_{u11}, [i_{u2}, i_{u3}, i_{u4}, ...i_{u10}])$, the dimension of which respectively denote the target user, the target item to be predicted, and the most recent nine interactions before the recommendation time. Then we followed the popular 80/20 rule to split historical data samples into the training/testing dataset, and all the survey data were treated as testing data. The goal was to recommend items users are likely to purchase, so records with $p = 1$ (for historical records) or purchase intention > 3 (for survey data) are labeled as positive samples.

4.2 Compared Methods

There are in total nine compared methods, and eight variations by respectively integrating PURS and TUR with the four accuracy-oriented approaches (e.g., "DIN+TUR" refers to the integration of TUR with the accuracy-oriented approach DIN). Concretely, we compared our method TUR with 5 unexpectedness-oriented methods:

- **Full-Auralist** [15], a personalized algorithm injecting novelty, diversity and serendipity into the learning process;
- **HOM-LIN** [1], a utility-based model to estimate the overall preference a user holds for an item;
- **UNEXP-AUG** [16], a modification of PureSVD by including the unexpectedness as a penalty factor to model both usefulness and unexpectedness;
- **SOG** [6] that introduces feature diversification to promote the recommendation serendipity; and
- **PURS** [8], an advanced framework that unifies relevance and unexpectedness into a hybrid utility function as we described before.

Moreover, we implemented four state-of-the-art accuracy-oriented approaches, in order to see whether the accuracy of our method could be comparable to theirs, and furthermore whether it would be feasible to enhance their unexpectedness by integrating TUR into their framework.

- **DIN** [17] that introduces a local activation unit to adaptively learn representation vector for each user to capture her interests;
- **PNN** [12] that extracts high-order feature interactions by introducing a product layer between the embedding layer and the fully connected layer;
- **Wide&Deep** [3] that jointly trains a linear model for feature processing and a feed-forward neural network for feature learning; and
- **DeepFM** [4] that combines the factorization machine and a feed-forward neural network to learn feature interactions.

Each method was trained and tested three times and the means of their accuracy and unexpectedness performance are reported in Tables 2 and 3. More details on codes and parameters can be found in https://github.com/greenblue96/TUR.

Table 2. Comparison of TUR with unexpectedness-oriented and accuracy-oriented baselines

Method	Accuracy (AUC)	Unexpectedness (MAE)	(RMSE)
Full-Auralist	0.5660	0.5048	0.6087
HOM-LIN	0.5352	0.4963	0.5978
UNEXP-AUG	0.4991	0.4157	0.5236
SOG	0.5142	0.3831	0.4716
PURS	0.6273	0.5260	0.6373
DIN	0.6186	–	–
PNN	0.5950	–	–
Wide&Deep	0.5930	–	–
DeepFM	**0.6305**	–	–
TUR	0.5920	**0.3267**	**0.4083**
Improvement	–	14.72%	15.50%

Note: The improvement is against the second-best performed method ($p < 0.001$ by Student's t-test).

Table 3. Comparison between TUR and PURS being integrated with other accuracy-oriented methods

Method		Accuracy (AUC)	Unexpectedness (MAE)	(RMSE)
DIN	+PURS	0.6857	0.5234	0.6337
	+TUR	0.6854	↑**0.3338**	↑**0.4183**
PNN	+PURS	0.6859	0.5234	0.6337
	+TUR	0.6852	↑**0.3350**	↑**0.4199**
Wide&Deep	+PURS	0.6854	0.5181	0.6269
	+TUR	0.6815	↑**0.3411**	↑**0.4278**
DeepFM	+PURS	0.6807	0.5209	0.6306
	+TUR	0.6799	↑**0.3251**	↑**0.4053**
Average improvement		–	35.99%	33.80%

Note: ↑ indicates that xxx+TUR (e.g., DIN+TUR) achieves significantly better prediction than xxx+PURS regarding the corresponding unexpectedness metric ($p < 0.001$ by Student's t-test).

5 Results

Metrics. To evaluate *accuracy*, we adopted the weighted **AUC**, the same as that used in PURS [8]. To evaluate *unexpectedness*, we calculated **MAE** and **RMSE** between the predicted unexpectedness and the user's real unexpectedness feedback after performing min-max normalization. For TUR and PURS, the predicted unexpectedness is the unexpectedness score. For HOM-LIN, it is the linear distance from i to u's expectation set. For UNEXP-AUG, it is the linear combination of i's rareness and its dissimilarity to u's profile. For Auralist [15] and SOG [6], we only use components except the relevance estimation for unexpectedness prediction.

Comparison with Baselines. There are several interesting observations (see Table 2): *First*, regarding recommendation accuracy, TUR outperforms four unexpectedness-oriented baselines, with 4.59% significant improvement ($p < 0.001$ by Student's t-test) than the second-best baseline Full-Auralist in terms of AUC. We also find that the accuracy of TUR can be comparable to those of the state-of-the-art accuracy-oriented algorithms (e.g., PNN and Wide&Deep), but be slightly lower than DIN and DeepFM. *Second*, as for unexpectedness, TUR performs significantly better than all the unexpectedness-oriented baselines, with 14.72% and 15.50% improvements on the second-best baseline SOG in terms of MAE and RMSE respectively, and 37.89% and 35.93% against PURS that TUR extends.

Integration with Accuracy-Oriented Method. Given that both TUR and PURS can act as a utility-based framework to be integrated with other accuracy-oriented methods, we are interested in comparing the two frameworks in this regard. Note that the integration can be simply done by replacing the relevance estimation (e.g., $Rel(u, i)$ in Equation (3) for TUR) with the output of an accuracy-oriented algorithm (i.e., DIN, PNN, Wide&Deep, or DeepFM).

From Table 3 we can see that all the combinations are basically equivalent regarding accuracy (with AUC ranging from 0.6799 to 0.6859), and the results are obviously better than those in Table 2 (in which the best accuracy is 0.6305 by DeepFM). More notably, the comparison between TUR and PURS shows that, when being integrated with the same accuracy-oriented algorithm, the former always significantly outperforms the latter regarding the unexpectedness metrics, with the best MAE and RMSE (0.3251 and 0.4053 respectively) obtained by DeepFM+TUR among all. On average, TUR shows an improvement of 35.99% w.r.t. MAE and 33.80% w.r.t. RMSE compared to to PURS. The results indicate that TUR can be more effective than PURS in terms of boosting the recommendation unexpectedness, while not compromising accuracy (and even increasing) when it is integrated with the accuracy-oriented method.

Table 4. Results of the ablation study

Method	Accuracy	Unexpectedness		Method	Accuracy	Unexpectedness	
	(AUC)	(MAE)	(RMSE)		(AUC)	(MAE)	(RMSE)
TUR^0	0.6854	**0.3338$^{1-6}$**	**0.4183$^{1-6}$**				
TUR$_I{}^1$	0.6855	0.5191	0.6281	TUR$_{IE}{}^4$	0.6856^0	0.4193$^{1-3}$	0.5282$^{1-3}$
TUR$_E{}^2$	0.6856^{0,6}	0.4386^{1,3}	0.5545^{1,3}	TUR$_{IT}{}^5$	0.6873^{0,2,4,6}	0.4988^1	0.6010^1
TUR$_T{}^3$	**0.6874**	0.4960^{1,5}	0.5973^{1,5}	TUR$_{ET}{}^6$	0.6854	0.3443$^{1-5}$	0.4320$^{1-5}$

Note: The superscript indicates that the corresponding method is significantly better than the numbered one.

Ablation Study. As shown above, DIN+TUR's overall performance is more satisfactory regarding both accuracy and unexpectedness, we therefore conducted ablation study on this version that is abbreviated as TUR henceforth. Six variants were implemented: TUR$_I$, TUR$_E$, TUR$_T$, TUR$_{IE}$, TUR$_{IT}$, and TUR$_{ET}$, where the subscript letter indicates the component considered by the variant (i.e., I, E, and T for implicit distance, explicit distance, and timeliness, respectively). Results show that all the six variants are inferior to the complete version of TUR (i.e., DIN+TUR) in capturing users' unexpectedness perception, with at least 3.15% worse w.r.t. MAE and 3.28% worse w.r.t. RMSE than TUR (see Table 4). It hence suggests that these three components, i.e., *implicit distance, explicit distance*, and *recommendation timeliness*, all contribute to TUR's unexpectedness prediction to a certain extent. We also notice that the timeliness module can help largely increase unexpectedness. For instance, the comparison of TUR with TUR$_{IE}$ reveals that the former obtains 25.61% and 26.27% improvements on unexpectedness in terms of MAE and RMSE respectively. Another interesting finding is that, the differences of TUR$_{IE}$ from TUR$_I$ and TUR$_E$ are both significant ($p < 0.001$), which verifies our assumption of taking into account their complementarity for enhancing unexpectedness prediction.

6 Conclusions

In this work, we propose the Temporal Unexpected Recommendation (TUR) approach. Specifically, grounded on the utility theory, we model user preference as a utility function accommodating both recommendation relevance and unexpectedness. For the latter, we particularly unify three components, i.e., *implicit distance* defined in the latent space, *explicit distance* computed over hierarchical category taxonomy, and *timeliness* learned through the time-aware GRU. Experiments on an e-commerce dataset containing users' real feedback show the superiority of our method to several baselines by significantly improving unexpectedness, while not compromising accuracy. In the future, we will be engaged in generalizing the findings to other domains, and considering leveraging users' personal characteristics (e.g., curiosity [13]) to further enhance unexpectedness.

Acknowledgements. This work was supported by Hong Kong Research Grants Council (RGC) (project RGC/HKBU12201620).

References

1. Adamopoulos, P., Tuzhilin, A.: On unexpectedness in recommender systems: or how to better expect the unexpected. TIST **5**(4), 1–32 (2014)
2. Chen, L., Yang, Y., Wang, N., Yang, K., Yuan, Q.: How serendipity improves user satisfaction with recommendations? a large-scale user evaluation. In: WWW, pp. 240–250 (2019)
3. Cheng, H.T., et al.: Wide & deep learning for recommender systems. In: DLRS, pp. 7–10 (2016)
4. Guo, H., Tang, R., Ye, Y., Li, Z., He, X.: DeepFM: a factorization-machine based neural network for CTR prediction. arXiv preprint arXiv:1703.04247 (2017)
5. Karpus, A., Vagliano, I., Goczyła, K.: Serendipitous recommendations through ontology-based contextual pre-filtering. In: BDAS, pp. 246–259 (2017)
6. Kotkov, D., Veijalainen, J., Wang, S.: How does serendipity affect diversity in recommender systems? a serendipity-oriented greedy algorithm. Computing **102**(2), 393–411 (2020)
7. Kotkov, D., Wang, S., Veijalainen, J.: A survey of serendipity in recommender systems. Knowl.-Based Syst. **111**, 180–192 (2016)
8. Li, P., Que, M., Jiang, Z., Hu, Y., Tuzhilin, A.: PURS: personalized unexpected recommender system for improving user satisfaction. In: RecSys, pp. 279–288 (2020)
9. Li, X., Jiang, W., Chen, W., Wu, J., Wang, G.: Haes: a new hybrid approach for movie recommendation with elastic serendipity. In: CIKM, pp. 1503–1512 (2019)
10. Li, X., Jiang, W., Chen, W., Wu, J., Wang, G., Li, K.: Directional and explainable serendipity recommendation. In: WWW, pp. 122–132 (2020)
11. Onuma, K., Tong, H., Faloutsos, C.: Tangent: a novel, surprise me, recommendation algorithm. In: KDD, pp. 657–666 (2009)
12. Qu, Y., et al.: Product-based neural networks for user response prediction. In: ICDM, pp. 1149–1154 (2016)
13. Wang, N., Chen, L., Yang, Y.: The impacts of item features and user characteristics on users' perceived serendipity of recommendations. In: UMAP, pp. 266–274 (2020)

14. Yu, Z., Lian, J., Mahmoody, A., Liu, G., Xie, X.: Adaptive user modeling with long and short-term preferences for personalized recommendation. In: IJCAI, pp. 4213–4219 (2019)
15. Zhang, Y.C., Séaghdha, D.Ó., Quercia, D., Jambor, T.: Auralist: introducing serendipity into music recommendation. In: WSDM, pp. 13–22 (2012)
16. Zheng, Q., Chan, C.K., Ip, H.H.: An unexpectedness-augmented utility model for making serendipitous recommendation. In: ICDM, pp. 216–230 (2015)
17. Zhou, G., et al.: Deep interest network for click-through rate prediction. In: KDD, pp. 1059–1068 (2018)

Towards Robust Recommender Systems via Triple Cooperative Defense

Qingyang Wang, Defu Lian$^{(\boxtimes)}$, Chenwang Wu, and Enhong Chen

University of Science and Technology of China, 96 Jinzhai Road,
Hefei, Anhui, China
{greensun,wcw1996}@mail.ustc.edu.cn, {liandefu,cheneh}@ustc.edu.cn

Abstract. Recommender systems are often susceptible to well-crafted fake profiles, leading to biased recommendations. The wide application of recommender systems makes studying the defense against attack necessary. Among existing defense methods, data-processing-based methods inevitably exclude normal samples, while model-based methods struggle to enjoy both generalization and robustness. Considering the above limitations, we suggest integrating data processing and robust model and propose a general framework, Triple Cooperative Defense (TCD), which cooperates to improve model robustness through the co-training of three models. Specifically, in each round of training, we sequentially use the high-confidence prediction ratings (consistent ratings) of any two models as auxiliary training data for the remaining model, and the three models cooperatively improve recommendation robustness. Notably, TCD adds pseudo label data instead of deleting abnormal data, which avoids the cleaning of normal data, and the cooperative training of the three models is also beneficial to model generalization. Through extensive experiments with five poisoning attacks on three real-world datasets, the results show that the robustness improvement of TCD significantly outperforms baselines. It is worth mentioning that TCD is also beneficial for model generalizations.

Keywords: Recommender systems · Model robustness · Poisoning attacks

1 Introduction

In recent years, with the rapid development of Internet technology, the amount of information on the Internet has shown explosive growth. To obtain valuable information from massive data information more quickly and effectively, "recommender systems" [2] came into being and quickly gained extensive attention and practical application in academia and industry. Recommender algorithms mine the content that the user is interested in from a large amount of data by using information such as user behavior and item characteristics and presenting it to the user in a list [15]. Their superiority and commercial background make them widely used in various industries [2,5,20].

R. Chbeir et al. (Eds.): WISE 2022, LNCS 13724, pp. 564–578, 2022.
https://doi.org/10.1007/978-3-031-20891-1_40

However, the recommender system also faces the test of severe security problems while providing convenience for our lives. Since the collaborative filtering method works based on user profile information, it is easily affected by false user profile information. Studies [18,21,33] have long shown that recommender systems, especially those in the field of sales and scoring, systematically interfere with the user ratings included in the system, which will also impact users' purchase behavior and system recommendation results [5]. And even if attackers do not know the algorithm or implementation details used by the recommendation system, only using small-scale misleading data, can also have obvious interference effects on the normal recommendation behavior of the system, (e.g., in 2002, after receiving a complaint, Amazon found that when a website recommends a Christian classic, another irrelevant book will be recommended simultaneously, which is caused by malicious users using deceptive means [22]).

Two main defense methods against poisoning attacks are data-processing-based defense and model-based defense [7,34]. Data-based defense tries to study the characteristics of poisoning attacks, strip fake profiles, and purify datasets before the training of recommender systems. However, to pursue high recall, these methods will inevitably delete normal data, which will lead to biased recommendations. Model-based defense improves the robustness of the recommendation algorithm itself, and adversarial training [24] is recognized as the most popular and effective model-based defense method to enhance recommendation robustness [34]. This method maximizes recommendation error while minimizing the model's empirical risk by adding adversarial perturbations to the model parameters, eventually building robust models in adversarial games. Although adversarial training can significantly improve the robustness of the recommender system, it is difficult to control the strength of adversarial noise, which results in reducing the generalization of the recommendation to a certain extent. Besides, a recent study has shown that adversarial training with perturbations added to model parameters cannot well resist poisoning attacks [34]. Therefore, it is very needed to design a suitable means to integrate them and make use of their strengths and avoid weaknesses.

Based on the shortcomings mentioned above, we propose a novel defense method that integrates data processing and model robustness boosting, Triple Cooperative Defense(TCD), to enhance the robustness of recommender systems. Specifically, in each round of training, we sequentially use the high-confidence prediction ratings (consistent ratings) of any two models as auxiliary training data for the remaining models, and the three models cooperatively improve recommendation robustness. The proposed strategy is based on the following considerations. In the recommender system, extremely sparse user-item interactions are difficult to support good model training, leading to models that are easily misled by malicious profiles. Besides, recent work also emphasizes that the model's robustness requires more real data [34]. Therefore, we make reasonable use of cheap pseudo-labels. Obviously, pseudo-labels must be guaranteed by high-confidence ratings, but in the explicit feedback-based recommender system that we focus on, the predicted value is the rating, not the confidence. To this end, we suggest training with three models and any two models' consistent prediction ratings as auxiliary training data for the third model. Model robustness is improved in data augmentation and co-training of the three models. Notably, we do not cull the data nor modify the individual model structure, which can overcome the shortcomings of existing defense methods. Through extensive experiments with five poisoning attacks on three real-world datasets, the results show that the robustness improvement of TCD significantly outperforms baselines. It is worth mentioning that TCD also improves model generalization.

The main contributions of this work are summarized as follows:

- the proposal of a novel robust training strategy, named Triple Cooperative Defense, by generating pseudo labels into the recommender system for eliminating the damage of malicious profiles to models, and training three models cooperatively for improving model robustness. It is noteworthy that this is the first algorithm to combine data-processing-based defense and model-based defense in recommender systems.
- an extensive study of co-training (defensive) methods to robustify the recommendation performance through the analysis of five attacks and three recommendation datasets. The results verify that our method enhances the robustness of the recommendation while ensuring generalization.

2   Related Work

2.1   Security of Recommender Systems

Many issues about security and privacy have been studied in recommender systems, which suggest that recommender systems are vulnerable [8,29], which leads to developing a toolkit for evaluating robustness [27]. Earlier attacks injected malicious profiles manually generated with little knowledge about the recommender system, so it could not achieve satisfactory attack performance, e.g., random attack [17] and average attack [17]. The training of model-based recommendation algorithms usually used backpropagation [12,14], so perturbations were added along the gradient direction to perform the attack [10,11,18,31]. Inspired by the GAN's application [16] in the recommendation, some work [6,21] used GAN to generate real-like fake ratings to bypass the detection. With the development of optimization algorithms, many works focused on attack specific types of recommender systems and turned attacks into optimization problems of deciding appropriate rating scores for users [11,17,18,26,36]. Moreover, some works [9,30] treated the items' ratings as actions and used reinforcement learning to generate real-like fake ratings. Such optimization-based methods have strong attack performance, so defense is needed to mitigate the harm of attack.

2.2   Defense Against Poisoning Attacks

According to the defense objective, a defense can be (i) reactive attack detection [7] or (ii) proactive robust model construction, which will be listed below.

Many researchers used KNN, C4.5, and SVM [3]to supervise the statistical attributes to detect attacks. In most practical recommendation systems, due to the small number of labeled users and the lack of prior knowledge, unsupervised learning [38,40] and semi-supervised learning [4] were used to detect attacks. However, to pursue high recall, these methods inevitably delete normal data, which lead to biased recommendations. Conversely, for our proposed TCD to enrich high-confidence data rather than remove outliers, it can avoid cleaning normal data and train a more accurate and robust model.

Athalye et al. [1] proposed defenses based on gradient masking produce models containing smoother gradients that hinder optimization-based attack algorithms from finding the wrong directions in space [23]. More recently, many works [8,13,19,28,32] have focused on adversarial training. Assuming that each instance may be the target of attacks [23], adversarial training adds perturbations to the inputs or model parameters that force the model to learn fragile perturbations. Although adversarial training can significantly improve the robustness of recommender systems, it is difficult to control the strength of adversarial data, which results in reducing the generalization of the recommendation. Instead, the proposed TCD does not need to add sensitive noise and is trained cooperatively to facilitate generalization, and we will prove it in Sect. 4.

3   Methodology

3.1   Threat Model

Attack Goal. Different shilling attacks may have different intents, but the eventual goal of an attacker may be one of several alternatives. We can divide the attack intents into three types, including push attacks, nude attacks, and random vandalism [29]. The push attack (nude attack) typically aims to increase (decrease) the popularity of the target item. For the random vandalism, the attacker combines push attack and null attack to maximize the error of the recommendation making users stop trusting the recommendation model and finally stop using it. We mainly focus on the defense against push attack, while nude attacks can be achieved by increasing the popularity of non-target items until the target item is not in the user's recommendation list [36], which in a sense is equivalent to push attacks.

Attack Knowledge-Cost. Attacker's knowledge-cost can be divided into high-knowledge attacks and low-knowledge attacks [29]. The former requires the attackers to know detailed knowledge of the rating distribution in a recommender system's database, such as the algorithm used, specific parameter settings, and even the users' historical behavior, the latter only knows system-independent knowledge such as knowledge might be obtained by consulting public information sources. Obviously, low-knowledge attacks are more practical because it is difficult for attackers to obtain detailed data and models. Therefore, we study the robust defense against low-knowledge attacks.

Attack Size. Attack size is the number of fake profiles injected into the system by the attackers [35]. Obviously, the model robustness and attack size cannot be decoupled. Considering that most users only rate a small number of items, the greater the attack intensity, the more likely it is to be detected [25]. Similar to [34], we limit the attacker size to 5%, and the limit of the number of ratings for each attacker is the average number of ratings.

3.2 Triple Cooperative Defense

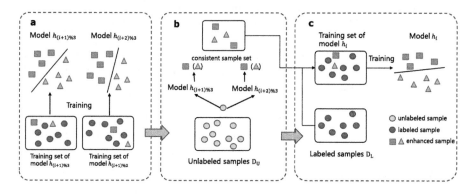

Fig. 1. The training of model h_i in each round. a: The other two models use the same collaborative training. b: The labels predicted the same by the two models are taken as consistent samples. c: Model i is trained on labeled samples D_L and consistent samples.

As discussed in Sect. 1, data-processing-based defense inevitably removes normal data altogether to achieve high recall rates, while model-based defense is difficult to enjoy both robustness and generalization [39]. Therefore, it is crucial to combine them effectively and design a defense algorithm that maximizes their strengths and circumvents their weaknesses. Recent studies [7] demonstrated that robust models require more labeled data [34]. Besides, the recommender system is extremely sparse, that is, there is little interactive information about users and items, making a small amount of normal data difficult to support good training of the model, and maybe misled easily by malicious data and produce biased recommendations. This finding makes us reasonably believe that the vulnerability of the recommendation system is largely due to the lack of data. However, it takes a lot of manpower and material resources to get labeled data, and using a small number of "expensive" labeled data instead of a large number of "cheap" unlabeled data is a huge waste of data resources. Considering the reasons mentioned above, we constructively propose adding pseudo ratings with high confidence improves the recommender robustness.

Unfortunately, in the implicit recommendation system concerned in this paper, it is challenging to obtain high confidence pseudo scores. This is because the output of recommender systems is prediction scores, not confidence, unlike other areas of machine learning (e.g., in the image field, the output is the prediction probability). So we develop TCD, which uses three models and takes the prediction consistency ratings of any two models as the high confidence pseudo ratings of the remaining model. Moreover, the use of three models can not only provide confidence scores but also improve the robustness of the model through the collaborative training of three models. The framework is shown in Fig. 1. In theory, more models with majority votes are more beneficial to obtain high-confidence data. However, the training of the model is linearly positively related to the number of models. We found that the performance of the three models is satisfactory and the training delay is tolerable. Now we provide details of the proposed TCD for defending against poisoning attacks.

Let D denote the dataset, D_L denotes the scoring samples of D, where each sample $(u, i, r_{i,j})$ denotes that the user u's rating on item i is $r_{i,j}$, and D_U denotes the no scoring samples of D, where each sample is like (u, i). The goal of the recommendation system h is to predict accurate scores $\hat{r}_{u,i} = h(u, i)$ of each sample $(u, i) \in D_U$.

In TCD, we denote the three models as h_0, h_1, and h_2, respectively. For any model, if the predicted scores of the other two models are consistent, then we have reason to believe that the predicted scores are high-confident and reliable to be added to the training set which addresses the difficulty to measure rating confidence. For instance, if h_0 and h_1 agree on the labeling $r_{i,j}$ of (u, i) in D_U, then $(u, i, r_{i,j})$ will be put into the training set for h_2 as auxiliary training data. It is obvious that in such a scheme if the prediction of h_0 and h_1 on (u, i) is correct, then h_2 will receive a new sample with high confidence for further training. This strategy takes into account that it is difficult for attackers to learn the real rating distribution, causing the poisoning profiles to deviate from the real data [21], which is reflected in the instability of their training. Therefore, cooperative training will magnify the influence of real profiles and relatively weaken the harm of false profiles.

Besides, the predicted ratings are floating points, making it impractical to judge based on the consistent rating. So we define a projection function $\Pi(\cdot)$ to project continuous scores onto reasonable discrete scores. In this way, only when two models give the same rating on (u, i) after projection, do we take the rating as the pseudo label and put $(u, i, \Pi(\hat{h}_j(u, i)))$ into the training set $D_L^{(k)}$.

The algorithm of TCD is shown in Algorithm 1. Each model is pre-trained from lines 1 to 5. Then, for each round of training for each model, an unlabeled prediction will be labeled if any two models agree on the labeling, as shown in lines 6 through 10. These pseudo labels with high confidence will be put into the third model's training dataset to reduce the harm that poisoning data do to the model, as shown in lines 11 through 16. After the training, we can perform the recommendation task using any model. Since the structure of each model is unchanged, the proposed strategy does not have inference delay, which is of more concern to practical applications.

Algorithm 1: Triple Cooperative Defense

Input: The epochs of training T, the epochs of pre-training T_{pre}, three models $h_1(u, i), h_2(u, i), h_3(u, i)$, labeled data D_L, unlabeled data D_U, projection function $\Pi(x)$

1 **for** T_{pre} *epochs* **do**
2   **for** $j \in [0, 1, 2]$ **do**
3 | Train h_j based on the training set D_L
4   **end**
5 **end**
6 **for** $T - T_{pre}$ *epochs* **do**
7   **for** $j \in [0, 1, 2]$ **do**
8      $D_L^{(j)} \leftarrow D_L$
9   **for** *every* $(u, i) \in D_U$ **do**
10   **if** $\Pi(\hat{h}_{(j+1)mod3}(u, i)) = \Pi(\hat{h}_{(j+2)mod3}(u, i))$ **then**
11 | $D_L^{(j)} \leftarrow D_L^{(j)} \cup \{(u, i, \Pi(\hat{h}_{(j+1)mod3}(u, i)))\}$
12   **end**
13   **end**
14   Train h_j based on training set $D_L^{(j)}$
15   **end**
16 **end**

It is worth noting that in the pre-training phase, we used the same dataset D_L for all models. Theoretically, we need to choose different training subsets to ensure the diversity of the model. This is necessary for other domains, such as computer version, because the number of parameters in a classifier is independent of the number of samples. However, in the recommender systems with extremely sparse data, selecting a subset means that a large number of users are cold-start users, and the parameters of these users cannot be trained, which directly leads to unsatisfactory recommendation performance. Therefore, all label data are selected for pre-training, while the models' diversity is guaranteed by different pseudo-labels in collaborative training.

4   EXPERIMENT

4.1   Settings

Datasets. We use three real-world datasets commonly used in the security studies [6,37] of the recommender system, including FilmTrust[1], ML-100K[2] (MovieLens-100K), and ML-1M[3](MovieLens-1M). ML-100K includes 943 users who have rated 1,682 movies for 100,000 ratings. ML-1M comprises 6,040 users who have rated 3,706 movies about one million times. For FilmTrust, the same

---

[1] https://www.librec.net/datasets/flmtrust.zip.
[2] https://grouplens.org/datasets/movielens.
[3] https://grouplens.org/datasets/movielens.

pretreatment as [21] is used to filter cold-start users who seriously affect the recommender system (the rating number is less than 15), leaving 796 users with trust ratings for 2011 movies. Table 1 lists the detailed statistics of these datasets. All ratings are from 1 to 5, and we normalized them to [0, 1] in the experiments. For each dataset, we randomly select a positive sample from each user for testing, and the rest are used as the training set and verification set in a 9:1 ratio.

Table 1. Statistics of datasets

Dataset	Users	Items	Ratings	Sparsity
FilmTrust	796	2011	30880	98.07
ML-100K	943	1682	100000	93.70
ML-1M	6040	3706	1000209	95.53

Attack Methods. In the low-knowledge attacks studied in this paper, the attacker uses captured partial data to rebuild a local simulator which is similar to the target model. Then, the attacker take the local simulator as a white box for attacking. The validity of this setting is guaranteed by the transferability of the attack. Here we use the following attacks for robustness validation:

– **Random Attack** [17]: This attack assigns the maximum rating to the target item and rates selected items according to the normal distribution of all user ratings at random.
– **Average Attack** [17]: The only difference from Random Attack is that the non-target selected item is randomly rated with the normal rating distribution of items.
– **AUSH Attack** [21]: This attack uses GAN to generate fake users to carry out attacks imperceptibly and assigns the highest rating to the target item.
– **PGA Attack** [18]: This attack builds an attack objective and uses SGD to update the poisoned user's ratings to optimize the objective. Finally, the first items with the largest ratings are selected as the fake user's filler items.
– **TNA Attack** [10]: This attack selects a subset of the most influential users in the dataset and optimizes the rating gap between the target item and top-K items in the user subset. Here we use S-TNA.

Baselines. We compare the proposed TCD with the following robust algorithms:

– **Adversarial Training (AT)** [14]: In each training step, it first uses SGD to optimize the inner objective to generate small perturbations, adds them to the parameters, and then performs training.
– **Random Adversarial Training (RAT)** [14]: In each training step, it first uses the truncated normal distribution $N(0,0.01)$ to generate small perturbations, adds them to the parameters, and then performs training.

These methods cannot enjoy both generalization and robustness. The larger the noise is, the better the robustness will be, but the generalization will decrease significantly. Therefore, 0.03 is selected as a compromise.

Evaluation Metric. We first use HR@50 (Hit Ratio), just like [34], which calculates the proportion of test items that appear in the user's top-50 recommendation list. Setting a large K helps make apparent comparisons between defense methods and collaborative filtering is often used for candidate selection in practical recommendations, so it is more instructive to select a larger K to ensure a high recall [13]. Besides, we use robustness improvement $RI = 1 - (HR_{defense} - HR_{orgin})/(HR_{attack} - HR_{orgin})$ defined in [34]. The closer the value is to 1, the better the robustness. We report the average results of 30 independent repeated experiments and perform paired t-test to judge the statistical significance when necessary.

Parameters Setting. We concern with the MF-based collaborative filtering method, and we set the latent factor dimension d to 128, the batch size to 2048, and the regularization parameter to 0.005. In FilmTrust, ML-100K, and ML-1M, $Tpre$ is set to 1, 4, 2, respectively. The model is trained for 40 epochs, the results are based on the choice of the smallest MSE, and the Adam optimizer is used for training. Besides, we set the attacker knowledge-cost to 0.4, the attack size to 3%, and the pseudo-label rate of ML-1M to 0.2. For the target items of attacks, we learn two types of items: (1) random items randomly selected from all items, and (2) unpopular items randomly selected from items with the number of rates less than 5. In each attack, we set the number of target items to 5 and set the number of filler items m' to the average number of ratings per user. The source code of TCD is available at https://github.com/greensun0830/TCD.

Table 2. Attack performance under different attack knowledge-cost.

Dataset	Random items							Unpopular items					
	Attack	Origin	Attack knowledge-cost					Origin	Attack knowledge-cost				
			0.2	0.4	0.6	0.8	1		0.2	0.4	0.6	0.8	1
Filmtrust	Average	0.1617	0.0889	0.1005	0.1612	0.1222	0.1303	0.0000	0.0016	0.0022	0.0013	0.0017	0.0024
	Random	0.1702	0.1376	0.1213	0.1622	0.1214	0.1404	0.0000	0.0034	0.0019	0.0012	0.0028	0.0023
	AUSH	0.1629	0.1132	0.1403	0.1625	0.2540	0.2675	0.0000	0.0152	0.0296	0.0285	0.0283	0.0461
	PGA	0.1574	0.0983	0.1031	0.1625	0.1471	0.1396	0.0000	0.0028	0.0013	0.0040	0.0049	0.0080
	TNA	0.1628	0.5619	0.5463	0.1446	0.5435	0.3380	0.0000	0.3054	0.4059	0.1839	0.0899	0.0807
ML-100K	Average	0.0233	0.1829	0.1579	0.2193	0.2237	0.2209	0.0000	0.0255	0.1572	0.5094	0.5943	0.4694
	Random	0.0234	0.0519	0.0956	0.0812	0.1099	0.0870	0.0000	0.1101	0.1056	0.1186	0.0906	0.0874
	AUSH	0.0233	0.1676	0.2819	0.3112	0.3667	0.3013	0.0000	0.0756	0.2320	0.7809	0.7942	0.8150
	PGA	0.0237	0.0855	0.1583	0.1673	0.1194	0.1667	0.0000	0.4558	0.2828	0.3912	0.3113	0.2809
	TNA	0.0244	0.0735	0.2355	0.2786	0.2512	0.2714	0.0000	0.6925	0.3934	0.6932	0.5628	0.7511
ML-1M	Average	0.0000	0.1829	0.2390	0.2812	0.2674	0.3116	0.0000	0.9029	0.9326	0.9261	0.9408	0.9434
	Random	0.0000	0.0519	0.0568	0.0563	0.0596	0.0608	0.0000	0.7213	0.7184	0.6471	0.7014	0.7588
	AUSH	0.0000	0.1676	0.2829	0.3145	0.3061	0.3278	0.0000	0.9680	0.9712	0.9767	0.9759	0.9803
	PGA	0.0000	0.0855	0.1027	0.1036	0.0418	0.0336	0.0000	0.9569	0.9433	0.9243	0.9034	0.9118
	TNA	0.0000	0.0735	0.2622	0.3046	0.3114	0.3406	0.0000	0.9068	0.9325	0.9395	0.9508	0.9496

4.2 Result Analysis

In this section, we compare the robustness and generalization of the model configured with TCD and other defense methods.

Attack Threat. Different attack knowledge-cost leads to different attack performances, as shown in Table 2. We can find that a larger attack knowledge-cost does not have better attack performance, even when attackers only know 20% of the model knowledge, they can achieve a good attack effect, and in most cases, 40% attack knowledge performs well. Moreover, considering practical application scenarios, attacks cannot get full knowledge about recommender systems. So we choose to set the attack knowledge-cost to 0.4 to ensure its practicability while achieving a good attack performance. However, we also found that not all attacks are effective. For example, heuristic Random Attack and Average Attack are ineffective in FilmTrust and even reduce the exposure rate of target items, which emphasizes the significance of studying optimization-based attacks.

Robustness. We evaluate the hit ratio of target items in attack and defense, as shown in Table 3. The Origin denotes the unperturbed model, and the Attack represents the perturbed model with no defense. Consistent with the findings in Table 3, We have the following finds:

Table 3. The performance in target items (robustness). *, ** and *** indicate that the improvements over the best results of baselines are statistically significant for $p < 0.05, p < 0.01$ and $p < 0.001$, respectively.

Dataset	Attack	Random items					Unpopular items				
		Origin	Attack	AT	RAT	TCD	Origin	Attack	AT	RAT	TCD
FilmTrust	Average	0.1617	0.1005	0.0961	0.1001	**0.1093****	0.0000	0.0016	0.0010	0.0008	**0.0009*****
	Random	0.1702	0.1213	0.1187	0.1257	0.1123	0.0000	0.0016	0.0020	0.0019	**0.0016*****
	AUSH	0.1629	0.1403	0.1345	0.1454	0.2204	0.0000	0.0323	0.0284	0.0330	**0.0024*****
	PGA	0.1574	0.1031	0.1008	0.1075	**0.1101****	0.0000	0.0012	0.0015	0.0016	**0.0009*****
	TNA	0.1628	0.5463	0.5346	0.5489	**0.4086*****	0.0000	0.4276	0.4251	0.4444	**0.0416*****
ML-100K	Average	0.0233	0.1579	0.1741	0.1525	**0.0340*****	0.0000	0.1694	0.1796	0.1421	**0.0009*****
	Random	0.0234	0.0956	0.0932	0.0889	**0.0353*****	0.0000	0.1105	0.1277	0.0965	**0.0010*****
	AUSH	0.0233	0.2819	0.2665	0.2773	**0.0355*****	0.0000	0.1478	0.1869	0.1714	**0.0009*****
	PGA	0.0237	0.1583	0.1654	0.1471	**0.0385*****	0.0000	0.3486	0.4656	0.4108	**0.0015*****
	TNA	0.0244	0.2355	0.2411	0.2369	**0.0334*****	0.0000	0.3011	0.3624	0.2986	**0.0015*****
ML-1M	Average	0.0000	0.2390	0.1547	0.2364	**0.0048*****	0.0000	0.8604	0.8593	0.8633	**0.0309*****
	Random	0.0000	0.0568	0.0455	0.0517	**0.0072*****	0.0000	0.6513	0.6450	0.6064	**0.0254*****
	AUSH	0.0000	0.2829	0.1395	0.2518	**0.0031*****	0.0000	0.9056	0.8845	0.8999	**0.0353*****
	PGA	0.0000	0.1027	0.0832	0.0968	**0.0191*****	0.0000	0.8577	0.8501	0.8498	**0.0236*****
	TNA	0.0000	0.2622	0.1663	0.2403	**0.0042*****	0.0000	0.8654	0.8525	0.8650	**0.0269*****

– These defense methods are positive in weakening the attack's damage concerning HR in most cases.

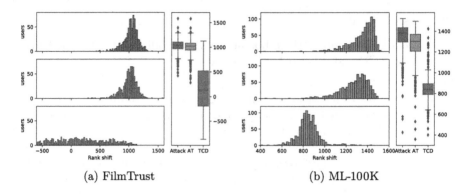

(a) FilmTrust   (b) ML-100K

Fig. 2. The distribution of rank shift. In FilmTrust and Ml-100k, top: TNA attack; middle: AT on TNA attack; bottom: TCD on TNA attack; boxplot: statistical distributions of rank shift. The closer the rank shift is to 0, the smaller the damage of the attack

- The proposed TCD achieves remarkable defense results, almost close to the unperturbed model performance. On average, we reduce the impact of attacks on random items by over 88% and unpopular items by over 82%, which effortlessly outperforms baselines.
- We notice that the performance of TCD against Average and Random on FilmTrust's unpopular items is slightly inferior when compared with the defense against other attacks while almost every performance of TCD on ML-100k and ML-1M is better than that of baselines. We suspect that Filmtrust is too small to represent real data, making it easier for adversarial training to discover and learn adversary data non-robust features while making it more formidable for TCD to find data's non-robust features.

Besides, Fig. 2 shows the Rank shift distribution of target items (unpopular items) under the TNA attack. The attack significantly promotes the target item's rank among all users. After using adversarial training, the rank change caused by the attack can be eased, but it is only slight. On the contrary, TCD impels the distribution of rank shift obviously tends to 0, which means that applying TCD can produce more stable recommendations in a disturbed environment. In conclusion, these results confirm the positive effect of TCD in boosting recommendation robustness against poisoning attacks.

Generalization. It is meaningless to improve the robustness at the cost of apparently sacrificing the generalization of standard recommendations. Table 4 records the HR of various defense methods in the holdout test set. We have the following finds:

- TCD surprisingly improves the generalization of the three datasets and the improvement is above 0.02 in terms of HR.

Table 4. The performance in test set (generalization). *, ** and *** indicate that the improvements over the unperturbed model are statistically significant for $p < 0.05, p < 0.01$ and $p < 0.001$, respectively.

Dataset	Attack	Random items					Unpopular items				
		Origin	Attack	AT	RAT	TCD	Origin	Attack	AT	RAT	TCD
Filmtrust	Average	0.8253	0.8196	0.8086	0.8187	**0.8640***	0.8273	0.8258	0.8096	0.8160	**0.8648***
	Random	0.8266	0.8245	0.8010	0.8179	**0.8635***	0.8275	0.8221	0.8085	0.8185	**0.8651***
	AUSH	0.8252	0.8240	0.8170	0.8193	**0.8660***	0.8256	0.8196	0.8053	0.8184	**0.8639***
	PGA	0.8257	0.8222	0.8046	0.8181	**0.8643***	0.8266	0.8212	0.8088	0.8205	**0.8636***
	TNA	0.8264	0.8079	0.7840	0.8021	**0.8639***	0.8273	0.8054	0.7824	0.8002	**0.8622***
ML-100K	Average	0.2006	0.1985	0.1907	0.1995	**0.2875***	0.2020	0.1998	0.1924	0.1970	**0.2836***
	Random	0.1988	0.2025	0.2003	0.2005	**0.2898***	0.1969	0.2058	0.1973	0.2003	**0.2804***
	AUSH	0.1998	0.1978	0.1894	0.1940	**0.2824***	0.2007	0.1971	0.1904	0.1951	**0.2797***
	PGA	0.2005	0.1960	0.1872	0.1920	**0.2851***	0.2022	0.1887	0.1848	0.1905	**0.2858***
	TNA	0.1995	0.1990	0.1933	0.1967	**0.2897***	0.2003	0.1970	0.1873	0.1911	**0.2785***
ML-1M	Average	0.0834	0.0748	0.0542	0.0718	**0.1097***	0.0843	0.0718	0.0519	0.0695	**0.1094***
	Random	0.0844	0.0877	0.0850	0.0860	**0.1097***	0.0833	0.0827	0.0816	0.0830	**0.1097***
	AUSH	0.0837	0.0733	0.0523	0.0689	**0.1105***	0.0832	0.0685	0.0448	0.0639	**0.1103***
	PGA	0.0837	0.0842	0.0805	0.0818	**0.1092***	0.0831	0.0774	0.0731	0.0767	**0.1105***
	TNA	0.0827	0.0748	0.0540	0.0713	**0.1101***	0.0846	0.0743	0.0539	0.0719	**0.1096***

These results confirm that TCD effectively guarantees the model's generalization while performing high-quality defense.

4.3   Parameter Analysis

Performance Under Different Attack Knowledge-Cost We conduct the robustness improvement test of TCD under different attack knowledge-cost, as illustrated in Fig. 3. On the one hand, the overall defense performance of TCD remains at a high level, although there will be individual cases on FilmTrust where it performs not that well. On the other hand, as the attack intensity increases, the robustness against attacks is still satisfactory. Especially in ML-100K and ML-1M, RI is almost clear 100%!

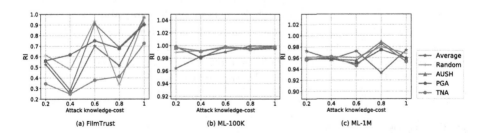

Fig. 3. Robustness improvement under different attack knowledge-cost

Performance Under Different Pseudo-label Ratios. The training time of TCD is directly proportional to the training set. Considering the size and sparsity of ML-1M, we decide to put only part of pseudo labels into the training set, and we denote the pseudo labels rate as the proportion of the pseudo labels which is put into the training set. We conduct the robustness test of TCD under different pseudo-label ratios, as illustrated in Fig. 4. With the injected pseudo-label ratio increases, the robustness of the model is improved accordingly, and 0 on the abscissa means attack without any defense. When the pseudo-label ratio is only 0.2, TCD can significantly improve the robustness of the model, which emphasizes its practicality in large datasets.

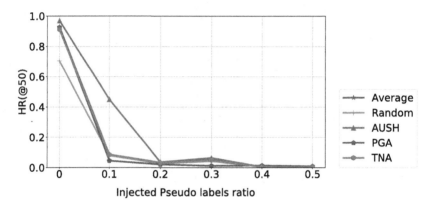

Fig. 4. The defense performance of the target items on ML-1M under different injected pseudo-label ratio

5   Conclusion and Outlook

In this paper, we proposed the TCD method to defend against attacks on recommender systems. It is noteworthy that TCD is the first algorithm to combine data-processing-based defense with model-based defense in recommender systems. Specifically, we sequentially use the high-confidence prediction ratings of any two models as auxiliary training data for the remaining models. Since TCD enhances data by adding pseudo labels instead of deleting abnormal data, it can avoid cleaning normal data and train a more accurate and robust model. Moreover, the cooperative training of the three models makes it beneficial for model generalization. Moreover, TCD is a general framework, so it can be combined with other defense methods. In the future, we plan to apply TCD in non-recommendation fields.

References

1. Athalye, A., Carlini, N., Wagner, D.: Obfuscated gradients give a false sense of security: circumventing defenses to adversarial examples. In: ICML, pp. 274–283. PMLR (2018)

2. Bobadilla, J., Ortega, F., Hernando, A., Gutiérrez, A.: Recommender systems survey. Knowl.-Based Syst. **46**, 109–132 (2013)
3. Burke, R., Mobasher, B., Williams, C., Bhaumik, R.: Classification features for attack detection in collaborative recommender systems. In: KDD, pp. 542–547 (2006)
4. Cao, J., Wu, Z., Mao, B., Zhang, Y.: Shilling attack detection utilizing semi-supervised learning method for collaborative recommender system. WWW **16**(5–6), 729–748 (2013). https://doi.org/10.1007/s11280-012-0164-6
5. Chevalier, J.A., Mayzlin, D.: The effect of word of mouth on sales: Online book reviews. J. Mark. Res. **43**(3), 345–354 (2006)
6. Christakopoulou, K., Banerjee, A.: Adversarial attacks on an oblivious recommender. In: RecSys, pp. 322–330 (2019)
7. Deldjoo, Y., Noia, T.D., Merra, F.A.: A survey on adversarial recommender systems: from attack/defense strategies to generative adversarial networks. CSUR **54**(2), 1–38 (2021)
8. Du, Y., Fang, M., Yi, J., Xu, C., Cheng, J., Tao, D.: Enhancing the robustness of neural collaborative filtering systems under malicious attacks. IEEE Trans. Multimedia **21**(3), 555–565 (2018)
9. Fan, W., et al.: Attacking black-box recommendations via copying cross-domain user profiles. In: ICDE, pp. 1583–1594. IEEE (2021)
10. Fang, M., Gong, N.Z., Liu, J.: Influence function based data poisoning attacks to top-n recommender systems. In: Proceedings of the Web Conference 2020, pp. 3019–3025 (2020)
11. Fang, M., Yang, G., Gong, N.Z., Liu, J.: Poisoning attacks to graph-based recommender systems. In: ACSAC, pp. 381–392 (2018)
12. Guo, H., Tang, R., Ye, Y., Li, Z., He, X.: DeepFM: a factorization-machine based neural network for CTR prediction. arXiv (2017)
13. He, X., He, Z., Du, X., Chua, T.S.: Adversarial personalized ranking for recommendation. In: SIGIR, pp. 355–364 (2018)
14. He, X., Liao, L., Zhang, H., Nie, L., Hu, X., Chua, T.S.: Neural collaborative filtering. In: WWW, pp. 173–182 (2017)
15. Himeur, Y., et al.: Blockchain-based recommender systems: applications, challenges and future opportunities. Comput. Sci. Rev. **43**, 100439 (2022)
16. Jin, B., et al.: Sampling-decomposable generative adversarial recommender. In: Advances in Neural Information Processing Systems, vol. 33, pp. 22629-22639 (2020)
17. Lam, S.K., Riedl, J.: Shilling recommender systems for fun and profit. In: WWW, pp. 393–402 (2004)
18. Li, B., Wang, Y., Singh, A., Vorobeychik, Y.: Data poisoning attacks on factorization-based collaborative filtering. NIPS **29**, 1885–1893 (2016)
19. Li, R., Wu, X., Wang, W.: Adversarial learning to compare: Self-attentive prospective customer recommendation in location based social networks. In: WSDM, pp. 349–357 (2020)
20. Lian, D., Wu, Y., Ge, Y., Xie, X., Chen, E.: Geography-aware sequential location recommendation. In: Proceedings of KDD 2020, pp. 2009–2019 (2020)
21. Lin, C., Chen, S., Li, H., Xiao, Y., Li, L., Yang, Q.: Attacking recommender systems with augmented user profiles. In: CIKM, pp. 855–864 (2020)
22. Liu, H., Hu, Z., Mian, A., Tian, H., Zhu, X.: A new user similarity model to improve the accuracy of collaborative filtering. KBS **56**, 156–166 (2014)

23. Machado, G.R., Silva, E., Goldschmidt, R.R.: Adversarial machine learning in image classification: a survey toward the defender's perspective. CSUR **1**, 1–38 (2021)
24. Madry, A., Makelov, A., Schmidt, L., Tsipras, D., Vladu, A.: Towards deep learning models resistant to adversarial attacks. arXiv (2017)
25. Mobasher, B., Burke, R., Bhaumik, R., Williams, C.: Toward trustworthy recommender systems: an analysis of attack models and algorithm robustness. TOIT **7**(4), 23-es (2007)
26. Oh, S., Kumar, S.: Robustness of deep recommendation systems to untargeted interaction perturbations. arXiv (2022)
27. Ovaisi, Z., Heinecke, S., Li, J., Zhang, Y., Zheleva, E., Xiong, C.: RGRecSys: a toolkit for robustness evaluation of recommender systems. arXiv (2022)
28. Park, D.H., Chang, Y.: Adversarial sampling and training for semi-supervised information retrieval. In: The World Wide Web Conference, pp. 1443–1453 (2019)
29. Si, M., Li, Q.: Shilling attacks against collaborative recommender systems: a review. Artif. Intell. Rev. **53**(1), 291–319 (2020). https://doi.org/10.1007/s10462-018-9655-x
30. Song, J., et al.: PoisonRec: an adaptive data poisoning framework for attacking black-box recommender systems. In: ICDE, pp. 157–168. IEEE (2020)
31. Tang, J., Wen, H., Wang, K.: Revisiting adversarially learned injection attacks against recommender systems. In: RecSys, pp. 318–327 (2020)
32. Tang, J., Du, X., He, X., Yuan, F., Tian, Q., Chua, T.S.: Adversarial training towards robust multimedia recommender system. IEEE Trans. Knowl. Data Eng. **32**(5), 855–867 (2019)
33. Wu, C., Lian, D., Ge, Y., Zhu, Z., Chen, E.: Triple adversarial learning for influence based poisoning attack in recommender systems. In: Proceedings of KDD 2021, pp. 1830–1840 (2021)
34. Wu, C., Lian, D., Ge, Y., Zhu, Z., Chen, E., Yuan, S.: Fight fire with fire: towards robust recommender systems via adversarial poisoning training. In: SIGIR, pp. 1074–1083 (2021)
35. Wu, Z., Wang, Y., Cao, J.: A survey on shilling attack models and detection techniques for recommender systems. Chin. Sci. Bull. **59**(7), 551–560 (2014)
36. Yang, G., Gong, N.Z., Cai, Y.: Fake co-visitation injection attacks to recommender systems. In: NDSS (2017)
37. Yuan, F., Yao, L., Benatallah, B.: Adversarial collaborative neural network for robust recommendation. In: SIGIR, pp. 1065–1068 (2019)
38. Zhang, F., Zhang, Z., Zhang, P., Wang, S.: UD-HMM: an unsupervised method for shilling attack detection based on hidden Markov model and hierarchical clustering. Knowl.-Based Syst. **148**, 146–166 (2018)
39. Zhang, J., et al.: Attacks which do not kill training make adversarial learning stronger. In: ICML, pp. 11278–11287. PMLR (2020)
40. Zhang, Z., Kulkarni, S.R.: Detection of shilling attacks in recommender systems via spectral clustering. In: FUSION, pp. 1–8. IEEE (2014)

Graph Collaborative Filtering
for Recommendation in Complex
and Quaternion Spaces

Longcan Wu[1], Daling Wang[1(✉)], Shi Feng[1], Xiangmin Zhou[2], Yifei Zhang[1],
and Ge Yu[1]

[1] Northeastern University, Shenyang, China
{wangdaling,fengshi,zhangyifei,yuge}@cse.neu.edu.cn
[2] RMIT University, Melbourne, Australia
xiangmin.zhou@rmit.edu.au

Abstract. With the development of graph neural network, researchers begin to use bipartite graph to model user-item interactions for recommendation. It is worth noting that most of graph recommendation models represent users and items in the real-valued space, which ignore the rich representational capacity of the non-real space. Besides, the simplicity and symmetry of the inner product make it ineffectively capture the intricate antisymmetric relations between users and items in interaction modeling. In this paper, we propose **G**raph **C**ollaborative **F**iltering for recommendation in **C**omplex and **Q**uaternion space (**GCFC** and **GCFQ** respectively). Specifically, we first use complex embeddings or quaternion embeddings to initialize users and items. Then, the Hermitian product (for GCFC) or Hamilton product (for GCFQ) and embedding propagation layers are used to further enrich the embeddings of users and items. As such, we can obtain both latent inter-dependencies and intra-dependencies between components of users and items. Finally, we aggregate the embeddings of different propagation layers and use the Hermitian or Hamilton product to obtain the intricate antisymmetric relations between users and items. We have carried out extensive experiments on three real-world datasets to verify the effectiveness of GCFC and GCFQ.

Keywords: Recommendation · Graph collaborative filtering · Non-real space

1 Introduction

Most of the current recommendation models are based on collaborative filtering (CF). Model-based CF methods are basically divided into two parts: embedding representation and interaction modeling. Model-based CF methods often use inner product to model interaction between users and items [11,15]. With the development of deep learning, nonlinear neural networks are introduced to

R. Chbeir et al. (Eds.): WISE 2022, LNCS 13724, pp. 579–594, 2022.
https://doi.org/10.1007/978-3-031-20891-1_41

capture the nonlinear relations between users and items [8,23]. Besides, the user-item interactions have rich high-order collaborative signals. If we can integrate the high-order collaborative signals into the embedding of users and items, we can get better embedding representation. Based on this, some studies [2,22] constructed a bipartite graph by user-item interactions, and used graph-related methods to capture the high-order collaborative signals between users and items in embedding representation process.

Despite the effectiveness of above models, we argue that these models have the following limitations. Firstly, the above models are based on real-valued operation and representations. Compared with representations in non-real space, such as complex space and quaternion space [14,20], real-valued representations have less representation capacity. The complex number $C = r + a\mathbf{i}$ and the quaternion $Q = r + a\mathbf{i} + b\mathbf{j} + c\mathbf{k}$ contain a real component and multiple imaginary components, so they have a richer representational capacity than the real number. Secondly, the above models tend to use nonlinear neural networks in the interaction modeling. Some studies have shown that the simple inner product can better model user preferences than nonlinear neural networks [5,16,17]. However, the complex relationships between users and items cannot be captured effectively using a simple inner product. Therefore, the interaction modeling based on inner product is still worth studying and exploring. Thirdly, in the general recommendation, users and items belong to different sets and there are obvious antisymmetric relations between them [28]. Neither inner product nor nonlinear neural network can model the antisymmetric relations between users and items in interaction modeling.

In order to solve above limitations, we propose **G**raph **C**ollaborative **F**iltering for recommendation in **C**omplex and **Q**uaternion space (**GCFC** and **GCFQ**). Specifically, we first use complex representations or quaternion representations to initialize users and items, which endow users and items representations with a richer representational capacity. Then, based on Hermitian product (for GCFC) or Hamilton product (for GCFQ) and embedding propagation layers, we can further enrich the embeddings of users and items. Benefiting from the Hermitian or Hamilton product, we can obtain both latent inter-dependencies and intra-dependencies between components of users and items. By embedding propagation layers, we can obtain high-order connectivities between users and items. Finally, in interaction modeling layer, we aggregate the embeddings of different propagation layers and use the Hermitian or Hamilton product to capture the intricate antisymmetric relations between users and items. We apply GCFC and GCFQ on three real datasets, and the experimental results clearly demonstrate the superiority and effectiveness of our proposed model.

In summary, we make the following contributions: (1) We propose to model recommendation in complex and quaternion spaces from the perspective of graph. This work expands the research of recommendation in non-real space. (2) We propose two novel graph neural network models for recommendation in complex and quaternion spaces, GCFC and GCFQ, respectively. Based on Hermitian or Hamilton product and embedding propagation layers, we enrich embeddings of users and items, and capture the intricate antisymmetric relations between users and items as well. (3) We conduct extensive experiments on three commonly used real-world datasets. Experiment results show that GCFC and GCFQ achieve better performance than state-of-art recommendation solutions.

2   Related Work

2.1   Model-Based Collaborative Filtering Methods

Matrix factorization (MF) [11,15] is the most representative model-based CF method, which maps the ID of users and items to real-valued embeddings, and then uses the inner product as the interaction function. In order to capture the nonlinear relationship between users and items, nonlinear neural network is introduced into the interaction function [8,23]. From the perspective of graph, the interactions between users and items in the recommendation can be seen as a bipartite graph. Early work used random walks on the bipartite graph to obtain high-order connectivities of users and items to improve the performance [3,24]. With the development of graph neural networks (GNN) [10], more and more researches begin to use GNN in the recommendation field [2,21,26]. NGCF [22] conducts multiple embedding propagation on user-item graph and concatenates multiple representations as the final embedding. Although the above work have achieved promising performance, they are all running in the real space, ignoring the rich representational capacity of complex space and quaternion space. Therefore, we propose to model recommender systems in complex and quaternion spaces from the perspective of graph.

2.2   Application of Complex and Quaternion Neural Networks

Due to its richer representational capacity, complex-valued deep neural network has been applied in many domains [1]. Yang et al. [25] proposed a complex transformer for sequence modeling. Quaternion, as an extension of complex number, can consider up to four-dimensional information. Therefore, quaternion neural networks have attracted the attention of researchers [14]. Nguyen et al. [13] employed graph neural network in quaternion space for node classification. Zhang et al. [27] used quaternion space to model entities and relations in knowledge graph (KG). Tay et al. [18] proposed quaternion transformer for many natural language processing tasks. As far as we know, only a few researches currently use complex number or quaternion to represent users and items in recommendations. Zhang et al. [28] directly employed complex embedding and quaternion embedding to model recommendation on the basis of MF. Fang et al. [6] modeled users and items in quaternion space and propagate them with quaternion feature transformation. Tran et al. [19] used attention and RNN to model user's long-term and short-term preferences for sequential recommendation in quaternion space. Inspired by the modeling of KG in quaternion space, Li et al. [12]

proposed to model unified user-item KG in quaternion space for KG-aware recommendation. The above researches show that modeling recommendation in complex and quaternion spaces can achieve better performance. Different from the above studies, we are the first to use GNN to model user-item interaction in complex and quaternion spaces.

3 Background of Complex and Quaternion Algebra

In this section, we give the necessary mathematical background about complex and quaternion algebra. For more details, please refer to [1,14].

Complex Algebra. A complex number C, belonging to complex space $\mathbb{C}$, contains a real part and an imaginary part: $C = r + a\mathbf{i}$, where r and a are real numbers and the imaginary unit $\mathbf{i}$ satisfies $\mathbf{i}^2 = -1$. We can expand the real and imaginary parts into real-valued vectors to obtain a complex vector. Similarly, we can obtain a complex matrix. The Hermitian product [20] of two complex number is defined as:

$$\langle C_1, C_2 \rangle = \overline{C_1} C_2 = (r_1 - a_1\mathbf{i})(r_2 + a_2\mathbf{i}) = (r_1 r_2 + a_1 a_2) + (r_1 a_2 - r_2 a_1)\mathbf{i} \quad (1)$$

where $\overline{C_1} = r_1 - a_1\mathbf{i}$ represents the complex conjugate of C_1. From above formula, we can find the Hermitian product of two complex number is asymmetrical, that is $\langle C_1, C_2 \rangle \neq \langle C_2, C_1 \rangle$. Many operations in real space can be applied to complex number. Suppose f is an operator in the real number space, we can use f in two complex numbers as follows: $f(C_1, C_2) = f(r_1, r_2) + f(a_1, a_2)\mathbf{i}$.

Quaternion Algebra. A quaternion Q is an extension of complex number, belonging to quaternion space $\mathbb{Q}$. Q contains one real part and three imaginary parts: $Q = r + a\mathbf{i} + b\mathbf{j} + c\mathbf{k}$, where $r, a, b,$ and c are all real numbers and the imaginary units $\mathbf{i}, \mathbf{j}$ and $\mathbf{k}$ satisfy: $\mathbf{i}^2 = \mathbf{j}^2 = \mathbf{k}^2 = \mathbf{ijk} = -1; \mathbf{ij} = \mathbf{k}, \mathbf{jk} = \mathbf{i}, \mathbf{ki} = \mathbf{j}, \mathbf{ji} = -\mathbf{k}, \mathbf{kj} = -\mathbf{i}, \mathbf{ik} = -\mathbf{j}$. We can expand the real and imaginary parts into real-valued vectors to obtain a quaternion vector. Similarly, we can obtain a quaternion matrix. The Hamilton product of two quaternion is also quaternion:

$$\begin{aligned}
Q_1 \otimes Q_2 &= (r_1 + a_1\mathbf{i} + b_1\mathbf{j} + c_1\mathbf{k}) \otimes (r_2 + a_2\mathbf{i} + b_2\mathbf{j} + c_2\mathbf{k}) \\
&= (r_1 r_2 - a_1 a_2 - b_1 b_2 - c_1 c_2) + (r_1 a_2 + a_1 r_2 + b_1 c_2 - c_1 b_2)\mathbf{i} \\
&\quad + (r_1 b_2 - a_1 c_2 + b_1 r_2 + c_1 a_2)\mathbf{j} + (r_1 c_2 + a_1 b_2 - b_1 a_2 + c_1 r_2)\mathbf{k} \quad (2)
\end{aligned}$$

From above formula, we can find that the Hamilton product is not commutative, that is $Q_1 \otimes Q_2 \neq Q_2 \otimes Q_1$. Many operations in real space can be applied to quaternion. Suppose f is an operator in the real number space, we can use f in two quaternions as follows: $f(Q_1, Q_2) = f(r_1, r_2) + f(a_1, a_2)\mathbf{i} + f(b_1, b_2)\mathbf{j} + f(c_1, c_2)\mathbf{k}$.

4   Methodology

In this section, we will introduce the proposed GCFC and GCFQ models in detail. Before that, we first give the definition of the problem. Then we give an explanation of the model overall framework. Next, we will detail each part of models.

4.1   Problem Formulation

Given user set $\mathcal{U} = \{u_1, u_2, ..., u_m\}$, item set $\mathcal{V} = \{v_1, v_2, v_3, , v_n\}$, and user-item interaction matrix $R \in \mathbb{R}^{m \times n}$, we can construct the user-item bipartite graph $G = (\{\mathcal{U}, \mathcal{V}\}, A)$. In user-item interaction matrix R, if there is implicit feedback between user u and item v, such as purchasing, clicking, watching, then $R_{uv} = 1$, otherwise $R_{uv} = 0$. $A \in \mathbb{R}^{(m+n) \times (m+n)}$ is the adjacency matrix of the user-item graph, which is constructed from user-item interaction matrix R:

$$A = \begin{bmatrix} 0^{(m \times m)} & R \\ R^T & 0^{(n \times n)} \end{bmatrix} \tag{3}$$

Our task is to learn the low-dimensional vector representations of users and items on the bipartite graph G, design the prediction functions to calculate the probabilities of each user engaging an item in complex and quaternion spaces, and make Top-K recommendations for a target user based on the probability scores.

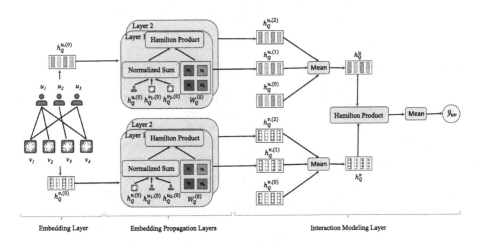

Fig. 1. Overall architecture of the proposed model GCFQ.

4.2   Framework Overview

Since GCFC and GCFQ have similar framework, we only give the overall framework of GCFQ as shown in Fig. 1. The GCFQ is mainly composed of three parts: (1) In the embedding layer, we randomly initialize quaternion vectors as the embeddings of users and items. (2) In the embedding propagation layers, by continuously gathering information from neighbors, the high-order connectivity between users and items are integrated into the embeddings of users and items. Thanks to the Hamilton product, we can get both latent inter-dependencies and intra-dependencies between components of users and items. (3) In the interaction modeling layer, we aggregate the embeddings of different propagation layers as the final embeddings of users and items, and then use Hamilton product to calculate the affinity score between users and items.

4.3   GCFC

Embedding Layer. In the embedding layer, we use complex vectors as embeddings of users and items. Note that we use real vectors to represent the real and imaginary part of complex vector, and then use real operations to simulate complex operations [25]. So, we have two initial complex embedding matrices $H_C^{U,(0)} \in \mathbb{C}^{m \times d}$ and $H_C^{V,(0)} \in \mathbb{C}^{n \times d}$, where m and n are the number of users and that of items respectively, d is the embedding size. Specifically, the initial complex embedding of user u is $h_C^{u,(0)} = h_{C,r}^{u,(0)} + h_{C,i}^{u,(0)} \mathbf{i}$, where $h_{C,r}^{u,(0)}, h_{C,i}^{u,(0)} \in \mathbb{R}^{d/2}, \mathbf{i}$ is an imaginary unit. Similarly, the initial complex embedding of item v is $h_C^{v,(0)}$. Thanks to complex embeddings, the user and item representations have two parts with a richer representational capacity.

Embedding Propagation Layer. The user-item interaction graph contains the high-order collaborative signals [4,7,22]. The collaborative signals reflect the similarity between users and items. In order to integrate the high-order collaborative signals into the embeddings of users and items, with the help of message-passing architecture in GNN [10], we introduce embedding propagation in the user-item graph. Specifically, the embedding propagation layer includes two steps: feature propagation and nonlinear transformation. In feature propagation process, when user u performs feature propagation in l_{th} layer, u aggregates the message from graph neighbors N_u and itself embeddings in layer $l - 1$. We take feature aggregation function in matrix form used in GCN [10]:

$$L = \widetilde{D}^{-\frac{1}{2}} \widetilde{A} \widetilde{D}^{-\frac{1}{2}} \tag{4}$$

$$H_C^{(l)} = \langle L, H_C^{(l-1)} \rangle = LH_{C,r}^{(l-1)} + LH_{C,i}^{(l-1)} \mathbf{i} \tag{5}$$

where A is the adjacency matrix of the user-item graph G, $\tilde{A} = A + I$ and I is the identity matrix; $\widetilde{D}$ is the degree matrix of $\tilde{A}$; $L \in \mathbb{R}^{(m+n) \times (m+n)}$ represents the normalized adjacency matrix; $\langle , \rangle$ denotes the Hermitian product; $H_C^{(l-1)} =$

$H_{C,r}^{(l-1)} + H_{C,i}^{(l-1)} \mathbf{i}$ is the embeddings of users and items after $l-1$ step of embedding propagation and $H_C^{(l-1)} \in \mathbb{C}^{(m+n) \times d_{l-1}}$, $H_C^{(0)} = \left[H_C^{U,(0)}; H_C^{V,(0)} \right]$. In nonlinear transformation process, after obtaining information from neighbors, we perform feature transformation in formula (6) and nonlinear activation in formula (7):

$$
\begin{aligned}
H_C^{(l)} &= \langle H_C^{(l)}, W_C^{(l)} \rangle \\
&= \left(H_{C,r}^{(l)} - H_{C,i}^{(l)} \mathbf{i} \right) \left(W_{C,r}^{(l)} + W_{C,i}^{(l)} \mathbf{i} \right) \\
&= \left(H_{C,r}^{(l)} W_{C,r}^{(l)} + H_{C,i}^{(l)} W_{C,i}^{(l)} \right) + \left(H_{C,r}^{(l)} W_{C,i}^{(l)} - H_{C,i}^{(l)} W_{C,r}^{(l)} \right) \mathbf{i}
\end{aligned}
\tag{6}
$$

$$
H_C^{(l)} = \sigma \left(H_C^{(l)} \right) = \sigma \left(H_{C,r}^{(l)} \right) + \sigma \left(H_{C,i}^{(l)} \right) \mathbf{i}
\tag{7}
$$

where $W_C^{(l)} = W_{C,r}^{(l)} + W_{C,i}^{(l)} \mathbf{i}$ is the trainable complex weight matrix and $W_C^{(l)} \in \mathbb{C}^{(d_{l-1}/2) \times d_l}$; $\sigma(x)$ is a nonlinear activation function. From above formula, we can find that $W_{C,r}^{(l)}$ and $W_{C,i}^{(l)}$ are shared by the real and an imaginary parts of $H_C^{(l)}$ in Hermitian product. Weight sharing enables the model to obtain both latent inter-dependencies and intra-dependencies between the components of user and item, leading to a higher expressive model.

Interaction Modeling Layer. After L layers, we will obtain $L+1$ representations at different layers for user u and item v. We take the mean of $L+1$ representations to get the final representation h_C^u and h_C^v for user and item. For example, the calculation formula for h_C^u is as follows:

$$
\begin{aligned}
h_C^u &= \text{mean} \left(h_C^{u,(0)}, h_C^{u,(1)}, \ldots h_C^{u,(L)} \right) \\
&= \text{mean} \left(h_{C,r}^{u,(0)}, \ldots, h_{C,r}^{u,(L)} \right) + \text{mean} \left(h_{C,i}^{u,(0)}, \ldots, h_{C,i}^{u,(L)} \right) \mathbf{i}
\end{aligned}
\tag{8}
$$

Then we use the Hermitian product to model the interaction between users and items:

$$
\begin{aligned}
r_C &= \langle h_C^u, h_C^v \rangle \\
&= \left(h_{C,r}^u - h_{C,i}^u \mathbf{i} \right) \left(h_{C,r}^v + h_{C,i}^v \mathbf{i} \right) \\
&= \left(h_{C,r}^u \cdot h_{C,r}^v + h_{C,i}^u \cdot h_{C,i}^v \right) + \left(h_{C,r}^u \cdot h_{C,i}^v - h_{C,i}^u \cdot h_{C,r}^v \right) \mathbf{i}
\end{aligned}
\tag{9}
$$

where "$\cdot$" denotes dot product. Through Hermitian product, we can further obtain inter-dependencies between components of user and item. In addition, Hermitian product is asymmetrical, which well captures the asymmetric relationship between user and item. Finally we take mean of all components of r_C as the prediction score:

$$
\hat{y}_{uv} = (r_{C,r} + r_{C,i}) / 2
\tag{10}
$$

4.4   GCFQ

Embedding Layer. In the embedding layer, we use quaternion vectors as the embeddings of users and items. Thus, we have two initial quaternion embedding matrices $H_Q^{U,(0)} \in \mathbb{Q}^{m \times d}$ and $H_Q^{V,(0)} \in \mathbb{Q}^{n \times d}$. Specifically, the initial quaternion embedding of user u is $h_Q^{u,(0)} = h_{Q,r}^{u,(0)} + h_{Q,i}^{u,(0)}\mathbf{i} + h_{Q,j}^{u,(0)}\mathbf{j} + h_{Q,k}^{u,(0)}\mathbf{k}$, where $h_{Q,r}^{u,(0)}, h_{Q,i}^{u,(0)}, h_{Q,j}^{u,(0)}, h_{Q,k}^{u,(0)} \in \mathbb{R}^{d/4}, \mathbf{i}, \mathbf{j}, \mathbf{k}$ are imaginary units. Similarly, the initial quaternion embedding of item v is $h_Q^{v,(0)}$. Using quaternion embeddings, the user and item representations have four parts with a richer representational capacity.

Embedding Propagation Layer. References to GCFC model above, we provide the matrix form of the embedding propagation layer in GCFQ. The embedding propagation consists of two steps: feature propagation and nonlinear transformation. In feature propagation process, we take feature aggregation function in matrix form used in GCN [10]:

$$H_Q^{(l)} = L \otimes H_Q^{(l-1)} = LH_{Q,r}^{(l-1)} + LH_{Q,i}^{(l-1)}\mathbf{i} + LH_{Q,j}^{(l-1)}\mathbf{j} + LH_{Q,k}^{(l-1)}\mathbf{k} \quad (11)$$

where L represents the normalized adjacency matrix; $\otimes$ denotes the Hamilton product; $H_Q^{(l-1)} = H_{Q,r}^{(l-1)} + H_{Q,i}^{(l-1)}\mathbf{i} + H_{Q,j}^{(l-1)}\mathbf{j} + H_{Q,k}^{(l-1)}\mathbf{k}$ is the embedding of users and items after $l-1$ step of embedding propagation and $H_Q^{(l-1)} \in \mathbb{Q}^{(m+n) \times d_{l-1}}, H_Q^{(0)} = \left[H_Q^{U,(0)}; H_Q^{V,(0)}\right]$. In nonlinear transformation process, after obtaining the information from neighbors, we perform feature transformation in formula (12) and nonlinear activation in formula (13):

$$\begin{aligned}
H_Q^{(l)} &= H_Q^{(l)} \otimes W_Q^{(l)} \\
&= \left(H_{Q,r}^{(l)}W_{Q,r}^{(l)} - H_{Q,i}^{(l)}W_{Q,i}^{(l)} - H_{Q,j}^{(l)}W_{Q,j}^{(l)} - H_{Q,k}^{(l)}W_{Q,k}^{(l)}\right) \\
&+ \left(H_{Q,r}^{(l)}W_{Q,i}^{(l)} + H_{Q,i}^{(l)}W_{Q,r}^{(l)} + H_{Q,j}^{(l)}W_{Q,k}^{(l)} - H_{Q,k}^{(l)}W_{Q,j}^{(l)}\right)\mathbf{i} \\
&+ \left(H_{Q,r}^{(l)}W_{Q,j}^{(l)} - H_{Q,i}^{(l)}W_{Q,k}^{(l)} + H_{Q,j}^{(l)}W_{Q,r}^{(l)} + H_{Q,k}^{(l)}W_{Q,i}^{(l)}\right)\mathbf{j} \\
&+ \left(H_{Q,r}^{(l)}W_{Q,k}^{(l)} + H_{Q,i}^{(l)}W_{Q,j}^{(l)} - H_{Q,j}^{(l)}W_{Q,i}^{(l)} + H_{Q,k}^{(l)}W_{Q,r}^{(l)}\right)\mathbf{k}
\end{aligned} \quad (12)$$

$$H_Q^{(l)} = \sigma\left(H_Q^{(l)}\right) = \sigma\left(H_{Q,r}^{(l)}\right) + \sigma\left(H_{Q,i}^{(l)}\right)\mathbf{i} + \sigma\left(H_{Q,j}^{(l)}\right)\mathbf{j} + \sigma\left(H_{Q,k}^{(l)}\right)\mathbf{k} \quad (13)$$

where $W_Q^{(l)} = W_{Q,r}^{(l)} + W_{Q,i}^{(l)}\mathbf{i} + W_{Q,j}^{(l)}\mathbf{j} + W_{Q,k}^{(l)}\mathbf{k}$ is the trainable quaternion weight matrix and $W_Q^{(l)} \in \mathbb{Q}^{(d_{l-1}/4) \times d_l}$; $\sigma(x)$ is a nonlinear activation function. From above formulas, we can find that $W_{Q,r}^{(l)}, W_{Q,i}^{(l)}, W_{Q,j}^{(l)}, W_{Q,k}^{(l)}$ are shared by the real and three imaginary parts of $H_Q^{(l)}$ in Hamilton product. Weight sharing enables the model to obtain both latent inter-dependencies and intra-dependencies between components of user and item, leading to a higher expressive model.

Interaction Modeling Layer. After L layers, we take the mean of $L + 1$ representations to get the final representation h_Q^u and h_Q^v for user and item. Then we use the Hamilton product to model the interaction between users and items:

$$
\begin{aligned}
r_Q &= h_Q^u \otimes h_Q^v \\
&= \left(h_{Q,r}^u \cdot h_{Q,r}^v - h_{Q,i}^u \cdot h_{Q,i}^v - h_{Q,j}^u \cdot h_{Q,j}^v - h_{Q,k}^u \cdot h_{Q,k}^v \right) \\
&\quad + \left(h_{Q,r}^u . h_{Q,i}^v + h_{Q,i}^u \cdot h_{Q,r}^v + h_{Q,j}^u \cdot h_{Q,k}^v - h_{Q,k}^u \cdot h_{Q,j}^v \right) \mathbf{i} \\
&\quad + \left(h_{Q,r}^u . h_{Q,j}^v - h_{Q,i}^u \cdot h_{Q,k}^v + h_{Q,j}^u \cdot h_{Q,r}^v + h_{Q,k}^u \cdot h_{Q,i}^v \right) \mathbf{j} \\
&\quad + \left(h_{Q,r}^u . h_{Q,k}^v + h_{Q,i}^u \cdot h_{Q,j}^v - h_{Q,j}^u \cdot h_{Q,i}^v + h_{Q,k}^u \cdot h_{Q,r}^v \right) \mathbf{k} \qquad (14)
\end{aligned}
$$

where "·" denotes dot product. Through Hamilton product, we can further obtain the inter-dependencies between the components of user and item. In addition, Hamilton product is asymmetrical, which well captures the asymmetric relationship between user and item. Finally we take mean of all components of r_Q as the prediction score:

$$
\hat{y}_{ui} = \left(r_{Q,r} + r_{Q,i} + r_{Q,j} + r_{Q,k} \right) / 4 \qquad (15)
$$

4.5 Model Training

This work mainly focuses on the top-K recommendation task, and we optimize the model using Bayesian Personalized Ranking (BPR) loss function [11]. Specifically, BPR loss function is formulated as:

$$
Loss = \sum_{(u,i,j) \in T} - \ln \sigma \left(\hat{y}_{ui} - \hat{y}_{uj} \right) + \lambda \| \Theta \|_2^2 \qquad (16)
$$

where $T = \{(u,i,j) | (u,i) \in \mathcal{R}_+, (u,j) \in \mathcal{R}_- \}$ is training dataset with observed interactions set $\mathcal{R}_+$ and the unobserved interactions set $\mathcal{R}_-$; $\sigma(x)$ is sigmoid function; $\hat{y}_{ui}$ and $\hat{y}_{uj}$ are the learned prediction score; λ is the L_2 regularization coefficient; Θ denotes trainable parameters, including $H_{C/Q}^{U,(0)}, H_{C/Q}^{V,(0)}, W_{C/Q}^{(k+1)}$.

Table 1. Datasets statistics.

Dataset	#User	#Item	#Interactions	Density
Amazon-Cloth	4,810	3,368	31,122	0.0019
Amazon-Electronic	9,279	6,065	158,979	0.0028
Book-Crossing	6,754	13,670	374,325	0.0040

5 Experiments

In this section, we conduct extensive experiments over three real-world datasets. We first give detailed experimental settings. Then we give model performance, hyper-parameter studies and model analysis.

5.1   Experimental Settings

Datasets. We conduct experiments on three widely used benchmark datasets [17], including Amazon-Cloth, Amazon-Electronic, and Book-Crossing. Information about these datasets is shown in Table 1. Amazon-Cloth and Amazon-Electronic are datasets that users rate items on Amazon, respectively corresponding to two categories: clothing and electronics. For each user, we take score greater than 3 as positive feedback. For Amazon-Cloth and Amazon-Electronic, we use 5-core setting and 10-core setting [22] to ensure the quality of the data. Book-Crossing is the dataset of user ratings about books. For each user, we take score greater than 0 as positive feedback and use 10-core setting to ensure the quality of data.

Baselines. We choose seven representative baselines to perform comparison experiments. These models not only include MF [11], NeuMF [8], GCMC [2], PinSage [26], NGCF [22] in real space, but also CCF and QCF [28] in non-real space. Since this work focuses on general recommendation, we do not use sequential recommendation model [19] and KG aware recommendation model [12] in non-real space as baselines.

Parameter Settings and Evaluation Setup. For all baselines, batch size is set to 1024, embedding dimensionality is set to 64, adam optimizer [9] is used to optimize all models, Xavier initializer is used to initialize the model parameters, and the loss function is BPR loss. For other hyperparameters, we refer to the original paper of baselines. Note that, the dimensionality of complex embeddings of users and items is 64 for GCFC, which means that each component of complex embedding is a vector with size $64/2 = 32$ as we mentioned in Sect. 4.3. Similarly, each component of quaternion embedding is a vector with size $64/4 = 16$ for GCFQ. The number of embedding propagation layer of GCFC and GCFQ is searched in $\{1, 2, 3, 4\}$. Finally, for all baselines, Bayesian HyperOpt [17] is used to perform hyper-parameter optimization on learning rate and coefficients of L_2 regularization term w.r.t. NDCG@20 on each dataset for 30 trails. In the experiment, we randomly select 80% of the historical interactions between users and items as the training set, 10% as the validation set, and 10% as the test set. The evaluation metrics use Recall@K and NDCG@K by the all-ranking protocol [7]. The above process is executed 10 times and the final average result is presented.

5.2   Overall Performance Comparison

The comparison results of all models are shown in Table 2 with the best result hightlighted in bold. We can draw the following conclusions:

- GCFQ performs best in all datasets, which shows the effectiveness of using graph neural network to model recommendation in quaternion space. Compared with GCFC, GCFQ uses quaternion embeddings, which have four components and enhance the representational capacity of model. Thus, GCFQ

Table 2. Overall performance of baselines on all datasets with the best result hightlighted in bold.

	Amazon-Cloth				Amazon-Electronic				Book-Crossing			
	Recall@K		NDCG@K		Recall@K		NDCG@K		Recall@K		NDCG@K	
	K = 20	K = 30	K = 20	K = 30	K = 20	K = 30	K = 20	K = 30	K = 20	K = 30	K=20	K = 30
MF	0.0760	0.0903	0.0327	0.0358	0.0301	0.0387	0.0125	0.0144	0.0020	0.0024	0.0009	0.0010
NeuMF	0.0384	0.0466	0.0153	0.0171	0.0339	0.0444	0.0142	0.0165	0.0017	0.0021	0.0008	0.0009
GCMC	0.0686	0.0883	0.0321	0.0363	0.0423	0.0559	0.0184	0.0214	0.0027	0.0033	0.0014	0.0015
PinSage	0.0709	0.0878	0.0356	0.0393	0.0458	0.0587	0.0197	0.0225	0.0025	0.0030	0.0014	0.0015
NGCF	0.0878	0.1021	0.0363	0.0390	0.0436	0.0555	0.0186	0.0212	0.0024	0.0030	0.0013	0.0014
CCF	0.0702	0.0896	0.0298	0.0339	0.0309	0.0402	0.0143	0.0164	0.0026	0.0031	0.0011	0.0013
QCF	0.0874	0.1058	0.0397	0.0436	0.0455	0.0578	0.0197	0.0225	0.0028	0.0034	0.0014	0.0015
GCFC	0.0815	0.0962	0.0393	0.0425	0.0450	0.0581	0.0193	0.0222	0.0033	0.0039	0.0016	0.0018
GCFQ	**0.0881**	**0.1074**	**0.0405**	**0.0437**	**0.0471**	**0.0592**	**0.0205**	**0.0233**	**0.0034**	**0.0041**	**0.0018**	**0.0020**

performs better than GCFC. The performance of GCFC in some cases is better than NGCF, which shows the potential of modeling recommendation in complex space.

- Compared with the models MF and NeuMF in real space, the models (CCF, QCF, GCFC, GCFQ) in the non-real space can achieve better performance. This is because the non-real embeddings have the rich representational capacity and Hamilton product and Hermitian product can capture the intricate antisymmetric relation between users and items.
- Compared with MF, CCF and QCF, the models that use bipartite graphs to model the interactions between users and items (NGCF, GCFC, GCFQ, etc.) can achieve better performance. The user-item interaction graph contains the high-order collaborative signals, which reflect the similarity between users and items. By performing message-passing on the bipartite graph, the high-order collaborative signals can be integrated into the embedings of users and items.

5.3   Hyper-parameter Studies

Number of Embedding Propagation Layer. In this section, we explore the influence of embedding propagation layer numbers on GCFC and GCFQ. We search layer numbers in $\{1, 2, 3, 4\}$ for GCFC and GCFQ on three datasests. The experimental results are shown in Fig. 2, and we can draw the following conclusions: (1) For the dataset Amazon-Cloth, the best number of layer is 1. This is because the Amazon-Cloth dataset is small, and one embedding propagation layer enables the node to obtain enough information from one-hop neighbors. (2) For the dataset Amazon-Electronic, the best number of layers is 3 for GCFC and 1 for GCFQ. Amazon-Electronic has more interaction information than Amazon-Cloth. Therefore, GCFC needs 3 layers to enhance the representation ability of model. Compared with GCFC, GCFQ has stronger modeling ability, so it only needs 1 layer for Amazon-Electronic. (3) The Book-Crossing is the largest in

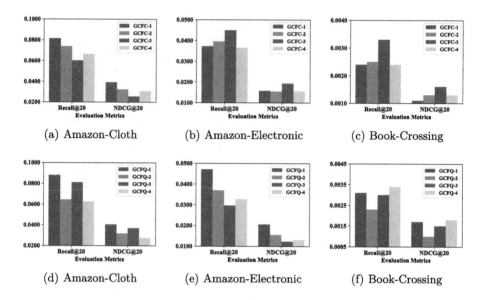

Fig. 2. Effect of number of embedding propagation layer on GCFC and GCFQ.

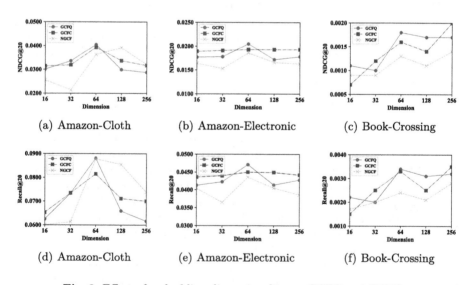

Fig. 3. Effect of embedding dimensionality on GCFC and GCFQ.

Table 3. Effect of Hermitian and Hamilton products.

	Amazon-Cloth		Amazon-Electronic		Book-Crossing	
	Recall@20	NDCG@20	Recall@20	NDCG@20	Recall@20	NDCG@20
GCFC	**0.0815**	**0.0393**	**0.0450**	**0.0193**	**0.0033**	**0.0016**
GCFC-in	0.0807	0.0390	0.0435	0.0190	0.0029	0.0015
GCFC-sys	0.0802	0.0392	0.0439	0.0192	0.0030	0.0015
GCFQ	**0.0881**	**0.0405**	**0.0471**	**0.0205**	**0.0034**	**0.0018**
GCFQ-in	0.0820	0.0401	0.0413	0.0174	0.0029	0.0015
GCFQ-sys	0.0808	0.0346	0.0433	0.0186	0.0028	0.0014

the three datasets and has more abundant interaction information. Therefore, GCFC and GCFQ need 3 and 4 embedding propagation layers respectively.

Effect of Embedding Dimensionality. In order to study the impact of embedding dimensionality on models, we search the embedding dimensionality in $\{16, 32, 64, 128, 256\}$ for GCFC and GCFQ on three datasests. The experimental results are shown in Fig. 3. From the figure, we can find that for Amazon-Cloth and Amazon-Electronic datasets, the best embedding dimensionality is 64. Higher dimensionality will lead to overfitting. For Book-Crossing, performance is improved as the dimensionality increase. This is because Book-Crossing has more interaction information than Amazon-Cloth and Amazon-Electronic, and requires a higher embedding dimensionality to represent users and items.

5.4   Model Analysis

Compared with the inner product, Hermitian and Hamilton products enable the components of embeddings of user and item to interact with each other, which endows them with better modeling capability while maintaining the simplicity. In addition, the Hermitian and Hamilton products are inherently asymmetrical, which enables them to capture the asymmetry in the recommendation. In order to verify the effectiveness of Hermitian and Hamilton products, we propose two variants of model: Model-in and Model-sys. Model-in replaces Hermitian or Hamilton product in interaction modeling layer with inner product. Model-sys redefines the prediction function in models. Specifically, when calculating the products between user and item in formulas 9 and 14, we redefine the products in GCFC and GCFQ as follows:

$$r_C = (\langle h_C^u, h_C^v \rangle + \langle h_C^v, h_C^u \rangle)/2 \tag{17}$$

$$r_Q = (h_Q^u \otimes h_Q^v + h_Q^v \otimes h_Q^u)/2 \tag{18}$$

Through above formula, we can eliminate the influence of asymmetry property of Hermitian product and Hamilton product on the model.

We conduct experiments on three datasets and the experimental results are shown in Table 3, from which we can draw the following conclusions: (1)

Eliminating the Hermitian and Hamilton products in interaction modeling layer reduces the performance of model. This is because both latent inter-dependencies and intra-dependencies between the components of embeddings of user and item can be obtained through Hermitian and Hamilton products. The inner product only models the interaction of the corresponding components between user and item. Therefore, compared with Hermitian or Hamilton product, the inner product has a weaker modeling ability. (2) Eliminating the asymmetry of Hermitian and Hamilton products reduces the performance of model. In the recommendation system, users and items belong to different sets, and there is obvious asymmetry between them. If this asymmetry is not considered, the performance of the model will decrease. From Table 1, we can see that the asymmetry of the dataset Book-Crossing is very strong, and there are more than twice as many items as users. So, compared with the other two datasets, the performance of GCFC-sys and GCFQ-sys drop more in Book-Crossing.

6   Conclusion

In this paper, we apply graph neural network to recommendation in complex and quaternion spaces, and propose two specific models GCFC and GCFQ respectively. These two models respectively employ complex and quaternion embeddings to represent users and items. Then based on Hermitian product (for GCFC) or Hamilton product (for GCFQ) and embedding propagation layers, we can obtain the intricate relations between users and items. Finally, in interaction modeling layer, we aggregate the embedding representations of different propagation layers and use Hermitian or Hamilton product to obtain the final prediction score between users and items. Extensive experimental results on three widely used datasets show the effectiveness of GCFC and GCFQ.

Acknowledgement. The work was supported by National Natural Science Foundation of China (62172086, 61872074, 62106039)

References

1. Bassey, J., Qian, L., Li, X.: A survey of complex-valued neural networks. arXiv preprint arXiv:2101.12249 (2021)
2. van den Berg, R., Kipf, T.N., Welling, M.: Graph convolutional matrix completion. arXiv preprint arXiv:1706.02263 (2017)
3. Chen, C., Wang, C., Tsai, M., Yang, Y.: Collaborative similarity embedding for recommender systems. In: Proceedings of the 28th International Conference on World Wide Web, pp. 2637–2643 (2019)
4. Chen, L., Wu, L., Hong, R., Zhang, K., Wang, M.: Revisiting graph based collaborative filtering: a linear residual graph convolutional network approach. In: Proceedings of the 24th International Joint Conference on Artificial Intelligence, pp. 27–34 (2020)
5. Dacrema, M.F., Cremonesi, P., Jannach, D.: Are we really making much progress? A worrying analysis of recent neural recommendation approaches. In: Proceedings of the 13th ACM Conference on Recommender Systems, pp. 101–109 (2019)

6. Fang, Y., et al.: Quaternion-based graph convolution network for recommendation. arXiv preprint arXiv:2111.10536 (2021)
7. He, X., Deng, K., Wang, X., Li, Y., Zhang, Y., Wang, M.: Lightgcn: simplifying and powering graph convolution network for recommendation. In: Proceedings of the 43rd International ACM SIGIR conference on Research and Development in Information Retrieval, pp. 639–648 (2020)
8. He, X., Liao, L., Zhang, H., Nie, L., Hu, X., Chua, T.: Neural collaborative filtering. In: Proceedings of the 26th International Conference on World Wide Web, pp. 173–182 (2017)
9. Kingma, D.P., Ba, J.: Adam: a method for stochastic optimization. In: Proceedings of the 3rd International Conference on Learning Representations (2015)
10. Kipf, T.N., Welling, M.: Semi-supervised classification with graph convolutional networks. In: Proceedings of the 5th International Conference on Learning Representations (2017)
11. Koren, Y., Bell, R.M., Volinsky, C.: Matrix factorization techniques for recommender systems. Computer **42**(8), 30–37 (2009)
12. Li, Z., Xu, Q., Jiang, Y., Cao, X., Huang, Q.: Quaternion-based knowledge graph network for recommendation. In: Proceedings of the 28th ACM International Conference on Multimedia, pp. 880–888 (2020)
13. Nguyen, D.Q., Nguyen, T.D., Phung, D.Q.: Quaternion graph neural networks. In: Asian Conference on Machine Learning, ACML 2021, 17–19 November 2021, Virtual Event. Proceedings of Machine Learning Research, vol. 157, pp. 236–251 (2021)
14. Parcollet, T., Morchid, M., Linarès, G.: A survey of quaternion neural networks. Artif. Intell. Rev. **53**(4), 2957–2982 (2020). https://doi.org/10.1007/s10462-019-09752-1
15. Rendle, S., Freudenthaler, C., Gantner, Z., Schmidt-Thieme, L.: BPR: bayesian personalized ranking from implicit feedback. In: Proceedings of the 25th Conference on Uncertainty in Artificial Intelligence, pp. 452–461 (2009)
16. Rendle, S., Krichene, W., Zhang, L., Anderson, J.R.: Neural collaborative filtering vs. matrix factorization revisited. In: Proceedings of the 14th ACM Conference on Recommender Systems, pp. 240–248 (2020)
17. Sun, Z., et al.: Are we evaluating rigorously? benchmarking recommendation for reproducible evaluation and fair comparison. In: Proceedings of the 14th ACM Conference on Recommender Systems, pp. 23–32 (2020)
18. Tay, Y., et al.: Lightweight and efficient neural natural language processing with quaternion networks. In: Proceedings of the 57th Conference of the Association for Computational Linguistics, pp. 1494–1503 (2019)
19. Tran, T., You, D., Lee, K.: Quaternion-based self-attentive long short-term user preference encoding for recommendation. In: Proceedings of the 29th ACM International Conference on Information and Knowledge Management, pp. 1455–1464 (2020)
20. Trouillon, T., Welbl, J., Riedel, S., Gaussier, É., Bouchard, G.: Complex embeddings for simple link prediction. In: Proceedings of the 33nd International Conference on Machine Learning, pp. 2071–2080 (2016)
21. Wang, S., et al.: Graph learning approaches to recommender systems: a review. arXiv preprint arXiv:2004.11718 (2020)
22. Wang, X., He, X., Wang, M., Feng, F., Chua, T.: Neural graph collaborative filtering. In: Proceedings of the 42nd International ACM Conference on Research and Development in Information Retrieval, pp. 165–174 (2019)

23. Xue, H., Dai, X., Zhang, J., Huang, S., Chen, J.: Deep matrix factorization models for recommender systems. In: Proceedings of the 26th International Joint Conference on Artificial Intelligence, pp. 3203–3209 (2017)

24. Yang, J., Chen, C., Wang, C., Tsai, M.: Hop-rec: high-order proximity for implicit recommendation. In: Proceedings of the 12th ACM Conference on Recommender Systems, pp. 140–144 (2018)

25. Yang, M., Ma, M.Q., Li, D., Tsai, Y.H., Salakhutdinov, R.: Complex transformer: a framework for modeling complex-valued sequence. In: Proceedings of the 2020 IEEE International Conference on Acoustics, Speech and Signal Processing, pp. 4232–4236 (2020)

26. Ying, R., He, R., Chen, K., Eksombatchai, P., Hamilton, W.L., Leskovec, J.: Graph convolutional neural networks for web-scale recommender systems. In: Proceedings of the 24th ACM International Conference on Knowledge Discovery & Data Mining, pp. 974–983 (2018)

27. Zhang, S., Tay, Y., Yao, L., Liu, Q.: Quaternion knowledge graph embeddings. In: Advances in Neural Information Processing Systems, pp. 2731–2741 (2019)

28. Zhang, S., Yao, L., Tran, L.V., Zhang, A., Tay, Y.: Quaternion collaborative filtering for recommendation. In: Proceedings of the 28th International Joint Conference on Artificial Intelligence, pp. 4313–4319 (2019)

Neural Networks

Event Source Page Discovery via Policy-Based RL with Multi-task Neural Sequence Model

Chia-Hui Chang[(✉)] [iD], Yu-Ching Liao, and Ting Yeh

National Central University, Taoyuan, Taiwan
chia@csie.ncu.edu.tw

Abstract. The problem of finding event announcement pages for any given website is called event source page discovery. In this paper, we show a policy-based deep reinforcement learning (RL) model for the event source page discovery agent. We use two stages to train our agent, pre-training and fine-tuning. In the pre-training phase, the model is trained with limited labeled data, where each episode has a fixed number of steps. In the fine-tuning phase, the agent is trained using unlabeled data and a reward system based on an event source page classifier. The agent learns whether to continue exploring or stop exploring through an adaptive threshold. The proposed agent achieves 74% precision with a 1.28 unit cost (the average number of clicks for each event source page) on the real word data set.

Keywords: Web mining · Event source page discovery · Reinforcement learning · Multi-task neural model

1 Introduction

For most people, looking for local events is a common need when traveling or moving to a new city. However, finding local events is not always easy. While a simple Google search could provide many search results, often they are mixed with non-event information, making it difficult to compare the results by locations and times. Therefore, Google research teams [1,10] propose the problem of mining events from the Web for event database construction. However, crawling the entire Web to filter event pages are too expensive. As most event organizers such as governments, schools, and businesses update event information on their websites, therefore, we propose the idea of monitoring the websites of potential event organizers from their latest news posts for event collection.

In this paper, we define the task of event source page discovery to find event announcement pages from the website of potential event organizers. As shown in Fig. 1, we use the URL links in Facebook event posts to locate event organizers'

This project is supported by Ministry of Science and Technology, Taiwan under grant MOST-109-2221-E-008-060-MY3.

R. Chbeir et al. (Eds.): WISE 2022, LNCS 13724, pp. 597–606, 2022.
https://doi.org/10.1007/978-3-031-20891-1_42

websites and use their homepages as the starting pages for the event source page
discovery task. With such event source pages, we can design automatic webpage
scraping modules to fetch these event source pages and apply unsupervised web
data extraction to build data APIs.

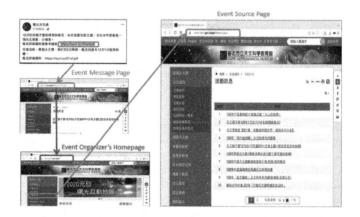

Fig. 1. An event post from Facebook Event with link to its event message page (green
link). We can derive its homepage URL from their domain names (red link) and use
them as the starting page to find event source or data-rich page. (Color figure online)

We proposed a two-stage reinforcement learning (RL) framework to train
our agent. In the first phase, the agent is trained by interacting with the reward
system based on limited labeled data using a fixed number of trials. In the second
phase, the model is fine-tuned using unlabeled data with rewards given by an
event source page classifier. The number of trials for each episode is controlled by
an adaptive threshold, so the agent knows whether to continue or stop exploring.
The proposed agent achieves 74% Return-On-Investment (i.e. precision) with 1.3
unit cost (the number of clicks for each event source page) on the real world data
set.

2   Related Work

Many previous works have applied reinforcement learning to focused crawling
[2,5,6,8,9] with different settings. For example, Rennie and McCallum [9] first
use reinforcement learning in Web crawling. Since the state space is huge and
difficult to generalize, they disregard states and employ a pre-trained naive Bayes
classifier to predict the value of each action to be taken based on the neighborhood text for the hyperlink.

Grigoriadis and Paliouras [2], on the other hand, consider each page as a state
and model a page as a feature vector of 500 binary values to reduce the size of
the state-action space. They adopt temporal difference learning with eligibility

traces TD(λ) to estimate the state-value of a Web page on a path to a relevant page. To avoid lookahead pre-fetching, they do not estimate scores for outlinks but inherit the values from their parents.

Han, et al. [3] also model each page as a state but use contextual and the link structure (e.g. relevance of target topic, average relevance of all parents) to represent Web pages as well as hyperlinks. They investigate the trade-off between synchronous and asynchronous methods, and propose an improved asynchronous method to update action-values at different time steps.

Anthelion [7] is a focused crawler specifically designed for collecting data-rich pages, which is closest to our goal. It first uses bandit-based approaches to choose a host with the highest score and decide which links to follow using online classification based on the context of the page and the feedback from the extraction of metadata from previously seen pages. For the evaluation of links in a host, they adopt a Hash-Trick to map all tokens of URLs and anchor texts into a fixed feature space of 5K to 20K, and use Naive Bayes and Hoeffding Trees for classification.

3   Problem Definition

An important component in reinforcement learning is the feedback mechanism. Through a reward (or cost) function that ranks an chosen action, the agent can learn to select the right actions. The agent's interaction with the environment results in a sequence of states, actions and rewards. The concatenation of the state-action-reward triplet ($<$s, a, r$>$) at each time point is called an *episode*, denoted by $\tau = (<s_1, a_1, r_1>, <s_2, a_2, r_2>, ..., <s_T, a_T, r_T>)$. The goal of RL is to learn a policy $\pi_\theta : S \rightarrow A$ to maximize the expected return $\bar{R}_\theta$ over all episodes.

$$\bar{R}_\theta = E_{\tau \sim p_\theta(\tau)}[\sum_{t=1}^{T} r_t] \tag{1}$$

For web crawlers, the current visited link a_t contains a set of out-going anchors, denoted by $L(a_t)$, to be explored. Let $Action(s_{t-1})$ be the link set that has not been explored at the previous step ($Action(s_0) = \emptyset$). Thus, the set of candidate actions that the crawler agent can choose at time t is the union of $L(a_t)$ and $Action(s_t)$, i.e., $Action(s_t) = Action(s_{t-1}) \cup L(a_t)$. If the crawler agent chooses a link a_{t+1} from $Action(s_t)$ for time step $t + 1$, then the Action set is updated by $Action(s_t) = Action(s_t) - \{a_{t+1}\}$ and the agent will move to a new page denoted by the link a_{t+1}. Thus, the number of actions in each state is changing all the time.

4   Methodology

We choose policy-based RL to implement our event source page discovery agent. Unlike other focused crawling tasks, the goal of the event source page discovery agent is to find event source pages within a given website. Therefore, the agent also needs to decide when to stop an episode to save costs.

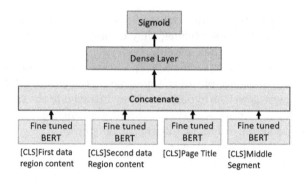

Fig. 2. The event source page scoring model

4.1 Reward Function

Since the cost to label all pages to differentiate whether a page contains structured data set is too high, and a pre-trained event source page classifier may not always give the correct guidance, we propose a two-step architecture to train our agent, including the pre-training phase and the fine-tuning phase. In the pre-training stage, the agent is trained on a small set of labeled websites, meaning that we need to manually label the event source pages within the domain specified in the input URL set $Seed_1$.

In the fine-tune stage, we designed a neural network model ϕ with four input segments. Although deep learning can automatically extract the most important features for classification tasks, when the training data is insufficient, proper input data filtering can help the model focus on the important content. As shown in Fig. 2, we used the first and second largest data segments from the output of MDR [4] as well as the page title and the middle region containing half the text nodes from the first percentile to the third percentile as input. We use BERT to encode each text segment, then concatenate them for the fully connected layer to learn the page representation. Finally, a sigmoid function is used to predict the probability that the input page is an event source page.

Pre-training Phase with Labeled Data. Since the reward function ϕ is trained from a small set of training data and may not be perfect, we employ the labeled training data in the pre-training phase to speed up the training process.

$$r(a) = \begin{cases} 1 & \text{if } a.p \text{ is an event source page} \\ max(-0.5, -0.1 * (\lfloor \frac{epoch}{2} \rfloor + 1)) & \text{otherwise} \end{cases} \quad (2)$$

Fine-Tuning Training Phase Without Labeled Data. In the fine-tuning stage, the agent is trained on a new URL set $Seed_2$ without labeled pages. Therefore, the reward of an action a is given by the event source page classifier ϕ.

$$r(p) = \phi(MDR(p).L1, MDR(p).L2, Title(p), Middle(p)) \quad (3)$$

where p denotes the downloaded page of the action a; $MDR(p).L1$ and $MDR(p).L2$ denote the first and second largest segment extracted by MDR.

4.2   Action Evaluation Model Based on Multi-task Learning

Let $L(s) = \{l_1, l_2, ..., l_K\}$ denote the ordered list of anchor links in the current web page s, where each anchor node $l_k = \{AT_k, TP_k\}$ consists of anchor text AT_k and tag path TP_k. The main task of the model π_θ is to output the probability of each anchor node to lead us to an event source page based on the concatenation of the vectors from Tag-Net and Anchor-Net. We propose a neural sequence model $\pi_\theta(s) \rightarrow [0,1]^K$ to evaluate the score of each anchor link in the current page and use $\pi_\theta(s,l) \rightarrow [0,1]$ to denote the prediction of the model for a link l in the current page s. As we can see on the left hand side of Fig. 3.

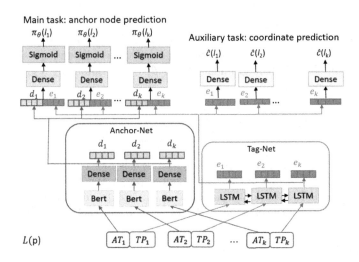

Fig. 3. Action evaluation model

To better represent the tag embedding, we also design an auxiliary task to predict the node coordinates (x_k, y_k) and size (w_k, h_k) of the node in the browser, that is, $pos(l_k) = (x_k, y_k, w_k, h_k)$. The auxiliary task not only considers the position of a single node, but also predict the position of the previous node and following nodes.

$$c(l_k) = \{pos(l_{k-1}), pos(l_k), pos(l_{k+1})\} \tag{4}$$

Objective Function. The objective function includes two parts. For auxiliary tasks, we use the mean square error as shown in Eq. (5), where T_n is the horizon of episode n and K_t is the number of anchor nodes in the page after taking action a_t (ignoring episode index n for brevity).

$$L_c = \frac{1}{N} \sum_{i=1}^{N} \sum_{t=1}^{T_n} \sum_{k=1}^{K_t} mse(c(l_k), \hat{c}(l_k)) \tag{5}$$

The goal of reinforcement learning is to maximize the expected accumulated reward $R(\tau)$, so the loss function is the negative average reward as shown in Eq. (6).

$$L_a = -\frac{1}{N} \sum_{n=1}^{N} R(\tau^n) * P(\tau^n|\theta) \tag{6}$$

where $P(\tau|\theta)$ denotes the probability of seeing episode τ. Combined with auxiliary tasks, the overall objective function is L as shown below.

$$L = \alpha * L_c + (1 - \alpha) * L_a, \ 0 < \alpha \le 1 \tag{7}$$

Implementation. Suppose N episodes $\{\tau^1, \tau^2, \ldots, \tau^N\}$ are collected with the same policy π_θ in each batch. Since the reward $R(\tau)$ is independent of the parameter θ, we can compute the gradient of $P(\tau|\theta)$ by decomposing $\nabla_\theta P(\tau|\theta)$ based on Markov property into

$$\nabla_\theta P(\tau^n|\theta) = \sum_{t=1}^{T_n} log \left[\frac{\exp^{\pi_\theta(f(a_t), a_t)}}{\sum_{a \in Action(s_t)} \exp^{\pi_\theta(f(a), a)}} \right] \tag{8}$$

where $f(a)$ returns the parent page where link a is first extracted.

Since the average number of event source pages and the average depth are usually very small, we adopt synchronous update to re-estimate each visited pages $\pi_\theta(s'_t)$, $t' < t$ in the episode to obtain $\pi_\theta(s'_t, a)$ for each action in $Action(s_t)$.

4.3   Fixed or Variable Horizon

In the pre-training phase, we set the maximum step T to 3 since there are an average of 3.47 event source pages per website and the average depth is 1.36 for domains in $Seed_p$. In the fine-tuning stage or testing phase, the number of steps is controlled by a threshold defined by a weighted average of the action scores using the current action evaluation model π_θ:

$$\eta_\theta = \frac{1}{|Seed_p|} \sum_{n \in Seed_p} \frac{1}{R(\tau_n)} \sum_{t=1}^{T_n} \pi_\theta(f(a_t), a_t) * r(a_t) \tag{9}$$

We use the episodes $\mathcal{T} = \{\tau_n | n \in Seed_p\}$ collected in the last epoch of the pre-training process to calculate the threshold η_θ of the current model π_θ. This is because the episodes collected in the last epoch of the pre-training process usually represent potential links to the event source page. By using $r(a_t)$ as weight, we only average the $\pi(f(a_t), a_t)$ value of event source pages, ignoring values of non-event source pages.

5   Experiment

For the following experiments, we collect potential event organizers from Facebook event posts and use the homepages of the mentioned URLs as the starting page for event source page discovery. We divided the labeled seed URLs into 40, 20, and 100 URLs for pre-training, validation, and testing (called TESW), respectively. In addition to the above labeled data, we also used an additional 300 URLs for fine-tuning (Phase II training).

The three evaluation metrics we use are page-wise precision, site-level recall and unit cost per event source page as shown in Eqs. (10), (11) and (12), respectively.

$$Precision = \frac{\# \ of \ event \ source \ pages \ found}{\# \ of \ total \ clicks} \qquad (10)$$

$$Recall = \frac{\# \ of \ episodes \ reaching \ event \ source \ pages}{\# \ of \ episodes} \qquad (11)$$

$$UnitCost = \frac{\Sigma_\tau Cost(\tau)}{\# \ of \ event \ source \ pages} \qquad (12)$$

5.1   Evaluation of the Pre-trained Model

Figure 4 shows the precision and unit cost of the pre-trained model on TESW dataset. Since the evaluation on test data adopts a variable horizon, we also calculated performance for the first, second, and third actions performed by the crawler agent. In the labeled test dataset, the model precision decreases from 0.75 to 0.57 and the unit cost increases from 3.85 to 1.75 using fixed step from 1 to 3, while the recall increases from 0.64 to 0.74. When using the variable Horizon, the performance achieves 0.72 precision and 0.64 recall with 1.40 unit cost, suggesting that the variable horizon mechanism is effective in determining whether to continue crawling in each website.

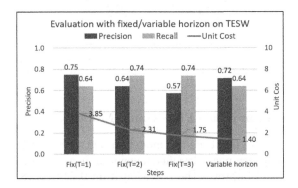

Fig. 4. Evaluation of the pre-trained model using fixed/variable horizon

Figure 5 shows the results of the pre-trained models with or without multitasking design. As can be seen from the figure, the precision and recall via the pure model has lower (0.63) precision and higher (0.73) recall, showing a comparative performance. However, the unit cost of the model trained without multitasking rises to 1.59.

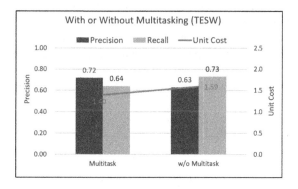

Fig. 5. Model design comparison with or without multitasking mechanism

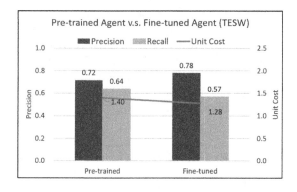

Fig. 6. Performance comparison of the pre-trained and fine-tuning model

5.2   The Evaluation of the Fine-Tuned Model

In the second stage, we fine-tune the model on 300 starting URLs with rewards given by an event source page classifier (shown in Sect. 5.3). As shown in Fig. 6, the fine-tuned model improves the precision from 0.72 to 0.78 but reduces the recall from 0.64 to 0.57 with an unit cost decrease from 1.40 to 1.28 on labeled test data.

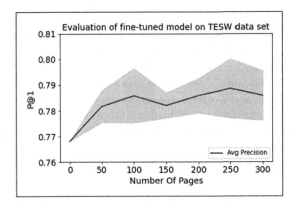

Fig. 7. The learning curve of the fine-tuning stage

Note that fine-tune model has its uncertainty during training because of the reward function is an estimation. As shown in Fig. 7, we conduct the experiment five times and show the learning curve of the fine-tuned model on the TESW dataset. We can see P@1 sometimes drops as the number of training pages increases.

5.3   Evaluation of the Event Source Page Classification

Finally, we present the performance of the event source page classification model. We conducted 4-fold cross-validation to show the performance of the event source page classification model using the labeled pages from a total of 1,863 training webpages and the 583 test webpages are labeled for the experiment. The event source pages to non-event source pages ratio is about 1/2. As shown in Table 1, the performance of our proposed model achieves 74.8% F1, while the baseline model which uses a complete web page as input, achieves only 63.4% F1. We can see the performance has been greatly improved with the selection of the first and second largest data-rich sections extracted by MDR.

Table 1. Performance comparison of event source page classification

Model	Accuracy	Precision	Recall	F1
Baseline	76.3%	64.6%	62.2%	63.4%
MDR filtered	83.7%	76.6%	73.0%	74.8%
MDR filtered (1863 + 40websites)	71.?%	57.1%	49.7%	53.2%

6   Conclusion and Future Work

In this paper, we proposed the task of event source page discovery for efficient event mining on the Web. We apply policy-based reinforcement learning to build a crawler agent and design a deep neural network with a multi-task design to predict the goodness of an anchor link. Meanwhile, two-stage training is used to speed up the procedure. The proposed multi-task model improves the precision from 0.63 (without multitasking) to 0.72 and reduces the unit cost from 1.59 to 1.40 on labeled test data. Finally, the fine-tuning model further increases the precision to 0.78 but also decrease the unit cost to 1.28. Since discovering each event source page is our goal, recall is more important than precision. Therefore, improving recall while maintaining high precision is our next research direction.

References

1. Foley, J., Bendersky, M., Josifovski, V.: Learning to extract local events from the web. In: Proceedings of the 38th International ACM SIGIR Conference on Research and Development in Information Retrieval, pp. 423–432. No. 09–13 in SIGIR15, ACM, Santiago, Chile (2015). https://doi.org/10.1145/2766462.2767739

2. Grigoriadis, A., Paliouras, G.: Focused crawling using temporal difference-learning. In: Vouros, G.A., Panayiotopoulos, T. (eds.) SETN 2004. LNCS (LNAI), vol. 3025, pp. 142–153. Springer, Heidelberg (2004). https://doi.org/10.1007/978-3-540-24674-9_16

3. Han, M., Wuillemin, P.-H., Senellart, P.: Focused crawling through reinforcement learning. In: Mikkonen, T., Klamma, R., Hernández, J. (eds.) ICWE 2018. LNCS, vol. 10845, pp. 261–278. Springer, Cham (2018). https://doi.org/10.1007/978-3-319-91662-0_20

4. Liu, B., Grossman, R., Zhai, Y.: Mining data records in web pages. In: Proceedings of the Ninth ACM SIGKDD International Conference on Knowledge Discovery and Data Mining, pp. 601–606. ACM, New York (2003). https://doi.org/10.1145/956750.956826

5. Menczer, F., Belew, R.K.: Adaptive retrieval agents: internalizing local context and scaling up to the web. Mach. Learn. **39**(2/3), 203–242 (2000). https://doi.org/10.1023/A:1007653114902

6. Menczer, F., Pant, G., Srinivasan, P.: Topical web crawlers: evaluating adaptive algorithms. ACM Trans. Internet Technol. **4**(4), 378–419 (2004)

7. Meusel, R., Mika, P., Blanco, R.: Focused crawling for structured data. In: Proceedings of the 23rd ACM International Conference on Conference on Information and Knowledge Management, pp. 1039–1048. CIKM 2014, Association for Computing Machinery, New York, NY, USA (2014). https://doi.org/10.1145/2661829.2661902

8. Partalas, I., Paliouras, G., Vlahavas, I.: Reinforcement learning with classifier selection for focused crawling. In: Proceedings of the 2008 Conference on ECAI 2008: 18th European Conference on Artificial Intelligence, pp. 759–760. IOS Press, NLD (2008)

9. Rennie, J., McCallum, A.: Using reinforcement learning to spider the web efficiently. In: Proceedings of the Sixteenth International Conference on Machine Learning, pp. 335–343. ICML 1999, Morgan Kaufmann Publishers Inc., San Francisco, CA, USA (1999)

10. Wang, Q., Kanagal, B., Garg, V., Sivakumar, D.: Constructing a comprehensive events database from the web. In: Proceedings of the 28th ACM International Conference on Information and Knowledge Management, pp. 229–238. CIKM 2019, Association for Computing Machinery, New York, NY, USA (2019)

Triplet Embedding Convolutional Recurrent Neural Network for Long Text Semantic Analysis

Jingxuan Liu[1], Ming Zhu[2], Huajiang Ouyang[3], Guozi Sun[2], and Huakang Li[1(✉)]

[1] School of AI and Advanced Computing, Xi'an Jiaotong-Liverpool University, 111 Ren'ai Road, Suzhou Industrial Park, Suzhou 215123, Jiangsu, China
`Huakang.Li@xjtlu.edu.cn`

[2] School of Computer Science, Nanjing University of Posts and Telecommuncations, Nanjing 210003, China
`sun@njupt.edu.cn`

[3] School of Engineering, University of Liverpool, Liverpool L69 3GH, UK
`H.Ouyang@liverpool.ac.uk`

Abstract. Deep Recurrent Neural Network has an excellent performance in sentence semantic analysis. However, due to the curse of the computational dimensionality, the application in the long text is minimal. Therefore, we propose a Triplet Embedding Convolutional Recurrent Neural Network for long text analysis. Firstly, a triplet from each sentence of the long text. Then the most crucial head entity into the CRNN network, composed of CNN and Bi-GRU networks. Both relation and tail entities are input to a CNN network through three splicing layers. Finally, the output results into the global pooling layer to get the final results. Entity fusion and entity replacement are also used to retain the text's structural and semantic information before triplet extraction in sentences. We have conducted experiments on a large-scale criminal case dataset. The results show our model significantly improves the judgment prediction task.

Keywords: Long text analysis · CRNN · Triplet embedding · Entity fusion and entity replacement

1 Introduction

Text analysis refers to various methods to learn and understand the meaning of the text, including analysis of long and short texts [1]. Although long text analysis has been quite effective in some domains, like social and financial, there are specific domains, like the judicial domain, where the application of artificial intelligence is lacking. So we propose a model for triplet embedding Convolutional Recurrent Neural Network (CRNN), which can be applied in crime and relevant legal long text prediction. Long text analysis can assist professionals in

© The Author(s), under exclusive license to Springer Nature Switzerland AG 2022
R. Chbeir et al. (Eds.): WISE 2022, LNCS 13724, pp. 607–615, 2022.
https://doi.org/10.1007/978-3-031-20891-1_43

making judgments and can facilitate domain intelligence and has specific research implications.

To solve the problem of long text identification, researchers have adopted a variety of approaches to achieve more accurate results in long text semantic analysis, which include: statistical rules [2], machine learning [3] and deep learning using neural networks [4]. Still, statistical rules lack practicality and robustness. Meanwhile, machine learning is still based on shallow text features and cannot judge complex texts.

To sum up, this paper uses multi-entity fusion and entity replacement (EFR) from the characteristics of long text data to reduce the dimensionality of the word vector space. Use the specified person's name to replace the corresponding victim and perpetrator's name in different texts, and the experimental results show that the EFR is better than the remaining approaches. Meanwhile, this paper uses semantic dependency analysis to obtain the semantic structure tree information of text and combines the sequences of its dependency triples as features and proposes a TeCRNN model based on dependency relations. The experimental results show that the TeCRNN model has better robustness. In summary, the main contributions of this paper are the following:

1. The use of entity recognition techniques to identify entities in text and the use of predefined entities to replace the recognition results, which to some extent acts as a dimensionality reduction and preserves the semantic structure of the text.
2. The use of dependency triples to obtain the semantic as well as structural relationships of factual text. The input text sequence is changed into a sequence of dependent triples, and then the semantic and structural features of the sequence are automatically obtained.

The rest of the paper is organized as follows. Section 2 includes a short review of related work. Section 3 describes the details of the proposed model. Section 4 presents the experimental design. Finally, we conclude the paper and discuss future work in Sect. 5.

2   Related Work

The literature related to this paper is reviewed regarding two aspects: core sentence matching of long text and full text matching of long text.

2.1   Core Sentence Matching

Long text analysis can be studied in some ways, one of which is to determine the degree of similarity of text content by looking at the core sentences of the text. Kim et al. proposed a word-level representation and fed it into a Convolutional Neural Network (CNN) [5] for classification [6]. Long et al. extracted the textual features of the different contents using a pairwise mutual attention mechanism to capture the interactive features between different texts [7]. In addition,

Yang et al. proposed to use Long-Short Term Memory (LSTM) [8] and a self-attentive mechanism [9] to embed the law definition and fact description into a low-dimensional space and then capture multiple repetitive interaction features between the fact description and the law [10].

2.2 Full Text Matching

Due to the complexity and diversity of long texts, covering many different topics and domains, full text matching is required to determine the degree of similarity of text content.. Yang et al. modeled the text-level and introduced a hierarchical attention mechanism into the model for computation [11]. Wei et al. use deep learning models, including CNN, Gated Recurrent Unit (GRU) [12], and attention mechanisms to obtain feature vectors and combine the predicted number of labels of the dataset with the output probability to get the result of label classification [13]. Besides, Li et al. proposed a multi-channel attention neural network model, which learns semantic representations of different features from long text and performs integrated tasks in a unified framework. The model further improves the performance of long text analysis [14].

3 Methodology and Model Design

3.1 Framework of EFR

Chinese is semantically focused, this paper mainly uses semantic dependency analysis [15] for long text analysis, which describes the dependency relationships between individual words. We use the dependency syntactic analysis of the Language Technology Platform (LTP) [16]. Specifically, segmentation of factual texts, different annotations are added to the relationships between words, and the dependency triad is obtained by LTP dependency analysis. The flow of data preprocessing is shown in Fig. 1.

Fig. 1. Data processing flow

First of all, the resampling method [17] was selected for data augmentation. Then the results of word segmentation of authentic judicial texts are analyzed statistically, and each different word is numbered and mapped one by one. The results of word separation are input into the Word2vec tool, and the word vectors are trained using CBOW. After that, interconversion of the results of the judicial text segmentation with the numbers in the factual dictionary, transforming the word sequences into numerical sequences. Then select a threshold value of the text length, using forward truncation and backward completion. Finally, the label is initialized, whose length is the number of categories of the label, and the corresponding position value of the label is changed.

3.2 SCRNN

The long text has many entities, so the choice was made to fuse the names of non-key persons, normalize them into a unified entity, and then replace all place names with entity nouns, which reduces the errors due to the segmentation of words. The model architecture designed in this section is the SCRNN model.

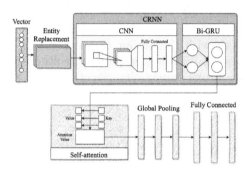

Fig. 2. Framework diagram of SCRNN model

As shown from Fig. 2, the model has three main parts: entity replacement and word vector representation, CRNN, and Self-attention.

Entity replacement and word vector representation: First, a regular expression replaces the determined result with a common entity name. Next, the new text is segmented into words using a custom dictionary with a word splitting tool. Finally, the new word vector is trained using the CBOW method in Word2vec.

CRNN: Use the CNN layer to extract the text surface features. The Bi-GRU is used to obtain the discourse order features.

Self-attention layer: It is less dependent on external data and better at capturing the internal relevance of data. In addition, there are also multiple events in the judicial fact text, and the inherent causal links between multiple events can also affect the final verdict.

3.3 TeCRNN

The TeCRNN model consists mainly of the CRNN model with auxiliary vectors based on the dependency triad, and the use of CRNN after the head vector allows for more sequential features to be obtained. The architecture is shown in Fig. 3.

In the model in Fig. 3, the head vector (A vector) is the sequence union of the head in the input triplet sequence, the tail vector is the set of sequences of

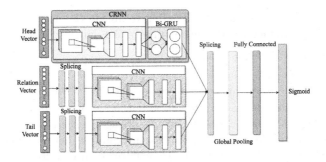

Fig. 3. Framework diagram of TeCRNN model

the tail, and the relation vector is the set of dependency vectors. In this paper, the A vector is spliced with the relation vector and denoted as the B vector, and the B vector is spliced with the tail vector and denoted as the C vector.

$$A = head \tag{1}$$

$$B = [head; relation] \tag{2}$$

$$C = [head; relation; tail] \tag{3}$$

In the first step, the A, B and C vectors are passed through the CNN layer respectively to extract the textual multivariate features $ConV_A$, $ConV_B$, $ConV_C$.

$$ConV_A = f(W_A \cdot A + b_A) \tag{4}$$

$$ConV_B = f(W_B \cdot B + b_B) \tag{5}$$

$$ConV_C = f(W_C \cdot C + b_C) \tag{6}$$

where f is the activation function, W_A, W_B, W_C are the convolution kernels, resulting in the output of 3 classes of convolutional features.

In the second step, the vector $ConV_A$ as the input to the Bi-GRU.

$$\overrightarrow{h} = \overrightarrow{GRU}(ConV_A) \tag{7}$$

$$\overleftarrow{h} = \overleftarrow{GRU}(ConV_A) \tag{8}$$

$$H = [\overrightarrow{h}; \overleftarrow{h}] \tag{9}$$

$\overrightarrow{h}$ represents the forward network and $\overleftarrow{h}$ represents the backward network. $GRU()$ represents the calculation of the GRU model to obtain the hidden layer output H.

In the third step, H, $ConV_B$, $ConV_C$ are stitched together through the splicing layer to obtain the fusion vector D.

$$D = [H; ConV_B; ConV_C] \tag{10}$$

In the fourth step, Global Max Pooling to obtain the most obvious features of the model and reduce the dimensionality of the data.

$$P = GlobalMaxPooling(D) \tag{11}$$

Finally, the first fully connected layer uses the ReLU function, which implements the non-linear feature transformation. Tthe second layer uses the Sigmoid function as the final classification function, setting the corresponding threshold-considering probabilities greater than this threshold as actual labels and those less than this threshold as non-labels, to achieve the prediction of the result.

4   Experimental Results and Analysis

4.1   Experimental Environment

The model runs mainly in a Linux environment with 32G of RAM and 6G of video memory, using the Keras 2.1.2 deep learning framework based on Tensor-Flow 1.4.0. The programming language is Python 3.6.

4.2   Dataset Statistic

In this paper, we use the dataset of CAIL2018 [18], which includes 154,592 train set, 17,131 valid set, and 32,508 test set.

4.3   Baselines

For comparison, we used several models as baselines, including the base CNN, Bi-LSTM, Bi-GRU, the CNN model with Self-attention added, and the main SCRNN and TeCRNN models proposed in this paper. Meanwhile, we remove the Bi-GRU layer from the TeCRNN model, denoted as the TeCNN model, and add Self- attention to the TeCNN model. In summary, this paper selected eight models for experiment.

4.4   Experiment Parameters Setting

The CNN model has 128 convolutional kernels, the convolution kernel size is 3, the stride is 1, the activation function is ReLU, the Pooling method is Global Max Pooling for CNN. Based on a combination of operational efficiency and effects, the number of neurons used is chosen to be 64 for Bi-GRU.

Due to the imbalance data nature of the dataset used in this paper. In view of this, we employ $F_1 - micro$, $F_1 - macro$ and $Accuracy$ [19], which are more suitable for imbalance datasets, as evaluation metrics.

4.5   The Impact of the EFR Method

To verify the effectiveness of the EFR method, this section uses a single-layer CNN, Bi-GRU, and Bi-LSTM model as the base model. The experimental results are shown in Table 1.

Table 1. Results for different text processing methods on different models

Pre-processing method	Type of model	$F_1 - micro$	$F_1 - macro$	Accuracy
Segmentation word	CNN	80.51	63.78	72.15
	Bi-LSTM	81.10	67.03	74.07
	Bi-GRU	81.09	67.01	74.05
	CNN	80.49	63.90	72.20
Stop word list	Bi-LSTM	81.04	66.93	73.99
	Bi-GRU	81.33	66.89	74.11
	CNN	81.15	65.91	73.53
EFR	Bi-LSTM	81.78	67.83	74.81
	Bi-GRU	**81.98**	**67.95**	**74.97**

As shown in the Table 1, the EFR method proposed in this paper also reduces the dimensionality of the data in the actual prediction process and retains the structural features of the text, laying a solid foundation for further analysis of the text. The EFR method shows some improvement compared to using only segmentation or the stop word list.

4.6   Experimental Results of All Models Comparison

To verify the validity of dependencies on judicial decisions, this section conducts experiments on all models; the results are shown in Table 2.

Table 2. Comparison of all related models

Type of model	Related legal articles prediction			Crime prediction		
	$F_1 - micro$	$F_1 - macro$	Accuracy	$F_1 - micro$	$F_1 - macro$	Accuracy
CNN	81.15	65.91	73.53	83.71	73.73	78.72
Bi-LSTM	81.78	67.83	/	/	/	/
Bi-GRU	81.98	67.95	/	/	/	/
CNN+Self-attention	81.99	69.21	75.60	84.52	75.13	79.83
SCRNN	**83.41**	69.98	76.70	**86.13**	75.12	80.63
TeCNN	81.97	71.49	76.73	84.81	75.76	80.29
TeCNN+Self-attention	81.83	71.01	76.42	84.84	75.31	80.08
TeCRNN	81.51	**72.45**	**76.98**	85.65	**76.25**	**80.95**

As can be seen in the Table 2, in the related legal articles prediction task. The TeCRNN model outperformed the SCRNN model by 0.28% in the *Accuracy* and improved by 2.47% in $F_1 - macro$, fully reflecting the role of dependencies in the small class. TeCRNN model enhanced by 0.25% of *Accuracy* compared to the TeCNN model. TeCRNN improved all evaluation metrics in the crime prediction task compared to the TeCNN model.

Overall, the SCRNN model outperformed the other models in terms of $F_1 - micro$, while the $F_1 - macro$ and *Accuracy* of the TeCRNN model are higher than other models. As we can see, our model has better generalization performance on the judicial decision prediction task of long text semantic analysis.

5   Conclusion

This paper proposes using EFR as an alternative to stop word lists to retain the structural and semantic information of the text to the greatest extent possible and reduce the dimensionality of the data. The model's results using standard stop word lists for the data are similar to those without processing, further illustrating the disadvantages of non-proprietary stop word lists. In addition, the model that uses dependencies has a significant advantage in acquiring features, even when compared to models that incorporate Recurrent Neural Networks or Self-attention, and has a competitive advantage.

Acknowledgements. This work was supported by the "Six talent peaks" High Level Talents of Jiangsu Province (XYDXX-204), Province Key R&D Program of Jiangsu (BE2020026), XJTLU Research Development Funding (RDF-20-02-10), Suzhou Science and Technology Development Planning Programme-Key Industrial Technology Innovation-Prospective Applied Basic Research Project (SGC2021086), Special Patent Research Project of China National Intellectual Property Office (Y220702).

References

1. Hassan, A., Mahmood, A.: Deep learning approach for sentiment analysis of short texts. In: 2017 3rd International Conference on Control, Automation and Robotics (ICCAR), pp. 705–710 (2022)
2. Lauderdale, B.E., Clark, T.S.: The Supreme Court's many median justices. Am. Polit. Sci. Rev. **106**(4), 847–866 (2012)
3. Gonçalves, T., Quaresma, P.: Is linguistic information relevant for the classification of legal texts? In: Proceedings of the 10th International Conference on Artificial Intelligence and Law, pp. 168–176 (2005)
4. Liu, P., Qiu, X., Huang, X.: Recurrent neural network for text classification with multi-task learning. arXiv preprint arXiv:1605.05101. (2016)
5. He, K., Zhang, X., Ren, S., Sun, J.: Deep residual learning for image recognition. In: Proceedings of the IEEE Conference on Computer Vision and Pattern Recognition, pp. 770–778 (2016)
6. Kim, Y.: Convolutional neural networks for sentence classification. arXiv: 1408.5882. (2014)
7. Long, S., Tu, C., Liu, Z., Sun, M.: Automatic judgment prediction via legal reading comprehension. In: Sun, M., Huang, X., Ji, H., Liu, Z., Liu, Y. (eds.) CCL 2019. LNCS (LNAI), vol. 11856, pp. 558–572. Springer, Cham (2019). https://doi.org/10.1007/978-3-030-32381-3_45

8. Ma, X., Tao, Z., Wang, Y., Yu, H., Wang, Y.: Long short-term memory neural network for traffic speed prediction using remote microwave sensor data. Transp. Res. Part C: Emerg. Technol. **54**, 187–197 (2015)
9. Chung, J., Gulcehre, C., Cho, K., Bengio, Y.: Empirical evaluation of gated recurrent neural networks on sequence modeling. arXiv preprint arXiv:1412.3555. (2014)
10. Yang, Z., Wang, P., Zhang, L., Shou, L., Xu, W.: A recurrent attention network for judgment prediction. In: Tetko, I.V., Kůrková, V., Karpov, P., Theis, F. (eds.) ICANN 2019. LNCS, vol. 11730, pp. 253–266. Springer, Cham (2019). https://doi.org/10.1007/978-3-030-30490-4_21
11. Yang, Z., Yang, D., Dyer, C., He, X., Smola, A., Hovy, E.: Hierarchical attention networks for document classification. In: Proceedings of the 2016 conference of the North American chapter of the association for computational linguistics: human language technologies, pp. 1480–1489 (2016)
12. Cho, K., et al.: Learning phrase representations using RNN encoder-decoder for statistical machine translation. arXiv preprint arXiv:1406.1078. (2014)
13. Wei, D., Lin, L.: An external knowledge enhanced multi-label charge prediction approach with label number learning. arXiv preprint arXiv:1907.02205. (2019)
14. Li, S., Zhang, H., Ye, L., Guo, X., Fang, B.: Mann: a multichannel attentive neural network for legal judgment prediction. IEEE Access **7**, 151144–151155 (2019)
15. Koopman, H., Sportiche, D., Stabler, E.: An Introduction to Syntactic Analysis and Theory. Wiley, Hoboken (2013)
16. Che, W., Li, Z., Liu, T.: LTP: A Chinese language technology platform. In: Coling 2010: Demonstrations, pp. 13–16 (2010)
17. Li, K.W., Yang, L., Liu, W.Y., Liu, L., Liu, H.T.: Classification method of imbalanced data based on RSBoost. Comput. Sci. **42**(9), 249–252 (2015)
18. Xiao, C., et al.: Cail 2018: a large-scale legal dataset for judgment prediction. arXiv preprint arXiv:1807.02478. (2018)
19. Li, Q., et al.: A text classification survey: from shallow to deep learning. arXiv preprint. arXiv:2008.00364. (2020)

Graph Neural Network with Self-attention and Multi-task Learning for Credit Default Risk Prediction

Zihao Li[1], Xianzhi Wang[1(✉)], Lina Yao[2], Yakun Chen[1], Guandong Xu[1], and Ee-Peng Lim[3]

[1] University of Technology Sydney, Sydney, NSW 2007, Australia
{zihao.li,yakun.chen}@student.uts.edu.au,
{xianzhi.wang,guandong.xu}@uts.edu.au
[2] University of New South Wales, Sydney, NSW 2052, Australia
lina.yao@unsw.edu.au
[3] Singapore Management University, Singapore 188065, Singapore
eplim@smu.edu.sg

Abstract. We propose a graph neural network with self-attention and multi-task learning (SaM-GNN) to leverage the advantages of deep learning for credit default risk prediction. Our approach incorporates two parallel tasks based on shared intermediate vectors for input vector reconstruction and credit default risk prediction, respectively. To better leverage supervised data, we use self-attention layers for feature representation of categorical and numeric data; we further link raw data into a graph and use a graph convolution module to aggregate similar information and cope with missing values during constructing intermediate vectors. Our method does not heavily rely on feature engineering work and the experiments show our approach outperforms several types of baseline methods; the intermediate vector obtained by our approach also helps improve the performance of ensemble learning methods.

Keywords: Credit default risk prediction · Graph neural network · Self-attention · Multi-task learning

1 Introduction

Credit default risk refers to the possibility of a loss resulting from a borrower's failure to repay a loan or meet contractual obligations. It is a major concern for any bank and financial institution in making loan decisions [1]. Bad loans can cause banks problems with their capital adequacy and, at worst, lead to default. Bad loans also risk impairing the long-term economic growth and lead to greater uncertainty and instability in the banking and financial systems. Therefore, it is highly necessary to assess borrowers' repayment abilities before authorizing a loan, which calls for accurate credit default risk prediction.

© The Author(s), under exclusive license to Springer Nature Switzerland AG 2022
R. Chbeir et al. (Eds.): WISE 2022, LNCS 13724, pp. 616–629, 2022.
https://doi.org/10.1007/978-3-031-20891-1_44

Traditional risk assessment highly relies on experts with professional knowledge and relevant experience to assess loan requests against specific business models and rules, which is labor-intensive and prone to personal bias. For example, the widely adopted '5C principle' [1] requires domain professionals to evaluate borrowers' default risk by manually evaluating borrowers on five aspects: *character, capital, capacity, collateral* and *conditions*. It helps to incorporate both qualitative or quantitative measures in the '5C principle'; however, this makes credit default risk assessment even more complicated and time-consuming.

The availability of big financial data related to personal and home credit offers the opportunity for automating credit default risk assessment with predictive models. Such models need to address several challenges for accurate credit default risk prediction. First, it requires incorporating all sources of clues about users' backgrounds, credit histories, investments, etc., to make accurate predictions. Second, certain users may have insufficient or incomplete information (e.g., non-existence of credit histories) for the prediction task, making it necessary to leverage the information about other users who have more useful information to help improve the prediction results. Until recently, the related research has been focusing on traditional machine learning techniques, e.g., Support Vector Machine (SVM) [11], decision tree [20], Random Forest (RF) [17], and XGBoost [15]. These models' performance highly depends on the quality of feature engineering, which requires high domain expertise to incorporate diverse sources and forms of data.

Recently, deep learning has shown great potential in addressing the above challenges, thanks to its capability to capture complex, non-linear relations from massive data [21,22]. It has proven successful in various domains, such as computer vision natural language processing, speech recognition, and recommendation systems [9,14,26]. However, there have been limited studies on credit default risk prediction based on deep learning techniques. Moreover, the current studies cannot effectively leverage multiple aspects of clues (e.g., heterogeneous information in applicants' profiles, relations among loan applications) to overcome the challenges posed by incomplete profiles and missing values, which greatly impair the prediction accuracy [29]. To cover this knowledge gap, a loan application graph can be designed based on raw application records. Intuitively, similar application records are likely to incur similar risk levels; so the similar neighbors can be considered as the auxiliary information to enrich the nodes (loan application records) containing missing values for credit default risk prediction. As shown in Fig. 1, we could construct a loan application graph based on the similarity between each client's historical records first. Hence, the neighbors information can be introduced as the external information to alleviate the missing values problem. And the credit default risk of each record is able to be predicted via node classification techniques.

Overall, we propose a novel Graph neural network with input attributes Self-attention and Multi-task learning (SaM-GNN), which comprehensively incorporates self-attention, graph neural networks, and multitask learning for accurate credit default risk prediction. In a nutshell, we make the following contributions:

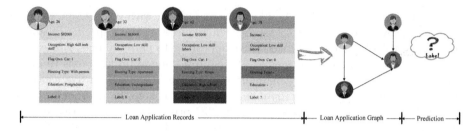

Fig. 1. A toy example. Loan application records are represented as nodes in a loan application graph. Then, credit default risk prediction can be transformed into a node classification problem.

- We construct an undirected graph for loan applications and combine self-attention and graph convolution networks for representation learning in our model. The self-attention mechanism enables effective feature representation, and graph convolution networks allow for aggregating similar information via a graph structure to improve the model's robustness to missing values in the input.
- We design two parallel tasks for multi-task learning based on shared feature representation: a decoder module for input reconstruction and a classification module for credit default risk prediction. The two tasks are jointly trained to optimize feature representation and prediction results simultaneously.
- We conducted experiments on two real-world credit default risk prediction datasets. Our experimental results show a significant performance improvement of our approach over state-of-the-art methods. Besides, the feature representations of loan applications output by our approach helps improve the performance of existing ensemble methods.
- We will make our data and code public, including detailed parameter configurations for all the methods, to ensure reproducibility[1].

The rest of the paper is organized as follows. Section 2 overviews existing methods for credit default risk prediction. Section 3 introduces our self-attention graph neural network for credit default prediction and multi-task training strategy. Section 4 reports our experiments to evaluate our model on two real-world datasets, and finally, Sect. 5 concludes the paper.

2   Related Work

There has been many studies based on single-model machine learning methods like decision tree for credit default risk prediction in various contexts [3,8,20]. But until now, most existing machine learning techniques for credit default risk prediction are based on ensemble models, which take either bagging and boosting approaches. Bagging methods (e.g., Random Forest [4]) train multiple classifiers

---

[1] https://github.com/ZihaoLi97/SAGM-for-Credit-Risk-Prediction.

simultaneously and then combine them to make the final prediction [19]. In contrast, boosting methods (e.g., XGBoost [6], LightGBM [12]) apply individual models in a chain, where each model takes as input the result of the previous model [15,16]. As a typical model of bagging strategy, Random Forest selects samples and attributes randomly to construct and integrate decision trees. Uddin et al. [24] leverage Random Forest in micro-enterprises credit default risk modeling for accuracy and interpretability. Zhu et al. [28] conclude that Random Forest has better accuracy than other machine learning methods like logistic regression, decision trees, and SVM. Li et al. [16] use the XGBoost algorithm to identify customers who do not pay back from good customers. Li et al. [15] further design a stacking framework for XGBoost, SVM, and Random Forest for P2P default risk prediction and experimentally show that the model fusion algorithm has better adaptability and accuracy. Aleksandrova et al. [3] evaluate several popular machine learning algorithms for P2P credit scoring; they conclude that ensemble classifiers (e.g., XGBoost, GBM, and Random Forest) outperform non-ensemble models (e.g., logistic regression, decision tree, and multilayer perceptron). Differing from Aleksandrova's conclusion, Coser et al. [8] point out that logistic regression and Random Forest obtain the best results among various models for default risk prediction.

There has been limited work on deep learning for credit default risk analysis [10]. Wang et al. [25] use LSTM for P2P lending risk prediction, and Maria et al. [29] build connections between borrowers based on their geographic locations or economic activities and develop a multi-layer personalized PageRank model for credit default risk prediction. Since there is limited historical lending data, it is difficult to make an accurate prediction. Suryanto et al. [23] apply transfer learning to alleviate the issue of insufficient historical data. In summary, existing deep learning models rarely comprehensively use the full-spectrum multi-source, heterogeneous data for risk assessment. And none of them establishes effective approach to learning effective representations of loan applications or explicit connections among the applications. They commonly face challenges in dealing with incomplete profiles of applicants and missing information in loan applications. In this regard, we apply self-attention with multi-task learning for application record representation, and also consider graph neural network to capture the connection among similar applications and alleviate the missing values problem. To the best of our knowledge, we are the first to apply graph neural networks and multi-task learning simultaneously to improve the robustness of credit default risk prediction.

3   Proposed Method

Our proposed model (shown in Fig. 2) works as follows: it first generates embedding of categorical data (e.g., gender, suite type, education) and applies self-attention mechanism to the embedding and numeric data (e.g., income total and goods price) for feature representation; Then, the resulting representations are concatenated and updated via graph convolution constructed based on the similarity between loan applications to alleviate the impact of missing values. Finally, a decoder module and a classification module (consisting of multiple fully connected layers) are jointly trained to generate feature representation and simultaneously predict credit default risk.

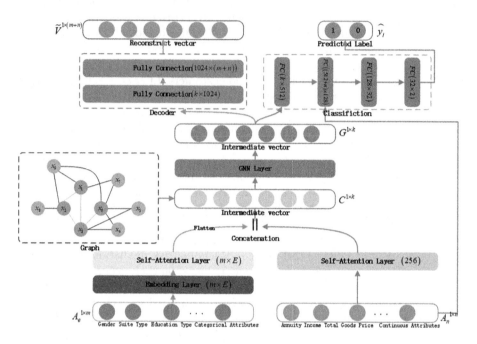

Fig. 2. The framework of SaM-GNN. $A_e^{1\times m}$. $A_n^{1\times n}$ are categorical attributes and numeric attributes, respectively, where m, n are the corresponding numbers. E is the embedding size, and $k = m \times E + 256$. C and G are intermediate vectors before and after similar information aggregation via graph convolution block. $\tilde{V}$ is the reconstructed input, and $\hat{y}$ is the predicted label.

3.1   Self-attention Module

This module aims for generating feature representation for categorical and numeric inputs. Let $X_e = \{x_{e_0}, x_{e_1}, ..., x_{e_m}\}$ be categorical attributes and $X_n = \{x_{e_0}, x_{e_1}, ..., x_{e_n}\}$ be numeric attributes in the input. Suppose $\mathbf{E_i} \in \mathbb{R}^{1\times d}$ is the embedding of categorical attribute x_{e_i}, where d is the embedding size. The feature representations of categorical attributes are as follows:

$$\begin{cases} \mathbf{Q_e} & = \mathbf{E_e W_q} + \mathbf{b_q} \\ \mathbf{K_e} & = \mathbf{E_e W_k} + \mathbf{b_k} \\ \mathbf{V_e} & = \mathbf{E_e W_v} + \mathbf{b_v} \\ \text{Attention}(\mathbf{Q_e}, \mathbf{K_e}, \mathbf{V_e}) & = \text{softmax}(\frac{\mathbf{Q_e K_e^T}}{\sqrt{d_k}})\mathbf{V_e} \end{cases} \quad (1)$$

where $\mathbf{E_e} \in \mathbb{R}^{m \times d}$ is the embedding of categorical attributes. $\mathbf{W_q}, \mathbf{W_k}, \mathbf{W_v} \in \mathbb{R}^{d \times d}$ and $\mathbf{b_q}, \mathbf{b_k}, \mathbf{b_v} \in \mathbb{R}^{1 \times d}$ are learning weight matrices. $1/\sqrt{d_k}$ is the scaling factor. Similarly, the feature representations of numeric attributes is as follows:

$$
\begin{cases}
\mathbf{Q_n} & = \mathbf{X_n}\mathbf{W'_q} + b'_q \\
\mathbf{K_n} & = \mathbf{X_n}\mathbf{W'_k} + b'_k \\
\mathbf{V_n} & = \mathbf{X_n}\mathbf{W'_v} + b'_v \\
\text{Attention}(\mathbf{Q_n}, \mathbf{K_n}, \mathbf{V_n}) & = \text{softmax}(\frac{\mathbf{Q_n^T} \cdot \mathbf{K_n}}{\sqrt{d_k}})\mathbf{V_n}^T
\end{cases}
\tag{2}
$$

where $\mathbf{X_n} \in \mathbb{R}^{1 \times n}$ is the numerical attributes value after normalization. $\mathbf{W'_q}, \mathbf{W'_k}, \mathbf{W'_v} \in \mathbb{R}^{n \times n}$ and $b'_q, b'_k, b'_v \in \mathbb{R}^{1 \times n}$ are learning weight matrices. $1/\sqrt{d_k}$ is the scaling factor.

We concatenate the representations of categorical attributes and numeric attributes to construct the intermediate vector $\mathbf{C} \in \mathbb{R}^{1 \times (m \times d + n)}$.

$$
\mathbf{C} = \overset{m}{\underset{i=0}{\|}} \text{Attention}(\mathbf{Q_{e_i}}, \mathbf{K_{e_i}}, \mathbf{V_{e_i}})
$$
$$
\| \text{Attention}(\mathbf{Q_n}, \mathbf{K_n}, \mathbf{V_n})
\tag{3}
$$

where $\|$ represents concatenation operation.

3.2 Graph Convolution Module

We construct an undirected graph by regarding each loan application as a node and adding weighted edges between nodes. Considering there are numerous attributes in raw data, we first select a subset of attributes to decrease the computational complexity. And then for every pair of nodes, we add an edge between them if they bear the same value on at least one attribute. We set the edge's weight to the number of attributes on which the two nodes share the same values.

To be specific, we define two thresholds, θ_m and θ_u, to select the attributes to participate in the graph construction. We choose an attribute if and only if 1) the proportion of loan applications that have missing values on the attribute in all the applications is smaller than θ_m and 2) the number of distinct values for the attribute is fewer than θ_u. These two thresholds should be appropriately configured to avoid it being excessively large (which introduces more noise) or small (which limits the auxiliary information usable to guide graph construction). We will study the impact of these thresholds in our experiments (Sect. 4.7).

Once the graph is constructed, we can apply graph convolution to aggregate neighbors' information and update the intermediate vector $\mathbf{C}$ [13]:

$$
\mathbf{C}^{(l+1)} = \text{ReLU}(\tilde{D}^{-\frac{1}{2}} \tilde{A} \tilde{D}^{-\frac{1}{2}} \mathbf{C}^{(l)} \mathbf{W}^{(l)})
\tag{4}
$$

where $\mathbf{C}^{(l+1)}$ is the intermediate vector after $l+1$ layers of graph convolution; $A \in \mathbb{R}^{N \times N}$ is the adjacency matrix for graph $\mathcal{G}$, $\tilde{A} = A + I$, and $\tilde{D}_{ii} = \sum_j \tilde{A}_{ij}$.

$\tilde{D}$ is the degree matrix of $\tilde{A}$; $\mathbf{W}$ is the learned weight. We denote the last layer of graph convolution as $\mathbf{C^{(L)}}$

Finally, we define a λ to determine how much information to aggregate from neighbors:

$$\mathbf{G} = \lambda\mathbf{C} + (1-\lambda)\mathbf{C^{(L)}} \tag{5}$$

where $\mathbf{G}$ is the final representation of the intermediate vector; $\mathbf{C}, \mathbf{C^{(L)}}$ are the intermediate vector before and after graph convolution; λ is a learned parameter that controls how much raw information to remember.

3.3   Decoder Module

The decoder module (shown in the top-left of Fig. 2) uses two fully connected layers to reconstruct the input and to capture a better representation of raw data.

$$\tilde{\mathbf{V}} = \text{ReLU}(\mathbf{W_{d_2}}\text{ReLU}(\mathbf{W_{d_1}}\mathbf{G^T} + \mathbf{d_1}^{\mathbf{T}}) + \mathbf{d_2}^{\mathbf{T}}) \tag{6}$$

where $\tilde{\mathbf{V}}$ is the reconstructed inputs, $\mathbf{W_{d_1}}, \mathbf{W_{d_2}}, \mathbf{d_1}, \mathbf{d_2}$ are the weight matrix for linear transformation.

3.4   Classification Module

The classification module uses fully connected layers to make predictions on whether or not to authorize a loan or not (the top-right of Fig. 2 shows the detailed specification of the module, e.g., the number of layers and the number of neurons of each layer). Although the intermediate vector $\mathbf{G}$ can capture semantic information from raw data (based on a stack of layers in our framework), it is prone to losing the shallow information in original data. To make up for the information loss, we concatenate the original numeric input (i.e., a numeric vector) and the intermediate vector as the combined input for predicting the risk probability. The prediction result can be represented as:

$$\hat{y} = \sigma(\mathbf{MLP}(\mathbf{G}||\mathbf{A_n})) \tag{7}$$

where σ denotes the sigmoid activation function.

3.5   Joint Learning

We apply a joint learning strategy for input vector reconstruction and credit default risk prediction. The loss function includes mean square loss and cross-entropy loss for the two learning tasks, respectively:

$$L = \frac{1}{|N|}\sum_{i \in N}(-\alpha(y_i log\hat{y}_i + (1-y_i)log(1-\hat{y}_i))$$

$$+ \beta\frac{1}{m+n}\sum_{j=1}^{m+n}(\mathbf{V_{ij}} - \tilde{\mathbf{V}}_{\mathbf{ij}})^2) + \lambda||\boldsymbol{\Theta}||_2 \tag{8}$$

where $\alpha, \beta \in [0,1]$ balances the loss between the classification task and the reconstruction task. $y_i = 1$ indicates a positive case while $y_i = 0$ indicates otherwise. $\hat{y}_i$ is the predicted probability, i.e., the network's output after the softmax layer. $\mathbf{V_{ij}}, \tilde{\mathbf{V}}_{ij}$ represent the original and reconstructed input vectors, respectively. Θ denotes the set of trainable parameters. The last term is $L2$ regularization to mitigate overfitting.

4   Experiments

In this section, we report our experiments for evaluating our approach against several competitive baselines. Besides, we provide a further evaluation of our model under different configurations and parameter settings.

4.1   Datasets

We conduct experiments on two public datasets, which are representative of high-dimensionality and high-volume features of credit default risk data, respectively.

- **Home Credit Default Risk dataset**[2] covers various information about applicants, such as family information, income and expenditure, credit records, loan records, and repayment history. There are 307,511 train samples and 48,744 test samples, each having 477 numeric attributes and 55 categorical attributes in the raw data. The ratio of positive to negative samples in the train set is approximately 1:11. Values are missing for half of those attributes. We randomly draw 10% of the train data as the validation set.
- **Lending Club dataset**[3] contains millions of loan records with 151 attributes from 2007 to 2018. Following previous work [3], we remove meaningless attributes (e.g., URL, member_id), together with those attributes with more than 30% missing values, and then fill the remaining missing values with zeros. Each sample has 7 categorical attributes and 16 numeric attributes after preprocessing. The ratio of positive to negative samples is approximately 1:4. We use the most recent 10% records for testing and the rest for training.

4.2   Baseline Methods and Evaluation Metric

We select several recent competitive methods, which reflect the state-of-the-art research, to compare with our approach:

- **Logistic Regression** [18]: a simple and efficient linear model for binary classification.
- **Decision Tree** [28]: a technique that classifies samples following an ordering of attributes with a tree structure.

---

[2] https://www.kaggle.com/c/home-credit-default-risk/overview.
[3] https://www.kaggle.com/wordsforthewise/lending-club.

- **Random Forest** [18]: an ensemble learning method that trains a multitude of decision trees and determines the label via majority voting.
- **XGBoost** [3]: a decision-tree-based ensemble machine learning algorithm that uses a gradient boosting framework.
- **Fully Connected Deep Network** [3]: a network with fully connected layers. We choose ReLU as the activation function and cross-entropy loss for optimization.
- **Convolution Neural Network** [27]: a network that feeds the concatenation of the representation of categorical data (obtained by convolution operations) and numeric attributes to fully connected layers for making predictions.
- **Wide & Deep Neural Network** [7] applies a linear model to improve the sparsity of categorical features and robustness of models via cross-product feature transformations. For the deep module, a feed-forward neural network is applied for feature representation, while the wide module is endeavored to improve the memory of the network.

For SaM-GNN, we set the embedding size $E = 5$, $\alpha = 0.5, \beta = 0.5$ for the loss function. For graph construction, we set $\theta_m = 0.3$ and $\theta_u = 20$ for attributes selection. The learning rate of the Adam optimizer is initialized to 0.001, which decays by 0.1 after every 50 epochs. Batch size and L2 penalty are set to 500 and 10^{-5}, respectively. For the classification module in SaM-GNN, we apply cross-entropy loss, use ReLU as the activation function, and set the dropout rate to 0.35 for all the fully connected layers except the last. The number of neurons in the layers are 512, 256, 128, 64, 32, 2 for Home Credit Default Risk dataset and 32, 16, 16, 2 for Lending Club dataset. More details about parameter configurations of methods can be found in our public code repository (see Sect. 1).

Following previous studies [2], we use *Area under the ROC Curve (AUC)* as the evaluation metric to evaluate models' performance. AUC has the characteristic of signifying the probability that positive samples receive higher scores than negative samples. Therefore, it can effectively reduce false alarms (or false positive rate) and decrease potential financial loss, making it especially suitable for the credit default risk prediction problem.

4.3   Comparisons with Baselines and Ablation Study

Table 1 shows the performance (with respect to AUC) of different methods. Generally, deep neural networks and ensemble methods outperform traditional models (Decision Tree, Logistic Regression), which has limited feature representation ability for high-dimensional data, while Boosting methods (XGBoost) outperform the Bagging method (Random Forest). Neural network-based models generally perform better than shallow models (traditional models, Bagging method) thanks to their strong feature representation and non-linear learning ability. Regarding Home Credit Default Risk dataset, SaM-GNN, outperform all the other methods. XGBoost and Random Forest achieve a remarkable improving

Table 1. Performance (AUC) of different models. The best three results are highlighted in boldface. ↑ and ↓ denote improvement and drop in performance, respectively. The numbers besides up/down arrows indicate the percentages by which the models improve their original versions.

Method	Home Credit	Lending Club
Logistic Regression	0.71739	0.69017
Decision Tree	0.72383	0.69925
Random Forest	0.74657	0.70380
XGBoost	0.76869	0.71616
Fully Connected Neural Network	0.76908	0.70448
Convolution Neural Network	0.77070	0.70961
Wide & Deep Neural Network	0.75824	0.70207
SaM-GNN	**0.78605**	**0.96982**
SaM-GNN w/o Decoder Module	0.77395 (↓ 1.54%)	0.96347 (↓ 0.65%)
SaM-GNN w/o Decoder & Graph Convolution	0.77026 (↓ 2.01 %)	0.71253 (↓ 26.05%)
Random Forest + Intermediate Vector	0.75270 (↑ 0.82%)	0.86833 (↑ 23.38%)
XGBoost + Intermediate Vector	0.77289 (↑ 0.55%)	0.87326 (↑ 21.94%)

after incorporating the intermediate vector generated by SaM-GNN, demonstrating the effectiveness of SaM-GNN in improving existing methods. As for Lending Club dataset, SaM-GNN and its variant without the Decoder module achieve a significant improvement (over 26%) over most of the other methods; they outperform the third-best method (i.e., XGBoost + Intermediate Vector) by a large margin of 0.1 in AUC, which reconfirms the superiority of our approach.

Our ablation study (based on comparisons between SaM-GNN and its variants, as shown in Table 1) demonstrates the effectiveness of considering the auxiliary information, i.e., similar credit application records, via graph convolution. While the Decoder module avails SaM-GNN's performance on Home Credit Default Risk dataset, it does not significantly impact the performance on Lending Club dataset—SaM-GNN obtains similar results regardless of whether it incorporates the Decoder module; this suggests the Decoder module is more effective on challenging tasks than easy ones—the classification task on Lending Club Dataset is not liable to overfit even without the Decoder module, given that the dataset contains millions of loan records but only 23 attributes.

4.4   Impact of Sampling Methods

Our datasets have imbalanced distributions over classes, with the ratios of positive to negative samples being 1:11 and 1:4 for Home Credit Default Risk and Lending Club datasets, respectively. Therefore, we test the effectiveness of three sampling strategies [3] in overcoming the class imbalance issue:

Table 2. Performance (AUC) of SaM-GNN under different sampling strategies. δ is the ratio of positive to negative samples after resampling. The best result under each ratio setting is highlighted in boldface.

Dataset	Home Credit			Lending Club		
Ratio (δ)	0.5	0.75	1.0	0.5	0.75	1.0
Upsamping	**0.78665**	**0.78529**	0.76584	**0.96390**	**0.95482**	**0.95394**
Downsampling	0.77398	0.77425	**0.77825**	0.93928	0.91154	0.89367
SMOTE	0.76134	0.76130	0.76307	0.93250	0.95238	0.94642

- **Upsampling**: Upsampling the positive samples and balance the data distribution. Let δ_{up} as the desired ratio of the number of samples in the minority class over the number of samples in the majority class after resampling.
- **Downsampling**: Downsampling the negative samples and balance the data distribution. Let δ_{down} as the ratio of the number of negative samples to the original number after resampling.
- **SMOTE** [5]: Selecting k nearest neighbors in the feature space for the minority class samples, drawing a line between the neighbors in the feature space, and drawing a new sample at a point along that line. Let δ_{smote} as the desired ratio of the number of samples in the minority class over the number of samples in the majority class after resampling.

Specifically, we study the performance of SaM-GNN under varying δ (the ratio of positive to negative samples after resampling). Our results (Table 2) suggest that among the three sampling methods, *upsampling* consistently results in the best AUC on both datasets. Also, for both datasets, the performance of sampling methods tends to fluctuate under varying values of the ratio (δ), indicating the best configurations of δ should be determined empirically rather than by following certain rules.

4.5   Impact of Vector-Fusion Methods

Vector-fusion methods are for fusing the feature representations of categorical and numeric inputs to construct the intermediate vector. We study the impact of two commonly used vector-fusion methods, *concatenation* and *mean-pooling*, on the performance of SaM-GNN.

Our results (Fig. 3) show that *concatenation* (i.e., what we use in SaM-GNN) generally leads to better performance than *mean-pooling*—while both methods result in similar results on Home Credit dataset, *concatenation* consistently outperforms *mean-pooling* on Lending Club dataset. *Mean-pooling* tends to favor larger embedding sizes, obtaining two out of the top-three best results under embedding-size = 50 and 100 on the datasets—larger embedding sizes help improve the network's feature representation ability when *mean-pooling* is applied. The optimal embedding size for *concatenation* is more data-specific. Specifically, *concatenation* requires smaller embedding sizes (e.g., 5, 15, 20) for

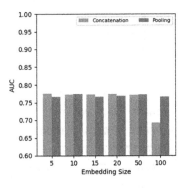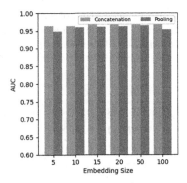

Fig. 3. Performance (AUC) of SaM-GNN with different vector-fusion methods on Home Credit (left) and Lending Club (right) Datasets.

smaller datasets (e.g., Home Credit) yet larger embedding sizes (e.g., 20, 50, 100) for larger datasets (e.g., Lending Club) to deliver best results. This makes sense as Lending Club contains more training samples with lower-dimensionallity, allowing for a 'wider' neural network to excel without overfitting.

4.6 Impact of Multi-task Learning Parameters

We study the performance of our model (i.e., SaM-GNN without the graph convolution module) under varying parameters for multi-task learning α and β while keep the other hyperparameters the same as SaM-GNN. The results on Home Credit Default Risk dataset (Table 3) show the AUC values above the diagonal are generally greater than below, indicating it improves the performance to force the network to pay more attention to obtaining a better intermediate vector representation. We omit to show the results on Lending Club dataset, on which the impact of multi-task learning is less evident.

4.7 Impact of Graph Construction Parameters

We further study the impact of θ_m and θ_u, which affect attribute selection during graph construction and, in turn, determine the final graph structure. To this end, we test the performance of SaM-GNN (without the Decoder module) under $\theta_u \in \{20, 30, 50, 100, 200, 500, 1000\}$ for Home Credit dataset, $\theta_u \in \{5, 10, 20, 30, 50\}$ for Lending Club dataset, and $\theta_m \in \{0.05, 0.1, 0.15, 0.2, 0.25, 0.3\}$. Intuitively, the graph contains more edges under smaller values of θ_u and θ_m. Our results show our model favors denser graphs derived from the datasets—SaM-GNN achieves the best AUC (0.78002 and 0.96652) under the smallest θ_u values (20 and 5) for Home Credit and Lending Club datasets, respectively. θ_m has a slighter impact on the results when compared with θ_u.

Table 3. Performance (AUC) of SaM-GNN (without considering the graph convolution module) under different parameter settings of multi-task learning on Home Credit Default Risk dataset. The best result in each row/column is highlighted in boldface.

α	β					
	0.0	0.2	0.4	0.6	0.8	1.0
0.2	0.74548	0.76145	**0.77629**	0.76835	0.76600	0.75980
0.4	0.75684	0.76086	0.76550	0.76078	0.75654	**0.76702**
0.6	0.74604	0.75617	0.76626	**0.77077**	0.76352	0.76245
0.8	0.75136	0.75099	0.75422	0.76565	**0.76814**	0.76579
1.0	**0.76426**	**0.77107**	0.75140	0.76066	0.75738	**0.77991**

5   Conclusion

In this paper, we propose a self-attention graph neural network with multi-task learning for credit default risk prediction. The network features self-attention and graph convolution to represent heterogeneous data with missing values, along with multi-task learning of classification and decoder modules for model training. Extensive experiments on two real credit default risk prediction datasets demonstrate the superiority of our approach to existing models. Besides, feature representations from our approach help improve the performance of Bagging and Boosting methods.

References

1. Abrahams, C.R., Zhang, M.: Fair Lending Compliance: Intelligence and Implications for Credit Risk Management. Wiley, Hoboken (2008)
2. Addo, P.M., Guegan, D., Hassani, B.: Credit risk analysis using machine and deep learning models. Risks **6**(2), 38 (2018)
3. Aleksandrova, Y.: Comparing performance of machine learning algorithms for default risk prediction in peer to peer lending. TEM J. **10**(1), 133–143 (2021)
4. Breiman, L.: Random forests. Mach. Learn. Arch. **45**(1), 5–32 (2001). https://doi.org/10.1023/a:1010933404324
5. Chawla, N.V., Bowyer, K.W., Hall, L.O., Kegelmeyer, W.P.: Smote: synthetic minority over-sampling technique. J. Artif. Intell. Res. **16**, 321–357 (2002)
6. Chen, T., Guestrin, C.: Xgboost: a scalable tree boosting system. In: 22nd ACM SIGKDD International Conference on Knowledge Discovery and Data Mining, pp. 785–794 (2016)
7. Cheng, H.T., et al.: Wide & deep learning for recommender systems. In: 1st workshop on Deep Learning for Recommender Systems, pp. 7–10 (2016)
8. Coser, A., Maer-Matei, M.M., Albu, C.: Predictive models for loan default risk assessment. Econom. Comput. Econom. Cybernet. Stud. Res. **53**, 149–165 (2019)
9. Cui, Z., et al.: Reinforced KGS reasoning for explainable sequential recommendation. World Wide Web **25**(2), 631–654 (2022)

10. Duan, J.: Financial system modeling using deep neural networks (DNNs) for effective risk assessment and prediction. J. Franklin Inst.-Eng. Appl. Math. **356**(8), 4716–4731 (2019)
11. Huang, C.L., Chen, M.C., Wang, C.J.: Credit scoring with a data mining approach based on support vector machines. Expert Syst. Appl. **33**(4), 847–856 (2007)
12. Ke, G., et al.: LightGBM: a highly efficient gradient boosting decision tree. In: 31st International Conference on Neural Information Processing Systems, vol. 30, pp. 3149–3157 (2017)
13. Kipf, T.N., Welling, M.: Semi-supervised classification with graph convolutional networks. arXiv preprint arXiv:1609.02907 (2016)
14. LeCun, Y., Bengio, Y., Hinton, G.: Deep learning. Nature **521**(7553), 436–444 (2015)
15. Li, G., Shi, Y., Zhang, Z.: P2P default risk prediction based on XGBoost, SVM and RF fusion model. In: 1st International Conference on Business, Economics, Management Science, pp. 470–475 (2019)
16. Li, Y.: Credit risk prediction based on machine learning methods. In: 14th International Conference on Computer Science & Education, pp. 1011–1013. IEEE (2019)
17. Malekipirbazari, M., Aksakalli, V.: Risk assessment in social lending via random forests. Expert Syst. Appl. **42**(10), 4621–4631 (2015)
18. Qiu, Z., Li, Y., Ni, P., Li, G.: Credit risk scoring analysis based on machine learning models. In: 6th International Conference on Information Science and Control Engineering (2019)
19. Schapire, R.E.: The strength of weak learnability. Mach. Learn. **5**(2), 197–227 (1990)
20. Sohn, S.Y., Kim, J.W.: Decision tree-based technology credit scoring for start-up firms: Korean case. Expert Syst. Appl. **39**(4), 4007–4012 (2012)
21. Song, X., Li, J., Lei, Q., Zhao, W., Chen, Y., Mian, A.: Bi-CLKT: bi-graph contrastive learning based knowledge tracing. Knowl.-Based Syst. **241**, 108274 (2022)
22. Song, X., Li, J., Tang, Y., Zhao, T., Chen, Y., Guan, Z.: JKT: a joint graph convolutional network based deep knowledge tracing. Inf. Sci. **580**, 510–523 (2021)
23. Suryanto, H., Guan, C., Voumard, A., Beydoun, G.: Transfer learning in credit risk. In: Brefeld, U., Fromont, E., Hotho, A., Knobbe, A., Maathuis, M., Robardet, C. (eds.) ECML PKDD 2019. LNCS (LNAI), vol. 11908, pp. 483–498. Springer, Cham (2020). https://doi.org/10.1007/978-3-030-46133-1_29
24. Uddin, M.S., Chi, G., Al Janabi, M.A., Habib, T.: Leveraging random forest in micro-enterprises credit risk modelling for accuracy and interpretability. Int. J. Finance Econ. **27**(3), 3713–3729 (2020)
25. Wang, Y., Ni, X.S.: Risk prediction of peer-to-peer lending market by a LSTM model with macroeconomic factor. In: ACM Southeast Conference, pp. 181–187 (2020)
26. Ying, H., et al.: Time-aware metric embedding with asymmetric projection for successive poi recommendation. World Wide Web **22**(5), 2209–2224 (2019)
27. Zhou, X., Zhang, W., Jiang, Y.: Personal credit default prediction model based on convolution neural network. Math. Prob. Eng. (2020)
28. Zhu, L., Qiu, D., Ergu, D., Ying, C., Liu, K.: A study on predicting loan default based on the random forest algorithm. Procedia Comput. Sci. **162**, 503–513 (2019)
29. Óskarsdóttir, M., Bravo, C.: Multilayer network analysis for improved credit risk prediction. Omega-Int. J. Manag. Sci. **105**, 102520 (2021)

Demo Papers

RDF_QDAG in Action: Efficient RDF Data Querying at Scale

Boumediene Saidi[1,2], Houssameddine Yousfi[1,2], Amin Mesmoudi[3(✉)],
Seif-Eddine Benkabou[3], Allel Hadjali[1], and Houcine Matallah[2]

[1] LIAS/ENSMA, Poitiers, France
[2] LIAS/Poitiers University, Poitiers, France
[3] LRIT/Tlemcen University, Tlemcen, Algeria
amin.mesmoudi@univ-poitiers.fr

Abstract. Querying large scale RDF data remains a challenging task, despite the development of several approaches to manage this type of data. Indeed, the "Schemaless" nature of this data prevents from taking advantage of the optimization techniques developed by the database community for decades.

Recently, we introduced RDF_QDAG, a new data management system for RDF, that relies on physical predicate-oriented fragmentation and logical graph exploration. RDF_QDAG offers a good compromise between scalability and performance. It also enables spatial queries to be processed thanks to a suitable extension that improves not only data access but also query evaluation.

In this demonstration, we present through a comprehensible GUI the main features and enhancements of RDF_QDAG. We assist the user in the formulation of queries, and also the interpretation of results according to the type (spatial, graph patterns, etc.) of data processed. We also show the different optimization techniques offered and their impact on performance. We also give the user the possibility to compare RDF_QDAG with a well known and commonly used RDF data management system.

Keywords: RDF · SPARQL · Scalability · Performance · Spatial RDF

1 Introduction

In recent years, we have entered a new era in which our view of data access has completely changed. Indeed, with a new movement called Open data, government services are forced to publish their data in order to give citizens the possibility to evaluate the politics of states in different fields. Open Data is considered today as a very important democratic tool. The Web has also become the privileged space for publishing government data, which is in line with W3C's vision that consists in transforming the classical Web of "documents" into a Web of "data". W3C even recommends tools to make it easier to publish and use data on the Web. Moreover, RDF and SPARQL are considered as "the standards" for

R. Chbeir et al. (Eds.): WISE 2022, LNCS 13724, pp. 633–640, 2022.
https://doi.org/10.1007/978-3-031-20891-1_45

data representation and querying in this new Web. In this vein, we are seeing a proliferation of RDF data sources on the Web. According to the cloud LOD, the number of RDF datasets increased from 12 in 2007 to 1,301 in 2021. This success is related to the ease of data representation in RDF.

In order to ensure efficient management of large-scale RDF data, we have proposed RDF_QDAG [5,11]. It relies on logical graph exploration, which avoids reconstructing query results using very expensive joins. In an effort to support large scale datasets without losing the very important notion of neighborhood, predicate-based fragmentation has also been adopted [5]. On top of graph matching, RDF_QDAG supports the processing of other operators such as Wildcard filtering, Spatial filtering, aggregation and sorting.

In this work, we demonstrate RDF_QDAG through a comprehensible GUI that illustrates different features alongside the performance and the scalability. We also discuss several key design decisions. The contributions of this work are as follows:

- We offer to the user the ability to run rich and complex SPARQL queries that cover the Basic Graph Pattern Matching, Aggregation, Wild Cards and Spatial operators on large scale data.
- We enable users to conduct comprehensive evaluation of RDF_QDAG and its optimization strategies. We give the user the possibility to compare RDF_QDAG with existing RDF data management systems.
- We simplify the process of formulating queries and interpreting data with a complete graphical interface, adapted to different types of data.

The system is publicly available at https://qdag.lias-lab.fr and the demonstration video is available at https://youtu.be/IIJTWwnxfEI.

The rest of the paper is organized as follows. We first provide an overview of RDF_QDAG in Sect. 2. We then present our proposed demonstration scenarios in Sect. 3, followed by a short discussion on related work (Sect. 4).

2   Main Features of RDF_QDAG

In this section we describe key concepts and techniques used in RDF_QDAG. Full details can be found in our paper by Khelil et al. [5].

2.1   Data Loading

Our goal was to take advantage of the notion of neighborhood between the nodes of the RDF logical graph, which avoids the use of intensive joins when evaluating queries. We decided to rely on a predicate-based fragmentation technique. In particular the graph is partitioned into Data Stars. A Data Star regroups triples with the same object or subject (head of the Data Star). Data Stars with the same characteristic set [6] are grouped in a fragment that is indexed and compressed separately.

Data loading is performed through several stages: Fragmentation, Entity linking, dictionary construction and statistics collection. The fragmenter ensures the extraction of Data Stars and groups them into fragments. The entity linker allows associating to each node the id of the fragment that groups its incoming arcs and the id of the fragment that groups its outgoing arcs. These links are necessary for our evaluation strategy that relies on logical graph exploration. The dictionary constructor allows to replace strings associated to the graph nodes with ids. Finally, statistics on fragments are collected to be used later for optimization strategies we propose.

2.2   Data Storage

Each fragment is stored as a clustered B+Tree. We rely also on an Rtree for spatial data. Our indexes are implemented using C++ in order to offer the best possible performance. A Fragment manager is integrated in order to manage the access to fragments. Finally, the dictionary engine manages the encoding/decoding of String values. It also offers the possibility to search String values using regular expressions.

2.3   Query Processing

On top of queries with BGP (Basic Graph Pattern), RDF_QDAG supports a wide variety of processing such as Wildcard filtering, Spatial filtering, grouping and sorting. Query evaluation relies on logical graph exploration. Same as the partitioning of the data into stars, the query is also fragmented into star queries based on the predicate set. The logical exploration consists firstly on finding Data Stars that match the first star query, then exploring the graph outward to match the following star queries. Based on this logic, the execution plan is an ordered list of star queries. An execution plan does not only contain matching operators related to star queries, but also filtering operators (numerical, wildcard and spatial), sorting and grouping operators.

For query evaluation, we have opted for personalized processing for each query. RDF_QDAG selects a set of operators to create a flow allowing to answer the query. For each star query, we create a data extractor and a Star query matcher. Data extractor allows to interact with the fragments in order to load relevant Data Stars. The star query matcher on the other hand allows to find mappings for the variables mentioned in the Star query. Numerical filters are taken into account by the star query matcher. Spatial and wildcard operators are added to the flow in the case of spatial or regular expression filtering. A Spatial operator needs to communicate with the geographical engine and the dictionary. We rely on CGAL[1] and JTS[2] as geo-engines. The wildcard filter interacts with the dictionary to decode the String values. In the case of the Group By (or Order By) clause, a grouping (or sorting) component is added to

---

[1]   https://www.cgal.org/.

[2]   https://github.com/locationtech/jts.

the flow. We have also added three write operators (file, network and console) to send results to the client.

2.4   Query Scheduling

RDF_QDAG brings together several execution and optimization strategies. With respect to query evaluation, we rely on a handler, based on the Volcano model [4]. It manages the execution of evaluation operators based on rules related to buffers fill rates. Indeed, RDF_QDAG associates buffers to each operator, which can be both producer/consumer. For spatial data, we propose two execution strategies. The first one "RDF first" consists in processing the BGP part first, the spatial filters are applied after finding mapping of the variables. On the other hand, the "Spatial first" strategy allows to take advantage of the Rtree index by applying a spatial filter before processing the BGP part of the query.

RDF_QDAG also offers several optimization strategies. First of all, we decide on the order of star queries evaluation. Overall, this order makes it possible to guide the exploration of the graph. We propose two strategies allowing to choose this order: a Heuristics one based on the work by Tsialiamanis et al. [9] and GoFast [11]. We also propose a pruning algorithm allowing to eliminate the fragments that do not contribute to the construction of the final results.

3   Demonstration Overview

We now describe how we plan to show to the attendees the main advantages of RDF_QDAG. First, we focus on the different strategies allowing RDF_QDAG to leverage a good compromise between scalabilty and performance. We provide an intuitive GUI to show the impact of the different strategies on performance. Then, we introduce RDF_QDAG's spatial query processing, backed by the different evaluation and optimization strategies.

3.1   Scenario 1: Large Scale Query Processing

In this scenario we show how the user can interact with the system. We particularly discuss the utilization of the Command line and the Web interfaces. We also present an interpretation of our findings.

Part 1: Command Line Data Loading and Query Execution. A user can rely on the "rdf_loader" script to load a new database. This script takes two parameters, namely the location of raw data (the RDF NT file) and the eventual location of the binary data after loading. We will show the different stages of loading: fragmentation, Entity linking, dictionary construction and statistics collection. For demonstration purposes, we will rely on a small dataset, i.e., Watdiv with 100k triples. To run queries in this mode, we make use of the java program gquery.jar, which takes the data location and the SPARQL query file as parameters. This program takes other optional parameters like the name of the optimizer and the use of the pruning technique.

Part 2: Selection of Evaluation Parameters. Figure 1 shows the GUI allowing to run a query using certain parameters. We give the user the possibility to choose a dataset. We preloaded three datasets: Yago (a real dataset with 210 million triples), Watdiv100M (a synthetic dataset with 100 million triples) and Watdiv1B (a synthetic dataset with 1 billion triples). A user can use a predefined query or define a custom one using the provided text area. We offer the possibility to visualize the BGP part of the query as shown in Fig. 1. The user can also choose between two optimizers, i.e., heuristic and GoFast, and to enable the pruner. For this demonstration, we offer the possibility to compare the different strategies of RDF_QDAG with an existing system (Virtuoso), a commercial triple store that supports BGP, WildCard, Aggregation, Sorting and Spatial queries.

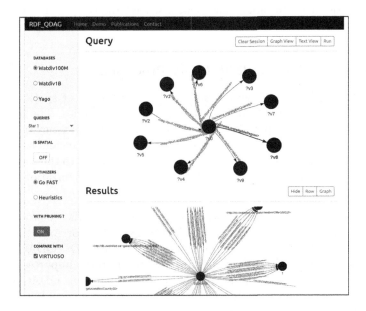

Fig. 1. Screenshot of visualization of a query and its results using RDF_QDAG

Part 3: Presentation of Results. By clicking on the run button, the user can both view the query results and also compare the performance against the Virtuoso system or with other RDF_QDAG optimization strategies. The user can choose the type of results visualization he wants. We offer to display the results in the form of a graph, table or Map (see Fig. 3). In the same visual representation, we plot different runs of the same query using different execution parameters (optimizers and pruning) to easily compare between them. Figure 2 shows execution time comparison for the Complex_1 query on Watdiv100M. We considered four (4) configurations for RDF_QDAG with a comparison with Virtuoso. One can see that RDF_QDAG outperforms Virtuoso even when we disable pruning and rely on the heuristic-based optimizer.

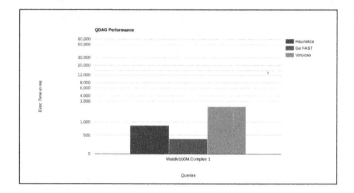

Fig. 2. Screenshot of execution time comparison for the complex_1 query on Watdiv(100M) using RDF_QDAG and Virtuoso

3.2 Scenario 2: Spatial RDF Query Processing

We enhanced RDF_QDAG with a spatial extension to inject spatial awareness into the system and enable support for spatial RDF queries. The focus is not only on the support of spatial operators but also on the efficiency of processing them while keeping a good compromise between performance and scalability. In what follows, we present the tools provided by RDF_QDAG to the users enabling them to process spatial data. We will also present the optimization techniques used for a better user experience.

Part 1: Spatial RDF Data Loading. We present in this scenario, the additional spatial files generated in the loading process. Similar to Scenario 1, the user selects the database file to import into the system. RDF_QDAG will automatically detect the existence of spatial information in the imported files based on the presence of spatial predicates. Using this logic, RDF_QDAG saves spatial objects separately in an R-Tree index. This R-tree is an additional access method that can be used to improve performance while running spatial queries. Relevant statistics and information about the data are also collected in the loading process to serve the same purpose. All the additional spatial processing steps are transparent to the user leading to a simplified loading process.

Part 2: GeoSPARQL Query Processing. Once the data is successfully loaded, the user can run spatial RDF queries. In this context, RDF_QDAG provides support for GeoSPARQL queries. Figure 3 gives an example of a GeoSparql intersection query. This query is composed of two parts: the BGP part and the spatial filter part.

RDF_QDAG uses two different strategies to evaluate GeoSPARQL queries (RDF-first strategy and Spatial first strategy). Depending on the selectivity of each part of the query, one strategy can perform better than the other. RDF_QDAG supports both of them to ensure the best possible performance in each case. In the RDF-first strategy, RDF_QDAG starts by performing graph matching operations. Then the spatial objects are retrieved and the spatial filter is evaluated. On the other hand, in the spatial-first strategy, the spatial filter is evaluated first. In this case, we utilize the R-tree index to optimize spatial data access. The results of the spatial filter are considered the start points for the graph exploration.

In the user interface, the user can enable pruning while processing complex queries as shown in Fig. 1. We give the user control over this parameter since pruning is not necessary for simple queries and light workloads. If this option is enabled, an additional pruning step is performed to eliminate non-relevant intermediary results early on in the process. On top of graph pruning, in the case of GeoSparql queries, spatial object distribution and other collected information are used in the pruning.

Part 3: Presentation of Results. RDF-QDAG provides a table view and a graph view of the results. In the case of GeoSPARQL queries, the spatial objects can be part of the results depending on the query provided by the user. As is the case in the earlier example query, mappings of the variable "?g" are spatial objects. Due to this, RDF-QDAG offers a map view to display the spatial objects as shown in Fig. 3.

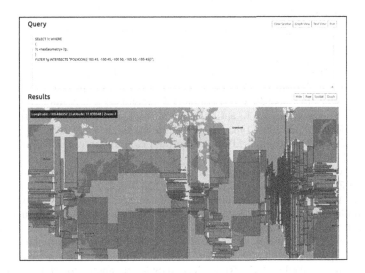

Fig. 3. Screenshot of spatial data visualization

The performance is one of the strong points of RDF-QDAG. In the case of GeoSparql, the user can plot the results of both evaluation strategies and compare them with Virtuoso.

4   Related Work

Many systems were then proposed to respond effectively to SPARQL queries. First approaches (e.g., Virtuoso [3]) tried to take advantage of existing systems (mainly relational) to quickly respond to RDF data management needs. Such solutions could not provide acceptable performance. The following generation approaches (e.g., RDF-3X [7] and gStore [10]) are built "from scratch" by revisiting traditional storage, query evaluation and optimization strategies. Although such approaches may have improved performance, they suffer from Scalability issues. On top of that, they are designed to take into account only the BGP (Basic Graph Pattern) of SPARQL queries. Although native systems have been designed especially for RDF data management, most approaches can hardly be extended to take into account advanced operators of SPARQL.

In order to guarantee scalability, systems (e.g., MIDAS-RDF [8], CliqueSquare [2] and SparkRDF [1]) based on distributed architectures have been proposed. The major drawback of distributed approaches is their inability to respond effectively to certain queries due to the network overhead.

RDF_QDAG is the system we propose to ensure both performance and scalability. It is built on top of the formal framework presented firstly by Khelil et al. [5]. On the other hand, the optimization techniques used are presented in our previous paper by Zouaghi et al. [11].

References

1. Chen, X., Chen, H., Zhang, N., Zhang, S.: SparkRDF: elastic discreted RDF graph processing engine with distributed memory. In: WI-IAT, pp. 292–300 (2015)
2. Djahandideh, B., Goasdoué, F., Kaoudi, Z., Manolescu, I., Quiané-Ruiz, J., Zampetakis, S.: CliqueSquare in action: flat plans for massively parallel RDF queries. In: ICDE 2015, pp. 1432–1435. IEEE Computer Society (2015)
3. Erling, O.: Virtuoso, a hybrid RDBMS/graph column store. IEEE Data Eng. Bull. **35**(1), 3–8 (2012)
4. Graefe, G.: Volcano/SPL minus/an extensible and parallel query evaluation system. IEEE Trans. Knowl. Data Eng. **6**(1), 120–135 (1994)
5. Khelil, A., Mesmoudi, A., Galicia, J., Bellatreche, L., Hacid, M.S., Coquery, E.: Combining graph exploration and fragmentation for scalable RDF query processing. Inf. Syst. Front. **23**(1), 165–183 (2021)
6. Neumann, T., Moerkotte, G.: Characteristic sets: accurate cardinality estimation for RDF queries with multiple joins. In: Proceedings of ICDE, pp. 984–994 (2011)
7. Neumann, T., Weikum, G.: RDF-3X: a RISC-style engine for RDF. Proc. VLDB Endow. **1**(1), 647–659 (2008)
8. Tsatsanifos, G., Sacharidis, D., Sellis, T.K.: On enhancing scalability for distributed RDF/S stores. In: EDBT 2011, pp. 141–152. ACM (2011)
9. Tsialiamanis, P., Sidirourgos, L., Fundulaki, I., Christophides, V., Boncz, P.A.: Heuristics-based query optimisation for SPARQL. In: EDBT, pp. 324–335 (2012)
10. Zou, L., Mo, J., Chen, L., Özsu, M.T., Zhao, D.: gStore: answering SPARQL queries via subgraph matching. Proc. VLDB Endow. **4**(8), 482–493 (2011)
11. Zouaghi, I., Mesmoudi, A., Galicia, J., Bellatreche, L., Aguili, T.: GoFast: graph-based optimization for efficient and scalable query evaluation. Inf. Syst. **99**, 101738 (2021)

Multi-source Logistics Data Management Architecture

Rongtao Qian, Tao Zou, Jiali Mao$^{(\boxtimes)}$, and Kaixuan Zhu

East China Normal University, Shanghai, China
{51215903010,51205903036,51215903072}@stu.ecnu.edu.cn,
jlmao@dase.ecnu.edu.cn

Abstract. As the logistics platform gained in popularity, extreme volume of logistics data has been generated and is continuously growing in size. It becomes a pain point to efficiently query and analyze for different sources of logistics. However, most of the existing distributed methods aim at managing a single-source data like spatial data or trajectory data and build spatial-temporal indexes to improve query efficiency. Thus it is in urgent need of designing an efficient data management architecture for supporting query or analysis on multi-source logistics data. On the basis of distributed environment, we first split massive logistics data into partitions in terms of time dimension, and apply hash algorithm and broadcast mechanism for each partition to accelerate data fusion. Further, we obtain multi-attribute trajectories by regarding the property of other sources of data as the attributes related to the trajectories, and build a distributed index to proliferate the efficiency of querying for logistics data. Finally, comparative experiments are conducted to demonstrate the advantages of our proposal, and a demo system is built for a logistics platform to showcase the effectiveness of our proposal.

Keywords: Data fusion · Multi-attributes trajectories · Spatio-temporal attribute index

1 Introduction

With the extensive application of logistics platform, a large amount of logistics data like waybill data and trucks' trajectory data has been generated and kept growing. Based upon querying and analyzing for these logistics data, various decision tasks such as vehicle scheduling and the matching between cargoes and trucks, can be finished. Take a logistics platform of an Iron and steel Group (or *JCZH* for short) as an example, *JCZH* has more than 80,000 registered trucks, and transports 14 million tons of steel products every year. To finish more than 1200 cargo transporting tasks (i.e. waybills) each day, *JCZH* needs to schedule sufficient number of trucks in advance, and handles more than 1000 requests for the trajectory of truck that transports cargoes. It not only involves spatial-temporal joining operations for trajectory data of GB level, but also needs to join with other source of data like waybill data multiple times.

© The Author(s), under exclusive license to Springer Nature Switzerland AG 2022
R. Chbeir et al. (Eds.): WISE 2022, LNCS 13724, pp. 641–649, 2022.
https://doi.org/10.1007/978-3-031-20891-1_46

How to effectively manage multi-source logistics data to guarantee high-efficiency implementing of querying or analysis task. Since the existing methods tend to manage a single-source data like spatial data or trajectory data [2,5,7,9], there are no ready-made solutions for logistics data management. Therefore, it necessitates to design an appropriate method to manage multi-source logistics data, including storing, joining and indexing for them. Recently, such distributed frameworks as Apache Hadoop and Apache Spark have been proved effective for handling a large amount of data. Compared with Hadoop that stores intermediate result on the disk, Spark provides an efficient in-memory data structure for data processing, called Resilient Distributed Datasets (or RDDs for short), which reduces lots of I/O and achieve greater performance. Till now, there are some spatial data management system based on Spark like GeoSpark [9] and Simba [7], but they only support spatial operations. We use Spark engine and implement spatial-temporal queries for logistics data. To support high-frequency query requests for multi-source logistics data, we need to fuse trajectory data with other sources of data including waybill data, truck data and cargo data. To this end, there are some unique challenges we need to address.

Challenge I: How to fuse multiple sources of logistics data? For instance, to answer the query request for the waybill of one given trajectory, we have to scan whole waybill dataset to find the waybill corresponding to that trajectory. It takes a significant amount of query time especially when the number of waybill data and trajectory data is huge. Intuitively, it can be solved by implementing joining operations for different data sets, but it is computationally expensive to directly join different massive data sets. The existing spatial-temporal join methods based on Spark [4,6] did not consider joining trajectory data with other sources of logistics data. Based upon analyzing the characteristics of logistics data, we introduce the strategy of divide-and-conquer and divide the logistics data into partitions according to the time dimension. For each partition, we leverage hash algorithm [3] and broadcast mechanism [1] to accelerate data fusion in a distributed environment.

Challenge II: How to efficiently query the fused logistics data? The existing methods [5,7,9] built indexes such as R-tree and Quad-tree based on Spark to improve efficiency of querying for trajectory data. Yet they do not focus on proliferating efficiency of associative querying for trajectory data and other sources of data. Xu [8] proposed a hybrid index to answer range query on multi-attributes trajectories. But it only supports relational databases and is not scalable for dealing with large amount of data. To tackle the issue of querying for the fused logistics data, we treat the information of other sources of data as the attributes related to the trajectories. In addition, to query huge amount of trajectories with attributes, we propose a novel spatial-temporal attribute index.

2   System Overview

The framework of our system is shown in Fig. 1. It has four modules including data source, preprocessing, indexing and querying. In data source module, collected data is stored on distributed system. In data preprocessing module, point data is converted into trajectory data and joined with waybill data, and then we can obtain trajectory with its corresponding attributes. In index module, spatio-temporal index is built for multi-attribute trajectories. At last, different types of query are supported in query module.

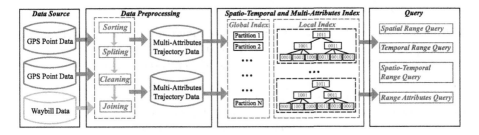

Fig. 1. Architecture of our logistics data management system.

2.1   Data Source

GPS Point Data. As shown in Fig. 2(a), GPS point data contains longitude, latitude, timestamp and truck ID.

Row No.	Truck ID	Longitude	Latitude	Timestamp
1	LU123	119.325842	35.698741	2021-08-31 12:32:12
2	HU223	118.125863	36.013321	2021-08-31 12:32:17
4	LU123	119.325745	35.702587	2021-08-31 12:30:54
...	...	...	...	...
125698	LU123	120.368934	36.366987	2021-09-07 09:13:52
...	...	...	...	...

(a)

Row No.	Waybill No.	Truck ID	Product Name	Starting City	Ending City	Loading Date	Return Bill Date
1	DD2743	LU123	Steal	RiZhao	QingDao	2021-07-18 09:30:12	2021-07-20 07:06:54
2	DD7842	HU887	Steel	RiZhao	JiNan	2021-07-19 15:00:01	2021-07-21 16:02:58
3	CG3231	LU123	Coal	QingDao	RiZhao	2021-08-03 09:32:12	2021-08-06 12:14:29
4	CG1234	HU223	Conch	WeiFang	RiZhao	2021-08-31 12:32:12	2021-09-01 21:18:45
...	...	...	...	...	...	...	...

(b)

Fig. 2. Samples of trajectory data and waybill data.

Waybill Data. As shown in Fig. 2(b), waybill data contains textual attributes, temporal attributes and truck ID. Textual attributes are the detail information of the waybill, including type of product the truck transported, starting city, destination city and so on. Temporal attributes record the start time and end time of this transportation task.

Trajectory Data. A trajectory is a sequence of GPS points sorted by timestamp. Besides truck ID, there is no other waybill data information.

Logistics Multi-attributes Trajectory Data. It refers to the data after fusing trajectory data with waybill data. Logistics multi-attributes trajectories contain not only trajectory point list, but also its corresponding logistic waybill information such as the product type, departure city, destination city, company and so on. In the following, we call it as multi-attributes trajectories for short.

In data source module, considering the large scale of these data, we use distributed database such as HBase or Hadoop Distributed File System (HDFS) directly to store them. APIs are supported by Spark to read data from HBase or HDFS conveniently.

2.2 Data Preprocessing

We can see from Fig. 2(a) that GPS points of different trucks are distributed in disorder, so we have to process these data and convert them into trajectories. Specifically, firstly we aggregate these points by their truck ID and then sort them by their timestamp, so that we obtain the trajectory point sequence of each truck. Secondly, we split the sequence into many trajectories if the timestamp interval between two trajectory points is too long. Thirdly, for each split trajectory, we will detect and remove outliers. After cleaning, we get trajectories with no waybill information. Next, we will join trajectory data with waybill data and generate multi-attributes trajectories.

Commonly, because trajectory data does not contain waybill ID, joining trajectory data and waybill data should consider both temporal range and truck ID. Applying existing distributed join algorithm directly cannot avoid linear scanning. In order to improve the efficiency of joining the trajectory corresponding to the waybill, we propose a novel joining algorithm. Firstly, we obtain the truck ID of the trajectory to be joined and generate a truck ID set by applying *aggregate* operator in Spark. Secondly, we filter waybill data according to whether the truck ID of the waybill in the truck ID set by hash algorithm. Thirdly, we broadcast these filtered waybill to each partition. Then we can make join in each partition locally without data transmission between partitions. Fourthly, for trajectory in each partition, we utilize a hash function again to find the list of waybills with the same truck ID of the trajectory. Lastly, we use a binary search algorithm to find the corresponding waybill according to the start time of the trajectory and the loading time of the waybill.

The reasons why our join method is efficient are following. Firstly, we filter the irrelevant waybill data through hash algorithm. The size of the remaining waybill data used for further join is greatly small. Secondly, broadcasting these smaller amount of waybill data can avoid time-consuming shuffle operation. Lastly, with hash technology and binary search in each partition, we can efficiently join trajectories with the smaller amount of waybills.

2.3 Indexing

Multi-attributes trajectories are generated after processing. Our system will build a two level index on them.

The temporal dimension is chosen as the global index. Because the temporal dimension has stronger filtering properties than the space dimension. Truck drivers often travel a long distance, so many trajectories are distributed in the same spatial region. Using the spatial global index cannot filter out trajectories that are not related to the query. If we firstly search according to temporal

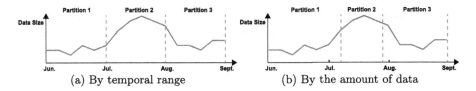

(a) By temporal range   (b) By the amount of data

Fig. 3. An example of how to partition a global index

dimension, larger amount of data will be filtered, which will greatly improve our query efficiency. We partition trajectories according their start time. For example, we store three months of trajectories and plan to store them into three partitions. A common strategy is distribute each month of data to one partition. However, in reality, the amount of data varies greatly each month. As shown in Fig. 3(a) the amount of trajectory data in July is larger than that in June and August. If we just distribute data according which month it belongs may cause skew. Data skew will lead to inefficiency in distributed systems, so we have to optimize the distribution of trajectory data. If data of one month is larger and that of its neighbouring months is smaller than average, we will distribute the temporal adjacent part of data to its neighbouring partitions. As shown in Fig 3(b), we distribute parts of trajectory data of July to partition 1 and partition 3, and the temporal range of data in each partition is continuous. Base on our proposed partition policy, when a temporal query comes, we will firstly find the partitions whose temporal range intersect with the temporal range of the query.

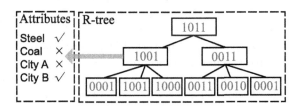

Fig. 4. Spatio-temporal attribute local index.

In each partition, we build local index to accelerate query. We use 3D R-tree to index trajectory data. We modify the data structure of R-tree to make it able to preserve attributes information. In the R-tree node, besides its spatio-temporal range, we add a bitset maintaining its attributes. Every bit in the bitset corresponds to an attribute, 1 indicates including the attribute and 0 indicates excluding the attribute. For example, as shown in Fig. 4, the bitset of the left node in second level encodes as 1001, which means including attributes of steel and city B. It indicates that there are trajectories containing these attributes in the leaf node of this node. Corresponding to the information in the waybill, these trajectories were transporting steel and their destination is city B.

The reason why we use bitset to indicate attributes are as follows. Firstly, bitset needs less storage space. Instead of using words of attributes directly, using bitset can save a lot of storage. For example, supposing that we have 256 attributes including types of products, names of destination cities and so on, we only need 32 byte storage space, which is only 8 size of int type. Secondly, we can prune by spatio-temporal range and attributes information at the same time. By this way, we can prune more nodes when searching the tree and accelerate the query process. The detail of query process will be explained in the next section. Last but not least, with bitset, we can prune more effectively and efficiently based on attributes. In the next step, we can easily judge whether nodes of R-tree contains attributes of queries by making a bitset intersection of the query and R-tree nodes. Compared by scanning each trajectory to find those meeting query conditions, using bitset can be effective. The intersection base on bits is a fast operation for computers, which makes our index more efficient.

2.4 Querying

In the beginning, we give the definition of the queries supported by our logistics data management system. We make T represents the universal set of multi-attributes trajectories.

Spatio-Temporal Range Query. Given a spatial range Q_s and a temporal range Q_t, the query returns a set of trajectories $T_q \subseteq T$, such that $\forall t \in T_q$: (i) spatial range of t is in Q_s; (ii) temporal range of t is in Q_t.

Range Attributes Query. Based on range queries with a spatio-temporal range Q_{st}, given a set of attributes Q_a, the query returns a set of trajectories $T_q \subseteq T$, such that $\forall t \in T_q$: (i) attributes of t is in Q_a; (ii) spatio-temporal range of t is in Q_{st}.

Here, we take spatio-temporal range attributes query for example to illustrate the query process with the index we propose.

Firstly, global index will find the partitions for further search according to the temporal range of the query. If users does not set temporal range, we have to search every partition to get the results. Next, in each partition, breadth first search is applied to search the R-tree. When searching the R-tree, we will prune nodes by not only spatio-temporal range but also bitsets of attributes. Specifically, if there is no intersection between the spatio-temporal range of the R-tree node and that of the query, we will prune this node and its children nodes. And if the intersection of the bitset of the query and that of R-tree node is all 0, we prune too. Lastly, the results in each partition are collected and sent to the client.

3 Demonstration

The web user interface of our logistics data management system is shown and the efficiency is evaluated by comparison experiments in the section.

Fig. 5. Web user interface of our logistics data management system.

3.1   User Interface

The web user interface is shown in Fig. 5. Users can input spatial range, temporal range and waybill information of the query. Note that the attributes can be added or reduced according the demand of users. If users doesn't set any attribute, system will search according to the spatio-temporal range by default. Our global index and local index still work, just not pruning according to attributes. Also, if user doesn't input spatial or temporal range, the query range is the corresponding minimum or maximum value. We support download function so that users can download the results as files and use them as data source for other tasks.

3.2   Comparison Experiment

We compare our join method and multi-attributes query with others to prove high performance of our system. The dataset we use is from *JCZH*. The temporal range of data is from May 2021 to February 2022. The size of waybill data is 1.5 GB and the size of GPS point data is up to 7.3 GB. The experimental environment consists of 3 cloud server nodes with 8 cores, 32 GB memory. Each node runs CentOS 7.5 with Java 1.8 and Spark 3.0.0.

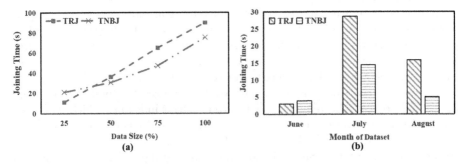

Fig. 6. The comparative results of join methods.

We compare our TNBJ (truck number broadcast join) method with [6], which we call TRJ (Temporal Range Join). TRJ divides trajectory data and waybill data into different partitions based on temporal range. Then it joins those trajectory data and waybill data, the temporal range of whose partitions is intersecting.

As we can see from Fig. 6(a), when data size is relatively small, like 25%, TRJ needs less time to finish joining. While with the increasing of data size, the joining time of TRJ grows faster than our method. This confirms that our method is more effective to deal with large amounts of data. Figure 6(b) shows the joining time of the two methods for different months. The data size of the trajectory data in June, July and August is 901 MB, 2.11 G and 852 MB respectively. The data size for June and August is similar, but their joining time by TRJ is quite different. Because in the real logistics scenario, the temporal distribution of trajectory data is uneven, partitioning by temporal range will induce data skew, which causes the low performance of TRJ. Moreover, with the data size growing, the amounts of truck numbers may not increase, which is limited for a logistics company. Therefore, the broadcast value in our method will not occupy more memory.

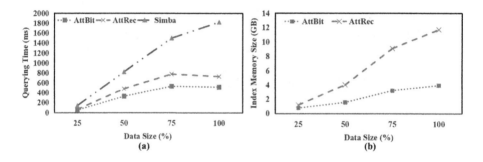

Fig. 7. The comparative results of range attributes queries.

Also, we compare the performance of our range attributes query method with that of other two methods. One method we compare is Simba [7]. Since Simba can only support spatial index, it has to apply *filter* operator in Spark when dealing with temporal range and attributes queries. Another method we compare is AttRec [8]. However AttRec is based on relational database. If we compare our method with AttRec directly, there is no doubt that our system based on Spark has a better performance than AttRec due to the power of distributed process ability. We apply AttRec in our local index to make a comparison. Note that, AttBit shown in Fig. 7 refers to our proposed method.

As we observe from Fig. 7(a), our AttBit achieves the best performance. Simba has to scan the remaining data after spatial indexing, which causes its low performance. Since AttRec is outside of R-tree and has larger memory size, it doesn't perform better than AttBit. Figure 7(b) shows the memory size of AttRec and our AttBit. Simba is not shown in the figure because it does not contain attribute index. With the data size increasing, AttRec needs more memory space because it stores bitmaps of all nodes for each attribute, while our method only uses one bitset for each node to maintain all attributes.

References

1. Chowdhury, M., Zaharia, M., Stoica, I.: Performance and scalability of broadcast in spark (2014)
2. Li, R. and He, H., Wang, R., Huang, Y., Zheng, Y.: JUST: JD urban spatio-temporal data engine. In: ICDE, pp. 1558–1569 (2020)
3. Liu, H., Xiao, J., Peng, F.: Scalable hash ripple join on spark. In: ICPADS, pp. 419–428 (2017)
4. Qiao, B., Hu, B., Zhu, J., Wu, G., Giraud-Carrier, C., Wang, G.: A top-k spatial join querying processing algorithm based on spark. Inf. Syst. **87**, 101419 (2020)
5. Shang, Z., Li, G., Bao, Z.: DITA: distributed in-memory trajectory analytics. In: SIGMOD, pp. 725–740 (2018)
6. Whitman, R.T., Marsh, B.G., Park, M.B., Hoel, E.G.: Distributed spatial and spatio-temporal join on apache spark. ACM Trans. Spat. Algorithms Syst. **5**(1), 1–28 (2019)
7. Xie, D., Li, F., Yao, B., Li, G., Zhou, L., Guo, M.: Simba: efficient in-memory spatial analytics. In: SIGMOD, pp. 1071–1085 (2016)
8. Xu, J., Lu, H., Güting, R.H.: Range queries on multi-attribute trajectories. IEEE Trans. Knowl. Data Eng. **30**(6), 1206–1211 (2017)
9. Yu, J., Wu, J., Sarwat, M.: A demonstration of GeoSpark: a cluster computing framework for processing big spatial data. In: ICDE, pp. 1410–1413 (2016)

TCPMS-FCP: A Traffic Congestion Pattern Mining System Based on Spatio-Temporal Fuzzy Co-location Patterns

Xiaoxu Wang[1], Jialong Wang[2], Lizhen Wang[1,2(✉)], Shan Wang[1], and Lei Ding[1]

[1] Department of Computer Science and Engineering, Dianchi College of Yunnan University, Kunming 650100, China
lzhwang@ynu.edu.cn
[2] School of Information Science and Engineering, Yunnan University, Kunming 650500, China

Abstract. Mining traffic congestion patterns is important for planning travel routes and optimizing traffic control in urban areas. However, existing methods ignore the spatio-temporal attributes of traffic flow data and the fuzziness of the concept of congestion itself, leading to defects and inaccuracies in the definition of traffic congestion. To this end, a novel traffic congestion pattern on the basis of spatio-temporal fuzzy co-location pattern is proposed, and a traffic congestion pattern mining system, named TCPMS-FCP, is developed. With TCPMS-FCP, travelers can choose appropriate travel routes to reduce travel time, while traffic management agencies can use the mined congestion patterns to improve the efficiency of traffic management and the level of traffic congestion control.

Keywords: Traffic congestion pattern mining · TCPMS-FCP · Spatio-temporal · Fuzzy

1 Introduction

Traffic congestion has received much attention in recent years due to its great impact on people's daily life [1]. The widely available sensors, such as GPS receivers and traffic cameras, provide rich data for mobile data analysis in urban areas. Fine grained traffic congestion pattern discovery on roads in urban cities can help people schedule travel routes in advance, and assist traffic control to relieve traffic pressure [2, 3]. Most existing methods are based on deep learning models, which cannot provide good interpretability [4, 5]. And also, the existing definition of traffic congestion is defective and inaccurate due to ignoring the spatio-temporal attributes of traffic flow data and the fuzziness of the concept of congestion itself, which leads to discovering unsatisfactory results [6].

Spatial co-location pattern mining, as one of the most important topics in the field of spatial data mining, aims to discover a subset of spatial features whose instances are frequently located together in geographic space. Spatial co-location patterns can be applied in all aspects of society, such as transportation, public health, and various location-based services [7, 8].

R. Chbeir et al. (Eds.): WISE 2022, LNCS 13724, pp. 650–657, 2022.
https://doi.org/10.1007/978-3-031-20891-1_47

In this paper, we propose a traffic congestion pattern named spatio-temporal co-location fuzzy congestion pattern (FuConPattern in short) by considering the "time", "space" and "fuzziness" of traffic flow data. Traffic congestion patterns take each road and the road speed in each time slice as features and instances, respectively. It computes the proximity in time as well as geographic space based on spatial co-location patterns, and fuzzes traffic congestion by a fuzzy membership function, making the analysis of road congestion more objective and accurate. Two algorithms, prevalent FuConPattern mining algorithm (STF) and maximal prevalent FuConPattern compress algorithm (MP), are proposed. STF can discover all traffic congestion patterns from traffic flow data within a time period specified by the user. MP can discover all maximal traffic congestion patterns from the traffic congestion patterns found by STF.

In order to visually display road congestion coming from the traffic flow data, we design and develop a Traffic Congestion Pattern Mining System (TCPMS-FCP) to mine and show the mined traffic congestion patterns to reflect the congestion state of each road over time. This system provides users with a concise interactive interface. Users can input relevant parameters according to their own requirements and clearly see the resulting congestion patterns displayed dynamically over the time period. Obviously, TCPMS-FCP can provide decision support and guidance for congestion prediction.

2 System Overview

Figure 1 shows the framework description of TCPMS-FCP and its details are as follows. Firstly, the user inputs traffic flow data into TCPMS-FCP, and sets three mining parameters: the fuzziness threshold $f\_threshold$, the time threshold $t\_threshold$, and the minimum prevalence threshold min_prev. Then, TCPMS-FCP performs STF and MP to get all maximal prevalent FuConPatterns in the background of the system. Finally, TCPMS-FCP outputs mining results, which are dynamically displayed according to the divided time periods. Each module of the system is described as below.

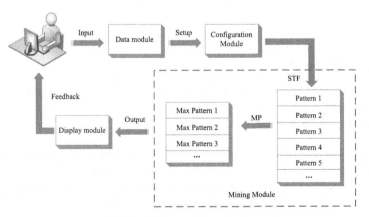

Fig. 1. Framework description

2.1 Data Module

The data module is responsible for obtaining road network information files and road topology relationship files, and then parsing the information stored in these files, such as latitude and longitude of GPS, road topology, time series, the speed collected by sensors, etc.

2.2 Configuration Module

The configuration module allows the user to input the traffic flow data and set the parameters *f_threshold*, *t_threshold*, and *min_prev* required for the subsequent mining process. Some definitions about fuzzy congestion patterns are as follows.

Spatio-Temporal Feature: Given a set of spatial features $F = \{f_1, f_2, ..., f_m\}$ and a set of temporal features $T = \{t_1, t_2, ..., t_n\}$, where spatial feature $f_i (1 \leq i \leq m)$ represents a road in the space, time feature $t_j (1 \leq j \leq n)$ represents a time period. A spatial feature f_i combines with a time feature t_j to form a spatio-temporal feature f_i-t_j which represents the state of road f_i within time period t_j. All spatio-temporal features form a set $FT = \{f_1 - t_1, f_1 - t_2, ..., f_m - t_{n-1}, f_m - t_n\}$.

Spatio-Temporal Instance: A specific object of the spatio-temporal feature f-t is called a spatio-temporal instance which refers to a speed record captured by a sensor in the road f under a specific time slice within the time period t.

f_threshold: Because of the fuzziness of traffic congestion itself, we propose a calculation method of the fuzzy membership degree based on the fuzzy set theory. This method can measure the traffic congestion state more accurately. The fuzzy membership degree $\mu(o)$ represents the degree to congestion state of a spatio-temporal instance o, and the value is in range of $[0, 1]$. The formula of $\mu(o)$ is as below.

$$\mu(o) = \begin{cases} 0, & v_f < \overline{v_o} \\ (v_f - \overline{v_o})/v_f, & \text{otherwise} \end{cases} \tag{1}$$

where v_f denotes the free-flow speed of road f, $\overline{v_o}$ denotes the instantaneous speed of the spatio-temporal instance o.

Spatio-Temporal Congestion Instance: Given a fuzziness threshold *f_threshold*, if a spatio-temporal instance o satisfies $\mu(o) \geq$ *f_threshold*, then o is said to be a spatio-temporal congestion instance.

t_threshold: When the time span between two spatio-temporal congestion instances with different spatial features (roads) under the same time period is less than or equal to *t_threshold* specified by the user, the two spatio-temporal congestion instances satisfies the time proximity relationship.

FPR (Fuzzy Participation Rate): Given a FuConPattern $c = \{f_1 - t, f_2 - t, ..., f_k - t\}$, the FPR of a spatio-temporal feature $f_i - t (1 \leq i \leq k)$ is defined as follows.

$$FPR(c, f_i - t) = \sum_{o \in I(c, f_i - t)} \mu(o) \Bigg/ |I(f_i - t)| \qquad (2)$$

where $I(c, f_i - t)$ represents the set of participating spatio-temporal congestion instances of $f_i - t$ within c, and $|I(f_i - t)|$ represents the number of all spatio-temporal congestion instances of $f_i - t$.

FPI (Fuzzy Participation Index): FPI is defined as the minimum FPR of all spatio-temporal features within c.

$$FPI(c) = \min_{i=1}^{k}\{FPR(c, f_i - t)\} \qquad (3)$$

Prevalent FuConPattern: Given a prevalence threshold min_prev, if a FuConPattern c satisfies $FPI(c) \geq min\_prev$, then c is said to be a prevalent FuConPattern.

2.3 Mining Module

The mining module contains two algorithms STF and MP, where STF discovers all prevalent FuConPatterns from the inputting traffic flow data according to the given parameters, and then MP finds all maximal prevalent FuConPatterns from the prevalent FuConPatterns. After that, the module outputs all maximal prevalent FuConPatterns. MP guarantees reasonable compression rate on FuConPatterns and the maximal FuConPatterns with little redundancy found by MP are convenient for the user to choose. The details of STF and MP are shown as follows.

Algorithm STF: Mining Prevalent FuConPatterns

Input: spatio-temporal feature set $FT=\{f_1\text{-}t, f_2\text{-}t, ..., f_m\text{-}t\}$, Spatial topological relations $TP=\{f_i{\rightarrow}f_j|1{\leq}i, j{\leq}m$ and $i{\neq}j\}$, spatio-temporal instance set S, the fuzziness threshold $f\_threshold$, the time threshold $t\_threshold$, the minimum prevalence threshold min_prev

Output: Prevalent FuConPatterns

1 $S_{f\_threshold}$=get_f($S, f\_threshold$);
2 SN=gen_time_neighborhoods($FT, S_{f\_threshold}, t\_threshold$);
3 generate 1-size prevalent fuzzy congestion patterns P_1 with FT, SN and min_prev;
4 **while**(P_{k-1} is not empty) **do**
5   C_k=gen_candidate_pattern(P_{k-1}, TP);
6   I_k=gen_participating_instance(C_k, SN);
7   P_k=select_prevalent_pattern(C_k, I_k, min_prev);
8    $k=k+1$;
9 **end do**
10 **return** $\bigcup (P_1, P_2, ..., P_k)$;

Algorithm STF details how the prevalent FuConPatterns are mined. At first, the instances satisfying $f\_threshold$ are filtered from the spatio-temporal instance set S (Step 1), then it generates a temporal proximity table SN according to the time proximity relationship (Step 2). With FT, SN and min_prev, it generates 1-size prevalent FuConPatterns stored in P_1 (Step 3). After that, it iteratively generates k-size candidate FuConPatterns C_k based on $(k-1)$-size prevalent FuConPatterns P_{k-1}, generates participating instances of any spatio-temporal features within C_k, calculates FPR and FPI of C_k, and selects k-size prevalent FuConPatterns which meets $FPI(c) \geq min\_prev$ (Step 4–9). STF will be terminated and return mined prevalent FuConPatterns when P_{k-1} is empty (Step 10).

The time complexity of STF is $O(\sum_{k=1}^{w} |SN||C_k|)$, the space complexity of STF is $O(|SN| + |I_k|)$, where w represents the maximum size of FuConPatterns.

Algorithm MP: Mining Maximal Prevalent FuConPatterns

Input: the set of all prevalent FuConPatterns P, the maximum pattern size mk
Output: Maximal Prevalent FuConPatterns
1 **if** mk=2 **then return** P;
2 **for** i **in** mk **to** 3 **do**
3     $highPatterns$=select_patterns(P, i);
4   **for** j **in** mk-1 **to** 2 **do**
5         $lowPatterns$=select_patterns(P, j);
6   P=select_max_patterns(P, $highPatterns$, $lowPatterns$);
7   **end do**
8 **end do**
9 **return** P;

Algorithm MP is used to find maximal prevalent FuConPatterns based on the set relation operation.

The time complexity of MP is $O(mk^2)$, the space of MP algorithm is $O(P)$.

Evaluation. Figure 2 shows the number of patterns mined by STF and MP, and the compression rate of maximal FuConPatterns. It can be seen that the number of maximal prevalent FuConPatterns mined by MP is far less than the number of prevalent FuConPatterns discovered by STF. A smaller number of maximal FuConPatterns means a higher compression ratio which can reach more than 84% shown in Fig. 2. In addition, maximal FuConPatterns can be more convenient for users to choose for its smaller number. Meanwhile, it can be seen from Fig. 3 that the response time of the system is within a reasonable range acceptable to people which implies that the system has a high availability.

2.4 Display Module

The display module can display three parts of information, including maximal FuConPatterns output by the mining module, the urban road network information, and the real-time congestion information labelled on the road network. Users can intuitively

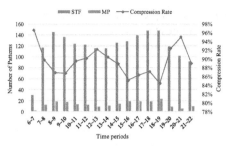

Fig. 2. The number of patterns mined by STF and MP, and the compression rate of maximal FuConPatterns

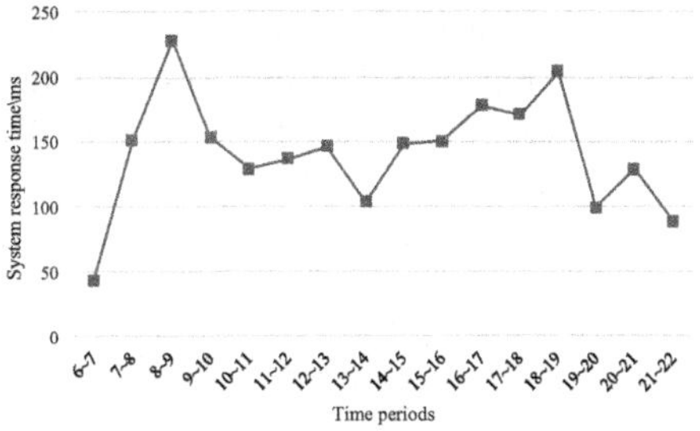

Fig. 3. System response time

understand traffic conditions from congestion information fed back by the display module, thus they could plan travel routes reasonably. Also, it can provide decision-making support and guidance for researchers with traffic congestion research.

3 Demonstration Scenarios

The system TCPMS-FCP has friendly interface with easy operation for users. In this demonstration, we use a real-world traffic dataset provided by the Big Data Development Administration and the Department of Transportation of Guizhou Province to show the interactive and running process of TCPMS-FCP. This traffic dataset is divided into data files by day, and each data file stores the data collected by sensors on that day. It uses a unique road ID to represent each road and sensors collect the speed of the road every two minutes. TCPMS-FCP takes one hour as a time period by default, and can dynamically discover and display urban traffic congestion patterns within 16 time periods from 6:00 to 22:00 for one day.

Figure 4 shows the user interface of TCPMS-FCP which includes Fig. 4(a) Menu, Fig. 4(b) Text Area and Fig. 4(c) Road Map. Menu contains an *open* button, a showing selected filename field, three text fields for inputting parameters and a *mining* button. When the user clicks the *open* button, a file dialog occurs and the users can choose a traffic data file of any day from it for mining. That process is shown in Fig. 4(d). Text Area is used to show the text of maximal prevalent FuConPatterns and any other information about the running process. Road Map uses directed line segment marked with road ID to represent each urban road and initially they are gray. After inputting a traffic data file and three mining parameters, clicking *mining* button to start the system, the Road Map dynamically displays mined traffic congestion patterns by using red color to label congested roads and using green color to label unblocked roads within 16 time periods. Figure 4(e) shows the results for 8:00–9:00 with a set of parameters. The mined maximal prevalent FuConPatterns are presented on the Text Area and corresponding congestion information are shown on the Road Map.

Figure 5 shows the mining results with the traffic data file of March 1, 2016 for given parameters $f\_threshold = 0.5$, $t\_threshold = 6$ and $min\_prev = 0.5$. We can see that during the dynamically mining process according to the time periods, the number of prevalent FuConPatterns and maximal prevalent FuConPatterns are 154 and only 26 respectively within the time period 8:00–9:00, so its compression ratio is as high as 83% shown in Fig. 5(a). The compression ratio demonstrates the high reliability of TCPMS-FCP. In Fig. 5(b), these maximal prevalent FuConPatterns are displayed on the Road Map of Guiyang City, in which these red line segments are crowded roads.

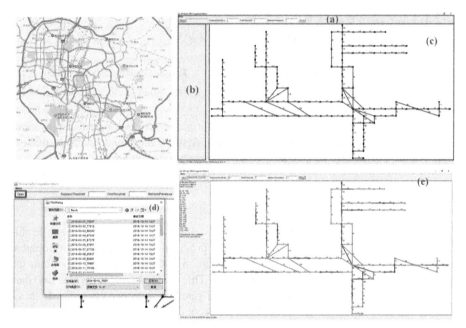

Fig. 4. Interface of TCPMS-FCP (Color figure online)

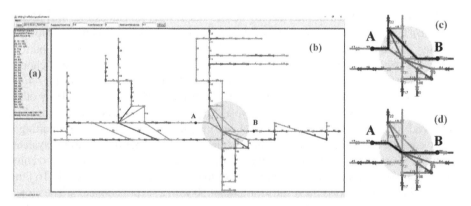

Fig. 5. Result display and analysis (Color figure online)

The TCPMS-FCP can help people schedule travel routes in advance and assist traffic control to relieve traffic congestion. For example, we can see that there are many different paths for the user to drive from point A to point B in yellow area in Fig. 5(b). According to the mining results, this yellow area has maximal FuConPatterns {84,120}, {22, 54}, {22, 23, 122} and {77, 115, 125}. The TCPMS-FCP provides this user with two optimal travel routes, one route is completely unblocked without any congestion in Fig. 5(c), and the other is the shortest route with congestion in Fig. 5(d). From that, this user can choose the most time-saving route to drive from A to B.

4 Conclusion

In this demonstration, we design and develop a traffic congestion pattern mining system based on spatio-temporal fuzzy co-location patterns, namely TCPMS-FCP. This system can discover all traffic congestion patterns from traffic flow data and display congested conditions about urban roads. It could give guidance for people choosing appropriate travel routes and also assist traffic control to relieve traffic congestion.

Acknowledgements. This work is supported by the National Natural Science Foundation of China (61966036), the Project of Innovative Research Team of Yunnan Province (2018HC019), the Yunnan Fundamental Research Project (202201AS070015), the Scientific Research Fund Project of Yunnan Provincial Department of Education (2021J0797), and the Scientific Research Fund Project of Dianchi College of Yunnan University (2022XYB12).

References

1. Di, X., Yu, X., Zhu, C.: Traffic congestion prediction by spatiotemporal propagation patterns. In: 20th IEEE International Conference on Mobile Data Management (MDM), pp. 298–303 (2019)
2. Song, J., Zhao, C., Zhong, S., Nielsen, T., Prishchepov, A.: Mapping spatio-temporal patterns and detecting the factors of traffic congestion with multi-source data fusion and mining techniques. Comput. Environ. Urban Syst. **77**, 101364 (2019)
3. Abbas, Z., Sottovia, P., Hassan, M., Foroni, D., Bortoli, S.: Real-time traffic jam detection and congestion reduction using streaming graph analytics. In: 8th IEEE International Conference on Big Data (IEEE BigData), pp. 3109–3118 (2020)
4. Zhang, J., Zheng, Y., Sun, J., Qi, D.: Flow prediction in spatio-temporal networks based on multitask deep learning. IEEE Trans. Knowl. Data Eng. **32**(3), 468–478 (2020)
5. Pan, Z., et al.: Spatio-temporal meta learning for urban traffic prediction. IEEE Trans. Knowl. Data Eng. **34**(3), 1462–1476 (2022)
6. He, Y., Wang, L., Fang, Y., Li, Y.: Discovering congestion propagation patterns by co-location pattern mining. In: U, L.H., Xie, H. (eds.) APWeb-WAIM 2018. LNCS, vol. 11268, pp. 46–55. Springer, Cham (2018). https://doi.org/10.1007/978-3-030-01298-4_5
7. Wang, L., Bao, X., Zhou, L.: Redundancy reduction for prevalent co-location patterns. IEEE Trans. Knowl. Data Eng. **30**(1), 142–155 (2018)
8. Hu, Z., Wang, L., Tran, V., Chen, H.: Efficiently mining spatial co-location patterns utilizing fuzzy grid cliques. Inf. Sci. **592**, 361–388 (2022)

Author Index

Printed in the United States
by Baker & Taylor Publisher Services